BEST PLACES®

NORTHWEST

**The Locals' Guide to the Best Restaurants,
Lodgings, Sights, Shopping, and More!**

*917.95
BEST PL
2007*

**Edited by
JO OSTGARDEN**

EDITION

SASQUATCH BOOKS
SEATTLE

Printed in the United States of America
Published by Sasquatch Books
Distributed by PGW/Perseus

Seventeenth edition
15 14 13 12 11 10 09   10 9 8 7 6 5 4 3 2 1

ISBN-13: 978-1-57061-575-7
ISBN-10: 1-57061-575-6
ISSN 1041-2484

Cover design: Sasquatch Books
Interior design: Scott Taylor/FILTER/Talent
Interior composition: Sarah Plein
Interior maps: Lisa Brower/GreenEye Design
Indexer: Michael Ferreira
Project editor: Rachelle Longé

SPECIAL SALES

Best Places guidebooks are available at special discounts on bulk purchases
for corporate, club, or organization sales promotions, premiums, and gifts. For
more information, contact your local bookseller or Special Sales, Best Places
Guidebooks, 119 South Main Street, Suite 400, Seattle, Washington, 98104,
800/775-0817.

SASQUATCH BOOKS

119 South Main Street, Suite 400
Seattle, Washington 98104
206/467-4300
www.sasquatchbooks.com
custserv@sasquatchbooks.com

Praise for Best Places® Guidebooks

"Best Places *are the best regional restaurant and guide books in America.*"
—THE SEATTLE TIMES

"Best Places *covers must-see portions of the West Coast with style and authority. In-the-know locals offer thorough info on restaurants, lodgings, and the sights.*"
—NATIONAL GEOGRAPHIC TRAVELER

"*Travelers swear by the recommendations in the* Best Places *guidebooks.*"
—SUNSET MAGAZINE

"*For travel collections covering the Northwest, the* Best Places *series takes precedence over all similar guides.*"
—BOOKLIST

"Best Places Northwest *is the bible of discriminating travelers to BC, Washington, and Oregon. It promises, and delivers, the best of everything in the region.*"
—THE VANCOUVER SUN

"*Not only the best travel guide in the region, but maybe one of the most definitive guides in the country, which many look forward to with the anticipation usually sparked by a best-selling novel. A browser's delight,* Best Places Northwest *should be chained to dashboards throughout the Northwest.*"
—THE OREGONIAN

"*Still the region's undisputed heavyweight champ of guidebooks.*"
—SEATTLE POST-INTELLIGENCER

"*Visitors to Washington, Oregon, and British Columbia would do well to pick up* Best Places Northwest *for an exhaustive review of food and lodging in the region. . . . An indispensable glove-compartment companion.*"
—TRAVEL AND LEISURE

"*Whether you're a Seattleite facing the winter doldrums or a visitor wondering what to see next, guidance is close at hand in* Best Places Seattle.*"
—SUNSET MAGAZINE

"*This tome [Best Places Seattle] is one of the best practical guides to any city in North America.*"
—TRAVEL BOOKS WORLDWIDE

"*Funny, conversational writing and clever sidebars make* Best Places Vancouver *an enjoyable read.*"
—VANCOUVER MAGAZINE

TRUST THE LOCALS

The original insider's guides, written by local experts

EVERY PLACE STAR-RATED & RECOMMENDED

★★★★ The very best in the region

★★★ Distinguished; many outstanding features

★★ Excellent; some wonderful qualities

★ A good place

HELPFUL ICONS

Watch for these quick-reference symbols throughout the book:

 FAMILY FUN

 GOOD VALUE

 ROMANTIC

 EDITORS' CHOICE

CONTENTS

CONTENTS

British Columbia

Introduction and Acknowledgments

Working on this travel guide, I was struck by the scope of this project. A guide like this requires obsessive attention to detail, a discerning eagle eye (many of them actually), and the ability to distil otherwise vast amounts of information into a practical but fun resource for independent tourists and travelers (both leisure and business) alike. But it also serves as a vital resource for new and established residents of the region.

The job would have been incredibly difficult without the help of Rachelle Longé at Sasquatch Books, who shepherded the visual and logistical aspects of this project, and all of the contributing writers whose keen eyes and intrepid research were invaluable. This project also benefits from the *seanachie* (Irish storyteller) genes inherited from my mother and the voracious reading habits of my father—which equally inspired me—as well as the 11 brothers and sisters who made me the person I am today. Credit also goes out to Mr. Richard O'Brien and Ms. Jo Lawson, whom I count among the two most inspiring English teachers on the planet. A note of deep gratitude to Ivy Manning, who introduced me to this challenging project, and to my son, Sam, and my husband, Michole, both of whom endured months of my distraction and fixation. Finally, extra treats for my constant canine office companion, Bodhi, who made the long days tenable.

—Jo Ostgarden

Contributors

MARIAN BUECHERT is a freelance writer, editor, and photographer who currently edits *Modern Dog* magazine. A lifelong resident of the Pacific Northwest, she has traveled extensively on five continents and has the remaining two on her "to do" list.

JULIA CATTRAL is a native-born Oregonian who grew up on an organic vineyard in Yamhill County. A Reed College graduate, she has lived and worked on Oregon's North Coast, produced pinot noir at a Willamette Valley winery, and has traveled extensively, including to Ecuador and Peru.

An avid traveler and outdoor enthusiast, **LISA FLOOD** moved to Oregon in 1996 and instantly fell in love with the Northwest. Her base camp is Portland, where she lives with her dog, Yogi, and her husband, Randy, as well as a steady stream of foster dogs. A marketing consultant, freelance writer, and columnist for *Fitness Plus* magazine, Lisa is a keen observer of life and dear friend to all who know her.

Travel adventures and a master's degree in clinical nutrition fueled **WENDY GORDON**'s interest in food and dining. The avid cook, organic gardener, and hiker began writing for local newspapers and magazines after moving to Portland, Oregon, in 1993. She writes regular columns for *The Northwest Examiner*, *Front Lines*, and *At the Wedge* newsletters, as well as feature articles for *Northwest Palate* magazine, *Portland Tribune*, and *The Oregonian*, among others.

LORI HENRY is a globe-trekking writer who calls Vancouver, British Columbia, home. Her column on traveling Western Canada fuses local insider knowledge with the curious eye of an explorer. You can find her work in, among others, *The Vancouver Sun*, *Vancouver View*, *BC Jazz Magazine*, Martiniboys.com nightlife magazine, and at Suite101.com Media Inc.

Kirsten Lawson is a Washington native and a freelance writer and photographer. She works and travels with her husband, James (Eric) Lawson, who immigrated to the Pacific Northwest 18 years ago to continue his career in publications editing, nature, and travel writing. Together **TEAM LAWSON-LAWSON** enjoy photographing and writing about their adventures and mishaps in the western United States.

Oregon native **JOANNA MILLER** is a freelance production coordinator who also writes about bakeries, chocolate, ice cream, and coffee shops for www.portland foodanddrink.com and the local weekly. Armed with a Willy Wonka–like sweet tooth, she is a regular contributor to www.sugarsavvy.com, an online forum of candy reviews.

Originally hailing from Ketchikan, Alaska, **GINNY MOREY** has called Seattle "home" for more than two decades. She writes primarily about bars, restaurants, shopping, and travel for a wide variety of publications, both online and in print. An avid reader and acknowledged superfluous-information buff, she spent 10 years hosting pub trivia quizzes and has appeared on the TV game shows *Jeopardy* and *Who Wants to Be a Millionaire*, yet finds herself unable to give up her lucrative freelancing career.

JO OSTGARDEN has traveled around the world—half of it by bicycle—and has called Portland, Oregon, home base for two decades. She has a master's degree in journalism and has worked as a writer and editor for newspapers, journals, magazines, and an online travel website for 30 years. She has written for *Bicycling*, *Shape*, and *Healthy Woman*, among many other national magazines; she also edited a book on reflexology and another on spiritual quests. Her favorite assignments are the one's she most passionate about: food, the environment, health, fitness, and travel.

MARY STEWART has lived and worked as a professional writer in Portland for 20 years. An avid traveler, a fearless cook, and a wine lover, she and her husband, Ron, have combed four continents, explored the country's east and west coasts, and hiked Portland's hills and back streets in search of culinary fortuity.

A FINAL TRIBUTE: *Nick Gallo was a longtime writer for the Best Places guidebooks, as well as more recently for* Travel & Leisure, Alaska Airlines Magazine, United Airlines' *Hemispheres*, Private Clubs, *and* NWA WorldTraveler. *We were sad to learn of his passing in October 2007. We are forever grateful for his contribution to this series.*

About Best Places® Guidebooks

People trust us. Best Places guidebooks, which have been published continuously since 1975, represent one of the most respected regional travel series in the country. Our reviewers know their territory, and seek out the very best a city or region has to offer. We provide tough, candid reports about places that have rested too long on their laurels, and delight in new places that deserve recognition. We describe the true strengths, foibles, and unique characteristics of each establishment listed.

Best Places Northwest is written by and for locals, and is therefore coveted by travelers. It's written for people who live here and who enjoy exploring the region's bounty and its out-of-the-way places of high character and individualism. It's these very characteristics that make *Best Places Northwest* ideal for tourists, too. The best places in and around the region are the ones that denizens favor: independently owned establishments of good value, touched with local history, run by lively individuals, and graced with natural beauty. With this seventeenth edition of *Best Places Northwest*, travelers will find the information they need: where to go and when; what to order; which rooms to request (and which to avoid); where the best skiing, hiking, wilderness getaways, and local attractions are; and how to find the region's hidden secrets.

NOTE: *The reviews in this edition are based on information available at press time and are subject to change. Readers are advised that places listed in previous editions may have closed or changed management or may no longer be recommended by this series. The editors welcome information conveyed by users of this book. A report form is provided at the end of the book, and feedback is also welcome via e-mail: BPFeedback@sasquatchbooks.com.*

How to Use This Book

This book is divided into 20 regional chapters covering a wide range of establishments, destinations, and activities. All evaluations are based on numerous reports from local and traveling inspectors. Final judgments are made by Sasquatch editors. **EVERY PLACE FEATURED IN THIS BOOK IS RECOMMENDED.**

STAR RATINGS *(for restaurants and lodgings only)* Restaurants and lodgings are rated on a scale of one to four stars (with half stars in between), based on uniqueness, loyalty of local clientele, performance measured against the establishment's goals, excellence of cooking, cleanliness, value, and professionalism of service. Reviews are listed alphabetically by region, and every place is recommended.

    ★★★★   The very best in the region

     ★★★   Distinguished; many outstanding features

      ★★   Excellent; some wonderful qualities

       ★   A good place

(For more on how we rate places, see "Best Places Star Ratings" on page xiv.)

BEST PLACES® STAR RATINGS

Any travel guide that rates establishments is inherently subjective—and Best Places is no exception. We rely on our professional experience, yes, but also on a gut feeling. And, occasionally, we even give in to soft spot for a favorite neighborhood hangout. Our star-rating system is not simply a checklist; it's judgmental, critical, sometimes fickle, and highly personal.

For each new edition, we send local food and travel experts out to review restaurants and lodgings, and then to rate them on a scale of one to four, based on uniqueness, loyalty of local clientele, performance measured against the establishment's goals, excellence of cooking, cleanliness, value, and professionalism or service. That doesn't mean a one-star establishment isn't worth dining or sleeping at. Far from it! When we say that all the places listed in our books are recommended, we mean it. That one-star pizza joint may be just the ticket for the end of a whirlwind day of shopping with the kids. But if you're planning something more special, the star ratings can help you choose an eatery or hotel that will wow your new clients or be a

PRICE RANGE (*for restaurants and lodgings only*) Prices for restaurants are based primarily on dinner for two, including dessert and tip, but not alcohol. Prices for lodgings are based on peak season rates for one night's lodging for two people (i.e., double occupancy). Peak season is typically Memorial Day to Labor Day for summer destinations, or November through March for winter destinations; off-season rates vary but often can be significantly less. Call ahead to verify, as all prices are subject to change. *Note:* Prices in British Columbia chapters are given in Canadian dollars.

$$$$ Very expensive (more than $100 for dinner for two; more than $200 for one night's lodging for two)

$$$ Expensive (between $65 and $100 for dinner for two; between $120 and $200 for one night's lodging for two)

$$ Moderate (between $35 and $65 for dinner for two; between $80 and $120 for one night's lodging for two)

$ Inexpensive (less than $35 for dinner for two; less than $80 for one night's lodging for two)

RESERVATIONS (*for restaurants only*) For each dining establishment listed in the book, we used one of the following terms for its reservations policy: reservations required, reservations recommended, or no reservations.

ADDRESSES AND PHONE NUMBERS Every attempt has been made to provide accurate information on an establishment's location and phone number, but it's always a good idea to call ahead and confirm.

stunning, romantic place to celebrate an anniversary or impress a first date.

We award four-star ratings sparingly, reserving them for what we consider truly the best. And once an establishment has earned our highest rating, everyone's expectations seem to rise. Readers often write us specifically to point out the faults in four-star establishments. With changes in chefs, management, styles, and trends, it's always easier to get knocked off the pedestal than to ascend it. Three-star establishments, on the other hand, seem to generate healthy praise. They exhibit outstanding qualities, and we get lots of love letters about them. The difference between two and three stars can sometimes be a very fine line. Two-star establishments are doing a good, solid job and are gaining attention, while one-star places are often dependable spots that have been around forever.

The restaurants and lodgings described in *Best Places Northwest* have earned their stars from hard work and good service (and good food). They're proud to be included in this book: look for our Best Places sticker in their windows. And we're proud to honor them in this, the seventeenth edition of *Best Places Northwest*.

WEB SITE/E-MAIL ADDRESSES Web site or e-mail addresses have been included where available. Please note that the Web is a fluid and evolving medium, and that Web pages are often "under construction" or, as with all time-sensitive information, may no longer be valid.

CHECKS AND CREDIT CARDS Many establishments that accept checks also require a major credit card for identification. Note that some accept only local checks. Credit cards are abbreviated in this book as follows: American Express (AE), Carte Blanche (CB), Diners Club (DC), Discover (DIS), Enroute (E), Japanese credit card (JCB), MasterCard (MC), Visa (V).

ACCESS AND INFORMATION At the beginning of each chapter, you'll find general guidelines about how to get to a particular region and what types of transportation are available, as well as basic sources for any additional tourist information. Also check individual town listings for specifics about visiting those places.

MAPS AND DIRECTIONS Each chapter in the book begins with a regional map that shows the general area being covered. Throughout the book, basic directions are provided with each entry. Whenever possible, call ahead to confirm hours and location.

THREE-DAY TOURS In every chapter, we've included a quick-reference, three-day itinerary designed for travelers with a short amount of time. Perfect for weekend getaways, these tours outline the highlights of a region or town; each of the establishments or attractions that appear in boldface within the tour are discussed in greater detail elsewhere in the chapter.

THE DETAILS Most bed and breakfasts don't allow children, or have age limits. Most don't allow pets, either. Some places require two-night stays during weekends or busy seasons. Ask about these topics when you make reservations.

HELPFUL ICONS Watch for these quick-reference symbols throughout the book:

 FAMILY FUN Places that are fun, easy, and great for kids.

 GOOD VALUE While not necessarily cheap, these places offer a good deal within the context of the region.

 ROMANTIC These spots offer candlelight, atmosphere, intimacy, or other romantic qualities—kisses and proposals are encouraged!

 EDITORS' CHOICE These are places we especially love.

 Appears after listings for establishments that have wheelchair-accessible facilities.

INDEX All restaurants, lodgings, town names, and major tourist attractions are listed alphabetically at the back of the book.

READER REPORTS At the end of the book is a report form. We receive hundreds of reports from readers suggesting new places or agreeing or disagreeing with our assessments. They greatly help in our evaluations, and we encourage you to respond.

PORTLAND AND ENVIRONS

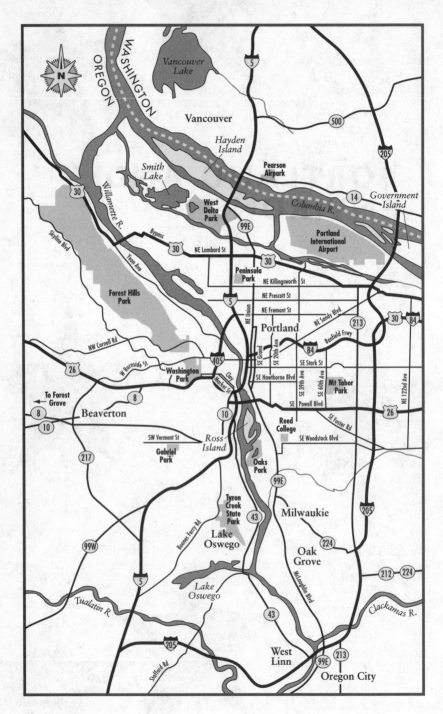

PORTLAND AND ENVIRONS

On the ever-changing list of the nation's Most Livable cities, Portland is a consistent contender. Few others cities of Portland's size match its intensity of "green," literally or in terms of the community's commitment to the environment. Culturally diverse and inclusive, Portlanders possess a do-it-yourself ethos, along with a renowned creative drive. The city, with a vibrant culinary scene, is well established as a foodie destination. It's also known as the leader, nationally, for the number of microbrew pubs—last count 36—stationed here.

Portland is also well known for its friendliness, its civic progressiveness—in 2008 it was the first city in the nation to elect an avowedly gay mayor—and its active citizenry, both politically and in terms of sports and lifestyle proclivities. Its manageable size provides many of the same amenities as those found in other large cities, but it still feels small enough to be safe and easy to get around in, thanks in part to being a national leader in comprehensive alternative transportation systems. It also consistently ranks as the best bicycling city in the nation.

And it does all this pretty much under the radar, without a Fortune 500–driven economy.

Located at the intersection of the Willamette and Columbia rivers, in close proximity to both the Pacific coast and Mount Hood (each about an hour and a half away), outdoor adventure is just a heartbeat away. While the waterfront and downtown core's open-air plaza are often called the city's playground and living room, respectively, dozens of urban parks and green spaces embrace the overflow.

When it comes to climate, Portland is at its best in midsummer to early fall (mid-June–early October), when the frequent rain abates to reveal blooming roses, dogwoods, rhododendrons, and a vividly green city bustling with festivals and outdoor events. Other times of the year, frequent but gentle showers set a laid-back pace—perfect cappuccino- or microbrew-sipping weather. Spandex and microfleece, depending on the season, are pretty much de rigueur fashion in Portland. You actually can get away with wearing the latter even to upscale restaurants.

ACCESS AND INFORMATION

PORTLAND INTERNATIONAL AIRPORT, or PDX (7000 NE Airport Wy; 503/460-4040; www.flypdx.com), is served by most major airlines. Allow at least 30 minutes to get from the airport to downtown. All major **CAR RENTAL** companies operate from the airport. Taxis and shuttles are readily available; expect to pay at least $26–$30 for the trip downtown. The most economical ride ($2.05) is via the airport **METROPOLITAN AREA EXPRESS,** aka **MAX.** Catch the sleek MAX light-rail train just outside the baggage claim area; the ride to the center of downtown at Pioneer Courthouse Square takes approximately 38 minutes. Another mode of transportation is the BLUESTAR **AIRPORTER** (503/249-1837) for $14; buses leave every 30 minutes. Many hotels provide free pickup service; check the reservation board in the baggage claim area to see if yours does.

Most drivers reach Portland via either **INTERSTATE 5**, which runs north-south, or **INTERSTATE 84**, running east-west. **US HIGHWAY 26**, "the Sunset Highway," runs west to Beaverton and the coast; **INTERSTATE 205** loops east off I-5 from Vancouver, Washington, to Lake Oswego and points south.

AMTRAK (503/273-4866 or 800/USA-RAIL; www.amtrak.com) operates out of the historic **UNION STATION** (800 NW 6th Ave) just 12 blocks north of downtown. This romantic red-brick structure stands in memory to the bygone era of the great railways. The nearby **GREYHOUND** station (550 NW 6th Ave; 503/243-2361 or 800/231-2222; www.greyhound.com) has a complete daily schedule.

TRI-MET (503/238-7433; www.trimet.org) operates the city bus and MAX systems; tickets for the two are interchangeable. Almost all bus lines run through the **PORTLAND TRANSIT MALL** (SW 5th and 6th aves); MAX lines also pass through downtown. Ride free downtown in the "Fareless Square," which extends from points downtown to the Convention Center. To ride to the most outlying neighborhoods, you'll need a two-zone ticket ($1.75), which you can purchase from the bus driver (exact change only) or at MAX stops. Another popular option is the **PORTLAND STREETCAR** (www.portlandstreetcar.org), which travels from the South Park Blocks through the Pearl District to NW 23rd Avenue.

If you're driving and want to cut some expenses—for example, the pesky high cost of parking charged by downtown Portland hotels, ask the **PORTLAND OREGON VISITORS ASSOCIATION** (www.travelportland.com) about their year-round **PORTLAND BIG DEAL** promotion.

Portland

Though Portland is a manageable size with or without a car, it's helpful to remember that the city is ruled by east-west bridges and divided into four segments: the Willamette River and Interstate 5 divide the city into an east side and a west side; Burnside Street divides the city into north and south sections. Downtown addresses generally begin with the prefix "SW," while the streets of the northwest quadrant, including the **PEARL DISTRICT**, have the NW prefix and run alphabetically starting at Burnside, moving north to NW Couch Street, NW Davis Street, and so on.

Portland is a city of neighborhoods, each with its own cultural leanings and represented by a volunteer-based neighborhood association and a district coalition, which serve as liaisons between neighborhood residents and city government. The southeast encompasses the city's densest collection of neighborhoods, from **ARDENWALD**, Portland's most southern neighborhood, bordering the coveted **SPRINGWATER CORRIDOR TRAIL** (a paved 19-mile trail from downtown's inner eastside esplanade to Boring), to laid-back **HAWTHORNE**, a neighborhood of progressive liberals and bohemians. The northeast section of the city, bordered by the Columbia River on the north, includes up-and-coming areas like the **NOPO** (North Mississippi) and the **ALBERTA STREET ARTS DISTRICT**. Both onetime decaying, marginalized neighborhoods have blossomed into two of the city's favorite cultural spots, with shops, restaurants, and galleries.

The downtown core is home to the performing arts center complex, a first-class art museum, and a historical museum, all located along a several-blocks-long greenbelt called the **SOUTH PARK BLOCKS**, which begin at **PORTLAND STATE UNIVERSITY** to the south and extend to north Salmon Street. At the very heart of the downtown core, **PIONEER COURTHOUSE SQUARE** (SW Broadway and SW Yamhill sts) has been called Portland's living room, featuring the public art Weather Machine, which predicts the weather at noon, plus food carts and places to sit and enjoy the weekday lunchtime concerts and events.

MAJOR ATTRACTIONS

While visiting Pioneer Courthouse Square, stop in at the **VISITOR CENTER** (503/275-8355; www.travelportland.com). Pick up excellent maps and talk to a city concierge for help with city navigation, dinner reservations, and event tickets.

An iconic Portland element to keep an eye out for is the Benson Bubblers. For nearly a century, Portlanders and visitors have sipped pure, unadulterated, naturally filtered drinking water—from a natural reservoir on the flanks of Mount Hood—from these elegant bronze drinking fountains. Look for them around downtown, in the University District, in Old Town/Chinatown, and in the lower half of the Pearl District; by all means, take a drink.

The **OREGON MUSEUM OF SCIENCE AND INDUSTRY**, or OMSI (1945 SE Water Ave; 503/797-4000; www.omsi.edu), is just across the river from downtown. It's anything but your typical museum; pick from planetarium shows, tours of an authentic U.S. Navy submarine, and movies at the IMAX theater. The **OREGON HISTORY CENTER** (1200 SW Park Ave; 503/222-1741) pays tribute to the Native Americans, pioneers, and others who have lived on the banks of the Willamette. Reachable by the MAX train, the **OREGON ZOO** (4001 SW Canyon Rd; 503/226-1561; www.oregonzoo.org) includes exhibits of Pacific Northwest creatures and train rides for the little ones. The **PORTLAND CHILDREN'S MUSEUM** (503/223-6500; www.portlandcm.org) is just across the parking lot.

PITTOCK MANSION (3229 NW Pittock Dr; 503/823-3624), overlooking the city on its northwest side, was built by Henry Lewis Pittock. The founder of *The Oregonian* daily newspaper rode a wagon train from Pennsylvania to the Oregon Territory in 1853 at age 17. The mansion, completed in 1914, is one of the city's landmarks. Stand on the front lawn for a better than 180-degree view of the city, the Willamette and Columbia rivers, and five Cascade Range peaks. The view of Mount Hood from the mansion's lawn is the one you see on most postcards.

Portland is often called the City of Roses for good reason. The **INTERNATIONAL ROSE TEST GARDEN** (www.rosegardenstore.com/thegardens.cfm) in **WASHINGTON PARK** (400 SW Kingston Ave; www.portlandonline.com/parks) first opened in 1917, serving as a sanctuary during World War I for European hybrid roses in danger of being bombed out of existence. An estimated 6,800

PORTLAND THREE-DAY TOUR

DAY ONE: Start the day downtown with an Americano and pastry at **STUMP-TOWN COFFEE ROASTERS** (1022 SW Stark St; 503/224-9060), Portland's—and some say the country's—best coffee. Turn the corner and head up the beautiful **SOUTH PARK BLOCKS** to either the **PORTLAND ART MUSEUM** or the **ORE-GON HISTORY CENTER**. Shoppers will want to detour to the multilevel **PIO-NEER PLACE MALL**. For lunch, grab the streetcar over to the **PEARL DISTRICT** for lunch at **BLUEHOUR**. From there, head just around the corner to the stacks at **POWELL'S CITY OF BOOKS** or to posh shopping in the Pearl. Late afternoon, check in to the **HOTEL DELUXE**, enjoy a cocktail in the hotel's swanky retro lounge, the **DRIFTWOOD ROOM**, and then step over to dinner at **GRACIE'S**.

DAY TWO: After breakfast at **50 PLATES** (333 NW 13th Ave; 503/228-5050), head farther west to explore some of Portland's best parks. Stop to smell the roses and see sweeping views up the street at the **WASHINGTON PARK INTERNATIONAL ROSE TEST GARDEN**; take in the **JAPANESE GARDEN** or **PITTOCK MANSION** on your way to the **OREGON ZOO**. When your stomach starts rumbling, head down the hill to the hip shopping district of NW 23rd and NW 21st avenues and spend the rest of the day browsing the boutiques of **NW 23RD AVENUE**. Afterward, head to nearby **23HOYT** for an early dinner before checking into the Andy Warhol–themed suite at the **HEATHMAN**.

DAY THREE: Begin the day with a **HEATHMAN** power breakfast. Take a right as you exit the front doors and head up Broadway a half block to check out the Italian Rocco Revival architecture of the 1928-built **ARLENE SCHNITZER**

rose bushes, representing some 550 varieties, can be seen and smelled, along with new rose varieties deemed "Official All-America Rose Selections" not yet available anywhere else. The 4.5-acre garden also includes footpaths, public art, fountains, and statues. In June the city's roses and its annual **ROSE FESTIVAL** (www.rosefestival.org) are in full bloom. This month-long extravaganza includes three parades—one is floral, natch—a riverfront carnival, and a rose show.

Portlanders flock to the banks of **TOM MCCALL WATERFRONT PARK**, on the west side of the Willamette River, for a run or stroll or to enjoy one of the city's many waterfront festivals. The waterfront is also the docking platform for the **PORTLAND SPIRIT** riverboat (503/226-2517; www.portlandspirit.com).

SOUTH WATERFRONT is Portland's newest, still-emerging neighborhood, showcasing sophisticated urban living in an inspired natural setting along the Willamette River. Incorporating green building practices, a variety of alternative modes of transportation, mixed-use retail, and green space, South Waterfront demonstrates Portland's vitality, progressive thinking, and commitment to livability. One of the area's key attractions is the Portland **AERIAL**

CONCERT HALL (corner of Main St and SW Broadway) and note the hall's 65-foot "Portland" marquee with its more than 6,000 theatrical lights. Turn back north and walk a couple of blocks to PIONEER COURTHOUSE SQUARE (SW Morrison St), the 40,000-square-foot plaza known as "PORTLAND'S LIVING ROOM." Check out the plaza sculptures and the architecture of PIONEER COURTHOUSE; built in 1875, it's the oldest federal building in the Pacific Northwest and the second oldest west of the Mississippi River. If it's a weekend, head west one block to stroll through the PORTLAND FARMERS MARKET (open Saturdays at North Park Blocks) or east five blocks to the outdoor crafts shopping extravaganza at PORTLAND SATURDAY MARKET (open Saturdays and Sundays). On weekdays, if you're up for walk, take the loop trail around the Willamette River from TOM MCCALL WATERFRONT PARK, stopping by the BAKERY BAR (1028 SE Water Ave; 503/546-8110) one block east of the EASTSIDE ESPLANADE for one the city's best sweet treats. Otherwise, head across the HAWTHORNE BRIDGE for some eclectic shopping in the laid-back HAWTHORNE DISTRICT or a hike around the extinct volcano that comprises MOUNT TABOR PARK (SE 60th Ave at SE Salmon St; 503/823-2223). For lunch, enjoy one of Portland's top burgers at CAFÉ CASTAGNA (1758 SE Hawthorne Blvd; 503/231-9959; next to Castagna Restaurant), then head to Laurelhurst Park (between SE Stark and Ankeny sts) and stroll around the park's pond under towering fir trees. On your way to dinner at KEN'S ARTISAN PIZZA and an art-house movie at the LAURELHURST THEATER (corner of SE Burnside Ave and SE 28th St), drive by the amazing gilded JOAN OF ARC statue in the NE 39th St and NE Glisan Avenue roundabout.

TRAM (503/494-8283; www.portlandtram.org), which travels 3,300 linear feet from South Waterfront over I-5, the Lair Hill neighborhood, and the SW Terwilliger Parkway to connect with Marquam Hill—also known locally as "Pill Hill." Workers and clients of Oregon Health Sciences University hospital, physician clinics, research labs, and medical and dental schools commute on the tram, while cyclists travel with their bikes on it to access the Sam Jackson Park road and Marquam Hill, where hiking and biking trails connect to the Hoyt Arboretum and Forest Park. The tram's cabins, which offer stunning views of the city and Mount Hood, depart approximately every five minutes daily and cost $4 round-trip. Biannually (typically in even years) in the South Waterfront, CIRQUE DU SOLEIL (www.cirquedusoleil.com) erects its exciting 2,600-seat big top, the GRAND CHAPITEAU (2750 SW Moody Ave) for Northwest debuts of many of their best sellers, like *Allegria*, *Varkai*, and *Corteo*.

The gentrified warehouse district known as the PEARL DISTRICT (between NW 9th and NW 15th aves and NW Burnside and NW Lovejoy sts) is the home of art galleries, hip upscale restaurants, and lots of shopping.

GALLERIES AND MUSEUMS

The **PORTLAND ART MUSEUM** (1219 SW Park Ave; 503/226-2811; www. portlandartmuseum.org) is the place to go for art exhibits with national acclaim. Other artsy options include picking up the "Public Art: Walking Tour" brochure at the visitor center at Pioneer Courthouse Square, visiting Pearl District destinations such as the Pacific Northwest College of Arts' **FELDMAN GALLERY** (1241 NW Johnson St; 503/226-4391) or the campy **3-D CENTER OF ART AND PHOTOGRAPHY** (1928 NW Lovejoy St; 503/227-6667; www.3dcenter.us), or taking part in the First Thursday or Last Thursday gallery walks.

PARKS AND GARDENS

Besides the semiwilderness of **FOREST PARK** (see Sports and Recreation), the West Hills are also home to **WASHINGTON PARK**, which includes the **HOYT ARBORETUM** (4000 SW Fairview Blvd; 503/865-8733; www.hoytarboretum. org). The arboretum visitor center offers maps of their native and exotic flora and pleasant hikes. Also in the park is the comprehensive collection of rose bushes and excellent views of the city at the **INTERNATIONAL ROSE TEST GARDEN** (see Major Attractions). Don't miss the serene **JAPANESE GARDEN** (503/223-1324; www.japanesegarden.com) across the street. Five formal garden styles are laid out on 5½ acres of photogenic serenity. The garden is especially beautiful in the fall, when the maple leaves turn brilliant red. A short drive up the hill is the **VIETNAM VETERANS' LIVING MEMORIAL**, an inspiring monument with an introspective garden featuring a wall engraved with the names of fallen Oregon soldiers.

Downtown you'll find the **CLASSICAL CHINESE GARDEN—THE GARDEN OF THE AWAKENING ORCHIDS** (NW Everett St and NW 3rd Ave; 503/228-8131; www.portlandchinesegarden.org), which offers insight into the world of urban Chinese flora and a place for quiet contemplation in the midst of city hustle and bustle. Guided tours are at noon and 1pm. Stop at the Tao of Tea within the garden; the upper level has the best views.

Tom McCall Waterfront Park is directly adjacent to the **VERA KATZ EASTBANK ESPLANADE**, which includes the nation's longest floating walkway (1,200 feet). Walking, biking, and in-line skating are popular ways to experience the 3-mile loop. The paved trail continues beyond SE Hawthorne Street, past OMSI and the Portland Opera building as the Springwater on the Willamette Trail, to **OAKS BOTTOM WILDLIFE REFUGE**, a rare urban sanctuary for ospreys, eagles, and great blue herons. Here, the pavement gives way to a dirt trail around the seasonal lakes at Oaks Bottom and continues beyond to the old railroad bed that was converted into the **SPRINGWATER CORRIDOR TRAIL** in Sellwood 17 miles out to the city of Boring.

SHOPPING

Portland possesses a plethora of unique shops downtown, in the Pearl and Northwest districts, and in many outlying neighborhoods' business districts.

Nike Headquarters may be in Beaverton, but their flagship **NIKETOWN** (SW 6th and Salmon sts; 503/221-6453) is downtown. The **COLUMBIA SPORTSWEAR** flagship store (911 SW Broadway; 503/226-6800), also known as "the Mother of All Stores," is located in the historic 1898 United Carriage Company building. The **PIONEER PLACE MALL** (700 SW 5th Ave) houses three square blocks of retail therapy, a better-than-average food court, and a movie theater. The largest longest-running open-air market for handcrafted goods in the United States, **SATURDAY MARKET** (10am–5pm Sat–Sun, closed Jan–Feb), is just under the Burnside Bridge near Skidmore Fountain in Portland's Old Town district on the west side of the Willamette River. In addition to hundreds of local artisans selling goods and arts, you'll find food and free live music.

The **PEARL DISTRICT** is home to another Portland icon, **POWELL'S CITY OF BOOKS** (1005 W Burnside Ave; 503/228-4651; www.powells.com), the main store all of 77,000 square feet, with satellites throughout the city. Gourmet cooks will love **SUR LA TABLE** (1102 NW Couch St; 503/295-9679) and **IN GOOD TASTE** (231 NW 11th Ave; 503/248-2015). The trendy **NW 23RD STREET** neighborhood, reachable by streetcar, is a shopper's paradise with major upscale chains like **POTTERY BARN** (310 NW 23rd; 503/525-0280), locally made **MOONSTRUCK CHOCOLATES** (526 NW 23rd; 503/542-3400), and oodles of charming clothing boutiques like the **ENGLISH DEPARTMENT** (1124 SW Alder St; 503/224-0724).

SE HAWTHORNE BOULEVARD has a laid-back, bohemian feel and offers some of the city's most distinctive shopping. Belmont Street, just to the north, continues the Hawthorne vibe with secondhand, music, and retro-oriented shops. Jewelry and antiques are sold at the **GOLD DOOR** (1434 SE 37th Ave; 503/232-6069), while cookbook fans love **POWELL'S BOOKS FOR HOME AND GARDEN** (3747 SE Hawthorne Blvd; 503/235-3802). Shoe lovers find heaven at **IMELDA'S SHOES** (3426 SE Hawthorne Blvd; 503/233-7476), and kids love the fascinating **KIDS AT HEART** (3445 SE Hawthorne Blvd; 503/231-2954) toy store.

The **DIVISION-CLINTON** neighborhood was once considered part of the Hawthorne District but has emerged with its own identity, particularly as a food destination. The majority of its commerce occurs along SE Clinton and SE Division Street from SE 25th Street to SE 36th Avenue. Buy the world's best motorcycle leathers—or get yours repaired—at **LANGLITZ LEATHERS** (2443 SE Division St; 503/235-0959), where the motorcycle jacket was literally first designed and produced in 1947. **URBAN FLORA PLANT OASIS** (3029 SE Division St; 503/236-3344) offers cut flowers, exotic plants, cacti, ornamentals, and gifts.

SELLWOOD in far southeast is one of the city's oldest and, at one time, most popular neighborhood—before gentrification reclaimed grittier neighborhoods. It's a vibrant, friendly place where people hang out at the coffee shops on the weekend and couples push strollers and walk their dogs to the area's two big parks: **WESTMORELAND** and the unparalleled wilderness in the city, **OAKS BOTTOM WILDLIFE REFUGE**. Sellwood-Westmoreland offers an eclectic mix of galleries, art studios, antiques, and boutiques.

The **ALBERTA ARTS DISTRICT** is located along NE Alberta Street in the Vernon, Concordia, and King neighborhoods. Indie shops rule here. **MABEL AND ZORA** (1468 NE Alberta St; 503/335-6169) showcases local designers, including Woolie Originals, Kiersten Crowley jewelry, Kicklit Kreations, Ida Green handbags, Paige Saez designs, and Amy Olson jewelry designs. Next door at **COLLAGE** and the **DIY LOUNGE** (1639 NE Alberta St; 503/249-2190), buy art supplies and try your hand at creative business, arts, and crafts classes taught by local experts, led by the woman who kick-started Portland's DIY movement, Jen Neitzel.

The area called the **NORTHWEST DISTRICT**—also dubbed **NOB HILL** and Trendy-first (or third) Avenue—shares some similarity with San Francisco's Haight Street. Turn-of-the-20th-century Victorians stand shoulder to shoulder on narrow alphabet streets intersecting the main avenues. Bookstores are pressed between quirky shops purveying gifts, kitchenware, bed and bath furnishings, and clothing. The shopping area—connected to downtown with a streetcar line—is bordered on the south by West Burnside Avenue and on the north by NW Thurman Street, from 21st to 23rd avenues.

NEW RENAISSANCE BOOK SHOP (1338 NW 23rd Ave; 503/224-4929) is Portland's largest metaphysical book and gift store. Pick up artisan bread and authentic French pastries at **ST. HONORÉ BOULANGERIE** (2335 NW Thurman St; 503/445-4342).

PERFORMING ARTS

Portlanders come to the **ARLENE SCHNITZER CONCERT HALL** (1037 SW Broadway) 52 weeks a year for concerts, lectures, and comedy performances; tickets are across the street at the **PORTLAND CENTER FOR THE PERFORM-ING ARTS**, or PCPA (1111 SW Broadway; www.pcpa.com), or from **TICKETS-WEST** (503/224-8499; www.ticketswest.com). The **OREGON SYMPHONY ORCHESTRA** (503/228-1353; www.orsymphony.org) performs regularly at "the Schnitz." Classical music fans appreciate the events put on by **CHAMBER MUSIC NORTHWEST** (503/294-6400; www.cmnw.org) at various venues.

The PCPA also has a resident theater company, **PORTLAND CENTER STAGE** (www.pcs.org), located in the **GERDING THEATER AT THE ARMORY** (128 NW 11th Ave; 503/445-3700). Opened in 2004, the facility houses a world-class 599-seat main-stage theater, a smaller 200-seat black-box theater, a rehearsal hall, production facilities, and a café. Gerding Theater (in the historic Portland Armory) has the distinction of being the first historic rehabilitation on the National Historic Register and the first performing arts venue to achieve a LEED (Leadership in Energy and Environmental Design) Platinum rating for efficient use of energy, water, and building materials to reduce operating expenses and the building's impact on the environment.

The **ARTISTS REPERTORY THEATER** (1515 SW Morrison St; 503/241-1278; www.artistsrep.org) garners lavish critical praise for their intimate "theater on the edge."

The **KELLER AUDITORIUM** (222 SW Clay St) hosts the **OREGON BALLET THEATER** (503/222-5538; www.obt.org) and musicals throughout the year.

Contemporary arts fans are energetically served by the performances and exhibitions of **PICA**, the Portland Institute of Contemporary Art (503/242-1419; www.pica.org), including its 10-day Time-Based Arts Festival.

FOOD AND WINE

Part of Portland's status as a stellar dining destination can be attributed to the local and regional farmers, ranchers, and fishers committed to bringing sustainable foods to the market. Equal credit goes to the interest, creativity, skill, and willingness of so many chefs to support these local suppliers by integrating these foods into their menus.

But the Oregon wine industry deserves a lot of the credit. Whether wine curious or wine connoisseur, many visitors who come to check out Oregon's world-class wine scene at its epicenter in the Willamette Valley, less than an hour west of Portland, also visit city restaurants to enjoy elite Portland farm-to-table and sea-to-table meals. Many of these meals are paired with the state's unrivalled pinot noirs and other notable wines, bringing the wine buzz effect full circle.

Winemaker and wine pairing dinners at some of the top restaurants have also helped educate palates and increase wine and culinary acumen. Some of the more interesting of these dinners take place at the **HEATHMAN**, **CASTAGNA**, and **PALEY'S PLACE** (see reviews). The Heathman's ongoing **DUELING SOMMELIER DINNER SERIES** pairs sommeliers and guest chefs with diners who vote for which mystery wine best pairs with each course.

The **BITE OF OREGON** (503/248-0600; www.biteoforegon.com), held at Waterfront Park, showcases more than two dozen Oregon restaurants, along with local wine and craft beer. The **INDIE WINE FESTIVAL**, held at Urban Wineworks and Chown Garage (on NW 16th and 17th aves, between Flanders and Everett sts; 503/827-6564; www.indiewinefestival.com) brings 40 small independent wine producers into the city to meet wine aficionados at an exciting two-day wine tasting event.

Even though wine is highly revered in Oregon, beer gets a fair share of affection. While the city has 36 microbreweries in the metropolitan area, more than any other city in the nation, it's the **OREGON BREWERS FESTIVAL**, on the waterfront in July (503/778-5917; www.oregonbrewfest.com), that gets the most buzz. Considered the world's premier craft beer event, the four-day annual festival draws about 73 breweries and 60,000 brew fans.

SPORTS AND RECREATION

Catch the NBA's **PORTLAND TRAIL BLAZERS** (503/797-9600; www.nba.com/blazers) and the Western Hockey League's youthful **PORTLAND WINTER HAWKS** hockey team (Ticketmaster: 503/224-4400; www.winterhawks.com) at the huge, domed **ROSE GARDEN ARENA** (One Center Ct; 503/797-9600). Triple-A **PORTLAND BEAVERS** play at **PGE PARK** (1844 SW Morrison St; 503/553-5400; www.pgepark.com). The United Soccer League's **PORTLAND TIMBERS** (503/553-5400; www.portlandtimbers.com) also play here to energetic, loyal crowds.

Individual sports thrive in Portland too: runners, hikers, and mountain bikers have access to more than 50 miles of trails in the 5,100 acres of **FOREST PARK** (www.portlandonline.com/parks), with trailheads easily accessed throughout the West Hills. **POWELL BUTTE** (503/823-1616 for daily access status), in far southeast Portland, is a 608-acre extinct cinder cone volcano that rises above the headwaters of Johnson Creek—an urban stream with remnant populations of native salmon and steelhead—and a portion of the **SPRINGWATER CORRIDOR TRAIL**. Trailheads, at 148th and Center sts, and 162nd and Powell sts, take hikers, runners, and mountain bikers to a huge meadow offering knockout views of area peaks. Birders and naturalists head to the trails around the **AUDUBON SOCIETY OF PORTLAND** (5151 NW Cornell Rd; 503/292-9453; www.audubonportland.org), while rowers are guaranteed miles of flatwater on the Willamette.

Portland is the only major city in the country to receive the Platinum Award for cycling, the highest rating by the League of American Bicyclists. The city boasts the highest percentage of bike commuters of any large city in the country, according to the U.S. Census Bureau. Part of the reason is designated bike lanes, as well as an active bicycling citizenry and love of the sport. Cycling has surpassed running as the top sport in the city. One of the most popular mass bicycle events in the city is the **PROVIDENCE BRIDGE PEDAL** (503/281-9198; www.providence.org/bridgepedal), which annually attracts more than 10,000 cyclists, who come to ride over the city's Willamette River bridges. The **NIGHT RIDE** (503/459 4508; www.thenightride.com) is a 15-mile event that attracts more than 2,000 cyclists who circumnavigate the city on closed streets and back roads.

NIGHTLIFE

Check the calendar listings in Portland's two free weekly papers, the *Willamette Week* and the *Portland Mercury*, for club and music goings-on. National acts play the **ALADDIN THEATER** (3017 SE Milwaukie Ave; 503/233-1994), **MCMENAMIN'S CRYSTAL BALLROOM** (1332 W Burnside St; 503/225-0047), and the **ROSELAND THEATER** (8 NW 6th Ave; 503/224-2038).

The minimalist-chic club **HOLOCENE** (1001 SE Morrison St; 503/239-7639) hosts electronica DJs and theme dance parties. Indie rockers flock to the retro–ski lodge interior of **DOUG FIR** (830 E Burnside St; 503/231-9663) for live music and a happening lounge scene; discounted rooms are offered after midnight at the adjacent Jupiter Hotel if you party too hard. And **MISSISSIPPI STUDIOS** (3939 N Mississippi Ave; 503/288-3895) hosts grassroots performances by folk and rock acts in an intimate theater setting.

The locally produced *BarFly* is a free listing of Portland's bars; you can find it online (503/813-9999; www.barflymag.com).

RESTAURANTS

Alberta Street Oyster Bar & Grill / ★★

2926 NE ALBERTA ST, PORTLAND; 503/284-9600

This handsome bistro's storefront windows give diners a glimpse of the action out on Alberta Street. Its masculine feel—black chairs and banquettes—combines with glowy red pendant lighting to anchor the focus inside. While oysters get the headlines (seven or eight on the daily fresh list), the menu leans toward locally grown ingredients and French-Italian techniques: pan-roasted black cod paired with marrow bean, wild arugula, fennel, green olives, and preserved Meyer lemon; English pea risotto spiked with tiny cipolline onions, truffle butter, pea shoots, and Parmesan. If the burnt caramel custard with smoked salt pretzel and candied orange is on the menu, save room for it. You'll find some eclectic wine picks, but the house cocktails absolutely rock. *$$–$$$; AE, DIS, MC, V; no checks; dinner Wed–Sun; full bar; reservations recommended; www.albertaoyster.com; at NE 29th.* &

Andina / ★★★

1314 NW GLISAN ST, PORTLAND; 503/228-9535

At one of Portland's most alluring restaurants, the warm terra-cotta color scheme, the *nuevo* Peruvian menu, the knowledgeable staff, the affable owner, and the lively Latin music in the bar combine to create an energy that's simply magnetic. After you make your way through small-plate appetizers like citrus-marinated seafood ceviche and potato-smoked trout *causa*, dive into entrées like lamb shank with salsa criolla and quinoa-crusted scallops with passion-fruit reduction. Cozy and colorful Bar Mestizo next door is great for drinks and small plates. Don't leave without indulging in the Peruvian national drink—the tart, mind-blowing Pisco Sour—or the ever-so-popular Sacsayhuamán (pronounced "sexy woman")—habanero pepper–infused vodka with passion fruit purée, topped with a cilantro sprig. Everything at Andina is tasty and exhilarating. *$$–$$$; AE, DIS, MC, V; no checks; lunch, dinner every day; full bar; reservations recommended; www.andinarestaurant. com; at NW 13th.* &

Aquariva / ★★

470 SW HAMILTON CT, PORTLAND; 503/802-5850

The floor-to-ceiling windows in the lower level of the dining room offer serene through-the-trees views of the Willamette River; stunning art glass frames overhead lighting. Only seven minutes by car from downtown, the restaurant has complimentary valet service that offers a pleasant escape from parking hassles. The kitchen, under chef Drew Lockett's direction, issues Italian-inspired small and sharable plates like tart-fried artichokes with tangy aioli, pan-seared Pacific black cod with earthy Oregon truffles, and an arugula salad laced with salt-cod crostini. Other good bets include crispy fried polenta or house-made gnocchi or pasta tossed in white truffle oil, tomato-basil fonduta, and morels. The wine list's straightforward and rotating selections

13

are seasonally appropriate and chosen to complement Lockett's ever-changing farm-to-table fare. *$$$–$$$$; AE, DIS, MC, V; local checks only; lunch Mon–Fri, dinner every day, brunch Sun; full bar; reservations recommended; www.aquarivaportland.com; end of SW Hamilton Ct.* &

Bay 13 Restaurant / ★★

701 NW 13TH ST, PORTLAND; 503/227-1133

Located in the historic 1909 Crane Warehouse building in Portland's Pearl District, this restaurant has a lot going for it. Unfortunately, enough Portlanders have a huge aversion to anything corporate that it hasn't been a big hit like other Pearl-area restaurants. The sleek, minimalist space, with warm walnut banquettes and a zinc bar, and its mission to serve only fish from sustainable sources are appealing. The Oyster Bar offers a daily selection of fresh shellfish; the Crudo Bar includes ceviche, *hamachi*, and ahi *poke*. The beet and pickled apple salad with chèvre, the asparagus and nettle risotto, the black cod, and the braised short ribs are all excellent alternatives to oysters and raw dishes. A list of tasty creative cocktails rounds out the mostly regional wine list. *$$–$$$; AE, DIS, MC, V; no checks; dinner every day; full bar; reservations recommended; www.bay13restaurant.com; corner of NW Johnson St.*

Biwa / ★★

215 SE 9TH AVE, PORTLAND; 503/239-8830

Step down into this tiny subterranean noodle house for Portland's version of Japanese bar food, and while you wait—and you will—check out the linear art gallery to your right. Once seated, dive into near-perfect house-made ramen noodles in savory broth or succulent yakitori meat skewers. Udon noodles, made fresh and hand-cut daily, are also masterful. You'll also discover a few Korean-inspired bites on the menu as well, including vegetable *chijimi* (a savory, onion-riddled pancake) and piquant kimchee. Other top choices include miso soup, pork-filled *gyoza* dumplings, and a curry rice concoction that sings with flavor. Ask the knowledgeable waitstaff for advice on their extensive sake menu. *$$; AE, MC, V; local checks only; dinner Mon–Sat; full bar; reservations recommended for 6 or more; www.biwarestaurant.com; corner of SE 9th and SE Ash.*

Bluehour / ★★★★

250 NW 13TH AVE, PORTLAND; 503/226-3394

If dining at expensive, ultramodern restaurants sounds intimidating, you're in for a surprising welcome at Bluehour. The gracious waitstaff greets and seats each guest with an unpretentious friendliness. Just baked, irresistibly fragrant hot rolls arrive immediately to assuage hunger while you peruse the menu. Choose chef Kenny Giambalvo's recommended dinner menu—salad, entrée, a selection from the decadent cheese menu, and dessert—meticulously crafted around Oregon fresh seafood and a handful of exceptional wines by the glass. It's all absolutely ambrosial: the seared sea scallops wrapped with smoked bacon; tender, buttery bites of pan-roasted quail paired with deeply satisfying sweet and tart warm rhubarb galette. Alternatively, experience a bit of luxury with a sumptuous burger and a signature Bluehour cocktail in the bar. *$$$–$$$$; AE, DIS, MC, V; no checks; lunch Mon–Sat, dinner every day, brunch Sun; full bar; reservations recommended; www.bluehouronline. com; at NW Everett.* &

Caffé Mingo / ★★★

807 NW 21ST AVE, PORTLAND; 503/226-4646
At this small trattoria, you're likely to share a large, rustic table with locals digging into huge plates of *caprese* or bread-and-tomato *panzanella* salad, homemade pastas tossed with rich Chianti-braised beef ragù, or polpettone— and Italian style meat loaf served with mashed potatoes and carmelized onion sauce. The tiramisu here is the city's dreamiest version; the all-Italian wine list is foolproof. The restaurant recently expanded into the space next door with a dedicated bar: Bar Mingo (503/456-4646). Waiting diners can now tuck into small bites from a new antipasto menu or dine on small plates in the bar while sipping cocktails. *$$; AE, DIS, MC, V; no checks; dinner every day; beer and wine; reservations recommended for 6 or more; www.caffemingonw.com; between NW Johnson and NW Kearny sts.* &

Carafe / ★★★

200 SW MARKET ST, PORTLAND; 503/248-0004
This Parisian-style bistro is a favorite with theatergoers and politicos alike (there's little chance of getting a table on nights there's a show across the street at the Keller Auditorium). The small dining room with tin ceiling and red leather booths is absolutely charming, despite its location in the ground floor of an office building. Paris native chef Pascal Sauton makes authentic French food accessible, with delicious versions of classics like foie gras terrine, cassoulet, and excellent steak *frites*. The wine list is extensive, and—as the restaurant's name implies—some options are available by the carafe and half carafe. *$$; AE, DIS, MC, V; no checks; lunch Mon–Fri, dinner Mon–Sat; full bar; reservations recommended; www.carafebistro.com; at SW 2nd Ave.* &

Carlyle / ★★★

1632 NW THURMAN ST, PORTLAND; 503/595-1782
Tucked into the far west end of the Pearl District, this sleek, upscale restaurant's location adds to its intrigue and appeal. The dining room is elegant and serene, while the chic, lively bar delivers snappy cocktails and reasonably priced bar food. Both venues indulge, with exquisite food and excellent service. Local, seasonal produce and specialty meats are prepared with layers of complementary flavors and textures. Try the crunchy butter lettuce salad spiked with piquant blue cheese, salt and pepper walnuts, and crisped parma ham; lightly seared tuna on a savory *maitake* mushroom–pearl onion bed; or moist and tender pistachio-encrusted venison fillet paired with banana-maple sweet potato purée, fresh herbs, and a swirl of sweet-and-sour blackberry

gastrique. Top it all off with molten chocolate cake from the creative dessert menu. *$$$; AE, DIS, MC, V; no checks; dinner every day; full bar; reservations recommended; www.carlylerestaurant.com; under I-405 at NW 16th.*

Castagna / ★★★★
Café Castagna / ★★

1752 SE HAWTHORNE BLVD, PORTLAND; 503/231-7373
1758 SE HAWTHORNE BLVD, PORTLAND; 503/231-9959

This ultraminimalist, serene dining room helps steer your focus to the plate and your companion(s). Aided by some of the best service in Portland, the kitchen consistently delivers super fresh, locally sourced seasonal dishes with strong Mediterranean influence: fresh pasta with Dungeness crab and Meyer lemon, perfectly seared scallops with asparagus, or semolina gnocchi with artichokes and chanterelles. Desserts, like the nearly perfect wine list—depth and breadth, with French, Italian, and Northwest bottles and by-the-glass—are flavor forward instead of cloyingly sweet. Convivial Café Castagna next door offers a counterpoint to the steadied ambience of the mother ship, with a bistro-style menu of salads, pastas, seasonal pizzas, and one of the city's top burgers: a thick, hefty patty of ground chuck between a house-baked sesame bun—served with perfect crispy fries. *$$–$$$; $$; AE, DIS, MC, V; local checks only; dinner Wed–Sat (Castagna), dinner every day (Café Castagna); full bar; reservations recommended; www.castagnarestaurant.com; at SE 17th Ave. &*

Clarklewis / ★★★½

1001 SE WATER AVE, PORTLAND; 503/235-2294

Set in a sophisticated industrial space in the heart of Portland's commercial east side, clarklewis feels like a modern refuge. Hearty dishes from the wood-fired hearth and rotisserie complement the fresh, locally sourced ingredients. Start your meal with the Cortez Bay scallop ceviche and a fresh and invigorating salad like the Rogue Creamery blue cheese terrine with glazed walnuts on a bed of red oak leaf lettuce dressed with Bing cherry–and–port vinaigrette. Pasta dishes feature creative blends, like orecchiette with green beans, gold potatoes, and pesto. Seasonal main courses include Pacific halibut wrapped in pancetta and spit-roasted local chicken with Mulino Marino polenta. *$$–$$$; AE, MC, V; no checks; dinner Tues–Sat; full bar; reservations recommended; www.clarklewispdx.com; at SE Yamhill St. &*

Clyde Common / ★★★

1014 SW STARK ST, PORTLAND; 503/228-3333

If the two-tops (foodie-speak meaning "tables for two") on the mezzanine level are filled, head to the zinc-topped bar, or buck up and graciously accept a seat at the communal table. Chances are, Clyde's magnetic energy will quickly seduce you. From an open kitchen in a stylish, refurbed industrial space, adept chefs prepare an innovative, ever-changing menu of European and *nuevo* American dishes. Start with salt cod croquettes, marinated olives, or a sideboard of sardines with a vodka chaser before moving on to creative salads, tender braised pork, or pasta dishes with accentuated, rather than smothered, flavors. The cocktails are among the best in the city—with a bar scene to match. There's also a short list of good wines and microbrews to round out the sumptuous menu printed on faux lined notepaper. *$$; AE, DIS, MC, V; no checks; lunch Mon–Fri, dinner every day; full bar; reservations recommended for 6 or more; www.clydecommon.com; corner of SW 10th and Stark.* &

East India Grill / ★★★

821 SW 11TH AVE, PORTLAND; 503/227-8815

Never before has an Indian restaurant in Portland put all of the elements into place to such great effect. Careful attention has been paid to every element—from the restaurant's inspired romantic interior with its beautiful lighting and dramatic stained-glass mandala in the ceiling to the impeccable service and authentic classic Indian cuisine with a contemporary flair. You'll recognize many of the dishes by name, but most are elevated by uncanny freshness, innovative combinations, and stunning presentation. From the perfectly paper-thin pappadams and savory garlic *kulcha* (a sumptuous naan) to the *saag paneer*—roasted homemade cheese spiking the spiced spinach—to the *tandoori murg*—chicken marinated in thick yogurt, spices, and Kashmiri cayenne—East India Grill feels like a magnificent culinary journey. Ask the in-the-know waitstaff to recommend a beverage pairing. *$$; AE, DIS, MC, V; checks OK; lunch, dinner every day; full bar; reservations recommended; www. eastindiacopdx.com; between SW Taylor and SW Yamhill.*

El Gaucho / ★★

319 SW BROADWAY (BENSON HOTEL), PORTLAND; 503/227-8794

The dining room here is the very picture of an elegant steak house, with huge velveteen chairs, tableside preparations of caesar salad, and expense-account prices. No surprises here; just American classics like oysters Rockefeller, meaty crab cakes, and grain-fed dry-aged steaks. The signature Gaucho Steak, an 8-ounce sirloin with a lobster tail and béarnaise sauce, is the ultimate artery clogger. A great bar menu, live jazz, and a cigar room draw the suit-and-tie crowd to the bar. *$$$; AE, DC, MC, V; no checks; dinner every day; full bar; reservations recommended; www.elgaucho.com; at SW Washington St.* &

Fenouil / ★★★

900 NW 11TH AVE, PORTLAND; 503/525-2225

The two-level dining room with stone accents, fireplaces, and floor-to-ceiling glass windows overlooking Jamison Square conjures images of a posh French brasserie. Tuck into butter lettuce, manchego, and hearts of palm, or lobster beignets with an anise-infused pastis aioli. For dinner, try seared scallops with smoked bacon stacked on a green pillow of mashed leeks, or the morel mushroom risotto with garlic confit, micro arugula, and fresh-shaved Oregon white truffles. Must-try accompaniments include *pommes frites* with a splash of truffle oil or au gratin potatoes with blue cheese, and crème brûlée to finish. Local ingredients and hints of fennel are pretty much the standard here. A short but sweet list of wines from Italy, France, and the Northwest are available by the glass, more by the bottle. *$$$; AE, DIS, MC, V; no checks; lunch, dinner Mon–Sat, brunch Sun; full bar; reservations recommended; www. fenouilinthepearl.com; corner of 11th and Kearney.* &

Fife / ★★

4440 NE FREMONT ST, PORTLAND; 971/222-3433

The open dining room awash in woodsy neutral colors and warm lighting lends a convivial feel to this neighborhood eatery, though its popularity means the decibel level is frequently high. The cooking is straightforward, modern American fare. The menu changes daily, with exceptional dishes like heirloom-carrot bisque, crisp-skinned free-range chicken cooked in a cast-iron skillet, and grilled hanger steak. Vegetable lovers may want to order side dishes—the entrées are often devoid of extras. Don't miss the desserts; the Chocolate Four Ways dessert plate is among one of the many sweet ways to indulge. *$$–$$$; DIS, MC, V; no checks; dinner Tues–Sat; full bar; reservations recommended; www.fiferestaurant.com; at NE 44th Ave.* &

Fratelli Cucina / Bar Dué / ★★★

1230 NW HOYT ST, PORTLAND; 503/241-8800

Fratelli took a chance on the Pearl District before anyone else and ignited a dining revolution. Reminiscent of the numerous tiny *cucinas* tucked into narrow streets in Italy, the eatery has a deceptive entrance: follow a long passage to the door near the kitchen to the rear of the dining room. Sparse furnishings and candlelight infuse a romantic air. The Venetian-inspired menu takes a traditional four-course approach with mains that include oven-baked risotto, fish specials, beef, and chicken and lamb dishes. Fratelli was also one of the first to work with local farmers, which means excellent vegetarian options. Service here is smart, the mostly Italian wine list excellent, and the location unbeatable. The accompanying Bar Dué offers terrific happy hour options. *$$; AE, DC, MC, V; no checks; dinner Tues–Sun; beer and wine; reservations recommended; www. fratellicucina.com; midblock, south side of street between 11th and 12th.* &

Gracie's / ★★★

729 SW 15TH AVE (HOTEL DELUXE), PORTLAND; 503/222-2171

Like the hotel it's located in, this beautiful dining room pays homage to Hollywood's golden era. You half expect to see George Clooney and the gang from *Ocean's 11* waltzing past the flowing drapes to one of the quilted leather banquettes. But the food is definitely the star attraction. The menu offers knockout pairings of ultrafresh ingredients and unadulterated flavors. Small plates on the seasonally changing menu include saffron mussels and clams, and creamy fava bean risotto. Show-stopping entrées include the shrimp and fontina gnocchi, the hanger steak with oven-roasted beets, or seared Alaskan halibut with a chowder-style sauce of steamed clams. The *pot de crème* is just one of the fine desserts you'll encounter, along with a short but excellent wine pairing list. *$$–$$$; AE, DIS, MC, V; checks OK; breakfast, lunch, dinner every day; full bar; reservations recommended; www.graciesdining.com; between SW Morrison and SW Yamhill sts.*

The Heathman Restaurant and Bar / ★★★☆

1001 SW BROADWAY, PORTLAND; 503/790-7752

This formal dining room, decorated with cream-colored marble and luxurious fabrics, has been the center of Portland power lunches and presymphony suppers for decades. At the helm is Philippe Boulot, a James Beard Best Chef in the Pacific Northwest award winner (among many other international honors). Combining seasonal and regional ingredients with classic French techniques results in small plates of rustic pork pâté with pistachios and Roquefort; the best onion soup this side of France; and curried crab cakes. For dinner, try bouillabaisse of regional seafood, Oregon black truffle, and king crab leg risotto; or elk chops. The voluminous wine list could keep an avid oenophile riveted for hours. Afternoon tea is served daily in the opulent Tea Court, with its marble fireplace and Austrian-cut crystal chandelier. *$$$–$$$$; AE, DC, DIS, MC, V; checks OK; breakfast, lunch, dinner every day; full bar; reservations recommended; www.heathmanrestaurantandbar.com; at SW Salmon St.* &

Higgins / ★★

1239 SW BROADWAY, PORTLAND; 503/222-9070

Pioneering chef Greg Higgins has been an outspoken advocate for organic and sustainable food production since the opening of his upscale restaurant in 1994. He continues to garner a loyal following for cooking that is the very picture of Pacific Northwest cuisine. The menu, which changes weekly, may include a generous house-made charcuterie plate, local mussels in garlic broth, and local albacore tuna with Meyer-lemon marmalade. The casual bar features excellent burgers and a legendary beer menu. *$$$; AE, DC, DIS, MC, V; local checks only; lunch Mon–Fri, dinner every day; full bar; reservations recommended; www.higgins.citysearch.com; at SE Jefferson St.* &

Ken's Artisan Pizza / ★★★

304 SE 28TH AVE, PORTLAND; 503/517-9951

Diners seem happy to stand in line sipping wine for up to an hour to score a table in the combined kitchen–dining room of this artisan pizza outpost of Ken's Artisan Bakery. The eatery has a Northwest brew-pub feel with recycled old-growth Douglas fir tables, some of them large farmhouse–communal style. Starters and salads are fresh and seasonal, from a zesty full-leaf caesar, plates of roasted veggies, and prosciutto. The large clay wood-fired oven cranks out pizzas (11 to chose from) that have a crackly yet chewy crust with just enough char to impart a wood-fired flavor. Top picks include fennel sausage with onion, the Margherita, and spicy *soppressata*. The small wine list, excellent brews, and trio of gelato/sorbetto—cherry, vanilla, raspberry—make dining here worth the wait. *$; MC, V; no checks; dinner Tues–Sat; beer and wine; no reservations; www.kensartisan.com/pizza.html; at NE Pine St.* &

Lauro Kitchen / ★★★

3377 SE DIVISION ST, PORTLAND; 503/239-7000

Chef-owner David Machado brings a magic touch to all his dining ventures. Lauro (like Vindahlo) are coveted by neighborhood diners, though foodies come from across the city to partake of the meals. Lauro is the go-to place for deep and, more recently, far-reaching Mediterranean cuisines, including flavors from Spain, Portugal, Morocco, and Lebanon. But there are also burgers and wonderful, crackly wood-fire-oven pizzas. The kitchen's standout, however, is a chicken *tagine*—with green olives, fennel, house-preserved lemons, and almond couscous—like none other. The same goes for the Portuguese port flan. Excellent affordable house wine and a short list of other wines—plus a list of crafty cocktails—adds up to a neighborhood legacy. *$$; AE, DC, DIS, MC, V; no checks; lunch, dinner Tues–Sat; full bar; reservations recommended; www.laurokitchen.com; SE corner of 34th and Division St.* &

Le Pigeon / ★★

738 E BURNSIDE ST, PORTLAND; 503/546-8796

This tiny French-influenced bistro on Lower Burnside elicits strong feelings from Portlanders, sometimes in the same circle. Some hate its communal dining, while others—the vegetarian-leaning crowd—are put off by the wild game meat, foie gras, and offal-centric menu. Meat eaters love the place, for good reason. The laid-back ambience is an interesting counterpoint to the culinary risk taking. Chef Gabe Rucker elevates beef bourguignon and seared flatiron steak to the heavens. But he also has a way with polarized elements like seasonal fruit and rich fats: apricot corn bread topped with maple ice cream and bacon bits; cherry tart with marrow and balsamic vinegar; earthy foie terrine with truffled apricots. Pork tongue dishes and the foie gras peanut butter–and–jelly sandwich are harder to fathom. *$$$; MC, V; no checks; dinner every day; full bar; reservations recommended; www.lepigeon.com; north side of Burnside between SE 7th and SE 8th sts.* &

Lovely Hula Hands / ★★

4057 N MISSISSIPPI AVE, PORTLAND; 503/445-9910

This is without a doubt one of the top dining spots in NoPo. Starters like Sauvie Island organic greens with fried chickpeas, cardoons, and manchego demonstrate the way this innovative kitchen handles standard and seasonal ingredients. Buttermilk fried chicken gets a chile oil treatment with a baby turnip, roasted cauliflower, rapini, and chickpea ragout. Grilled Strawberry Mountain rib eye is paired with sweet cherry tomato salsa and fried green tomatoes. The burger is a half pound of ground chuck with caramelized onion served on a brioche bun. The wine list is fairly deep in French and Italian picks, with a few excellent regional varietals thrown in for comfort. Save room for the nut and rosemary tart with candied kumquats. *$$; MC, V; no checks; dinner Tues–Sun; full bar; no reservations; www.lovelyhulahands.com; between N Mason and N Shaver sts.* &

Lucy's Table / ★★★

704 NW 21ST AVE, PORTLAND; 503/226-6126

This intimate dining room's rich palette of colors and big storefront windows make it feel big. The menu changes to reflect seasonal availability, but some intriguing combos you're likely to encounter include pomegranate-glazed baby-back pork ribs and wild-boar ravioli; oven-roasted chicken breast stuffed with prosciutto and *taleggio*; and wild mushroom and sweet pea risotto with camembert cheese and earthy truffle oil finish. It's all incredibly delectable. Menu standards (nearly always available) include goat cheese ravioli with crispy shallots and pancetta; roasted red beet and pear salad; and braised rabbit with crispy polenta. Save room for the flourless chocolate cake; it's worth every calorie spent. The wine list includes a deep and broad selection from Europe, South America, and Australia, with some excellent regional picks as well. *$$; AE, DC, MC, V; checks OK; dinner Mon–Sat; full bar; reservations recommended; www.lucystable.com; corner of NW 21st Ave and NW Irving St.*

McCormick & Schmicks / ★★★

235 SW 1ST AVE, PORTLAND; 503/224-7522

The founding first location of this corporate chain, this is the one that set the standard high. Located in a historic landmark building, it has a sophisticated, clubby feel that makes it perfect for power lunches, romantic dinners, and happy hour. In addition to tables, there are high-back booths—some partially enclosed—draped with white linens. The seasonally inspired menu is largely anchored in Northwest waters, but when it's not, it's duly noted on the daily fresh sheet. Good bets: oysters on the half shell; seared yellowfin tuna with wasabi, soy, and ginger; Dungeness crab cakes; and cedar plank–roasted salmon. At happy hour, hunker down in the art deco–era bar for the best classic cocktails in the city (the Blood and Sand is stunning) and low-priced pub food. *$$–$$$; AE, DIS, MC, V; checks OK; lunch, dinner every day; full bar; reservations recommended; www.mccormickandschmicks.com; between SW Pine and SW Oak sts.* &

Nostrana / ★★★

1401 SE MORRISON ST, PORTLAND; 503/234-2427

Soaring ceilings and stylish accents give this dining room a modern feel, but it's the ultrafresh (and mostly local, organic) food that is the real standout. You can't go wrong with any of the Italian-leaning menu regulars: Nostrana salad—radicchio spiked with Parmigiano-Reggiano, rosemary, and sage croutons in a caesar-style dressing; the charcuterie plate with chicken liver pâté and spicy onion relish on huge hunks of bruschetta; the wood-fired Margherita pizza piled high with fresh, snappy arugula; or the artisan cheese plate with homemade walnut bread and a fig "salami." Pastas and grilled seafood and meats round out the entrée selections, though servings of some items are small-plate sized. The excellent wine list encompasses most Italian regions, with a few picks from Oregon. *$$–$$$; AE, MC, V; checks OK; lunch Mon–Fri, dinner every day; full bar; reservations recommended; www.nostrana.com.* &

PORTLAND NEIGHBORHOOD TOUR DE FOODIE

Portland's evolving culinary scene is at its most creative out in the neighborhoods. Here are four to venture into to enjoy top-notch wine and innovative dishes. At most places, local, seasonal, and often organic fare are givens.

In far southeast, the Sellwood neighborhood is home to **GINO'S** (8051 SE 13th Ave; 503/233-4613) and **PORTOFINO CAFFE ITALIANO** (8075 SE 13th Ave; 503/234-8259), two longtime favorite Italian restaurants just steps away from each other. A few blocks north is Italian newcomer **A CENA** (7742 SE 13th St; 503/206-3291), dishing up more refined dishes in a warm, inviting space. **SABURO'S SUSHI HOUSE** (1667 SE Bybee Blvd; 503/236-4237) draws lines of diners from across Portland every night for its innovative rolls and ample servings of Japanese cuisine.

Some of the best restaurants in Southeast Portland are located in the **HAWTHORNE DISTRICT**, which extends as far south as SE Division Street. **POK POK AND THE WHISKEY SODA LOUNGE** (3584 SE Division St; 503/233-3656; www.pokpokpdx.com) serves some of the city's best Thai street food, along with beer and cocktails. The chicken *tagine* with fennel, preserved Meyer lemons, olives, and almond couscous at **LAURO KITCHEN** will keep you returning again and again. Head to **PIX PATISSERIE** (3402 SE Division St; 503/232-4407) for dessert, but be forewarned: the tortes and cakes are almost too fancy-looking to eat. The

Olea / ★★★★

1338 NW HOYT ST, PORTLAND; 503/274-0800

The modern interior with soaring ceilings and a neutral color palette set the scene for bold and daring yet subtly nuanced Mediterranean-influenced cuisine. Indulgence is the word of the day here, so plan on multiple courses. Start with seared ahi tuna with fennel-apple *panzanella* and brown butter vinaigrette. Continue with wild mushroom *strozzapreti* with garlic, arugula, tarragon, and Pernod cream; or try the pan-seared chicken with roasted grapes, tiny cipolline onions, prosciutto, and new potatoes. Finish with an intriguing butternut squash baklava with pomegranate and chilled *affogad*. The wine list has some excellent offerings, but the cocktails are exceptional; on-site infusions make for creative drinks. *$$$; AE, CB, DIS, DC, MC, V; no checks; dinner Mon–Sat; full bar; reservations recommended; www.olearestaurant.com; at 14th Ave.* &

Paley's Place / ★★★★

1204 NW 21ST AVE, PORTLAND; 503/243-2403

Chef Vitaly Paley—named best chef of the Pacific Northwest by the James Beard Foundation in 2005—along with his wife, Kim, runs this intimate 50-seat restaurant with passion and expertise. The seasonally influenced French

fabulously retro **VICTORY WINE BAR** (3652 SE Division St; 503/236-8755) is the place to hit at happy hour for awesome small plates of comfort food to match an excellent beer, wine, and cocktail list.

NE 28TH STREET is another foodie destination. Tuck into the affordable Mediterranean prix-fixe dinner at **TABLA MEDITERRANEAN BISTRO**. **NAVARRE** (10 NE 28th Ave; 503/232-3555) offers 50-plus wines by the glass to match their farm-to-table menu of Italian, Spanish, and French small and large plates. Choose a bottle from **NOBLE ROT'S** (2724 SE Ankeny St; 503/233-1999) 400-bottle cellar to pair with petite local, seasonal dishes. You'll have to grin and bear the long line at **KEN'S ARTISAN PIZZA**, but it's worth it for the city's best artisan pizza.

In the rapidly gentrified **NORTH MISSISSIPPI AVENUE AREA**, head to **TREBOL** (830 N Shaver St; 503/517-9347) for Oaxacan cuisine made with fresh, seasonal, and local ingredients. There's no Hawaiian but lots of fresh local dishes at **LOVELY HULA HANDS**. At **LUPA WINE BAR** (3955 N Mississippi Ave; 503/287-5872), you can sip your way around the world while snacking on delectable bites of olives, almonds, and *boquerones*.

Quirky **ALBERTA ARTS DISTRICT** has three must-hits: **LOLO** (2940 NE Alberta St; 503/288-3400) for tapas; **CIAO VITO** for fresh rustic Italian; and **ALBERTA STREET OYSTER BAR & GRILL** for burgers, and, of course, oysters.

—Jo Ostgarden

menu presents delicacies like grilled diver scallops with leek fondue and caviar butter, crispy veal sweetbreads with mushroom-chestnut relish, and grilled Kobe beef with seared foie gras. Their chocolate soufflé cake with honey-vanilla ice cream is the most sensuous dessert in town. *$$$; AE, MC, V; no checks; dinner every day; full bar; reservations recommended; www.paleysplace.net; at NW Northrup St.*

Pambiche / ★★

2811 NE GLISAN ST, PORTLAND; 503/233-0511

Bold flavors, authentic cuisine—what's not to love about this brightly painted, award-winning Cuban eatery? Regardless of the facts that they have only 10 tables inside and a few seats at the counter and that the prices are a bit high on some dishes, lines are long on weekends. Hungry crowds clamor for Cuban-American chef John Connell Maribona's fried plantains, fried yucca root, grilled Cuban sandwiches, bacalao (sautéed salt cod with fresh vegetables), and empanadas—all based on traditional recipes passed through generations of great family cooks from prerevolutionary Cuba. On summer nights, snag a table on Pambiche's patio, and you'll feel like you've been zipped off to a sidewalk café in Old Havana. During the day, pop in for café con leche and breakfast, or take home one of their house-baked cakes, cheesecakes, classic tortes, or tarts. *$–$$; MC, V; no checks; lunch, dinner every day; beer and wine; no reservations; www.pambiche.com; at NE 28th.* &

Park Kitchen / ★★

422 NW 8TH AVE, PORTLAND; 503/223-7275

This tiny bistro and bar is so popular that in warm weather they raise the garage-door wall and seat people at sidewalk tables looking out over the North Park blocks. Don't miss the excellent lunches, which include homey, creative fare like homemade hot dogs and duck confit Reubens. The dinner menu offers small plates like salt-cod fritters and green-bean tempura, along-side creative entrées like Berkshire pork with pickled watermelon or duck with root-beer spices and corn-bread pudding. Desserts are especially good during berry season. *$$–$$$; AE, MC, V; no checks; lunch Mon–Fri, dinner Mon–Sat; full bar; reservations recommended; www.parkkitchen.com; at NW Glisan St.* &

Portland City Grill / ★★★

111 SW 5TH AVE (UNICO US BANK TOWER), PORTLAND; 503/450-0030

This penthouse restaurant puts you literally on top of Portland with sweep-ing vistas of downtown and the Cascades. The dinner menu is bona fide cor-porate America, however, promising prime steaks; lobster; pork, veal, and lamb chops; and few surprises. The kitchen spices things up with Asian and Hawaiian twists, but often the miso, shiitake, and ponzu glazes overwhelm the original dishes. The gorgeous steaks are outstanding. If you love rare meat, the crew here listens, delivering a New York strip that is red and fleshy in the middle and pink throughout. The full sushi menu, incongruous though it may be, is a highlight. *Maki are exemplary and affordable. $$–$$$; AE, DC, DIS, MC, V; no checks; lunch Mon–Fri, dinner every day; full bar; reservations recommended; www.portlandcitygrill.com; on 30th floor.* &

Saucebox / ★★★

214 SW BROADWAY, PORTLAND; 503/241-3393

The chic modern interior, edgy and gorgeous art, hip DJs, and inventive cocktail list draw a wide swath of Portlanders to the boisterous bar. The new dining room offers a more serene yet hip modern setting where the pan-Asian menu and Pacific Island cuisine becomes the focus rather than the people. It's an easy choice: Thai green curry Draper Valley chicken breast spiked with coconut milk and Chinese eggplant; or founding chef Chris Isra-el's signature Javanese roasted salmon with its sweet, spicy lime and palm sugar glaze and the fun pupu platter that lets you sample everything from shrimp dumplings to baby back ribs. The cocktail menu is as entertaining to read as it is to drink from; housemade elixirs and fruit infusions add to the appeal. *$$–$$$; AE, DC, MC, V; no checks; dinner Tues–Sat; full bar; reservations recommended; www.saucebox.com; at SW Ankeny St.* &

Salty's on the Columbia / ★★★

3839 NE MARINE DR, PORTLAND; 503/288-4444

Salty's is like an old, reliable friend: always there for you, with the added bonuses of gracious service, succulent seafood and juicy steaks, and the best, all-encompassing views of the mighty Columbia River. Fresh, local seafood is at the heart of the menu, but you'll also find some excellent casual appetizers to nosh on while watching ospreys dive for fish on the river as the sun goes down, with live jazz playing in the background. An award-winning wine list complements the big menu, and the award-winning weekend brunch harkens back to a bygone era of grand, all-you-can-eat feasts. Salty's is a favorite among locals and a place to wow out-of-towners. Desserts are out of this world, so save room. *$$$; AE, DC, DIS, MC, V; no checks; lunch Mon–Fri, dinner every day, brunch Sat–Sun; full bar; reservations recommended; www. saltys.com; north side of Marine Dr ½ mile east of NE 33rd Ave.* &

Tabla Mediterranean Bistro / ★★★

200 NE 28TH AVE, PORTLAND; 503/238-3777

Glance into the kitchen, see the busy chefs, and get a subtle whiff of savory soups and perfectly seared, herb-wrapped New York steak. The restaurant has a retro-modern look with an unpretentious feel, and its prix-fixe three-course dinner is the best deal in town. Start with silky, luscious duck pâté served with spicy house-made pickles. Choose a middle of *tajarin*—simple house-made pasta—perfectly cooked and tossed with a savory blend of truffle butter and *grana padano*. Entrées include duck confit—salty and crunchy on the outside, moist and tender on the inside. Braised boar shoulder is fork-tender in a rich, spicy sauce. Stuffed? Desserts can be packed to go. The wine list, which is full of undiscovered gems, includes wine flights. *$$–$$$; AE, DIS, MC, V; no checks; dinner Tues–Sun; full bar; reservations recommended; www.tabla-restaurant.com; at Davis St.* &

Ten 01 / ★★

1001 NW COUCH ST, PORTLAND; 503/226-3463

Ultramodern and softly lit, this purely Pearl District restaurant has a stylized industrial look; the mezzanine level subtly hovers over a rear open bar and kitchen. A classic Northwest theme—all-natural meats, regional and local ingredients—permeates throughout the menu's seasonal changes. Chef Jack Yoss uses a refined touch to coax out pure flavors. Small plates include *hamachi* sashimi with slightly sharp apple-celeriac vinaigrette, or clams steamed in sherry-spiked chile broth with a pinch of garlic. Half chicken au jus is paired with heirloom tomato–olive bread salad. Grilled New York steak with harissa bordelaise is paired with fingerling potato salad. An extensive, deep, and well-defined wine list and classy cocktail offerings are Pearl perfect. Classic desserts like crème brûlée and a trio of chocolates are an excellent conclusion. *$$$; AE, DIS, MC, V; checks OK; lunch Mon–Sat, dinner every day; full bar; reservations recommended; www.ten-01.com; at NW Couch St.*

23Hoyt / ★★★

529 NW 23RD ST, PORTLAND; 503/445-7400

Floor-to-ceiling windows provide full views of the boisterous, busy shopping district from the comfortable, contemporary dining room. Grilled chèvre in radicchio, served with olive tapenade, is a good place to start. The Greek-inspired spinach salad combines cucumber, feta, red onion, and chickpeas. Entrées are presented simply. Four generous lamb chops are served with sautéed brussel sprouts and creamy potato gratin. Zarzuela, a rich fish stew, is full of fat mussels that melt in your mouth and has just the right balance of seafood. When your gracious, attentive server arrives to tempt you with the dessert menu, try the pear tartlet. It arrives in a pond of luscious huckleberry sauce and is garnished with whipped crème fraîche. The wine list and cocktail list are fun and adventurous. *$$-$$$; AE, DIS, MC, V; no checks; dinner Tues–Sat; full bar; reservations recommended; www.23hoyt.com; at NW Hoyt.* &

Vindahlo / ★★

2038 SE CLINTON ST, PORTLAND; 503/467-4550

There is something indescribably quixotic about David Machado's "spice route" bistro. There's the bilevel loft that pulls your eyes upward as your olfactory senses lean toward the open kitchen on the main level. Sage and curry color on the walls and cobalt blue lights enliven the industrial space. But more than anything it's the flavors that move you toward higher realms. Not everything is perfect; you'll wish some dishes had more heat, or not. But overall there's much to satisfy here as you lean your elbows into bamboo tabletops. Try minted spring vegetable Samosas with yogurt chutney; chile-spiked Moan-style mussels steamed in coconut curry; or Draper Valley chicken tikka in classic Moghul marinade with garlic naan for leverage. Cool off with a Mumbai Mule or a cold beer. *$$; AE, MC, V; no checks; dinner Tues–Sat; full bar; reservations recommended (online only); www.vindahlo.com; at SE 20th.* &

LODGINGS

The Benson Hotel / ★★★

309 SW BROADWAY, PORTLAND; 503/228-2000 OR 888/523-6766

The grande dame of luxury hotels in Portland, the Benson has been operating since 1913. The palatial lobby features a stamped-tin ceiling, sparkling chandeliers, stately columns, and a huge fireplace. The service is impeccable, if sometimes a bit impersonally formal. The rooms are done up in conservative colonial style with heavenly memory-foam beds. The suites, with beds longer than usual, are a favorite among NBA players. *$$$-$$$$; AE, DC, DIS, MC, V; checks OK; www.bensonhotel.com; exit 299A off I-5.* &

Embassy Suites Portland–Downtown / ★★☆

319 SW PINE ST, PORTLAND; 503/279-9000

The Embassy Suites chain bought the languishing, once-grand, historic Mult-nomah Hotel in 1997 and brought it back to its former glory. The massive lobby boasts a soaring two-story ceiling with gilded columns, luxurious fur-niture, and a fountain. All rooms are suites, done up in a somewhat stuffy contemporary style, with living rooms, refrigerators, and microwaves. The indoor pool, free hot breakfasts, and game room with pool table and video games make this a good bet when traveling with kids. The Portland Steak and Chophouse offers a fresh seafood menu that changes daily and average American fare at steeper-than-average prices. *$$$; AE, DC, DIS, MC, V; no checks; www.embassysuites.com; between 2nd and 3rd aves.* &

The Governor Hotel / ★★

614 SW 11TH AVE, PORTLAND; 503/224-3400 OR 800/554-3456

Opened in 1909, in the heady days following the centennial 1905 Lewis and Clark Exposition, this hotel lives and breathes Pacific Northwest history. Arts and Crafts–style furnishings, murals depicting local Native American tribes, and a wood-burning fireplace give the lobby a clubby feel. The adjoin-ing Jake's Grill, with its cigar-friendly bar and great happy-hour menu, is a popular watering hole for locals. Rooms are decorated in rather bland earth tones; suites feature jetted tubs, and some have sky-lit rooms. Take a peek at the meeting rooms and ballrooms, which are modeled after palatial Italian villas. Maid and room service are available 24 hours a day. *$$$; AE, DIS, MC, V; no checks; www.governorhotel.com; at SW Alder St.* &

The Heathman Hotel / ★★★★

1001 SW BROADWAY, PORTLAND;
503/241-4100 OR 800/551-0011

This intimate boutique hotel's exceptional service and enduring commitment to the local arts and theater scene are legendary. The art deco–style lobby is incredibly inviting, as is the opulent tearoom, where you can enjoy afternoon tea service, as well as reading, lounging, and nightly live jazz. Premium perks include your own personal concierge and your choice of luxury mattress and pillows from the hotel's the Art of Sleep menu. Original art—some famous, some by celebrities—is displayed on the mezzanine level and in rooms like the Andy Warhol suite. Bathrooms are small but gorgeous, and the rooms have real windows that open wide. The Heathman Restaurant and Bar feature some of the city's best French and Northwest focused cuisine, plus an amazing wine and cocktail menu. *$$$–$$$$; AE, DC, DIS, MC, V; checks OK; www. heathmanhotel.com; at SW Salmon St.* &

Hotel deLuxe / ★★★

729 SW 15TH AVE, PORTLAND; 866/895-2094
Formerly the Hotel Mallory, this 1912 hotel saw an $8 million renovation in 2006. The air of 1940s Hollywood glamour prevails, with each floor dedicated to a film director or movie genre, with film stills on the walls. Each of the 130 rooms are decorated in bright blues and greens, with marble-floored bathrooms, flat-screen TVs, and MP3 listening docks. The rooms ending in "03" have sweeping northern views of the city. There's also a fitness center, the brat pack–style Driftwood Room lounge, and Gracie's, which offers worldly cuisine and 24-hour room service. *$$$–$$$$; AE, DC, DIS, MC, V; no checks; www.hoteldeluxeportland.com; between SW Morrison and SW Yamhill sts.* &

Hotel Lucia / ★★☆

400 SW BROADWAY, PORTLAND; 503/225-1717 OR 877/225-1717
This is one of the most stylish of all of Portland's boutique hotels, rivaling anything the W chain might offer in larger cities, for much less money. The white and black minimalism of the lobby is softened by splashy modern art, unusual fresh flowers, and a seating area warmed by a fireplace. The hip staff are good guides to what's hot in the city. The pet-friendly rooms, while not exactly spacious, do offer amenities like a pillow menu, feathertop beds, and 24-hour room service from Bar Restobar, a small-plates fusion kitchen and cocktail bar, next door. *$$$; AE, DC, DIS, MC, V; checks OK; www.hotellucia.com; at Stark St.* &

Hotel Monaco / ★★★

506 SW WASHINGTON ST, PORTLAND;
503/222-0001 OR 800/711-2971
This elegant 10-story hotel is part of the Pacific Northwest–owned Kimpton Boutique Hotels chain and is newly refurbished. The Fifth Avenue property features a cozy lobby with a large corner fireplace, complimentary Starbucks coffee, and evening wine tastings. Nearly two-thirds of the 221 rooms are spacious suites with contemporary lemon-yellow striped walls, sofas, cushy animal-print bathrobes, live goldfish, hip magazines, and Aveda bath products. The corner rooms are smaller; if you're looking for space, request another room in advance. The fitness room is open all hours. The staff is attentive and gracious, especially to your four-legged companions, who get their names entered on a lobby chalkboard. *$$$; AE, DIS, MC, V; checks OK; www.monaco-portland.com; at 5th Ave.* &

Hotel Vintage Plaza / ★★☆

422 SW BROADWAY, PORTLAND; 503/228-1212 OR 800/263-2305
This intimate 107-room boutique hotel of the Kimpton group is both playful and elegant. The 10-story hotel resides in an 1894 restored building, with upscale antique furnishings in the lobby and wine tastings in the evenings. The rooms vary from double-bed rooms with intense jewel-toned bedding

PORTLAND SPA TOUR

Whether weary from travel or sore from life's pursuits, everybody needs a good massage from time to time. No matter where you are in Portland, there's a day spa offering relief.

NORTHEAST: A comprehensive menu of face and body treatments can be found at **SPA WILLIAMINA** (2223 NE 43rd St; 503/287-2787), but the unique fragrant stone massage combining the best of two treatments—hot stones and healing essential oils—will nourish your skin, relax your mind, and relieve tight muscles.

NORTHWEST: Jump-start your lymphatic system with a seaweed body-detox treatment designed especially for active or frequent travelers at **BELLINI'S EUROPEAN DAY SPA** (2326 NW Irving St; 503/226-1526).

NORTH: Relieve aching travel or hiker's feet with a foot massage and aqua chi footbath at **EXODUS** (4211 Interstate Ave; 503/288-3110).

SOUTHEAST: Head to Scandinavian-inspired **LÖYLY** (2713 SE 21st Ave; 503/236-6850) for gender-specific and communal saunas, steam baths, and massages.

SOUTHWEST: REJUVENATION DAY SPA (6333 SW Macadam Ave, Ste 105; 503/293-5699) performs manual lymph drainage treatments that help stimulate the immune system, calm the nervous system, and relax the muscles.

DOWNTOWN: At the sensuous **AEQUIS SPA** (419 SW 11th Ave, Penthouse; 503/223-7847), take an island trip without leaving Portland: Hawaiian Lomi Lomi massage—long, rhythmic strokes and joint mobilization—relieves sore bodies.

—Jo Ostgarden

and curtains to the more modern top-floor "Starlight" rooms with conservatory windows and star-themed decor. The best suites are the three "Garden Spa" rooms with balconies equipped with two-person spa tubs. Pets are welcomed upon check-in and are treated to gourmet treats and springwater. *$$–$$$; AE, DC, DIS, MC, V; no checks; www.vintageplaza.com; at SW Washington St.* &

The Jupiter Hotel / ★

800 E BURNSIDE ST, PORTLAND; 503/230-9200 OR 877/800-0004

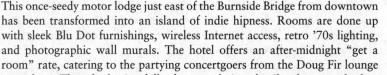

This once-seedy motor lodge just east of the Burnside Bridge from downtown has been transformed into an island of indie hipness. Rooms are done up with sleek Blu Dot furnishings, wireless Internet access, retro '70s lighting, and photographic wall murals. The hotel offers an after-midnight "get a room" rate, catering to the partying concertgoers from the Doug Fir lounge next door. Though they're full of smart design details, these are budget accommodations—linens and bathrooms aren't luxurious, and the clientele is young and noisy. Ask for a room on the "quiet side" if you're not up for all-hours partying. They also have a fleet of five authentic Parisian bicycles guests can reserve. *$–$$; AE, DIS, MC, V; no checks; www.jupiterhotel.com; between SE 8th and 9th aves.* &

The Lion and the Rose / ★★☆

1810 NW 15TH AVE, PORTLAND; 503/287-9245 OR 800/955-1647
This Queen Anne mansion built in 1906 is set in the historic Irvington District, just blocks from the bustling Lloyd Center Mall. It may be close to the modern world outside, but once you're inside, you're surrounded by the romance of another era. This stately house features seven guest rooms done in Victorian-Edwardian style with floral prints and massive antiques, augmented with convenient amenities like data ports and modern marble bathrooms. The lavish two-course breakfasts are excellent. The friendly innkeepers also serve snacks in the late afternoon in the parlor. *$$$; AE, DC, DIS, MC, V; no checks; www.lionrose.com; north of NE Broadway.*

The Nines / ★★★★

525 SW MORRISON ST, PORTLAND; 877/229-9995
Its central location—across from Pioneer Square—and stunning city and inner atrium views from the rooms in this just-opened hotel make it a must-visit Portland destination. Sitting atop the landmark Meier & Frank Building, the Nines' striking contemporary decor and impeccable level of service are just two of the standouts that push this hotel into the stratosphere of luxury. Its 331 guest rooms (including 13 suites) feature local art, plush bedding with Egyptian sateen sheets, 42-inch HD TVs, and other premium amenities. Guests can also enjoy a cutting-edge fitness center and club lounge in addition to two upscale dining and bar options (the eclectic, pan-Asian Departure and the local, seasonal and steak-house cuisine of Urban Farmer). *$$$–$$$$; AE, DC, DIS, MC, V; checks OK; www.thenines.com; at SW Salmon St.* &

The Paramount Hotel / ★★☆

808 SW TAYLOR ST, PORTLAND; 503/223-9900
This 15-story luxury hotel opened in 2000, just one block from the Arlene Schnitzer Concert Hall downtown, to much acclaim. Each of the 154 rooms is decorated with restrained elegance in beige fabrics, Biedermeier furniture, and granite-topped bathroom counters. The executive rooms include either jetted tubs or private balconies with views of peaceful Park Street. All guest rooms include large desks equipped with two phone lines and data ports. The elegant marble lobby is flanked by Dragonfish, a Japanese restaurant, on one side and their lively bar on the other. Try their excellent sushi deals at happy hour. *$$$–$$$$; AE, DC, DIS, MC, V; checks OK; www.portland paramount.com; at Park Ave.* &

Portland's White House / ★★★

1914 NE 22ND AVE, PORTLAND; 503/287-7131

On the outside, this 1911 Greek Revival mansion with circular driveway, carriage house, and fountain is almost as grand as its namesake in Washington, DC. Inside this six-room B and B, you'll find rooms with tasteful antiques, heavenly feather beds, wireless Internet access, and updated bathrooms. Every room boasts either a jetted tub, an original claw-foot bathtub, or a six-head steam shower. A full gourmet breakfast with local hormone-free meats and espresso is served daily. Weddings are frequently held in the beautiful garden. *$$$–$$$$; AE, DIS, MC, V; no checks; www.portlandswhitehouse. com; 2 blocks north of NE Broadway.*

RiverPlace Hotel / ★★★

1510 SW HARBOR WY, PORTLAND;
503/228-3233 OR 800/227-1333

Located directly on the busy Willamette River downtown, this casually elegant hotel is known for its optimal river views and warm service. The best rooms among the 74 kings, doubles, and suites face the water. Decor echoes the river, with Cape Cod–style beige and powder blues and Craftsman-style furniture. Plush furnishings include feather beds and CD players in every room. The concierge service is among the best in the city; complimentary continental breakfast, as well as 24-hour room service from 3 Degrees Restaurant, can be brought to your room. *$$$–$$$$; AE, DC, DIS, MC, V; no checks; www. riverplacehotel.com; south end of Tom McCall Waterfront Park.* &

Portland Environs

Oregon's emphasis on proactive land-use planning and transit-oriented development has lessened the distance—both geographically and culturally—between Portland and its suburbs. Businesses like Intel, Nike, and Columbia Sportswear have made the western suburbs of Washington County (which primarily includes Hillsboro, Sherwood, Tigard, Tualatin and Wilsonville, and Beaverton) more attractive to visitors and Portlanders. Two of the state's most notable wineries, Ponzi and Cooper Mountain (one of the state's first certified biodynamic and organic vineyards), are located in Beaverton. Gresham lies just east of Portland and is the state's fourth largest city. Also known as "the city of music," it hosts the annual Mt. Hood Jazz Festival each summer. Suburbs to the south include Milwaukie, Oregon City, West Linn, and Lake Oswego—each offering an abundance of green spaces and parks, dining hot spots, and historical points worth exploring.

Lake Oswego

Although it's located adjacent to the Willamette River, most of Lake Oswego's downtown core snugs against the shores of its namesake lake, Oswego Lake, or stretches out to the I-5 freeway. This mostly wealthy enclave is like a tiny big city, both culturally and in outlook. City parks, downtown art, and lush, forested lake vistas typify the city of Lake Oswego.

Downtown Lake Oswego has galleries, restaurants, and gift, flower, and clothing boutiques. Tree-lined streets, along with captivating art sculptures and hanging flower baskets, give the city a warm and arty appeal.

Nearby, board the **WILLAMETTE SHORE TROLLEY** (503/697-7436; www.trainweb.org/oerhs/wst.htm) for a 6-mile run from Lake Oswego to Portland along the west bank of the river.

The **LAKE OSWEGO FARMERS MARKET** is held every Saturday from mid-May to mid-October. The European-style market includes a wide variety of regional produce, baked goods, and nursery stock, as well as live entertainment.

LAKE OSWEGO FESTIVAL OF THE ARTS (www.lakewood-center.org) features a juried craft fair in George Rogers Park, a Visual Arts Open Show with 1,100 pieces of art submitted by regional artists, and a special juried exhibit of fine artwork; both are held at the Lakewood Center for the Arts (368 S State St; www.lakewood-center.org).

A historic walking tour guide, available from the **LAKE OSWEGO CHAMBER OF COMMERCE** (242 B Ave; 503/636-3634; www.lake-oswego.com), showcases LO's First Addition, one of the city's oldest neighborhoods, where many of the houses were built in distinctive architectural styles, including Gothic, Craftsman, Colonial Revival, Vernacular, and English Cottage.

Nearby, **TRYON CREEK STATE PARK**, a 645-acre nature park, offers superb hiking and horseback riding trails, a bike path, and a nature center and public art space.

RESTAURANTS

Clarke's Restaurant / ★★★

455 SECOND ST, LAKE OSWEGO; 503/636-2667
Chef Jonathan Clarke offers a seasonally changing menu of simply prepared, fresh local ingredients with Northwest, French, and Italian influences. Cozy and comfortable, yet simply elegant, Clarke's eatery has all the elements in place that make it a perfect neighborhood spot. Starters include artisan cheese plates, flaked duck confit and sweet pea flan, and caesar salad. Entrées include seafood, chicken, and specialties like wild boar pasta or lobster and shrimp risotto. Top side picks include truffled fries and creamed Swiss chard with pancetta. Tarts, seasonal sorbets, cakes, panna cotta, and classic crème brûlée are all knockouts. *$$–$$$ AE, DIS, MC, V; local checks only; dinner every day; full bar; reservations recommended; www.clarkes.ypguides.net; between Aves A and B.* &

FiveSpice Bistro / ★★

315 FIRST ST, LAKE OSWEGO; 503/697-8889

This medium-sized bistro's large European-style windows, covered fireside patio, and large deck overlooking Oswego Lake lend maximum appeal to this intimate dining experience. A mix of glass tile and wood accents give the dining room and wine bar a stylish but relaxed feel. The local seasonal menu features innovative dishes that combine classic French technique with a sophisticated blending of vibrant flavors. Dishes range from a trio of tartares (beef with balsamic teriyaki, ahi with spicy aioli, edamame with rosemary-orange oil) to a duet of free-range chicken (roasted breast or miso braised leg) to a Strawberry Mountain New York steak with truffled fingerling potatoes in a black vinegar veal reduction. An extensive wine list—125 French, Oregon, and Washington wines, 25 by the glass—along with creative cocktails, make an impressiion. *$$; AE, DIS, MC, V; local checks only; lunch, dinner every day; full bar; reservations recommended for 6 or more; www.fivespicerestaurant. com; ½ block from Millennium Plaza.* &

Tucci / ★★

220 A AVE, LAKE OSWEGO; 503/697-3383

Spearheaded by Pascal Chureau of Fenouil and Lucier, this neighborhood trattori offers modern Italian cuisine prepared with fresh local ingredients. Bronze and olive drapes contrast with a faux tortoise-backed bar for a chic, luxurious feel. The open kitchen gives it a warm, welcoming effect. Enjoy antipasto or wood-fired pizza starters. *Secondis* include beef, seafood, and fowl. The mesquite-roasted free-range chicken with Gorgonzola-spiked braised black kale and creamy Reggiano polenta; the seared sea scallops paired with pork–spaghetti squash roulade; and wild boar sausage pizza with roasted fennel, caramelized red onion, and fresh mozzarella are all standouts. Save room for house-made gelato in a perfect trifecta of flavors—fig, sambuca, and cinnamon espresso. The Lido Bar inside Tucci is ideal for small plates and wine from their exclusively Italian list. *$$$$; AE, MC, V; no checks; lunch, dinner Tues–Sun; full bar; reservations recommended for 6 or more; www.tucci.biz; between 2nd and 3rd sts.* &

Beaverton

Located in the heart of the Tualatin Valley, midway between Mount Hood and the Oregon Coast, and just 7 miles from Portland, Beaverton is best known as the home of Nike. Beaverton's metro area encompasses rolling green hills, forests, rivers, wetlands, and a sea of traffic. Despite the dominant car culture—light rail helps you get east or west, but it's the north-to-south boulevards and I-217 that get really jammed up—a 25-mile network of bike paths helps keep people moving. There are also 100 parks encompassing 1,000 acres, more designated "green space" than most cities of its size, to help take the load off. There's a park located within a half mile of every home, plus 30 miles of hiking trails.

Abundant shopping malls, swimming pools, tennis courts, softball fields, and golf courses, as well as access to backcountry biking roads, keep residents on the move.

RESTAURANTS

Mingo / ★★

12600 SW CRESCENT AVE, BEAVERTON; 503/646-6464
The rustic Italian dishes that made Caffe Mingo so popular in Northwest Portland get an added boost from this suburban outpost's vibrant industrial space. In summer, a wall of garage doors open to the Beaverton Round's central piazza, with a beautiful water fountain adding to the ambience. Depending on the season, tuck into caramelized onion ravioli with light cream sauce, *penne al sugo di carne*, *caprese* and Mingo salads, spiedini with prawns and croutons, Gorgonzola and walnut *raviolini*, and the grilled portobello mushrooms. The dessert menu expands on Caffe Mingo's classic theme, but you'll still find that silky panna cotta and surprising prunes in Nebbiolo. They also offer winemaker dinners here; call for a schedule. *$$–$$$; AE, DC, DIS, MC, V; local checks only; lunch Mon–Fri, dinner every day; beer and wine; reservations recommended; across MAX line tracks from parking structure.*

Pho Van / ★

11651 SW BEAVERTON HILLSDALE HWY,
BEAVERTON; 503/627-0822
Pho Van is one of the best-loved cheap-eats options in Portland, but it's just as popular out in Beaverton, where long waits can ensue on weekends. Something about the steaming-hot beef noodle soup with heaps of herbs seems to warm even the rainiest of days. It's not all Vietnamese noodles and broth at this outpost, though; the giant bowls overflowing with rice vermicelli noodles and grilled chicken, herb-packed salad rolls with spicy peanut sauce, and the multicourse beef lunch are excellent options, as is the Vietnamese chicken with yams and onions in yellow curry sauce. For excellent warm-weather quaffing, choose from nine international beers. A selection of aromatic teas takes the edge off cooler nights. *$; DIS, MC, V; no checks; lunch, dinner Mon–Sat; beer and wine; reservations recommended; www.phovanrestaurant. com; across from Fred Meyer.*

COLUMBIA RIVER GORGE AND MOUNT HOOD

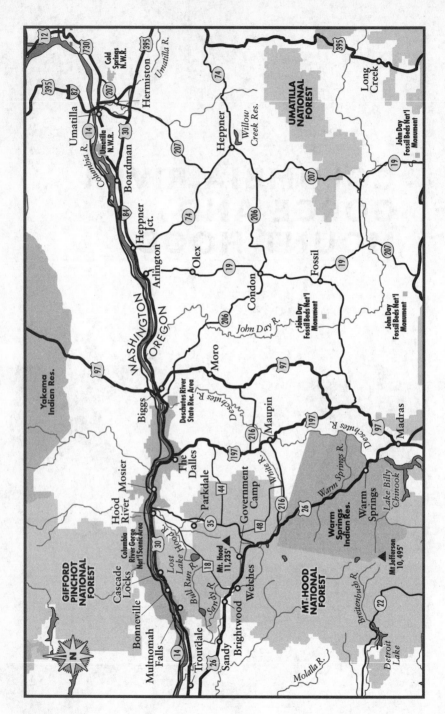

COLUMBIA RIVER GORGE AND MOUNT HOOD

Sculpted by the catastrophic floodwaters of the last ice age, the Columbia River Gorge stretches 80 miles east and west, cut 4,200 feet deep below the crest of the Cascade Range. Ribbons of snowmelt spill over the canyon's edges, creating a wall of intermittent waterfalls—77 of them named—most of which are easily viewed from the Historic Columbia River Highway and Interstate 5. Established as the nation's first national scenic area, it also has the distinction of being the nation's most awe-inspiring natural area located near a large urban district.

The two largest cities in the Columbia River Gorge—Hood River and The Dalles—are magnets for outdoor enthusiasts and adventure seekers, thanks to ideal wind conditions for kiteboarding and windsurfing, as well as proximity to the Cascades. The range's dominant peak in Oregon, Mount Hood, draws skiers, climbers, and hikers to its snowy flanks.

ACCESS AND INFORMATION

The Columbia River Gorge and Mount Hood are most commonly approached from Portland on **INTERSTATE 84**, the main highway through the gorge. I-84 connects to both **INTERSTATE 5** and **INTERSTATE 205**. For the scenic route, exit at Troutdale to the **HISTORIC COLUMBIA RIVER HIGHWAY**. Much of the narrow, winding road is unsuitable to big rigs (RVers, take note), and cautious, slow driving is always called for as it's frequently used by touring and training cyclists. **US HIGHWAY 26**, also called the Mt. Hood Scenic Byway, is the main inland road from Portland to Mount Hood.

In the winter, traction devices are often required on Mount Hood. The **OREGON DEPARTMENT OF TRANSPORTATION** (503/588-2941 outside Oregon, or 800/977-6368; www.tripcheck.com) issues daily reports. Winter sports on the mountain require an **ODOT WINTER SNO-PARK PERMIT** ($3 per day, $7 for 3 days, $20 per year); they also are sold at state **DEPARTMENT OF MOTOR VEHICLE** offices and (typically with an added fee) at resorts, service stations, and retailers.

GREYHOUND (503/243-2357 or 800/231-2222; www.greyhound.com) provides daily service to Hood River and The Dalles. The **AMTRAK EMPIRE BUILDER** (800/872-7245; www.amtrak.com) has a daily train to Bingen, Washington, just across the Columbia River from Hood River, and to Wishram, Washington, 15 miles east of The Dalles.

Local tourist information is available from the **HOOD RIVER COUNTY CHAMBER OF COMMERCE** (720 E Port Marina Dr, Hood River; 541/386-2000 or 800/366-3530; www.hoodriver.org) and **THE DALLES AREA CHAMBER OF COMMERCE** (404 W 2nd St, The Dalles; 541/296-2231 or 800/255-3385; www.thedalleschamber.com).

Columbia River Gorge National Scenic Area

To protect the gorge's 292,500 acres of natural beauty from the perils of development, Congress established it as the Columbia River Gorge National Scenic Area in 1986. The scenic area is bounded by the Columbia's confluence with the Sandy River near Troutdale in the west and the Deschutes River near The Dalles in the east.

Troutdale

Despite the strip-mall feel and truck-stop blight along I-84, Troutdale, founded in the 1850s, has a tucked-away historic downtown that makes an interesting stop. Much of Troutdale's land was purchased by Captain John Harlow, a former sea captain and successful Portland businessman who gave the town its name after putting some trout ponds in a small dale near his home. Today the city serves as the eastern gateway to the **HISTORIC COLUMBIA RIVER HIGHWAY**, the **MOUNT HOOD SCENIC BYWAY**, and the **COLUMBIA RIVER GORGE**.

Historic downtown Troutdale offers several blocks of specialty garden, gift, wine, art, and antique stores, as well as galleries and cafés. A must-stop for nostalgia and coffee is **TROUTDALE GENERAL STORE** (289 E Historic Columbia River Hwy, Troutdale; 503/492-7912), where, in addition to unique souvenirs and gifts, you can get a quick cup of coffee or breakfast, deli-type lunch, or soda from the old-fashioned soda fountain. In July, the **TROUTDALE BITE & BLUEGRASS** (503/491-8407; www.troutdalebiteandbluegrass.com) is an all-day event held downtown in **MAYOR'S SQUARE**, showcasing local and regional bluegrass bands.

Three miles of sandy beach bring the crowds out to nearby **ROOSTER ROCK STATE PARK** (800/551-6949; www.oregonstateparks.org), which offers one of the largest swimming areas in the Portland region. Head east along the beach, and you'll wind up in official designated "clothing-optional" territory. By design, it's not visible from the clothing-required area of the large park; the two spaces coexist in harmony. Two disc-golf courses are also available for use at the park, and in July, crowds of stargazers arrive at night with their telescopes. Tourist information is available at **WEST COLUMBIA GORGE CHAMBER OF COMMERCE** (107 E Historic Columbia River Hwy, Troutdale; 503/669-7473; www.westcolumbiagorgechamber.com).

RESTAURANTS

Riverview Restaurant / ★★

29311 SE STARK ST, TROUTDALE; 503/661-3663

Modern and airy, with soaring ceilings and an expansive wall of windows, this eponymously named restaurant is a charmer. Warmed by the glow of slate-tiled fireplaces and hardwood floors, the ambience dovetails nicely with

the Northwest-focused menu punctuated by multicultural influences. Starters include Indian curry with naan, *insalata caprese*, and steamed chicken
wontons served with a reduction of Yoshida's gourmet sauce. The menu's
classics also shine: excellent seared scallops, crab cakes, wild salmon with a
miso glaze, butternut ravioli, and Kobe burgers with Oregon blue cheese fill
out the menu. A fun dessert menu, including amazing banana and chocolate
spring rolls, a well-selected wine list, tasty cocktails, and original artwork
from the Yoshidas' private collection adorning the walls make this place a
real treat. *$–$$; AE, MC, V; no checks; dinner every day; full bar; reservations
recommended; www.riverviewrestaurant.com; I-84 exit 18, left onto Columbia
River Hwy, 3 miles to Stark St Bridge.* &

LODGINGS

McMenamin's Edgefield / ★

2127 SW HALSEY ST, TROUTDALE; 503/669-8610 OR 800/669-8610
Built in 1911 as the Multnomah County Poor Farm, this property has gone
through several incarnations, including a nursing home for 20 years before
it was shuttered in 1982. The McMenamin brothers, master renovators and
microbrew specialists, bought the 38-acre complex in 1990 and transformed
it into a European-style village complete with a winery, a brewery, gardens,
a pub, a movie theater, and restaurants. Lodgings are located in a 100-room
hotel with 1930s furnishings, wall murals, and door art. Most rooms are
basic, turn-of-the-20th-century European-style with vintage furniture and
porcelain sinks. Most have shared baths and no TVs. For those on very low
budgets, there's hostel-style bunk-bed lodging. Complimentary breakfast is
served onsite at the Black Rabbit Restaurant. *$–$$; AE, MC, V; checks OK;
www.mcmenamins.com; I-84 exit at Wood Village, south to Halsey St, turn left,
drive ¼ mile to Edgefield sign on right.* &

Columbia River Highway:
Corbett and Bridal Veil

Follow Troutdale's main street east across the narrow Sandy River bridge, bear
right, and you're on the **HISTORIC COLUMBIA RIVER HIGHWAY**, an intact 22-
mile stretch of nearly century-old highway. The road climbs past Dabney State
Park before arriving in **CORBETT**, a tiny burg named for Senator Henry Winslow
Corbett, a prominent Oregon pioneer who lived in Portland and also had a farm
nearby. Artists, musicians, and organic farmers call this area home.

VISTA HOUSE (40700 E Historic Columbia River Hwy, Corbett; 503/695-
2230; www.vistahouse.com; every day Mar–Oct, weekends Nov–Feb) sits at the
spectacular viewpoint of **CROWN POINT**, overlooking a 733-foot-high cliff. The
recently restored 1918 building with its stone-flanked facade and rotunda, gleaming marble floors, ornate carvings, historic displays, and breathtaking views of

the gorge is worth the drive up the long, winding road (take valuables with you and lock your car).

Named after nearby **BRIDAL VEIL FALLS,** the next town to the east still exists largely because of its highly sought-after postmark. Each year, thousands of brides bring their wedding invitations to **BRIDAL VEIL** for its coveted postmark.

As you continue east along the historic road lined with ornate railings built by Italian stonemasons, you'll begin to see more waterfalls. Some 2 million visitors a year visit **MULTNOMAH FALLS,** the second-highest year-round waterfall in the United States. The 620-foot gusher brings overwhelming crowds in spring, summer, and fall, but just as stunning is the less-crowded winter view of the frozen cascade. The U.S. Forest Service staffs an interpretive center on the ground floor of the **MULTNOMAH FALLS LODGE** (see review), located at the beginning of a footpath that takes travelers to the **MULTNOMAH FALLS FOOTBRIDGE,** up nearly a mile of switchbacks to a lookout near the top of the falls, and eventually another 6 miles to the top of Larch Mountain.

The **ONEONTA BOTANICAL AREA** 2 miles east of Multnomah Falls is home to many wildflowers endemic to the gorge. It's also where you'll find **ONEONTA GORGE,** a narrow canyon filled with hanging gardens.

HORSETAIL FALLS PICNIC AREA is a half mile east of Oneonta, and it's another mile east to **AINSWORTH STATE PARK,** which offers a fully equipped campground for tent campers and RVs. Its proximity to the freeway makes it a convenient choice rather than a quiet one, but it is nonetheless very popular.

RESTAURANTS

Multnomah Falls Lodge / ★

**50000 HISTORIC COLUMBIA RIVER HWY (US HWY 30 E),
BRIDAL VEIL; 503/695-2376**
Designed in the "Cascadian" style, this lodge was built in 1925 with native split fieldstone in varying shades of black, gray, brown, and red, irregularly laid, with a steeply pitched cedar-shingled gable roof, dormers, and massive chimneys. It's since undergone several changes, yet the original charm and character remain intact. Sitting at the base of Multnomah Falls, the lodge no longer serves overnighters. Instead, you get meals with spectacular views from every table. The main dining room has floor-to-ceiling windows, while a new annex has glass walls and ceiling for maximum waterfall viewing. The menu is Northwest-inspired, with salmon and oyster omelets at breakfast, fish-and-chips for lunch, and a more formal dinner selection—but most dine here for the view. *$$; AE, DIS, MC, V; no checks; breakfast, lunch, dinner every day, brunch Sun; full bar; reservations recommended; www.multnomahfallslodge. com; I-84 exit 31.* &

The View Point Inn Restaurant / ★★

40301 E LARCH MOUNTAIN RD, CORBETT; 503/695-5811
With French doors to a sunset-oriented veranda, wall sconce lighting, and a Rumford-designed fireplace (massive, stone-built, and shallow, it throws a lot

of heat along with ambience), this place is romantic to the nth degree. Add elegantly presented dishes infused with old-world tastes and fresh Northwest ingredients, and it's a lock. The seasonal dinner menu includes a selection of fresh seafood and meats like pan-seared halibut and fillet of Cascade Natural (free-range) beef, along with at least one exceptional meat-free dish (for example, herbed gnocchi). At lunch, the Crown Point burger (Cascade Beef) smothered in either Tillamook cheddar or Rogue blue cheese gets a double thumbs-up. At Sunday brunch, try the mascarpone-stuffed French toast. The well-sourced wine list is exceptional. *$$–$$$; AE, MC, V; no checks; lunch, dinner Tues–Sat, Sun brunch; full bar; reservations required; www.theview pointinn.com; 3 miles east of Crown Point, right on Larch Mt. Rd.* &

LODGINGS

The View Point Inn / ★★★

40301 E LARCH MOUNTAIN RD, CORBETT; 503/695-5811
Built in 1924 as a world-class boutique hotel, the inn has had guests including presidents, Hollywood stars, and European royalty. Listed on the National Register of Historic Places, the landmark inn and restaurant (see review) were recently renovated with great effort by Geoff Thompson and Angelo Simione. It's a glorious retreat in an exceptional natural setting. Choose from five accommodations options, including a luxury suite, a queen bedroom with shared bath, the twin-bed Innkeeper's room, a gorgeous queen sleeping loft, and the summer-only remodeled Chicken Coop, which sleeps two. A lavish breakfast is included. *$$–$$$; AE, MC, V; no checks; www.thviewpointinn. com; 3 miles east of Crown Point, right on Larch Mt. Rd.* &

Cascade Locks

Once the site of a boomtown called Whiskey Flats, **CASCADE LOCKS** took its official name from a set of navigational locks built in 1896 to improve navigation through Columbia River rapids. Early river travelers were in for a challenge when they encountered the fierce rapids, and most boats had to be portaged around them. In 1864 the first steam locomotive in the Pacific Northwest—the Oregon Pony—pulled cars on a portage railroad next to the river. When Bonneville Dam was built in 1937, the water behind it rose 60 feet. The locks were submerged and not rebuilt until 1993. The city is located just upstream from the **BRIDGE OF THE GODS**, a 1926 cantilever toll bridge that spans the Columbia River—the only bridge that crosses the river between Portland and Hood River, linking Oregon and Washington. It's named after a mysterious geologic event that left a land bridge elevated above the Columbia rapids. Learn more about it at the **CASCADE LOCKS VISITOR CENTER** (Cascade Locks Marina Park, 355 Wa-Na-Pa St, Cascade Locks; 541/374-8619 or 800-643-1354; www.cascade-locks.or.us). Just upriver from the old locks, the 600-passenger **STERNWHEELER COLUMBIA GORGE** (Cascade Locks Marina Park, 355 Wa-Na-Pa St, Cascade Locks;

> ## COLUMBIA RIVER GORGE THREE-DAY TOUR
>
> **DAY ONE:** Grab a cup of coffee and light breakfast at the **TROUTDALE GEN-ERAL STORE** and head east on the Historic Columbia River Highway to **CROWN POINT**. Stop for photos and tour Vista House, then head to **MULTNOMAH FALLS LODGE** for lunch. Back on the old highway, pull off in a few miles to tour **CASCADE LOCKS** and **BONNEVILLE DAM**; pause at Cascade Locks for a ride on the **STERNWHEELER COLUMBIA GORGE** or enjoy an ice cream cone at the **EAST WIND DRIVE-IN**. Continue east to Hood River, then check in to and freshen up at the **COLUMBIA GORGE HOTEL** before taking a leisurely drive through the "**FRUIT LOOP**," a 45-mile drive through the valley's orchards. Head back to Hood River for dinner at **BRIAN'S POURHOUSE**.
>
> **DAY TWO:** Enjoy a grand breakfast at the hotel, then choose between trains, scenery, and shopping or recreation on the river for your morning itinerary: take a ride on the **MOUNT HOOD RAILROAD**, then walk around the shops on **OAK STREET** in downtown Hood River, or visit **BIG WINDS** to take a windsurfing lesson on the Columbia River. Stop for lunch at the **PANZANELLA ARTISAN BAKERY AND ITALIAN DELI**. In the afternoon, take in the area's

541/374-8427 or 800/643-1354; www.sternwheeler.com) is moored. The 140-foot replica makes daily excursions on the Columbia summer through autumn, with weekend brunch and dinner cruises year-round.

On a hot summer day, don't miss the fabulous blueberry malt milk shakes and mile-high ice cream cones at **EAST WIND DRIVE-IN** (395 NW Wa-Na-Pa St, Cascade Locks; 541/374-8380; on downtown loop). **CHARBURGER** (745 NW Wa-Na-Pa St, Cascade Locks; 541/374-8477) offers gut-bomb burgers, a fresh salad bar, and good milk shakes. Call it a night at the **BEST WESTERN COLUMBIA RIVER INN** (735 Wa-Na-Pa St, Cascade Locks; 541/374-8777; www.bestwesternoregon.com), which has an indoor pool and free breakfast and is pet friendly, or at the **COLUMBIA GORGE INN** (404 SW Wa-Na-Pa St, Cascade Locks; www.columbiagorgemotel.net), which offers 30 units and newly renovated kitchenettes.

Just east of Cascade Locks is **BONNEVILLE DAM**, (I-84 exit 40; 541/374-8820; www.nwp.usace.army.mil/op/b/), a New Deal project started in 1934, along with Grand Coulee Dam on the upper Columbia in Washington. The main attractions here are the fish ladders and visitor center on Bradford Island. The **BONNEVILLE FISH HATCHERY** (541/374-8393) features tree-shaded ponds that hold large trout and giant, prehistoric-looking sturgeon.

At the next exit eastbound is **EAGLE CREEK GORGE** (exit 41), a popular scenic area that doubles as an alternate route for the **PACIFIC CREST TRAIL**. A moderate 4.2-mile hike takes you to **PUNCHBOWL FALLS** (400 feet elevation gain).

history with a visit to the **HOOD RIVER COUNTY HISTORICAL MUSEUM**, then head east to The Dalles to see the **COLUMBIA GORGE DISCOVERY CENTER** and the **WASCO COUNTY HISTORICAL MUSEUM**. Have dinner at the **WINDSEEKER**, or if you're running out of time, grab a bite at **BIG JIM'S DRIVE INN**. Head south on Hwy 197 and check in to your room at the **BALCH HOTEL** in Durfur.

DAY THREE: Get up early and enjoy a complimentary breakfast at the hotel before heading west 12 miles on Durfur Valley Road and connecting with Forest Road 44. Continue driving a couple miles west to where the road meets SR 35, the **MOUNT HOOD SCENIC HIGHWAY**. Head south and enjoy the various pullouts and scenic opportunities. (Less adventurous drivers may prefer to head back to I-84 and follow SR 35 south out of Hood River.) Eventually, SR 35 connects to Hwy 26 west. Continue on it to Government Camp and grab lunch at the **ICE AXE GRILL** or further west at **EL BURRO LOCO** in Welches. Finally, check in at the **TIMBERLINE LODGE**. Swim in the outdoor pool or have a hot toddy in the bar offering in-your-face-views of the summit before enjoying dinner in the **CASCADE DINING ROOM**.

RESTAURANTS

Pacific Crest Pub / ★

500 WA-NA-PA ST, CASCADE LOCKS; 541/374-9310

Enjoy views of the Columbia River and Cascade mountains from the dining room, bar, or outdoor patio of this pub café. Built in the early 1920s as a boardinghouse for Bonneville Dam workers and restored in 2007, the pub café offers a menu of regionally oriented, handcrafted pizzas and roadhouse standards like a plowman's platter, burgers, salads, baked chicken, and hot sandwiches. Choose from 10 beers on tap, including regional brews from Walking Man (Stevenson, Washington) and Full Sail (Hood River). They also rent GPS units with preset waypoints that lead to geo caches hidden in the gorge. A dormitory-style hostel with shared baths is scheduled to open on the upper floors of the three-story building in 2009. *$; MC, V; no checks; lunch, dinner Tues–Sun; beer and wine; no reservations; www.pacificcrestpub. com; I-84 exit 44, east edge of downtown loop.*

Hood River

Hood River was once a quiet riverside town with a bucolic orchard backdrop. All that changed when windsurfers discovered the area's wind power, and it wasn't long before it became the windsurfing capital of the world. Even if you don't windsurf, it's still an ideal base camp for cycling, hiking, or even wine tasting. The town's increasing popularity has brought a string of new developments, rising real estate prices, and the lively buzz of restaurants, breweries, gear shops, and outfitters.

Windsurfing lessons and rental gear are available at **BIG WINDS** (207 Front St, Hood River; 541/386-6086 or 888/509-4210; www.bigwinds.com/lessons). The **NEW WIND KITE SCHOOL** (13 Oak St, Hood River; 541/387-2440; www. newwindkiteboarding.com) offers kiteboarding lessons. **GORGE PADDLING** (2070 Freedom Loop, Hood River; 541/490-9404; www.gorgepaddling.com) offers kayaking.

It's not just the outdoors crowd that flocks to Hood River. **OAK STREET**, the town's main drag, is filled with specialty shops, and the tour of the **FULL SAIL BREWERY AND PUB** (506 Columbia St, Hood River; 541/386-2247; www.fullsail brewing.com) is widely popular. The area also hosts a variety of festivals celebrating both food and recreation (see "Hood River's Fruit Loop").

A great way to experience the **HOOD RIVER VALLEY** is to take the **FRUIT LOOP TOUR** (541/386-7697; www.hoodriverfruitloop.com), which showcases the county's diversity of sustainable agriculture. An hour's drive from Portland, the 45-mile scenic drive takes you into orchards, vineyards, farmlands, and small communities, with 36 designated stops. Depending on the season, you can sample and buy (or pick your own) fresh cherries, strawberries, pears, and apples. You can also buy country bakery goods and sachets of local lavender. Several farms also raise alpacas (see "Hood River's Fruit Loop"). Additionally, there are more than 22 wineries in the area. **COLUMBIA GORGE WINEGROWERS ASSOCIATION** (www. columbiagorgewine.com) has tours and tastings. For a comprehensive overview, visit **MOUNT HOOD WINERY** (3189 SR 35, Hood River; 541/386-8333).

The **MOUNT HOOD RAILROAD** (110 Railroad Ave, Hood River; 541/386-3556 or 800/872-4661; www.mthoodrr.com; Mar–mid-Dec) hauls freight and passengers in historic railcars from Hood River south to Parkdale. The company offers a **FRUIT BLOSSOM SPECIAL**, which tours through spring orchards, as well as scenic brunch and dinner trains. The railroad's headquarters are in the former Union Pacific depot, built in 1911.

Local artists exhibit downtown on the **FIRST FRIDAY** of each month (Hood River Downtown Business Association; 541/490-0022; www.downtownhood river.com; May–Dec). At the **HOOD RIVER SATURDAY MARKET** (5th and Columbia sts, Hood River; 9am–3pm May–Sept), there's often live music as well as the usual produce.

Hood River history is on display at the **HOOD RIVER COUNTY HISTORICAL MUSEUM** (300 E Port Marina Dr, Hood River; 541/386-6772; open every day summer–early fall). The **HOOD RIVER COUNTY CHAMBER OF COMMERCE** (720 E Port Marina Dr, Hood River; 541/386-2000 or 800/366-3530; www.hoodriver. org) is a good resource.

RESTAURANTS

Abruzzo Italian Grill / ★★

1810 W CASCADE ST, HOOD RIVER; 541/386-7779
The smell of fresh pasta and the sound of happy chatter waft down the street from this small olive-green building a few blocks from downtown. This local favorite features generous dishes from the Abruzzo region of Italy. It's not unusual to wait for a table; the homemade gnocchi, rich pancetta sauces, and fresh berry panna cotta often draw a crowd. The cement floors and wood tabletops lend an informal note, and the atmosphere can be noisy. Opt for the outdoor seating in summer. *$; MC, V; local checks only; dinner Tues–Sat; full bar; no reservations; west of downtown on north side of st.* &

Brian's Pourhouse / ★★

606 OAK ST, HOOD RIVER; 541/387-4344
This one-story white-clapboard house feels like a beach vacation home. The setting, like the menu, has something for everyone. Just don't go looking for brewpub fare. The front-room bar is often packed with a louder singles crowd drinking beer, wine, and cocktails, but the back dining room is family friendly, complete with crayons. More casual fare includes pizzas, fish tacos, and gourmet burgers, but Brian's true culinary specialties are innovative fish dishes, such as jerk salmon, sesame ahi tuna, and crispy oyster starters. *$$; MC, V; local checks only; dinner every day; full bar; reservations recommended; www.brianspourhouse.com; between 6th and 7th sts.* &

Panzanella Artisan Bakery and Italian Deli / ★

102 5TH ST, HOOD RIVER; 541/386-2048
Providing Hood River with the stuff of life, Panzanella sells artisan breads, sandwiches, and picnic-ready goodies. Grab a stool at the high counter and enjoy the paintings by local artists, or take out your lunch—which most folks do. Breakfasts are light, such as toast with preserves. *$; MC, V; checks OK; breakfast, lunch Mon–Sat; no alcohol; no reservations; at Cascade Ave.* &

Stonehedge Gardens / ★★

3405 CASCADE AVE, HOOD RIVER; 541/386-3940
The winding road to Stonehedge Gardens is mined with potholes, but the century-old clapboard house—originally a summer cottage—sits amid trees and gardens, making it a winner for romantic outdoor dining. The fire-warmed interior has walls and ceilings paneled with age-darkened Douglas fir. The bistro-style menu could be better, but it's the charming setting that makes this place worth visiting. In winter, try bargain entrées like portobello mushroom ravioli or spicy Thai chicken in peanut sauce. *$$; AE, DC, DIS, MC, V; checks OK; dinner every day; full bar; reservations recommended; wwwstonehedgegardens.com; I-84 exit 62, look for sign on south side of Cascade Ave, follow gravel road 1/3 mile.*

HOOD RIVER'S FRUIT LOOP

Download a map of the **FRUIT LOOP** (www.hoodriverfruitloop.com) in advance, or pick one up at the **HOOD RIVER VISITOR CENTER** (405 Portway Ave, Hood River; 800/366-3530; I-84 exit 64), at **FRUIT LOOP LOCATIONS**, or at the **MT. HOOD COUNTRY STORE** (6545 Cooper Spur Rd, Mt Hood; 503/352-6024; on Hwy 35 at south end of Hood River Valley).

Buy a fresh-baked 4-pound apple pie and sip pear-dumpling-and-huckleberry milk shakes at the **APPLE VALLEY COUNTRY STORE** (2363 Tucker Rd, Hood River; 541/386-1971). Edible keepsakes include handcrafted fruit jams, pepper jellies, syrups, and pie fillings. Weekends, July–October, the store hosts an old-fashioned barbecue daily. Starting in early spring and continuing through December, you can pick up greenhouse plants, including more than 40 types of pansies, herbs, and hanging baskets, at **RASMUSSEN FARMS** (3020 Thomsen Rd, Hood River; 800/548-2243; www.rasmussenfarms.com). By June, they also have u-pick and ready-picked berries; the produce selection grows exponentially with the season. **DOUBLE DUTCH FARMS** (3057 Lingren Rd, Odell; 541/354-6262; www.alpacasdoubledutch.com), a full-service alpaca ranch, offers on-site alpaca oogling and alpaca fiber goods at its accompanying Accent on Alpacas country store. With picnic tables and awesome views, the **HOOD RIVER VINEYARDS AND WINERY** (4693 Westwood Dr, Hood River; 541/386-3772; www.hoodrivervineyards.us)—the oldest winery in the gorge—is an ideal place to sip fine estate-grown red wines, ports, or Gewürztraminers. Buy jams, honey, and freshly picked fruit during the harvest season at **MCCURDY FARMS FRUIT STAND** (2080 Tucker Rd, Hood River; 541/386-1628). Call ahead to arrange to see **CLEAR CREEK DISTILLERY'S** (in Portland) *Eau de Vie de Poire*: pears growing in bottles in orchard trees.

—Jo Ostgarden

LODGINGS

Columbia Gorge Hotel / ★★☆

4000 WESTCLIFF DR, HOOD RIVER; 541/386-5566 OR 800/345-1921

Opened in 1921 as a destination on the then-new Columbia River Highway, the Columbia Gorge Hotel scores big for history and setting. The grand stuccoed building with a red tile roof and green shutters is surrounded by fabulous flower gardens and overlooks the Columbia River and Wah Gwin Gwin Falls. Visited in its heyday by presidents and cultural luminaries, the hotel offers opulent, view-filled common areas. Designed for another era, some of the rooms are quite small if not a bit dated (depending on your taste), but all are unique—some have brass or canopy beds, and some of the larger rooms have fireplaces. Most have excellent gorge views. The room rate includes turndown service and the trademarked, titanic-sized "World Famous Farm Breakfast." Spa services are also available. *$$$; AE, DIS, MC, V; checks OK; www.columbiagorgehotel.com; I-84 exit 62.* &

Hood River BnB / ★

918 OAK ST, HOOD RIVER; 541/387-2997

Hardwood floors and cozy, light-filled rooms make Hood River BnB a relaxing respite with a river view. Built in 1909, the sunny house sits just a few blocks from downtown; each of its four guest rooms has wi-fi Internet access and a gear storage area. Well-behaved dogs are allowed in the Sun room, and children are welcome in the Sky room and Sun room, both with en suite bathrooms and futon couches. The upstairs River and Mountain rooms share a bath. The River room has, by far, the best view of Mount Adams, across the river in Washington. *$$; MC, V; checks OK; www.hoodriverbnb.com; between 9th and 10th sts.*

Vagabond Lodge / ★

**4070 WESTCLIFF DR, HOOD RIVER;
541/386-2992 OR 877/386-2992**

For the informed traveler on a budget, this place can be a money-saving convenience. The rooms in the hackneyed front part of the motel are spartan and nondescript; request one in the new three-story riverside building. Some have balconies overlooking the Columbia River, some have fireplaces, and a few have kitchens. Families will appreciate the hideaway sleeper sofas, which stretch capacity to six to a room. *$$; AE, DC, DIS, MC, V; no checks; www.vagabondlodge.com; I-84 exit 62, west on Westcliff Dr past Columbia Gorge Hotel.*

Mosier

Mosier doesn't look like much from the highway, but drive in and you'll see why it has quietly attracted a fair share of big-city transplants. Set in one of Oregon's sunniest locales, it has a mix of historic buildings and new homes—and a mere 400 residents.

Mosier is located between two stretches of the **HISTORIC COLUMBIA RIVER HIGHWAY**; the one on the west, about a half mile up Rock Creek Drive, is open to hikers and bicyclists only. Called the **HISTORIC COLUMBIA RIVER HIGHWAY STATE TRAIL**, it runs 4½ miles through the historic Mosier Twin Tunnels, affording stunning views of the river and the gorge. It ends just east of Hood River. The Mosier area is also known as a good birding destination and includes two segments of the **OREGON CASCADES BIRDING TRAIL** (www.oregonbirdingtrails. org), one at Mosier Waterfront and the other at the Twin Tunnels.

Take the old highway to the east, and about midway to The Dalles, the road climbs to the scenic viewpoint at **ROWENA CREST**, which overlooks the Nature Conservancy's **TOM MCCALL PRESERVE** (just beyond milepost 6; www.nature. org), with stunning wildflower fields amid a mound-and-swale topography. To take one or two short interpretive hikes, park at the Rowena Crest viewpoint or at the trailhead on US Highway 30.

RESTAURANTS

The Good River Restaurant / ★★☆

904 2ND AVE, MOSIER; 541/478-0199
This classy downtown restaurant is a pleasant surprise. In addition to seasonal salads prepared with local ingredients and classic standards like fresh seafood, rib eye, and pork tenderloin, the menu offers several unexpected multicultural options, like Cuban pulled pork and chicken korma—a northern Indian dish. Creative gourmet pizzas also shine with decidedly local flavors. Try the Mosier Pizza, made with smoked bacon, caramelized pears, blue cheese, and mozzarella, or the Kinsey Farm pizza, topped with white sauce, Gruyère, Brie, dried local cherries, spinach, and ancho peppers. Even meat loaf gets an upgrade here with Black Angus beef. Along with a short but noteworthy list of regional wines, they also serve creative cocktails and an ever-changing list of microbrews. *$$; AE, DIS, MC, V; local checks only; breakfast Sun, lunch Wed–Fri, dinner Wed–Sun; full bar; reservations recommended; www.goodriverrestaurant.com; just east of "downtown."* &

LODGINGS

Mosier House Bed & Breakfast / ★

704 3RD AVE, MOSIER; 541/478-3640 OR 877/328-0351
The town's founder, Jefferson Newton Mosier, built this Queen Anne Victorian house in 1904 overlooking the Columbia River, and it's now on the National Register of Historic Places. Present owner Matt Koerner carefully restored it over several years. The house features period furnishings throughout, four guest rooms with shared baths upstairs, and a master guest room with a claw-foot tub, private entrance, and porch. The full breakfast sometimes includes crepes. *$$; MC, V; checks OK; www.mosierhouse.com; turn up Washington St and go left on 3rd Ave.*

The Dalles

The **COLUMBIA GORGE DISCOVERY CENTER** and **WASCO COUNTY HISTORICAL MUSEUM** complex, about 3 miles west of town (5000 Discovery Dr, The Dalles; 541/296-8600; www.gorgediscovery.org), chronicle the area's natural and human history.

In terms of both landscape and culture, this is the town where the West begins in Oregon. One of the state's oldest cities, The Dalles sits on land that for centuries was one of the main indigenous trading centers in North America. Tribes from as far away as North Dakota and California came here to barter and fish. Explorers Lewis and Clark, and their Corps of Discovery, also camped here—at **ROCK FORT** (northeast of 2nd and Webber sts, The Dalles; 541/296-2231 for directions)—in October 1805 and again in April 1806 on their way home from a cold winter on the Pacific coast.

The town's name originated with French voyageurs traveling the Columbia River in the early 1800s. The French term for "flagstone"—*le dalle*—suggests a gutter or a trough, or in this case, river rapids flowing swiftly through a narrow channel over flat, basaltic rocks. The town rose in status in the 1850s when it became the seat of Wasco County, the largest county ever formed in the United States, stretching to Wyoming.

During the Great Migration, the town site marked the place where pioneers had to decide whether to take their wagons around Mount Hood by the Barlow Trail—a steep and treacherous route—or lash wagon and belongings onto crude rafts and brave the Columbia's rapids. Today the rapids and the falls—from the Big Eddy west of the city to Celilo village in the east—along with the subsistence fishing grounds of many tribes, are gone, inundated in 1957 after completion of The Dalles Dam.

Dozens of elegant 19th- and early-20th-century buildings from the city's heyday have been preserved, including the **FORT DALLES MUSEUM** (15th and Garrison sts, The Dalles; 541/296-4547), in the 1857 surgeon's quarters of the former fort, and **OLD ST. PETER'S LANDMARK** (3rd and Lincoln sts, The Dalles; 541/296-5686), built in 1898 as a Roman Catholic church and saved by preservationists when the parish moved to a modern building. Its 176-foot-high spire has been a landmark since 1897. Inside, there's a rare tigerwood pipe organ and a life-size statue of the Madonna, carved from the keel of an 1850s shipwreck.

The original **WASCO COUNTY COURTHOUSE** (420 W 2nd Pl, The Dalles; www.wascochs.org) was built in 1859; a second, in 1884. The third and current one (5th and Washington sts, The Dalles), resplendent in golden oak and marble, dates from 1914. Outside, a bronze statue of a pronghorn antelope serves as a reminder and a tribute to a more recent past; it is dedicated to local residents who helped oust the followers of Bhagwan Shree Rajneesh, who from their compound in nearby Antelope, waged a political coup against the county government in the 1980s.

In 1891 a large area of The Dalles was leveled by fire. A flood hit three years later, and you can see water marks on the front of **KLINDT'S BOOKSELLERS** (315 E 2nd St, The Dalles; 541/296-3355), founded in 1870 and still the oldest continually operating bookstore in Oregon. It moved to its Second Street location in 1893, the year before the flood.

Now a market center for the region's cherry growing, wheat farming, and cattle ranching, The Dalles loves parades, determinedly throwing two big ones each year: **THE DALLES CHERRY FESTIVAL PARADE** in late April and the **FORT DALLES RODEO PARADE** (lots of cowboys and horses!) in mid-July. Parts of The Dalles are also being revitalized, including the waterfront, which is ripe for the undertaking. Currently, the **LEWIS AND CLARK RIVERFRONT TRAIL** runs 6½ miles along the river. Eventually, the paved trail will run a full 9½ miles between the Discovery Center and The Dalles Dam. Visitor information is available from **THE DALLES AREA CHAMBER OF COMMERCE** (404 W 2nd St, The Dalles; 541/296-2231; www. thedalleschamber.com).

Hamburgers are "made with love" at **BIG JIM'S DRIVE INN** (2938 E 2nd St, The Dalles; 541/298-5051; www.bigjimsdrivein.com.); the place has a long history in the city under several different owners but offers yesteryear classic drive-in fare—old-fashioned milk shakes, banana splits, and sundaes—the locals love.

RESTAURANTS

Baldwin Saloon / ★

205 COURT ST, THE DALLES; 541/296-5666

The 1876 Baldwin Saloon has seen a bit of everything between its brick walls. In the span of a century, it's been a steamboat navigational office, a coffin storage site, an employment office, and a saddlery before finally returning to its origins as a bar and restaurant. Recent restorations added an impressive collection of early 20th-century Northwest oil paintings. The American food is consistently good, with noteworthy oysters Rockefeller and rich desserts (the walnut tart, especially). *$$; MC, V; local checks only; lunch, dinner Mon–Sat; full bar; reservations recommended; www.baldwin saloon.com; at 1st St.* &

Petite Provence / ★

408 E 2ND ST, THE DALLES; 541/506-0037

This is a place where eggs are beaten to just the right froth, poured into a pan at just the right temperature, then served up fresh and hot as omelets. Herbed potato pancakes and perfect toast take breakfast or brunch up another notch. But it's the beautiful and glistening breads and pastries—with tastes straight out of the French countryside—that'll make you want to pack up and move here. A display case filled with goodies conspires to blow your diet big-time. *$; MC, V; no checks; breakfast, lunch Mon–Sat; full bar; reservations recommended; 1 block north of Hwy 30, downtown.* &

Windseeker Restaurant & Portside Pub / ★

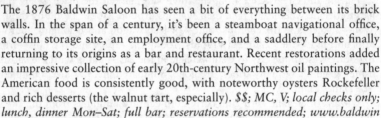

1535 BARGEWAY RD, THE DALLES; 541/298-7171

Perched alongside the Columbia River and framed by tended gardens, the Windseeker offers panoramic views of the gorge. Chef David Worley, a Le Cordon Bleu award winner, crafts regional dishes that incorporate the region's bounty. Try the hazelnut-coated halibut, fried razor clams, poached salmon with peach citrus sauce, tender filet mignon, or jumbo sea scallops *en croute* in mushroom cream sauce. If you can't make dinner, hit Sunday brunch for crispy Belgian waffles, made-to-order omelets, and an extensive array of weekly rotating entrées, including homemade chicken and dumplings or seafood sauté with crab claws. The extensive wine list highlights varietals from local wineries. Most nights, you'll need a reservation to get one of the coveted window seats. *$$; MC, V; no checks; lunch, dinner every day, brunch Sun; full bar; reservations recommended; www.windseekerrestaurant. com; near the port.* &

LODGINGS

The Balch Hotel / ★★

40 S HEIMRICH ST, DUFUR; 541/467-2277
Proximity to The Dalles, and a back route connection to the Mt. Hood Scenic Byway, make this restored 100-year-old hotel an option for adventurous travelers who want to poke around Oregon's Wild West and are looking for a serene, off-the-beaten-track base camp. Surrounded by spectacular views of Mount Hood and rolling fields of golden wheat and green alfalfa, all 19 rooms are furnished with period antiques that convey the elegance of the era in which the historic hotel was built. Some rooms have baths; others have sinks and share a bath across or down the hall. There are no elevators or lifts, no televisions or phones, but there is free wireless Internet access. A sumptuous breakfast for two is included. *$$; MC, V; no checks; www.balchhotel.com; on Hwy 197 12 miles south of The Dalles.*

Mount Hood

Perpetually snowcapped, 11,245-foot Mount Hood is the highest place in Oregon and one of the most frequently climbed glaciated mountains in the world. Mount Hood has 12 named glaciers, the most visited of which is **PALMER GLACIER**, located partially within the Timberline Lodge ski area and along the most popular climbing route. With a chairlift and ski slope at 10,000 feet, the Palmer makes skiing possible year-round. Aspiring young Olympians, including the U.S. Ski Team, come from all over the world for summer training.

Encompassing more than 1 million acres, the **MOUNT HOOD NATIONAL FOREST** (www.fs.fed.us/r6/mthood/) is Portlanders' primary outdoor playground and retreat from urban life. Pick up maps and detailed information on wilderness regulations at **MOUNT HOOD INFORMATION CENTER** (65000 E Hwy 26, Welches; 503/622-3017; www.mthood.org), the **HOOD RIVER RANGER STATION** (6780 SR 35, Parkdale; 541/352-6002), or the **ZIGZAG RANGER STATION** (70220 E Hwy 26, Zigzag; 503/622-3191).

Mount Hood has five main ski areas. **COOPER SPUR** (11000 Cloud Cap Rd, Mount Hood; 541/352-7803; www.cooper_spur.com), 27 miles south of Hood River on **STATE ROUTE 35**, is an affordable day-ski area at 4,500 feet, with 10 runs, a chairlift, three rope tows, and a T-bar. The biggest one, **MOUNT HOOD MEADOWS** (2 miles north of SR 35 on FR 3555, Mount Hood; 503/337-2222; www.skihood.com), is at 7,300 feet elevation. It has a day lodge, 87 runs, four high-speed quads, six double chairlifts, and a Nordic ski center. Meadows, as it's known, teams with many lodgings in the Mount Hood–Hood River area to offer bargain lift tickets.

GOVERNMENT CAMP, 53 miles east of Portland on Hwy 26, is the village center of the inexpensive and popular **SUMMIT SKI AREA** (near the rest area at east end of Government Camp; 503/272-0256; www.summitskiarea.com). Founded in 1927, it is the oldest ski and sledding area on Mount Hood. Ski and tube rentals are available. The **MOUNT HOOD CULTURAL CENTER AND MUSEUM** (88900 E Hwy 26, Government Camp; 503/272-3301; www.mthoodmuseum.org) displays a photo collection and exhibits of Mount Hood winter sports history.

MOUNT HOOD SKIBOWL (87000 E Hwy 26, Government Camp; 503/272-3206; www.skibowl.com), at 5,026 feet, bills itself as America's largest night-ski area, with 34 lighted runs, four double chairlifts, and a tubing hill. In the summer, it's transformed into the **MOUNT HOOD SKIBOWL SUMMER ACTION PARK**, with 25-plus activities, including a dual alpine slide, Indy Karts, miniature golf, bungee jumping, batting cages, croquet, and a 40-mile mountain-bike park.

SNOW BUNNY (about 2 miles east of Government Camp on Hwy 26) is a small snow-play area, elevation 3,816 feet, and a popular trailhead for cross-country skiers, snowshoers, and snowmobilers.

At the top of the hill is **TIMBERLINE** (4 miles north of Hwy 26, just east of Government Camp; 503/622-7979; www.timberlinelodge.com). It offers six lifts; four are high-speed quads, including the Palmer Lift, which takes skiers up to the Palmer Glacier. In the summer, the **MAGIC MILE SUPER EXPRESS** lift carries riders 1,000 feet to **PALMER JUNCTION**, where the **MAGIC MILE INTERPRETIVE TRAIL** leads to **TIMBERLINE LODGE**.

Climbers who want to scale Mount Hood must register and obtain a free but mandatory wilderness permit in the 24-hour climbing room at Timberline's **WY'EAST DAY LODGE. TIMBERLINE MOUNTAIN GUIDES** (541/312-9242) does guided climbs. The relative easiest route up the mountain is on the south side; it takes most climbers 8 to 10 hours to scale it and requires crossing a crevasse during the warmer months and some potentially technical rope work near the Pearly Gates. Check with the Zigzag Ranger Station for conditions.

RESTAURANTS

Cascade Dining Room / ★★★

TIMBERLINE LODGE, TIMBERLINE; 503/622-0700
The rustic, carved wood of the main lodge provides a warm, casual setting for some of the most sophisticated food in the region. Executive chef Leif Eric Benson has presided here for almost three decades, winning a steady stream of awards for his deftly prepared Cascadian cuisine, which samples liberally from fresh Northwest-grown, -gathered, and -caught ingredients. Sweeping views of the mountain make this a special-occasion favorite. Diners can tour the downstairs wine vault. *$$$; AE, MC, V; checks OK; breakfast, lunch, dinner every day; full bar; reservations recommended; www.timberlinelodge.com; 60 miles east of Portland off US Hwy 26.* &

Ice Axe Grill / Mount Hood Brewing Company / ★

87304 GOVERNMENT CAMP LOOP,
GOVERNMENT CAMP; 503/622-0724

This brew-pub café's mountain-lodge ambience matches its après-ski menu. Dig into deli sandwiches, burgers, pizzas, and an assortment of entrées, including Cajun blue flatiron steak and beer-battered fish-and-chips; vegetarians can tuck into a mélange of gnocchi and sautéed veggies in a light cream sauce topped with honey-roasted hazelnuts and Gorgonzola. On Sundays, if you can finish the "Dare" burger, you get a $2 rebate. For desserts, go for the molten lava cake—a dark chocolate Bundt cake served with Tillamook ice cream. The grill is also home to the Mount Hood Brewing Company's house-brewed Ice Axe India Pale Ale and Hogsback Oatmeal Stout, as well as other cask-conditioned ales and nitro taps. $–$$; AE, DIS, MC, V; checks OK; lunch, dinner every day; beer and wine; reservations recommended; www. iceaxegrill.com; just off Hwy 26. &

Rendezvous Grill & Tap Room / ★

67149 E HWY 26, WELCHES; 503/622-6837

In Welches, the "Vous," as locals call it, serves up regional cuisine without the pretense found in Portland. The kitchen relies on fresh, in-season ingredients—chanterelle mushrooms, huckleberries, Dungeness crab, Willapa Bay oysters—as basic ingredients in their dishes. House-made desserts are widely raved about. The congenial Tap Room, open from early afternoon to evening, offers drinks, snacks, and meals, including a portobello sandwich and a burger on an onion bun with aioli sauce—accompanied, of course, by perfectly crisp French fries. $–$$; AE, DIS, MC, V; local checks only; lunch, dinner every day June–Sept, Wed–Sun Oct–May; beer and wine; reservations recommended; just east of traffic signal in Welches on north side of hwy. &

LODGINGS

The Hidden Woods Bed & Breakfast / ★★★

19380 E SUMMERTIME DR, SANDY; 503/622-5754

Originally built in 1929, this elegantly updated, hand-hewn-fir log cabin is located in a tiny forest community on the Sandy River with quick access to mountain activities. Surrounded by towering firs and whimsical gardens, the two-story, two-bedroom cabin's rustic, woodsy theme—black bears, fly-fishing—provides a charming counterpoint to its modern conveniences: fully equipped kitchen, bath, washer and dryer. Guests get the private cabin, with an outdoor grilling area and hot tub/spa, to themselves. Ski, bike, or flip a fly in the river, then climb into the hot tub and listen to the *snap, crackle,* and *pop* of the fire in the fire pit while you unwind. A hearty, sumptuous breakfast awaits at Coni and Terry's 3,000-square-foot log home, down the path next door. $$–$$$; no credit cards; checks OK; www.thehiddenwoods. com; at milepost 33, about 20 miles from Timberline turnoff.

Mount Hood Hamlet Bed & Breakfast / ★★

6741 SR 35, MOUNT HOOD; 541/352-3574 OR 800/407-0570

Retired teachers Paul and Diane Romans built this colonial-style house—inspired by an ancestral home in Rhode Island—on farmland on the northeast side of Mount Hood (closer to Hood River), where Paul was raised. Decor is tasteful early American, and the bed-and-breakfast has a spectacular, up-close view of Mount Hood. All guest rooms have private baths, fireplaces, Jacuzzis, and TVs. Families should ask for the larger Orchard Room. The outdoor hot tub, heated year-round, sits among the inn's "Backyard Habitat" designed by the National Wildlife Federation; more than 45 bird species have been identified on the property. The inn also has a strong environmental ethic, composting, recycling, heating with a geothermal exchange, and serving locally sourced foods at breakfast. *$$$; DIS, MC, V; checks OK; www. mthoodhamlet.com; 20 miles north of Mount Hood Meadows.* &

Timberline Lodge / ★★★☆

**TIMBERLINE SKI AREA, TIMBERLINE;
503/622-7979 OR 800/547-1406**

Designated as a national historic landmark, this gorgeous lodge is nothing short of a national treasure. Built during the depression as a New Deal Work Progress Administration project, the lodge also served as a backdrop for the 1980 Stanley Kubrick film *The Shining*. Perched at an elevation of 5,960 feet, the expansive building incorporates massive old-growth timbers and local stone. Intricately carved decorative elements appear throughout the lodge, along with handcrafted furniture, original art, and historical dioramas. Since it's federally owned, discounted rates are mandated, fulfilled by European-style chalet rooms with bunk beds that sleep up to 10 people, plus shared baths. More expensive rooms have stone fireplaces and views. Ask specifically about room views, as deep snow can disappointingly obscure vistas. *$–$$$; AE, MC, V; checks OK; www.timberlinelodge.com; 60 miles east of Portland off US Hwy 26.* &

WILLAMETTE VALLEY

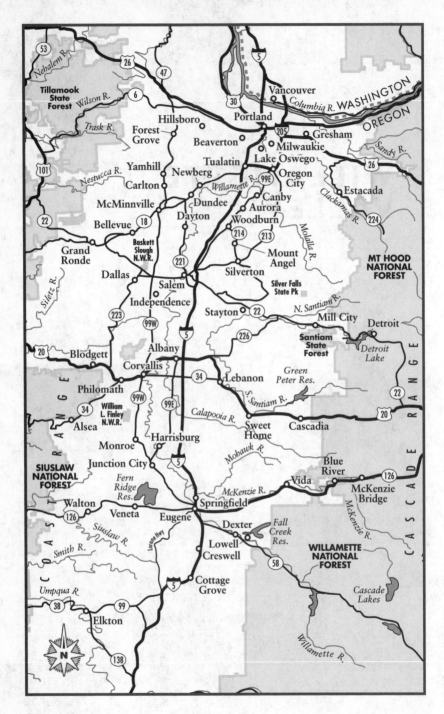

WILLAMETTE VALLEY

The Missoula Floods, which inundated the Northwest from Montana to the Pacific dozens of times at the end of the last ice age, left in their wake Oregon's agricultural heartland: the Willamette Valley. Rich volcanic and glacial soils from western Montana through Eastern Washington that were deposited across the valley floor when the waters subsided left behind, in some areas, fertile soil a half mile deep. The valley—a broad plain and rolling hills—is bound on the west by the Oregon Coast Range, on the east by the Cascade Range, on the north by bluffs above the Columbia River, and on the south by the Calapooya Mountains, which separate the headwaters of the Willamette from the Umpqua River valley.

During spring and summer growing seasons, roadside stands dot the country lanes, and farmers markets roll into the valley's historic towns. Covered bridges beckon drivers to explore a vast network of back roads, and the valley's flat terrain and year-round temperate weather draw cyclists from the cities. The climate and gentle rolling hills also contribute to the valley's success as a major wine-producing region, widely known as **OREGON WINE COUNTRY**, with multiple American viticultural areas. Today more than 13,000 acres of vineyards and more than 300 wineries—many of them notably committed to sustainable-farming practices—produce some of the world's finest pinot noir and pinot gris, as well as other varietals. The expansion of vineyards and the popularity of area wineries bring a growing collection of tantalizing restaurants and places to stay.

ACCESS AND INFORMATION

Commuter airlines serve the **PORTLAND INTERNATIONAL AIRPORT** (off I-84, northeast Portland; 503/460-4040; www.flypdx.com) and the **EUGENE AIRPORT** (off Route 99W, northwest Eugene; 541/682-5430; www.eugeneairport. com). Car rentals are available at both airports and in Eugene and Portland.

Most travelers arrive via **INTERSTATE 5**, which parallels the Willamette River from Portland to Eugene. This is the express route through the Willamette Valley. It typically takes about two hours to drive from Portland to Eugene. **ROUTE 99W** parallels I-5 west of the Willamette and makes for a more leisurely north-south commute through agricultural fields, small country towns, and the wine country of Yamhill County. Contact the **OREGON DEPARTMENT OF TRANSPORTATION** (503/588-2941 or 800/977-6368) for road conditions. **TRAVEL ADVISOR** (www.tripcheck.com) also has helpful information.

AMTRAK (800/USA-RAIL; www.amtrak.com) commutes from Portland to Eugene and stops in Salem, Albany, and Eugene. The **WILLAMETTE VALLEY VISITOR'S ASSOCIATION** (866/548-5018; www.oregonwinecountry.org) is a good, general source; check out the **WILLAMETTE VALLEY WINERIES ASSOCIATION** (503/646-2985; www.willamettewines.com) for extensive and up-to-date listings of the area's lodgings, restaurants, special events, and, of course, 200-plus wineries.

Newberg

Located in the northwest part of the valley, Newberg, along with neighboring towns, attracts wine seekers. Others come to visit the Hoover-Minthorn House Museum (115 S River St; 503/538-6629): In 1885 an 11-year-old boy named Herbert Hoover came to Newberg to live with his aunt and uncle—the Minthorns—and remained there until he was in his mid-teens. In 1929 he was elected president of the United States. The museum is open to visitors February through December.

RESTAURANTS

The Painted Lady / ★★★

201 S COLLEGE ST, NEWBERG; 503/538-3850

Avoiding the cluttered mishmash that is often the result of restaurants in houses, chefs/co-owners Allen Routt and Jessica Bagley-Routt have created a space that maintains elegance, serving a (seasonally rotating) prix-fixe menu that fuses the local bounty of the Northwest with classic European culinary techniques. First-course options range from delicately composed salads like butter lettuce, fresh crab, avocado, and pine nuts in a tarragon citrus vinaigrette to wild mushroom ragout over light and pillowy gnocchi. Entrées include slow-roasted steelhead fillet over a fennel bacon slaw with carrot purée; Niman Ranch New York steak treated with caramelized onions, blue cheese butter, and silky mashed potatoes; and vegetarian crepes stuffed with roasted winter vegetables and tomato cream. Desserts are inspired, especially the chèvre cheesecake with poached pear. *$$$–$$$$; AE, DIS, MC, V; no checks; dinner every day; full bar; reservations recommended; www.thepainted ladyrestaurant.com; just off 1st St.*

LODGINGS

Springbrook Hazelnut Farm / ★★

30295 N RTE 99W, NEWBERG; 503/538-4606 OR 800/793-8528

In the heart of Oregon wine country, this landmark farmhouse is not only an exquisitely decorated B and B but a working hazelnut farm as well. Wicker furnishings decorate two upstairs rooms, which share a bathroom; downstairs, two others are furnished with antiques and have half baths, sharing a full bath down the hall. Rose Cottage and the Carriage House, each with a kitchen, are behind the main house. The old barn is now a small winery, and the hazelnut stand is open in the fall. Visitors can explore the orchards, swim in the pool, play tennis, and explore wine country. *$$–$$$; DIS, MC, V; checks OK; www. nutfarm.com; just off Rte 99W north of town.*

Dundee

Dundee is easily the culinary epicenter of the northern Oregon wine country. Several notable restaurants are strung along Rte 99W, many in former early 20th-century homes, but the area also has a high concentration of wineries. In fact, the Dundee locale has its own subappellation: Dundee Hills. Much of the acreage is owned by many of Oregon's pioneer winemakers, who continue to grow and make beautiful wines. **SOKOL BLOSSER WINERY** (see "Oregon's Growing Cadre of Green Wineries") is one of the key leaders in sustainability. Wines produced in this area include pinot noir, pinot gris, white Riesling, chardonnay, pinot blanc, pinot meunière, muscat Ottonel, Müller Thurgau, and dolcetto. Later comers have added to the bounty as well, with wineries like **VISTA HILLS VINEYARD** (see "Oregon's Growing Cadre of Green Wineries"), which produces premium pinots and donates 10 percent of all wine profits to students working their way through college.

RESTAURANTS

The Dundee Bistro / ★★★

100-A SE 7TH ST, DUNDEE; 503/554-1650
This bustling bistro-pizzeria-bar built by the Ponzi family, respected Oregon winemaking pioneers, features large windows and a lovely courtyard. Sage- and pumpkin-tinted walls and floor give the space a Tuscan ambience, but the food is distinctively Northwestern. A seasonal menu might feature Dungeness crab or a roasted beet and applewood-smoked bacon salad, lemon- and garlic-braised Draper Valley chicken, or Oregon petrale sole with tortellini. Desserts include molten chocolate cake, brown sugar–infused pear crisp topped with house-made vanilla ice cream, and refreshing fruit sorbets. The adjacent Ponzi Wine Bar showcases small-production north Willamette Valley wines, with a 90 percent focus on pinot noirs. *$$; AE, MC, V; local checks only; lunch, dinner every day; full bar; reservations recommended; www. dundeebistro.com; on Rte 99 W.* &

Red Hills Provincial Dining / ★★★

276 ROUTE 99W, DUNDEE; 503/538-8224
The reception at this enchanting 1912 Craftsman-style house-turned-restaurant is warm and inviting. The simple European-country dinner menu is ever changing and intriguing: veal osso buco with creamy polenta, perhaps, or fricasee of game hen with chanterelles. All the details are just right, whether it's bread dusted with fresh rosemary or poached pears with caramel sauce. The deep and wide wine list is worldly. A private dining room seats up to 12. *$$; AE, MC, V; checks OK; dinner Tues–Sun; full bar; reservations recommended; www.redhillsdining.com; north edge of town.*

Tina's / ★★★

760 ROUTE 99W, DUNDEE; 503/538-8880
Very much a local gathering place, this small, unassuming house on the side of the highway belies the treasures inside. The space sparkles with stylish decor, bright white walls, and a fireplace. The cuisine is contemporary European with a focus on seasonal local ingredients, including Oregon lamb and Harris Ranch beef tenderloin. The sea scallops in a thyme-infused sauce are

exceptional, as is the purée of corn soup, creamy without cream. Surprises include salmon spring rolls served with hazelnut sauce. The list of house-made desserts is short, and the wine list is long: the right proportion in these parts. *$$; AE, DIS, MC, V; checks OK; lunch Tues–Fri, dinner every day; full bar; reservations recommended; center of town, across from fire station.* &

Dayton

A small town mostly known for its wine-country connection, Dayton is home to several landmark buildings. The most historic, perhaps, is the **FORT YAMHILL BLOCK HOUSE** (in the city park). Built by Willamette Valley settlers on Fort Hill, in the Grand Ronde Valley in 1855–1856, it was later moved here to save it. Several high-profile wineries are also in the area, including **DROMAINE DROUHIN** (6750 Breyman Orchards Rd; 503/864-2700; www. domainedrouhin.com), one of the few vineyards in the country to cultivate their own rootstock. The winery sits snug into the highest slopes of Oregon's Red Hills, sharing a nearly identical climate, latitude, and aspect with its counterparts in the Burgundy area of France.

RESTAURANTS

Joel Palmer House / ★★★

600 FERRY ST, DAYTON; 503/864-2995
No trip to Oregon wine country is complete without a visit to the Joel Palmer House, headed by chef Jack Czarnecki, an authority on mushrooms and their culinary uses. Rare is the dish here that emerges without some play on that theme. Starters include a three-mushroom tart, escargots with black chanterelles, and corn chowder. Complex and yet perfectly nuanced entrées might feature a rack of lamb with rich pinot noir–hazelnut sauce or wild mushroom duxelles and a Creole–pinot gris sauce side by tender sautéed scallops. Or consider Jack's Mushroom Madness, a prix-fixe, multicourse dinner emphasizing—what else?—wild mushrooms. Housed in town cofounder General Joel Palmer's former home, the restaurant has an air of romance and formality. *$$–$$$; AE, DIS, MC, V; local checks only; dinner Tues–Sat; full bar; reservations required; www.joelpalmerhouse.com; downtown.* &

LODGINGS

Wine Country Farm / ★

6855 BREYMAN ORCHARDS RD, DAYTON; 503/864-3446 OR 800/261-3446
Wine Country Farm is nestled into the Red Hills of Dundee, where the soil is indeed red and the expansive vineyards are spectacular. The nine colorful and vibrant guest rooms in the white stucco 1910 house have private bathrooms; two have fireplaces. A hot tub, sauna, and on-site massages are available. A large wine-tasting room is right next door so you can sip to your heart's delight before retiring to your room. Owners of the 13-acre farm also own Arabian horses and offer guided trail rides as well as buggy rides to other wineries. Enjoy

the farm breakfast on a sun-washed deck with a spectacular view. *$$–$$$; MC, V; checks OK; www.winecountryfarm.com; right onto McDugal Rd just past Sokol Blosser Winery, then right to Breyman Orchards Rd.*

Carlton

Carlton's 19th-century brick and stone storefronts make for a nostalgic, pleasant stroll through an interesting downtown. Small quilting, gardening, and art shops provide local small-town ambience. Several tasting rooms and wine cellars tempt you in.

The **TASTING ROOM** (105 W Main St; 503/852-6733; www.pinotnoir.com) features wines from several local wineries that are typically closed to the public. **CARLTON WINEMAKER STUDIO AND TASTING ROOM** (see "Oregon's Growing Cadre of Green Wineries") is a wine cooperative led by Eric Hamacher.

The **HORSE RADISH** (211 W Main St; 503/852-6656; www.thehorse radish.com) is a casual wine bar and specialty food shop selling locally bottled condiments, artisan cheeses, meats, and chocolates, in addition to bottles from small-production wineries. Dine in or take away, but do enjoy the live music on weekend evenings. The **FILLING STATION** (305 W Main St; 503/852-6687; www.fillingstationdeli.com) has free wi-fi, in addition to breakfast, lunch, and Portland's famous Stumptown coffee.

RESTAURANTS

Cuvée / ★★★

214 W MAIN ST, CARLTON; 503/852-6555
Indulge in traditional French-country cuisine in the heart of downtown Carlton. Chef Gilbert Henry sources fresh, local vegetables, fish, and meat to create classic dishes, including escargots in a shallot and garlic butter sauce, chicken liver mousse, coquilles St. Jacques, and steak *frites*. The concise menu puts a fresh twist on local and international fare as well: Try the Dungeness crab and pear port reduction over basmati rice or Moroccan lamb *tagine* rich with spices, dried apricots, and garbanzo beans. The wine list is broad, while desserts, happily, stray not much farther than simple and perfect *mousse au chocolat*, crème caramel, and chocolate cake. *$$–$$$; AE, DIS, MC, V; local checks only; dinner Wed–Sun; full bar; reservations recommended; www.cuveedining.com; downtown.*

LODGINGS

Abbey Road Farms / ★★★

10501 NE ABBEY RD, CARLTON; 503/852-6278
Make no mistake: the accommodations in this B and B's converted grain silos are far from rough. Five separate suites offer radiant-floor heat, private baths, Jacuzzis, and sweeping views of the sustainable-focused working farm. Owners Judi and John Stuart, who opened Abbey Road in 2005,

---

WILLAMETTE VALLEY THREE-DAY TOUR

DAY ONE: Starting in Eugene, enjoy eggs Benedict or thick French toast at STUDIO ONE CAFÉ (1473 E 19th Ave, Eugene; 541/342-8596; 11am–4pm Mon–Fri). Then take I-5 to exit 182 at Creswell and visit KING ESTATE (80854 Territorial Rd, Eugene; 541/942-9874 or 800/884-4441; www.kingestate.com; noon–5pm every day) for a tour of the winery, a walk in the garden, and small-plate wine pairings on the patio. Take the winding back roads about 20 miles to Eugene, following the Lorane Highway north. In the afternoon, if weather permits, stop at SPENCER'S BUTTE (on S Willamette St, Eugene) for a steep 1-mile hike to a viewpoint, or walk the PREFONTAINE TRAIL along the Willamette River. For an indoor option, check out crafts and shopping at the FIFTH AVENUE PUBLIC MARKET, or visit the JORDAN SCHNITZER MUSEUM OF ART at the University of Oregon campus. Check in to the CAMPBELL HOUSE near the public market, then dine at CAFÉ SORIAH for Mediterranean-inspired specialties.

DAY TWO: Enjoy your breakfast at the B and B, then take a two-hour drive north to Silverton. Stop to explore landscaped acres at the OREGON GARDEN before checking in to the WATER STREET INN BED AND BREAKFAST in

---

maintain lush, English-style gardens, plus alpacas, llamas, donkeys, and dairy goats, from which Judi crafts several varieties of fresh chèvre that make frequent appearances on the breakfast table. In fact, meals include many seasonal products of the farm: Queen Anne cherries, fresh eggs, vegetables, and herbs, in addition to meats from nearby Carlton Farms. The Stuarts' most recent accomplishment is the on-site AgriVino Wine Center, using an innovative Italian wine-preservation system that allows guests to taste 1-ounce pours from 56 different Willamette Valley wines. *$$$; MC, V; no checks; www.abbeyroadfarm.com; just off NE Kuehne Rd west of downtown.*

McMinnville

This once drive-through strip town has been nudged into the high life by thriving wine and agriculture industries. Get off the main thoroughfare and wander through a shaded town center humming with wine shops, cafés, and boutiques—many inhabiting buildings erected at the turn of the 20th century. McMinnville's central location makes it a good base for wine touring, but be aware that the area is especially bustling around Memorial Day, Thanksgiving, and late July or early August during the INTERNATIONAL PINOT NOIR CELEBRATION (503/472-8964 or 800/775-4762; www.inpc.org) at Linfield College. Purchase tickets a year in advance if you're determined to attend. Pick up

downtown Silverton. Walk a block to **O'BRIAN'S CAFE** for lunch, and sit on the patio overlooking **SILVER CREEK** to enjoy the best country cooking. Either tour the wineries around Silverton (see "Oregon's Growing Cadre of Green Wineries") or drive to **SILVER FALLS STATE PARK** to view the falls. Dine at **SILVER GRILLE CAFÉ & WINES** in downtown Silverton.

DAY THREE: Have breakfast at the inn and then drive west to Mount Angel to tour the **MOUNT ANGEL ABBEY**. Then continue northwest to Newberg, the heart of **OREGON WINE COUNTRY**. Begin by driving south on **RTE 99W**, stopping for tastings at **SOKOL BLOSSER WINERY** (5000 Sokol Blosser Ln, Dundee; 503/864-2282 or 800/582-6668; www.sokolblosser.com), one of the very first Oregon wine producers, and **ARGYLE WINERY** (691 Rte 99W, Dundee; 503/538-8520; www.argylewinery.com) for the state's best sparkling wine. For lunch, either pack a picnic to enjoy at a winery or drive to McMinnville and partake of fine French cuisine at **BISTRO MAISON**. Continue visiting wineries as you drive north to Carlton, stopping at the **CARLTON WINEMAKER STUDIO AND TASTING ROOM** and enjoying the shops along Main Street. For dinner, take the short drive to Dayton to enjoy a meal at the **JOEL PALMER HOUSE** and then tuck into bed at the **WINE COUNTRY FARM**.

information at the **MCMINNVILLE CHAMBER OF COMMERCE** (417 N Adams St; 503/472-6196; www.mcminnville.org). Right off the main drag, Third Street, is an area known as the "Pinot Quarter": eight wineries clustered in a few blocks. **PANTHER CREEK CELLARS** (455 NE Irvine St; 503/472-8080) was one of the first and also one of the stars.

The **EVERGREEN AVIATION MUSEUM** (500 NE Capt Michael King Smith Wy; 503/434-4180; www.sprucegoose.org) features Howard Hughes' *Flying Boat*. Every spring, the **HOTEL OREGON** (see review) hosts a **UFO FESTIVAL**, welcoming believers, skeptics, noted experts, and everyone in between, from near and far, for a weekend of fun, enlightenment, and entertainment.

RESTAURANTS

Bistro Maison / ★★

729 E 3RD ST, MCMINNVILLE; 503/474-1888
This inviting French café, owned by chef Jean-Jacques and his wife, Deborah, is located in a historic bungalow decorated with cheery wallpaper and leather-backed booths. A good place to start is the *moules*, mussels cooked in three different styles. Entrées include classic coq au vin in a rich pinot noir sauce and *confit de canard*, braised duck crisped with orange Cognac. The *profiteroles au chocolat* are an awesome way to top off dinner. On warm summer days, outdoor seating in the courtyard is pleasant. Sample single

pours or flights at the wine bar at the front. *$$; DIS, MC, V; local checks only; lunch Wed–Fri, dinner Wed–Sun, late brunch Sun; full bar; reservations recommended; www.bistromaison.com; next to train station.*

La Rambla / ★★☆

238 NE 3RD ST, MCMINNVILLE; 503/435-2126

La Rambla serves as a warm beacon, offering Northwest-inspired Spanish cuisine. Tucked into an 1898 building that was originally a bar, the cozy yet sophisticated restaurant has won awards for restoration and beautification. Entrées run from traditional paella to house-cured, grilled Carlton Farms pork chops. A varied list of tasty, amply sized cold and hot tapas ($6–$14) includes baked goat cheese with hazelnuts and smoky paprika tomato sauce, skewers of lamb from a local farm, and mini free-range buffalo burgers. The astounding wine list includes more than 300 local and Spanish bottles. *$$–$$$; AE, DIS, MC, V; checks OK; lunch, dinner every day; full bar; reservations recommended; www.laramblaonthird.com; between Cowels and Baker sts.* &

Nick's Italian Café / ★★

521 E 3RD ST, MCMINNVILLE; 503/434-4471

Nick Peirano's daughter Carmen and her husband, Eric Ferguson, have recently taken over the helm of this Oregon wine country original—the culinary leader of the pack. Featuring locally sourced products and house-made charcuterie, the café offers a five-course, prix-fixe menu. Start with an appetizer, perhaps fresh melon and pears with prosciutto or an artichoke with tarragon mayonnaise. Follow with garlic minestrone—Nick's grandmother's recipe. The creative pasta course might include Nick's famous smoked-salmon or Dungeness crab and pine nuts lasagnes. Entrées range from salt-grilled wild salmon steaks to rabbit braised in local pinot gris with Gorgonzola polenta. Desserts are difficult to resist. Try the dense chocolate brandy hazelnut torte with a refreshing gin and tonic ice. *$$$; AE, MC, V; checks OK; dinner Tues–Sun; beer and wine; reservations recommended; www. nicksitaliancafe.com; next to Hotel Oregon.* &

LODGINGS

Hotel Oregon / ★

310 NE EVANS ST, MCMINNVILLE; 503/472-8427 OR 888/472-8427

Mike and Brian McMenamin—the kingpins of Oregon's microbrew empire—restored a 1905 hotel in the center of McMinnville, and it's now one of the most popular places to stay for wine country tours, as well as during wine festivals. Most of the 42 rooms are small with colorful decor; only a few have private baths. A pub and restaurant downstairs definitely contribute to the noise, so bring your earplugs. The Rooftop Bar is spectacular during good weather—an excellent place to relax at the top of the town while enjoying McMenamin's famous ales. *$$; AE, DIS, MC, V; checks OK; www.hotel oregon.com; at 3rd St.* &

Youngberg Hill Vineyards & Inn / ★★★

**10660 YOUNGBERG HILL RD, MCMINNVILLE;
503/472-2727 OR 888/657-8668**

Set on the crest of a 700-foot hill, this quiet inn is distinguished by its views of the Willamette Valley. A large wraparound porch beckons, even on cold days, for gazing at the rolling hills. Owners Wayne and Nicolette Bailey have recently added 5 acres to the original 12-acre vineyard. The seven spacious guest rooms and suites have private baths; three have fireplaces. A cozy music room, living room, and gift shop add to the appeal. Guava juice and muffins, baked apples, and eggs Florentine with grilled salmon are typical selections at the breakfast table. *$$$; MC, V; checks OK; www.youngberghill.com; 12 miles southwest of town.* &

Amity

Established in the mid-1800s by two brothers who were Oregon Trail pioneers, Amity holds one of the region's best flower festivals, the **AMITY DAFFODIL FESTIVAL**. Festival central is **AMITY ELEMENTARY SCHOOL** (300 Rice Ln; 503/835-2181 ext 287; www.amitydaffodil.org). One of Oregon's first wineries and several other top ones are in the area, including **AMITY VINEYARDS** (18150 SE Amity Vineyards Rd; 503/835-2362) and **COHELO WINERY** (111 5th St; 503/835-9305), in the heart of town. The town is also home to the **BRIGITTINE MONKS' PRIORY OF OUR LADY OF CONSOLATION** (23300 Walker Ln; 503/835-8080), where you can buy their nationally lauded Chocolate Fudge Royal and Chocolate Truffles Royale by the pound. Chuck and Glenda Lawrence started **EOLA HILLS MINATURE DONKEY FARM** (9055 SE Eola Hills Rd; 503/835-9929) after retiring and building their dream home in Amity. The adorable donkeys are a must-see.

Bellevue

Primarily an intersection, 8 miles southwest of McMinnville on Route 18, this small village is home to Oregon's largest art gallery: **LAWRENCE GALLERY** (19700 SW Rte 18; 503/843-3633), complete with a water and sculpture garden outside. The attached **OREGON WINE TASTING ROOM** (19690 SW SR 18; 503/843-3787; www.winesnw.com/oregonwinetastingroom.htm) features samplings from about two dozen wineries, while the **FRESH PALATE CAFÉ**, in the same space, offers (19700 SW Rte 18; 503/843-4400) fresh produce, homemade breads and dressings, and scrumptious desserts.

Woodburn

Get off I-5 and head east for about 1½ miles, following signs to the city center. It's like a trip south of the border: several Latino-owned businesses are on the main drag. Make **SALVADOR'S BAKERY** (405 N 1st St; 503/981-4595) your first stop for *carnitas* or queso cotija. **LUPITA'S RESTAURANT** (311 N Front St; 503/982-0483) is a good choice for a sit-down meal with an English-Spanish menu. Several inexpensive taquerias with fast service are spread throughout downtown; **TAQUERIA EL REY** (966 N Pacific Hwy; 503/982-1303) offers traditional versions of tacos, made with beef *cabeza* (head), *tripa* (tripe), and *lengua* (tongue).

Silverton

Iris farmers surrounding this small country town cultivate acres of these delicate blooms. The effect, particularly in the spring, is a splash of vibrant colors on an otherwise green canvas. If flowers, east valley wineries, or hiking trails have brought you here, Silverton works well as a centralized base camp. Two noteworthy wineries are **MERIDIAN ESTATE VINEYARDS** (6685 Meridian Rd NE, Silverton; 503/910-7253) and **VITIS RIDGE WINES** (6685 Meridian Rd NE, Silverton; 503/873-8304; www.vitisridge.com).

In the can't-miss **SILVER FALLS STATE PARK** (off SR 214, 26 miles east of Salem; 503/873-8681; www.oregonstateparks.org/park_211), a 5-mile, moderately difficult hiking trail circles several spectacular waterfalls ranging from 10 to 200 feet. Several of the falls in this park just southeast of town are accessible by car or a short walk.

The **OREGON GARDEN** (on SR 213, 2 miles southwest of Silverton; 503/874-8100; www.oregongarden.org) is a 240-acre wonderland of flora and birds. Stroll through more than 20 specialty gardens, among waterfalls, ponds, and fountains, to gather ideas. Don't miss the unique conifer garden or the 400-year-old Signature Oak. The fascinating Gordon House, designed by legendary architect Frank Lloyd Wright, is also on the premises.

One of the valley's best farmers market sets up shop 9am–1pm on Saturdays through mid-October at **TOWNE SQUARE PARK** (Main St, Silverton; 503/390-7276). You'll find an incredible variety of flowers, including irises and lavender, other plants, and fresh fruits (truly the world's best strawberries) and vegetables.

RESTAURANTS

Silver Grille Café & Wines / ★★★

206 E MAIN ST, SILVERTON; 503/873-4035
Chef Jeff Nizlek runs this well-known contemporary bistro and wine shop in downtown Silverton. The elegant interior is dimly lit, with dark wood wainscoting below red grass-paper walls. The chef sources the majority of the café's seafood from the coast and works with local farms to create seasonal menus. Entrées include wild-caught salmon with garden dill sauce and wild rice pilaf and Oregon buffalo served with basil sauce and tomatoes. Finish with a cassis-infused Scharffenberger chocolate mousse made with local black currants, swimming in Willamette Valley berry sauce and crème anglaise. *$$; AE, MC, V; checks OK; dinner Wed–Sun; full bar; reservations recommended; www.silvergrille.com; at 1st St.* &

LODGINGS

Water Street Inn Bed and Breakfast / ★★

421 WATER ST, SILVERTON; 503/873-3344 OR 866/873-3344
This beautifully appointed B and B reflects the renovation of a mother and
daughter-in-law team. The spacious historic home, originally built in 1890
as the Wolfard Hotel, boasts five immensely comfortable, unique—though
not huge—guest rooms, all with private baths, several with double whirlpool tubs, and one with a double shower. Attention to detail, from the
added period crown sconces to the exquisite decor and linens in the rooms,
is evident. Favorites on the breakfast menu include Grand Marnier–infused
French toast and perfect eggs Benedict. *$$–$$$; AE, MC, V; checks OK; www.*
thewaterstreetinn.com; downtown, 1 block off Silver Creek.

Stayton and Sublimity

These small communities are close enough to Salem to capture some of that city's
hustle, yet both are infused with plenty of country ambience. Stayton's historic
downtown core has a very small-town feel. **SANTIAM HISTORICAL MUSEUM** (260
N 2nd Ave, Stayton; 503/769-1406) houses artifacts from the Willamette Valley.
The covered **STAYTON-JORDAN BRIDGE** and short walking trails can be found at
PIONEER PARK (7th and Pioneer sts, Stayton).

Salem

The Indian name for this town, one of Oregon's oldest communities, was
Chemeketa—the "meeting or resting place." It's also the state's seat of government and its second-biggest city—and ever-growing. The handsome parks of the
state capital grounds invite a stroll. Several points of interest encourage longer
looks: historic homes and buildings along with a fair amount of shopping and
intriguing restaurants. If you're drawn to Oregon history and architecture, a free
tour of the **1938 CAPITOL BUILDING** (900 Court St NE; 503/986-1388; www.
leg.state.or.us/capinfo)—topped by a tall statue of a pioneer sheathed in gold—is
worth your time.

The **SALEM VISITOR INFORMATION CENTER** (503/581-4325 or 800/874-
7012; www.scva.org) is located at the **HISTORIC MISSION MILL VILLAGE** (1313
Mill St SE; 503/585-7012; www.missionmill.org), a large cluster of restored
buildings from the 1800s that includes several homes, a Presbyterian church, and
a woolen mill. The Northwest's oldest remaining frame house is here: the **JASON
LEE HOUSE**, dating from 1841. The **SALEM CHAMBER OF COMMERCE** (1110
Commercial St NE; 503/581-1466; www.salemchamber.org) is a useful resource.

BUSH HOUSE (600 Mission St SE; 503/363-4714; www.oregonlink.com/
bush_house; tours Tues–Sun, noon–5pm May–Sept, 2–5pm Oct–Apr) is an 1877
Victorian home built by Aashal Bush, a pioneer newspaper publisher. The house

OREGON'S GROWING CADRE OF GREEN WINERIES

Warm summers, wet and mild winters, and rainy springs make for ideal growing conditions for cool-climate grapes. Yamhill County has more than 175 wineries, mostly between Newberg and McMinnville on **RTE 99W**, accessible from Interstate 5 south of Portland. Most of the area's wineries are open year-round, but on summer weekends, Memorial Day, and Thanksgiving, they get crowded. Expect traffic and congestion, and take it slow. The **WILLAMETTE VALLEY WINERIES ASSOCIATION** (503/646-2985; www.willamettewines.com) brochure and map are a good place to start.

With the vital watersheds of the Pacific Northwest at risk from agricultural pollution, several of the 300-plus wineries in the Willamette Valley practice varying degrees of organic and low-impact farming in their vineyards. Beyond the elimination of fungicides, these wineries have made an environmental commitment that extends to the overall operations of the business, employing recycled materials in their buildings and, in some cases, glass ceilings, as well as minimizing the use of electricity and other resources. On wine tours, make a point of visiting the northern Willamette Valley vineyards noted not only for their "green" practices, but also for exceptional wines.

Head south on **RTE 99W** toward McMinnville. At the town of Newberg, veer onto Hwy 240, continuing west. Make your first stop at **PENNER ASH** (15771 NE Ribbon Ridge Rd, Newberg; 503/554-6696; www.pennerash.com) to sample a pinot noir or viognier in their LEED (Leadership in Energy and Environmental Design) certified tasting room. Continue west to the town of

is situated in Bush's Pasture Park, complete with rose gardens, hiking trails, a conservatory, and an art gallery.

The oldest university in the West, **WILLAMETTE UNIVERSITY** (900 State St; 503/370-6300; www.willamette.edu), is a pleasant place to stroll. Stop at the botanical gardens and the **HALLIE FORD MUSEUM OF ART** (700 State St; 503/370-6855; www.willamette.edu/museum_of_art), the second-largest museum in the state, with 3,000 pieces. Nearby **SASS WINERY** (9092 Jackson Hill Rd; 503/391-9991) produces small amounts of amazing handcrafted pinots and chardonnay.

Summer brings the **WORLD BEAT FESTIVAL** (503/581-2004; www.world beatfestival.org), held in late June. Around Labor Day, the **OREGON STATE FAIR** (503/947-3247; www.oregonstatefair.org), the largest in the state, runs for 10 days.

Carlton; the **CARLTON WINEMAKER STUDIO AND TASTING ROOM** (801 N Scott St, Carlton; 503/852-6100; www.winemakersstudio.com) is Oregon's first solar-heated, gravity-flow, eco-conscious wine cooperative, housing up to 10 wine producers, also in a LEED-certified building with a tasting room attached. Sample red varietals (tempranillos, Syrahs, and pinot noirs) from Dominio IV winery, in addition to Andrew Rich, Hamacher, and others.

Return to Rte 99, looping east again toward Portland. Just west of Dundee is **SOKOL BLOSSER WINERY** (5000 Sokol Blosser Ln, Dundee; 503/864-2282; www.sokolblosser.com), established in 1971. One of the first Oregon wineries, as well as one of the first to farm organically using solar power and B50 biodiesel in their tractors, the winery produces premium pinot noir, pinot gris, and proprietary blends. Another winery in the area employing sustainability practice include **VISTA HILLS VINEYARDS** (6700 Hilltop Ln, Dundee; 503/864-3200; www.vistahillsvineyard.com), a Low Input Viticulture & Enology, Inc. (LIVE) program promoting agricultural and environmental sustainability through responsible holistic vineyard management. East of Salem and worth the drive is **VAN DUZER VINEYARDS** (11975 Smithfield Rd, Dallas; 800/884-1927), which unveiled their state-of-the-art and energy-efficient winery in the fall of 2008; the unique growing conditions of the Van Duzer corridor combine with sustainably grown grapes to become luscious pinots. Farther south, **BENTON-LANE WINERY** (23924 Territorial Hwy, Monroe; 541/847-5792; www.benton-lane.com) produces certified, sustainably farmed estate wines.

—Jo Ostgarden

RESTAURANTS

Alessandro's 120 / ★★

120 COMMERCIAL ST NE, SALEM; 503/370-9951
Simple, elegant pasta and seafood are the top picks at this longtime favorite. The menu isn't particularly original, but the classics are mostly done well, starting with fresh ingredients. But the most interesting may be the multicourse dinner. The staff asks if there's a particular dish you don't like, then surprises you with the rest. Enjoy live jazz on Friday and Saturday evenings. *$$; AE, DIS, MC, V; no checks; lunch Mon–Fri, dinner Mon–Sat; full bar; reservations recommended; www.alessandros.net; downtown near Court St.* ⅚

Bentley's Grill / ★★☆

291 LIBERTY ST SE (PHOENIX GRAND HOTEL), SALEM; 503/779-1660

This upscale grill serves small plates, from a rotisserie chicken quesadilla to an Italian deli platter. Entrées include traditional grill fare: grilled flatiron steak with garlic mashed potatoes and vegetables, rotisserie chicken, smoked prime rib, seared halibut. Sandwiches and pizza are available all day. *$–$$$; AE, DIS, MC, V; checks OK; lunch, dinner every day; full bar; reservations recommended; www.bentleysgrill.com; downtown between Trade and Ferry sts.* ♿

j. james restaurant / ★★

325 HIGH ST SE, SALEM; 503/362-0888

An Oregon native and James Beard invitational chef, owner Jeff James makes simple but creative seasonal dishes, sourced from quality local and regional ingredients. Each plate is unique in presentation and distinct in flavor. The ever-changing menu features an array of enticing appetizers like figs with blue cheese. Entrées include herb-roasted chicken breast, smoked-salmon gnocchi, panfried Willapa Bay oysters, and molasses-cured pork loin. White linens and big windows give it an upscale but comfortable ambience. *$$; AE, MC, V; checks OK; lunch Tues–Fri, dinner Tues–Sat; full bar; reservations recommended; www.jjamesrestaurant.com; downtown in Pringle Park Plaza.* ♿

Morton's Bistro Northwest / ★★★

1128 EDGEWATER ST NW, SALEM; 503/585-1113

A clever design located this diner below roadway level, looking out on an attractive courtyard backed by an ivy-covered wall. The interior is intimate, with dark wood beams and soft lighting. Hints of international influences can be seen in the solidly Northwestern menu: salmon fillet accompanied by a potato-pumpkin mash; vegetarian lasagne that surprises with its freshness; a luscious mixed grill; delicious cioppino. *$$; MC, V; checks OK; dinner Tues–Sat; full bar; reservations recommended; www.mortonsbistronw.com; between Gerth and McNary aves in West Salem.* ♿

LODGINGS

Phoenix Grand Hotel / ★★★

201 LIBERTY ST SE, SALEM; 503/540-7800 OR 877/540-7800

This contemporary hotel attached to the Salem Conference Center features an expansive lobby and 193 modern, spacious, and inviting guest rooms, with suites as well. Suites have kitchenettes and separate living and sleeping areas; some have Jacuzzis. No need to worry if you get a room that doesn't have one: the hotel has a spa, along with a pool and fitness room. The central location makes for an easy walk to the capitol building, downtown shops, and parks. *$$$–$$$$; AE, DIS, MC, V; checks OK; www.phoenixgrandhotel.com; between Trade and Ferry sts.* ♿

Independence

Nominated for the prestigious All-America City award, this historic town has a remarkable wealth of 19th-century architecture. Bypassed by major highways in the 1960s (much to its benefit), Independence today possesses a beautiful revitalized historic district. This riverside town may appear to be untouched by modern time, but its proximity to Salem has made it popular for commuters. The **RIVER GALLERY** (184 S Main St; 503/838-6171; www.oregonlink.com/rivergallery) exhibits work of local artists. Southeast of town is the four-car **BUENA VISTA FERRY** (503/588-7979; Wed–Sun Apr–Oct), which will take you and your car across the Willamette.

RESTAURANTS

Buena Vista House Café and Lodging / ★

11265 RIVERVIEW ST, INDEPENDENCE; 503/838-6364

Located 6 miles south of the Independence Bridge—near the Buena Vista Ferry—this well-known café and B and B are a little tricky to find. But as proprietor Claudia Prevost (co-owner with her husband, David) assures potential visitors, it's well worth the effort. The café posts on a blackboard a weekly menu that reflects Claudia's commitment to sustainably grown local ingredients. She bakes her own bread and scones, smokes her own meats, and grows some of the fruits, vegetables, and herbs she uses in her dishes. House specialties include smoked sausages, salmon croquettes, wild-mushroom quiche, and home-smoked pork loin. On every other Friday, they fire up the earthen oven for artisan pizzas. More often than not, the couple—both are accomplished musicians who have played professionally—entertain. Upstairs in the B and B–style lodging, antiques decorate three bedrooms in a refreshingly spare country style. *$–$$; no credit cards; checks OK; dinner Fri, brunch Sat–Sun; beer and wine; reservations required; south of town on ferry access rd.*

Albany

Albany—once an important transportation hub for the Willamette Valley—is another town that was, fortunately, bypassed during the construction of I-5.

Most of the remaining covered bridges characteristic of the mid-1900s Willamette Valley—there were once about 300 throughout Oregon, and today there are fewer than 50—are in Linn and Lane counties. Six are near Scio, just northeast of Albany, and several cross the rivers around Eugene and Cottage Grove. For maps, contact the **ALBANY CONVENTION AND VISITORS CENTER** (300 SW 2nd Ave; 800/526-2256; www.albanyvisitors.com) or the **COVERED BRIDGE SOCIETY OF OREGON** (541/265-2934; www.coveredbridges.stateoforegon.com).

RESTAURANTS

Sybaris / ★★★

442 SW IST AVE, ALBANY; 541/928-8157
This elegant and eclectic restaurant is located on First Avenue downtown. Exposed brick walls, large windows, and high ceilings dominates the historic space, but a fireplace helps warm it. The menu changes monthly with picks like steamed halibut with a spicy lemon-wasabi sauce on a sushi-rice "puck" (think hockey) or a roasted venison loin with vegetables and a huckleberry-port sauce. The entrées are generous, but save room for the amazing chocolate hazelnut cake. *$$; AE, MC, V; checks OK; dinner Tues–Sat; full bar; reservations recommended; www.sybarisbistro.com; downtown between Washington and Ferry sts.* &

Corvallis

An annual influx of young people heading to **OREGON STATE UNIVERSITY** (15th and Jefferson sts; 541/737-0123; www.orst.edu) imparts a youthful exuberance to this compact, medium-sized city. Surrounded by natural beauty, the downtown area holds an array of interesting shops and cafés, including the **BEANERY**, serving fresh-roasted **ALLAN BROS. COFFEE** (500 SW 2nd St; 541/753-7442). The vibrant **RIVERFRONT PARK** (1st and Madison sts), a paved esplanade along the Willamette River, features a fountain, stone benches, picnic tables, and sculptures, including a pair of adorable metal bronze otters, by five local and regional artists. The **SATURDAY FARMERS MARKET** runs mid-April–October; get information at **CORVALLIS TOURISM** (553 NW Harrison Blvd; 541/757-1544 or 800/334-8118; www.visitcorvallis.com).

MARY'S PEAK (on SR 34, west of Corvallis) is the tallest point in the Coast Range, at 4,097 feet. Excellent hiking is accessible from **MCDONALD STATE FOREST** (off Route 99W, 6 miles north of Corvallis), or you can take shorter interpretive hikes at the **PEAVY ARBORETUM** (on Arboretum Rd 8 miles north of Corvallis, right off Hwy 99W; free; open every day), operated by Oregon State University. The 40-acre arboretum holds a variety of native and exotic plant species. **TYEE WINE CELLARS** (26335 Greenberry Rd, Corvallis; 541/753-8754; www.tyeewine.com) is tucked in dense, rolling foothills, with winding roads and fantastic views.

RESTAURANTS

Gathering Together Farm / ★★

25159 GRANGE HALL RD, PHILOMATH; 541/929-6007
Five miles west of Corvallis, you'll find a farm stand that also serves lunches made from their own freshly grown organic produce. The seasonally changing menu features salads (a recent one included roasted beets and goat cheeses from local creameries) and more creative picks like duck confit pizza with pickled apples, Black Forest stew with beer-braised wild mushrooms and sage

bread pudding, and house-made pastries. Breakfasts include omelets made with the farm's own eggs and vegetables, bread pudding French toast studded with dried cherries and pistachios, house-made sausages, and organic coffee and juices. The farm also offers monthly wine dinners. *$; AE, DIS, MC, V; local checks only; breakfast Sat, lunch Tues–Sat, dinner Fri, brunch first and third Sunday of every month; wine only; reservations recommended; www. gatheringtogetherfarm.com; right off Main St in Philomath to S 13th St to Fern Dr, then right on Grange Hall Rd for ⅓ mile.*

Iovino's / ★★★

136 SW WASHINGTON ST, CORVALLIS; 541/738-9015

Iovino's, located in a multimillion-dollar condo project in downtown Corvallis, offers five levels of dining and seats up to 250. The bank of windows—with views that overlook the river—and stylish red banquettes with white and black linens give the restaurant a sophisticated feel. The kitchen puts out *nuovo* Italian to match, with intriguing twists like caramelized onions and capers on bruschetta or sweet marsala sauce over turkey scallops and mashed ricotta potatoes. *$$; AE, MC, V; checks OK; lunch Mon–Sat, dinner every day; full bar; reservations recommended; at Monroe Ave.* &

LODGINGS

Hanson Country Inn / ★★

795 SW HANSON ST, CORVALLIS; 541/752-2919

Book a room at this former poultry ranch, and you'll feel like you're in the country—yet you're just minutes from town. Like any ranch, the inn has expansive grounds. The 1928 wood-and-brick farmhouse is a registered historic home with a trove of antiques. Each of the two suites have a private bath, cable TV, telephone, Internet access, and private deck. The cottage, with two bedrooms and a kitchen, is perfect for families. Breakfasts include crepes with blackberries or a frittata. After breakfast, explore the formal garden and the original egg house. *$$–$$$; AE, DIS, MC, V; checks OK; www.hcinn.com; 5 minutes west of town.*

Harrison House Bed and Breakfast / ★

2310 NW HARRISON BLVD, CORVALLIS; 541/752-6248 OR 800/233-6248

Just a few blocks from campus, this B and B has simply decorated guest rooms—nothing innovative—and a pleasant lounging space. Owners Maria and Charlie Tomlinson, who moved from New York, are gracious. Talk local politics with Charlie; he's on the city council. All four guest rooms have private baths. The English Garden Cottage, with a kitchenette and sitting area, is available only when the hosts' sons are out of town. Enjoy a microbrew or a glass of wine when you arrive, and let Maria know your preferences for the next morning: fruit with muffins, eggs Benedict, stuffed crepes. *$$; AE, DC, DIS, JCB, MC, V; checks OK; www.corvallis-lodging.com; at 23rd St.*

Eugene and Springfield

Located at the southern end of the Willamette Valley, at the confluence of the McKenzie and Willamette rivers and about 60 miles east of the Oregon Coast, Eugene is in many ways Oregon's cultural hub. Though less loud and audacious than Portland, Eugene was working on being green long before the state's largest city took the title.

Eugene's vibrant social matrix is an intriguing mix of intellectuals, students, athletes, manufacturing workers, organic farmers, retirees, and many who came here in pursuit of alternative lifestyles back in the 1960s. It's also the hometown of the late "Merry Prankster" Ken Kesey, best known as the author of *One Flew Over the Cuckoo's Nest* and *Sometimes a Great Notion*—and perhaps the man who put Eugene on the counterculture map.

But embracing its conventional cultural sensibilities equally, Eugene has a thriving arts scene with a respected symphony, ballet, opera, and small theater companies. The **HULT CENTER FOR THE PERFORMING ARTS** (7th Ave and Willamette St; 541/342-5746; www.hultcenter.org) is the city's world-class concert facility.

The **UNIVERSITY OF OREGON** (13th Ave and University St; 541/346-3111; www.uoregon.edu) is the state's flagship institution, featuring a natural history museum and the **JORDAN SCHNITZER MUSEUM OF ART** (on UO campus; 541/346-3027; www.uoma.uoregon.edu), with Japanese, Chinese, and European exhibits.

Several unique and earthy coffeehouses, bakeries, and brew pubs are scattered throughout the city. **SWEET LIFE PATISSERIE** (755 Monroe St; 541/683-5676) is a local favorite, providing many vegan options among a vast selection of exceedingly good pastry, both sweet and savory. For microbrews, **MCMENAMIN'S HIGH STREET BREWERY & CAFE** (1243 High St; 541/345-4905) is near the university, or try **STEELHEAD BREWERY** (199 E 5th Ave; 541/686-2739) near the train station. **STUDIO ONE CAFÉ** (1473 E 19th St; 541/342-8596) offers an original breakfast and lunch menu, complete with old favorites and reflecting the alternative style of Eugene with vegan and vegetarian options. If you prefer wine, **OREGON WINE WAREHOUSE** (943 Olive St; 541/342-8598) is worth a visit. Also, several local wineries, such as **TERRITORIAL VINEYARDS & WINE COMPANY** (907 W 3rd Ave; 541/684-9463; www.territorialvineyards.com) and **KING ESTATE** (80854 Territorial Rd; 541/942-9874 or 800/884-4441; www.kingestate.com), have opened tasting rooms.

At the **FIFTH AVENUE PUBLIC MARKET** (5th Ave and High St), you can peruse boutiques and import shops and choose from several indie cafés for quick and casual refreshment. The **SATURDAY MARKET** (Oak St at 8th Ave; 541/686-8885; Apr–fall) is the state's oldest outdoor fair and farmers market; don't miss **TOBY'S TOFU PALACE** and other unique, Eugene-style food vendors. In September, the **EUGENE CELEBRATION** (www.eugenecelebration.com) takes over the downtown blocks with music, food booths, and crafts.

HENDRICKS PARK (follow signs from Fairmount Blvd east of UO) is a great place to walk or run; it also features a 10-acre rhododendron garden that blooms

CYCLING THE WILLAMETTE VALLEY

Scenic roads zigzag past orchards, vineyards, oak forests, covered bridges, and fields, all of which make cycling the Willamette Valley a lot of fun. The best months are May through mid-October, though you should pack rain gear if you're riding in May through mid-June and during all of October. Whether you do a two- or three-day tour or ride for an afternoon, for most of the riding season you can count on refueling at farm stands selling locally grown berries and produce, but there are also plenty of small-town cafés and markets along the way. Most wineries are open to the cycling public and offer tastings free or for a nominal fee. Get a brochure with maps and a trip planner from the **OREGON WINE CENTER** (503/228-8336; www.oregonwine.org).

BIKE OREGON WINE COUNTRY (503/623-2405 or 800/291-6730; www. eolahillswinery.com) is a fully supported ride of anywhere from 30 to 70 miles through the scenic Eola Hills and mid–Willamette Valley wine country. All rides start and end at Eola Hills Wine Cellars in Amity. Lunch is provided at one of many participating wineries, and all wine purchased en route is transported back to Eola Hills by support vehicles.

The **WILLAMETTE VALLEY SCENIC BIKEWAY ROUTE** spans 130 miles. Starting in Champoeg State Park just south of Newberg and ending at Armitage County Park in Eugene, the route follows country roads along the Willamette River. Get details from **OREGON PARKS AND RECREATION** (800/551-6949; www.oregon.gov/oprd/parks/bike). Bike rentals are available in Salem at **SOUTH SALEM CYCLEWORKS** (4071 Liberty Rd S, Salem; 503/399-9848) and in Eugene at **PAUL'S BICYCLE WAY OF LIFE** (152 W 5th Ave, Eugene; 541/344-4105).

—Jo Ostgarden

in May and June. The **PREFONTAINE TRAIL** along the Willamette River is accessible from several locations, including **ALTON BAKER PARK** (off Centennial Blvd).

Springfield is the gateway to the McKenzie River, one of the coldest rivers in Oregon; it flows out of the Cascades.

RESTAURANTS

Adam's Place / ★★★

30 E BROADWAY, EUGENE; 541/344-6948
Adam Bernstein, a third-generation restaurateur, has tastefully dressed this intimate downtown spot with arches, pillars, sconces, and a lovely fireplace. The result is quietly sophisticated, unpretentious yet classy. Entrées include terrific wild salmon topped with a sweet, tangy orange glaze. Vegetarian

options are always interesting, and desserts are yummy, especially the crème brûlée. Attached is Luna, featuring Spanish tapas—this is the spot to hear live jazz. *$$–$$$; AE, MC, V; checks OK; dinner Tues–Sat; full bar; reservations recommended; www.adamsplacerestaurant.com; on downtown mall.* &

Ambrosia / ★★☆

174 E BROADWAY, EUGENE; 541/342-4141

A pizzeria with modern pizzazz and a menu filled out with a selection of entrées, this place hits mostly high notes. Low lighting creates an intimate atmosphere, and tables are tucked into "rooms" or scattered in an airy mezzanine; sit at the wooden bar to take in the chefs' action. Try the ravioli San Remo, handmade and stuffed with veal, chicken, and ricotta, or the crepes filled with smoked salmon, spinach, and ricotta. End the evening with homemade gelato. *$$; MC, V; local checks only; lunch Mon–Fri, dinner every day; full bar; reservations recommended for 6 or more; www.ambrosiarestaurant.com; at Pearl St.* &

Beppe and Gianni's Trattoria / ★★

1646 E 19TH AVE, EUGENE; 541/683-6661

This neighborhood trattoria, created by John Barofsky and Beppe Macchi, reflects the spirit and flavor of Beppe's homeland, Italy. Located in an old house, the restaurant is often jam-packed. The small menu covers the bases. Antipasto choices include roasted garlic and warm cheese. *Primi* dishes— mostly pasta—are generous enough to serve as a main course. *Secondi* entrées include sautéed chicken with wild mushrooms or marsala- and rosemary-perfumed lamb chops. *$$; MC, V; checks OK; dinner every day; beer and wine; reservations recommended for 8 or more; east of Agate St.* &

Café Soriah / ★★★

384 W 13TH AVE, EUGENE; 541/342-4410

In this smart and sophisticated restaurant, chef-owner Ibrahim Hamide has created an exciting and irresistible Mediterranean and Middle Eastern menu. The space and menu are comfortable enough for casual dining, but the flavors merit special occasions. The tiny bar in the front is a work of art in wood. A leafy, walled terrace offers comfortable outdoor seating. Stellar appetizers include baked feta, baba gannoujh, and stuffed grape leaves. The menu changes monthly, with entrées like roasted salmon, herbed chicken breast, marinated beef skewer, potato kibbeh, and eggplant and tomato dhal. Save room for baklava. *$$; AE, MC, V; checks OK; lunch Mon–Fri, dinner every day; full bar; reservations recommended; www.soriah.com; at Lawrence St.* &

Café Yumm! / ★

730 E BROADWAY, EUGENE (AND BRANCHES); 541/344-9866

This casual but so-much-better-than-fast-food joint has embraced the "less is more" approach to eating, with delightful results. Starting with a list of fresh and organic ingredients—brown or white rice, black beans, field greens, cheese, avocado, cilantro, olives, tempeh, tofu, chicken—Café Yumm! manages to take a mundane tostada or taco salad and transform it into something more wholesome and memorable. Hearty house-made cookies round out soul-satisfying meals. *$; MC, V; checks OK; lunch, dinner every day; beer and wine; no reservations; www.cafeyumm.com; SW corner of E Broadway and Hilyard St.*

Chanterelle / ★★

207 E 5TH ST, EUGENE; 541/484-4065
Consistently singled out as one of the area's best, this intimate dining room is sophisticated and unfussy, with a small menu that continues to reflect the classical French culinary sensibilities and Austrian roots upon which the restaurant was founded. Escargots and oysters Rockefeller are among a handful of appetizers. The traditional baked French onion soup is a standout. A dozen entrées start with prawns, chicken, lamb, halibut, salmon, or beef as the main ingredient, with a variety of flavor add-ons. The wine list is tightly focused with some excellent regional and international picks, while the bar knocks out tasty creative and classic cocktails. *$$$; AE, DC, MC, V; checks OK; dinner Tues–Sat; full bar; reservations recommended; www.chanterelleres-tauranteugene.net; across from public market.* &

Koho Bistro / ★★★

2101 BAILEY HILL RD, EUGENE; 541/681-9335
If you drive by the Churchill Shopping Center, you might miss this low-profile establishment. Koho Bistro is Eugene's neighborhood gathering place for relaxed fine dining. Its location about 10 minutes from downtown deters the usual crowds. The ever-changing menu is Northwest focused, with a wide range of options, from meat to seafood to vegetarian, and a nod to the local farmers who provide the ingredients. Top starters include Guinness Stout battered Brie wedge, carmelized onion and bacon tart, and New England seafood chowder. For an entrée, try the grilled sea scallops, pan-roasted halibut with black truffle risotto, or rich seafood cannelloni. The fairly deep wine list represents a wide spectrum of varietals and regions. *$$; AE, DIS, MC, V; local checks only; lunch Mon–Fri, dinner Mon–Sat; full bar; reservations recommended; www.kohobistro.com; from W 11th Ave, across from athletic field, south on Bailey Hill Rd.* &

Marché / ★★★

296 E 5TH AVE, EUGENE; 541/342-3612
With seating for up to 80, an exhibition kitchen with a wood-fired oven, a stylish bar, and a large outdoor dining area, this elegant bistro has a lot to offer. The menu is based on food you might find at a farmers market: fresh, seasonal, local, and regional—changing with the seasons. Quality ingredients, as organic and free range as they can find, are combined with French-based culinary techniques to deliver dishes that are intensely flavored and beautifully presented. For starters, choose from Willapa Bay oysters or a rich and diverse charcuterie

plate, among others. For dinner, meats and seafood reign, with a bouillabaisse with grilled bread that's an absolute knockout. In a hurry with less money to spend? Head upstairs to Cafe Marché. *$$–$$$; AE, DC, DIS, MC, V; checks OK; lunch, dinner every day, brunch Sun; full bar; reservations recommended; www.marcherestaurant.com; in public market.* &

Ring of Fire / ★★

1099 CHAMBERS ST, EUGENE; 541/344-6475

Exotic fragrances and elegant decor will transport you far, far away from the sprawling strip malls of W 11th Avenue. Thai, Indonesian, and Korean cuisines are the stars, with reliable favorites such as phad thai and vegetable tempura. Try one of the specialties like crispy ginger red snapper or Thai coconut curry. For dessert, don't miss the tempura bananas with cool coconut ice cream. Portions are generous; takeout is available late. *$$; MC, V; no checks; lunch, dinner every day; full bar; reservations recommended; www.ringoffirerestaurant.com; off W 11th Ave.*

LODGINGS

Campbell House / ★★★

252 PEARL ST, EUGENE; 541/343-1119

Built in 1892 and restored as a huge and luxurious bed-and-breakfast inn, the Campbell House has 18 guest rooms that shine with old-world charm (four-poster beds, high ceilings, dormer windows) and include private baths and modern amenities. For a special occasion, reserve the Dr. Eva Johnson Suite, with a bathroom alcove and a two-person jetted tub. The Celeste Cottage is a house next door. If you like the personalized service of a B and B but don't like to feel hovered over, this inn is for you. *$$–$$$$; AE, DC, DIS, MC, V; no checks; www.campbellhouse.com; 2 blocks north of public market.* &

Hilton Eugene and Conference Center / ★

66 E 6TH AVE, EUGENE; 541/342-2000 OR 800/937-6660

The Hilton works well as a convenient home base for exploring Eugene. Most rooms have views of either the city or Skinner Butte. Also on-site are a small indoor pool and sauna, Jacuzzi, fitness room, bike rentals, and Hertz rental car office. The lobby, bar, and attached Big River Grille, which specializes in seafood, have tastefully playful art and decor. *$$–$$$; AE, DC, DIS, MC, V; checks OK; www.eugene.hilton.com; I-5 exit 194B, next to Hult Center.* &

NORTHERN
OREGON COAST

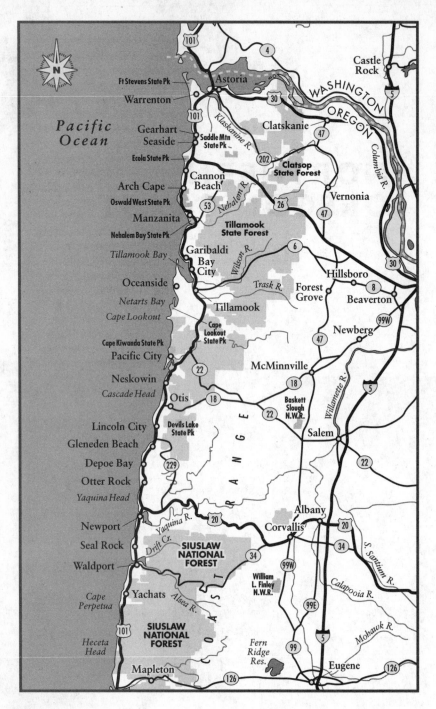

NORTHERN OREGON COAST

From Astoria to Yachats—the mouth of the Columbia River to Cape Perpetua—the Northern Oregon Coast is consider one of the most scenic coastal drives in the United States. Ask an Oregonian about "the Coast," and they'll tell you it's more than just a place they play. Part of the pull is its beauty, its promise of relaxation, the endless horizon, the sound of crashing waves, and the long, arching beaches that call out for walking.

But there's something subtler here, too; an intriguing mystique permeates. Tales of lost treasures have long endured, thanks in part to the Spanish galleons that plied the coast from the 15th through the 18th centuries.

The coast's most tangible treasure, however, is its mostly unfettered natural beauty. At nearly every town or viewpoint along the way, a picturesque scene unfolds: towering rock sentinels, striking sandstone cliffs, sweeping endless beaches bordered by tufted grass dunes, quiet bird-filled estuaries, and many unmarked beaches and isolated wonders waiting to be discovered. And, thanks to Oregon's unique "beach bill," public access to the shoreline is guaranteed.

Unfortunately, fast-food franchises, big-box retailers, and corporate chains have infiltrated the bigger towns along the coast, and the coast highway, as locals call US Highway 101, doubles as the main drag in most cities. Summer traffic through Seaside and Cannon Beach, and between Lincoln City and Newport, is particularly challenging; visitors would be wise to avoid rushed travel.

ACCESS AND INFORMATION

US HIGHWAY 101 runs along the coast, detouring into and around towns, rivers, jetties, and estuaries in some areas. It is connected to **INTERSTATE 5** by several east-to-west highways that run along rivers. The only commercial airport at this time—a proposal is currently under review for service to Newport and Astoria—on the coast is in North Bend on the southern coast. That airport is serviced with daily flights to and from **PORTLAND INTERNATIONAL AIRPORT. AMTRAK THRUWAY MOTORCOACH SERVICE** (800/872-7245; www.amtrak.com) is available daily to Astoria, Seaside, and Cannon Beach from **PORTLAND UNION STATION. SUNSET EMPIRE TRANSIT** (800/776-6406; www.ridethebus.org), also called "the Bus," offers service between Astoria and Portland via Cannon Beach.

If you're coming from the north in Astoria, be sure to stop in the **STATE WELCOME CENTER** (111 W Marine Dr, Astoria; 503/325-6311 or 800/875-6807).

Weather on the Northern Oregon Coast is variable. Plan for rain in winter and intermittent showers and sunshine in summer (July–Sept), but it's rarely hot. Tourist season runs from spring break in late March to the onset of the wet season, usually mid- to late October.

Astoria

Surrounded by water—the Columbia River to the north, Youngs Bay to the south, and just a few miles from the Pacific Ocean—Astoria is the oldest American settlement west of the Rockies, a town steeped in history. It boasts more buildings per square foot on the National Historic Register than anywhere else in Oregon. Lewis and Clark spent a winter 200 years ago at a spot just southwest of modern-day Astoria. Several years later, in 1811, John Jacob Astor's Pacific Fur Company made Fort Astoria its primary fur-trading post in the Northwest and established American claims on the land. By the late 1800s, salmon canneries, forestry, and shipping had turned Astoria into a boomtown.

Boasting a genuine sense of time and place, Astoria has several worthy historical attractions, including **FORT CLATSOP NATIONAL MEMORIAL** (92343 Fort Clatsop Rd; 503/861-2471), where Lewis and Clark built their winter encampment; the **COLUMBIA RIVER MARITIME MUSEUM** (1792 Marine Dr; 503/325-2323), a first-rate museum depicting the maritime history of the area known as the "graveyard of the Pacific" (including the Cape Disappointment lighthouse); the **CAPTAIN GEORGE FLAVEL HOUSE** (8th and Duane St; 503/325-2563), which showcases the city's ornate Queen Anne architecture; the **ASTORIA COLUMN** (follow signs to top of 16th St), which stands 125 feet tall and has 164 steps, offering the city's best views; and the **ASTORIA RIVERFRONT TROLLEY** (trolley barn; 503/325-6311), a refurbished 1913 streetcar—for only $1, passengers can ride from the Port of Astoria to the East Mooring Basin.

But for all its noteworthy past, this town isn't just for history buffs. A city of 10,000 residents, Astoria is undergoing a renaissance. New restaurants, hotels, and boutiques line the historic 1920s-era downtown, while the steep, wooded hillsides are peppered with renovated Victorian homes. The once-lagging Commercial Street boasts renovated spaces, including the **LIBERTY THEATRE** (1203 Commercial St; 503/325-8108), an Italian Renaissance–style structure back in business after an $8.5 million restoration.

Though Astoria has a storied past, its present is equally alluring. Local events include the beloved and busy **ASTORIA SUNDAY MARKET** (on 12th St waterfront; May–Oct) and the **FISHER POETS GATHERING** (Feb), which celebrates the fishing life.

RESTAURANTS

Blue Scorcher Café / ★★

1493 DUANE ST, ASTORIA; 503/338-7473

Located on the eastside of downtown in the historic Fort George building, Blue Scorcher Café takes its name from the 1885 precursor to the modern road bike. But it's the high-quality artisan breads; pastries; handcrafted seasonal, organic menu; and Columbia River views that are the draw. Cooperatively owned and run, the collective spirit shows in the attention to detail. Tasty breakfast menu items include eggs dishes, granola, and French toast, accompanied by organic coffee. At lunch try the sweet potato burger or pizza with beer made at the brew pub next door. Added bonuses: free wi-fi, a variety of periodicals for purchase, and a children's play area that offers parents a chance to savor it all. Pastry and chill cases hold meals-to-go. *$; MC, V; local checks only; breakfast, lunch Tues–Sun; beer and wine; no reservations; www. bluescorcher.com; corner of 15th and Duane sts.*

Schooner 12th Street Bistro / ★★

360 12TH ST, ASTORIA; 503/325-7882
Husband-and-wife entrepreneurs Chris and Jennifer Holen made their mark with two highly regarded Astoria restaurants. Baked Alaska, a popular waterfront spot, was doing so well that in 2004 they opened the Schooner, a casually cosmopolitan restaurant-lounge. Serving as restaurant for the Hotel Elliott (see review) across the street, Schooner attracts a blend of tourists and locals. Warm red hues and mahogany wood play nicely against a bank of windows. Fish tacos, buffalo burgers, and crab cakes—all generously portioned—are notable, but it's the martinis that earn the real buzz. *$$–$$$; AE, MC, V; checks OK; lunch, dinner every day; full bar; reservations recommended; www.schoonerbistro.com; downtown.* &

Silver Salmon Grille / ★★

1105 COMMERCIAL ST, ASTORIA; 503/338-6640
Jeff and Laurie Martin remodeled the historic Fisher Building and created an upscale destination downtown. With an intimate white tablecloth–and–candles elegance, the grill is a top-tier choice garnering consistent accolades. Salmon, of course, takes center stage, including the popular Silver Salmon Supreme—salmon stuffed with Dungeness crab, bay shrimp, and smoked Gouda. Want more? Head next door to Silver Salmon Cellars, a wine bar. *$$–$$$; AE, MC, V; checks OK; lunch, dinner every day; full bar; reservations recommended; www.silversalmongrille.com; downtown at 11th St.* &

T. Paul's Urban Café / ★★

1119 COMMERCIAL ST, ASTORIA; 503/338-5133
On the sleepy Oregon Coast, "urban" is relative. But T. Paul's delivers a hip and urbane vibe to counter the predictable lull of the coast. Both eclectic and original, this comfy bistro-coffeehouse blend has a loyal, if not diverse, following of artsy locals and buttoned-down professionals. Meals range from routine salads, soups, and chowder to more adventurous dishes like crab-stuffed ravioli and chipotle pesto pasta. Linger over coffee and dessert (caramel-apple pie or creamy cheesecake). On weekends, sink into a music groove and people-peeping as local bands take the stage. *$–$$; MC, V; checks OK; lunch, dinner Mon–Sat; beer and wine; no reservations; downtown at 11th St.* &

LODGINGS

Cannery Pier Hotel / ★★★

NO. 10 BASIN ST, ASTORIA; 503/325-4996 OR 800/325-4996

Astoria's newest and most ambitious hotel is built on the site of the former Union Fish Cannery. The hotel is literally on the Columbia River, at the end of a 600-foot pier directly below the soaring Astoria-Megler Bridge. The hotel deftly juxtaposes grit with luxe: exposed steel beams and wooden trusses blend seamlessly with contemporary furnishings and plush linens. All 46 rooms boast fireplaces, balconies, hardwood floors, and eye-popping river views. Book one of the deluxe rooms; these spacious studios surpass the boxy feel—and higher rates—of the one-bedroom suites. *$$$–$$$$; AE, DIS, MC, V; checks OK; www.cannerypierhotel.com; beneath Astoria-Megler Bridge.* &

Hotel Elliott / ★★★

357 12TH ST, ASTORIA; 503/325-2222 OR 877/378-1924

A massive $4 million renovation transformed downtown's historic Hotel Elliott into a 32-room jewel. The recent restoration of the 1924 hotel retained the warm mahogany details and original lobby desk but vamped up the old girl with an underground wine bar, a cigar lounge, and a rooftop garden providing panoramic views of the Columbia River and the manicured Victorians peppering the hillside. Typical of early 1900s hotels, the rooms are snug but made cozy with plump duvets and heated bathroom floors. *$$–$$$$; AE, DIS, MC, V; checks OK; www.hotelelliott.com; between Commercial and Duane sts.*

Gearhart

The first planned resort community on the Oregon Coast, Gearhart early on enacted zoning restrictions that keep development at bay. This means no neon signage or fast-food joints—just 2 miles of fine, sandy beach fringed with golden grassy dunes, pine trees, and weather-beaten shingle cottages. The community of residents and vacation homeowners from Portland and Seattle prefer to keep it that way, but that doesn't make it dullsville. "Downtown" Gearhart may be an overstatement, but main street is home to a few businesses, most notably the gourmet market **GEARHART GROCERY** (599 Pacific Wy, Gearhart; 503/738-7312). **PACIFIC CREST COTTAGE** (726 Pacific Wy, Gearhart; 503/738-6560) offers a unique blend of interior designs, linens, and housewares. **FITZGERALD'S** (738 Pacific Wy, Gearhart; 503/717-9748), a few steps away, has arty dinnerware, glassware, lamps, and other specialized home and garden furnishings. Also worth a visit is glassblower **JOHN COOK'S STUDIO** (3427 Hwy 101 N; 503/738-5122). The **HISTORIC RIDGE PATH TRAIL**, a short three-quarter-mile link in the **OREGON COAST TRAIL**, wends north and south behind many of the village's classic homes and dunes. For breakfast, head to **GRANDMA'S COUNTRY KITCHEN** (4030 Hwy 101, Gearhart; 503/738-7098), or get your fill of burgers at **RECREATION LANES**

RESTAURANT & LOUNGE (3518 Hwy 101, Gearhart; 503/738-5333) or fish-and-chips at the **MCMENAMINS SAND TRAP BAR & GRILL** (1157 N Marion Ave, Astoria; 503/717-8150). **GEARHART GOLF LINKS** (503/738-3538), the oldest golf course in the Northwest, is an 18-hole public adventure carefully placed among the coastal dunes.

RESTAURANTS

Pacific Way Cafe & Bakery / ★★☆

601 PACIFIC WY, GEARHART; 503/738-0245
At this local favorite, lines spill out the door for bread-by-the-loaf, marion-berry scones, pastries, and java. Housed in an old storefront with a vintage vibe, three dining areas feature handcrafted alderwood tables, refinished fir floors, wainscoting, and old photos. A covered patio in the beautiful back-yard flower garden provides an ideal setting for dinner in summer. For lunch, the sandwiches are your best bet (it's a bakery, right?). The dinner menu includes classic caesar salads, gourmet pizzas, and sophisticated regional surf and turf dishes. The wine list offers a good selection of regional and inter-national picks. *$$–$$$; MC, V; checks OK; lunch, dinner Thurs–Mon; beer and wine; reservations recommended; www.pacificwaybakery.com; corner of Pacific Wy and Cottage Ave.* &

LODGINGS

Gearhart Ocean Inn / ★★★

67 N COTTAGE AVE, GEARHART; 503/738-7373
This surprisingly affordable and newly refurbished inn, just two blocks from the beach, has an upscale ambience with an old-time motor-inn feel. You can pull up to the doorstep and park at each of the 12 New England–style attached cottages, offering one- and two-bedroom suites plus king and queen studios. Rooms are painted in muted modern tones with period beadboard accents, but it's the extras that really appeal: luxury linens; plush robes; TV/DVD and stereo; gas fireplace or gas Franklin stove; captain's galley or fully equipped kitchen with organic Sleepy Monk coffee awaiting you. In the large, private communal backyard, you'll find comfy Adirondack chairs, a croquet set, a picnic table, a gas barbecue, and room for the kids or pets to play. *$$–$$$; AE, MC, V, checks OK; www.gearhartoceaninn.com; in heart of town.*

Seaside

Seaside is the quintessential beach town serving as an affordable, family-friendly vacation destination. Long considered the rowdy cousin of its classy, quiet Gear-hart neighbor, Seaside, like a rough pearl, is slowly gaining respect as its down-town becomes more polished. New condos and luxury timeshares bookend the increasingly revitalized historic core.

To be sure, Seaside still sports plenty of reminders of its Coney Island–like past, but it also possesses some wonderful landmarks. The early 1900s boardwalk, known as the **PROM**, is a 2-mile pedestrian walkway that parallels the beach. At its center is the automobile roundabout known as the Turnaround. In addition, downtown's historic Gilbert District is experiencing an overhaul.

Other outdoor attractions include the **NECANICUM RIVER**, which flows through town, where steelhead and salmon can be caught, and the nearby **QUA-TAT MARINE PARK** (downtown, along the Necanicum) for picnicking and free summer concerts. **SURFERS** are often spotted at "the Point" at the south edge of town. And, best of all, there's always a stretch of wide, sandy, and very **WALKABLE BEACH**—the hallmark of Oregon beaches.

RESTAURANTS

Taste of Tuscany / ★★

1815 S ROOSEVELT DR (HWY 101), SEASIDE; 503/738-5377
This 4,500-square-foot eatery just off Hwy 101 encompasses two dining areas, a lounge, an extensive wine cellar, and an intimate wine bar. Pendant lights, wall sconces, candlelight, and an arched gas fireplace lend a Tuscan villa ambience. The cuisine, like that of Tuscany, is "back to basics" fare incorporating simple, ultrafresh ingredients. Top picks on the menu include seven-layer lasagne, chicken and white-bean cassoulet, eggplant Parmesan, and bruschetta topped with sun-dried tomatoes and black olive tapenade. Other standouts include traditional sandwiches, a salad of greens, grilled veggies, olives, and garlic crostinnis topped with a maple and basil balsamic dressing, and the tiramisu for dessert. *$$; AE, MC, V; local checks only; lunch, dinner Wed–Sun; full bar; reservations recommended; corner of Avenue T and S Roosevelt Dr.* &

LODGINGS

Inn of the Four Winds / ★★

820 N PROMENADE, SEASIDE; 503/738-9524 OR 800/818-9524
Amid the clatter of kitschy Seaside, Inn of the Four Winds is a quiet, under-stated find. A major renovation of this stately 1940s-era home created a fresh-scrubbed, two-story, 14-room hotel. All rooms have typical hotel amenities, along with ocean-view decks. Deluxe rooms sport bay windows but are just a bit larger than the standard rooms. For families, the first-floor suites sleep up to five and feature grassy patios for seaside lazing. But it's the location—oceanfront, on the Prom, on the sedate north end of town—that seals the deal. *$$–$$$; AE, MC, V; no checks; www.innofthefourwinds.com; 8th Ave and Downing St.*

NORTHERN OREGON COAST THREE-DAY TOUR

DAY ONE: Enjoy breakfast with a view at the Blue Scorcher Café, then spend the day exploring Astoria. Drive to the **ASTORIA COLUMN** to see the lay of the land, and then tour several of the restored Victorian homes, such as **CAPTAIN GEORGE FLAVEL HOUSE**. Grab lunch at **T. PAUL'S URBAN CAFÉ**, and then head to the **COLUMBIA RIVER MARITIME MUSEUM**. Check in at the **CANNERY PIER HOTEL** and freshen up before dinner at the **SILVER SALMON GRILLE**.

DAY TWO: Head south, stopping briefly in Gearhart at **PACIFIC WAY CAFE & BAKERY** for coffee and pastries. Continue to Cannon Beach and take a stroll on the beach to **HAYSTACK ROCK** or along Hemlock Street to check out the galleries. Next, head toward Newport, stopping in Bay City for lunch at **PACIFIC OYSTER COMPANY**'s grill. Continuing south, take a detour to **THREE CAPES SCENIC DRIVE** and marvel at the views. In Newport, have dinner at **BLU CORK** before retiring to **TYEE LODGE**.

DAY THREE: After your candlelit breakfast at Tyee, take a hike around the **YAQUINA HEAD OUTSTANDING NATURAL AREA**, home to Oregon's tallest lighthouse. The area has paved hiking trails, stunning ocean vistas, and an interpretive center. Cross town to the historic bay front and stroll through the shops before enjoying lunch at **LA MAISON BAKERY AND CAFÉ**. Afterward, drive south to Yachats, stopping at **CAPE PERPETUA SCENIC AREA** for the views, and then tour the **SEA LION CAVES**. Head back to Yachats to catch sunset cocktails at the oceanfront lounge at the **ADOBE RESORT** (1555 Hwy 101, Yachats; 541/547-3141), followed by dinner and music at the **DRIFT INN**. Call it a day in a cabin at the **SHAMROCK LODGETTES**.

Cannon Beach

Oregon's upscale seaside town is flush with expensive restaurants, cozy cafés, trendy boutiques, world-class art galleries, affordable and high-end lodging, and, well, tourists. Still, the wide, white-sand beach remains the most compelling draw. It can be raining sideways in Portland and be sunny here. **HAYSTACK ROCK**, one of the world's largest coastal monoliths, is the town's most prominent natural wonder. Rising 235 feet out of the sea, Haystack Rock is a protected marine garden. At low tide, it's filled with sea urchins and purple and sunflower sea stars.

ECOLA STATE PARK (north end of Cannon Beach; www.oregonstateparks.org) is where to go for big views, picnic areas, and hiking trails—including a portion of the Oregon Coast Trail. A mile offshore rests the **TILLAMOOK ROCK LIGHTHOUSE**, built more than a century ago and decommissioned in 1957. Today the lighthouse stores cremated remains.

Galleries are too many to mention, but highlights include **DRAGONFIRE GAL-LERY** (123 S Hemlock St; 503/436-1533), showing contemporary art, and **NORTH-WEST BY NORTHWEST GALLERY** (232 N Spruce St; 503/436-0741), exhibiting fine art and crafts.

"Evoo" is the acronym for extra virgin olive oil, a key ingredient in Northwest and Mediterranean cuisines, as well as for the **EVOO CANNON BEACH COOKING SCHOOL** (188 S Hemlock St; 503/436-8555 or 877-436-EVOO; www.evoo.biz; corner of Taft and Hemlock sts), which features a gorgeous, state-of-the-art demonstration kitchen and instructional meals overseen by a team of culinary experts: Bob Neroni and Lenore Emery. One of the star attractions in Cannon Beach, the chef-instructors parlayed their expert culinary skills into hands-on classes and demos that draw student-guests close to the action. Afterward, everyone digs into the finale, often paired with wine. Limited seatings of just 18 guarantee fun food adventures. They also sell kitchen goods and gifts.

There's plenty of fine dining in Cannon Beach, but for food that doesn't max out your budget, try **LOCAL GRILL AND SCOOP** (156 N Hemlock St; 503/436-9551) for excellent clam chowder, a small but fresh salad bar, and Tillamook ice cream, from a rotating list of intriguing flavors, piled mile high in a cone. One block north, **PIZZA FETTA** (231 N Hemlock St; 503/436-0333) turns out artisan pies that draw lines out the door. Buy by the slice to save money; the whole pies are spendy. **ECOLA SEAFOODS RESTAURANT AND MARKET** (208 N Spruce St; 503/436-9130; www.ecolaseafoods.com) is a good place to pick up the fresh catch or takeaway meals.

RESTAURANTS

Gower St Bistro / ★★

1116 S HEMLOCK ST, TOLOVANA PARK; 503/436-2729
Dine in or fill a picnic basket at this charming European-style charcuterie. Cruise the cases and select cured meats, artisan cheeses, and seasonal salads. Another case nearby holds seductively rich desserts—try the beautiful Pyramide du Louvre, coffee mousse, mango, coconut biscuit—and pastries. The table service is as charming as the space—pressed-tin ceilings, nice ambient and accent lighting, circular tables covered in butcher paper and white linens. For brunch, tuck into Dungeness crab cakes, ultrafresh gazpacho, delicate fried calamari with chipotle aioli, crispy *pommes frites*, grilled polenta cakes, or curried chicken salad. For dinner, try the wine-braised chicken Marbella, Gower Street meat loaf, or a lusty Bistro burger. Crafty cocktails and an excellent wine list complete the deal. *$$; AE, MC, V; checks OK; dinner, brunch every day; full bar; reservations recommended (dinner); www.gowerstbistro. com; corner of Hemlock and Gower sts, downtown.*

Newmans at 988 / ★★★☆

988 S HEMLOCK ST, CANNON BEACH; 503/436-1151
Chef John Newman, a Culinary Institute of America grad with a notable resume, heads the kitchen of this intimate dining room, inconspicuously

tucked inside a small yellow 1920s cottage. White linens, dark wood, and candlelight set the scene for standout dishes showcasing French and Italian cuisines. Tuck into small plates of lusty wild mushroom polenta, crab cakes with a hint of fresh herbs, or a roasted beet and chèvre salad. Nosh on entrées of chicken piccata with wild mushroom risotto cake or fresh seafood du jour with seasonal veggies. The sharp wine list offers Italian and French reds and whites, along with an excellent list of regional picks. Save room for the amazing *pot de crème* or the artisan cheese plate. An ever-changing nightly prix-fixe menu is also available. *$$–$$$; MC, V; local checks only; dinner every day July–Sept, Tues–Sun Oct–June; beer and wine; reservations recommended; www.newmansat988.com; midtown at Harrison St.*

Sweet Basil's Café / ★

271 N HEMLOCK ST, CANNON BEACH; 503/436-1539
Order lunches crafted from local and organic ingredients, including a terrific selection of vegetarian, vegan, seafood, poultry, and pork dishes. There is also good selection of salads, cold and hot sandwiches, wraps, paninis, and fusion dishes. Seasonal offerings mean there are ever-changing daily specials like mussels in chipotle cream or artichokes and oyster casserole. *$–$$; MC, V; no checks; lunch Wed–Mon, dinner Fri–Sat; no alcohol; reservations required (dinner); www.cafesweetbasils.com; downtown.* &

LODGINGS

Hallmark Suites / ★★

1400 S HEMLOCK ST, CANNON BEACH;
503/436-1566 OR 800/448-4449
Located one block east of the beach, these suites don't provide much of a view, but they are perfect in every other way. The comfortable living area features a galley-style kitchenette, gas fireplace, sitting area, and balcony patio. There's a separate bedroom in back with a king bed and TV/video player. In between the living area and the bedroom is a sleeping area with a queen bed and a bath with a jetted tub. Enjoy a dip in the indoor heated pool and spa in the small building housing this complex of suites. Many rooms are dog friendly. Hallmark also has a larger oceanfront resort complex one block south, but the suites are the real treat. *$$–$$$; AE, MC, V; no checks; www.halmarkinns.com; ½ mile south of town center.* &

The Inn at Cannon Beach / ★★

3215 S HEMLOCK ST, CANNON BEACH;
503/436-9085 OR 800/321-6304
Cottage-style architecture and simple, comfortable, modern rooms and suites make this an excellent choice for travelers who like the convenience of suite-style hotel accommodations but prefer something more inspired. The extras add to the appeal: hummingbirds in the garden courtyard, cookies in the lobby, welcome gifts in every room—including sand buckets for the kids and

pet baskets for dogs—plus gas fireplaces, flat-screen TVs, minifridges, coffee-makers, microwaves, free wireless connectivity, free fitness club passes, and a light breakfast buffet in a room off the lobby. *$$$; AE, DC, DIS, MC, V; checks OK; www.innatcannonbeach.com; 1.5 miles south of Cannon Beach.* &

The Ocean Lodge / ★★★

**2864 SOUTH PACIFIC ST, CANNON BEACH;
503/436-2241 OR 888/777-4047**

Located on the oceanfront just south of Cannon Beach, this beautifully crafted lodge offers close-up views of Haystack Rock and immediate access to the incredibly long walking beach that sweeps around it. Reminiscent of a 1940s-style beach lodge, it's warm and comfortable. Rooms feature fireplaces, minifridges, and wireless Internet access; semiprivate decks with Adirondack chairs; and a library reading nook. Suites across from the entrance are spacious, romantic aeries. Complimentary light breakfast is served in the dining room on the second level. Pets are welcome. *$$$–$$$$; AE, DIS, MC, V; no checks; www.theoceanlodge.com; 1.5 miles south of Cannon Beach.* &

Arch Cape

When former Governor Oswald West first proposed designating the Oregon Coast a public highway, his suggestion wasn't as radical as some thought. In fact, it was in keeping with its original use. Native Americans had blazed trails across most of the coastline, and settlers later followed. In the late 1800s, a roadway was carved into the base of the headland at Hug Point, between Arcadia Beach and Arch Cape, to allow travel at high tide. Settlers came down this road from Cannon Beach, 4 miles north, to make land claims at Arch Cape.

By the late 1930s, the only thing holding back the opening of a newer and higher roadway (US Highway 101) from north to south was several creeks in the vicinity of Arch Cape—Necarney, Short Sand, and Arch Cape creeks. A tunnel was blasted through the ridge and high steel bridges were erected to span all of them, completing, in 1940, the final missing link in the Oregon Coast Highway.

Today southbound travelers pass through this tunnel just before they reach the enclave of manicured vacation homes that comprise the pocket community of Arch Cape. Tucked between **HUG POINT STATE PARK** (along Hwy 101; 800/551-6949; www.oregonstateparks.org) and **OSWALD WEST STATE PARK** (along Hwy 101; 800/551-6949; www.oregonstateparks.org), this hideaway nestles against an uncrowded coastline and has just a deli, a post office, and several excellent lodging options. At low tide, a stony beach turns into a soft, sandy shore with dark and dramatic sea stacks in the distance. A pair of corroded cannons was discovered in 2008 after storms eroded the beach. Archaeologists called it an extremely uncommon level of discovery and have speculated that they were likely from the USS *Shark*, an 1846 shipwreck.

LODGINGS

The Inn at Arch Cape / ★★

**79340 HWY 101, ARCH CAPE; 503/738-7373
OR 800/352-8034**

Located in the heart of Arch Cape, this lovely inn offers a serene '30s-style ocean retreat. Enjoy an intimate central courtyard, beautiful gardens, and easy access to 7 miles of walking beach (at low tide). The six guest rooms are uniquely appointed with a mix of modern and rustic elegance—some with warm tongue-and-groove pine interiors and all with gorgeous wood-burning fireplaces constructed of beach rock, along with TVs and DVD players and luxurious bedding. They also have fully equipped kitchens and private baths. The inn is completely nonsmoking and pet friendly. If they're full, try one of their cottages and suites in Gearhart. *$$–$$$; AE, DIS, MC, V; no checks; www.innatarchcape.com; corner of Ocean Rd and Hwy 101.* &

Manzanita, Nehalem, and Wheeler

This trio of waterfront towns—Manzanita on the beach, Nehalem on the river, and Wheeler on the bay—makes for an interesting trifecta of adventure, solitude, and easy retreat. Increasingly upscale Manzanita abuts the proletarian **NEHALEM BAY STATE PARK** (off Hwy 101, south of Manzanita; 503/368-5154; www.oregonstateparks.org), sharing 7 miles of sand dune–bordered beach. In recent years, tranquil Manzanita has become a magnet for urban refugees. Just a few miles south of Manzanita, the quiet towns of Nehalem and Wheeler sit tucked against the beautiful Nehalem River and Bay. Both villages are experiencing fits and starts of rejuvenation.

Before heading into Manzanita, get your bearings at **NEAHKAHNIE MOUN-TAIN WAYSIDE** (1 mile north of town, along Hwy 101), taking in the majestic vistas of the area's gracefully arching shoreline. **MANZANITA BEACH** (on Ocean Rd in Manzanita; www.iwindsurf.com) is a popular windsurfing site, known for its reliable 18–24mph summer winds. Rent bikes, skim boards, or surfboards at **MANZANITA BIKES AND BOARDS** (170 Laneda Ave, Manzanita; 503/368-3337; manzanitabikesandboards.com). Golfing is available at **MANZA-NITA GOLF COURSE** (Lakeview Dr, Manzanita; 503/368-5744), a public 9-hole course. Nehalem Bay State Park is a fun-packed site, offering an airstrip, a horse camp with corrals and campsites, and yurt rentals. Entry to the park is off Hwy 101 at the Bayshore junction south of Manzanita.

The **NEHALEM RIVER**, particularly the estuary and bay adjacent to the state park, is a challenging and serene place to kayak. Rent equipment at **WHEELER ON THE BAY LODGE AND MARINA** (580 Marine Dr, Wheeler; 503/368-5858 or 800/469-3204). **NEHALEM BAY** is a great fishing and crabbing spot. Rent boats and tackle at the **WHEELER MARINA** (278 Marine Dr, Wheeler; 503/368-5780). For fresh seafood dinners with a bay view, visit **SEA SHACK RESTAURANT AND LOUNGE** (380 Marine Dr, Wheeler; 503/368-7897). For pizzas and casual Italian fare, try **GUIDO'S** (675 Hwy 101, Wheeler; 503/368-7778).

RESTAURANTS

Marzano's Pizza Pie / ★

60 LANEDA AVE, MANZANITA; 503/368-3663
Located along Manzanita's main street, with a vaguely classic Italian ambience (with some great posters on the walls), Marzano's is the best pizza you'll find south of Cannon Beach. Of course, you'll wish the pies were bigger—the 18-inch large feeds two hungry adults but isn't particularly hearty. Still, the made-fresh-daily New York–style crust and fresh, high-quality sauces and toppings, including freshly grated mozzarella, provolone, Parmesan, and other specialty imported Italian cheeses and hand-selected quality meats, are a cut above most pizza available farther south. They also serve calzones, soup and salads, a few wines by the glass, and beer. *$; MC, V; local checks only; dinner every day; beer and wine; no reservations; on main drag 2 blocks east of beach.*

Nehalem River Inn Restaurant / ★★

341910 HWY 53, NEHALEM; 503/368-7780
Views of the Nehalem River are part of the charm here whether you're in the dining room or on the patio. Combining traditional techniques with quality local and organic ingredients, the kitchen here turns out seasonally changing, French-inspired fare. A typical salad might be the wild arugula with pepitas, black currants, couscous, and tarragon aioli. For entrées, look for steak or an elaborate seafood dish, like seared local diver scallops served with crème fraiche and goat cheese grits, *edamame*, organic tomatoes, and roasted red pepper coulis. The wine list includes a good selection of local and international offerings. The downside for parents of well-mannered kids? Children under 12 are banned from the dining room. Restaurant hours vary by season, so be sure to call ahead. *$$–$$$; MC, V; no checks; dinner Fri–Mon; beer and wine; reservations recommended; www.nehalemriverinn.com; 3 miles east of Hwy 101.*

Wanda's Cafe & Bakery / ★★

12870 HWY 101, NEHALEM; 503/368-8100
Wanda's Cafe is all wink and kitsch. Decorated with a wacky collection of Americana—formica tables, dozens of old toasters, and a fish tank dressed as a television and labeled "telefishin," for example—this diner-bakery is an entertaining spot at the Nehalem bend. But it's not all show; the eats are consistently good. Breakfast and lunch feature fresh and bountiful omelets, quiches, salads, homemade soups, and an assortment of fresh baked goods. With its good value, great sense of humor, and relaxed vibe, Wanda already has out-of-town regulars. *$; no credit cards; checks OK; breakfast, lunch every day; no alcohol; no reservations; center of town.*

LODGINGS

The Inn at Manzanita / ★★

32 LANEDA AVE, MANZANITA; 503/368-7701
Infused with light and ocean views, this getaway located just 200 feet from the ocean and in the heart of downtown Manzanita is tranquility itself. The soothing sounds of surf lull and satisfy, proving that location really does matter. A mix of shingled, multilevel structures provides 13 guest rooms, each complete with spa tub, fireplace, and deck (as well as standard amenities such as robes, coffee, and wet bar). Securing a reservation at this popular spot lauded by several national publications requires long-range planning. *$$$–$$$$; MC, V; checks OK; www.oceaninnatmanzanita.com; at the beach.*

Old Wheeler Hotel / ★★

495 HWY 101, WHEELER; 503/368-6000 OR 877/653-4683
Housed on the second floor of a storefront in the center of undiscovered Wheeler, this historic jewel experienced massive restoration in 2004. Owners Maranne Doyle-Laszlo and Winston Laszlo took great pains to turn the 1920s structure into a charming but comfy bay-front bed-and-breakfast, and all five guest rooms overlook Nehalem Bay. Guests have free access to a collection of American Film Institute's top 10 movies (a nod to Winston's father, who was a Hollywood screenwriter). With its hardwood floors, clawfoot tubs, and ornate chandeliers, the hotel is a Victorian vacation—without the steep rates. *$–$$; AE, DIS, MC, V; no checks; www.oldwheelerhotel.com; across from bay and train depot.*

Rockaway Beach

A seaside escape for Portlanders in the 1920s, Rockaway's allure dimmed over the years as the offerings of trendier beach towns outshined this one, which lacks a town center and is more like a strip of beach homes and barely surviving businesses. Still, what Rockaway doesn't offer in upscale boutiques or fine dining, it makes up for with 7 miles of wide, sandy beach. Several old school–style big-box motels line the shore, and dozens of oceanfront homes serve as vacation rentals. A unique vintage train runs through town. Untapped and mostly undeveloped, Rockaway Beach is still—but likely not for long—an uncrowded and affordable beach retreat.

To fuel your body for a day of beachcombing or paddling Spring Lake, just across the road, try takeout Southern-style barbecue at **D'MAX BBQ** (2010 Hwy 101; 503/312-4120), offering house-made barbecued baked beans, coleslaw, ribs, pulled pork sandwiches, beef brisket, and made-fresh-daily sweet potato pie. At **DRAGONFLY SISTERS ESPRESSO & CAFÉ** (107 S Miller St; 503/355-2300; www. dragonflysisters.com), sip lattes while tucking into homemade scones, bran muffins, soup, and sandwiches, or cool off with Tillamook ice cream cones, milk shakes, and sundaes. Located on the beach at the downtown wayside park, the **BLUEWATER GRILL** (210 S 1st Ave; 503/355-3111) offers close-up ocean views and a menu of seafood, steaks, and comfort food favorites.

LODGINGS

Twin Rocks Motel / ★

7925 MINNEHAHA ST, ROCKAWAY BEACH; 503/355-2391 OR 877-355-2391
Although billed as a motel, this oceanfront lodging is really a set of five fresh-scrubbed cottages. Each individual cottage has two bedrooms and a kitchen; all but Cottage 4 have fireplaces. Best of all, this low-fuss spot is on the beach, with the sun and surf lapping at the door. Fronting a 7-mile stretch of sandy beach, this place was made for walking. Stock up on groceries and fire up the barbie. *$$–$$$; no credit cards; checks OK; www.twinrocksmotel.net; 1 mile south of Rockaway, on beach.* &

Garibaldi, Bay City, and Tillamook

The Tillamook, Trask, Wilson, and Kilchis rivers and Dougherty Slough all pass through or near the town of Tillamook—part of a network of more than 20 rivers and streams that feed into Tillamook Bay and out to the Pacific Ocean. Garibaldi and Bay City, small towns nestled on the bay, are peppered with proof of water-based industry: fishing boats and oyster-shell mounds. **PACIFIC OYSTER COMPANY** (5150 Oyster Dr, Bay City; 503/377-2323) is a good stop for oysters and a view. The food concession at the oyster processing plant in Bay City, just past Garibaldi, features a sit-down deli/oyster bar, offering outrageously good oyster stew, oyster burgers and shooters, an excellent Dungeness crab melt sandwich, and a whole crab dinner.

Tillamook, with its broad expanse of green pastures, is best known as dairy land. It is home to the world-famous **TILLAMOOK COUNTY CREAMERY ASSOCIATION** plant and visitor center (4175 Hwy 101, Tillamook; 503/815-1300 or 800/542-7290; www.tillamookcheese.com), which offers self-guided tours and tastes. Across town, check out the **TILLAMOOK AIR MUSEUM** (6030 Hangar Rd, Tillamook; 503/842-1130), a former blimp hangar showcasing restored aircraft. Visit the **TILLAMOOK COUNTY MUSEUM** (2106 2nd St, Tillamook; 503/842-4553, near intersection of Hwy 101 and 2nd St) to see the rocks bearing cryptic symbols that were found on Neahkahnie Mountain. They also display blocks of beeswax from the 1600s bearing stamped trade markings, which native inhabitants later used as trade currency.

Oceanside

Carved from a cliff, Oceanside is 8 miles west of Tillamook along **THREE CAPES SCENIC DRIVE**, a gorgeous 34-mile loop traversing a changing landscape of ocean vistas, green pastures, rolling dunes, and thickets of alder, birch, and spruce. It's a little confusing trying to find this spot because it's largely isolated from Hwy 101. Head west through downtown Tillamook on Third Street, then turn right on Bay Ocean Road toward Cape Meares or left toward Netarts. The road loops in both directions to Oceanside.

CAPE MEARES STATE PARK (800/551-6949; www.oregonstateparks.org; on Three Capes Scenic Dr, just north of Oceanside) offers hiking and scenic views of Tillamook Bay and the Pacific. Walk up to and inside **CAPE MEARES LIGHTHOUSE** (503/842-2244). At only 38 feet tall, it's the shortest lighthouse in Oregon, though it stands more than 200 feet above the ocean. The Three Capes route winds along Netarts Bay before reaching **CAPE LOOKOUT STATE PARK** (13000 Whiskey Creek Rd, 11 miles southwest of Tillamook; 503/842-4981; www.oregonstateparks. org), with 212 campsites and a huge expanse of beach. The hike out to the lookout point through an old-growth forest is one of the state's best hikes.

Oceanside itself is a quiet residential town with a variety of vacation homes woven into its landscape. Plan ahead to secure a rental. With scant restaurants, shops, or lodging, this town is all about the ocean. A good option if you plan ahead is the **OCEANSIDE HISTORIC ANCHOR INN** (1505 Pacific Hwy, Oceanside; 503/842-2041; www.oceansideshistoricanchorinn.com). If you can't get a room, at least try the **ANCHOR INN GRILL**, where you can tuck into burgers, Oregon Coast seafood dishes, including salmon, crab, oysters, and clams, and many other traditional Oregon beef and fish entrées, while sipping exclusively regional wines.

RESTAURANTS

Roseanna's Oceanside Café / ★

1490 PACIFIC ST, OCEANSIDE; 503/842-7351

Roseanna's is massively popular, as evidenced by long lines and the number of locals lining the bar. The secret to success? Stunning tableside views of the crashing Pacific and its enchanting sea stacks, along with an extensive list of homemade desserts. It's expensive, but for those willing to fork over $10 for grilled cheese sandwiches and much more for dinner entrées, this small and cheery eatery is thoroughly enjoyable. Try seasonal dishes made with crab, lingcod, sturgeon, and razor clams; Willapa Bay oysters are nearly always available. The wine list has good depth, but cocktails are fairly limited. *$$–$$$; MC, V; no checks; lunch, dinner, brunch every day; full bar; no reservations; www.roseannascafe.com; on the main street.* &

Pacific City

Just off the main drag of Hwy 101, Pacific City is a secret spot gaining momentum. With the Big Nestucca River running through it, the small town is experiencing a rush of residential development. Pacific City has three beach accesses: **ROBERT STRAUB PARK** (800/551-6949) to the south, **PACIFIC AVENUE** in the center of town, and the most popular, **CAPE KIWANDA**—a dramatic sandstone headland— at the north end of town, a popular spot for hang gliding, surfing, and kite flying. The dory fleets (classic fishing boats) launch here, and surfers ride the waves. It's here that you can also see the "other" Haystack Rock offshore (the most well-known one is in Cannon Beach).

Open to the public only for special events, the **NESTUCCA BAY NATIONAL WILDLIFE REFUGE** (just off Hwy 101 south of Pacific City; 541/867-4550) is habitat for rare wildlife, including the world's small population of Semidi Islands Aleutian cackling geese, and is the only coastal wintering spot for dusky Canada geese.

In the center of town you'll find boutiques, including **VILLAGE MERCHANTS** (at River Pl, 34950 Brooten Rd, Pacific City; 503/965-6911) for clothing and gifts and **PACIFIC CITY GALLERY** (35350 Brooten Rd, Pacific City; 503/965-7181) for art.

Go gourmet at **HARVEST FRESH RIVER PLACE DELI** (at River Pl, 34950 Brooten Rd, Pacific City; 503/965-0090), or settle into a comfy overstuffed chair at **STIMULUS** (33105 Cape Kiwanda Dr, Pacific City; www.stimuluscafe.com), an eclectic café and bistro. Enjoy lattes or cappuccinos along with light breakfast and lunch items, including muffins, pastries, and paninis, while perusing periodicals and listening to jazz. The homey **VILLAGE COFFEE SHOPPE RESTAURANT AND BAKERY** (34910 Brooten Rd, Pacific City; 503/965-7635) serves budget breakfasts. **LOS CAPORALES MEXICAN RESTAURANT** (35025 Brooten Rd, Pacific City; 503/965-6999) serves up authentic Mexican dishes at reasonable prices.

RESTAURANTS

Delicate Palate Bistro / ★★

35280 BROOTEN RD (PACIFIC CITY INN), PACIFIC CITY; 503/965-6464 OR 866/567-3466

Fine wines and excellent service complement a menu of innovative starters, salads, and entrées at this upscale bistro. Make it all small plates, or start with the Dungeness crab cakes; sesame-seared Kare ahi tuna with Asian slaw; roasted beet salad with mandarin oranges and goat cheese fritters; or Fuji apple and Gorgonzola salad with baby greens, candied walnuts, and champagne vinaigrette. Entrées are equally gourmet. Try the seafood risotto or king salmon served with a Mediterranean ragout. The wine list is phenomenal, the martinis a good alternative. The house seats 46, but there are also tables outside on the deck, in the bar, and in the garden. *$$; AE, DIS, MC, V; checks OK; dinner Wed–Sun; full bar; reservations recommended; www.delicate palate.com; 2 blocks south of Pacific Ave.* &

Grateful Bread Bakery & Restaurant / ★

34805 BROOTEN RD, PACIFIC CITY; 503/965-7337

A local institution, this bright and cheery bakery-restaurant consistently dishes up excellent and affordable meals. At the bakery counter, old-fashioned glass-topped platters hold beautiful berry pies, massive cinnamon buns, and man-hand-sized cookies and chocolate cheesecake brownies. Though the restaurant's ambience is very basic, the fare is hearty and interesting. Breakfast standouts include challah French toast, gingerbread pancakes, and a hearty scramble of oysters, eggs, and veggies. Robust sandwiches on fresh bread highlight the lunch menu; pizzas, pastas, and vegetarian dishes dominate dinner. The Tillamook cheddar cheese and corn chowder is a must-have. Eat in, linger on the deck, or pack a picnic for the beach. *$–$$; MC, V;*

checks OK; breakfast, lunch, dinner Thurs–Mon; no alcohol; no reservations; north end of Brooten Rd.

Pelican Pub & Brewery / ★

33180 CAPE KIWANDA DR, PACIFIC CITY; 503/965-7007
Surfboards hanging from wood beams, a young laid-back staff, and the smell of hops give this brew pub a chill-on-the-beach vibe. The fare is basic sports-bar grub, but it's the brews and views that helped Pelican win Small Brewpub of the Year from the prestigious Great American Beer Festival. The pub consistently earns top honors for its Kiwanda Cream Ale, MacPelican Scottish Style Ale, and Doryman's Dark Ale. Sampling in-house brewed beer here is serious fun; there are even beer-dessert pairings on the menu. Perched on the windswept beach, it's the perfect spot to kick back and watch surfers and dory fleets. *$–$$; AE, MC, V; local checks only; breakfast, lunch, dinner every day; full bar; no reservations; www.pelicanbrewery.com; on Brooten Rd.*

LODGINGS

Inn at Cape Kiwanda / ★★

33105 CAPE KIWANDA DR, PACIFIC CITY; 503/965-7001 OR 888/965-7001
Earth tones and fireplaces create a Northwestern ambience throughout this 35-room hotel. Though it's not exactly oceanfront, every room has a Pacific view, with the commanding Haystack Rock at the forefront. The Haystack Suite offers a romantic tub with an ocean view, two private balconies, and all the goods to entertain: espresso machine, wine chiller, and full sets of dishes and glassware. *$$$–$$$$; AE, DIS, MC, V; no checks; www.innatcapekiwanda. com; across street from Pelican Pub.*

Neskowin

Boasting just 300 full-time residents (the population swells to 2,000 in summer), Neskowin is a small town with a concentration of tidy cottages in the center village and motels-turned-condos on its south edge. Signs of growth are evident, especially north of town on the east side of Hwy 101, where large homes spread across the hillside. Still, the diminutive town boasts just a few hotels and vacation rentals and one restaurant: **HAWK CREEK CAFÉ** (4505 Salem Ave; 503/392-3838). In the center village, colorful homemade yard signs plead drivers to "slow down." And that sentiment best sums this slow and sleepy coastal town with an unspoiled coastline.

The white-sandy beach, though narrow, is walkable, and **PROPOSAL ROCK** stands as a sentinel just offshore. **CASCADE HEAD** (trailhead 2 miles south of Hwy 101) is a temperate rain forest with miles of trails through old-growth forest. And the nearby **SITKA CENTER FOR ART AND ECOLOGY** (503/994-5485), at the southern base of Cascade Head, offers workshops.

Lincoln City

Unlike many Oregon Coast destinations, Lincoln City demands car travel. Spread along both sides of bustling Hwy 101, Lincoln City is actually several towns (Cutler City, Taft, Nelscott, Delake, and Oceanlake) joined in one long sprawl. Lodging is plentiful, with a mix of dated and new big-box motels. Upscale digs are rare. It's the beach that redeems the bustle. Seven miles of wide, sandy, walkable shore stretch from Road's End (north end of town) to the peaceful shores of Siletz Bay.

Lincoln City has some real treasures; it's just that the quality spots can get lost in the din of development. **BIJOU THEATRE** (1624 NE Hwy 101; 541/994-8255) is a historic theater showing art-house films; **BOB'S BEACH BOOKS** (1747 NW Hwy 101; 541/994-4467) is an independent bookshop in the Oceanlake district; **CATCH THE WIND KITES** (240 SE Hwy 101, 130 SE Hwy 101; 541/994-9500) sells hundreds of varieties for breezy shores.

Art galleries are plentiful, **FREED GALLERY** (6119 SW Hwy 101; 541/994-5600) among them. The **JENNIFER SEARS GLASS ART STUDIO** (4821 SW Hwy 101; 541/996-2569) offers free glassblowing demos. Lincoln City has a lot to digest. Stop by the **LINCOLN CITY VISITORS & CONVENTION BUREAU** (801 SW Hwy 101; 503/996-1274 or 800/452-2151) for an overview.

RESTAURANTS

Bay House / ★★★★

5911 SE HWY 101, LINCOLN CITY; 541/996-3222
Set on the banks of Siletz Bay, this enduring restaurant tacks along traditional lines, with tabletop candlesticks providing just enough light to read the inspired menu of Pacific Northwest meals. The menu changes daily, spotlighting tender beef, local fish, and organic veggies in preparations that are fresh flavored and elegant. As always, the wine list is book-thick and Wine Spectator–approved. The newest addition to the restaurant is a separate wine bar and cocktail lounge. *$$$–$$$$; AE, DIS, MC, V; no checks; lunch, dinner every day; full bar; reservations recommended; www.thebayhouse.org; south end of town.* &

Blackfish Café / ★★★

2733 NE HWY 101, LINCOLN CITY; 541/996-1007
Since opening in 1999, this coastal treasure has offered an unusual blend of affordable, first-rate meals without the foodie fuss. Blackfish keeps it real with a stylish but comfy dining-room ambience. The menu, which changes seasonally, focuses on fresh catches, vegetables, and fresh baked bread from the owners' Rockfish Bakery. *$$–$$$; AE, MC, V; no checks; lunch, dinner Wed–Mon (Thurs–Mon in winter), brunch on holidays; beer and wine; reservations recommended; www.blackfishcafe.com; north end of town.* &

LODGINGS

Inn at Spanish Head / ★

4009 SW HWY 101, LINCOLN CITY; 541/996-2162 OR 800/452-8127
Carved from a steep cliff side, this resort hotel boasts great views and premium beach access. These 125 individually owned condo units serve as vacation rentals, meaning each has its own style and decor. All are fresh and tidy, with floor-to-ceiling windows and access to an outdoor pool, a Jacuzzi, a small gym, and a game room. One-bedroom suites are the roomiest, though the smaller bedroom and studio units have kitchenettes and elbow room. Check out the top-floor restaurant and lounge for curve-of-the-earth views stretching from Cascade Head to Siletz Bay. *$$$–$$$$; AE, DC, DIS, MC, V; checks OK; www.spanishhead.com; south end of town.*

Olivia Beach Cottage Rentals / ★★★

4741 NW HWY 101, LINCOLN CITY; 866/994-7026
Beach houses and cottages, located in the Historic Nelscott District, offer the feel of a real neighborhood with parks, preserved wetlands, and wooded paths—all within walking distance of the beach. The self-contained community, designed by acclaimed New Urbanist architect Laurence Qamar, is incredibly well priced; the smallest home sleeps four and the largest 12. Modern sophistication is the rule, with luxury furnishings, jetted tubs, and gourmet kitchens with granite countertops. Nearly every part of your stay is equipped, including everything you need in a kitchen (except food), a washer and dryer, a gas barbecue, high-speed Internet access, a TV, and DVD and CD players. Some even have hot tubs and bicycles. *$$$; AE, MC, V; no checks; www.oliviabeach.com; enter at corner of SW 28th St & SW Beach Ave.* &

Gleneden Beach

More an oversize wayside than a thriving town, Gleneden Beach is mostly known as the site of Salishan, a well-heeled resort accompanied by tony boutiques and art galleries. **EDEN HALL** (6675 Gleneden Beach Loop Rd; 541/764-3825) is a stage for local music and theater, and the adjoining **SIDE DOOR CAFE** (541/764-3825), a bistro housed in Gleneden's old brick and tile factory.

RESTAURANTS

The Dining Room / ★★★

7760 N HWY 101 (SALISHAN SPA & GOLF RESORT),
GLENEDEN BEACH; 541/764-3600 OR 800/452-2300
The split-level design and floor-to-ceiling windows bring the outdoors into this expansive dining room. Despite the casual feel, the space is warm, modern, and elegant with white table linens, fine china, and vibrant carpeting. It's also very expensive, an indulgent splurge. In the foyer, there's a temperature-controlled, 750-bottle wine showcase, one of the state's largest. The menu is

NORTHERN OREGON COAST SPAS

Make the most of your trip to the Oregon Coast by indulging in some true downtime. The North Coast's growing cadre of luxury spas provides the impetus; here, they're listed north to south.

CANNON BEACH SPA (232 N Spruce St, Cannon Beach; 503/436-8772; www.cannonbeachspa.com) is a top-tier spot for the ultimate unwind. During cool and rainy weather, schedule a hot stone massage. Smooth black rocks are gathered from Ecola State Park's Indian Beach, heated in a big crocklike cooker, and used by the therapist to transfer radiant warmth to tight and sore muscles. After a full day of activity, schedule a deep tissue massage, an indulgent release aided by deft hands and old-fashioned liniment rub.

SPA MANZANITA (144 Laneda Ave, Manzanita; 503/368-4777; www.spa manzanita.com) offers same-day and reserved appointments at their beautiful spa one block from the ocean. Choose from nine types of massage using organic, nut-free oils, in addition to reflexology, wraps, waxing, facials, salt glows, peels, and massage lessons for couples.

Northwest regional with a strong seasonal and fresh local focus, including seafood, wild game, Kobe beef, and pastas. *$$$–$$$$; AE, DIS, MC, V; no checks; dinner every day; full bar; reservations recommended; www.salishan. com; east side of hwy.* &

LODGINGS

Salishan Spa & Golf Resort / ★★★

7760 N HWY 101, GLENEDEN BEACH; 541/764-3600 OR 800/452-2300
A pioneer in swanky coastal lodging, this sprawling resort—built in 1965—spans 750 acres on both sides of Hwy 101. Although Salishan has seen both heydays and decline, a multimillion-dollar renovation in 2004 brought upgrades to the 205 guest rooms and suites—from basic to posh, including fireplaces, minifridges, and more modern amenities like flat-panel TVs, plush robes, and luxury baths—all with Northwest styling. Other amenities include a Scottish-style golf course, tennis courts, boutiques, art galleries, three restaurants, a 10,000-bottle wine cellar, an indoor pool, a 24-hour fitness facility, and a full-service spa (see "Northern Oregon Coast Spas"). When booking, try for a second-floor room; most have fireplaces, and they're much quieter. The only downside to Salishan? Uneven service. *$$$–$$$$; AE, DC, DIS, MC, V; checks OK; www.salishan.com; east side of hwy.* &

The gorgeous 9,000-square-foot $3.5 million **SPA AT SALISHAN** (7760 Hwy 101, Gleneden Beach; 541/764-4300; www.salishan.com) is stunning and serene. Overlooking Siletz Bay, the contemporary building blends cedar, stone, and natural light. The indulgent menu includes seven types of massage, wraps, scrubs, manicures, and pedicures.

At **DESERT SPRINGS NATURAL HEALING SPA** (422 SW 10th St, Newport; 541/574-9887; www.dshealing.com), overlooking Yaquina Bay, owner and herbalist Norma Anderson delivers unique treatments, often even hard to find in the big city, including ear candling, energy release, Reiki, and raindrop therapy.

The 3,000-square-foot **OVERLEAF SPA** (280 Overleaf Lodge Ln, Yachats; 541/547-4880; www.overleaflodge.com), north of town above the rocky coastline, offers revitalizing and relaxation treatments with a view. The third-story facility provides extraordinary views of the ocean, particularly from the immersion pool. The menu includes massages, Vichy showers, Jacuzzis, saunas, steam baths, and a fitness center.

—Jo Ostgarden

Depoe Bay

Small but mighty, Depoe Bay has the world's smallest harbor: 350 feet wide, 750 feet long, and only 8 feet deep at mean low tide. Roughly 100 vessels moor here year-round, with many more boats visiting during the summer. Navigating the short and narrow basalt channel is daunting at best, and the journey to sea is tricky for even the most skilled sailor. A huge seawall runs the length of the downtown core, providing optimum ocean views and seaspray experiences. Waves run beneath lava beds, building enough pressure to spout water as high as 60 feet into the air.

Depoe Bay is billed as the whale-watching capital of the world, and a resident pod of gray whales call these waters home. The **DEPOE WHALE WATCHING CENTER** (119 SW Hwy 101, Depoe Bay; 541/765-3304) is in the center of town. **DOCKSIDE CHARTERS** (541/765-2545 or 800/733-8915) offers fishing expeditions and whale-watching tours.

A line of shops along Hwy 101 peddles the typical tourist jumble of taffy and T-shirts. Skip the clutter and look to the sea. With limited lodging in Depot Bay, consider **BELLA BEACH VACATION RENTALS** (24 Bella Beach Dr, Depoe Bay; 866/994-7026; www.bellabeach.com) for a range of affordable upscale cottages and houses just off Hwy 101 north of Depot Bay. For casual dining with a view of the harbor, try the **SPOUTING HORN** (10 SE Hwy 101, Depoe Bay; 541/765-2261). A local institution, they offer a good but inexpensive buffet on Thursday and Saturday nights and seafood dinners every night except Tuesdays.

RESTAURANTS

Tidal Raves / ★★

279 NW HWY 101, DEPOE BAY; 541/765-2995

Straddling the gap between flip-flop casual and highbrow fussy, Tidal Raves fills the niche for moderately priced, fresh seafood in a picturesque setting carved out of a cliff side cove. The views alone are worth the stop. Swirling surf crashes against rocks below, and at sunset the beauty is blinding. Thankfully, the food—chockablock with seafood choices—hits the mark. Thai-grilled tiger shrimp is a signature dish, and the cioppino earns accolades too. It's easily the best restaurant in town, so reservations are critical. *$$–$$$; AE, MC, V; local checks only; lunch, dinner every day (winter hours vary); beer and wine; reservations recommended; on west side of hwy.*

LODGINGS

Channel House Inn / ★★

35 ELLINGSON ST, DEPOE BAY; 541/765-2140 OR 800/447-2140

It's not especially luxurious, and the boxy exterior isn't a real charmer, but Channel House scores points for sheer drama. A true cliffhanger, the 12-room inn overlooks the narrow channel into Depoe Bay harbor. Waves crash against the rocky shoreline, and every room boasts ocean views. All rooms—ranging from singles to more spacious suites—have private baths, and most have private decks and fireplaces. *$$$–$$$$; AE, DIS, MC, V; checks OK; www.channel_house.com; south end of town.*

Newport

One of the Oregon Coast's most popular tourist destinations, Newport—at first glance—is an unending stream of strip malls and stoplights. Wade through the commercial chaos to uncover the coastal gems tucked on side streets and out-of-the-way spots. In short, avoid Hwy 101. Instead, check out the artsy **NYE BEACH HISTORIC DISTRICT** (on 3rd St west of Hwy 101), where boutiques share the neighborhood with the **NEWPORT PERFORMING ARTS CENTER** (777 W Olive St, Newport; 541/265-2787) and the **NEWPORT VISUAL ARTS CENTER** (777 NW Beach Dr, Newport; 541/265-6540). As the name implies, this area offers easy access to an expansive stretch of unspoiled but popular beach.

Head to the east side of Hwy 101 for the **HISTORIC BAYFRONT**, where a working harbor bustles with a dizzying array of fishing fleets, souvenir shops, seafood markets, chowder houses, and a (cheesy) wax museum. A lovely bridge and two lighthouses grace this town: **YAQUINA HEAD OUTSTANDING NATURAL AREA AND LIGHTHOUSE** (off Hwy 101 to the north; 541/574-3100) and **YAQUINA BAY LIGHTHOUSE** (access via SW 9th St; 541/265-5679) to the south. Newport also boasts two aquariums: **HATFIELD MARINE SCIENCE CENTER** (2030 SE Marine Science Dr, Newport; 541/867-0100), an Oregon State University marine research

facility, and the world-class 29-acre **OREGON COAST AQUARIUM** (2820 SE Ferry
Slip Rd, Newport; 541/867-3474).

RESTAURANTS

Blu Cork / ★★★

613 SW 3RD ST, NEWPORT; 541/265-2257
Warm, earthy hues, white tablecloths, a granite bar, and live music have
made this hip wine bar a coastal hit. Every weekend, the casually classy spot
packs guests enjoying mid- to high-end wines, live music (local, polished jazz
ensembles and folk artists), and delicious small-plate appetizers. They serve
35 to 40 wines by the glass along with small plates featuring bold Spanish and
French flavors at reasonable prices. The menu features flavors that go well
with wine (vanilla, berry, floral, citrus, almond). You can also sample artisan
cheeses, served with quince and flatbread, or their house-made pâtés or hand-
tossed grilled pizzas. *$–$$; MC, V; no checks; dinner Wed–Sat; beer and wine;
no reservations; corner of Coast Ave and Third St.* ⅃

La Maison Bakery and Café / ★★★

315 SW 9TH ST, NEWPORT; 541/265-8812
Fresh flowers, white linens, warm woods, and colorful walls set the mood
at this French-country café. Tucked a few blocks east of Hwy 101, this
intimate spot has just 10 tables and a bursting dessert case. Breakfast and
lunch are delicious surprises at this hidden find. Crepes are stuffed with
artichokes, tomatoes, and cheese. Breakfast sandwiches feature homemade
oversize English muffins. Lunch shines too. Feast on roast pork, grilled
chicken salad, or soups. *$–$$; MC, V; local checks only; breakfast, lunch
Tues–Sat; beer and wine; no reservations; east side of hwy, near 10th and
Lee sts.*

Local Ocean Seafoods / ★★★

213 SE BAY BLVD, NEWPORT; 541/574-7959
Zip past the clatter of tourist traps and head to Local Ocean Seafoods for
fresh, affordable seafood with a harbor view and relaxed, modern vibe. This
casually sophisticated fish market–restaurant serves simple but inspired headliners like fish tacos, teriyaki tuna kebabs, and roasted-garlic crab chowder.
This high-energy spot shines as Newport's only modern architecture. Postmodern meets industrial cool with glass walls, stainless-steel accents, and
exposed ductwork. In the summer, the glass doors slide open for alfresco
dining. *$–$$; MC, V; local checks only; lunch, dinner every day; beer and wine;
no reservations; www.localocean.net; east end of bay front.*

LODGINGS

Sylvia Beach Hotel / ★★

267 NW CLIFF ST, NEWPORT; 541/265-5428 OR 888/795-8422
Built in 1910 and last renovated in the 1980s, this hotel is like a favorite pair of well-worn jeans. With 33 guest rooms named after famous writers, this Nye Beach inn attracts writers and readers. There are no televisions, radios, or phones—just plenty of time to walk the beach, write, or draw. The three "classics" rooms feature decks, fireplaces, and ocean views. The four-story hotel is reminiscent of a huge old clapboard roadhouse. It's just steps from the lightly traveled beach as well as trendy restaurants and boutiques. Communal-style meals are served in the hotel's restaurant. *$$–$$$; AE, MC, V; checks OK; www.sylviabeachhotel.com; oceanfront.* &

Tyee Lodge / ★★★

4925 NW WOODY WY, NEWPORT; 541/265-8953 OR 888/553-8933
This secluded bed-and-breakfast skips the theme rooms and faux Victorian fuss in favor of relaxed, quiet comfort and great ocean views. Nestled in the trees on a cove overlooking Agate Beach, it has five guest rooms featuring ocean views, private baths, fireplaces, comfy chairs, and mints at the bedside. Guests are greeted with warm cookies and complimentary wine and beer, and breakfast is a candlelit, three-course affair. *$$$; AE, DIS, MC, V; checks OK; www.tyeelodge.com; very north end of town.*

Waldport

Overshadowed by busy Newport to the north and quirky Yachats to the south, Waldport is an unsung seaside town with its own quiet beauty. The lovely Alsea River Bay, for example, is an estuary offering great clamming and fishing. Boats and equipment can be rented at **DOCK OF THE BAY MARINA** (1245 Mill St; 541/563-2003). On sunny days, hundreds of sea lions sunbathe on the sand spit beneath the stately **ALSEA BAY BRIDGE** on Hwy 101. Built in 1937 and restored in 1991, the bridge is a beautiful example of the coast's many historic spans. At the south end of the bridge, the **ALSEA BAY BRIDGE INTERPRETIVE CENTER** (620 NW Spring St; 541/563-2002) presents museum-quality photos and displays of the area's transportation history. Near the port, stop at the **SALTY DAWG BAR & GRILL** (375 Port St; 541/563-2555) for Broasted chicken. Head to **ESPRESSO 101 BAKERY & DELI** (120 Hwy 101; 541/563-3621) for hot coffee, fresh doughnuts, and local gossip. For more substantial meals (but equally fast), try enduring favorite **VICKIE'S BIG WHEEL DRIVE IN** (Hwy 101 and Spring St; 541/563-3640). If you decide to stay overnight, find clean rooms and ocean views at both the **CLIFF HOUSE BED AND BREAKFAST** (1450 SW Adahi Rd; 541/563-2506; www.cliff-houseoregon.com) and the **CAPE COD COTTAGES** (4150 SW Pacific Coast Hwy; 541/563-2106; www.dreamwater.com/thecottages).

Yachats

Small but active, Yachats (pronounced "YA-hots") is a funky, inclusive town tucked between a lush forest and the rugged, rocky shore. Crashing waves can be heard from just about any place in this town nestled against the earth's edge.

This village of just 650 residents—and steadily growing—is surrounded by natural wonders, including three state parks: **YACHATS OCEAN ROAD STATE NATURAL SITE, YACHATS STATE PARK** (www.oregonstateparks.org), and **SMELT SANDS STATE RECREATION SITE**—here the **804 TRAIL** traverses north along rocky cliffs to spill onto an 8-mile stretch of wide, sandy beach. Just 2 miles south, **CAPE PERPETUA SCENIC AREA** (2400 Hwy 101, Yachats; 541/547-3289) is a temperate rain forest with 26 miles of hiking trails. Nearby **HECETA HEAD LIGHTHOUSE** (866/547-3696) shines as the brightest light on the Oregon Coast, with Cape Creek Bridge nearby. The neighboring **SEA LION CAVES** (91560 Hwy 101, Yachats; 541/547-3111) is the largest sea cave in the world. It plummets 208 feet below the ground and is as wide as a football field.

RESTAURANTS

The Drift Inn / ★★★

124 HWY 101, YACHATS; 541/547-4477

This place gets steadily packed at breakfast, lunch, and dinner. The down-to-earth spot (with a wonderfully attentive, if not hippy-esque, staff) is a cozy, family-friendly spot that's the centerpiece of counterculture Yachats. The eclectic menu—burgers, salads, pasta, steaks—is combined with nightly live music. Though weekends and summer season deliver crowds, the bar-side wait is bearable. *$–$$$; MC, V; checks OK; breakfast, lunch, dinner every day; full bar; no reservations; www.the-drift-inn.com; center of town.*

Green Salmon Coffee House / ★★

220 HWY 101, YACHATS; 541/547-3077

Deceptively named, the Green Salmon is nothing but plain-and-simple fresh and natural. "Green," of course, refers to environmentally friendly solar power and low-flush toilets, along with organic coffee, plus eggs and produce harvested from local farms. Owners Deb Gisetto and Dave Thomas keep this counter-service café earthy with standouts like panini sandwiches on hearty whole-grain bread and Deb's Famous Oats (a generous bowl of warm oats and granola drizzled with honey and steamed milk). *$; no credit cards; checks OK; breakfast, lunch Tues–Sun; no alcohol; no reservations; at 2nd St.* &

LODGINGS

Overleaf Lodge / ★★★

280 OVERLEAF LODGE LN, YACHATS; 541/547-4880 OR 800/338-0507

This three-story, 54-room hotel hugs the rocky coastline and offers ocean-front drama from every room. The surf practically churns at your bedside, and the neighboring walking trail yields tide-pool explorations. Easily the most modern of all Yachats accommodations, the Overleaf—with whirlpool tubs, soft robes, fireplaces, and picture windows—is targeted for couples seeking a seaside escape. While the rooms are all tastefully decorated in earth tones, there is a somewhat processed quality that feels more corporate chain than comfy lodge. An expansion in 2006 provided additional rooms, a fitness room, and a 3,000-square-foot spa (see "Northern Oregon Coast Spas"). *$$$–$$$$; AE, DIS, MC, V; no checks; www.overleaflodge.com; north end of town.* &

Shamrock Lodgettes / ★★★

105 HWY 101 S, YACHATS; 541/547-3312 OR 800/845-5028

The oceanfront setting with the feel of a park conspires to give this sweet inn its appeal. This gem is situated on 5 serene acres at the mouth of Yachats Bay, where the river meets the sea. Rooms spill onto a sandy beach and the picturesque bay. Accommodations are a mixed bag of 1950s-era knotty-pine cabins and modern motel rooms (many with kitchenettes). The guest-room decor is equally eclectic, ranging from kitschy cabin to colorful contemporary. An expansion in 2006 added two new cabins with large decks, kitchenettes, fireplaces, and peeks of the Pacific. *$$–$$$$; AE, MC, V; no checks; www. shamrocklodgettes.com; south of bridge.*

SOUTHERN
OREGON COAST

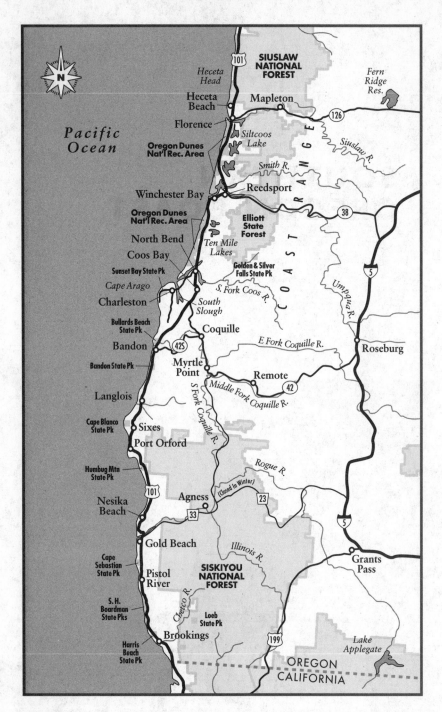

SOUTHERN OREGON COAST

Traveling along the southern coast of Oregon, spectacular windswept vistas unfold with every curve in the road, offering glimpses of beautiful coves tucked into sheer cliffs that drop to the sea, pounding surf swirling around dramatic clusters of eroded sentinel-like sea stacks, and intermittent stretches of mature forests reaching toward the sea's edge. Depending on the season, keen-eyed travelers might catch sight of migrating California gray whales from the various viewpoints strung along the coastal headlands. Just inland, bordering the southernmost Oregon Coast, giant redwoods in pockets of preserved wilderness press against the sky. Spawning salmon take their fated journey upstream through canyons cut by time and water.

Isolated from urban centers and largely undeveloped, this 150-mile stretch of breathtaking coastline is marked by just a handful of small communities. The eight major towns are historical seaports situated near the mouth of rivers. Given their distance from major cities (an eight-hour drive from San Francisco and at least a four-hour drive from Portland), these towns are not as focused on tourism as north coast towns are. The south coast both struggles and thrives in its beautiful yet remote location.

ACCESS AND INFORMATION

US HIGHWAY 101 follows the Pacific coastline from Washington to Southern California, linking most of the towns along the Southern Oregon Coast. From Interstate 5, four paved two-lane scenic roads follow rivers west to the South Coast: from Eugene STATE ROUTE 126 follows the Siuslaw River to Florence; from Drain, STATE ROUTE 38 follows the Umpqua River to Reedsport; from Roseburg, STATE ROUTE 42 follows the Coquille River to Coos Bay and Bandon; and from Grants Pass, US HIGHWAY 199 follows the Smith River, then cuts through the redwoods and dips into Northern California at the Oregon border south of Brookings.

Air service between Portland and North Bend is offered on HORIZON AIR (800/547-9308; www.alaskaair.com). GREYHOUND (800/231-2222; www.greyhound.com) offers service to Coos Bay and bus stops at Florence and Reedsport.

Florence

Florence marks the northern edge of a sweeping sand-dune landscape that is constantly being altered and reshaped by winds and ocean tides. The OREGON DUNES NATIONAL RECREATION AREA (541/750-7234) begins here, with 32,000 acres of mountainous coastal dunes—the largest expanse of such dunes in the United States—stretching 40 miles south to Coos Bay. Far from lifeless, the dunes are, in fact, home to a variety of ecosystems, from small pockets of forest to isolated marshes. And everywhere there are birds, including osprey, sanderling, and the snowy plover, a shorebird whose declining population has placed it on the

Audubon WatchList. In the spring and summer, wild strawberries, blackberries, and elderberries are ripe for the picking. To get the real flavor of this unique eco-system, head to the **OREGON DUNES OVERLOOK** (on Hwy 101, 11 miles south of Florence). A half-mile paved trail leads to the viewing area; for a closer look, sample the many trails that traverse both the dunes and the coastal forests.

SAND MASTER PARK (87542 Hwy 101, Florence; 541/997-6006)—the world's first sand-boarding park—offers 40 acres of wind-sculpted dunes and guided tours to remote dune areas. For the uninitiated, sand boarders (surfers or riders) traverse the dunes on a laminated plank in a manner nearly identical to big-wave surfing on ocean swells. **JESSIE HONEYMAN STATE PARK** (on US 101, 3 miles south of Florence; 800/551-6949), with 2 miles of sand dunes, is the second-largest overnight campground in the state. Two large freshwater lakes provide premium fishing, kayaking, and boating. Surf and diving instruction, as well as sand board and kayak rentals, are available at **CENTRAL COAST WATERSPORTS** (1901 Hwy 101, Florence; 541/997-1812 or 800/789-DIVE).

DARLINGTONIA BOTANICAL WAYSIDE (on east side of Hwy 101, 5 miles north of Florence) is dedicated to the protection of a single species: *Darlingtonia californica*, a carnivorous pitcher plant identified by its unusual burgundy flowers. The park features a boardwalk trail through 18 acres of bog.

A thriving commercial center serves an area-wide population of around 19,000 with a modern public library and several department stores. There's also a community college, a winter concert series, and even taxi service. At the same time, the town is emerging as an affordable, family-focused vacation spot. Florence is dotted with art galleries, antique stores, boutiques, and restaurants. The best of these are generally in **OLD TOWN**, with its views of the **SIUSLAW RIVER BRIDGE**.

RESTAURANTS

Pomodori's / ★★★

1415 7TH ST, FLORENCE; 541/902-2525
This charming spot, owned and operated by John Bartow and Jeffrey Lindow, enjoys a robust local following. Although *pomodori* is Italian for "tomatoes," you won't find any sloppy red sauce here. Chef John exercises a deliberate but delicious touch, turning out Mediterranean-style dishes that lean toward basil, pine nuts, sun-dried tomatoes, kalamata olives, and white-wine infusions. The focus is on pure fresh flavor, reflected in the use of organic ingredients and innovative preparations of surf and turf. Enjoy equally satisfying, though more casual, fare at lunch. *$$–$$$; MC, V; no checks; lunch, dinner Tues–Sat; full bar; reservations recommended; at Maple St.* &

Waterfront Depot Restaurant & Bar / ★★

1252 BAY ST, FLORENCE; 541/902-9100
Tucked along the Siuslaw River in Old Town, this local favorite once served as the train depot for nearby Mapleton. Transformed into a restaurant in 2004, it maintains a historic ambience with original wood flooring and walls painted in deep brown and purple hues. A comfy wood bar dominates nearly

half of the busy dining room, making it an ideal perch for sampling from a list of more than 30 wines or gourmet martinis. Reasonable prices and a sit-and-stay-awhile vibe entices area residents, who pack this place nightly to enjoy eclectic dishes ordered off a chalkboard menu. *$–$$; MC, V; local checks only; dinner every day; full bar; reservations recommended; ¾ block east of Hwy 101.*

LODGINGS

Heceta Lighthouse Bed and Breakfast / ★★★

92072 HWY 101, BETWEEN YACHATS AND FLORENCE; 541/547-3696

Set on a rugged cliff 400 feet above the ocean, Heceta Head's lighthouse beams the brightest beacon on the Oregon Coast. The lightkeeper's cottage, a beautiful old Victorian, now operates as an interpretative center by day and a B and B by night. It offers six cozy guest rooms, startlingly beautiful ocean views, and walking trails leading to the lighthouse and beach, guaranteeing that staying here is a rare and special experience. The Mariner rooms offer the best views and privacy. Breakfast is a decadent, two-hour, seven-course affair, and dinners are also available by arrangement. For private parties, you can rent the entire place. *$$$; AE, DIS, MC, V; no checks; no children under 10; www. hecetalighthouse.com; 1 mile north of Devils Elbow State Park.*

Lighthouse Inn / ★

155 HWY 101, FLORENCE; 866/997-3321

A lot of motels on the Oregon Coast tend to the shabby side, but the Lighthouse Inn, built in 1938, has been completely remodeled. Family-owned and -operated, it is within convenient walking distance of Old Town and offers spacious rooms (most with kitchenettes), Internet access, and a lobby with books and games. *$; MC, V; no checks; www.lighthouseinn.net; at 1st St.*

Gardiner, Reedsport, and Winchester Bay

Once bustling with mill activity, this trio of small towns has suffered the decline of the timber industry but is poised for a comeback with the development of a recreation-based economy. Its crowning glory is its proximity to the spectacular **OREGON DUNES NATIONAL RECREATION AREA** (see Florence section). As a "designated ATV area," this part of "the Dunes" is not exactly a place for quiet contemplation. Keep this in mind when rolling into the area's RV parks, which draw the majority of three- and four-wheel-vehicle enthusiasts. Those who prefer quieter pastimes can still enjoy boating, clamming, crabbing, hiking, whale watching, fishing, and swimming in the freshwater lakes.

In Reedsport, the **UMPQUA DISCOVERY CENTER MUSEUM** (409 Riverfront Wy, Reedsport; 541/271-4816) features exhibits that explore the natural and cultural history of lower Umpqua and the Oregon Coast. The **UMPQUA RIVER LIGHTHOUSE** (1020 Lighthouse Wy, Winchester Bay; 541/271-4631) looms above the

---

SOUTHERN OREGON COAST THREE-DAY TOUR

DAY ONE: After staying the night at **HECETA HEAD LIGHTHOUSE**, belly up for the seven-course breakfast, then head south toward Florence. Stop at **DARLING-TONIA BOTANICAL WAYSIDE** for a short stroll to view unusual bog flowers, then take in the riverfront shops in **OLD TOWN** Florence. Savor a light lunch of chowder or quiche on the riverfront deck at **TRAVELER'S COVE** (1362 Bay St, Florence; 541/997-6845) before hitting **JESSIE M. HONEYMAN STATE PARK** to sand board, hike, and swim. Tired but satisfied, enjoy an evening drive south along Hwy 101 toward Coos Bay, stopping in North Bend for dinner at **CAFÉ MEDITERRANEAN** before settling in at the **COOS BAY MANOR BED AND BREAKFAST**.

DAY TWO: After breakfast at Coos Bay Manor, continue south to the harbor village of Charleston, southwest of Coos Bay on Cape Arago Hwy. Pack some picnic fixings at **SEA BASKET** (3502 Kingfisher Rd, Charleston; 541/888-5711) before heading to **SUNSET BAY** and **SHORE ACRES STATE PARKS**. After your oceanside explorations and lunch, head south to Bandon, where golfers can play

---

entrance to Winchester Bay—a midsize working harbor. The 65-foot-tall tower features a historic Fresnel lens that emits a distinctive red and white flare. Tours of the lighthouse and museum are offered May through September. Four miles east of Reedsport, **DEAN CREEK ELK PRESERVE** offers visitors an up close look at elk, beaver, and local birds.

North Bend, Coos Bay, and Charleston

Known as Oregon's Bay Area, these three towns merge together into the Oregon Coast's largest urban area and what often is seen by outsiders as one long, nondescript industrialized strip. Yet the area also provides evidence of an active working coast, with industries ranging from lumber to shipping to salmon canning.

NORTH BEND—located on the "north bend" of the Coos Bay estuary—is an old sawmill town dating back to the 1850s. The downtown still has many of its original turn-of-the-20th-century fireproof masonry buildings. Slowly being restored, today they hold antique and collectibles shops and used bookstores. For a while, the town was home to Vern Gorst, who played an important role in developing the nation's first airmail and air transport systems. The daring aviation entrepreneur and pioneer founded Pacific Air Transport, the West Coast's first airmail carrier, in 1925.

With the largest natural harbor between Seattle and San Francisco, **COOS BAY** was once the largest timber shipping port in the world before the forest products industry took a dive in the early 1990s. Today travelers on Hwy 101 often see foreign vessels docked at the harbor, as the city of 15,000 is now a major shipping and manufacturing center. Located slightly inland with a bay that wraps around

the world-class courses at **BANDON DUNES GOLF RESORT**, while others can tool through **OLD TOWN** shops and riverfront or take in a tour of **FABER FARMS'** cranberry bogs. Enjoy an early dinner at **WILD ROSE**, then unwind at the **BANDON OCEAN GUESTHOUSE BED AND BREAKFAST** (87147 Beach Ln, Bandon; 541/347-2531 or 888/253-1777).

DAY THREE: Enjoy breakfast in the B and B's sunny dining room before heading south to Cape Blanco, the westernmost point along the Oregon Coast. On the way, stop at the **LANGLOIS MARKET & DELI** (48444 Hwy 101, Bandon; 541/348-2476) for picnic fixings: their famous hot dogs or a turkey sandwich made with local cranberry sauce. Hike at **CAPE BLANCO STATE PARK**, taking in the **LIGHTHOUSE**, historic **HUGHES HOUSE**, and rugged shoreline. Continue south, stopping in mystical Port Orford for a tour of the art galleries and a walk down to **BATTLE ROCK**. Then head to Gold Beach for a visit to **GOLD BEACH BOOKS** and dinner at the **CROW'S NEST** or **SPINNERS**. Cap off your trip with a night at the luxurious **TU TU' TUN LODGE**.

both sides of the city, Coos Bay has a beautiful bridge and an extensive waterfront, albeit one that's underutilized. Still, there is promise for a brighter future as high-end homes increasingly emerge along the highlands and shorelines of Coos Bay.

CHARLESTON, 9 miles west on Cape Arago Highway, is an old waterfront fishing village noted today for its premier sports fishing harbor and one of the state's busiest commercial fishing ports. The area's natural wonders are its prominent draw. A strip of state parks with a trail linking them all together lines the dramatic shore. Traveling south on the Cape Arago Hwy, your first stop is **SUNSET BAY STATE PARK** (89814 Cape Arago Hwy, Charleston; 541/888-4902), 12 miles southwest of Coos Bay. Fifty-foot cliffs frame a bowl-shaped cove, creating a natural stage for, as the name indicates, idyllic sunsets. Comfortable yurts with heat and electricity allow for year-round camping. A few miles south, **SHORE ACRES STATE PARK** (541/888-3732) is the former grand summer estate of pioneer lumberman and shipbuilder Louis J. Simpson. Native and exotic trees, shrubs, and flowering plants fill the beautiful botanical gardens. A fully enclosed observation building, the **SIMPSON REEF OVERLOOK** (4.3 miles south of Shore Acres, in Cape Arago State Park) offers magnificent views of pounding seas, rugged cliffs, towering sea stacks, and glimpses of migrating whales December through June. The observation building also overlooks the **OREGON ISLANDS NATIONAL WILDLIFE REFUGE** (541/867-4550), home to seabirds, seals, and sea lions. You can get a closer look at the wildlife **CAPE ARAGO STATE PARK** (15 miles southwest of Coos Bay; 800/551-6949), located on a 134-acre narrow coastal promontory jutting a half mile into the sea. Enjoy lunch at one of the picnic tables scattered about the bluffs, or follow hiking trails to numerous tide pools along the beach (beachside trails are closed March to June to protect seal pups).

RESTAURANTS

Café Mediterranean / ★★

955 S 5TH ST, COOS BAY; 541/269-1224 OR 800/269-1224
Celebrity chef Rachael Ray filmed her famed "$40 a Day" segment at this friendly, family-style café in the historic downtown of Coos Bay. And it's no wonder. Chef-owner Sami Abboud—a former Lebanese pop star who emigrated to the United States in the late 1990s—serves up the real deal: gyros, spanakopita, creamy lentil soup, and chicken shawerma sandwiches. This relaxed café is a welcome change from the typical coastal fish-and-chips fare. *$–$$; MC, V; no checks; lunch, dinner Mon–Sat; beer and wine; no reservations; www.cafemediterranean.net; between Johnson Ave and Ingersoll St.* &

LODGINGS

Coos Bay Manor Bed and Breakfast / ★★

955 S 5TH ST, COOS BAY; 541/269-1224 OR 800/269-1224
A family-friendly B and B is a rare find. This stately Victorian welcomes not only well-mannered children but also pets. This, however, doesn't make it a romper room. Set on a beautifully landscaped residential street with river-front views, the home sparkles with spacious, tall-ceilinged rooms, antique furnishings, and a baby grand piano. Of the five guest rooms, three have private baths and one "family suite" has a shared bath. Owners John and Felicia Noace serve a full breakfast. *$$; AE, MC; checks OK; www.coosbaymanor. com; between Johnson Ave and Ingersoll St.*

The Old Tower House Bed and Breakfast / ★★

476 NEWMARK AVE, COOS BAY; 541/888-6058
You'll find this historical Gothic Revival–style home, the oldest structure in Coos County, in the appealing Empire District, a once-bustling area slowly being revitalized. In the main house, the three guest rooms share two baths, while a cottage tucked behind the home provides additional space and privacy. Innkeepers Tom and Stephanie Kramer celebrate the past with decor heavy on antiques and lace. A continental breakfast is provided. *$$–$$$; DIS, MC, V; checks OK; www.oldtowerhouse.com; at Marple St.*

Bandon

To golf enthusiasts, Bandon means one thing: world-class golfing. Bandon Dunes is as close to an authentic Scottish or Irish golf experience as you can have without leaving the States. In addition to three courses at **BANDON DUNES GOLF RESORT** (see review) at the north end of town, there's a nine-holer at **BANDON FACE ROCK GOLF COURSE** (3235 Beach Loop Rd, Bandon; 541/347-3818). Together they have created a micro-economy within a town of not quite 3,000 residents.

But golf isn't everything that is happening here. Located at the mouth of the **COQUILLE RIVER**, Bandon is booming culturally. Top-tier hotels and specialized inns now cater to the sophisticated traveler. **OLD TOWN**, a historic district along the Coquille River, teems with bistros, cafés, and shops. Art galleries feature painting, woodcarving, glass, and fabric art. **BANDON CHAMBER OF COMMERCE** (300 2nd St, Bandon; 541/347-9616; www.bandon.com) has more information.

To the south, cranberries thrive in the sandy soil and mild climate. Bandon is the major producer of cranberries in the western United States; the berries are bigger, darker, and sweeter here than their eastern cousins. The annual **BANDON CRANBERRY FESTIVAL** (541/347-9616) is held in September. **FABER FARMS** (54980 Morrison Rd, Bandon; 541/347-1166; off SR 42) offers tours and tastings. And at the **GARDEN PARTY** (on SR 42S east of town; 541/347-3578), cranberry farmer Chris Holck serves tea and pie in an intimate, serene setting.

Along with its other attractions, Bandon boasts a majestic, moody coastline best accessed from the south jetty in town or from **FACE ROCK VIEWPOINT** on **BEACH LOOP ROAD**. This scenic route parallels the ocean with views of the wealth of sculpted rock formations, providing an excellent alternative to congested Hwy 101. Two miles north of Bandon, **BULLARDS BEACH STATE PARK** (541/347-2209) offers walking and biking trails to uncrowded beaches. From Bullards, stroll to **COQUILLE RIVER LIGHTHOUSE**, built in 1896, restored in 1978. Tours are offered on summer weekends.

RESTAURANTS

Alloro Wine Bar & Restaurant / ★★

375 2ND ST, BANDON; 541/347-1850
Debuting in 2006, snappy Alloro wows this seaside town with authentic Italian cuisine and top-shelf wines in a contemporary setting. Located in Old Town, this small but tony *enoteca* serves a bevy of homemade pastas and dishes such as *pesce spada alla griglia* (grilled swordfish) and *bistecca fiorentina*. Wine options include many of Oregon's best vintages. *$$–$$$; MC, V; local checks only; dinner Wed–Sun; beer and wine; reservations recommended; www.allorowinebar.com; at Oregon Ave SW.*

Wild Rose / ★★

130 CHICAGO AVE SE, BANDON; 541/347-4428
Like a garden in harvest, Wild Rose brims with fresh food in a small but lively space. You won't find any weeds in this tidy Old Town spot, but if you did they would be edible and organic. Lynn Flattley prepares the meals while her husband, Dan, works the front of the house. Everything is homemade here, from the breads and soups to desserts. Daily seafood specials, such as crab ravioli or grilled salmon, are fresh-caught and delicious. *$$–$$$; MC, V; local checks only; dinner Wed–Sun; full bar; reservations recommended; at 1st St.*

LODGINGS

Bandon Dunes Golf Resort / ★★★⯪

57744 ROUND LAKE DR, BANDON; 541/347-4380 OR 888/345-6008
Bandon Dunes' three Scottish-style courses—situated along 23 miles of wind-swept dunes—rank high on *Golf Magazine*'s list of Top 100 in the World. Golfers get a workout here, as carts aren't allowed and the wind is strong, but the challenge and beauty of the experience (as well as caddies who can pick up the load for those in need) more than make up for any discomfort. Three restaurants, two bars, and a variety of accommodations keep guests fed, rested, and on the green. Accommodations, geared toward foursomes of golfers, include a main lodge and a series of cottages tucked throughout the expansive grounds. Don't expect fluffy robes or Jacuzzi tubs; the focus here is totally golf. *$$$–$$$$; AE, DIS, MC, V; no checks; www.bandondunesgolf. com; at end of rd.* &

Sunset Oceanfront Motel / ★★⯪

1865 BEACH LOOP RD, BANDON; 541/347-2453 OR 800/842-2457
This complex offers a huge choice of beachfront accommodations, from basic single rooms to rustic cabins to beach houses with kitchens and fireplaces. Everyone gets to use the heated indoor pool and spa, and the friendly staff provides amenities such as wireless Internet access and portable cribs. *$–$$; AE, MC, DIS, V; no checks; 2-night minimum; www.sunsetmotel.com; just north of Face Rock Dr.*

Port Orford

Foggy and mystical, Port Orford seems to stand in its own private world of quiet. But even this remote village is facing development pressures as its majestic beauty gains recognition. Once a working town of lumbermen, ranchers, and fishermen, the area is steadily attracting second-home owners and retirees. The rugged isolation of Port Orford attracts artists, and the town boasts the impressive ratio of eight art galleries per 1,000 residents.

It's not difficult to see the appeal. **CAPE BLANCO LIGHTHOUSE** in rugged and windy **CAPE BLANCO STATE PARK** (5 miles west of Hwy 101; 800/547-7842) is the oldest lighthouse on the Oregon Coast and located at its most westerly point. The lighthouse, 245 feet above the ocean, is open seasonally to the public. West of the station, a path leads to the end of the cape. The nearby **HUGHES HOUSE** (541/382-0248; www.hugheshouse.org) was home to the ranchers who originally owned what is now the state park. Tours are offered April to October. **HUMBUG MOUNTAIN STATE PARK** (off Hwy 101, 5 miles south of Port Orford; 541/332-6774) features a steep switchback trail through old-growth forest.

Port Orford is one of Oregon's only true **OCEAN HARBORS**. Because the port is unprotected from strong southerly winds, fishing boats can't be moored in the harbor. Instead, they are lifted in and out of the turbulent ocean with a five-story hoist. Visitors are welcome to this unique open-water port with dramatic ocean views, and **FRESH SEAFOOD** is available right off the boat (on Dock Rd, 1 block west of Hwy 101, Port Orford).

The gigantic rock promontory of **BATTLE ROCK**, in the center of town, dominates the waterfront shoreline. The rock marks the site of the mid-19th-century battle between the first landing party of white settlers and local Native Americans. Past the rock, a trail winds down the hillside and to the beach.

LODGINGS

Wildspring Guest Habitat / ★★★★

92978 CEMETERY LOOP, PORT ORFORD;
541/332-0977 OR 866/333-9453
This secluded 5-acre resort induces a tranquil, reverent pace. With just five cabins, it is a getaway small in scale but large in spirit. Meander hiking trails through acres of forest, relax in meditation alcoves, stroll through the walking labyrinth, or unwind in the open-air slate spa overlooking the Pacific. If requested, the resort offers drum circles, guided meditation, and tai chi. Built in 2004, the cabins nestled under a canopy of trees boast an elegant mix of sumptuous bedding, warm woodwork, relaxing music, soft robes, and low light. There's a breakfast buffet and hot fudge sundae bar; guests can use the communal kitchen if desired. *$$–$$$$; MC, V; no checks; no children under 8; www.wildspring.com; at junction of County Rd 268.* &

Gold Beach

This small but sprawling city serves as gateway to some of the state's best fishing, hiking, and white-water recreation. Named for the gold found here in the 19th century, Gold Beach is renowned as the town at the ocean end of the Rogue River. The shiny nuggets are gone, but the **ROGUE RIVER** still provides plenty of riches for anglers. Today salmon, steelhead, and trout draw enthusiasts from all over the country.

Many visitors head inland to the harsh and rugged 180,000-acre **KALMIOPSIS WILDERNESS AREA** (in Siskiyou National Forest, between Gold Beach and Brookings). Maps are available at the **U.S. FOREST SERVICE** office (29279 S Ellensburg Ave, Gold Beach; 541/247-3600). Trails through the wilderness, always challenging due to steepness and narrow, rocky surfaces, have been made more difficult by the 2002 Biscuit Fire.

Jet-boat trips are a popular way to explore the backcountry. Guides offer insight and stop to observe wildlife during the 60- to 100-mile journey upriver. Two reputable boat companies service the Rogue: **JERRY'S ROGUE RIVER JETS** (800/451-3645) and **MAILBOAT HYDROJET TRIPS** (800/458-3511). Reservations are recommended.

The **OREGON COAST TRAIL** (800/525-2334) traverses headlands and remote beaches between Gold Beach and Brookings. A portion of the trail winds up and over the cape at **CAPE SEBASTIAN STATE PARK** (off Hwy 101, 3 miles south of Gold Beach; 800/551-6949).

BEACONS OF LIGHT

The Oregon Coast boasts numerous historic lighthouses standing as icons along the Pacific shore. In varying sizes, statures, and working conditions, the beacons serve as reminders of the state's treacherous maritime past. Most offer walking tours, interpretive trails, and—best of all—fantastic views.

CAPE DISAPPOINTMENT, near Astoria, is the oldest lighthouse in the Northwest, built to warn boaters of the dangerous entrance to the Columbia River. Even with the lighthouse's beacon, hundreds of ships were lost in what is called the "graveyard of the Pacific."

TILLAMOOK ROCK LIGHTHOUSE sits on a rock outcrop 2 miles offshore (the state's only offshore lighthouse) visible from both Seaside and Cannon Beach. Though decommissioned in 1957, the light has a second, er, life as a columbarium (a place where cremated remains are stored).

Standing just 38 feet tall, **CAPE MEARES LIGHTHOUSE** (10 miles west of Tillamook on Three Capes Scenic Loop) is the shortest in Oregon, though it sits more than 200 feet above the ocean. When it was lit, its beacon was visible for more than 23 miles. A modern beacon has replaced the old beacon (which sits just behind the new one), though the original sentinel still operates as an interpretive center.

Newport has two lighthouses. **YAQUINA HEAD LIGHTHOUSE**, rising a stately 93 feet, is the tallest on the Oregon Coast, standing 162 feet above sea level. A major face-lift in 2006 keeps it in working order. The nearby **YAQUINA BAY**

Shopping and dining options in town are limited, but **GOLD BEACH BOOKS** (29707 Ellensburg Ave, Gold Beach; 541/247-2495) offers two stories of new and used books, coffee, and a showcase for local musicians and artists.

RESTAURANTS

Spinner's Seafood, Steak, & Chophouse / ★★

29430 ELLENSBURG AVE (HWY 101), GOLD BEACH; 541/247-5160
In an attempt to hit all markets, Spinner's packs its menu with multiple choices: burgers, pasta, salmon, lobster, steaks, and more. Many times, the effort makes the mark, though often the results hover at average. But the setting is stellar, which no doubt explains the cars packing the lot every night. Every table boasts an ocean panorama. Wild abalone is an unusual specialty. *$$–$$$; AE, MC, V; checks OK; lunch, dinner every day; full bar; reservations recommended; just south of 8th St.*

LIGHTHOUSE, located on the north end of Yaquina Bay State Recreation Site, provides a nautical backdrop but was in service for only a few years before being replaced by Yaquina Head Lighthouse.

Located on a cliff side, the picturesque **HECETA HEAD LIGHTHOUSE** north of Florence shines the brightest light on the Oregon Coast. The historic assistant lightkeeper's house now operates as an interpretive center and bed-and-breakfast (see review).

The **UMPQUA RIVER LIGHTHOUSE** looms above the entrance to Winchester Bay—a midsize working harbor. The 65-foot tower contains a distinctive Fresnel lens that emits a red and white flash. Tours of the lighthouse and adjacent museum are offered in the summer.

CAPE ARAGO LIGHTHOUSE, located 12 miles southwest of North Bend and Coos Bay, emits a unique foghorn. Though the lighthouse is not open to the public, views are good from Sunset Bay State Park south of the lighthouse.

Although it was decommissioned in 1939, the **COQUILLE RIVER LIGHTHOUSE** near Bandon was restored in 1979 to serve as an interpretive center. Park staff and volunteers offer year-round tours of the tower watch room.

CAPE BLANCO LIGHTHOUSE, 9 miles north of Port Orford, towers as the most westerly point in the continental United States. The oldest standing lighthouse on the Oregon Coast, its dramatic cliff-top location provides a watchtower for wildlife viewing below.

—Drew Myron

LODGINGS

Tu Tu' Tun Lodge / ★★★★

96550 N BANK ROGUE, GOLD BEACH;
541/247-6664 OR 800/864-6357

Set on the grassy banks of the Rogue River 7 miles inland, Tu Tu' Tun (pronounced "too-TOOT-in") is a rare resort, perfectly balancing contemporary lodge decor with a tranquil outdoor setting. This is a second-generation family business: hosts Dirk and Laurie Van Zante lovingly tend the lodge built and designed by Dirk's stepfather in 1970. Among the coast's spendiest accommodations, the lodge offers 16 rooms, 2 suites, and 2 cottages—with nary a misstep among them. $$$–$$$$; MC, V, checks OK; www.tututun. com; at Krysten Ln.

Brookings

You know you're near the California border when palm trees dot the landscape. Just 6 miles north of California, Brookings is often referred to as the Banana Belt of the Pacific Northwest, thanks to its sunny and temperate year-round climate. Winter weather is noticeably milder here than elsewhere on the Oregon Coast. Retirees have flocked to this warm zone, and spendy new homes line the hillsides.

Brookings hums with an economy based on lumber, fishing, and service-oriented jobs. In addition, the temperate climate lends itself to flower production, and Brookings is North America's top provider of **EASTER LILY BULBS**. These factors create a bustling town that is sadly short on fine dining and lodging. Try **SUZIE Q'S FINE DINING** (613 Chetco Ave, Brookings; 541/412-7444) for excellent breakfast and lunch; dinner is ambitious but pricey.

The surrounding natural beauty makes the area worth a visit. To the north lie **SAMUEL H. BOARDMAN** and **HARRIS BEACH STATE PARKS** (541/469-2021). Both have beautiful, rugged coastlines and dramatic overlooks; Harris Beach offers camping, tide pooling, rock scrambling, and a great view of **BIRD ISLAND**, a national wildlife sanctuary. To the east are the lush **SISKIYOU MOUNTAINS**, divided by the Chetco and Winchuck rivers. Truly ancient redwood forests lie to the south.

AZALEA PARK (just east of Hwy 101, Brookings; 541/868-1100) is a great picnic spot and home to native azaleas—some two centuries old!—wild strawberries, fruit trees, and violets. **MYRTLEWOOD**, a broad-leaved evergreen that grows only in the Midwest and southernmost reaches of Oregon, is ideally suited for sculpting and carving, and shops selling these wares line the highway. You can see this wonderfully fresh-scented tree in its native habitat at **LOEB STATE PARK** (N Bank River Rd, Brookings; 541/469-2021; 8 miles east of town). **REDWOOD NATURE TRAIL**, a 1-mile loop just a half mile past the park on the north bank of the Chetco River, traverses the northernmost redwood grove in the United States, including some 350-foot-tall trees.

The **PORT OF BROOKINGS HARBOR** (16408 Lower Harbor Rd, Brookings; 541/469-2218) is home to commercial fishermen as well as **PLEASURE BOATERS** and **SPORT FISHERMEN**. Public boat ramps and slips are available. A small public fishing pier is located near the Coast Guard station on Boat Basin Road.

LODGINGS

Chetco River Inn / ★★

21202 HIGH PRAIRIE RD, BROOKINGS; 541/251-0087 OR 800/327-2688
Eighteen miles inland and a world away, this backcountry getaway commands peace and quiet. Situated on 35 acres of private forest bordered on three sides by the wild and scenic Chetco River, this lodge defines unplugged, operating entirely on solar power, a generator, batteries, and propane. The five guest rooms and two cottages are comfortably decorated and offer river and garden views. The inn's fragrant lavender gardens add to the serene atmosphere. A pristine outdoor setting and rare solitude make this inn a real find. *$$$; MC, V; checks OK; ww.chetcoriverinn.com; near intersection of NFD 1376 Rd.*

SOUTHERN AND CENTRAL OREGON AND THE CASCADES

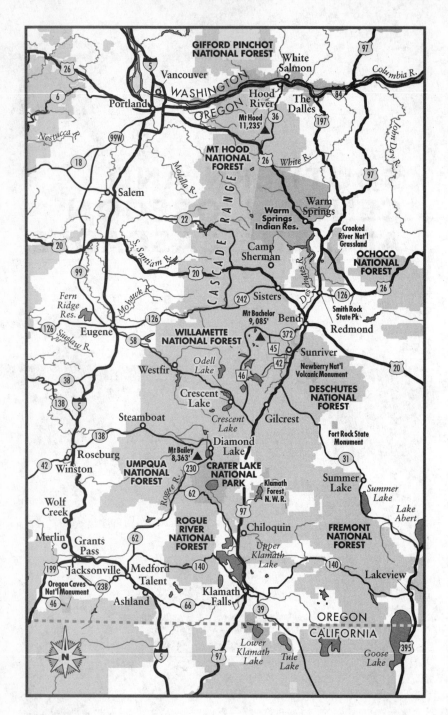

SOUTHERN AND CENTRAL OREGON AND THE CASCADES

Most pioneers traveling the Oregon Trail journeyed along the Columbia River and then south to the fertile Willamette River Valley. The ones who didn't—thousands of them—took the Applegate Trail via Nevada into Southern Oregon. Blazed in 1846 as an alternate, and potentially safer, route to Oregon, the Applegate Trail proved to be equally arduous. Once they arrived, though, the stalwart and determined pioneers worked in orchards, fields, and lumber mills—industries that would become the mainstay of the Southern Oregon economy well into the 20th century.

Other settlers continued north to the Willamette Valley and still others eventually went east of the Cascades—which in this region includes Mounts Jefferson, Washington, Bachelor, Sisters, and Broken Top—to a 10,000-square-mile area drained by the Deschutes River. Today this area is called Central Oregon, and what was once seen as an area of great promise but few resources is now the state's premier outdoor recreation hub—a base camp for mountain bikers, fishers, hikers, campers, rock climbers, white-water rafters, skiers, and golfers.

While snow and trails in the Cascades drive much of this new economy, the mountain range also divides the state into two distinct climates. On the lee (east) side of the range, ponderosa pine forests transition into the Great Basin's high desert plateau. Summers are typically very warm and dry (though snow in June isn't unheard of); winter brings snow more often than rain.

ACCESS AND INFORMATION

A major north-south highway runs along each side of the Cascades: **INTERSTATE 5** on the west, **US HIGHWAY 97** on the east. **US HIGHWAY 26**, the main east-west route between Portland and southeastern Oregon, crosses the Cascades south of Mount Hood and connects with Hwy 97 at Madras. Routes to Bend, the largest town on the east side of the Cascades, depart from Salem on **STATE ROUTE 22**, from Albany on **US HIGHWAY 20**, and from Eugene on **STATE ROUTE 126** (via McKenzie Pass). From Eugene, follow **STATE ROUTE 58** (via Willamette Pass) to Hwy 97 at the halfway point between Bend and Klamath Falls. The most scenic route to the east side of the mountains, open only in summer, is the narrow **OLD MCKENZIE HIGHWAY (SR 242)** from Eugene. Farther south, Crater Lake is accessible from Roseburg on **STATE ROUTE 138** (via Diamond Lake) and from Medford on **STATE ROUTE 62**, which loops east to Hwy 97 north of Klamath Falls. The most southerly east-west routes are from Medford on **STATE ROUTE 140** and from Ashland on the **GREEN SPRINGS HIGHWAY (SR 66)**, both to Hwy 97 at Klamath Falls.

Flights between Portland and Bend-Redmond, Klamath Falls, and Medford are offered daily on **HORIZON AIR** (800/547-9308; www.horizonair.com) and other carriers. **AMTRAK** (800/USA-RAIL; www.amtrak.com), bound for California from Portland, crosses Willamette Pass into Klamath Falls, bypassing Southern Oregon with the exception of a stop in tiny Chemult. **GREYHOUND** (800/231-2222; www.greyhound.com) offers bus service throughout Central and Southern Oregon.

Southern Oregon

Agriculture and wood products have long been the engine of this region's economy, but for the past decade, changes have been afoot. The area has seen an influx of urban refugees from California, and the arts, theater, and wine scenes are the richer for it.

While the Willamette Valley undoubtedly snags most of the wine industry headlines, winemaking in Southern Oregon has its own distinguished history and growing cadre of notable wineries. The wine grown here is not only surprisingly innovative but also of high quality—perhaps because the warmer climate and subsequent drier growing season permit an expanded range of grape cultivation. Many of the grapes grown here are established along stream terraces, free of coastal weather influences, and in granite soils that provide optimum drainage. But uniquely, there are also wider variations in climate within each of the region's appellations as well, which allows for greater variety and more diverse flavors within the same grape variety.

Roseburg and the Umpqua River Valley

Surrounded by scrub oak and possessing some of the state's mildest weather, Roseburg is the seat of Douglas County, which contains 100 miles of the Applegate Trail. When Jesse Applegate, Levi Scott, and other trailblazers mapped the trail in 1846, it followed the city's Winchester, Jackson, and Main streets. Later the trail became SR 99 until I-5 was built over it and split the city north to south. To locate the trail or for more information, contact the **ROSEBURG VISITORS AND CONVENTION BUREAU** (541/672-9731).

Roseburg's historic downtown was all but decimated in a fiery explosion in 1959. But some of the city's historic buildings, with architectural styles ranging from Queen Anne and Victorian Gothic to Craftsman and Prairie style, remain. The **WILLIS HOUSE** (744 SE Rose St, Roseburg), a two-story Victorian with a gabled roof and paired brackets, was built in 1874 and moved to its present location in 1911. The **FLOED-LANE HOUSE** (544 SE Douglas Ave, Roseburg), more commonly known as the **JOSEPH LANE HOUSE**, is an example of a Classical Revival and is the only surviving home linked to Joseph Lane, the first territorial governor of Oregon.

Roseburg has been home to many cultural luminaries, including **DAVID HUME KENNERLY**, the Pulitzer Prize–winning photographer for President Gerald Ford; **ART ALEXAKIS**, the lead singer of Everclear; and Flying Ace **MARION E. CARL**, the Marine Corps hero of Midway and Guadalcanal—ironically and tragically killed by an intruder in his home in 1988 at the age of 83.

Mr. Carl's achievements have not been forgotten. He is honored annually in late June when the skies over **ROSEBURG REGIONAL AIRPORT** (2251 NW Aviation Dr, Roseburg; 541/672-4425) showcase a number of airplanes flown during World Wars I and II and Vietnam at the **ROSEBURG AIR SHOW** held at **MARION E. CARL MEMORIAL FIELD**.

Keeping with the retro spirit, **K-R DRIVE-INN** (I-5 exit 148, 25 miles north of Roseburg; 541/849-2570) dishes up huge scoops of regionally famous Umpqua ice cream and incomparable malts—try the wild blackberry; the parking lot is full from before noon till after dark. Fittingly, the town's largest festival—the **GRAFFITI CRUISE-IN** (www.graffitiweekend.com)—takes place annually in July, drawing classic cars and hot rods.

DOUGLAS COUNTY MUSEUM OF HISTORY AND NATURAL HISTORY (Roseburg fairgrounds, I-5 exit 123; 541/957-7007; www.co.douglas.or.us/museum) offers an in-depth look at area history. Family-run **KRUSE FARMS** (532 Melrose Rd, Roseburg; 541/672-5697 or 888/575-4268; www.krusefarms.com; open Apr–Jan except holidays) sells fresh-baked marionberry pies, farm produce, and gifts at their farm market. You can also find a variety of locally produced salad greens, herbs, landscape plants, honey, fresh-cut flowers, home-baked goods, local eggs, and handicrafts at the **DOUGLAS COUNTY FARMERS MARKET** (1444 NW Garden Valley Blvd, Roseburg; 541/459-3067; 9am–1pm Sat during growing season; Roseburg Valley Mall in front of Rite Aid).

Nearly a dozen—many of them exceptional—wineries are located throughout this area. Some top producers to visit for tasting include **ABACELA WINERY** (12500 Lookingglass Rd, Roseburg; 541/679-6642; www.abacela.com), **GIRARDET** (895 Reston Rd, Roseburg; 541/679-7252; www.girardetwine.com), **HILL CREST VINEYARD** (240 Vineyard Ln, Roseburg; 541/673-3709; hillcrestvineyard.com), and **HENRY ESTATE WINERY** (687 Hubbard Creek Rd, Umpqua; 541/459-5120 or 800/782-2686; www.henryestate.com).

Humans are the only things actually caged at the **WILDLIFE SAFARI** (on SR 99, 4 miles west of I-5 exit 119; 541/679-6761 or 800/355-4848; www.wildlifesafari.org), where you cruise through 600 acres of sort-of free-roaming cheetahs and giraffes; in total there's 600 animals from around the world living on the reserve.

RESTAURANTS

Roseburg Station Pub & Brewery / ★

700 SE SHERIDAN ST, ROSEBURG; 541/672-1934

You know what you're going to get at McMenamins, and it is not much different in Roseburg, where the brothers have brought their robust ales, pub grub, and psychedelic art to yet another historic site: Roseburg's 90-year-old train depot. This brick fortress is an oasis in the summer heat, with its covered patio overlooking the tracks for the Southern Pacific Railroad's now-defunct Shasta Route. *$; AE, DIS, MC, V; local checks only; lunch, dinner every day; full bar; no reservations; www.mcmenamins.com; downtown.* ໒

LODGINGS

Seven Feathers Hotel and Casino Resort / ★★

146 CHIEF MIWALETA LN, CANYONVILLE; 800/548-8461

Owned by the Cow Creek Band of the Umpqua Tribe, this resort houses the most luxurious hotel on Oregon's I-5 corridor. Funded by 1,000-plus slots and gaming tables, the 147-room hotel (with indoor swimming pool and spa)

OREGON CASCADES THREE-DAY TOUR

DAY ONE: Begin with breakfast at **KAH-NEE-TA HIGH DESERT RESORT**, then head out to Hwy 26 for the **MUSEUM AT WARM SPRINGS** to learn about Native American history. Continue south to Bend for lunch at the **DESCHUTES BREWERY & PUBLIC HOUSE**. Take a quick stroll through downtown and **DRAKE PARK** overlooking **MIRROR POND** before checking in at **SEVENTH MOUNTAIN RESORT**. Pick up the **DESCHUTES RIVER TRAIL** from the inn's nature trail for a hike to Dillon or Benham Falls in summer, or venture up the road toward **MOUNT BACHELOR** for a late-afternoon Nordic ski at **VIRGINIA MEISSNER SNO-PARK** (on Cascade Lakes Hwy 14 miles west of Bend; get required permit at local ski shops) in winter. After a soak in the inn's hot tub, head downtown for drinks and dinner at **MERENDA RESTAURANT AND WINE BAR**. Groove on over to the **GROVE CANTINA** for dancing and dessert.

DAY TWO: After checking out, savor coffee and a pastry at **NANCY P'S BAKING COMPANY** (1054 NW Milwaukee Ave, Bend; 541/322-8778), then sprint across the street to grab a healthy assortment of organic deli food to go at **DEVORE'S GOOD FOOD STORE AND WINE SHOP**. In summer, drive the one-lane road off County Road 21 to **PAULINA PEAK** for a view of the **NEWBERRY CRATER, PAULINA AND EAST LAKES**, and the **BIG OBSIDIAN FLOW**; year-round, visit the **HIGH DESERT MUSEUM**. Continue south on Hwy 97 to either

---

is a bargain on weekdays. The dramatic crystal-chandeliered Camas Room (lunch, dinner every day) offers fine Northwest cuisine and an exceptional Sunday brunch. *$$; AE, DIS, MC, V; local checks only; www.sevenfeathers. com; 25 miles south of Roseburg.* &

Wolf Creek Inn / ★

100 FRONT ST, WOLF CREEK; 541/866-2474

The oldest continuous-use hotel in the state of Oregon—built in 1883 by pioneer merchant Henry Smith—the Wolf Creek Inn was billed as a "first-class traveler's hotel" for stagecoach riders. Hollywood actors flocked here in the 1920s, then the state purchased it in 1975, and now it is on the National Register of Historic Places. Nine rooms are decorated in historic period furnishings—phone- and TV-free in keeping with the era. One room on the second floor is dedicated to Jack London, who stayed here in 1911. The Clark Gable Suite has a veranda that extends along the front of the room. The downstairs dining room, open to nonguests for lunch and dinner, features the best of both coasts, with Northwest fare and New York–style pizza. *$$; MC, V; local checks only; closed Mon–Tues Oct–May; www.thewolfcreekinn. com; I-5 exit 76, 20 miles north of Grants Pass.* &

SR 138 in summer for the north entrance to **CRATER LAKE NATIONAL PARK** or to SR 62 just north of Klamath Falls in winter to the park's south entrance. Drink in the heady blue of Crater Lake as you enjoy a picnic on the rim. Drive westward on SR 62 and then I-5 to Ashland and check in at cozy **A COWSLIP'S BELLE**. Walk through **LITHIA PARK** on your way to an early dinner at **LELA'S CAFÉ** before making a mad dash to the **OREGON SHAKESPEARE FESTIVAL** for an eight o'clock performance. Walk the four blocks back to your turned-down bed, and fall into a deep slumber.

DAY THREE: Get some laps in at the Ashland Racquet Club swimming pool (courtesy of your inn) before a leisurely breakfast back at Cowslip's Belle. Then pack your cooler with ice before heading north on Hwy 99 for a self-guided wine and farm tour, starting with **RISING SUN FARMS** and **HARRY AND DAVID'S COUNTRY VILLAGE** in Medford. Detour north on I-5 to the **ROGUE CREAMERY**, then shoot south on Hanley Road to **VALLEY VIEW WINERY**'s tasting room in Jacksonville. Take a stroll through the shops on historic **CALIFORNIA STREET** and visit the **JACKSONVILLE MUSEUM**. Have a bite at **BELLA UNION** before heading west on SR 238 and south on Hwy 199 to **FORIS VINEYARDS WINERY**. Catch the last tour of the day at **OREGON CAVES NATIONAL MONUMENT** before returning north to Grants Pass for dinner at **RIVER'S EDGE** and the final night's stay at **FLERY MANOR**.

North Umpqua River

From Roseburg traveling east toward Diamond Lake and Crater Lake National Park, SR 138 follows the Wild and Scenic–designated **NORTH UMPQUA RIVER**. The emerald green waters of the North Umpqua are famous worldwide among fly fishers, attracting the rich and famous for nearly a century. Today the area also attracts hikers and mountain bikers to the **NORTH UMPQUA TRAIL**, which follows the river east for more than 70 miles. Spectacular hikes, like the one at **FALL CREEK FALLS** (SR 138 milepost 32), show off the North Umpqua Forest's old-growth canopy.

SR 138, commonly known as the Waterfall Highway, shows off the abundant waterfalls in the North Umpqua River drainage. **WATSON FALLS** (2.2 miles east of Toketee Lake to Fish Creek Rd No. 37) is the highest in southwest Oregon, cascading 272 feet; the falls are much more turbulent in the spring. **TOKETEE FALLS** (¼ mile past FR 34, 16 miles west of Diamond Lake) plunges 113 feet in two-tiered drops, attracting photographers from around the world. **OREGON RIDGE & RIVER EXCURSIONS** (Box 495, Glide; 541/496-3333 or 888/454-9696; www.umpquarivers.com) offers float trips on the river, followed by a salmon bake dinner on a private beach.

LODGINGS

Steamboat Inn / ★★

42705 SR 138, STEAMBOAT; 541/498-2230 OR 800/840-8825
This homey fishing lodge sits on the banks of the North Umpqua River. Eight small cabins share a common veranda that parallels the river; each (somewhat cramped) unit has knotty pine walls and a bathroom with a soaking tub. Remarkable family-style dinners are served in the main building by reservation; breakfast and lunch are in the café. In spring, winemakers and chefs make special meals. *$$$; MC, V; checks OK; Sat–Sun Mar–Apr and Nov–Dec, closed Jan–Feb; www.thesteamboatinn.com; 38 miles east of Roseburg.*

Steelhead Run Bed & Breakfast / ★

23049 NORTH UMPQUA HWY, GLIDE; 541/496-0563
Located on 5 acres on a bluff overlooking the North Umpqua River, the resort-style B and B boasts a breathtaking view and features one of the area's best swimming holes. Lodging options include three comfortably appointed theme-decorated guest rooms and three kitchen apartments with private bathrooms, some with river views and private entrances. Dogs are welcome in some rooms; partiers are not. Mornings get kick-started with a large country buffet breakfast in the river-view dining room. *$$; AE, DIS, MC, V; no checks; www.steelheadrun.com; 3 miles east of Glide.* &

The Rogue River Valley

The **ROGUE RIVER** is one of the wildest and most beautiful rivers in Southern Oregon. Percolating out of crystal-clear springs in Crater Lake National Park, the river flows west from the Cascades to the Coast Range through miles of wilderness. It forms canyons, rapids, and pools before spilling into the Pacific Ocean, carrying steelhead and king salmon along with it. Many rustic lodges along the river cater specifically to fly fishers and rafters. Grants Pass and nearby Merlin offer the best fishing and rafting.

Two companies offer guided river tours. **HELLGATE JETBOAT EXCURSIONS** (966 SW 6th St, Grants Pass; 541/479-7204 or 800/648-4874; www.hellgate.com) departs from the **RIVERSIDE INN** (986 SW 6th St, Grants Pass; 541/476-6873 or 800/334-4567; www.riverside-inn.com). **ORANGE TORPEDO TRIPS** (210 Merlin Rd, Merlin; 541/479-5061; www.orangetorpedo.com) conducts popular white-water trips.

Grants Pass

The town of Grants Pass may seem as though it offers little in the way of culture or charm. But take the time to stop in its historic downtown: you'll find some quaint and long-standing businesses, as well as a few upscale shops. Pop into the **BLUESTONE BAKERY & COFFEE CAFÉ** (corner of 6th and D sts; 541/471-1922) for intensely rich desserts. To find out about other fun activities, stop at the **GRANTS PASS & JOSEPHINE COUNTY CHAMBER OF COMMERCE** (198 SW 6th St; 541/955-7144) downtown.

RESTAURANTS

River's Edge / ★★★

1936 SR 99, GRANTS PASS; 541/479-3938

Kelly Hatch has graced the culinary scene with what she calls classic Pacific cuisine, which translates to Pacific Rim dishes: local, regional, Hawaiian, Japanese, and even Californian. Tuck into plates of macadamia nut–encrusted halibut, wasabi tenderloin, Monterey Bay calamari, and Pacific Northwest seafood. Upscale yet casual, the dining room is airy and modern with a fireplace, water wall, and a muted palette. On sunny days, the riverside seating with incredible river views is the obvious choice. The enthusiastic service and dependable wine list add to the appeal. *$$–$$$; AE, MC, V; no checks; lunch, dinner every day, brunch Sun; full bar; reservations recommended; www.riversedgerestaurant.net; I-5 exit at Grants Pass.* ᕼ

Summer Jo's / ★★

2315 UPPER RIVER RD LOOP, GRANTS PASS; 541/476-6882

Sitting on a 6-acre organic farm, this cheery country restaurant serves entrées like salmon with sorrel sauce or rosemary-encrusted rack of lamb with apple-mint chutney. Try the excellent Epicurean Adventure Tasting Menu and a selection from the Wine Spectator award-winning wine list. *$–$$; AE, MC, V; local checks only; breakfast, lunch, dinner Wed–Sat (closed Jan–mid-Feb); full bar; reservations recommended; www.summerjo.com; I-5 exit 58.* ᕼ

LODGINGS

Rogue Forest Bed & Breakfast / ★★☆

12035 GALICE RD, MERLIN; 541/472-1052

Built by Rogue river-rafting pioneers, this inn lies in a steep canyon 16 miles west of the interstate surrounded by forest, within earshot of Rocky Riffle, a Class II rapid. It has two B and B–style suites: a 375-square-foot one in the main house and a separate 550-square-foot cabin suite connected to it by a redwood walkway. Both offer retreatlike ambience and feature private decks, reserved time in the hot-spring-fed outdoor Jacuzzi, and luxurious linens. The on-site Rogue Forest River Company offers rafting trips. *$$$; MC, V; checks OK; www.rogueforest.com; I-5 exit 61 at Merlin.*

Cave Junction and Oregon Caves National Monument

Cave Junction, 28 miles southwest of Grants Pass on Hwy 199, is home to two premier Oregon wineries: **FORIS VINEYARDS WINERY** (654 Kendall Rd, Cave Junction; 541/592-3752 or 800/84FORIS; www.foriswine.com) and **BRIDGEVIEW VINEYARDS & WINERY** (4210 Holland Loop Rd, Cave Junction; 541/592-4688 or 877/273-4843; www.bridgeviewwine.com). Both have tasting rooms open every day.

About 20 miles east of Cave Junction, on SR 46, is **OREGON CAVES NATIONAL MONUMENT** (19000 Caves Hwy, Cave Junction; 541/592-2100; www.nps.gov/orca; tours every day, hourly mid-Mar–Nov, every 30 minutes late June–Aug). It's an active marble cave filled with glistening mineral formations and wet with moon milk, set among redwoods at 4,000 feet elevation. If you tour the caves, come prepared for cool temperatures and strenuous climbing up 500 steps.

OREGON CAVES CHATEAU (541/245-9022; May–Oct), a completely hand-built, shaggy 22-room lodge, is built across a ravine and has a stream running through the dining room.

LODGINGS

Out 'n' About Treesort / ★

300 PAGE CREEK RD, CAVE JUNCTION; 541/592-2208
This out-on-a-limb B and B has 18 structures swinging from the trees, including 12 lodging units ranging from the Tree Room Schoolhouse Suite for six to the Peacock Perch for two. Tree-musketeers can engage in ropes courses, horseback riding, and even craft making. Full breakfast is included. Book early; summer reservations go fast. The resort also offers tours and tree house–building workshops. *$$; MC, V; checks OK; www.treehouses.com; 10 miles southeast of Cave Junction near Takilma.*

Medford

While Southern Oregon's largest city may not win any beauty contests, Medford has achieved national recognition for its shapely pears, due to the efforts of Harry and David's, a local mail-order giant. **HARRY AND DAVID'S COUNTRY VILLAGE** (1314 Center Dr, Medford; 541/864-2277; www.harrydavid.com) offers "seconds" from gift packs; it's the departure point for **TOURS** (877/322-8000) of the complex, also home to **JACKSON & PERKINS** (www.jacksonandperkins.com), the world's largest rose growers.

The international award–winning cheeses of the **ROGUE CREAMERY** (311 N Front St, Central Point; 541/665-1155) can be tasted at their factory in Central Point, a small burg a couple miles north of Medford. Check out their new **ITALIAN MARKETPLACE & CAFÉ** (211 N Front St, Central Point), one block away. If you're heading toward Ashland from Medford, make one more stop, at the **RISING SUN FARMS** tasting room (5126 S Pacific Hwy, Phoenix; 541/535-8331), to stock up on picnic supplies, like their Pesto-Dried Tomato Cheese Torta.

The **CRATERIAN GINGER ROGERS THEATER** (23 S Central Ave, Medford; 541/779-3000; www.craterian.org) is Medford's showpiece, a downtown performing arts center with a 742-seat theater that opened in 1997. The 1924 building, originally called the Craterian, functioned as a vaudeville and silent-movie house. It is now named for Ginger Rogers—the actress owned a ranch on the nearby Rogue River for many years, once danced on the Craterian stage, and in the last years before her death helped raise money for the theater's $5.3 million renovation.

For dining in Medford proper, try **PORTERS** (147 N Front St, Medford; 541/857-1910) in the old train station, with patio dining. For fine dining, try **CAFÉ DEJEUNER** (1108 E Main St, Medford; 541/857-1290), and for Thai food go to **ALI'S THAI KITCHEN** (2392 N Pacific Hwy, Medford; 541/770-3104), a humble spot north of town with good, inexpensive fare. A good place to hang your hat is **UNDER THE GREENWOOD TREE** (3045 Bellinger Ln, Medford; 541/776-0000), a classy B and B that also serves a country-gourmet three-course breakfast.

Jacksonville

Located 4 miles west of Medford and a scenic drive from Ashland through vineyards and orchards, Jacksonville has a main street that looks like it's right out of a western movie set. Founded amid the frenzy of 1850s gold seekers, today it's picture-postcard perfect. The town relied heavily on its good looks and historic merit for survival since the Pacific Railroad bypassed it and laid rails through Medford, a few miles east. Because the **APPLEGATE VALLEY** was well suited for orchards, miners picked up their ploughs when the gold rush ended. Much of the original 19th-century town, declared a National Historic Landmark in 1966, has been restored; Jacksonville now boasts more than 100 historic homes and buildings, several along **CALIFORNIA STREET**.

The **JACKSONVILLE MUSEUM** (206 N 5th St, Jacksonville; 541/773-6536; www.sohs.org), in the stately 1883 Italianate courthouse, follows the history of the Rogue River Valley and displays works by **PETER BRITT** (see Britt Festival), a famous local photographer and horticulturist. In the adjacent children's museum, kids walk through miniature pioneer settings. Walking trails thread around old gold diggings in the hills; the longest (3 miles) is **RICH GULCH HISTORIC TRAIL** (trailhead off 1st and Fir sts), an easy climb to a panoramic view. Nowadays, you can gaze from afar at the 1875 "country Gothic" **BEEKMAN HOUSE AND GARDENS** (on east end of California St, Jacksonville; 541/773-6536); otherwise, you need to prearrange a private tour.

Taste award-winning wines from **VALLEY VIEW WINERY** (1000 Applegate Hwy, Jacksonville; 800/781-9463; www.valleyviewwinery.com; in Ruch, about 9 miles south of Jacksonville) at their on-site Wine Pavilion.

The **BRITT FESTIVAL** (541/773-6077 or 800/882-7488; www.brittfest.org; June–Sept), an outdoor music-and-arts series, is held on the hillside field where Peter Britt lived. It's now the area's biggest draw in summer, with 70,000 visitors.

RESTAURANTS

Jacksonville Inn Restaurant / ★★

175 E CALIFORNIA ST, JACKSONVILLE; 541/899-1900 OR 800/321-9344

Ask about the best restaurant in town, and this restaurant's name is the one you're most apt to hear. Located in a historic downtown storefront built in 1861 and listed on the National Register of Historic Places, it's a local treasure—careful eyes will spot specs of gold in the mortar of the quarried sandstone used to build it. The decor reflects early American West. Choose from a large selection of dishes, including fresh local seafood, stuffed hazelnut chicken, filet mignon, prime rib, and chèvre ravioli—often accompanied by salads or sides of fresh veggies, many grown organically in the inn's garden. The restaurant has received numerous awards, among them a nod from *Wine Spectator* for its comprehensive wine list (more than 2,000 bottles). Reserve in advance, especially during the Britt Festival. *$$$; DIS, MC, V; checks OK; breakfast, dinner every day, lunch Tues–Sat, brunch Sun; full bar; reservations recommended; www.jacksonvilleinn.com; downtown.*

LODGINGS

Jacksonville Inn / ★★

175 E CALIFORNIA ST, JACKSONVILLE;
541/899-1900 OR 800/321-9344
Snug into one of eight elegant hotel rooms, two named and decorated for local luminaries: the Reverend Francoise Zavious Blanchet and Peter Britt. Graciously appointed with authentic western antiques, the rooms are period accurate with modern comforts. Each has a private bath and air conditioning. The inn maintains four cottages down the street as well. All have a whirlpool tub, steam shower, entertainment center with full stereo system, fireplace, wet bar, king-sized canopy bed, sitting room, and private patio. All accommodations include breakfast at the inn's restaurant (see review). One of the cottages is wheelchair accessible. *$$; DIS, MC, V, no checks; www.jacksonville inn.com; downtown.*

Talent

Just 6 miles north of Ashland, this historic town nestled in the Bear Creek Valley possesses plenty of historical intrigue. The first settlers arrived in 1852 and 1853, most staking Donation Land Claims. The Table Rock Treaty of September 1853 temporarily stemmed a conflagration between whites and Indians in the region. That same year, John Beeson arrived from the Midwest via England. Beeson considered Indians to be equals and was one of the only whites to denounce the miners and settlers who advocated the complete extermination of Native people. His views were highly unpopular, and he headed back east rather than face assassination. There he met with then President Lincoln to advocate on behalf of Native American rights. He is now buried in the area next to his wife in Stearn's Cemetery. The town wasn't officially named until A. P. Talent arrived in 1875, set up a store and post office within it, and finally platted the present town site in 1880.

Today, Talent is the home of the Camelot Theatre, a popular year-round theater company, and several top-rated restaurants. It's also the home of **PASCHAL WINERY** (1122 Suncrest Rd, Talent; 800/446-6050; www.paschalwinery.com; 2 miles from I-5 exit 21); check out the full-bodied wines at the beautiful estate. Lodging is limited, but the **ASHLAND B&B NETWORK** (800/944-0329; www.abbnet.com) can arrange a stay in one of more than 30 nearby bed-and-breakfasts.

OREGON SHAKESPEARE FESTIVAL AND THE ASHLAND THEATER SCENE

Established in 1935, the **OREGON SHAKESPEARE FESTIVAL** is among the oldest and largest professional regional theater companies in the United States. OSF presents an eight-month season of 11 plays by Shakespeare, as well as classic and contemporary playwrights in repertory, in three unique theaters. In the outdoor **ELIZABETHAN THEATER**, which seats 1,200, famous and authentic nighttime productions of Shakespeare plays are staged (three each summer). The two indoor theaters—the intimate **NEW THEATRE** and the **ANGUS BOWMER THEATRE** (mid-Feb–late Oct)—include comedies, classics, romances, new works, and dramas. The festival is dark on Mondays.

Offstage, visit the **EXHIBIT CENTER**, where you can clown around in costumes from plays past. Company members give informal free **NOON TALKS** about life at OSF, as well as **BACKSTAGE TOURS** for a fee. Before the plays on the Elizabethan stage, the free **GREEN SHOW** (June–Oct) is a lively and colorful program of dance and music in the festival courtyard, with three different shows nightly, some with themes to match the night's outdoor play. Music and dance concerts are also held across the street in **CARPENTER HALL** (noon Wed and Sat in Aug).

Current playbill and ticket information for OSF (last-minute tickets in summer are very rare) are available at the **FESTIVAL BOX OFFICE** (15 S Pioneer St, Ashland; 541/482-4331; www.osfashland.org; open every day except holidays).

Ashland is also home to the **OREGON CABARET THEATER** (1st and Hargadine sts, Ashland; 541/488-2902; www.oregoncabaret.com; Feb–Dec), which presents musicals and comedies accompanied by a full dinner and dessert menu, beer, and wine. Opened in 2002, **OREGON STAGE WORKS** (191 A St, Ashland; 541/482-2334; www.oregonstageworks.org; Mar–Oct) stages creative and challenging productions of American playwrights.

—Annissa Anderson

RESTAURANTS

Avalon Bar & Grill / ★★

105 W VALLEY VIEW RD, TALENT; 541/512-8864

Owners Dal and Renee Carver got it right at their popular Wild Goose Café in Ashland and brought their experience to bear on this newer place. Don't let the nondescript shopping-center location and facade throw you. Inside, you'll find a warm and inviting dining room balanced with a touch of upscale sophistication. The menu follows the same note. Hearty bistro fare gets a gourmet touch with seriously delicious results. Try seafood frittata or eggs Benedict for breakfast; paninis, burgers, and sweet potato fries for lunch (served all day); and steaks, seafood, wild salmon, and pasta for dinner. The wine list offers both local and international picks by the bottle and some by the glass. *$–$$; MC, V; local checks only; breakfast, lunch, dinner every day; full bar; reservations recommended; www.avalonbarandgrill.com; near I-5 in Talent Plaza.* &

Ashland

The remarkable success of the **OREGON SHAKESPEARE FESTIVAL** (see "Oregon Shakespeare Festival and the Ashland Theater Scene") since 1935 has transformed this sleepy town into one with, per capita, the region's best tourist amenities. The festival draws more than 370,000 people throughout the eight-month season, filling its theaters to an extraordinary 85 percent capacity on average. The town of 20,000 still has its soul: for the most part, it seems a happy little college town, set amid lovely ranch country.

Designed by the creator of San Francisco's Golden Gate Park, **LITHIA PARK** (59 Winburn Wy; 541/488-5340), in the downtown hub, is a 93-acre expanse of emerald lawns, sports courts, colorful landscaping, playground equipment, a Japanese garden, duck ponds, a formal rose garden, groves of sycamore trees, and a number of secluded spots for picnicking. There's also an ice-skating rink in winter. **SCHNEIDER MUSEUM OF ART** (1250 Siskiyou Blvd; 541/552-6245) at the south end of the Southern Oregon University campus is the best art gallery in town. **WEISINGER'S OF ASHLAND WINERY** (3150 Siskiyou Blvd; 541/488-5989; www.weisingers.com) and **ASHLAND VINEYARDS** (I-5 exit 14; 541/488-0088; www.winenet.com) are worth a stop. Get picnic supplies at the **ASHLAND COMMUNITY FOOD STORE** (237 N 1st St; 541/482-2237; www.ashlandfood.coop), a busy member-owned co-op.

Swim at the **ROGUE RIVER RECREATION AREA** or **APPLEGATE RIVER. SKI ASHLAND** (1745 SR 66, Ashland; 541/482-2897; www.mtashland.com; typically open Thanksgiving–mid-Apr), on nearby Mount Ashland 18 miles south of town, offers 23 runs for all classes of skiers.

RESTAURANTS

Amuse Restaurant / ★★★

15 N 1ST ST, ASHLAND; 541/488-9000

The French expression *amuse-bouche*, or "fun for the mouth," appropriately provides the name for this elegant restaurant. Husband-and-wife team Erik Brown and Jamie North bring years of experience at notable Napa Valley restaurants. Their French-inspired dishes make extensive use of organic produce and meats, served in eye-appealing compositions. More than 150 wines represent the Northwest and France. For dessert, try North's deep-fried pastry lavished in whipped cream and berry jam. *$$$; AE, DC, DIS, MC, V; local checks only; dinner Tues–Sun summer, Wed–Sun off-season; beer and wine; reservations recommended; www.amuserestaurant.com; 1 block from plaza.* &

Breadboard Restaurant & Bakery / ★

744 N MAIN ST, ASHLAND; 541-488-0295
Diners return again and again to this unassuming eatery on the edge of town for dependable and hearty home cooking. Covered patios have gorgeous views of the rolling hills. The sizable menu appeals to vegetarians and carnivores alike. In the morning, try a tofu scramble with fresh salsa, a chicken-fried steak, or sourdough pancakes with a side of crispy bacon. Breads, muffins, and pastries are served with homemade jam. *$; MC, V; local checks only; breakfast, lunch every day (closed some holidays); no alcohol; no reservations; 1 mile north of town.* &

Cucina Biazzi / ★★

568 E MAIN ST, ASHLAND; 541-488-3739
Beasy McMillan has owned several successful restaurants in Ashland over the years, but this traditional Tuscan-style trattoria is her best-loved to date. Four-course dinners are served on white linen in what was once the living room in this former residence. As tempting as the antipasto may be, don't fill up on it—fresh pasta portions are substantial, followed by a fish or meat entrée, a perfectly dressed green salad, and a rich dessert. *$$$; MC, V; checks OK; dinner every day; full bar; reservations recommended; near fire station.*

Lela's Café / ★★★

258 A ST, NO. 3, ASHLAND; 541/482-1702
Owner Lela Sherdon originally started a bakery, which grew into a small café and is now one of the better places in Ashland. Each dish offers a series of delights to the tongue—chicken liver mousse with Calvados gelée, brioche, and sweet onion marmalade is just one delicious option. Ordering a smattering of small plates and wines is suggested, as is saving room for dessert. *$$–$$$; MC, V; local checks only; lunch, dinner Tues–Sat summer; beer and wine; reservations recommended; www.lelascafe.com; close to train tracks.* &

Monet / ★★★

36 S 2ND ST, ASHLAND; 541/482-1339
This gentrified French restaurant is the talk of Ashland. Favorite dishes include shrimp sautéed in white wine and Pernod or beef tenderloin flambéed in Cognac, then served in a four-peppercorn cream sauce. The chef goes out of his way to make interesting vegetarian choices, such as La Crique Ardechoise, a country potato dish with garlic and parsley. Dine outdoors if you can. *$$$; DIS, MC, V; local checks only; dinner Tues–Sun summer, Tues–Sat off-season (closed Jan–mid-Feb); full bar; reservations recommended; www.restaurant monet.com; just off Main St.* &

The Peerless Restaurant / ★★★

265 4TH ST, ASHLAND; 541/488-6067
Crissy Barnett's reputation for doing things in style can definitely be said about her restaurant, adjacent to her boutique hotel. The Peerless has the best

atmosphere in town. The menu is Northwest, with tropical influences. There's a daily happy hour, and you can also bring in your own wine on Wednesday nights with no corkage fee. *$$$; AE, DIS, MC, V; checks OK; dinner every day June–Oct, Tues–Sat off-season (closed Jan); full bar; reservations recommended; between A and B sts.* &

The Wild Goose Café / ★★

2365 ASHLAND ST, ASHLAND; 541/488-4103
This casual bistro's menu implements locally sourced Oregon ingredients whenever possible. Breakfast offers an extensive selection of egg dishes and French toast variations. For lunch, dine on sandwiches, fish tacos, fish-and-chips, chicken fried steak, or classic caesar salad. On the long dinner menu, choose from a variety of starters, pastas, and surf and turf entrées, including Umpqua oysters and petite hanger steak. The wine list is deep, wide, and enormous. There's nightly entertainment, and late diners can order lunch and dinner in the bar until 1am. *$–$$; AE, MC, V; no checks; breakfast, lunch, dinner every day; full bar; reservations recommended; www.wildgoosecafe. com; SR 66 at I-5 exit 14.* &

LODGINGS

Country Willows Inn / ★★★

1313 CLAY ST, ASHLAND; 541/488-1590 OR 800/945-5697
Set on 5 acres of farmland outside of town, this 1896 home affords peace and quiet, plus a lovely view of the hills. Chuck and Debbie Young offer a variety of rooms, suites, and cottages. Breakfast, presented on a pretty sunporch, features organic juices and unique egg dishes. Besides a hot tub and swimming pool, you'll see the Youngs' ducks, geese, and goats. *$$–$$$; AE, DIS, MC, V; checks OK; www.countrywillowsinn.com; 4 blocks south of Siskiyou Blvd.* &

A Cowslip's Belle / ★★★

159 N MAIN ST, ASHLAND; 541/488-2901 OR 800/888-6819
Named after a flower in *A Midsummer Night's Dream*, this 1913 Craftsman bungalow is cheery. Rooms in the main house are traditional, while a Craftsman-style addition offers more privacy. Request the suite with spa tub, twisted-juniper bed frame, and balcony overlooking the Cascade mountains. Turndown service, a full breakfast, and an Ashland Racquet Club pass complete a pretty picture. *$$$; MC, V; checks OK; www.cowslip.com; 3 blocks north of theaters.* &

Mount Ashland Inn / ★★★

550 MOUNT ASHLAND RD, ASHLAND;
541/482-8707 OR 800/830-8707
Wind your way up Mount Ashland Ski Road and discover a huge, two-story log cabin, crafted from incense cedars from the surrounding 40-acre property where Chuck and Laurel Biegert have created five suites for absolute comfort. Enjoy spectacular mountain views from the dining room. An outdoor spa and

sauna, cross-country skis, snowshoes, and mountain bikes are available, as is a multicourse breakfast (for extra). Expect snow November through April. *$$$; DIS, MC, V; checks OK (for deposit only); www.mtashlandinn.com; follow signs to Mount Ashland Ski Area.*

Peerless Hotel / ★★★

243 4TH ST, ASHLAND; 541/488-1082 OR 800/460-8758
In Ashland's Historic Railroad District, the original hotel that stood here was saved from disrepair and transformed into six B and B units decorated in an exotic style, with antiques and whimsical murals that make you feel as though you're in different continents. High ceilings and luxurious, oversize bathrooms are trademarks. Suite 3 features a bath with two claw-foot tubs and a glassed-in shower. A four-course gourmet breakfast is served at the owner's Peerless Restaurant (see review) across the garden. *$$$–$$$$; DIS, MC, V; checks OK; www.peerlesshotel.com; between A and B sts.* &

Klamath Falls

For decades, the wide-open spaces around this city of 19,000 (called "K Falls" by locals) attracted only ranchers and farmers lured by the 1902 Reclamation Act that offered homesteads to veterans. Recurring droughts throughout the late 1990s and into the early 2000s brought water issues to a boil, and enactment of the Endangered Species Act—drafted in part to protect coho salmon in Upper Klamath Lake—restricted irrigation, leaving farmers high and dry. While the feds work on creative solutions, Klamath Falls is hardly going down the drain. Oregon's "City of Sunshine" redeveloped downtown and is promoting the area's natural beauty, tourism and real estate are on the rise, and the town now sports several hotel chains.

The **FAVELL MUSEUM OF WESTERN ART AND INDIAN ARTIFACTS** (125 W Main St; 541/882-9996; www.favellmuseum.com) is a true Western museum. **KLAMATH COUNTY MUSEUM** (1451 Main St; 541/883-4208) exhibits the region's volcanic geology. The **BALDWIN HOTEL MUSEUM** (31 Main St; 541/883-4207; June–Sept), in a spooky 1906 hotel, retains many fixtures of the era. The **ROSS RAGLAND THEATER** (218 N 7th St; 541/884-0651 or 888/627-5484; www.rrtheater.org), a onetime art-deco movie theater, now presents more than 60 plays each year.

UPPER KLAMATH LAKE lies on the remains of a larger ancient lake system and, at 143 square miles, is the largest lake in Oregon; it's fine for fishing and serves as bird nesting grounds. The Williamson River, which flows into the lake, yields plenty of trout. The **VOLCANIC LEGACY SCENIC BYWAY** (SR 140) runs alongside the lake and through the beautiful Wood River Valley. The Klamath Indian Tribe, a confederation of the Klamath, Modoc, and Yahooskin Natives who have occupied the region for thousands of years, opened their **KLA-MO-YA CASINO** (on Hwy 97, Chiloquin; 541/783-7529 or 888/552-6692; www.klamoyacasino.com) just a few miles north of the Klamath Falls Airport.

RESTAURANTS

Bel Tramonto / ★

6139 SIMMERS AVE, KLAMATH FALLS; 541/884-8259

Located on an unlikely strip several minutes' drive from downtown, Bel Tramonto is nonetheless worth seeking out. The restaurant's previous interior was completely remodeled and redecorated to match the Tuscan-style menu. The four courses are offered à la carte, but there's also a prix-fixe option. Homemade pastas and hearty meat and fish dishes are complemented by a selection of affordable Italian wines. *$$–$$$; AE, DIS, MC, V; local checks only; dinner Tues–Sat; full bar; reservations recommended; corner of S 6th and Patterson sts.* &

LODGINGS

Running Y Ranch Resort / ★★

5500 RUNNING Y RD, KLAMATH FALLS;
541/850-5500 OR 888/850-0275

The $250 million Running Y Ranch Resort provides recreation and real estate services along with its 85-room lodge, Arnold Palmer 18-hole golf course, restaurant, café, and condo development on 9,000 acres on Klamath Lake. Though the ambience in the lodge rooms is spare, you get a lot of room to roam, and many have views onto the golf course and beautiful surrounds. Relaxation and recreation are easily had here. In addition to golf, there's a spa, a sports and fitness center, a pool, a sauna, a hot tub, and an ice rink, and biking trails are close by. *$$–$$$$; AE, DC, DIS, MC, V; checks OK; www. runningy.com; 10 miles west of town.*

Lakeview

At nearly 4,800 feet elevation, Lakeview calls itself the "tallest town in Oregon." While most of Lake County exceeds 4,300 feet elevation, this prehistoric lake basin is more noteworthy for its hot springs and fabulous hang gliding. **HUNTER'S HOT SPRINGS** (Hwy 395, 2 miles north of town; 800/858-8266; www.hunters resort.com) has two pools—the outdoor pool is perfect for stargazing—with direct hookups to geyser springs that blow every 40 seconds at Old Perpetual.

Paragliding championships are held above Lakeview at **BLACK CAP LAUNCH** (follow signs in Lakeview for Hang Glider Port), which offers tremendous views for those without wings. A popular gliding site is Tague's Butte on **ABERT RIM**, a massive fault scarp that stretches 30 miles long and towers 2,000 feet over Lake Abert. **WARNER CANYON SKI AREA** (10 miles north of Lakeview; 541/947-5001) offers 17 weeks of skiing each year, beginning in mid-December, with no lines for the 700-foot vertical chair lift. The modest ski lodge has a small restaurant.

For authentic campfire cuisine and western-style cabins, visit the **WILLOW SPRINGS GUEST RANCH** (Clover Flat Rd, Lakeview; 541/947-5499; www. willowspringsguestranch.com), a working cattle ranch that generates its own power. The wood-fired hot tub overlooks acres of meadows.

Summer Lake

In the heart of **OREGON'S OUTBACK** lies Summer Lake, bordered by the Fremont National Forest and marshland. Birders will find plenty of thrills at **SUMMER LAKE WILDLIFE AREA** (53447 SR 31; 541/943-3152), one of Oregon's largest bird refuges. Archaeology hounds will be happy too; there are more **PETROGLYPHS** found throughout Lake County than in the rest of Oregon and Washington combined. Hiking in the **GEARHART MOUNTAIN WILDERNESS** to the south, fly-fishing the many rivers and reservoirs, and cycling the almost-deserted paved roads in the **FREMONT NATIONAL FOREST** are just a few options.

Summer Lake itself mostly recedes in summer, but don't worry: you can still get wet. Head to **SUMMER LAKE HOT SPRINGS** (SR 31 milepost 92; 877/492-8554), a historic bathhouse where for $5 you can soak all day. The **LODGE AT SUMMER LAKE** (53460 SR 31; 541/943-3993), housed in Paisley's former dance hall, serves three home-style meals a day year-round. **SUMMER LAKE STORE** (877/492-8554; 541/943-3931), a mom-and-pop grocery store, and a small pioneer museum nearby are usually open.

Silver Lake

North of Silver Lake, watch for the cutoff to **FORT ROCK STATE MONUMENT** (off Hwy 31 26 miles north and east of Silver Lake; 541/536-6055). Here you'll find remnants of an ancient volcanic blast, where Klamath Indians found refuge when Mount Mazama exploded 6,800 years ago. In one of Fort Rock's caves, archaeologists found what they believe to be the oldest shoes on record: a pair of woven sandals that date back 10,000 years.

RESTAURANTS

Cowboy Dinner Tree / ★

50962 E BAY RD, SILVER LAKE; 541/576-2426
This rustic line shack–turned–steak house surprises many who first arrive on its doorstep, but word of the legendary cowboy dinner helps them through the creaky wooden doors. Come hungry, because the dinners truly are huge. Diners choose from either a whole smoked chicken or a hunk of aged and dry-rubbed grilled steak, served with a mountain of accompaniments. Basic, woodstove-heated cabins are also available for the weary. *$–$$; no credit cards; checks OK; dinner Fri–Sun Nov–May, Thurs–Sun June–Oct; no alcohol; reservations required; www.cowboydinnertree.com; 4 miles off SR 31 at milepost 47.*

Crater Lake National Park

Heading north from Klamath Falls on Hwy 97, then west on SR 62, you'll reach the south entrance to **CRATER LAKE NATIONAL PARK**. Some 7,700 years ago, 10,000- to 12,000-foot-high Mount Mazama was the Mount St. Helens of its day. It blew up and left behind a 4,000-foot-deep crater—now a lake filled by rainwater and snowmelt. With the water plunging to depths of 1,932 feet, it's the deepest lake in the United States—and probably the bluest. A prospector searching for gold found this treasure in 1853; in 1902 it was designated a national park, the only one in Oregon.

Crater Lake National Park is extraordinary: the impossibly blue lake, eerie volcanic formations, a vast geological wonderland. The **STEEL INFORMATION CENTER** (near south entrance at park headquarters; 541/594-3000; www.nps. gov/crla) is a good stop year-round; in summer, a second visitor center operates in **RIM VILLAGE**. Visitors can camp at **MAZAMA VILLAGE CAMPGROUND** or book a room at the 40-unit **MAZAMA VILLAGE MOTOR INN** (541/830-8700); plan early, as space fills fast. The 33-mile **RIM DRIVE** along the top of the caldera offers many vistas; the two-hour boat ride from Cleetwood Cove out to **WIZARD ISLAND** requires a short but strenuous hike back to the parking lot. In winter, only the south and west entrance roads are open. Then, cross-country skiing and snowshoe walks are popular.

LODGINGS

Crater Lake Lodge / ★★

RIM DR, CRATER LAKE NATIONAL PARK; 541/830-8700
Originally built in 1909, the historic wood-and-stone building, perched at 7,000 feet on the rim of the caldera, was weakened by decades of heavy snowfall. Now restored, the summer lodge has 71 guest rooms, all with great views. Best are the eight with claw-foot bathtubs in window alcoves. Guests should reserve right away in the lodge-style dining room; if it's full, choose between two restaurants: at nearby Rim Village or Mazama Village. *$$$; DIS, MC, V; checks OK; closed mid-Oct–mid-May; www.craterlakelodge.com; via SR 138 (north) or SR 62 (south).*

Diamond Lake and Mount Bailey

MOUNT BAILEY ALPINE SKI TOURS (off SR 138, just north of Crater Lake; 800/733-7593 or 800/446-4555; www.catskimountbailey.com) offers true back-country skiing, with experienced, safety-conscious guides and snow cats instead of helicopters to take you to the top of this 8,363-foot ancient volcano. **DIAMOND LAKE RESORT** (800/733-7593; www.diamondlake.net), headquarters for the guide service, is a top-notch recreation base camp.

Cascade Lakes Area

The 100-mile scenic **CASCADE LAKES HIGHWAY** (SR 58) tour requires several hours and a picnic lunch; mountain views and fishing resorts are tucked along the way. Most scenic are **SPARKS AND ELK LAKES**; both offer great boating and swimming. **HOSMER LAKE** is a favorite for canoeing and fishing (only with a fly), while **LAVA LAKE** offers fishermen live-bait options. **ODELL AND DAVIS LAKES**, near Willamette Pass on SR 58, mark the southern end of the tour that winds its way north, eventually following the Deschutes River on Century Drive to Bend.

Odell Lake

LODGINGS

Odell Lake Lodge and Resort / ★

21501 E ODELL LAKE ACCESS OFF SR 58, CRESCENT LAKE;
541/433-2540 OR 800/434-2540

This shoreside resort is ideal for the fisher, hiker, and skier. Cast for mackinaw, rainbow, or kokanee trout in summer, or sink into a good book in the library in winter. Request Room 3, a corner suite warmed with knotty pine paneling and lake and stream views, or spend the few additional dollars to get a lakeside cabin. The restaurant is open year-round for three meals a day. *$$; DIS, MC, V; checks OK; www.odelllakeresort.com; 30 miles from Oakridge on SR 58, take E Odell Lake exit.* &

Sunriver

More than a resort, Sunriver is an organized community with 1,500 residents. The unincorporated town sprawls over 3,300 acres, and its own runway for private air commuting does brisk business. Sunriver's specialty is big-time escapist vacationing, and the resort (see review) has all the facilities to keep you busy all week long, year-round. For members and resort guests, a two-level indoor club and spa provide tennis courts, a lap pool, and a full slate of services, from massages to aromatherapy. Summer offers golf (three 18-hole courses), tennis (28 courts), rafting, canoeing, fishing, swimming (three pools, two complexes of hot tubs), biking (30 miles of paved trails), and horseback riding. In winter, the resort is home base for skiing (Nordic and alpine), ice skating, and snowmobiling.

Because of strict light pollution control in Sunriver, you can see deep-sky objects through the large-scale public observatory at the **SUNRIVER NATURE CENTER AND OBSERVATORY** (541/593-4394 or 541/593-4442; www.sunriver naturecenter.org; open Tues–Sun). Join a star party or check out interpretive exhibits, botanical garden, and a nature trail.

Dining in Sunriver includes Meadows at the Lodge, a showplace for Sunday brunch. Seasonally, resort guests can make dinner reservations at the Grille at Crosswater, an exclusive members-only restaurant. **ZEPPA BISTRO** (on Obsidian Lake in Caldera Springs development; 541/593-4855) offers early-morning pastries and wood-fired pizzas and paninis for lunch and dinner. The Trout House at the Sunriver Marina (57235 River Rd, Sunriver; 541/593-8880) is a mainstay for dinner and Sunday brunch.

LODGINGS

Sunriver Lodge & Resort / ★★★⯪

17600 CENTER DR, SUNRIVER; 541/593-1000 OR 800/801-8765
Sunriver Resort has been a family and group vacation destination for more than two decades. The outdoor recreation options make it the perfect active getaway, with a vast range of accommodations. For the best bargain, request one of the large homes through the lodge reservation service and split expenses with another family; included are club and pool access. Couples choose Lodge Village rooms for an economical choice or splurge on luxurious River Lodge rooms. *$$$–$$$$; AE, DIS, MC, V; checks OK; www.sunriver-resort.com; 15 miles south of Bend.*

Bend and Mount Bachelor

For 12,000 years, only Native Americans inhabited what is now called Bend. But in 1824, Peter Skene Ogden and members of his fur-trapping party showed up. Next came John C. Frémont, John Strong Newberry, and other Army survey parties. Finally, pioneers heading west passed through, fording the Deschutes River at Farewell Bend. Today the formerly sleepy high-desert town, founded on timber a century ago, is the largest city on the sunny side of the Cascades. Many consider it Oregon's tourism showcase. Hundreds of travelers come to visit and end up staying, doubling the population of Bend in the last decade to its current population of more than 78,000.

If the long snow season on nearby Mount Bachelor, the centerpiece of Central Oregon's alpine playground, isn't enough to lure you in winter, then the more than 35 golf courses, plentiful hiking and bike trails, river rafting, access to more than 300 high lakes, and world-class fishing and climbing should suffice in summer. And with more than 220 days of sunshine and a mild climate, Bend and its environs afford some form of outdoor recreation year-round, attracting multisport enthusiasts and some of the nation's top triathletes (see Sports and Recreation).

Bend

Named after Farewell Bend, a designation used by early pioneers to refer to one of the few fordable points along the Deschutes River, the town literally sits at a bend in the river. Today, the **DESCHUTES RIVER TRAIL** has access points from downtown to well past the Seventh Mountain Resort (see review), providing access to more than 10 miles of trails, lava formations, and a series of waterfalls (see Parks). In warmer months, raft outfitters take customers through the more prominent sections of rapids, while do-it-yourselfers brave the calmer stretches.

The **BEND PARKWAY**, a raised highway that lets passers-through avoid 10 miles of uninspired strip development along Hwy 97, allows access to the historical town center, which thrives just to the west. To the southwest is the **OLD MILL DISTRICT** (see Shopping), a former timber mill torn down and replaced with a sleek glass-and-split-rail complex of restaurants, shops, and galleries on the Deschutes riverbank. Apropos to the "new" Bend, the mill district's previously abandoned smokestacks building, seen from higher spots around town, now houses an **REI** store (380 Powerhouse Dr; 541/385-0594; www.rei.com). Across the river, the **LES SCHWAB AMPHITHEATER** (see Performing Arts and Nightlife) seats 7,500 for concerts. To the east of downtown is the newly thriving **MIDTOWN** area surrounding **PILOT BUTTE**. Farther east, the ponderosas and deciduous plantings close to the river give way to juniper and sage, all but invisible for the quickly sprouted housing developments there.

ACCESS AND INFORMATION

Air service to Central Oregon is funneled into **ROBERTS FIELD AIRPORT** (15 miles north of Bend, in Redmond), which is serviced by Alaska/Horizon, United, and SkyWest airlines with direct flights from Portland, Seattle, San Francisco, Los Angeles, and Salt Lake City. There are also two private airports, one in Sunriver and one in Bend. Several national **CAR RENTAL** companies have locations in the airport, and a few more have Bend storefronts. **GREYHOUND** (1555 NE Forbes St, Bend; 541/382-2151) offers daily bus service to major Oregon cities.

Tourism information can be found at the **BEND VISITOR AND CONVENTION BUREAU** (917 NW Harriman St, Bend; 541/382-8048; www.visitbend.com) or at the **CENTRAL OREGON VISITORS ASSOCIATION** (661 SW Powerhouse Dr, Bend; 800/800-8334; www.visitcentraloregon.com).

MAJOR ATTRACTIONS

Heading north from Summer Lake on State Route 31 or from Klamath Falls on Hwy 97, the road to Bend passes through **NEWBERRY NATIONAL VOLCANIC MONUMENT** (on both sides of US Hwy 97 between La Pine and Bend; 541/593-2421 or 541/383-4771; www.fs.fed.us), a 56,000-acre monument in the Deschutes National Forest. Within the **NEWBERRY CRATER** (on FR 21, 13 miles east of Hwy 97) lie the Big Obsidian Flow, Paulina Falls, and East and Paulina lakes. The 7,985-foot **PAULINA PEAK**, accessible by road in summer, provides an excellent view of the collapsed caldera, which spans 500 square miles. Tour **LAVA RIVER CAVE** (on Hwy 97, 13 miles south of Bend), a mile-long lava tube. As you descend into the dark depths, you'll need a warm sweater. **LAVA LANDS VISITOR CENTER** (base of Lava Butte, 12 miles south of Bend; 541/593-2421; closed in winter) is the interpretive center for the miles of lava beds. Lava Butte, formed by a volcanic fissure, offers dramatic views. Seasons for Newberry attractions vary depending on snowfall (generally mid-May–Sept).

The **HIGH DESERT MUSEUM** (59800 S Hwy 97, 4 miles south of Bend; 541/382-4754; www.highdesertmuseum.org), built from pine and lava rocks, is set on 20 acres of natural trails. Outdoor exhibits offer replicas of covered wagons, a sheepherder's camp, a settlers' cabin, and an old sawmill. The museum also has an extensive collection of Columbia Plateau Indian artifacts.

MUSEUMS AND GALLERIES

The **MIRROR POND GALLERY** (875 NW Brooks St; 541/317-9324; www.
mirrorpondgallery.org) is a showcase for community art sponsored by **ARTS
CENTRAL** (www.artscentraloregon.org), the regional arts council for Central
Oregon. Several art galleries are scattered throughout the Old Mill District
(see Shopping).

Downtown, visit the **DESCHUTES HISTORICAL CENTER** (NW Idaho and
Wall sts; 541/389-1813), which features regional historical facts and interesting pioneer paraphernalia.

PARKS

The **BEND METRO PARKS & RECREATION DISTRICT** (www.bendparks
andrec.org) manages 2,375 acres of parks in Bend, including 48 miles of
trails. **DRAKE PARK** features 11 acres bordering the Deschutes River on **MIR-
ROR POND**. **SHEVLIN PARK** (less than 3 miles west of Bend) is perfect for
picnics and outdoor fun. The district also operates **JUNIPER SWIM & FITNESS**
(800 NE 6th St, Bend; 541/389-7665). Portions of the **DESCHUTES RIVER
TRAIL** are within the city limits. **BIG SKY PARK** (21690 Neff Rd, between
Neff and Hamby rds), Bend's newest sports park, features soccer and baseball
fields, a BMX track, walking trails, and a dog park.

PILOT BUTTE STATE SCENIC VIEWPOINT (Hwy 20 just east of Bend;
541/388-6055) is a red-cinder-cone park with a mile-long road to a knockout view on top. Just northwest, along the Deschutes River, **TUMALO STATE
PARK** (541/382-3586) offers both day-use and camping options with yurt,
tent, or RV spots.

SHOPPING

Bend is full of upscale shopping. **DOWNTOWN**, locally owned and unique
stores include art galleries; gift, clothing, and shoe boutiques; children's toy
and apparel shops; and specialty food, wine, and chocolate stores. There's an
outdoor promenade at the **SHOPS AT THE OLD MILL** (541/312-0131; www.
theoldmill.com) with top-of-the-line chain stores, just steps from the Deschutes
River. There are also a few small shops, restaurants, and a cinema.

PERFORMING ARTS AND NIGHTLIFE

Central Oregon's mild temperatures and many days of sunshine make it ideal
for outdoor concerts. The famous **CASCADE FESTIVAL OF MUSIC** (www.
cascademusic.org) is held in Drake Park every summer in late August. Musicians perform a different theme nightly under large tents.

The scenic **LES SCHWAB AMPHITHEATER** (www.bendconcerts.com),
overlooking the Deschutes River in the Old Mill District, is host to many
famous artists and offers the free **SUMMER SUNDAYS CONCERT SERIES**,
featuring local bands. The **ATHLETIC CLUB OF BEND** (61615 Athletic Club
Dr; 541/385-3062; www.athleticclubofbend.com) holds its **CLEAR SUMMER
NIGHTS** concerts every summer, bringing well-known artists to an intimate

setting. The renovated **TOWER THEATRE** (835 NW Wall St; www.tower
theatre.org) downtown regularly presents concerts, as well as the **BEND FILM
FESTIVAL** (www.bendfilm.org).

Bend's stage theaters offer an array of productions. The **CASCADES THE-
ATRICAL COMPANY** (148 NW Greenwood Ave; 541/389-0803) presents six
main-stage productions yearly, with an all-volunteer production crew and
cast. The **SECOND STREET THEATER** (220 NE Lafayette Ave; 541/312-9626) is
a local repertory company that produces seven professional shows annually.

For a complete listing, pick up the **SOURCE** (www.tsweekly.com), the local
alternative free weekly. Much of the indoor live music listed shows at either
the **DOMINO ROOM** (51 NW Greenwood Ave; 541/388-1106) or the **GROVE
CANTINA** (1033 NW Bond St; 541/318-8578).

SPORTS AND RECREATION

Bend is home to several annual sporting events that draw competitors and
spectators from all around the globe. **POLE PEDDLE PADDLE** (www.mbsef.org/
events/ppp), held every May, involves alternating between downhill and cross-
country skiing at Mount Bachelor, cycling, trail running, canoeing or kayaking,
and sprinting to the finish line at Les Schwab Amphitheater. The **PACIFIC CREST
TRIATHLON** (www.racecenter.com/pacificcrest) in June attracts top athletes
from across the nation to what is fast becoming one of the West's top training
grounds. The preeminent **CASCADE CYCLING CLASSIC** (www.cascade-classic.
org) in July is the longest-running stage racing event in North America.

The **BEND ELKS BASEBALL CLUB** (www.bendelks.com) excites fans all
summer long at their home games staged at **VINCE GENNA STADIUM** (SE 5th
St and Roosevelt Ave, Bend). **GOLF TOURNAMENTS** occur from midspring
to late fall every year at many of the more than 35 public and private courses
(www.visitbend.com) in Central Oregon.

RESTAURANTS

Alpenglow Café / ★

1133 NW WALL ST, BEND; 541/383-7676
The glow they're referring to is probably the warm feeling you'll have after eating their mountainous breakfast (served all day). Orange juice is fresh squeezed,
bacon and ham are locally smoked, and all breads are homemade. Chunky
potato pancakes, made with cheddar and bacon, are served with homemade
applesauce or sour cream. Entrées come with a pile of home fries and coffee cake
or fresh fruit. *$; AE, DIS, MC, V; local checks only; breakfast, lunch every day;
no alcohol; no reservations; www.alpenglowcafe.com; at Greenwood Ave.* &

Deschutes Brewery & Public House / ★★★

1044 BOND ST, BEND; 541/382-9242
The Deschutes Brewery, nationally recognized for its handcrafted ales, has
been a stop for most visitors since 1988. Nightly (and lunch) specials rival
those of the fancier restaurants, but here people share a table and also

MICROBREW COUNTRY

Microbrew fans traveling in Southern or Central Oregon have much to anticipate. Beyond Portland, the proliferation of great brew pubs lends credence to
Oregon's reputation as Beernirvana. Here's the evidence, from north to south:

At **THREE CREEKS BREWING COMPANY** on the FivePine campus (FivePine
Lodge, Sisters; 866/974-5900; www.fivepinelodge.com), look for the newly built
Old West–style livery stable. The 6,000-square-foot facility houses a 10-barrel
brewing system and a full restaurant and brew pub.

In Bend, the **DESCHUTES BREWERY & PUBLIC HOUSE** is the leader of the
pack. Brewers of award-winning Black Butte Porter, Bachelor Bitter, and Cascade
Golden Ale, they're the second-largest Oregon microbrew bottler. Knock back
a pint of their seasonal beer on tap or cask ale—it's akin to drinking estate wine.
Tour their **BREWING FACILITY AND MOUNTAIN ROOM** (901 SW Simpson
Ave, Bend; 541/385-8606) and snag some free samples.

BEND BREWING COMPANY's (1019 NW Brooks St, Bend; 541/383-1599) Elk
Lake India Pale Ale, Outback Old Ale, and Metolius Golden Ale are local favorites.
Use that to your advantage: fewer tourists mean more tables and shorter wait
times. In summer, take your beer out on the patio overlooking Mirror Pond. **SIL-
VER MOON BREWING** (24 NW Greenwood Ave, Bend; 541/388-8331) is what
might be called a micro-microbrewer. Don't miss their Bridge Creek Pilsner, Bad-
lands Bitter, or Snakebite Porter. The Brothers McMenamin most recently joined

munch on scrumptious Buffalo wings, a brewery burger, or sweet and spicy
baked mac and cheese. Impeccable service makes it all a joy. $–$$; AE, MC,
V; checks OK; lunch, dinner every day; beer and wine; no reservations; www.
deschutesbrewery.com; off Greenwood Ave. &

Hans / ★★

915 NW WALL ST, BEND; 541/389-9700
In Bend for 22 years, Hans is a tried-and-true favorite for both lunch and
dinner. A casual, bright café with hardwood floors and big windows, Hans
continues to offer a refreshingly low-key atmosphere and amazing consis-
tency in the selection of tasty pizzas, pastas, and German specialties. Look
for blackboard specials on the lunch menu, including the Hans burger and
high-quality deli sandwiches. A pastry case with layered cakes and cook-
ies sold separately tempts even the strong-willed. $$; MC, V; local checks
only; lunch, dinner Tues–Sat; full bar; reservations recommended; www.hans
restaurant.com; downtown. &

the fray in Bend with their renovation of the **MCMENAMINS OLD ST. FRANCIS SCHOOL** (700 NW Bond St, Bend; 541/382-5174).

Heading down from Mount Bachelor? Stop at the **LODGE AT CASCADES LAKES BREWING COMPANY** (1441 SW Chandler Ave, Bend; 541/388-4998) to sample Monkey Face Porter, Pine Marten Pale Ale, and 20-Inch Brown.

In Southern Oregon, you can visit a train station the McMenamins juggernaut brought back to life: the **ROSEBURG STATION PUB & BREWERY**. Sip brews and nosh pies at the **WILD RIVER BREWING & PIZZA COMPANY** (249 N Redwood Hwy, Cave Junction; 541/592-3556). At their Grants Pass pub (595 NE E St, Grants Pass; 541/471-7487), sample year-round as well as seasonal ales brewed on-site.

Wine isn't the only buzz in Ashland. Try **STANDING STONE BREWING COMPANY** (101 Oak St, Ashland; 541/482-2448). Besides brewing outstanding ales, they've created an energy-efficient and sustainable way to run a high-production brew pub.

In Klamath Falls, **MIA & PIA'S PIZZERIA & BREWHOUSE** (3545 Summers Ln, Klamath Falls; 541/884-4880) is a family-style brew pub with 13 micros on tap. The **CREAMERY BREW PUB & GRILL** (1320 Main St, Klamath Falls; 541/273-5222), with 12 of their own regular and seasonal ales on tap, is housed in a renovated creamery.

—Jo Ostgarden

Merenda Restaurant and Wine Bar / ★★★

900 NW WALL ST, BEND; 541/330-2304

Chef-owner Jody Denton offers rustic Riviera-inspired comfort food with simple, high-quality ingredients—at competitive prices. Though spacious, both the restaurant and the wine bar fill up quickly, so be prepared to wait if you don't have a reservation. The menu includes pasta, pizza, meat dishes, and a nightly wood-fired special. For starters, try the stuffed figs or Spanish white anchovies. Wine flights are popular here, as is happy hour. $$–$$$; AE, DC, DIS, MC, V; local checks only; lunch, dinner every day; full bar; reservations recommended; www.merendarestaurant.com; downtown. &

Pine Tavern / ★★

967 NW BROOKS ST, BEND; 541/382-5581

With 70 years of history and a reputation for quality, the Pine Tavern is all you want in a dinner house: good food, service, atmosphere, and value. Request a table by the window overlooking Mirror Pond, and marvel at the 200-year-old tree growing through the tavern floor; outdoor dining is also available. Oregon Country Beef prime rib is the restaurant's specialty. Save the hearty sourdough scones and honey butter for dessert. *$$; AE, DIS, MC, V; checks OK; lunch Mon–Sat, dinner every day; full bar; reservations recommended; www.pinetavern.com; downtown.* ⅰ

LODGINGS

Mount Bachelor Village Resort / ★★★

19717 MOUNT BACHELOR DR, BEND; 541/389-5900 OR 800/574-4204
The advantage this development has over some of its neighbors is spacious rooms. Go for the newer units, where the color scheme is modern and light and soundproofing helps mute the thud of ski boots. Some rooms look out at the busy road, but the River Ridge Suites overlook the spectacular Deschutes River. Amenities include outdoor Jacuzzis, a seasonal outdoor heated pool, tennis courts, a 2.2-mile nature trail, and complimentary access to the exclusive Athletic Club of Bend. *$$$; AE, DIS, MC, V; checks OK; www.mtbachelorvillage.com; off Century Dr toward Mount Bachelor.* ⅰ

Rock Springs Guest Ranch / ★★

64201 TYLER RD, BEND; 541/382-1957 OR 800/225-3833
From June through September and on holidays, the emphasis here is on family vacations, weddings, and reunions. The rest of the year, it's a top-notch conference center. In summer, day counselors supervise kids in day-long special programs while adults hit the trail, laze in the pool, play tennis or sand volleyball, or ride one of 70 horses stabled on-site. Digs are comfy knotty pine cottages with fireplaces set amid ponderosa pines alongside a small, secluded lake. *$$$; AE, MC, V; checks OK; www.rocksprings.com; off Hwy 20, 8 miles north of Bend.* ⅰ

Seventh Mountain Resort / ★★

18575 SW CENTURY DR, BEND; 541/382-8711 OR 800/452-6810
This resort, which offers the closest accommodations to Mount Bachelor, is popular with families, no doubt due to the vast choice of activities and the reasonable prices. An ice rink, a sauna, three hot tubs, a water slide, and a heated swimming pool vie for guests' attention, along with tennis, horseback riding, biking, skating, rafting—you get the picture. Seasons Restaurant gives guests a good reason to stay at the resort for dinner and the fantastic Sunday brunch. *$$–$$$; AE, DIS, MC, V; checks OK; www.seventhmountainresort.com; 7 miles west of downtown.* ⅰ

Mount Bachelor

MOUNT BACHELOR SKI AREA (on Century Dr 22 miles southwest of Bend; 541/382-7888 for ski report or 800/829-2442; www.mtbachelor.com) is one of the largest ski areas in the Pacific Northwest, with **SEVEN HIGH-SPEED LIFTS** (10 lifts in all) feeding skiers onto 3,100 vertical feet of groomed and dry-powder slopes. Snowboarders and skiers can enjoy a full park with rails and jumps, a minipark for beginners, and the **SUPERPIPE**—a 400-foot-long half-pipe with

17-foot walls. The **TUBING PARK** has a surface lift and five groomed runs. The **SKIER'S PALATE** (at midmountain Pine Marten Lodge) serves excellent lunches; **SCAPOLO'S** (on lodge's lower level) features Italian cuisine. Skiing usually closes in mid-May, and the slopes reopen July 1 for summer sightseeing. High-season amenities include a ski school, racing, a day care, rentals, and a Nordic lodge with trails groomed for both classic and skate skiing.

Sisters and the Deschutes River Area

From Bend, Hwy 20 heads northwest to Sisters, and from Sisters, State Route 126 goes east to Redmond; together with Hwy 97, these roads form a triangle in an area rich with rivers and parks. North from Madras on Hwy 26 is the Warm Springs Indian Reservation. And through it all runs the **DESCHUTES RIVER**, designated a scenic waterway north of the town of Warm Springs.

Redmond

Often overlooked in favor of Bend, its big sister to the south, Redmond offers a nice alternative base for exploring the Sisters region. About 6 miles north of Redmond, east of Terrebonne, experienced rock climbers gather to test their mettle and nerve on the buff and magenta tuff and rhyolite cliffs of **SMITH ROCK STATE PARK** (east of Hwy 97; 541/548-7501); year-round camping is available. **CHOCK-STONE CLIMBING GUIDES** (541/318-7170 or 877/254-6611; www.chockstone climbing.com) is a guide-owned outfitter that can show you the ropes.

LODGINGS

Inn at Eagle Crest / ★★

1522 CLINE FALLS RD, REDMOND; 541/923-2453 OR 800/682-4786
This would simply be yet another golf resort in Central Oregon if it weren't for the fact that golfers get to enjoy oddly milder weather just 20-some miles north of Bend. The effect is related to a microclimate influence. Private homes at this full resort rim the 18-hole golf course; visitors choose from hotel rooms or condominiums. The resort has two recreation centers with a variety of court sports, pools, and spa facilities, as well as trails, an equestrian center, and playfields. The food at the resort's formal Niblick & Greene's is apropos to its clubby atmosphere. $$; AE, MC, V; checks OK; www.eagle-crest.com; 5 miles west of Redmond. &

Sisters

Named after the three mountain peaks—Faith, Hope, and Charity—that dominate the horizon to the west, this little community is becoming a Mecca for stressed out urbanites looking for a taste of cowboy escapism. On a clear day (about 250 a year here), Sisters is exquisitely beautiful. Surrounded by mountains, trout streams, and pine and cedar forests, this small town capitalizes on the influx of winter skiers and summer camping and fishing enthusiasts. Though the town population is about 1,000, more than 7,500 live in the surrounding area on sage and ponderosa ranchettes.

In the early 1970s, Sisters developed its western theme, but it's grown much more sophisticated. The town, built on about 30 feet of pumice dust spewed over centuries from the nearby volcanoes, has added mini-mall shopping clusters with courtyards and sidewalks to eliminate blowing dust. There are several large art galleries, locally owned curio shops, an excellent fly-fishing shop—the **FLY FISHER'S PLACE** (151 W Main Ave; 541/549-3474; www.theflyfishersplace.com), and even freshly roasted coffee, at **SISTERS COFFEE COMPANY** (273 W Hood Ave; 541/549-0527; www.sisterscoffee.com).

Sisters' economy thrives on the attention of tourists, hosting 56,000 visitors for each of four shows during June's annual **SISTERS RODEO**. In July, the town also has the world's largest outdoor quilt show, the longtime **SISTERS OUTDOOR QUILT SHOW**, with 800 quilts hanging from balconies and storefronts. Call the **VISITOR CENTER** (541/549-0251) for information.

With an easy walk to every store in town, Sisters has become known as a great place to shop. Among many locally owned and unique stores is the famous quilt and gift shop **STITCHIN' POST/WILD HARE** (311 W Cascade St; 541/549-6061), a must-see for the crafts crowd, and eclectic **BEDOUIN** (141 E Hood Ave; 541/549-3079), with its walk-through neighbor **NAVIGATOR NEWS**, an art gallery–coffeehouse.

Though the restaurant-to-visitor ratio is unexpectedly low, two good bakeries can be found downtown. The **SISTERS BAKERY** (251 E Cascade St; 541/549-0361) makes old-fashioned doughnuts, pastries, and pies. For an ever-so-slightly healthier option, **ANGELINE'S BAKERY & CAFÉ** (121 W Main Ave; 541/549-9122) offers bagels and sandwiches.

RESTAURANTS

Bronco Billy's Ranch Grill and Saloon / ★

190 E CASCADE ST, SISTERS; 541/549-RIBS
Formerly known as the Hotel Sisters Restaurant, this bar and eatery serves, unsurprisingly, ranch cooking. Owners John Keenan and John Tehan have succeeded in re-creating the look of a first-class 1900 hotel, with a touch of *Hee Haw!* and haunted house thrown in for entertainment value; full-size straw-stuffed dolls in period dress occupy the corners. The upstairs hotel rooms are now private banquet rooms. The covered patio is a good hangout for drinks in summer. *$$; MC, V; checks OK; lunch, dinner every day summer, lunch Sat–Sun, dinner every day winter; full bar; reservations recommended; at Fir St.* ⅙

Jen's Garden / ★★

403 E HOOD AVE, SISTERS; 541/549-2699
When Jen's Garden first opened, food lovers from Black Butte Ranch to Tumalo got pretty excited. Chef-owners T. R. and Jennifer McCrystal fill a

previously empty niche of fine dining in Sisters with their French provincial–inspired restaurant. The intimate cottage cuisine stars finely prepared à la carte and prix-fixe menu options that change weekly, with items like grilled pork tenderloin with roasted shallot-applejack demi-glace over white beans and pears. $$$; MC, V; *local checks only; dinner Wed–Sun; beer and wine; reservations recommended; www.intimatecottagecuisine.com; at Larch St.*

Pleiades / ★★★

1021 DESPERADO TRAIL (FIVEPINE LODGE), SISTERS; 541/549-5900 OR 866/974-5900

Named after a cluster of stars alternatively known as the Seven Sisters, this sharp, sophisticated restaurant possesses a rich, warm ambience. Chefs prepare food to match, with a wide variety of Northwest-focused dishes featuring locally raised and organically grown ingredients. The menu changes with seasonal availability, but you can expect salads, sandwiches, and burgers for lunch and creatively presented chicken, beef, and seafood dishes for dinner. Top-shelf Oregon and California picks dominate the affordable wine list, with a few good French selections as well. The heated outdoor patio should entice you to take your meal outdoors. $$; *AE, DIS, MC, V; checks OK; lunch, dinner every day; full bar; reservations recommended; www.pleiadesatfivepine. com; next to Sisters Athletic Club.* &

LODGINGS

Black Butte Ranch / ★★★

HWY 20, SISTERS; 541/595-6211 OR 866/901-2961

With 1,800 acres, this recreation wonderland remains the darling of Northwest resorts. Rimmed by the Three Sisters mountains, the ranch draws families year-round to swim, ski, fish, golf, bike, boat, ride horses, and play tennis. The best way to make a reservation is to state the size of your party and whether you want a home or condo. Tables at the Lodge Restaurant (Wed–Sun in winter) are tiered so everyone can appreciate the meadow panorama beyond. $$$; *AE, DIS, MC, V; checks OK; www.blackbutteranch.com; 8 miles west of Sisters.* &

FivePine Lodge / ★★★★

1021 DESPERADO TRAIL, SISTERS; 541/549-5900 OR 866/974-5900

Marketed as one of the most romantic spa hotels in Oregon, FivePine definitely lives up to its intentions. Thirty-two classic Craftsman cottages and lodge rooms are nestled into a pine-forested meadow at the base of the Three Sisters range. Rooms and suites are furnished with handbuilt Amish hardwood furniture and warmed by tiled Arts and Craft–style fireplaces. Luxurious room amenities include 42-inch plasma-screen TVs. Baths feature Kohler tubs filled by a waterfall and separate Italian-tile showers. Complimentary breakfast, a hosted wine reception, and access to the on-campus Sisters Athletic Club are included. On-site Shibui Spa vies for the title of the state's finest hotel spa. Its beautiful design and highly skilled therapists offer massage, facials, waxing, and nail treatments. *$$$–$$$$; AE, DIS, MC, V; no checks; www.fivepine lodge.com; ½ mile southeast of Sisters.*

Camp Sherman

This tiny settlement midway between Sisters and Santiam Pass is located on the **METOLIUS RIVER**, a federally designated Wild and Scenic River that rises on the eastern slopes of the Cascade Mountains and flows north and eastward to **LAKE BILLY CHINOOK** before joining with the Deschutes River at **COVE PALISADES STATE PARK** (7300 SW Jordan Rd, Culver; 541/546-3412). The Camp Sherman area is known for its stunning mountain views, hiking trails, fly-fishing streams, wildflower meadows, and abundant wildlife and birds. Part of the **OREGON CAS-CADES BIRDING TRAIL** (www.oregonbirdingtrails.org), the area offer a chance to search for the elusive white-headed woodpecker and other bird species. Set in a cabin-style building surrounded by towering pines, the **KOKANEE CAFE** (25545 SW FR 1419, Camp Sherman; 541/595-6420; April–Oct) is so popular you had best make reservations if you want a table.

Warm Springs

Many travelers pass through the **WARM SPRINGS INDIAN RESERVATION** on their way south to Bend or north to Mount Hood. To visitors, the area is most well known for the sulfur-free hot springs near the Warm Springs River—the center of **KAH-NEE-TA HIGH DESERT RESORT & CASINO** (see review), on the reservation nestled below the barren Mutton Mountains. Even if you're not spending the night, be sure to stop and visit the incredible **MUSEUM AT WARM SPRINGS** (541/553-3331; www.warmsprings.biz/museum). It includes a stunning exhibit of a Wasco Indian wedding ceremony, a contemporary art gallery, and a gift shop.

LODGINGS

Kah-Nee-Ta High Desert Resort & Casino / ★★

6823 HWY 8, WARM SPRINGS; 541/553-1112 OR 800/554-4786

Sprawling across the high desert on the Warm Springs Reservation, this family-friendly resort has views and then some. It's a peaceful getaway 11 miles from Hwy 26. Accommodations range from luxury suites and private view-balcony rooms in the 139-room lodge to village suites, teepees, and a full-service RV park. Guests have access to an 18-hole golf course, tennis courts, a hot springs mineral pool, a fitness center, plus Spa Wanapine. The main lodge's fine dining room is the Juniper Room; the Chinook Room offers buffet service and food to go. *$$–$$$; AE, DC, DIS, MC, V; checks OK; www. kah-nee-taresort.com; on Hwy 8, 9.7 miles north of Warm Springs.* &

EASTERN OREGON

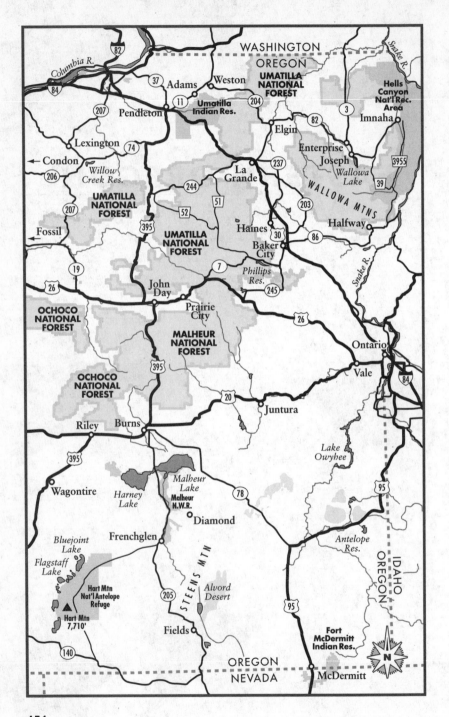

EASTERN OREGON

Eastern Oregon remains the last region of the state where Oregon's old license plate motto "Pacific wonderland" still applies. The beauty and isolation of the mountains, valleys, fields, rivers, and forests are complemented by towns where people know each other and rely on the land to survive. While enjoying the alpine meadows of the Wallowa Mountains, Hells Canyon (deeper than the Grand Canyon), the rugged Blue Mountains, stunning Steens Mountain, or the expansive Malheur National Wildlife Refuge, you'll find areas so off the beaten path that many lifelong Oregonians have never seen them.

The optimum word for climate in Eastern Oregon is "dry." Winters consist of snowstorms separated by dry days and stunning blue skies, the perfect climate for skiers and winter enthusiasts. Summers start cold and damp, then build into scorching days contrasted with beautiful evenings. Summer fades with cooler days that can easily be described as the perfect climate. Autumn is marked by frosty nights and warm days.

The outdoor possibilities are nearly endless throughout the region. For classic natural Oregon beauty, the northeast features mixed pine and fir forests, steep canyons, and beautiful rivers and streams. For sweeping vistas and wide-open spaces, head to the central and southeast sections.

ACCESS & INFORMATION

Accessing Eastern Oregon is primarily via **INTERSTATE 84, US HIGHWAY 395,** and **US HIGHWAY 26**. See them as big rivers flowing through the region. Follow them, and as you branch off onto state roads, county roads, and, ultimately, Forest Service roads and scenic byways, you'll find yourself at the source of what makes Eastern Oregon special.

I-84 runs through Pendleton, La Grande, and Baker City and ends at Ontario on the Idaho border. Hwy 395 connects Pendleton to Burns running north and south, providing access to Umatilla, Malheur, and Ochoco national forests. Pick up Hwy 26 at Prineville and take it through the center of the region to the Oregon-Idaho state line. **US HIGHWAY 20** runs from Bend and takes a slightly more southern route to Ontario.

In winter, check road conditions, especially in the passes and on any of the highways. A great way to actually anticipate what lies ahead are the camera links on the **OREGON DEPARTMENT OF TRANSPORTATION** (503/588-2941 or 800/977-6368; www.oregon.gov/ODOT) and **TRIP CHECK** (www.trip check.com) Web sites. Road reports are also available.

SEAPORT AIRLINES (888/573-2767; www.seaportair.com) replaced Horizon Air as the carrier for flights from Portland to Pendleton. Regular train service in the region was axed in 1997. **GREYHOUND** (800/231-2222; www. greyhound.com) travels I-84 east from Portland to Boise, Idaho. Several smaller carriers, such as **COMMUNITY CONNECTIONS** (541/523-6591; www. unioncountyccno.org) in Enterprise, Joseph, La Grande, and Baker City and **PEOPLE MOVER** (800/527-2370) in John Day, operate locally.

Pendleton

This is the Round-Up City, named for the world-famous rodeo that takes place in September (see "Pendleton Roundup: A Life List Item"). Pendleton is Eastern Oregon's "largest city," with 14,000 residents and a lively downtown. Many people have lived in this area for generations and are proud of their farms, ranches, and wool—all foundations of the local economy.

PENDLETON WOOLEN MILLS (1307 SE Court Pl, Pendleton; 541/276-6911; www.pendleton-usa.com) was founded here in 1909. Get a deal on discounted blankets or take a tour of the mills. **PENDLETON UNDERGROUND TOURS** (37 SW Emigrant Ave, Pendleton; 541/276-0730 or 800/226-6398) is a popular one-hour tour of the city's past, including its 1890s underground poker rooms and brothels.

ARMCHAIR BOOKS (39 SW Dorian Ave, Pendleton; 541/276-7323) has a great selection of books by regional authors. **HAMLEY'S AND COMPANY** (30 SE Court Ave, Pendleton; 541/278-1100; www.hamley.com), longtime makers of saddles and leather goods, also includes an art gallery and has expanded into dining.

The **TAMÁSTLIKT CULTURAL INSTITUTE** (72789 Hwy 331, Pendleton; 541/966-9748) tells the story of this part of Oregon from the Native point of view. In addition to enjoying fascinating exhibits, try your luck, relax, or enjoy a round of golf at the **WILDHORSE RESORT CASINO** (see Lodgings).

RESTAURANTS

Hamley Steak House / ★★★

8 SE COURT AVE, PENDLETON; 541/278-1100 OR 877/342-6539

Cowboys in Pendleton covet custom Hamley saddles, metalwork, and leather goods for their quality legacy, but they're just as likely to pick up their gear and head next door to enjoy high-quality steaks or French fries with their young 'uns. A multimillion-dollar renovation created a stunning restaurant. Enjoy the signature porterhouse or shrimp scampi with local veggies. Let little buckaroos order from the kids' menu, or grab some barbecue to go. An excellent wine list compliments the steak-focused menu. The late-night lounge offers a bargain bar menu. *$$; AE, DIS, MC, V; checks OK; lunch, dinner every day (fewer hours in winter); full bar; reservations recommended; www.thehamleysteakhouse.com; on Hwy 30.* &

Raphael's / ★★★

233 SE 4TH ST, PENDLETON; 541/276-8500 OR 888/944-CHEF

This place proves that you can find fine dining in a cow town. Raphael's, located in the historic Raley House—the home of Round-Up founder Roy Raley and, later, Pendleton mayor Joe McLaughlin—offers western food with a flair that makes your taste buds two-step. Whether you eat in front of the green marble fireplace or on the back deck, enjoy steaks and seafood, Oregon marionberry elk chops, or rattlesnake-and-rabbit sausage. *$$; AE,*

PENDLETON ROUND-UP: A LIFE LIST ITEM

Rarely does a world-class event take place in a small rural town out West. Rarer still is a successful world-class act that has taken place annually for nearly a century and has changed little since it started. The **PENDLETON ROUND-UP** has remained true to its roots: a classic cowboys-and-Indians event.

During Round-Up week, this small town of 15,000 swells to twice its size and little else gets done in town. When the party starts with the Saturday-night concert, Main Street shuts down and doesn't open up again for a week. During the next seven days, the excitement and crowds build, entertained by rodeos, live music, street shows, open-air barbecues and breakfasts, Indian beauty pageants, tribal dancing, parades, and the **HAPPY CANYON SHOW**: the world's most unique pageant. The youngsters are also part of the festivities with their own rodeo, junior pageant, and kids' day at the rodeo. Some of the world's best rodeo athletes compete for significant prize money. One of the more popular events is the **PROFESSIONAL BULL RIDERS CLASSIC**, which opens the rodeo.

The Pendleton Round-Up represents the history of much of Eastern Oregon, and the festivities mix the Native's view while also maintaining the flavor and mystique of the cowboy. This small-town event with a big heart is truly worthy of anyone's life list of must-dos.

—Michole Jensen

DIS, MC, V; checks OK; dinner Tues–Sat; full bar; reservations recommended; www.raphaelsrestaurant.com; between Court Pl and Dorian Ave. &

LODGINGS

The Pendleton House Bed & Breakfast / ★★★

311 N MAIN ST, PENDLETON; 541/276-8581 OR 800/700-8581
A great place to stay after a long drive or a big day at the rodeo, this pink stucco mansion overlooking the Umatilla River and Pendleton's downtown is, without a doubt, the nicest place in town. An English garden and front porch with white chairs are a major contrast to the wheat fields and cowboy rowdiness. Ask for the Gwendolyn or Mandarin Room, both of which have balcony access. *$$; MC, V; checks OK; www.pendletonhousebnb.com; cross Umatilla River to N Main St.*

Wildhorse Resort Casino / ★★

72777 HWY 331, PENDLETON; 800/654-9453
Owned and operated by the Confederated Tribes of the Umatilla Indian Reservation, Wildhorse offers golf, a museum, shopping, dining, and games for both adults and kids. Besides the casino, the main attraction is the Tamástslikt

Cultural Institute, which helps document and preserve the past, present, and future traditions and practices of the Cayuse, Umatilla, and Walla Walla tribes. Before or after your adventures, Wildhorse has a buffet for breakfast, lunch, and dinner, or for finer dining, try the newly opened Plateau Restaurant (casino users pack it, so reserve). *$$; AE, DIS, MC, V; checks OK; www.wildhorseresort.com; off I-84, 4 miles east of Pendleton.* &

Milton-Freewater

Locals have dubbed it **MUDDY FROGWATER COUNTRY**—and throw an annual festival (www.muddyfrogwaterfestival.com) to celebrate it, which just goes to show this small town in the foothills of the Blue Mountains has a sense of humor. Once two towns, Milton and Freewater, the communities merged in 1950.

The town sits on the edge of the acclaimed Walla Walla Valley Wine Appellation (Walla Walla is just 8 miles to the north) and is also known for its agricultural bounty. Plenty of sun in summer plus mild winters contribute to an almost perfect grape-growing climate for the varietals cultivated here. **SEVEN HILLS VINEYARD** (83501 Lower Dry Creek Rd, Milton-Freewater; 541/938-8941; www.sevenhillsvineyard.com), located just 4 miles west of Milton-Freewater, was originally planted in 1981 and has expanded to more than 200 acres of premium wine grapes.

Chocolate makes a natural wine accompaniment; sample flavors like thyme, lavender, clove, and cassis at **PETITS NOIRS** (622 S Main St, Milton-Freewater; 541/938-7118; www.petitsnoirs.com). Several artists' studios are located here.

Two motels offer overnight accommodations: the **MORGAN INN** (104 N Columbia St, Milton-Freewater; 541/938-5547) and **OUT WEST MOTEL** (84040 Hwy 11, Milton-Freewater; 541/938-6647). **LACASITAS** (6 S Columbia St, Milton-Freewater; 541/938-3508) offers reliably good Mexican food.

La Grande

Home to Eastern Oregon University, the only four-year university east of the Cascades, La Grande vacillates between sleepy and determined, with a variety of shops and restaurants catering to both out-of-town college students and local ranchers, and loggers. Enjoy wine, coffee, treats, and a stroll through several downtown galleries during the **THIRD THURSDAY ART WALK**. Search out a book or two at **SUNFLOWER BOOKS** (1114 Washington St, La Grande; 541/963-5242) or **EARTH-N-BOOK** (1118 Adams Ave, La Grande; 541/963-8057)—have some coffee and curl up and read.

For a look at the countryside, climb aboard the **EAGLE CAP EXCURSION TRAIN** (www.eaglecaptrain.com) and enjoy a 3.5-hour ride through country you won't see any other way except by horse or on foot. The train departs from Elgin and includes lunch or dessert and beverage. Rides are available Saturday mornings and Thursday afternoons April through October. A **FISH TRAIN** (see "Fish Train") is available in February and March.

RESTAURANTS

Foley Station / ★★

1114 ADAMS AVE, LA GRANDE; 541/963-7473

Housed in the historic Palmer Building, this casual bistro serves meals all day in a comfortable open-kitchen atmosphere. International influences add flair to dishes made with local, seasonal ingredients. The panfried halibut and organic beef burgers are a bargain; pair either with one of Oregon's many microbrews. But many locals come here for brunch and some of the best Belgian waffles and huevos rancheros you'll find anywhere. In April the restaurant puts *Titanic* artifacts on display and re-creates the menu from the *Titanic* to commemorate the ship's sinking. Hit the lounge for happy hour or a late evening when they roll out "Martinis and Munchies." Their regional microbrew list and a wide selection of international wines are formidable. *$$; AE, DIS, MC, V; checks OK; lunch, dinner, brunch every day; full bar; reservations recommended; www.foleystation.com; between 4th and Depot sts.* &

Ten Depot Street / ★★

10 DEPOT ST, LA GRANDE; 541/963-8766

This longtime local favorite serves up excellent food in a historic atmosphere. The dining room features antique furnishings to complement the restored landmark brick building. Try the bar if you want to savor the food and wine in a richer atmosphere, with a carved wood bar back. The blue plate specials are a deal and often include produce from the chef's own garden. Dinners range from a half-pound burger to chicken-and-pesto pasta to prime rib (the house specialty). *$$; AE, MC, V; checks OK; lunch, dinner Mon–Sat; full bar; reservations recommended; 2 blocks west of Adams Ave.* &

LODGINGS

Stange Manor Inn / ★

1612 WALNUT ST, LA GRANDE; 888/286-9463

Once owned by a lumber baron, this 1920s Georgian mansion features a stunning winding staircase and a sunroom perfect for plotting your next adventure or savoring your recent travels. The best choice is the master bedroom, but the maid's room and the guest room are fine too. This is La Grande's nicest place to stay, and chef-owner Carolyn Jensen's breakfast prepares you for the day, especially if you'll be eating lunch late. *$$; MC, V; checks OK; www.stangemanor.com; corner of Spring and Walnut sts.*

Wallowa Mountains and Hells Canyon

Known as the Oregon Alps, the Wallowa Mountains were the home of the legendary Chief Joseph, who fled from his homeland with a band of Nez Perce, only to make a last stand near the Canadian border in Montana. Although Chief Joseph's remains are far from his beloved land of the winding water, he saw to it that his father, Old Chief Joseph, was buried on the north shore of Wallowa Lake.

HELLS CANYON NATIONAL RECREATION AREA (35 miles east of Joseph; 541/426-5546; www.fs.fed.us/hellscanyon) encompasses the continent's deepest gorge. This recreation area provides stunning views and wild country that will never be tamed except by the Snake River that created this stunning landscape.

Enterprise

RESTAURANTS

Terminal Gravity Brewery / ★

803 SCHOOL ST, ENTERPRISE; 541/426-0158

Oregon is known for great microbrews, and this brew pub solidifies the state's reputation in Eastern Oregon. Their IPA is the company's most sought-after brew, but their stout and ESG (Extra Special Golden) are also great. Their breakfast stout receives high marks from beer aficionados and should be tasted, if not enjoyed, in a tall glass. The brewery itself is a traveler's haven, with pickup volleyball games in the summer and lively discussions in the winter. The food is better-than-average pub fare, with local produce and a revolving menu. *$; MC, V; checks OK; dinner Wed–Sun (hours vary in winter); beer and wine; no reservations; south end of town.* &

LODGINGS

1910 Historic Enterprise House Bed & Breakfast / ★★

508 1ST ST S, ENTERPRISE; 541/426-8825 OR 888/448-8825

Considered one of Oregon's largest and loveliest mansions, the Enterprise House offers a quiet, relaxed atmosphere, just minutes from Joseph and Wallowa Lake and within walking distance of Terminal Gravity Micro Brewery and Lear's Irish Pub. Enjoy a stroll through the orchard or gear up for something more adventurous such as hiking, backpacking, camping, swimming, boating, fishing, and backcountry skiing in nearby Eagle Cap Wilderness Area. When you're done, come back, kick off your boots, and relax or enjoy an awesome bubble bath. *$$; MC, V; checks OK; www.enterprisehousebnb. com; off Residence St.* &

Joseph

Located in the heart of a stunning valley within easy driving distance of both the Hells Canyon and the Eagle Cap Wilderness, Joseph is a great place to start or end adventures, as outdoor enthusiasts have always found. In the 1990s, Joseph gained a reputation as a world-class art center known for bronze casting and stunning sculptures. Joseph is now home to two working foundries and a dozen galleries, showcasing mostly traditional art.

FISH TRAIN

Oregon draws anglers from all over the world who come to experience the joy of fishing for steelhead, the prized fish of fly fishermen. Eastern Oregon offers a new twist with the **FISH TRAIN** (541/437-4475; www.minammotel. com or www.eaglecaptrain.com), operated by the Wallowa Union Railroad. The train travels down the Wallowa River Canyon, which is hailed as one of the best steelhead fly-fishing locations in the West. Fishermen can hop aboard the train in the early morning and get dropped off at any location of their choice along the route. At the end of the day, they hop back on board when the train comes back up the canyon.

The Wallowa River fish hatchery virtually ensures steelhead are running during the high season, and anglers won't have to worry about harming the native fish run. Only 25 fishermen are allowed each day on the train (available Sat–Sun Feb–Mar) for the 10-mile trip down the Wallowa Wild and Scenic Waterway, so reservations are suggested. Charter trains are also available. Although not a luxury ride, a hot lunch and beverages are included in the ticket cost. A half-day trip departs from the Minam Motel at 1:30pm and returns at 4:15pm. Sightseers, birders, and wildlife watchers are also welcome.

—Michole Jensen

Explore Joseph's art scene along Main Street, which also features local eating places and stores necessary for everyday life, such as hardware and lumber. The street is filled with lampposts, paving-stone sidewalks, and large bronze sculptures. Getting a real feel for the art requires trips to **KELLY'S GALLERY ON MAIN STREET** (103 N Main St, Joseph; 541/432-3116; www.kellysgalleryatjoseph.com), **ASPEN GROVE GALLERY** (602 N Main St, Joseph; 541/432-9222), **INDIGO GALLERY** (504 S Main St, Joseph; 541/432-5202), and **VALLEY BRONZE OF OREGON** (307 W Alder St, Joseph; 541/432-7551; www.valleybronze.com).

WALLOWA LAKE STATE PARK, located south of Joseph on the lakeshore, is one of the most beautiful state parks in the country. In addition to a swimming beach and a boat launch, the park is adjacent to trailheads leading into the **EAGLE CAP WILDERNESS AREA**. Also nearby is 8,200-foot Mount Howard, featuring the **WALLOWA LAKE TRAMWAY** (59919 Wallowa Lake Hwy, Joseph; 541/432-5331; www.wallowalaketramway.com), a gondola that ascends to 2 miles of hiking trails with views of Hells Canyon, the Wallowas, and Idaho's Seven Devils Mountains. Maps are available at the **WALLOWA MOUNTAINS VISITOR CENTER** (88401 Hwy 82, Enterprise; 541/426-5546).

Want a backpacking experience without hefting the load? Let a llama carry the gear, with **HURRICANE CREEK LLAMA TREKS** (866/386-8735 or 541/928-2850; www.hcltrek.com; June–Aug). A day's hike takes you 4 to 8 miles, and meals are included. Sign up for a morning horseback ride or an extended wilderness pack trip at the **EAGLE CAP WILDERNESS PACK STATION** (59761 Wallowa Lake Hwy, Joseph; 541/571-5893 or 800/681-6222).

If you prefer snow, explore the Wallowas by heading into the backcountry for a few days of guided telemark skiing with **WING RIDGE SKI TOURS** (541/426-4322 or 800/646-9050; www.wingski.com). The **EAGLE CAP SLED DOG RACE** (800/585-4121; www.eaglecapsleddograce.net), a qualifier race for the big Iditarod Race in Alaska, is unique to Oregon and occurs every January.

RESTAURANTS

Old Town Café / ★

8 S MAIN ST, JOSEPH; 541/432-9898
The café is often packed with locals and tourists alike. The mix creates a modern-day western watering-hole atmosphere. Try for a seat in the garden while enjoying your lunch or the breakfast burritos smothered in homemade salsa. *$; MC, V; checks OK; breakfast, lunch Fri–Wed; beer and wine; no reservations; downtown.* &

LODGINGS

The Bronze Antler Bed & Breakfast / ★★

309 S MAIN ST, JOSEPH; 541/432-0230 OR 866/520-9769
When Bill Finney and Heather Tyreman took over this cozy lodge, locals helped restore the interior to its past glory when giving it a comfortable Eastern Oregon feel. The Chief Joseph Room has a panoramic view of the Wallowa Mountains. When the sun sets, the Sawtooth Room is the place to be. The caretakers enjoy sharing their favorite hiking trails or the best dish at any restaurant in the county, giving guests a true insider's view into Joseph. Children over 12 are welcome. *$$; AE, DIS, MC, V; checks OK; www.bronzeantler.com; at 4th Ave.* &

Wallowa Lake Lodge / ★

60060 WALLOWA LAKE HWY, JOSEPH; 541/432-9821
Although many of the rooms at the Wallowa Lake Lodge are small, this is one instance where it's actually fine; visitors in the area mostly just need a shower and a bed. The stunning landscape and small-town attitude beckon for exploration, and evenings are often spent sprawled in front of the lobby's stone fireplace. To enjoy the beauty of the lake, try the lake-view rooms with balconies. If you plan to stay longer than a night, the lakeside cabins are best. *$$; DIS, MC, V; checks OK; www.wallowalake.com; near state park.*

Halfway

Located on the southern slopes of the Wallowas, Halfway is even more isolated than Joseph and nearly as pretty. The surreal, mountain-rimmed valley is filled with old barns and fields that are green in spring and into early summer. Outfitter

WALLOWA LLAMAS (36678 Allstead Ln, Halfway; 541/742-2961; www.wallowa llamas.com) leads three- to seven-day trips into the Eagle Cap Wilderness, with the animals lugging your gear.

HELLS CANYON begins at **OXBOW DAM**, 16 miles east of Halfway. For stunning views of the **SNAKE RIVER**, drive from Oxbow to Joseph (take Hwy 86 to FR 39, summers only). Get maps from the **U.S. FOREST SERVICE RANGER STATION** (541/742-7511) in Pine, 1 mile outside Halfway. For those who would rather experience the raging river up close, **HELLS CANYON ADVENTURES** (4200 Hells Canyon Dam Rd, Oxbow; 541/785-3352; www.hellscanyonadventures.com) arranges jet-boat or white-water raft tours leaving from Hells Canyon Dam.

Baker City and Haines

In 1861, gold was found in the Blue Mountains near Baker City. By the beginning of the 20th century, 6,700 people (more than lived in Boise at that time) had settled or tented in this raucous town. But as the mines died out, the population scattered. In the 1960s, the Geiser Grand Hotel shut its doors, and travelers often passed right through town.

In the early 1990s, Baker City had another run of luck. The Bureau of Land Management chose Flagstaff Hill, 4 miles north of town, for its **NATIONAL HISTORIC OREGON TRAIL INTERPRETIVE CENTER** (Hwy 86, Baker City; 541/523-1843; open every day; $5 per adult) in 1992. The museum drew more than 500,000 visitors in its first 18 months, kick-starting a small tourism boom. The popularity of the museum continued, and three years later, the Geiser Grand Hotel became a grand dame once again, thanks to a $6 million makeover.

Like many Eastern Oregon towns, Baker City is not touristy. There are no trendy restaurants, shopping is limited, and nightlife is sedate. But visitors don't come for the parties; they come for the history and scenery. After checking out the interpretive center, you can head to the trail, which is just a quick drive down the road. If you want your own Oregon Trail experience, take the 75-minute round-trip hike. Living-history camps outside the center give insight into one of the largest peacetime migrations ever. Plan on a half day or so to fully explore this gem.

If you find yourself downtown first, stop at **BELLA** (2023 Main St, Baker City; 541/523-7490), a popular downtown market. The architecture is unique to these small towns, with more than 100 buildings listed in the National Register of Historic Places.

A restored narrow-gauge steam train, the **SUMPTER VALLEY RAILWAY** (541/894-2268; www.svry.com), makes the short run between McEwen, just west of Phillips Lake, and Sumpter, Memorial Day through September. **ANTHONY LAKES SKI AREA** (on FR 73, 20 miles west of North Powder; 541/856-3277) has good powder snow, one chair lift, cross-country trails, and snow-cat skiing. In the same area, see elk on the horse-drawn wagon tours of the **ELKHORN WILDLIFE AREA**.

THREE-DAY BACKCOUNTRY TOUR
AND OREGON TRAIL DRIVE

DAY ONE: Start early with a cup of coffee and something sweet at Pendleton's **GREAT PACIFIC WINE AND COFFEE COMPANY**, then take a short drive east on I-84 to **WILDHORSE RESORT CASINO** and grab a filling breakfast. At the nearby **TAMÁSTLIKT CULTURAL INSTITUTE**, learn the story of Eastern Oregon from Native inhabitants' point of view. From here, head east again on I-84 to the **BLUE MOUNTAIN CROSSING OREGON TRAIL INTERPRETIVE PARK**, exit 248, where you can take a short walk in the ruts left by those traveling the Oregon Trail and get an idea of the difficulty of wagon-train travel. Travel east to La Grande and drop in to **FOLEY STATION** for Alaskan halibut fish-and-chips, fresh Pacific fried oyster stew, or a Reuben. Head out of town on SR 82 toward Elgin on the first leg of the **HELLS CANYON SCENIC BYWAY** (hellscanyonscenicbyway.com) to catch the **EAGLE CAP EXCURSION TRAIN** (www.eaglecaptrain.com); enjoy a 3.5-hour ride through country you otherwise could only see by horse or on foot; or take a 20-mile detour to Cove on Hwy 237 and visit **GILSTRAP BROTHERS WINERY** (69789 Antlers Ln, Cove; 541/568-4646), known for their merlot. Enjoy a taste or buy a bottle before heading to Enterprise. Stop at **TERMINAL GRAVITY BREWERY** for a microbrew and some delicious pub fare before continuing a few miles down the road to Joseph, where you check in

RESTAURANTS

Barley Brown's Brewpub / ★

2190 MAIN ST, BAKER CITY; 541/523-4266
This family-friendly restaurant serves downtown Baker City's biggest dinners; the menu features pasta and steak. Although only half the space is dedicated to the bar, the brewery makes and serves a full line of beers with cute names, including Tumble Off Pale Ale and seasonal brews such as Sled Wreck Winter Ale. Weekends often feature live music. *$; AE, DC, DIS, MC, V; checks OK; dinner Mon–Sat; full bar; no reservations; at Church St.* &

LODGINGS

Geiser Grand Hotel / ★★

1996 MAIN ST, BAKER CITY; 541/523-1889 OR 888/434-7374
An 1889 National Historic Landmark, the Geiser Grand was restored in 1993—but not everything changed, since locals swear the Geiser Grand is haunted, and a *New York Times* writer even reported that she felt a "presence" there sitting on her bed. But don't let that spook you. Each of the 30 rooms has a crystal chandelier and real class. The cupola suite is a splurge,

at the **BRONZE ANTLER BED & BREAKFAST** for a relaxing night's rest.

DAY TWO: Enjoy breakfast at the Bronze Antler and stroll down Main Street to check out the art galleries. Grab an early lunch at **OLD TOWN CAFÉ**, then take SR 350 toward Imnaha. Along the way, visit **WALLOWA LAKE STATE PARK**, located south of Joseph. Take the **WALLOWA LAKE TRAMWAY** to the top of 8,200-foot Mount Howard. Then continue to Halfway and check in to **PINE VALLEY LODGE**; if they say their **HALFWAY SUPPER CLUB** is serving dinner when you make your reservation, don't miss this opportunity. Otherwise, head to **THOMPSON'S HELLS CANYON INN** (Hwy 86, Halfway; 541/785-3383; 2 miles west of Oxbow Dam) for a steak or burger.

DAY THREE: Get breakfast at **MIMI'S CAFÉ** (241 Main St, Halfway; 541/742-4646), then hook up with **HELLS CANYON ADVENTURES** in Oxbow for a jet-boat or white-water raft tour. Afterward, it's back on SR 86 to Baker City and the **NATIONAL HISTORIC OREGON TRAIL INTERPRETIVE CENTER**, located at Flagstaff Hill, 4 miles north of town. The center has living-history camps that offer insight into one of the largest peacetime migrations. Have dinner at **BARLEY BROWN'S BREWPUB** or the **GEISER GRILL** in **GEISER GRAND HOTEL**. After dinner, enjoy a self-guided walking tour of the 100 buildings listed in the National Register of Historic Places before turning in at the Geiser Grand Hotel.

but the mountain and downtown views are worth it. The dining area, where you'll get mainly meat-and-potatoes fare, has a huge stained-glass skylight. *$$; AE, DIS, MC, V; checks OK; www.geisergrand.com; at Washington Ave.*

John Day

Located just off the Oregon Trail, this area was studded with gold and filled with gold seekers before the 1860s. **KAM WAH CHUNG MUSEUM** (125 NW Canton St, John Day; 541/575-2800; open every day May–Oct) was the stone-walled home of an early 20th-century Chinese herbalist and doctor who also had a general store.

For a prehistoric experience, head to the **JOHN DAY FOSSIL BEDS NATIONAL MONUMENT**, one of the world's greatest fossil collections, with three dispersed units. Colorfully banded hills are seen at the **PAINTED HILLS UNIT**; an ancient fossilized forest is viewable at the **CLARNO UNIT**. Fascinating geological layers can be seen at the **SHEEP ROCK UNIT**, along with the park's **VISITOR CENTER** and **FOSSIL MUSEUM** at the **THOMAS CONDON PALEONTOLOGY CENTER** (Hwy 19, 10 miles northwest of Dayville; 541/987-2333; open 9am–5pm every day; west of John Day). Peruse beautiful fossils, interactive displays, audiovisual presentations, and even a window into the park's paleontology lab, where scientists prepare and study fossil specimens.

Southeast High Desert

MALHEUR NATIONAL WILDLIFE REFUGE (on Hwy 205, 37 miles south of Burns; 541/493-2612) encompasses 187,000 acres of wetlands and lakes, one of the country's major bird refuges. Spring is the optimum time to see the widest variety of birds, as more than 130 species rest on the refuge during their migration. The **REFUGE HEADQUARTERS** (on south side of Malheur Lake 32 miles southeast of Burns; 541/493-2612) provides maps.

Burns

Once the center of expansive and impressive cattle kingdoms, Burns is still a market town, albeit a quieter one. **CRYSTAL CRANE HOT SPRINGS** (on Hwy 78, Crane; 541/493-2312; www.cranehotsprings.com; 25 miles southeast of Burns) is an excellent place to take a break from driving and swim in the hot-springs pond or soak in a water trough turned hot tub.

RESTAURANTS

Meat Hook Steak House / ★★

673 W MONROE ST, BURNS; 541/573-7698
Noted as serving the best steak in town, and likely the most expensive, the Meat Hook Steak House is only a couple years old, but its menu features beef from the local ranches, including the owner's cattle. The ribbons on the walls are a testimony to the champion line of beef. Come with a hearty appetite; if you opt for the desserts, you may be leaving with a to-go bag. *$$; MC, V; checks OK; dinner Mon–Sat; full bar; reservations recommended; on Hwy 20.* &

LODGINGS

Sage Country Inn / ★

351 W MONROE ST, BURNS; 541/573-7243
Located in the heart of town, allowing easy access to restaurants, shopping, or other modern amenities that come in handy after a long adventure. The three guest rooms in this 1907 Georgian Colonial are unique enough to satisfy a variety of tastes. For a shot of western testosterone, the Cattle Baron's Room is the obvious choice. The Court Street Room is more feminine; Kathreen's Room offers a nice mix. The rooms have antiques and books on local history and ranchers' witticisms. Read up, and save your questions for breakfast—the owners can tell you all about the history of southeastern Oregon. *$$; MC, V; checks OK; www.sagecountryinn.com; at S Court Ave.*

Frenchglen

A tiny town in southeastern Oregon (population about 15), Frenchglen is located 60 miles south of Burns and is a favorite stopover for visitors to the **MALHEUR NATIONAL WILDLIFE REFUGE** (see Southeast High Desert introduction) or Steens Mountain. In 1908 Presisdent Theodore Roosevelt set aside unclaimed lands encompassed by Malheur, Mud, and Harney lakes "as a preserve and breeding ground for native birds." Shaped like a lopsided T, the refuge spans an area 40 miles long and 39 miles wide. The more than 187,000 acres of habitat includes wetlands, riparian areas, meadows, and uplands. It's also known as a critical stop along the Pacific Flyway; in spring, some 130 species of birds nest on the refuge, while other waterfowl use it to refuel for their journey north. The refuge headquarters is located on the south side of Malheur Lake about 32 miles southeast of Burns. The refuge and museum are open daily from dawn until dusk. The **VISITORS CENTER** (36391 Sodhouse Ln, Princeton; 541/493-2612) is open 8am–4pm every day.

STEENS MOUNTAIN is a single gigantic fault block that rises gradually from the west to an elevation of 9,670 feet and then drops sharply to the Alvord Desert in the east. A road goes most of the way to the top (summers only), and another makes a long loop around the mountain. The latter passes the vast borax hardpan of the former Alvord Lake and numerous hot springs. Near the northeastern end of the route, Mann Lake offers some good fishing. Contact the **BUREAU OF LAND MANAGEMENT** (Hwy 20W, Hines; 541/573-4400) just southwest of Burns for information.

A rough but scenic ride from Frenchglen takes you to the 275,000-acre **HART MOUNTAIN NATIONAL ANTELOPE REFUGE** (541/947-3315). Turn west off Highway 205 and follow Rock Creek Road to the visitor center. Pronghorn antelope are frequently sighted, and bighorn sheep live east of the headquarters on the steep cliffs that form the western boundary of fault-block Hart Mountain. No visit here is complete without a long dip in the local hot spring. It's south of the visitor center in the campground—rustic but free.

LODGINGS

Frenchglen Hotel / ★

39184 HWY 205, FRENCHGLEN; 541/493-2825
Owned by the Oregon state parks department, the Frenchglen Hotel is a small, white frame American Foursquare–style building that dates back to the mid-1920s. Not much is square or level here, but that's part of the charm. Eight small, plain bedrooms don't have TVs or telephones; all rooms share baths. If you want your own, five units behind the hotel offer private baths. Many of the guests are birders, and the lobby is stocked with field guides. Ranch-style dinner is one seating only, with mandatory reservations; breakfast and lunch are offered off the menu. *$; MC, V; checks OK; closed mid-Nov–mid-Mar; ww.oregonstateparks.org/park_3.php; 60 miles south of Burns.* &

SEATTLE
AND ENVIRONS

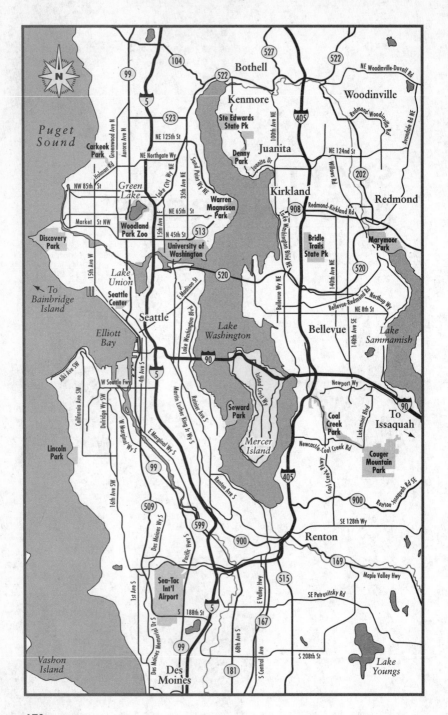

SEATTLE AND ENVIRONS

Seattle's natural beauty puts it in contention for one of *the* most beautiful cities in the United States, but it's the support the city receives for cultural venues from well-established Fortune 500 companies that has helped it achieve world-class status. From the Seattle Symphony, which host hundreds of concerts each year in Benaroya Hall, to Marion Oliver McCaw Hall—the gleaming home of internationally acclaimed Seattle Opera and Pacific Northwest Ballet—to the Frank O. Gehry–designed Experience Music Project, investment in the arts has helped the city live up to its reputation as cultural hub.

Many of downtown's newest buildings—including upscale hotels, boutiques, and high-end stores—are interspersed along the urban grid, bookended by two of the city's most colorful historic areas: the century-old Pike Place Market in the north and to the south, Pioneer Square, home to turn-of-the-19th-century architecture and Old West–style saloons.

Seattle's neighborhoods also display the yin and yang of historic-meets-modern. The fishing-industry stronghold of Ballard now boasts hipster lounges cheek to jowl with hole-in-the-wall dive bars; the eccentric and artistic "republic of Fremont"—complete with its famous sculpture of a troll eating a Volkswagen Beetle—hosts edgy boutiques and new apartments and condos. Other bustling 'hoods include Capitol Hill, where students and bohemian types populate coffee shops and funky secondhand stores; trendy Belltown, with expensive high-rise condos overlooking Elliott Bay, boutiques, and see-and-be-seen restaurants and clubs; and stately Queen Anne, with a charming hilltop avenue lined with shops and, on its southern slope, the city's most identifiable landmark, the 605-foot-tall Space Needle, erected for the 1962 World's Fair. Sprawling West Seattle is where Seattle history began, when settlers landed at Alki Point in 1851, and is also home to the city's official highest point: 520 feet above sea level. Alki Beach is a big draw year-round, but particularly when the sun brings out runners, cyclists, dog walkers, and in-line skaters.

Seattle's neighbors east of Lake Washington are also diverse, from old-guard Mercer Island to the minimetropolis of Bellevue—which continues to expand with upscale shopping centers and restaurants—to corporate Redmond (home to Microsoft), the spreading sprawl of Issaquah and the Sammamish Plateau, and the tony lakefront city of Kirkland.

But regardless of all of this growth and development, it's still the natural surroundings that keep natives from leaving and attract newcomers—especially those in pursuit of an active lifestyle. Puget Sound islands and the Olympic Mountains rise to the west across Puget Sound (for Bainbridge Island, see the Olympic and Kitsap Peninsula chapter); the Cascades rule the eastern horizon; on a clear day, Mount Rainier rises high in the south; and water—Elliott Bay, Lake Union, Lake Washington—embraces the city on three sides. Waterproof gear is regarded by some as a uniform from October to May, when the region lives up to its soggy, cloudy reputation. "Microclimate," "rain shadow," and "convergence zone" are familiar terms to locals: As they say, "If you don't like the weather, drive a few blocks." Still, even Seattleites are surprised to learn their home ranks substantially behind the likes of New York, Boston, Atlanta, Houston, Miami, and "the other Washington" in annual rainfall. That noted, this is the most overcast of all national major metropolitan areas, with an average of 227 cloudy days per year.

ACCESS AND INFORMATION

Telling nightmare traffic stories is something of a competitive sport in Seattle, but it has grown progressively more difficult to impress friends and coworkers with your tales of transport woe. Even with differing evaluation criteria, Seattle almost always makes the top five on worst-traffic-in-the-country lists. Aside from telecommuting and carpooling, the best defense is patience and street smarts.

INTERSTATE 5 is the main north-south arterial, and two east-west arterials connect it to Eastside communities (such as Bellevue) via two floating bridges: **INTERSTATE 90** (south of downtown) and **STATE ROUTE 520** (north of downtown). The major Eastside north-south highway is **INTERSTATE 405**. Numerous smaller highways connect the neighborhoods, such as **STATE ROUTE 99** (Pacific Highway S/Aurora Avenue N), which parallels I-5 to the west; **STATE ROUTE 522**, which connects I-5 and I-405 at the north end of Lake Washington; and **STATE ROUTES 509 AND 599**, alternate routes south to the airport.

Getting to downtown from **SEATTLE-TACOMA INTERNATIONAL AIRPORT** (17801 Pacific Hwy S, SeaTac; 206/431-4444; www.portseattle.org/seatac) is a 30-minute drive north on I-5, but try to avoid rush hours (7–9:30am and 3:30–7pm), when trip length can double—or worse. **GRAY LINE AIRPORT EXPRESS** (206/626-6088; www.graylineofseattle.com) runs airport passengers to and from major downtown hotels (about $10 one way, $17 round-trip). **SHUTTLE EXPRESS** (425/981-7000; www.shuttleexpress.com) is a good option for those staying outside the downtown core, but taxis are often not much more expensive. **TAXIS** from the airport cost $35–$40; by law, however, taxis *to* the airport from downtown Seattle charge a lower flat fee, around $28 plus fuel surcharges (although some cabbies might need reminding). Large **CAR RENTAL** agencies have locations near the airport, in downtown Seattle, and in the outlying neighborhoods and suburbs.

AMTRAK (King St Station, 3rd Ave S and S Jackson St, Seattle; 800/872-7245; www.amtrak.com) and **GREYHOUND** (811 Stewart St, Seattle; 800/231-2222; www.greyhound.com) are located downtown. **METRO TRANSIT** (206/553-3000; transit.metrokc.gov) has more than 300 bus routes and connects with bus services from greater Puget Sound to the north (Community Transit) and south (Pierce Transit and Sound Transit). Metro buses are free 6am–7pm downtown (between waterfront and 6th Ave, and Jackson and Battery sts). The vintage **WATERFRONT STREETCAR** trolley service (part of Metro) has been indefinitely suspended during "waterfront improvements," replaced by SR 99 serving the waterfront, Pioneer Square, and Chinatown–International District. The South Lake Union line of the **SEATTLE STREETCAR** (www.seattlestreetcar.org) runs between southeast Lake Union and Pacific Place Station, at the heart of the downtown shopping core. For off-road transport, ride the space-age **MONORAIL** (206/905-2620; www.seattlemonorail.com), which glides between downtown's **WESTLAKE CENTER** (Pine St and 4th Ave, 3rd floor, Seattle) and the Seattle Center in two minutes. For a scenic, water-focused day trip, catch a **WASHINGTON STATE FERRY** (Colman Dock, Pier 52, Seattle; 206/464-6400 or 888/808-7977; www.wsdot.wa.gov/ferries) to Bainbridge Island, Vashon Island, or Bremerton.

SEATTLE'S CONVENTION AND VISITORS BUREAU has a **CITYWIDE CONCIERGE AND VISITORS CENTER** at the Washington State Convention and Trade Center (7th Ave and Pike St, main floor next to escalators, Seattle; 206/461-5888; www.visitseattle.org), where you can find help with general information, buying tickets, and making reservations.

Seattle

Seattle possesses a thriving and diverse arts and entertainment scene. Venues host renowned musicians, contemporary artists, Broadway-bound plays and musicals, and acclaimed dance troupes. Seattle is also a bona fide food-lover's destination offering a wide range of global cuisines, with dozens of world-class restaurants and extraordinary, innovative chefs who take full advantage of the bounty of the region—including the state's burgeoning wine industry.

MAJOR ATTRACTIONS

Even first-time visitors can rattle off the must-sees in Seattle: **PIKE PLACE MARKET** (Pike Pl and 1st Ave between Virginia and Union sts, Seattle; 206/682-7453; www.pikeplacemarket.org), **PIONEER SQUARE** (along 1st and 2nd aves, between James and S Jackson sts, Seattle; www.pioneersquare.org), and the **SPACE NEEDLE**, which anchors a corner of another major attraction—**SEATTLE CENTER** (301 Harrison St, Seattle; 206/684-8582; www.seattlecenter.com), between Denny Way and Mercer Street, between First and Fifth avenues North. Born out of the 1962 World's Fair, the more than 80-acre park is home to arts and sports venues—such as **MARION OLIVER MCCAW HALL** and **KEY ARENA**—as well as museums, including the **PACIFIC SCIENCE CENTER** (200 2nd Ave N, Seattle; 206/443-2001; www.pacsci.org), with interactive, kid-friendly exhibits and an IMAX theater.

Life on and in Puget Sound is the focus of interactive exhibits at **ODYSSEY, THE MARITIME DISCOVERY CENTER** (2205 Alaskan Wy, Pier 66, Seattle; 206/374-4000; www.ody.org) and the impressive **SEATTLE AQUARIUM** (1483 Alaskan Wy, Pier 59, Seattle; 206/386-4320; www.seattleaquarium.org), which completed a $41 million expansion and renovation in 2007. Get close to more than 1,000 animal species at the acclaimed **WOODLAND PARK ZOO** (5500 Phinney Ave N, Seattle; 206/684-4800; www.zoo.org). In Pioneer Square, the hokey-but-fun **UNDERGROUND TOUR** (610 1st Ave, Seattle; 206/682-4646; www.undergroundtour.com) teaches visitors about Seattle's unusual and occasionally scandalous history.

SEATTLE THREE-DAY TOUR

DAY ONE: Start your day at **PIKE PLACE MARKET** with a stop at the original **STARBUCKS** to sample a cup of their fresh-brewed signature Pike Place Roast. You'll appreciate the fuel as you explore the market's fruits, teas, baked goodies, eclectic jewelry and gifts, and enormous, bargain-priced floral bouquets. Watch and listen to street performers of all descriptions, wander past Pike Place Fish Market to see salmon being tossed, then head to **TICKET/TICKET** to scout out half-price tickets to a same-day performance. Descend to the waterfront via the cobblestone section of Pike Street/Post Alley and lunch on fish-and-chips at **IVAR'S FISH BAR** (Pier 54, Seattle; 206/467-8063; www.ivars.net); be willing to share leftover fries with assertive seagulls. Head to the **SEATTLE AQUARIUM** and **SEATTLE ART MUSEUM**, or board an **ARGOSY CRUISE** (Pier 56, Seattle; 206/623-1445; www.argosycruises.com) to take in terrific city and mountain views. Rest awhile in your room at the **INN AT THE MARKET** before dinner at the nearby cozy **CHEZ SHEA** (94 Pike St, Seattle; 206/467-9990; www. chezshea.com). If you procured tickets to an evening performance, instead stop by **DELAURENTI** (1435 1st Ave, Seattle; 206/622-0141; www.delaurenti.com) or other market vendors to assemble an impromptu picnic, which you can enjoy on the inn's rooftop before heading out for the evening's entertainment. Either way, have a nightcap in **CAMPAGNE**'s chic bar before turning in.

DAY TWO: Wash down a house-baked crumpet in the market at the **CRUM- PET SHOP** (1502 1st Ave, Seattle; 206/682-1598) with a cup of tea. Pray for clear skies before heading to lower Queen Anne and **SEATTLE CENTER** for the quintessential Seattle vista from the top of the **SPACE NEEDLE**. Music fans should consider a visit to **EXPERIENCE MUSIC PROJECT**; grab a bite at **REVOLUTION**

MUSEUMS AND GALLERIES

The 42-foot-tall *Hammering Man* kinetic sculpture presides over **SEATTLE ART MUSEUM**, a.k.a. SAM (100 University St, Seattle; 206/654-3100; www. seattleartmuseum.org), home to impressive modern, Asian, African, and indigenous Northwest Coast art collections, as well as host of national and international traveling exhibits. SAM is even more of a destination since an elegant expansion was completed in 2007. Asian art fans shouldn't miss SAM's **SEATTLE ASIAN ART MUSEUM** (1400 E Prospect St, Seattle) in Capitol Hill's Volunteer Park. Also part of SAM, the 9-acre **OLYMPIC SCULPTURE PARK** (2901 Western Ave, Seattle) boasts oversize artwork, stunning views, and a somewhat puzzling superfluity of "do not touch" signs. All branches also boast clever museum shops and well-named **TASTE** eateries (www. tastesam.com), meriting visits on their own. On the University of Washington

BAR & GRILL (206/770-2777) on the premises. Outdoorsy types can rent a kayak and paddle around Lake Union or visit the CENTER FOR WOODEN BOATS (1010 Valley St, Seattle; 206/382-2628; www.cwb.org). Shoppers can head to BELLTOWN to find a chic new outfit for a night on the town. Refuel at lunchtime at JOEY'S (901 Fairview Ave N, Seattle; 206/749-5639): try the incredible rotisserie chicken or a huge salad. If you'd rather have a light lunch, go to MACRINA BAKERY & CAFÉ. No matter which option you choose, save room for dinner at UNION before a concert and drinks at the swanky TRIPLE DOOR. The dark, sultry SUITE 410 makes a perfect spot for a wind-down cocktail before you return to Inn at the Market.

DAY THREE: Grab a very French pastry at LE PANIER (1902 Pike Pl, Seattle; 206/441-3669; www.lepanier.com) in the market, then head to PIONEER SQUARE for an UNDERGROUND TOUR and a taste of Seattle's history. Browse the shelves at ELLIOTT BAY BOOK COMPANY. Hungry? SALUMI is just a couple blocks away, but if the line's too long, head south and east to CHINATOWN–INTERNATIONAL DISTRICT and the food court at UWAJIMAYA VILLAGE. To continue the Asian theme, drive or take a taxi to the SEATTLE ASIAN ART MUSEUM in VOLUNTEER PARK. VOLUNTEER PARK CAFÉ (1501 17th Ave E, Seattle; 206/328-3155; www.alwaysfreshgoodness.com) makes a charming spot for dinner; other fine Capitol Hill options include OSTERIA LA SPIGA, BOOM NOODLE, and TIDBIT BISTRO (2359 10th Ave E, Seattle; 206/323-0840; www.tidbitbistro.com). Finish the night in the ultrasexy bar IL BISTRO (93 Pike St, Seattle; 206/682-3049; www.ilbistro.net) right below the Pike Place Market entrance, or over a drink in the romantic Fireside Room in the SORRENTO HOTEL before staying for the night.

campus, the HENRY ART GALLERY (15th Ave NE and NE 41st St, Seattle; 206/543-2280; www.henryart.org) is known for its photography collection and excellent contemporary art exhibits. (Maya Lin presented her first West Coast exhibit here in 2006.) First Hill's once-stodgy FRYE ART MUSEUM (704 Terry Ave, Seattle; 206/622-9250; www.fryeart.org; free) has been redesigned and now includes edgy exhibits, music, and film events. Learn what it means to be African American in the Northwest and explore the continuing story at the NORTHWEST AFRICAN AMERICAN MUSEUM (2300 S Massachusetts St, Seattle; 206/518-6000).

To view work by glass pioneers like Dale Chihuly, visit FOSTER/WHITE GALLERY (220 3rd Ave S, Seattle; 206/622-2833; and 1331 5th Ave, Seattle; 206/583-0100; www.fosterwhite.com). STONINGTON GALLERY (119 S Jackson St, Seattle; 206/405-4040; www.stoningtongallery.com) exhibits contemporary Native American jewelry, textiles, and other artworks. For more galleries, see the Shopping section.

The **CHILDREN'S MUSEUM** (Seattle Center, 305 Harrison St, Seattle; 206/441-1768; www.thechildrensmuseum.org) encourages exploration of other cultures with exclusively hands-on exhibits, an arts and crafts studio, and two traveling shows per year. **WING LUKE ASIAN MUSEUM** (407 7th Ave S, Seattle; 206/623-5124; www.wingluke.org) examines the Asian-American experience in the Northwest, including the internment of Japanese Americans during World War II. Bankrolled by Microsoft cofounder Paul Allen, the eye- and ear-popping **EXPERIENCE MUSIC PROJECT** (Seattle Center, 325 5th Ave N, Seattle; 206/770-2700; www.empsfm.org) celebrates rock 'n' roll and its history, and the **SCIENCE FICTION MUSEUM** (206/724-3428; www.empsfm. org) opened in the same building in 2004. Twenty-six full-size airplanes are suspended in midair at the **MUSEUM OF FLIGHT** (9404 E Marginal Wy S, Seattle; 206/764-5720; www.museumofflight.org). The **BURKE MUSEUM OF NATURAL HISTORY AND CULTURE** (17th Ave NE and NE 45th St, Seattle; 206/543-5590; www.burkemuseum.org) on the UW campus harbors the Pacific Northwest's only real dinosaurs—snap a shot of Junior sitting on the 5-foot-tall sauropod thighbone. It is also home to a spectacular collection of Northwest Coast Indian art and artifacts. Nearby, on the north shore of Lake Union, lies the landmark restaurant **IVAR'S SALMON HOUSE** (401 NE Northlake Wy, Seattle; 206/632-0767; www.ivars.net). The art collection at this cedar longhouse replica is museum-worthy, making Ivar's an ideal desti- nation for a post-Burke repast.

PARKS AND GARDENS

Seattle offers hundreds of acres of picture-perfect vistas and scenic parks to explore. A local favorite, **DISCOVERY PARK** (3801 W Government Wy, Seattle; 206/386-4236; www.cityofseattle.net/parks) in Magnolia boasts the largest wilderness expanse in the city, with miles of trails, a beach, an 1881 lighthouse, and sweeping Sound views. **WASHINGTON PARK ARBORETUM** (2300 Arboretum Dr E, Seattle; 206/543-8800; www.depts.washington.edu/ wpa) has 200 wooded acres along Lake Washington's Ship Canal, with walking and running trails and a Japanese garden. **VOLUNTEER PARK** (1247 15th Ave E, Seattle; 206/684-4075; www.seattle.gov/parks) on Capitol Hill features a 1912 conservatory full of hothouse plants, a sculpture by Isamu Noguchi, and a view from the top of the water tower. **SEWARD PARK** (5902 Lake Washington Blvd S, Seattle; 206/684-4396; www.seattle.gov/parks) has a 2.4-mile trail looping its Bailey Peninsula, an art studio, and an old-growth forest on its 300 acres. **GAS WORKS PARK** (2101 N Northlake Wy, Seattle; 206/684-4075; www.seattle.gov/parks) on Lake Union is where Seattleites go to fly kites and to watch boaters crisscross the lake. Joggers, skaters and bladers, dog walkers, cyclists, and strollers all enjoy the 2.8-mile circuit around **GREEN LAKE** (7201 E Greenlake Dr N, Seattle; 206/684-4075; www. cityofseattle.gov/parks), a spot that feels as crowded as I-5 at rush hour on sunny or temperate days.

SHOPPING

While it's true that plenty of Seattleites favor fleece, Gore-Tex, and jeans over business suits, haute couture, and high heels, "casual" no longer automatically equates with "frumpy" in this cosmopolitan city. The downtown core along Fifth and Sixth avenues hosts fashionable outposts that include **BETSEY JOHNSON** (1429 5th Ave, Seattle; 206/624-2887; www.betseyjohnson.com), **BARNEYS NEW YORK** (600 Pine St, Seattle; 206/622-6300; www.barneys.com), and **MARIO'S** (1513 6th Ave, Seattle; 206/223-1461; www.marios.com), a huge designer store known for exemplary service and men's and women's top labels. Stunning couture by Seattle local **LULY YANG** can be found downtown (1218 4th Ave, Seattle; 206/623-8200; www.lulydesign.com).

The upscale shopping centers **PACIFIC PLACE** (600 Pine St, Seattle; 206/405-2655; www.pacificplace.com) and **RAINIER SQUARE** (between 4th and 5th aves and Union and University sts, Seattle; www.rainiersquare.com) house scores of national chains—Coach, Tiffany & Co., Louis Vuitton, Brooks Brothers, MaxMara—as does the more standard **WESTLAKE CENTER** (4th Ave and Pine St, Seattle; 206/467-1600; www.westlakecenter.com), which is home to Daiso, a Japanese "100 yen" chain store (like American dollar stores, only with better swag—some 30,000 items) with something for everyone, and local favorites such as Made in Washington and Fireworks. Founded-in-Seattle **NORDSTROM** (500 Pine St, Seattle; 206/628-2111; www.nordstrom.com) has a downtown flagship that offers floors of classy merchandise.

Mavens and hipsters of both genders flock to stylish boutiques like **NUVO MODA** (1307 1st Ave, Seattle; 206/684-6886), the **FINERIE** (1215 1st Ave, Seattle; 206/652-4664; www.thefinerie.com), **BABY & CO** (1936 1st Ave, Seattle; 206/448-4077), and **POLITE SOCIETY** (1924 1st Ave, Seattle; 206/441-4796; www.shoppolitesociety.com). **TULIP** (1201 1st Ave, Seattle; 206/223-1790; www.tulip-seattle.com) is a wonder-filled, stylish, girly haven.

Also downtown, visitors and locals alike head to **PIKE PLACE MARKET** (see Major Attractions) for photo ops, fresh produce, "flying" salmon, local crafts, great restaurants in all price ranges, and food-related goods, such as upscale kitchenware and gadgetry from the flagship **SUR LA TABLE** (84 Pine St, Seattle; 206/448-2244; www.surlatable.com) and ambrosial macaroni and cheese from **BEECHER'S HANDMADE CHEESE** (1600 Pike Pl, Seattle; 206/956-1964; www.beechershandmadecheese.com), not to mention coffee from the original **STARBUCKS** (1912 Pike Pl, Seattle; 206/448-8762; www.starbucks.com), open since 1971. To sample a range of other locally roasted coffees in one convenient location, head to **SEATTLE COFFEE WORKS** (111 Pike St, Seattle; 206/340-8867; www.seattlecoffeeworks.com). With area confectioners gaining national recognition, some are convinced chocolate has become the "new coffee": the **CHOCOLATE BOX** (108 Pine St, Seattle; 206/443-3900; www.sschocolatebox.com) carries sweet treats from around the world and offers three-hour guided tours.

Fashionistas shop the once gritty, now trendy **BELLTOWN** (www.belltown.org) just north of downtown, for its stylish boutiques and home decor stores such as **GREAT JONES HOME** (1921 2nd Ave, Seattle; 206/448-9405;

www.greatjoneshome.com), **KARAN DANNENBERG CLOTHIER** (2232 1st Ave, Seattle; 206/441-3442), and **J GILBERT FOOTWEAR** (2025 1st Ave, Seattle; 206/441-1182; www.jgilbertfootwear.com). Seattle's most saturated neighborhood for wining and dining, Belltown offers scores of restaurants, watering holes, and coffee shops for postshopping relief.

Historic **PIONEER SQUARE**, anchoring the south end of downtown, features an eclectic trove of **ART GALLERIES**; streets fill with art lovers each month during the popular **FIRST THURSDAY GALLERY WALK** (Pioneer Square Community Association; 206/667-0687; www.pioneersquare.org). The neighborhood also offers both niche and mainstream bookstores, including local independent **ELLIOTT BAY BOOK COMPANY** (101 S Main St, Seattle; 206/624-6600; www.elliottbaybook.com), which hosts popular author readings and houses more than 150,000 new and used tomes. Quirky and slightly martial **UTILIKILTS** (620 1st Ave, Seattle; 206/282-0322; www.utilikilts.com) has a wide array of legless bottoms for the self-assured gent.

Books in Japanese, Asian goods, and unusual foods (durian, anyone?) can be found just east of Pioneer Square in the **CHINATOWN–INTERNATIONAL DISTRICT'S UWAJIMAYA VILLAGE** (600 5th Ave S, Seattle; 206/624-6248; www.uwajimaya.com), the largest Asian grocer and gift store in the Pacific Northwest, which also has a large food court featuring all descriptions of Asian cuisine. **KOBO AT HIGO** (602-608 S Jackson St, Seattle; 206/381-3000; www.koboseattle.com), featuring the work of Japanese and Northwest artisans, is also a must-visit. If all that shopping makes you hungry, bargain eateries abound, including **SHANGHAI GARDEN** (524 6th Ave S, Seattle; 206/625-1688), with hand-shaved barley green noodle dishes; the historic Japanese favorite **MANEKI** (304 6th Ave S, Seattle; 206/622-2631; www.manekirestaurant.com), more than a century old; and **SEVEN STARS PEPPER SZECHUAN** (1207 S Jackson St, Seattle; 206/568-6446).

Capitol Hill also has its share of Asian-themed dining destinations, such as the boisterous **BOOM NOODLE** (1121 E Pike St, Seattle; 206/701-9130; www.boomnoodle.com), with communal table seating. **POPPY** (622 Broadway Ave E, Seattle; 206/324-1108), the new Indian-inspired *thali* restaurant from famed, longtime **HERBFARM** (see Restaurants) chef Jerry Traunfeld, is a must for food lovers, and it won't break the bank. Vintage clothing shop **RED LIGHT** (312 Broadway Ave E, Seattle; 206/329-2200; www.redlightvintage.com) and retro home-furnishing purveyor **AREA 51** (401 E Pine St, Seattle; 206/568-4782; www.area51seattle.com) are right at home on funky Capitol Hill; all types of pedestrians—students, tattooed musicians, young professionals—can be seen strolling the area's main drag of **EAST BROADWAY**.

The **UNIVERSITY DISTRICT**, surrounding the University of Washington campus, offers budget-priced eateries and shops carrying goods decorated with the school's Husky mascot. The upscale, open-air **UNIVERSITY VILLAGE** (NE 45th St and 25th Ave NE, Seattle; 206/523-0622; www.uvillage.com) is home to Crate & Barrel, Sephora, Anthropologie, Abercrombie & Fitch, Restoration Hardware, Barnes & Noble, Eddie Bauer, and PotteryBarn.

Quirky **FREMONT**, north of the Ship Canal, offers artsy shops, niche bookstores, and small boutiques along Fremont Avenue and 35th Street. Take a tour and sample chocolate goodies made from fair-trade and organic cocoa beans at **THEO CHOCOLATE** (3400 Phinney Ave N, Seattle; 206/632-5100; www.theochocolate.com). Bargain hunters shouldn't miss the year-round, Euro-style **FREMONT SUNDAY FLEA MARKET** (Evanston Ave N and N 34th St, Seattle; 206/781-6776; www.fremontmarket.com), with up to 150 vendors, including wood-fired pizza maker **VERACI** (206/535-1813; www.veracipizza.com), with some of the best thin-crust slices around.

The Scandinavian stronghold of **BALLARD** has unique boutiques like international folk art gallery **LA TIENDA** (2050 NW Market St, Seattle; 206/297-3605; www.latienda-folkart.com), while **ARCHIE MCPHEE** (2428 NW Market St, Seattle; 206/297-0240; www.mcphee.com) is the ultimate destination for quirky playthings for kids of all ages. **OLIVINE** (5344 Ballard Ave NW, Seattle; 206/706-4188; www.olivine.net), dubbed "the ultimate girl store," is countered by **BLACKBIRD** (5410 22nd Ave NW, Seattle; 206/547-2524; www.blackbirdballard.com), hawking hip attire for guys. Along Market Street and Ballard Avenue, numerous shops offer new and used furniture, books, and gifts for home and pets, plus wine bars, taverns, bars, and cafés reflect the neighborhood's heritage, with others catering to stylish locals now frequenting the area. A section of Ballard Avenue (between 20th and 22nd aves NW) shuts down every Sunday 10am–3pm for the popular **BALLARD FARMERS MARKET**. Snap up tasty treats there and take them to the **HIRAM M. CHITTENDEN LOCKS** and **CARL S. ENGLISH BOTANICAL GARDENS** (3015 NW 54th St, Seattle; 206/783-7059) for a picnic as you watch boats transition between saltwater Puget Sound and the freshwater Ship Canal. Make a side trip to the much-praised bakery **CAFÉ BESALU** (5909 24th Ave NW, Seattle; 206/789-1463), Tex-Mex **AUSTIN CANTINA** (5809 24th Ave NW, Seattle; 206/789-1277; www.austincantina.org), or **COPPER GATE** (6301 24th Ave NW, Seattle; 206/706-3292; www.thecoppergate.com), a cool restaurant-and-bar that pays homage to the neighborhood's Scandinavian roots.

The **PHINNEY** and **GREENWOOD** neighborhoods, north of Fremont, are home to several shopping destinations. Boutiques like **HIP ZEPHYR** (6241 Phinney Ave N, Seattle; 206/905-6069; www.hipzephyr.com), **FROCK SHOP** (6500 Phinney Ave N, Seattle; 206/297-1638; www.shopfrockshop.com), **LEMON MERINGUE** (7720 Greenwood Ave N, Seattle; 206/297-6071; www.lemonmeringue.us), and **TWEED** (424 N 85th St, Seattle; 206/784-4444; www.tweedboutique.com) offer fun and sophisticated fashions. Good, inexpensive bars, eateries, and coffeehouses are also numerous. **OLIVER'S TWIST** (6822 Greenwood Ave N, Seattle; 206/706-6673; www.oliverstwistseattle.com), a relaxed, atmospheric cocktail bar with small bites, makes a terrific postshopping destination.

Small boutiques and cozy coffeehouses, including the Latin American–inspired **EL DIABLO** (1811 Queen Anne Ave, Seattle; 206/285-0693; www.eldiablocoffee.com), line the top of **QUEEN ANNE**. The much busier Lower Queen Anne is home to bars, restaurants, scores of apartment buildings, and Seattle Center (see Major Attractions), but before exploring the bottom of the hill, drive by tiny **KERRY PARK** (211 W Highland Dr, Seattle; 206/684-4075; www.seattle.gov/parks), boasting one of the most photographed vistas in Seattle.

Eco-conscious shoppers head east to the up-and-coming **SOUTH LAKE UNION** (www.discoverslu.com) neighborhood. Check out the "green" at **GOODS FOR THE PLANET** (525 Dexter Ave N, Seattle; 206/652-2327; www.goodsfortheplanet.com) , and explore the edgy **VELOCITY ART AND DESIGN** (251 Yale Ave N, Seattle; 206/749-9575; www.velocityartanddesign.com; also downtown), across the street from the flagship **REI** (222 Yale Ave N, Seattle; 206/223-1944; www.rei.com), a magnet for outdoor enthusiasts of all abilities; in addition to being chock full of equipment, it has an indoor climbing wall and outdoor mountain bike–hiking test trail. Look for invigoration or relaxation at **BANYA 5** (217 9th Ave N, Seattle; 206/262-1234; www.banya5.com), a Russian-Turkish bath with sauna, steam room, hot tub, cold and warm-salt pools, a tea room, and massage and scrub services. Wind down at the attached infused-vodka bar-café, **VENIK LOUNGE** (206/223-3734; www.veniklounge.com). **DANIEL'S BROILER** (809 Fairview Pl N, Seattle; 206/621-8262) has lakefront seating, also on Lake Washington (200 Lake Washington Blvd, Seattle; 206/329-4191); **JOEY'S** (901 Fairview Ave N, Seattle; 206/749-5639) has reliable standards (also at Westfield Southcenter Mall).

WEST SEATTLE retail options continue to grow, particularly in the area known as the **JUNCTION** (California Ave SW and SW Alaska St, Seattle). It's home to the year-round **WEST SEATTLE FARMERS MARKET** (206/547-2278; www.seattlefarmersmarkets.org), numerous shops like the darling shoe boutique **CLEMENTINE** (4447 California Ave SW, Seattle; 206/935-9400; www.clementines.com). **BAKERY NOUVEAU** (4737 California Ave SW, Seattle; 206/923-0534; www.bakerynouveau.com) produces ethereal pastries and exemplary baguettes, a perfect postshopping respite.

PERFORMING ARTS

Theater/Dance

Seattleites avidly support the arts. Many New York producers try out shows here before taking them to Broadway. The big three playhouses are **A CONTEMPORARY THEATRE**, a.k.a. **ACT** (700 Union St, Seattle; 206/292-7676; www.acttheatre.org), **INTIMAN THEATRE** (201 Mercer St, Seattle Center; 206/269-1900; www.intiman.org), and **SEATTLE REPERTORY THEATRE** (155 Mercer St, Seattle Center; 206/443-2222; www.seattlerep.org). The musical toasts of Broadway, as well as those Broadway-bound, star at the ornate **5TH AVENUE THEATRE** (1308 5th Ave, Seattle; 206/625-1900; www.5thavenuetheatre.org). The historic **PARAMOUNT THEATRE** (911 Pine St, Seattle; 206/447-5510; www.theparamount.com) also hosts touring productions and national headliners. Imaginative, sophisticated productions play out at **SEATTLE CHILDREN'S THEATRE** (201 Thomas St, Seattle Center; 206/441-3322; www.sct.org). **TEATRO ZINZANNI** (222 Mercer St, Seattle; 206/802-0015;

http://dreams.zinzanni.org), which stages an entirely new show three to four times a year, pairs an extravagant cirque-meets-cabaret experience with a five-course meal designed by famed local chef Tom Douglas. Classics are the core of the city's premier dance company, the **PACIFIC NORTHWEST BALLET** (Seattle Center; 206/441-2424; www.pnb.org); an annual holiday tradition, *The Nutcracker* features spectacular Maurice Sendak–designed sets.

Music

Music of all genres—from alternative rock to reggae to chamber to classical—can be heard in Seattle, still remembered as the home of Pearl Jam, Nirvana, Soundgarden, and Alice in Chains. The **SEATTLE SYMPHONY** (200 University St, Seattle; 206/215-4747; www.seattlesymphony.org), under the baton of Gerard Schwarz, has an elegant downtown home in Benaroya Hall. The acclaimed **SEATTLE OPERA** (321 Mercer St, Seattle Center; 206/389-7676; www.seattleopera.org), guided by Speight Jenkins, brings first-rate productions to the state-of-the-art Marion Oliver McCaw Hall. The largest community chorus in the country, the outstanding **SEATTLE MEN'S CHORUS** (206/388-1400; www.flyinghouse.org), puts on full-scale productions that somewhat overshadow sister organization the **SEATTLE WOMEN'S CHORUS**.

Jazz clubs include classy **DIMITRIOU'S JAZZ ALLEY** (2033 6th Ave, Seattle; 206/441-9729; www.jazzalley.com), with one of the best sound systems around, and cozy **TULA'S** (2214 2nd Ave, Seattle; 206/443-4221; www.tulas.com). The chic, clubby **TRIPLE DOOR** (216 Union St, Seattle; 206/838-4333; www.tripledoor.com), underneath the popular **WILD GINGER** (see Restaurants), hosts a broad spectrum of musical acts; jazz is only part of the appeal. Aficionados looking for more intimate, jazz-specific venues should visit www.seattlejazzscene.com.

The city's most anticipated festivals revolve around music and the performing arts. The **NORTHWEST FOLKLIFE FESTIVAL** (Seattle Center; 206/684-7300; www.nwfolklife.org) showcases a melting pot of talent—from African marimba players to American fiddlers—over Memorial Day weekend. Held in mid-May, the **SEATTLE INTERNATIONAL CHILDREN'S FESTIVAL** (Seattle Center; 206/684-7336; www.seattleinternational.org) makes a good Folklife warm-up. The largest annual arts and music festival, **BUMBERSHOOT** (Seattle Center; 206/281-8111; www.bumbershoot.org), is named for the umbrellas that many locals stubbornly eschew. It takes place over Labor Day weekend, with headliners ranging from Beck to Tony Bennett to Black Rebel Motorcycle Club. Jazz artists make the rounds of local clubs for the **EARSHOT JAZZ FESTIVAL** (206/547-9787; www.earshot.org) in October.

Literature/Film

Perennially ranked as one of the most literate cities in the United States, Seattle's well-read populace enthusiastically supports the annual **SEATTLE ARTS AND LECTURES** Literary Lectures series (held at Benaroya Hall, 200 University St, Seattle; 206/621-2230; www.lectures.org), which books prominent authors. **TOWN HALL** (1119 8th Ave, Seattle; 206/652-4255;

www.townhallseattle.org) hosts international writers, politicians, journalists, and lecturers from all disciplines in a historic building with stained-glass windows and wooden benches.

Of the numerous **ANNUAL FILM FESTIVALS** and programs in Seattle (www.seattle.gov/filmoffice/festivals.htm), the largest is the world-class **SEATTLE INTERNATIONAL FILM FESTIVAL** (206/464-5830; www.seattlefilm.org), which features hundreds of international films at various theaters and venues in a packed three-week marquee that begins in late May. The well-attended event also includes discussions and panels with actors and filmmakers.

Check the local dailies and free weeklies for a range of event and entertainment listings. Most tickets are sold through **TICKETMASTER** (206/292-ARTS; www.ticketmaster.com), but **TICKET/TICKET** (206/324-2744) sells half-price, day-of-show tickets—and day-before matinees—in four locations (401 Broadway Ave E, 2nd level, Seattle; Pike Place Information Booth, 1st and Pike, Seattle; Pacific Place, 4th level, Seattle; and Meydenbauer Center, 11100 NE 6th St, Ste 2, Bellevue).

NIGHTLIFE

Some of the city's best night spots are in Belltown and on Capitol Hill, also a magnet for Seattle's gays and lesbians. Hot destinations on the hill range from the high-energy dance beats at **NEIGHBOURS** (1509 Broadway Ave, Seattle; 206/324-5358; www.neighboursnightclub.com) to the retro chic of the **BALTIC ROOM** (1207 Pine St, Seattle; 206/625-4444; www.thebalticroom.net) and the **CENTURY BALLROOM AND CAFÉ** (915 E Pine St, 2nd floor, Seattle; 206/324-7263; www.centuryballroom.com), a former theater offering swing and salsa dancing and dance instruction classes. Indie bands are the draw at **NEUMO'S** (925 E Pike St, Seattle; 206/709-9467; www.neumos.com), one of Seattle's most popular live-music venues.

In Belltown, popular lounges and hybrids include the high-tech dance floor and high-class pool hall of **BELLTOWN BILLIARDS** (90 Blanchard St, Seattle; 206/448-6779; www.belltownbilliards.net). On Queen Anne, **PARAGON RESTAURANT & BAR** (2125 Queen Anne Ave N, Seattle; 206/283-4548; www.paragonseattle.com) gets packed and often has live music, and the cavelike **TINI BIGS** (100 Denny Wy, Seattle; 206/284-0931; www.tinibigs.com), which straddles Belltown and lower Queen Anne, is famous for its voluminous, inventive cocktails and award-winning bartenders.

Have a good belly laugh at **COMEDY UNDERGROUND** (222 S Main St, Seattle; 206/628-0303; www.comedyunderground.com) and **GIGGLES** (5220 Roosevelt Wy NE, Seattle; 206/526-5653; www.gigglescomedyclub.com).

Near Seattle Center, all-ages rock shows are held at the largely volunteer-run **VERA PROJECT** (766 Thomas St, Seattle; 206/956-8372; www.theveraproject.org), which offers both music education and entertainment to the under-21 set. Downtown, national headliners pack in the crowds at the vintage **MOORE THEATRE** (1932 2nd Ave, Seattle; 206/467-5510; www.themoore.com) and have graced **SHOWBOX AT THE MARKET** (1426 1st Ave, Seattle; 206/628-3151; www.showboxonline.com) since 1938. In Fremont, hipsters listen to live music at **NECTAR** (412 N 36th St, Seattle; 206/632-2020; www.nectarlounge.com), **HIGH DIVE** (513 N 36th St, Ste G, Seattle; 206/632-0212; www.highdiveseattle.com), and **TOST** (513 N 36th St, Seattle; 206/547-0240; www.tostlounge.com). In Ballard, the **TRACTOR** (5213 Ballard Ave NW, Seattle; 206/789-3599; www.tractortavern.ypguides.net) books folk, alt-country, and bluegrass acts, among others.

For revelers who want to dance the night away, Belltown's futuristic **VENOM** (2218 Western Ave, Seattle; 206/448-8887; www.venomseattle.com), with a DJ who spins tunes from a capsule in the middle of the floor, and the massive **TRINITY NIGHTCLUB** (111 Yesler Wy, Seattle; 206/447-4140; www.trinitynightclub.com) in Pioneer Square both have a young, urban vibe. **RE-BAR** (1114 Howell St, Seattle; 206/233-9873; www.rebarseattle.com) offers dancing plus more offbeat diversions, and **CONTOUR** (807 1st Ave, Seattle; 206/447-7704; www.clubcontour.com) has a devoted following. One of the best destinations for burlesque, a medium that has been steadily gaining steam, is **CAN CAN** (94 Pike St, Seattle; 206/652-0832; www.thecancan.com).

Truly transcendent cocktails can be found at several notable locations: Near the Pike Place Market, **ZIG ZAG CAFÉ** (1501 Western Ave, Seattle; 206/625-1146; www.zigzagseattle.com) is famous for its extraordinary bartenders. **SUITE 410** (410 Stewart St, Seattle; 206/624-9911; www.suite410.com) is a sexy, classy, date-worthy den. Other notable downtown drink destinations include Viceroy, Del Rey, and Oliver's (in the Mayflower Park Hotel—see review). Travel farther to drink and nosh at Sambar and Licorous; attached, respectively, to **LE GOURMAND** and **LARK** (see Restaurants), these destinations are worth a visit on their own.

Beer has a loyal following in town, and brew pubs are aplenty. Try Elysian Brewing, Pyramid Alehouse (across from Safeco Field), and **PIKE PUB AND BREWERY** (1415 1st Ave, Seattle; 206/622-6044; www.pikebrewing.com). For more unusual, international selections, visit **BROUWER'S** (400 N 35th St, Seattle; 206/267-1200; www.brouwerscafe.com), with its enormous, largely Belgian selection; **FEIERABEND** (422 Yale Ave N, Seattle; 206/340-2528; www.feierabendseattle.com) for German brew (served in authentic glassware) and victuals; or **TAP HOUSE GRILL** (1506 6th Ave, Seattle; 206/816-3314; www.taphousegrill.com; also in Bellevue), which features a staggering 160 beers on tap.

Wine bars abound and help support the state's 550 wineries, and counting. For information on Washington wines, visit www.washingtonwine.org. **LOCAL VINE** (2520 2nd Ave, Seattle; 206/441-6000; www.thelocalvine.com) offers classes and a remarkable by-the-glass list; **SMASH WINE BAR & BISTRO** (1401 N 45th St, Seattle; 206/547-3232; www.smashwine.com); **IMPROMPTU WINE BAR** (4235 E Madison St, Seattle; 206/860-1569; www.impromptuwinebar.com), and **CELLAR 46** (7650 SE 27th St, Ste 120, Mercer Island; 206/407-3016; www.cellar46.com).

SPORTS AND RECREATION

Even when they don't win pennants, the **SEATTLE MARINERS** (206/346-4000; seattle.mariners.mlb.com) have a hit on their hands with the glorious open-air (plus retractable roof) **SAFECO FIELD** (1516 1st Ave S, between Royal Brougham Wy and S Atlantic St, Seattle), popular even with non-baseball fans, thanks to its public tours. The **SEATTLE SEAHAWKS** may be headquartered in Renton, but nearby **QWEST FIELD** (800 Occidental Ave S, Seattle; 206/682-2800; www.seahawks.com; www.qwestfield.com) is where the Paul Allen–owned NFL team plays their home games. The stadium has also hosted the **SEATTLE SOUNDERS** (206/622-3415 or 800/796-KICK; www.seattlesounders.net), a United Soccer League First Division team that, along with Seattle Sounders Women, now plays at **STARFIRE STADIUM** (www.starfiresports.com) in Tukwila. Beginning in 2009, Qwest Field will be home to the country's 15th Major League Soccer team, named **SEATTLE SOUNDERS FC** (877/657-4625; www.soundersfc.com); one of the franchise's minority owners is celeb and soccer fan Drew Carey. The **UNIVERSITY OF WASHINGTON HUSKIES** (Husky Stadium, 3800 Montlake Blvd NE, Seattle; 206/543-2200; www.gohuskies.com) thrill rabid fans from their aging Lake Washington–backed gridiron. The pro women's basketball team, the WNBA's **SEATTLE STORM** (206/283-DUNK; www.wnba.com/storm), which won the national championship in 2004, tips off in **KEY ARENA** (305 Harrison St, Seattle; 206/684-8582; www.seattlecenter.com) in summer.

Plenty of outdoor venues appeal to amateur athletes. Cyclists, in-line skaters, walkers, and runners work up a sweat along the 14-mile **BURKE-GILMAN TRAIL,** a paved rail-trail running from the north rim of Lake Union to the Eastside along the northwest shore of Lake Washington. Along the trail, the **BICYCLE CENTER** (4529 Sand Point Wy NE, Seattle; 206/523-8300) rents bikes and skates. For a map of Seattle bike routes, contact the city **BICYCLE AND PEDESTRIAN PROGRAM** (206/684-7583; www.seattle.gov/transportation/bikeprogram.htm). Kayakers, rowers, and canoeists ply the waters of **LAKE UNION** and **LAKE WASHINGTON**. Rent a kayak from **NORTHWEST OUTDOOR CENTER** (2100 Westlake Ave N, Ste 1, Seattle; 206/281-9694 or 800/683-0637; www.nwoc.com) or a canoe at the **UNIVERSITY OF WASHINGTON WATERFRONT ACTIVITIES CENTER** (206/543-9433; http://depts.washington.edu/ima/IMA_wac.php). Contact the U.S. Forest Service's **OUTDOOR RECREATION INFORMATION CENTER** (206/470-4060; www.nps.gov/ccso/oric.htm) for assistance with trip planning.

RESTAURANTS

Agua Verde Café & Paddle Club / ★★

1303 NE BOAT ST, SEATTLE; 206/545-8570
Even on the grayest days, this waterfront café feels like sun-drenched Baja, thanks to brightly colored walls and a deck overlooking Portage Bay. Around lunchtime expect a crowd; on sunny afternoons, paddlers who've rented kayaks from the club downstairs arrive for après-workout margaritas. The menu

features Baja classics—fish tacos, salads, ceviche—and plenty of vegetarian plates. We love the *tacos de mero*: grilled Alaskan halibut and shredded cabbage drizzled with avocado sauce. *$; DIS, MC, V; checks OK; lunch, dinner Mon–Sat; full bar; reservations recommended (dinner only); www.aguaverde. com; U District.*

Black Bottle / ★★↟

2600 1ST AVE, SEATTLE; 206/441-1500
Self-described as a "gastro-tavern," this popular 21-and-over Belltown joint is dim, loud, and a lot of fun, and they serve food late. An eclectic array of dishes—meats, seafood, flatbread—is intended for passing around the table, so the more friends you bring, the more you can sample. Don't miss the blasted broccoli: even George H. W. Bush might like this version. Scarf enough cruciferous greens, and ordering the peach-blueberry kettle tart drenched with fresh cream will feel almost guilt-free. *$$–$$$; AE, DC, DIS, MC, V; no checks; dinner every day; full bar; reservations recommended; www. blackbottleseattle.com; Belltown, at Vine St.*

Boat Street Cafe / ★★★

3131 WESTERN AVE, STE 301, SEATTLE; 206/632-4602
The name endures, even though this charming French-inspired restaurant hasn't been situated on Boat Street for many a year. Chef-owner Renee Erickson has a deservedly loyal following that trek to this unobtrusive location for a table inside her bright, shabby-chic dining room. Start with the pâté or famous Boat Street pickle plate, move on to roasted chicken with tarragon and vinegar sauce, and always save room for dessert, like the classic sour cherry clafoutis. *$$$; AE, DC, DIS, MC, V; no checks; brunch, lunch every day, dinner Tues–Sat; beer and wine; reservations recommended; www.boatstreetcafe.com; lower Queen Anne, between Denny Wy and Bay St.* &

BOKA Kitchen + Bar / ★★★

1010 1ST AVE (HOTEL 1000), SEATTLE; 206/357-9000
With walls that rotate through a range of muted colors, this too-too-sexy room in a high-tech hotel has a cool L.A. feel. Short rib sliders, truffle fries, and mac 'n' cheese—all irresistible—are served in sizes that won't ruin the calorie budget; on the entrée menu, look for the crispy Muscovy duck leg and wild salmon on lentils. If the bar's too scenesterish, cross the lobby to the laid-back Studio 1000 for more-sedate drinks and bites. The Vintimate wine dinners allow guests to sup with some of Washington's talented winemakers. *$$$; AE, DIS, MC, V; no checks; lunch Mon–Fri, dinner every day, brunch Sat–Sun; full bar; reservations recommended; www.bokaseattle.com; downtown, at Madison St.* &

Brasa / ★★★

2107 3RD AVE, SEATTLE; 206/728-4220
In a spacious, two-level dining room, James Beard Award–winning chef Tamara Murphy offers a broad Mediterranean menu with a big dollop of

integrity: she believes in local, organic ingredients and honoring the animals, such as Whistling Train Farm pigs, that give their lives to feed her guests. Also look for dishes like paella and Lopez Island Wagyu beef bolognese. During the daily happy hour, the lounge fills up with savvy diners supping on the entire bar menu at half price. *$$$; AE, DC, MC, V; no checks; dinner every day; full bar; reservations recommended; www.brasa.com; Belltown, near Lenora St.*&

Cactus / ★★☆

2820 ALKI AVE SW, SEATTLE (AND BRANCHES); 206/933-6000
Across from Alki Beach, the big, bustling Cactus is warm and inviting in cool-weather months and refreshingly breezy in summer, when the huge glass garage door–windows are rolled open. Favorite Mexican and Southwest dishes include the poblano *chile rellenos*, the Navajo *torta* made with Indian fry bread, and the butternut squash enchilada. Everything tastes a little better washed down with a salt-rimmed margarita. Other locations are in Madison Park (4220 E Madison St, Seattle; 206/324-4140) and the Eastside (121 Park Ln, Kirkland; 425/893-9799). *$$–$$$; AE, MC, V; no checks; lunch, dinner every day; full bar; reservations recommended for 6 or more; www.cactus restaurants.com; West Seattle, at 63rd Ave SW.* &

Café Flora / ★★☆

2901 E MADISON ST, SEATTLE; 206/325-9100
A meat-free vegetarian's delight, but even devout carnivores don't complain when they're served coconut tofu with sweet chile sauce, truffle pizza, or portobello Wellington, a mushroom version of the classic beef tenderloin preparation. At brunch, order beignets or gingerbread pancakes. Café Flora, known for giving back generously to the community, proudly supports local producers and businesses. And did we mention the beignets? *$$–$$$; MC, V; local checks only; lunch Mon–Fri, dinner every day, brunch Sat–Sun; beer and wine; reservations for large groups only (phone-in wait list); www.cafeflora. com; Madison Valley at 29th Ave E.* &

Campagne / ★★★

86 PINE ST, SEATTLE; 206/728-2800
Tucked away in a Pike Place Market courtyard, Campagne's candlelit dining room with cherry-wood floors and yellow walls evokes southern France. Chef Daisley Gordon blends Northwest influences into French fare—think wild mushrooms with house-made gnocchi or roasted leg of lamb with chickpea purée, red pepper, and artichoke and red-wine relish. Hazelnut crème brûlée with a Breton sable cookie is heaven. Downstairs is the more bistro-ish, slightly lower priced Café Campagne (1600 Post Alley, Seattle; 206/728-2233), also open for lunch and wildly popular weekend brunch. *$$$; AE, DC, MC, V; no checks; dinner every day; full bar; reservations recommended; www. campagnerestaurant.com; in courtyard of Inn at the Market.* &

Canlis / ★★★★

2576 AURORA AVE N, SEATTLE; 206/283-3313
A favorite for the most special occasions, thanks to its beautiful, elegant interior, impeccable service, and breathtaking Lake Union views, family-owned Canlis has been offering Seattle legendary, memorable dining since 1950. Even the parking valets astound. Dubbing itself the "birthplace of Northwest cuisine," Canlis serves dishes like escargot in puff pastry, oysters on the half shell, and wild king salmon with hazelnut-caper butter. The much-lauded wine list has bottles starting at around $20 and soaring to $12,500 (a 1990 Burgundy). Even without wine, dinner doesn't come cheap; for considerably less, soak in the Canlis ambience over a perfectly crafted cocktail and snacks in the piano bar. *$$$$; AE, DC, DIS, MC, V; checks OK; dinner Mon–Sat; full bar; reservations required; www.canlis.com; Queen Anne, just south of Aurora bridge.* &

Carmelita / ★★★

7314 GREENWOOD AVE N, SEATTLE; 206/706-7703
Here is a vegetarian restaurant that even a carnivore can love, thanks to innovative, seasonal menus and attention to detail. (On cool evenings, garden patio diners can wrap themselves in blankets provided by the restaurant.) Art fills this casually elegant restaurant owned by Kathryn Neumann and Michael Hughes. Find entrées like leek and Gruyère tart with frisée salad, caper vinaigrette, and potato *galette*, or pizza with cauliflower pesto, fresh mozzarella, Romano, pickled peppers, and broccoli sprouts. On "Wine Down" Wednesdays, all bottles are half price. *$$; MC, V; no checks; dinner Tues–Sun; beer and wine; reservations recommended; www.carmelita.net; Phinney Ridge, near 73rd St.* &

Cascadia Restaurant / ★★★

2328 1ST AVE, SEATTLE; 206/448-8884
Chef-owner Kerry Sear uses the finest ingredients and flavors to create deliciously simple fare that he serves in a lovely, serene dining room with a waterfall window. The menu, both regional and far-flung, features such à la carte options as ginger lobster spring rolls, caramelized spice-rubbed king salmon, and roasted organic chicken with black truffles. Six-course tasting menus, one vegetarian, are also available. Packed during happy hour, the bar is renowned for its addictive miniburgers. *$$$$; AE, DC, DIS, MC, V; no checks; dinner Mon–Sat; full bar; reservations recommended; www.cascadiarestaurant.com; Belltown, between Bell and Battery sts.* &

Crave / ★★★

1621 12TH AVE, SEATTLE; 206/388-0526
Modern comfort food rules the roost at this little laid-back eatery at the front of the Capitol Hill Arts Center. Chef-owner Robin Leventhal's eclectic menu is delectable, from puffy apple Dutch babies to the must-have Reuben to shiitake mac 'n' cheese. The kitchen uses free-range, grass-fed, organic meats; artisan breads and cheeses; and local produce when possible. At press time the

SEATTLE RESTAURANTS WITH A VIEW

SALTY'S ON ALKI offers the most all-encompassing view of the downtown skyline and waterfront and, in addition to being known for warm service, succulent seafood, and a wonderful wine list, puts on a weekend buffet brunch that is counted among the most spectacular in the nation. Hop on the **ELLIOTT BAY WATER TAXI** (Pier 55, 1101 Alaskan Wy, Seattle; 206/553-3000; transit.metrokc. gov; May–Oct), which, after a 12-minute crossing, drops you right next to Salty's at **SEACREST PARK** (1660 Harbor Ave SW, Seattle).

Across the bay, **ANTHONY'S PIER 66** (2201 Alaskan Wy, Seattle; 206/448-6688; www.anthonys.com) offers an elevated perch for panoramic views of Seattle's working waterfront and the Olympic Mountains. At this flagship of the Anthony's restaurant empire, the global menu features everything from Asian-influenced seafood, such as sake-steamed ginger Penn Cove mussels, to Pacific Northwest classics, like planked halibut and wild salmon. Downstairs, the casual **BELL STREET DINER** (2201 Alaskan Wy; 206/448-6688) is very family friendly, and there's a walk-up fish bar for to-go orders. Whichever you choose, dine outside in warm weather.

At Pier 70 to the north, right next to the **OLYMPIC SCULPTURE PARK**, lies **WATERFRONT SEAFOOD GRILL**, also offering spectacular bay-and-mountain views. Although it's seafood-centric, chops and steaks at this sister restaurant to El Gaucho are predictably excellent. Sit on the deck over the water if weather allows, and order the pyrotechnic Emerald City Volcano for dessert, only prepared after dark for maximum effect.

restaurant's future was unknown. *$$–$$$; AE, MC, V; no checks; breakfast, lunch Mon–Fri, dinner every day, brunch Sat–Sun; beer and wine; reservations recommended; www.cravefood.com; between Olive Wy and Pine St.*

Crémant / ★★★☆

1423 34TH AVE, SEATTLE; 206/322-4600
This French eatery appeals to Francophiles and foodies alike, with classic bistro fare from coq au vin to cassoulet, served in generous portions by a smooth, talented staff. Start with a glass of *crémant* (French sparkling wine from regions other than Champagne). Dive into divine French onion soup through a layer of bubbled, brown Gruyère; savor flavorful, bacon-wrapped country pâté or *salade d'endive* with Roquefort and walnuts. Whatever you do, get the *pommes frites*. Surroundings are modern, a bit whimsical, and on the loud side. *$$$; MC, V; no checks; dinner Tues–Sun; full bar; reservations recommended; www.cremantseattle.com/info.html; Madrona, near Union St.* ♿

To say that the reputation of the **SPACE NEEDLE**'s restaurant has been uneven, historically speaking, is putting it mildly: you can't count on the food being exceptionally good, but you *can* count on it being exceptionally expensive. That said, on a clear evening at sunset, **SKYCITY AT THE NEEDLE** (400 Broad St, Seattle Center; 206/905-2100; www.spaceneedle.com/restaurant) offers—at an elevation of 500 feet—some of the most spectacular vistas of any restaurant in the world; during the course of a two-hour meal, you get to see all of Seattle laid out before you, twice.

Popular with prom-goers and special-occasion celebrants, tourist-pleaser **PALISADE** (2601 W Marina Pl, Seattle; 206/285-1000; www.palisaderestaurant.com) in Magnolia, north and slightly west of downtown, offers an eye-catching interior—with oversize glass art, a Japanese garden, and a flowing, koi-stocked pond—that rivals the outside distractions. The menu sports a Polynesian theme. Downstairs is the casual, family-friendly **MAGGIE BLUFFS** (206/283-8322; www.r-u-i.com/mag), with a stellar patio. Insider's tip: For an even better look at downtown, during daylight hours the **ELLIOTT BAY MARINA** (www.elliottbaymarina.net) is obliged to provide free shuttle boat service between Pier G and the observation platform on the breakwater sheltering the marina.

Due to the front-row views of watercraft sailing to and from the Ship Canal via the **HIRAM M. CHITTENDEN LOCKS**, marine aficionados flock to stalwart **RAY'S BOATHOUSE** and the wildly popular **RAY'S CAFÉ** upstairs, whose long, narrow deck is a must-visit destination for throngs of Seattleites once warm weather arrives. (They even provide lap blankets for chilly evenings.)

—Ginny Morey

Crow / ★★☆

823 5TH AVE N, SEATTLE; 206/283-8800

A lively bistro with a clever, seasonal menu is definitely something to crow about. Pan-roasted chicken is delicious, as is the house lasagne. The best seats, especially for solo diners, are at the bar facing the open kitchen. Crows are part of the decor, but evidence of Crow's warehouse past remains: the room can get a bit loud. For a different scene, head to sister restaurant Betty (1507 Queen Anne Ave N, Seattle; 206/352-3773) at the top of the hill: some people like it even better. *$$$; MC, V; no checks; dinner every day; full bar; reservations recommended; www.crowandbetty.com; lower Queen Anne, at Valley St.* ♿

Crush / ★★★

2319 E MADISON ST, SEATTLE; 206/302-7874

In a stylishly renovated 1903 Tudor-Victorian house, chef Jason Wilson serves seasonal "modern American" fare. The menu is inspired by the freshest local, artisanal, organic ingredients and may include slow-braised short ribs with potato purée or peppered rare ahi tuna with pork belly–braised beans. Other specialties include house-made chocolates and gourmet cheeses. Crush is quite a scene, particularly on weekends. By all means, sip a delicious cocktail in the bar while you wait to be seated, but be wary of jostling elbows. *$$$; AE, DIS, MC, V; no checks; dinner Tues–Sat; full bar; reservations recommended; www.crushonmadison.com; Madison Valley, near 23rd Ave E.*

Dahlia Lounge / ★★★

2001 4TH AVE, SEATTLE; 206/682-4142
Sophisticated yet comfortable, Dahlia is regarded as celebrity chef Tom Douglas's flagship, though other destinations in his empire (Etta's Seafood, Palace Kitchen, Lola, Serious Pie) are equally praiseworthy. The menu changes daily, but expect the likes of roasted monkfish with sweet-corn sauce and chanterelle mushroom hash, squash ravioli, or Oregon Country Beef flatiron steak. Dungeness crab cakes and coconut cream pie merit their iconic status, as does the bag of doughnuts fried to order, served with vanilla mascarpone. If there's no room for a postlunch sweet, take home a treat from Dahlia Bakery (206/441-4540) next door. *$$$; AE, DC, DIS, MC, V; no checks; lunch Mon–Fri, dinner every day; full bar; reservations recommended; www.tomdouglas. com; downtown, at Virginia St.* &

El Gaucho / ★★★

2505 1ST AVE, SEATTLE; 206/728-1337
Swanky, sultry El Gaucho is one of the best steak houses in America. Patrons, seated on comfy, mink-lined banquettes, feast on prepared-tableside caesar salad or bananas Foster and any number of (trademarked) Angus beef prime cuts served with classic sides. In the bar, a well-dressed crowd sips cocktails and wine from a lauded list. The Pampas Room downstairs, open for dancing and drinking on Friday and Saturday, serves the full El Gaucho menu, and the boutique inn upstairs offers lodging. *$$$$; AE, MC, V; no checks; dinner every day; full bar; reservations recommended; www.elgaucho.com; Belltown, at Wall St.* &

Elliott's Oyster House / ★★★

1201 ALASKAN WY, PIER 56, SEATTLE; 206/623-4340
Elliott's annual Oyster New Year, observed the first Saturday in November, is a world-class all-you-can-slurp pig-out; they also serve 6,000 oysters weekly and have a progressive oyster happy hour on weekdays. But this 30-plus-year-old restaurant—with updated nautical decor and windows overlooking tourist-boat docks—offers much more than bivalves, appealing to locals and visitors alike. Wild salmon preparations and crab cakes are notably exceptional, as is their white wine list and prodigious rum collection. *$$$; AE, DC, DIS, MC, V; no checks; lunch, dinner every day; full bar; reservations recommended; www. elliottsoysterhouse.com; waterfront, at Seneca St.* &

Flying Fish / ★★★

2234 1ST AVE, SEATTLE; 206/728-8595
Even on nights when neighboring Belltown joints are quiet, the stylish Flying Fish usually seems busy. (For optimum people watching, request a table on the mezzanine level.) The seafood-dominated menu employs raw ingredients that are 100 percent organic or harvested in the wild for each order of lobster ravioli or crispy calamari with honey-jalapeño mayonnaise. Large parties opt for to-be-shared platters for family-style camaraderie. The restaurant also features a select late-night menu. *$$$; AE, MC, V; no checks; lunch Mon–Fri, dinner every day; full bar; reservations recommended; www.flyingfishseattle. com; Belltown, at Bell St.* &

Harvest Vine / ★★★☆

2701 E MADISON ST, SEATTLE; 206/320-9771
Joseba Jimenez de Jimenez's Spanish tapas draw raves from locals and visiting celeb chefs alike. Start with a glass of fino sherry and order *platitos* from more than two dozen seasonally inspired hot and cold options. Simply superb are the pan-seared duck breast and the caramelized chickpeas with cumin tomato sauce. The chef's wife and award-winning pastry *patrona*, Carolin Messier de Jimenez, innovates classic Spanish and Basque desserts. For a more casual and equally marvelous experience, check out their second venue, Txori (2207 2nd Ave, Seattle; 206/204-9771; www.txoribar.com), which features small bites from northern Spain (*pintxos*). *$$$–$$$$; MC, V; checks OK; dinner every day; beer and wine; reservations recommended; www.harvestvine.com; Madison Valley, at 27th Ave E.*

Hing Loon / ★★☆

628 S WELLER ST, SEATTLE; 206/682-2828
While the fluorescent-lit surroundings are the opposite of cozy, here the service is friendly and attentive, and the cheap Chinese food is delicious. Read from the handwritten paper menus on the walls to order specials like salt-and-pepper tofu, lamb and mushroom hot pots, and a myriad of excellent seafood. (The full menu exceeds seven pages.) Overwhelmed? You can't miss with any of Hing Loon's noodle dishes, green onion pancakes, or sizzling eggplant. *$; MC, V; no checks; lunch, dinner every day; beer and wine; no reservations; Chinatown–International District, near 6th Ave S.* &

How to Cook a Wolf / ★★☆

2208 QUEEN ANNE AVE N, SEATTLE; 206/838-8090
Named for the classic M. F. K. Fisher title, this extremely popular, clubby, cub-sized dining room is big on flavor. It's chef-owner Ethan Stowell's third venture (after Tavolata and Union—see review); he's clearly got a finger on Seattle's food pulse. The size means no reservations, but diners are willing to queue up for an array of mostly small plates, like roasted fingerling potatoes with fried duck egg or cauliflower agnolotti. Pop around the corner to Opal (2 Boston St, Seattle; 206/282-0142) for a drink while you wait. *$$–$$$; AE,*

MC, V; no checks; dinner Thurs–Mon; beer and wine; no reservations; www. howtocookawolf.com; Queen Anne, near W Boston St.

Il Terrazzo Carmine / ★★★

411 1ST AVE S, SEATTLE; 206/467-7797

Il Terrazzo boasts a loyal clientele that considers this Seattle's best Italian restaurant. The long-devoted sup and sip here, at discreetly spaced tables set against European draperies, while business types dominate lunch. Service is near impeccable, but the main attraction is the food: classic preparations like cannelloni filled with veal and spinach bubbling with ricotta, or fettuccine tossed with house-smoked salmon, mushrooms, and peas. Tiramisu is fittingly decadent. $$$; AE, DC, DIS, MC, V; no checks; lunch Mon–Fri, dinner Mon–Sat; full bar; reservations recommended; www.ilterrazzocarmine.com; Pioneer Square, near S Jackson St. &

Joule / ★★☆

1913 N 45TH ST, SEATTLE; 206/632-1913

Despite their youth, married chef-owners Seif Chirchi and Rachel Yang boast extensive restaurant experience, and their menu at this small jewel of a bistro, named after the unit of energy, is an intriguing mélange of Korean and French cuisines. Shiitake mushrooms and Bleu d'Auvergne cheese cozy up in lasagne, spicy beef soup with leeks is calmed by crème fraîche, and presentation is picture-perfect. This jolt is just what the neighborhood needs. $$–$$$; AE, DIS, MC, V; no checks; dinner Tues–Sun; beer and wine; reservations recommended; www.joulerestaurant.com; Wallingford, near Meridian Ave N. &

The Kingfish Café / ★★☆

602 19TH AVE E, SEATTLE; 206/320-8757

The Coaston sisters serve sassy Southern classics in a stylish, casual space with sepia-tinted photos from the family album—including one of distant cousin Langston Hughes—adorning the tall walls. Expect a wait, but it's worth it for the likes of "Jazz It Slow Gumbo," crab-and-catfish cakes with green-tomato tartar sauce, or the famous "My Way or the Highway" buttermilk fried chicken. Save room for red velvet cake, coconut cake, or strawberry shortcake. $$–$$$; MC, V; lunch Mon–Fri, dinner every day, brunch Sat–Sun; beer and wine; no reservations; www.thekingfishcafe.com; east Capitol Hill, at E Mercer St. &

La Carta de Oaxaca / ★★

5431 BALLARD AVE NW, SEATTLE; 206/782-8722

This small, bustling restaurant with crowded communal tables and black-and-white photographs on the walls serves some of the best Mexican food in Seattle. Start with chips and your pick of dips from the salsa bar. Entrée portions are just larger than tapas size; best bets include the halibut tacos, chiles rellenos, chicken in a sweet mole negro, and sausage and potato molotes (fried tortillas). Margaritas or cerveza from the tiny bar make the often-lengthy wait for a seat more sufferable. Parking can be a challenge. *$–$$; AE, DIS, MC, V; no checks; lunch Tues–Sat, dinner Mon–Sat; full bar; no reservations; www. lacartadeoaxaca.com; Ballard, south of Market St.*

La Medusa / ★★☆

4857 RAINIER AVE S, SEATTLE; 206/723-2192

In a neighborhood that's grown steadily more "gentri-funki-fied," this cozy family friendly restaurant has been a hit since it opened in 1997. The menu is Sicilian-inspired, using both imported ingredients and the finest from local purveyors. On Wednesdays, prix-fixe Market Dinners, sourced from the seasonal Columbia City Farmers Market a half block away, are a great bargain, but also look for roasted cauliflower *gratinata* (with pine nuts, raisins, and spicy butter), a fig-anchovy-garlic-stuffed double pork chop, and spaghetti with tuna meatballs. (Kids can get their own pizza or spaghetti marinara.) *$$–$$$; MC, V; no checks; dinner Tues–Sat; beer and wine; reservations recommended; www.lamedusarestaurant.com; near S Edmunds St.* &

Lampreia / ★★★

2400 1ST AVE, SEATTLE; 206/443-3301

This sparely appointed restaurant has a near-cultish following, largely deserved, though some admittedly just don't get it. From most seats, diners can observe chef-owner Scott Carsberg in the kitchen. Many consider Carsberg, often regarded as a minimalist, a genius, each plate's presentation a work of art. Menu descriptors reflect his simple approach: "lentils from Verona served as a salad with guinea hen terrine," "thin sheets of pasta filled with foie gras in beef consommé." Service is seamless. At press time the restaurant had announced plans to move a few blocks away. *$$$$; AE, MC, V; no checks; dinner Tues–Sat; full bar; reservations recommended; www.lampreia restaurant.com; Belltown, at Battery St.* &

Lark / ★★★☆

926 12TH AVE, SEATTLE; 206/323-5275

Bring a group to this subtly elegant Capitol Hill spot with exposed wood beams and sheer curtains, and plan to linger. The delicious seasonal offerings—made from largely organic, artisanal, or foraged ingredients—are intended for sharing, but you may want to hoard favorites, such as baby beets with sherry vinegar and tangerine oil, flatiron steak with parsley salad and blue cheese, or halibut cheeks with stone-ground grits. The no-reservations policy (except for large groups) can require patience; Lark's bar is tiny, partially why James Beard Award–winning chef John Sundstrom and partners opened the luscious Licorous (928 12th Ave, Seattle; 206/325-6947; www.licorous.com), a chic bar with small plates, right next door. *$$$; MC, V; checks OK; dinner Tues–Sun; full bar; no reservations; www.larkseattle.com; near E Spring St.* &

Le Gourmand / ★★★⯪

425 NW MARKET ST, SEATTLE; 206/784-3463
Le Gourmand's modest exterior doesn't broadcast "upscale restaurant," but, remodeled early in 2008, the streamlined, modern interior makes a serene backdrop for Bruce Naftaly's fine, rich French-Northwest fare, best appreciated at a leisurely pace. Naftaly is a king of foraged and organic ingredients; depending on the season, you might enjoy earthy nettle soup or delicate leek and onion tarts crowned with juniper berries. Cross your fingers for the presence of succulent Mangalitsa pork. Exceptional cocktails and small plates (*frites* are a must) can be had at the adjoining, postage-stamp-sized lounge, Sambar (206/781-4883), with its intimate warm-weather patio. *$$$–$$$$; AE, MC, V; no checks; dinner Wed–Sat; full bar; reservations recommended; Ballard, at 6th Ave NW.* ♿

Le Pichet / ★★★

1933 1ST AVE, SEATTLE; 206/256-1499
If you're longing to re-create your last stay in Paris' fifth arrondissement—*sans* the agonizing exchange rate—this narrow, cheek-to-jowl bistro is ideal. Avoid peak meal times (there's little space to spare), and you can relax with the newspaper over a repast of country-style pork pâté (with honey, walnuts, and crusty baguette), onion soup lyonnaise, or broiled eggs with ham and Gruyère. Chicken is roasted to order. Wines are available by the glass, *demi-pichet, pichet*, or bottle. Also visit *très charmant* sister restaurant Café Presse (1117 12th Ave, Seattle; 206/709-7674; www.cafepresseseattle.com) on Capitol Hill. *$$–$$$; MC, V; no checks; breakfast, lunch, dinner every day; full bar; reservations recommended (dinner only); www.lepichetseattle.com; Belltown, near Virginia St.*

Macrina Bakery & Café / ★★

2408 1ST AVE, SEATTLE (AND BRANCHES); 206/448-4032
Seattleites head here for extraordinary treats: fresh breads, pastries, cakes, and espresso. Homemade bread pudding with fresh fruit and cream or housemade granola make great starts to a day; lunch offerings include salads and sandwiches on fresh bread. The cozy café's founder and James Beard Award nominee, Leslie Mackie, reveals baking secrets in her *Macrina Bakery and Café Cookbook*. Other locations include Queen Anne (615 W McGraw St, Seattle; 206/283-5900). *$; MC, V; no checks; breakfast, lunch Mon–Fri, brunch Sat–Sun; beer and wine; no reservations; www.macrinabakery.com; Belltown, between Battery and Wall sts.* ♿

Malay Satay Hut / ★★

212 12TH AVE S, SEATTLE (AND BRANCHES); 206/324-4091
At this strip-mall joint in Seattle's Little Saigon, Malaysia meets China, India, and Thailand, and the tantalizing result is flavorful curries, wontons, stir-fries, and satays. Order the favorite *roti canai*, Indian flatbread served with a potato-chicken curry sauce, or Buddha's Yam Pot, a chicken, shrimp, and vegetable

stir-fry in a deep-fried basket of grated yams. *$–$$; MC, V; no checks; lunch, dinner every day; beer and wine; reservations recommended; www.malaysatay hut.com; Chinatown–International District, at Jackson St.* &

Matt's in the Market / ★★☆

94 PIKE ST, 3RD FLOOR, SEATTLE; 206/467-7909

Matt's expanded its once tiny space on the third floor of the Corner Market Building and has lost none of its popularity. There's hardly a more quintessential Seattle view than from a window table overlooking the Pike Place Market. The kitchen turns out well-crafted food that's some of downtown's freshest—chefs shop the market twice daily. Seafood is the best bet: try rare-seared albacore, filé gumbo, or clams and mussels in an ouzo-infused broth. *$$$; MC, V; no checks; lunch, dinner Mon–Sat; beer and wine; reservations recommended; www.mattsinthemarket.com; at 1st Ave.*

Monsoon / ★★☆

615 19TH AVE E, SEATTLE; 206/325-2111

Like the prevailing wind after which this restaurant is named, the menu changes seasonally, but look for signatures like spring rolls stuffed with Dungeness crab or tamarind soup with chicken and gulf shrimp. Share the five-spice flank steak with Chinese celery and hothouse tomatoes, the oven-baked Asian eggplant, or the seared scallops with bok choy and black-bean sauce. Waits can be long, and the dining room is noisy when full, somehow more fitting during the dim sum weekend brunch. *$$; AE, DC, DIS, MC, V; no checks; dinner every day, brunch Sat–Sun; beer and wine; reservations recommended; www.monsoonseattle.com; east Capitol Hill, near Mercer St.* &

Nell's Restaurant / ★★★

6804 E GREENLAKE WY N, SEATTLE; 206/524-4044

Near-northenders embrace Nell's, a calm, warmly elegant bilevel dining room that would look perfectly at home in Belltown. From a glassed-in kitchen, chef-owner Philip Mihalski marries classical training with fresh, seasonal simplicity, and the results are often marvelous. Look for dishes like sweetbreads, sweet onion tart, and pork tenderloin with roasted pears. In addition to a rotating tasting menu, the restaurant regularly hosts special multicourse dinners paying homage to famous chefs, from the likes of Julia Child to Vincent Price. *$$$; AE, DC, DIS, MC, V; no checks; dinner every day; full bar; reservations recommended; www.nellsrestaurant.com; at 2nd Ave NE.* &

Nishino / ★★★

3130 E MADISON ST, SEATTLE; 206/322-5800

A favorite among Japanese food lovers, this inviting dining room has high walls that are decorated with big, splashy paintings, a fine echo of the artistic composition of each plate. Chef Tatsu Nishino, who opened this restaurant near the arboretum in 1995, certainly has the chops: he helmed the kitchen at Nobu Matsuhisa's original L.A. restaurant. Adventurous diners can't go wrong with the *omakase* (Japanese for "leave it to me") dinner, in which the chef creates a memorable, multicourse extravaganza. *$$$; AE, MC, V; no checks; dinner every day; beer and wine; reservations recommended; www. nishinorestaurant.com; Madison Valley, near Lake Washington Blvd E.* &

The Oceanaire Seafood Room / ★★★

1700 7TH AVE, SEATTLE; 206/267-2277
Part of a national chain, this big dining room is a classic fish house with a long list of fresh-daily seafoods, an oyster bar, professional service, and decor inspired by a 1940s steamship. Expect traditional dishes—oysters Rockefeller, caviar, Dover sole, fish-and-chips—but don't overlook the inspired specials. Everything's à la carte, which can make for an expensive outing, but portions tend to be more than generous, including the towering inferno of a baked Alaska. *$$$–$$$$; AE, JCB, MC, V; no checks; lunch Mon–Fri, dinner every day; full bar; reservations recommended; www.theoceanaire.com; downtown, at Olive Wy.* &

Osteria La Spiga / ★★★

1429 12TH AVE, SEATTLE; 206/323-8881
A boisterous atmosphere makes it always seem like a party at la Spiga, a tall, spacious, L-shaped room serving dishes (some from treasured family recipes) from the Emilia-Romagna region of northern Italy. Making everyone feel like an old friend at the front of the house is Pietro Borghesi—who has also assembled a stellar Italian wine list—while his wife, Sabrina Tinsley, is the talented executive chef presiding over the kitchen, turning out favorites like Pietro's aunt Irene's eggplant, his mother Ida's tiramisu, and a bolognese ragù over tagliatelle that makes grown men weep for joy. *$$–$$$; AE, MC, V; no checks; dinner every day; full bar; reservations recommended; www.laspiga. com; Capitol Hill, between Pike and Union sts.* &

Palace Kitchen / ★★

2030 5TH AVE, SEATTLE; 206/448-2001
The mural on this restaurant's south wall is a tip-off to owner Tom Douglas's inspiration: the 17th-century image depicts scullery maids and servants feasting on roast meats and guzzling red wine in the "palace kitchen." Sit at the large horseshoe bar and order shareables like the spicy grilled chicken wings, or for a meal try the *plin*, tender raviolis with chard and sausage, their legendary burger, or one of the night's specials from the applewood grill. The full menu is served until 1am. *$$; AE, DC, DIS, MC, V; no checks; dinner every day; full bar; reservations recommended for 6 or more; www.tomdouglas.com; Belltown, at Lenora St.* &

Ponti Seafood Grill / ★★★

3014 3RD AVE N, SEATTLE; 206/284-3000
Open since 1990, Ponti is a class act. The restaurant's design is reminiscent of an Italian villa, a likeness most evident on warm summer evenings, when

you're relaxing on the sheltered patio with its delightful view of the Fremont Bridge. Seasonal offerings are creative, but signature favorites, such as Dungeness crab spring rolls and Thai curry penne (with crab, grilled scallops, and sweet-tart tomato-ginger chutney) are forever. For quality and price, their popular happy hour's one of the best in town: don't miss the wild salmon slider with absolutely perfect shoestring fries. *$$$; AE, JCB, MC, V; no checks; dinner every day; full bar; reservations recommended; www.pontiseafoodgrill. com; north Queen Anne, off Nickerson St.* &

Purple Café and Wine Bar / ★★
1225 4TH AVE, SEATTLE; 206/829-2280
This glam, impossibly tall room, dominated by a climate-controlled wine storage "tower" smack-dab in the middle, gives downtown Seattle a decided L.A./New York flavor. Take a love seat at the mezzanine level to spy on the action below. The best way to dine is by snacking, grazing, and sharing: look for terrific cheeses and the tapas-style tasting menu, including petite desserts. Even though the wine menu is huge, with around 90 by-the-glass choices alone, they're all about approachability—it's a snobbery-free zone. *$$–$$$; AE, DIS, MC, V; no checks; lunch, dinner every day; full bar; reservations recommended; www.thepurplecafe.com; at University St.* &

Racha Noodles & Thai Cuisine / ★★
23 MERCER ST, SEATTLE (AND BRANCHES); 206/281-8883
As implied in its name, this richly decorated dining room (and somewhat sexy lounge) serves an array of noodle types and widths on its broad menu: decision-making is a challenge, but nearly everything is delicious. Lunch combinations are offered, too, including the likes of catfish *panang* and or red curry chicken served with phad thai and the option of either brown rice or jasmine rice. Other locations are in Woodinville, Olympia, and at Southcenter (Westfield) shopping mall, in Woodinville, and in Olympia (see Web site for details). *$$; AE, MC, V; no checks; lunch, dinner every day; full bar; reservations recommended; www. rachathai.com; Queen Anne, at 1st Ave N.* &

Ray's Boathouse / ★★★
6049 SEAVIEW AVE NW, SEATTLE; 206/789-3770
Regional seafood dominates the menu at this bona fide institution on Shilshole Bay. Journeying to and from the Chittenden Locks, fishing vessels and pleasure craft glide by the windows of the candlelit dining room, enhancing the subtly nautical theme. Seafood, like the signature Chatham Strait sake *kasu* sablefish (black cod), is usually wild and always fresh. Upstairs, Ray's Café (206/782-0094), with its popular deck, serves lower-priced, lighter fare—fish-and-chips, burgers, clam linguine—and its bar hosts a bustling happy hour. *$$$; AE, DC, DIS, MC, V; checks OK; lunch, dinner every day; full bar; reservations recommended; www.rays.com; Ballard.* &

Restaurant Zoë / ★★☆

2137 2ND AVE, SEATTLE; 206/256-2060
Named after owners Scott and Heather Staples's daughter, Zoë is a lively (sometimes a bit too loud) urban bistro that runs like a well-oiled machine, front of house and back. Dishes rotate on the varied and inventive seasonal, meat-lovers' menus, but favorite ingredients like English peas, wild mushrooms, heirloom tomatoes, fingerling potatoes, and figs are regarded as old friends. For a slightly younger vibe, visit Chef Staples's more casual venture on Capitol Hill, the hip and edgy gastropub Quinn's (1001 E Pike St, Seattle; 206/325-7711; www.quinnspubseattle.com), named for his son, where guests sup on braised oxtails and wild boar sloppy joes. *$$$; AE, MC, V; checks OK; dinner every day; full bar; reservations recommended; www.restaurantzoe. com; Belltown, at Blanchard St.* &

Rover's / ★★★★

2808 E MADISON ST, SEATTLE; 206/325-7442
"Chef in the Hat" Thierry Rautureau has won the hearts of Seattleites with his divine French fare; foodies from afar also make pilgrimages to his nationally renowned restaurant tucked away in the tony Madison Valley retail district. Each plate is a perfectly composed work of art. Rautureau uses stocks, reductions, herb-infused oils, and purées to enhance steamed Maine lobster, breasts of quail, or the requisite foie gras—offerings that may appear on one of the extraordinary prix-fixe menus (except the vegetarian). The wine collection is nothing short of stunning. *$$$$; AE, MC, V; no checks; lunch Fri, dinner Tues–Sat; beer and wine; reservations required; www.rovers-seattle. com; near 28th Ave E.* &

Saito's Japanese Café & Bar / ★★★

2120 2ND AVE, SEATTLE; 206/728-1333
On any given night in this smart Belltown place, you might see the Japanese ambassador or Mariners superstar Ichiro Suzuki. They come for Saito-san's sushi, arguably the best in town, matched by an outstanding sake collection. The fish is fresh and cut thicker than you'll usually find in Seattle, and hot items are innovative. Try the butter *itame*, a geoduck sauté with sugar snap peas and shiitake mushrooms. Save room for the sampler of house-made green tea, mango, or sweet plum ice creams. *$$$; AE, DIS, E, MC, V; no checks; dinner Tues–Sat; full bar; reservations recommended; www.saitos-cafe. com; near Lenora St.* &

Salumi / ★★★

309 3RD AVE S, SEATTLE; 206/621-8772
In the late 1990s, Armandino Batali (father of celeb chef Mario Batali) opened up shop and began curing such delights as *coppa*, mole salami, lamb "prosciutto," flavor-filled *finocchiona*, spicy *soppressata*, lamb and orange sausage, and *culatello*, rare outside Italy. Eat in or take out; the meatball sandwich, piled high with sautéed peppers and onions, is a favorite. Expect

lines out the door of this narrow storefront and limited, communal seating at lunch. If the crowds are too daunting, look for Salumi's cured meats in restaurants all over the city. *$–$$; AE, MC, V; checks OK; lunch Tues–Fri, dinner Sat; beer and wine; reservations required; www.salumicuredmeats.com; Pioneer Square, near Main St.*

Sazerac / ★★☆

1101 4TH AVE, SEATTLE; 206/624-7755
Louisiana's a bit far to go for dinner, but Sazerac, named for the iconic N'awlins cocktail (and decorated in rich ruby hues to match), is happy to provide a little down-home hospitality. The dining room is big and lively, and the menu mixes Southern flavors with Northwest bounty and inspiration: crispy catfish—flavored with jalapeño-lime butter—farmed in neighboring Idaho. If available, the fall-off-the-bone, applewood-smoked ribs are fantastic. Gumbo? But of course. And the individual "oooey gooey chocolate cakes" speak for themselves. *$$$; AE, DC, DIS, MC, V; no checks; breakfast, lunch Mon–Fri, dinner every day, brunch Sat–Sun; full bar; reservations recommended; www.sazeracrestaurant.com; downtown, at Spring St.* &

Sitka & Spruce / ★★★

2238 EASTLAKE AVE E, SEATTLE; 206/324-0662
Chef Matthew Dillon's tiny storefront offers dining at its most convivial. There's but a handful of tables, and a communal table dominates the center of the room; sharing tastes with strangers is part of the fun. Dillon—dubbed a 2007 "Best New Chef" by *Food & Wine*—works his magic on the freshest of seasonal ingredients, from wild morels to halibut cheeks. Check the chalkboard for the day's fare, delivered at a leisurely pace. His latest venture is the Corson Building (5609 Corson Ave S, Seattle; 206/762-3330; www.thecorsonbuilding.com) in Georgetown. *$$–$$$; MC, V; no checks; breakfast Sat–Sun, dinner Tues–Sat; full bar; reservations recommended for 5 or more; www.sitkaandspruce.com; between E Lynn and E Boston sts.*

Steelhead Diner / ★★★

95 PINE ST, SEATTLE; 206/625-0129
There's a deserved buzz about chef Kevin Davis's quintessentially market-fresh menu, perhaps best described as elegant comfort food—fried cheese curds and *poutine* (fries laden with gravy) notwithstanding. The plump, tasty crab cake is so crabby it seems held together by faith alone. An outstanding "mocktail" menu complements the cocktail list. Wild steelhead (a seagoing trout) isn't currently a sustainable species; don't expect to find it on the menu. Do, however, expect a crowd of devoted diners, the diametric opposite of "endangered." *$$$; AE, DC, DIS, MC, V; local checks only; lunch Tue–Sat, dinner Tues–Sun, brunch Sun; full bar; reservations recommended; www.steelheaddiner.com; Pike Place Market, near 1st Ave.* &

Tamarind Tree / ★★½

1036 S JACKSON ST, STE A, SEATTLE; 206/860-1404
At this always-packed Vietnamese bistro, the upscale, contemporary decor and moody lighting make for a refined setting where you wouldn't think using fingers as utensils would be encouraged. But that's what makes it fun. When the *Thang Long* yellow catfish arrives with accompaniments—rice crackers, roasted peanuts, lettuce, carrots, and a mountain of fresh herbs—assemble a lettuce-leaf burrito and munch away. Fresh Tamarind Tree salad rolls are so good you'll order more for dessert; don't miss the piquant Tamarintini cocktail. *$–$$; MC, V; no checks; lunch, dinner every day; full bar; no reservations; www.tamarindtreerestaurant.com; Chinatown–International District, in Asian Plaza near 12th Ave.* &

Tilth / ★★★½

1411 N 45TH ST, SEATTLE; 206/633-0801
Housed on the main floor of a Craftsman bungalow, Tilth is a bit crowded and fittingly homey, a must for dyed-in-the-wool food aficionados. The second restaurant ever certified organic by the Oregon Tilth association, chef Maria Hines's sweet eatery gives vegetables, local and/or foraged, top billing with extraordinary meats and wild fishes. The mini duck burgers are a tasty twist on a trendy favorite. All main courses are available in two sizes, which facilitates sampling and sharing. *$$$; MC, V; no checks; brunch Sat–Sun, dinner Tues–Sun; full bar; reservations recommended; www.tilthrestaurant.com; Wallingford, near Interlake Ave N.*

Union / ★★★½

1400 1ST AVE, SEATTLE; 206/838-8000
Chef-owner Ethan Stowell's first—and most elegant—of three restaurants, Union brings together a wonderful wine selection and the finest and freshest of ingredients on a daily-changing menu that reads like a regional culinary tour. Start with geoduck or Totten Inlet *Crassostrea virgincas* (judged the best-tasting overall in a 2008 national oyster competition); share a plate of agnolotti with hazelnuts, sage, and brown butter; and fight over the last bite of seared sea scallops with parsnip-apple purée and red cabbage. For a more casual meal, check out Tavolata (2323 2nd Ave; 206/838-8008; www.tavolata.com) and How to Cook a Wolf (see review). *$$$; AE, MC, V; no checks; dinner every day; full bar; reservations recommended; www.union seattle.com; downtown, at Union St.* &

Waterfront Seafood Grill / ★★★

2801 ALASKAN WY, PIER 70, SEATTLE; 206/956-9171
A grand, sparkling waterside location makes a fitting setting for the splashy menu and award-winning wine list at this sister restaurant to El Gaucho (see review). Steaks are top-notch (and a bona fide splurge when accompanied by king crab or Australian lobster), but most people come here for wild salmon (such as the prized Yukon River king) and halibut or starters like

fiery "Wicked Shrimp." The "Seafood Bacchanalia for Two" is everything the name implies—and more. On a warm summer's eve, there's hardly a better spot for outdoor dining than the spacious deck. *$$$–$$$$; AE, MC, V; no checks; dinner every day, brunch Sun; full bar; reservations recommended; www.waterfrontpier7o.com; between Broad and Clay sts.* &

Wild Ginger Asian Restaurant and Satay Bar / ★★

1401 3RD AVE, SEATTLE; 206/623-4450
This landmark is wildly popular, though some maintain it's overhyped. Owners Rick and Ann Yoder's culinary vision, inspired by time spent in Southeast Asia, changed the Seattle restaurant scene and pan-Asian cuisine everywhere. Wild Ginger offers a wide range of dishes from Bangkok, Singapore, Saigon, and Jakarta. Order from skewered selections, like the mountain lamb and Saigon scallop satay, or opt for enduring favorites like monk's curry, black pepper scallops, and fragrant duck with steamed buns and plum sauce. *$$$; AE, DC, DIS, MC, V; no checks; lunch Mon–Sat, dinner every day; full bar; reservations recommended; www.wildginger.net; downtown, at Union St.* &

LODGINGS

Alexis Hotel / ★★★

1007 1ST AVE, SEATTLE; 206/624-4844 OR 866/356-8894
Given a $10 million face-lift (completed in 2007), this elegant Euro-boutique-style hotel has 121 guest rooms, including suites, and welcomes pets. The lobby and gallery showcase the Alexis "art walk" that changes quarterly, and every evening there's a wine reception for guests. North-facing rooms have a view of Elliott Bay; First Avenue rooms may be a little noisy. Perks include shoeshines, a fitness room, an on-call masseuse, and the Etherea Salon/Spa. The Library Bistro provides breakfast, brunch, and lunch; the pubby Bookstore Bar, popular with locals, boasts an impressive single-malt Scotch menu. *$$$–$$$$; AE, DC, DIS, JCB, MC, V; no checks; www.alexishotel.com; downtown, at Madison St.* &

Arctic Club Hotel / ★★★

700 3RD AVE, SEATTLE; 206/340-0340 OR 800/600-7775
Founded by a lucky few that struck it rich during the Klondike Gold Rush, the elite Arctic Club (established 1908) moved here in 1916; in 2008, this historic building was reintroduced as a grand boutique hotel: adorned with 27 distinctive walrus heads and a foyer and stairways lined in Alaskan marble, it's on the National Register of Historic Places. Art and artifacts abound. There are 120 spacious rooms and suites, 32 with jetted tubs, eight with rooftop terraces, plus a fitness room and business center. Dip into an icy beverage at the cool Polar Bar before dining in style at JUNO (206/631-8080; www.junorestaurant.com), featuring seasonal menus focused around organic, eco-friendly ingredients. *$$$$; AE, DC, DIS, MC, V; no checks; www.arcticclub hotel.com; downtown, at Cherry St.* &

The Edgewater / ★★★

2411 ALASKAN WY, PIER 67, SEATTLE; 206/728-7000 OR 800/624-0670
A waterfront landmark, the Edgewater is the only Seattle hotel that juts over the water, and it's the only venue that once allowed customers—including, most famously, the Beatles—to fish from its guest-room windows. (There's even a "Beatles Suite," ideal for Anglophiles.) All 223 rustic-chic rooms have fireplaces and log bed frames. The sleek Six Seven Restaurant & Lounge serves Northwest cuisine with pan-Asian influences amid stunning views of Elliott Bay, Puget Sound, and the Olympics. *$$$; AE, DC, DIS, JCB; MC, V; no checks; www.edgewaterhotel.com; south of Wall St.* &

Fairmont Olympic Hotel / ★★★★☆

411 UNIVERSITY ST, SEATTLE; 206/621-1700 OR 800/441-1414
On the site of the original University of Washington campus, the only AAA Five Diamond hotel in Seattle offers exceptional pampering in a 1924 Italian Renaissance icon. Luxury can be found in each of the 450 rooms and suites and in the venerable restaurant, the Georgian (206/621-7889). Amenities include twice-daily housekeeping service, full-service health club and indoor swimming pool, complimentary shoeshine, town-car service, and high-speed Internet access. The Fairmont doesn't pamper just adults; it goes out of its way for children, providing loaner Sony PlayStations, kid-sized bathrobes, and even babysitting services. *$$$$; AE, DC, DIS, JCB, MC, V; checks OK; www.fairmont.com/seattle; downtown, at 4th Ave.* &

Four Seasons Hotel / ★★★★

99 UNION ST, SEATTLE; 206/749-7000 OR 800/819-5053
The Emerald City hasn't had a Four Seasons since the Olympic Hotel (see review) was assumed by Fairmont Hotels & Resorts in 2003. Now, sited opposite the Seattle Art Museum, this sleek, modern hotel—with a full-service spa and 36 exclusive condos on the upper floors—is Seattle's hottest new lodging. State-of-the-art two-person tubs and televisions embedded in bathroom mirrors are found in each of the 149 guest rooms, 13 of which are suites. Sheltered by the building, the gorgeous pool deck, with whirlpool and fire pit, faces Elliott Bay and the Olympic Mountains. A restaurant and lounge reside on the lobby level. *$$$$; AE, DC, DIS, JCB, MC, V; no checks; www.fourseasons.com/seattle; downtown, at First Ave.* &

Hotel Ändra / ★★★

2000 4TH AVE, SEATTLE; 206/448-8600 OR 877/448-8600
This 1926 building was transformed into the contemporary Hotel Ändra, and it's luxurious yet simple: no spa, and a small gym. The 119 rooms and suites are spacious, but bathrooms tend to be tiny. Sleek and modern, rooms are decorated with a neutral-toned Swedish aesthetic. Celebrity chef Tom Douglas's Greek-inspired restaurant Lola (206/441-1430; www.tom douglas.com) is an added bonus, especially since you can sup on their food in Ändra's loft above the lobby. Popular Italian restaurant Assaggio

(2010 4th Ave, Seattle; 206/441-1399; www.assaggioseattle.com) is right downstairs as well. *$$$$; AE, DIS, MC, V; no checks; www.hotelandra.com; Belltown, near Virginia St.* &

Hotel Max / ★★★

620 STEWART ST, SEATTLE; 206/728-6299 OR 866/833-6299
This artsy, funky 163-room hotel in downtown Seattle has plenty of youth appeal. Each room has an original painting by a Northwest artist (read about them in the book in the honor bar) and a full-length photo on the door. Rock 'n' roll plays in the lobby; there's even a "grunge floor," if that says anything. Amenities are posh—a fitness center, 24-hour room service from Red Fin (206/441-4341; www.redfinsushi.com) downstairs, flat-screen LCD TVs, and special pillow and spiritual menus to personalize the experience. *$$$–$$$$; AE, DC, DIS, JCB, MC, V; no checks; www.hotelmaxseattle.com; near 6th Ave.* &

Hotel Monaco / ★★★

1101 4TH AVE, SEATTLE; 206/621-1770 OR 800/715-6513
The Monaco's 189 rooms are boldly decorated in a blend of colorful stripes and florals in Technicolor hues; Mediterranean suites feature bathrooms with two-person Fuji jet tubs. Amenities include 24-hour room and business service, leopard-print bathrobes, evening wine tastings, a fitness center, and privileges at a health club. Monaco's over-the-top personality extends to the Southern-inspired Sazerac restaurant (see review). Ask for a loaner goldfish to keep you company during your stay, or bring a four-legged friend; it's possibly the most pet-friendly hotel in town. *$$$–$$$$; AE, DC, DIS, MC, V; no checks; www.monaco-seattle.com; downtown, at Spring St.* &

Hotel 1000 / ★★★★☆

1000 1ST AVE, SEATTLE; 206/957-1000 OR 877/315-1088
This luxury hotel is high-tech and sophisticated. After your first visit, the hotel sets the preferred temperature and art preferences for your room. Just wave your key card to get in. Infrared-sensor technology tells staff if you're inside. The Golf Club "virtually" features more than 50 of the world's best courses. Decorated with an Asian-Northwest aesthetic, the 101 guest rooms and 19 suites are comfortable and soothing, and in the elegant bathrooms, fill-from-the-ceiling pedestal tubs are delightful. There's also a cozy spa, called Spaahh (206/357-9490), a reading area, a fitness center, and the inviting lounge Studio 1000, with an open fire pit, off the lobby. Be sure to dine at swanky-mod BOKA Kitchen + Bar (see review). *$$$$; AE, DIS, MC, V; no checks; www.hotel1000seattle.com; downtown, at Madison St.* &

Hotel Vintage Park / ★★★

1100 5TH AVE, SEATTLE; 206/624-8000 OR 800/624-4433
From the lobby's plush velvet settees and leather armchairs to the Chateau Ste. Michelle Suite's double-sided fireplace, the Vintage Park looks like an ideal spot to break out the smoking jacket and cravat. The 126 rooms are

named after Washington wineries and vineyards, and the hotel hosts a complimentary Northwest wine tasting every evening. Nice touches include in-room spa services, privileges at a local health club, and 24-hour room service, including lunch and dinner from the hotel's excellent Italian restaurant, Tulio (206/624-5500; www.tulio.com). The hotel sets a high standard for eco-friendly practices. *$$$; AE, DIS, MC, V; no checks; www.hotelvintagepark. com; downtown, at Spring St.* &

The Inn at El Gaucho / ★★★

2505 1ST AVE, SEATTLE; 206/728-1133 OR 866/354-2824
In a city full of multistory hotels, the Inn at El Gaucho, with its 18 cozy rooms on a single floor above the restaurant (see review), is masculine and clubby; it's a perfect urban hideaway. Have a steak and sides delivered to your room and savor each bite while reclining on a leather love seat, watching a movie on your flat-screen TV. Though rooms feel like upscale bachelor pads, both genders feel right at home. Cookies, a jazz CD, and bottled water are nice bonuses. *$$$– $$$$; AE, MC, V; no checks; www.inn.elgaucho.com; Belltown, at Wall St.*

Inn at the Market / ★★★★

86 PINE ST, SEATTLE; 206/443-3600 OR 800/446-4484
Everything about the Inn at the Market oozes quintessential Seattle atmosphere: views of Elliott Bay and the Olympics from most rooms; close proximity to bustling Pike Place Market; room service from country-French Campagne (see review). The 70 rooms are handsomely dressed in soft taupe, copper, and green and have floor-to-ceiling bay windows; four townhouse-style suites were remodeled in early 2008. The rooftop deck, a best-kept secret, is a must-see. *$$$–$$$$; AE, DC, DIS, MC, V; no checks; www.innatthemarket.com; near 1st Ave.* &

Mayflower Park Hotel / ★★

405 OLIVE WY, SEATTLE; 206/623-8700 OR 800/426-5100
Past and present come together at this handsome 1927 hotel set in the heart of the city's retail district. A member of the National Trust Historic Hotels of America, the Mayflower has a lobby decorated with antique Chinese artwork and furniture. The 171 rooms are mostly small (except suites), but offer elegant, European-style dark-wood furniture and deep tubs. Amenities include free high-speed wireless Internet access and a fitness studio. Cozy Andaluca (206/382-6999) serves outstanding Mediterranean-Northwest fare; you can also sip an award-winning martini at Oliver's, the elegant lounge. *$$–$$$; AE, DC, DIS, MC, V; checks OK; www.mayflowerpark.com; at 4th Ave.* &

Pan Pacific Hotel / ★★★

2125 TERRY AVE, SEATTLE; 206/264-8111 OR 877/324-4856
Located a short distance from the downtown core, this luxurious property of 160 rooms marries an "East meets West" design with an international standard of service: each guest is assigned a personal steward upon checking in.

Furnishings (Hypnos beds, Herman Miller chairs) and bed linens (Egyptian cotton) are top-notch. Visit the Vida Wellness Spa (888/865-2630; www. vidawellness.com) for pampered relaxation. In addition to the hotel's bar and restaurant on the lobby level, there's also a Whole Foods (206/621-9700; www.wholefoodsmarket.com) and an outpost of popular pizzeria Tutta Bella (206/624-4422; www.tuttabellapizza.com). *$$$$; AE, DC, DIS, JCB; MC, V; no checks; www.panpacific.com/seattle; South Lake Union, between Lenora St and Denny Wy.* &

Pensione Nichols / ★★☆

1923 1ST AVE, SEATTLE; 206/441-7125 OR 800/440-7125
The only bed-and-breakfast in Seattle's downtown core (just above Pike Place Market), Pensione Nichols is furnished with antiques from the 1920s and '30s; 10 guest rooms share four bathrooms. A large, appealing common room on the third floor has a spectacular view of Elliott Bay; a bountiful continental breakfast—including fresh treats from the market—is served here. Be warned: The stair climb from street level is steep. *$$; AE, DC, DIS, MC, V; checks OK; www.pensionenichols.com; between Stewart and Virginia sts.*

Sorrento Hotel / ★★★

900 MADISON ST, SEATTLE; 206/622-6400 OR 800/426/1265
When it opened in 1908, the Sorrento was a grand Italianate masterpiece holding court just east of downtown. Today, shadowed by modern, boxy buildings, the Sorrento's beauty is better appreciated in its sumptuous furnishings, marble bathrooms, and the plush, mahogany-lined Fireside Room, one of the best locales in the city for a romantic cocktail. The 76 rooms and suites are comfortably luxurious in an old-fashioned way, but offer amenities like free high-speed Internet access. The Hunt Club (206/343-6156) serves Northwest-Mediterranean cuisine and provides 24-hour in-room dining. The complimentary town car, an imported London black cab, transports guests to downtown locations. *$$$$; AE, DIS, MC, V; no checks; www.hotelsorrento. com; First Hill at Terry Ave.* &

W Seattle Hotel / ★★★

1112 4TH AVE, SEATTLE; 206/264-6000 OR 877/946-9357
Dressed in postmodern art, velvet drapes, and oversize chess sets, the W's two-story lobby is a see-and-be-seen kind of place; settle into the W Bar with a cocktail and people-watch for an hour or two. The rest of the hotel lives up to its eye-catching entryway. Taupe and black rooms are stylishly simple with stainless steel– and glass-accented bathrooms, goose-down comforters, and Zen-inspired water sculptures. In the "Extreme Wow" Suite, look out over Seattle from your Jacuzzi. You don't have to go far for great food—just cross the lobby to Earth & Ocean (206/264-6060; www.earthocean.net). *$$$$; AE, DC, DIS, JCB, MC, V; no checks; www.whotels.com; downtown, at Seneca St.* &

The Westin Seattle / ★★½

1900 5TH AVE, SEATTLE; 206/728-1000 OR 800/937-8461
The Westin's twin cylindrical towers have a '60s-era look, but the spacious guest rooms provide some of the best views in the city, especially above the 20th floor. The gargantuan size of the hotel (891 rooms and 34 suites) contributes to some lapses in service, but rooms are comfortable—after all, the Westin is renowned for the "Heavenly Bed" and "Heavenly Bath." *$$$$; AE, DC, DIS, JCB, MC, V; no checks; www.westin.com; downtown, at Stewart St.* &

The Eastside

The sprawling suburbs—and suburban cities—on the east side of Lake Washington across from Seattle are collectively known as "the Eastside." Although there's no formal designation, the primary cities are Bellevue, Redmond, Kirkland, Woodinville, and Issaquah; numerous towns and neighborhoods include Mercer Island, Clyde Hill, and Medina to the west of Bellevue; Newcastle and Sammamish to the east; even Bothell and Kenmore at the north end of Lake Washington and Renton to the south. Plenty of people, families in particular, love living on the Eastside enough to brave the harrowing daily commute between Seattle and points east (via SR 520, SR 522, I-90, and I-405). A useful resource, the magazine *425* is dedicated to promoting the Eastside's identity separate from Seattle proper.

Bellevue

Bellevue has somewhat balanced its shopping-mall image; after all, big companies such as Drugstore.com, T-Mobile USA, and Expedia.com are headquartered here. Washington's fifth-largest city now boasts an impressive downtown skyline populated by glass high-rises and upscale condo developments, as well as a few distinct cultural attractions. The **MEYDENBAUER CENTER** (11100 NE 6th St; 425/637-1020; www.meydenbauer.com) hosts myriad arts performances, and the **BELLEVUE ARTS MUSEUM** (510 Bellevue Wy NE; 425/519-0770; www.bellevuearts.org) presents exhibits of regional arts, crafts, and design. The **ROSALIE WHYEL MUSEUM OF DOLL ART** (1116 108th Ave NE; 425/455-1116; www.dollart.com) displays more than 3,000 dolls and also offers dolls for purchase.

Still, shopping and dining remain the main attractions of the downtown core—and the intersection at Bellevue Way and NE Eighth Street has the congestion to prove it. "The Bellevue Collection" is comprised of three high-end shopping centers with hundreds of destinations between them: **BELLEVUE SQUARE** (between Bellevue Wy NE and 100th Ave NE, and NE 4th and NE 8th sts; 425/454-8096; www.bellevuesquare.com), packed with a triple-decker Nordstrom store, Macy's, and Crate & Barrel, plus 200 shops and restaurants; kitty-corner is glitzy **BELLEVUE PLACE** (10500 NE 8th St; www.bellevueplace.com); and across the street is **LINCOLN SQUARE** (800 Bellevue Wy; www.lincoln-square.com), with popular chain restaurants like McCormick & Schmick's and Romano's Macaroni Grill, as well as a large, high-end billiards parlor, the region's only outpost of **LUCKY STRIKE LANES** (425/453-5137; www.bowlluckystrike.com), and a 16-screen movie theater. Farther east, find family-oriented **CROSSROADS SHOPPING CENTER** (15600 NE 8th St; 425/644-1111; www.crossroadsbellevue.com), much less crowded than its chic downtown Bellevue counterparts.

WASHINGTON SQUARE (425/974-7000; www.washingtonsquareliving.com) is under development: the first tower opened early in 2008, and construction is scheduled to continue over seven more years, blending retail and a luxury hotel with condominiums. Also under construction is a new office tower, City Center Plaza, where upscale steakhouse **EL GAUCHO** (110th Ave NE and NE 6th St; www.elgaucho.com) will debut new dishes and serve lunch. The **BRAVERN** (NE 8th St, between 110th and 112th aves NE) across the street will also be home to Neiman Marcus, Jimmy Choo, Wild Ginger, and John Howie Steak, a steak house from the founder of **SEASTAR** (see review). For more-intimate shopping, check out boutiques like the new **POSH ON MAIN** (10245 Main St, Ste 103; 425/454-2022; www.poshonmain.com) in Old Bellevue, which has luxe women's shoes, à la New York. **TAP HOUSE GRILL** (550 106th Ave NE; 425/467-1730; www.taphousegrill.com) features a staggering 160 beers on tap.

For nature in the city, head to the 19-acre **DOWNTOWN PARK** (10201 NE 4th St, just south of Bellevue Square, Bellevue), with a waterfall and promenade. Other parks include **BELLEVUE BOTANICAL GARDEN** (12001 Main St, Bellevue; 425/452-2750; www.bellevuebotanical.org); **ENATAI BEACH PARK** (3519 108th Ave SE, Bellevue; 425/452-6885), where you can go canoeing and kayaking; and **NEWCASTLE BEACH PARK** (4400 Lake Washington Blvd SE, Bellevue; 425/452-6885), with swings, slides, and swimming. Not far away, upscale, suburban Newcastle is home to the region's most exclusive golf course, also a popular wedding site: even if playing nine holes isn't in the cards, the **GOLF CLUB AT NEWCASTLE** (15500 Six Penny Ln, Newcastle; 425/793-5566; www.newcastlegolf.com) offers charming watering holes and a dining room, Calcutta Grill. At an elevation of about 1,000 feet, the club offers views of Seattle, Mount Rainier, the Cascades, and the Olympics that are nothing short of eye-popping. Visit www.bellevuewa.gov or www.ci.bellevue.wa.us for more Bellevue information.

RESTAURANTS

Bis on Main / ★★☆

10213 MAIN ST, BELLEVUE; 425/455-2033

A Bellevue classic, Bis on Main offers genteel dining in an area dominated by large chain eateries, but their French-Italian-American menu isn't for the faint of heart. Dip truffle fries into blue cheese aioli to double your pleasure. Luxuriate in crispy sweetbreads and black truffle gnocchi or a tangle of rich, wild mushroom tagliatelle. Savor roasted duck with *amarena* cherries, balsamic vinegar, and foie gras butter. Walls are adorned with contemporary art, lovely to look at if you can tear your gaze away from your plate. *$$$–$$$$; AE, DC, DIS, MC, V; checks OK; lunch Mon–Fri, dinner every day; full bar; reservations recommended; www.bisonmain.com; Old Bellevue, at 102nd Ave.* &

Daniel's Broiler / ★★★

10500 NE 8TH ST, 21ST FLOOR,
BELLEVUE (AND BRANCHES); 425/642-4662

If you're looking for a bird's-eye view in Bellevue, this is the spot. Daniel's is one of the most respected and beloved steak houses in the area, with two other locations in Seattle. Nonbeefy menu favorites include the crispy artichoke heart starter, served with garlic hollandaise, and a decadent lobster club salad. They also have a popular happy hour, a piano bar, and their clubby Vintage Lounge's 30 by-the-glass offerings—all rated 90 and above by *Wine Spectator*. *$$$–$$$$; AE, DC, DIS, MC, V; no checks; lunch Mon–Fri, dinner every day; full bar; reservations recommended; www.schwartzbros.com; Bellevue Place, at NE 8th.* &

Joeys / ★★☆

800 BELLEVUE WY NE, STE 118, BELLEVUE; 425/637-1177

A Canadian-based chain, this masculine, booth-heavy dining room is deceptive: staff often seem to be hired more for their "assets" than serving skills, but that doesn't change the fact that the food is often surprisingly good. The menu is globally eclectic, ranging from salads to sandwiches, fresh seafood to steaks, a Japanese bento box to Bombay butter chicken. Start with crunchy, crab-filled California sushi tacos and finish with fondue for two. Night owls, take note: they serve the full menu until 1:30am every day. *$$–$$$; AE, DC, MC, V; no checks; lunch, dinner every day; full bar; reservations recommended; www.joeysrestaurants.com; Bellevue Place, at NE 8th St.* &

Seastar Restaurant and Raw Bar / ★★★

205 108TH AVE NE, BELLEVUE; 425/456-0010

This fine-dining establishment is owned by chef John Howie, who also opened Sport Restaurant & Bar near Seattle Center. Try the multilevel raw-bar sampler: Hawaiian ahi *poke*, California roll, and scallop ceviche. On the hot side, look for flash-seared diver sea scallops with tropical fruit chutney or Kauai shrimp wrapped in *saifun* noodles. Howie is a pioneer of alder- and cedar-plank cooking, so the likes of salmon and halibut always shine. Offerings for red meat lovers are also delicious. *$$$; AE, DC, DIS, MC, V; no checks; lunch, dinner every day; full bar; reservations recommended; www. seastarrestaurant.com; at NE 2nd St.* &

0/8 Seafood Grill and Twisted Cork Wine Bar / ★★★

900 BELLEVUE WY NE (HYATT REGENCY BELLEVUE),
STE 100, BELLEVUE; 425/637-0808

When you're a hotel restaurant, you often have to be all things to all diners, but chef Dan Thiessen's great strength here is, indeed, seafood. The brandied Dungeness crab bisque and raw sashimi scallops are genius. Grilled salmon, halibut, prawns, and scallops are all fine choices. (Carnivores, fear not: There's plenty of turf to go with the surf.) Equally noteworthy is the innovative, award-winning wine program—approachable, broad, and Northwest-focused, with lots of sparkling wines and more than 80 choices by the glass alone. *$$$; AE, JCB, MC, V; no checks; breakfast, lunch, dinner every day, brunch Sat–Sun; full bar; reservations recommended; www.o8seafoodgrill.com; at NE 8th St.* &

LODGINGS

Bellevue Club Hotel / ★★★

11200 SE 6TH ST, BELLEVUE; 425/454-4424 OR 800/579-1110
One of the most elegant lodgings in the area, the Bellevue Club is part boutique hotel, part upscale athletic club. The 67 richly appointed rooms (and three suites) feature original Northwest artwork, as well as locally custom-made cherry-wood furniture. Some rooms overlook the tennis courts; others open to terra-cotta patios. Oversize limestone-and-marble bathrooms—with spalike tubs—are perfect for postworkout soaks. The club offers fine dining at Polaris Restaurant (425/637-4608), cocktails in the adjoining Cosmos Lounge, casual fare at Splash, and java from Luna espresso bar. *$$$–$$$$; AE, DC, DIS, MC, V; checks OK; www.bellevueclubhotel.com; at 112th Ave SE.* &

Hilton Hotel Bellevue / ★★

300 112TH AVE SE, BELLEVUE; 425/455-1300 OR 800/643-7907
A multimillion-dollar conversion from its former incarnation as a Doubletree Hotel has made this a fine option for business and leisure travelers alike. The 353 rooms are quiet and spacious, the bed linens luxurious, and bathrooms have deep soaking tubs. (Suites have Jacuzzis.) A rather elegant dining room, Basil's Kitchen, serves all meals, including Sunday brunch; the varied menu has a Mediterranean-Northwest focus. The adjoining Basil's Bar is a fine spot to wind down with a favorite cocktail; the Tully's Coffee in the atrium jump-starts your day. *$$–$$$; AE, DC, DIS, JCB, MC, V; checks OK; www.bellevuehilton.com; near SE 4th St.* &

Hyatt Regency Bellevue / ★★⯪

900 BELLEVUE WY NE, BELLEVUE; 425/462-1234 OR 800/233-1234
Conveniently located in Bellevue Place, in the heart of the Bellevue shopping and entertainment district, this 24-story hotel—imbued with a subtly Asian aesthetic—has plenty to offer guests. Bowling, billiards, a cinema multiplex, and more than 250 shops and department stores are across the street. The 382 rooms are contemporary and comfortable, though noise can be an issue. (Request a room on a higher floor.) More than 30 restaurants are within a block; on-site options include Daniel's Broiler, Joeys, and 0/8 Seafood Grill and Twisted Cork Wine Bar (see reviews). *$$$–$$$$; AE, DC, DIS, JCB, MC, V; checks OK; www.bellevue.hyatt.com; at NE 8th St.* &

Westin Bellevue / ★★★

600 BELLEVUE WY NE, BELLEVUE; 425/638-1000 OR 800/937-8461
Swanky, hip, sexy, and elegant: that's how people describe this new hotel in the buzzing Bellevue retail core. The 337 rooms have all the Westin

EASY SEATTLE GETAWAYS

VASHON ISLAND: It's a 15-minute car-ferry ride from West Seattle to this bucolic, rural island, which has no hotels, no stoplights, and one fast-food outlet. What it does have are beautiful parks, user-friendly B and Bs, miles of country roads for biking, an inner bay good for swimming in summer, and the charming, quirky restaurant **GUSTO GIRLS** (17629 Vashon Hwy SW, Vashon Island; 206/463-6626; www.gustogirls.com). See the Puget Sound chapter for information.

LEAVENWORTH: OK, it's kitschy (faux Tyrolean architecture, men in lederhosen), but the mountain air is invigorating, the hiking and biking is unsurpassed, and oompah bands and a little accordion music never hurt anyone—much. Special events include Oktoberfest and the Christmas Lighting Festival, and the drive there and back is a favorite for fall color. See the Central Cascades chapter for information.

VICTORIA: Hop on the *Victoria Clipper* for the three-hour catamaran ride to the Inner Harbour, then grab your overnight bags and walk to your room at the world-famous **FAIRMONT EMPRESS HOTEL** or one of dozens of quality hotels and B and Bs. Foot power takes you to all the attractions in this oft-visited small city, which has shed its one-note Olde England persona: no one will insist you have tea and scones. See the Victoria and Vancouver Island chapter for information.

SUNCADIA VILLAGE: For scenic surroundings and a "one-stop-shopping" resort getaway, Cle Elum's become a bona fide destination: **SUNCADIA RESORT** has opened a 254-suite lodge to go with their intimate, 18-room inn. There's first-rate dining, golfing, swimming, fitness activities, romance packages, boutique shopping, myriad outdoor activities, an on-site spa, and more. For more intimate pampering, visit the excellent **SISTER MOON SPA** (304 W 1st St, Suncadia; 509/674-7721; www.sistermoonspa.com). A side trip to **ROSLYN** is a must for fans of TV's quirky *Northern Exposure*. See the Central Cascades chapter for information.

YAKIMA VALLEY: Until recently, the world-class wines produced here were not matched by the valley's dining and lodging options, but a new generation of

amenities, including 32-inch flat-screen TVs and signature "Heavenly Beds." Take in views of Mount Rainier, the Seattle skyline, and Lake Washington. Sixteen grand deluxe rooms have big four-fixture bathrooms, high ceilings, and private decks. The indoor lap pool has an outdoor deck and a "powered by Reebok" gym. Dine in the Northwest-focused Manzana Rotisserie Grill (425/455-7600; www.manzanagrill.com), or have a drink in Cypress, the relaxing lounge. *$$$–$$$$; AE, DC, DIS, JCB, MC, V; no checks; www.westin.com/bellevuewa; in Lincoln Square.* &

small inns and bistros is changing that. It's just a two-hour drive from Seattle to Yakima and a bit more to the heart of wine country in Sunnyside, where the sun shines almost every day. Be sure to drive through **TOPPENISH** to view the town's remarkable collection of **MURALS**. See the Southeast Washington chapter for information.

TACOMA: Yes, Tacoma. The City Seattleites Love to Disparage has three museums—the **WASHINGTON STATE HISTORY MUSEUM, MUSEUM OF GLASS**, and **TACOMA ART MUSEUM**—well worth a visit. A drive along the bluffs facing **COMMENCEMENT BAY**, admiring the grand homes, is a reminder that Northwest fortunes were made here before Seattle prospered and that **POINT DEFIANCE PARK** is almost the equal of Vancouver's **STANLEY PARK**. The historic **SPAR TAVERN** (2121 N 30th St, Tacoma; 253/627-8215; www.the-spar.com) serves terrific pub grub. See the Puget Sound chapter for information.

PORT TOWNSEND: One of the West's finest collections of heritage Victorian homes, many of them B and Bs, beckons visitors to this artsy, somewhat bohemian community, as does the annual **WOODEN BOAT FESTIVAL**. Music is a summertime draw at **FORT WORDEN STATE PARK** and the **OLYMPIC MUSIC FESTIVAL** (in nearby Quilcene), and **SWEET LAURETTE CAFÉ AND BISTRO**'s charming provençal food and atmosphere are divine. See the Olympic and Kitsap Peninsulas chapter for information.

UNION: It takes only a couple of hours to get to the Hood Canal's "hook" via Tacoma or via two ferry routes: Fauntleroy-Southworth or Seattle Pier 52–Bremerton. Relax at the rustic-posh **ALDERBROOK RESORT**, whose spa offers first-rate treatments, or the cozy **HOOD CANAL COTTAGES AT ROBIN HOOD VILLAGE** (6780 E SR 106, Union; 360/898-2163; www.robinhood village.com); the historic **ROBIN HOOD RESTAURANT & PUB** (206/898-4400; therobinhood.com) is right next door. See the Olympic and Kitsap Peninsulas chapter for information.

—Ginny Morey

Redmond

Once a bucolic valley farming community, Redmond is today a sprawling McTown of freeway overpasses, offices (Microsoft, Nintendo of America, and Eddie Bauer are headquartered here), subdivisions, and retailers large and small, including the open-air, 100-plus-shop **REDMOND TOWN CENTER AND CINEMAS** (16495 NE 74th St, Redmond; 425/867-0808; www.redmondtowncenter.com). Shop till you drop or your growling stomach gets the best of you, then head to **MATT'S ROTIS-SERIE & OYSTER LOUNGE** (425/378-0909; www.mattsrotisserie.com), **SPAZZO**

ITALIAN GRILL & WINE BAR (425/881-4400; www.schwartzbros.com/spazzo), or **DESERT FIRE** (425/895-1500; www.desertfiremex.com), three of Redmond Town Center's best dining options. A lower-budget spot is **MALAY SATAY HUT** (15230 NE 24th St, Redmond; 425/564-0888). For 21-and-over entertainment, the **BIG PICTURE** (Redmond Town Center, 2nd floor; 425/556-0566; www.thebigpicture. net; also downtown at 2505 1st Ave, Redmond; 206/256-0566) offers movies, cocktails, and billiards in one plush location.

In summer, 522-acre **MARYMOOR PARK** (6046 W Lake Sammamish Pkwy NE, Redmond; 206/296-2966; www.metrokc.gov/parks/marymoor) draws crowds for picnics and other family-oriented activities. Redmond's not dubbed the bicycle capital of the Northwest for nothing: cyclists can pedal the 10-mile **SAMMAMISH RIVER TRAIL** (www.metrokc.gov/parks/trails) from Marymoor Park to Bothell, or check out races at the 400-meter **MARYMOOR VELODROME** (206/957-4555; www.marymoor.velodrome.org) in Marymoor Park. The **CONCERTS AT MARY-MOOR** (206/628-0888; www.concertsatmarymoor.com) is a popular summer program that has featured artists ranging from Norah Jones to Ringo Starr to the Doobie Brothers.

RESTAURANTS

Pomegranate Bistro / ★★★

> 18005 NE 68TH ST, REDMOND; 425/556-5972

Successful caterer Lisa Dupar and her husband opened this restaurant with families in mind, and they succeeded in making a place where both kids and adults can have fun (though kidless grown-ups never feel put out by the underage set). A huge catering kitchen adjoins the restaurant, the action visible through a large window. Parents drink Key lime pie martinis, kids drink alcohol-free *loco coladas*, and everyone feasts on inventive, seasonal dishes, including pizzalike flatbreads with a variety of toppings. The Espresso Bar (open every day from 7am) has delish baked goods. *$$–$$$; AE, DIS, MC, V; no checks; lunch every day, dinner Tues–Sat, brunch Sat–Sun; full bar; reservations recommended; www.pomegranatebistro.com; across from Chalet Grocery on Redmond Wy.* &

Typhoon! / ★★☆

> 8936 161ST AVE NE, REDMOND (AND BRANCHES); 425/558-7666

After great success in Oregon, chef Bo Cline blew into Washington with her spectacular array of complex and flavorful Thai dishes. *Miang kum*, a peasant dish, is toasted coconut, shallot, ginger, lime, peanut, dried shrimp, and chile placed atop a spinach leaf and finished with the chef's signature sauce: just try not inhaling these. Typhoon! is also known for its spectacular tea menu, with some exceptional loose leaves costing $3,000 per pound and higher. *$$$; AE, DC, DIS, MC, V; checks OK; lunch Mon–Sat, dinner every day; full bar; reservations recommended; www.typhoonrestaurants.com; near NE 90th St.* &

Kirkland

Sure, there's a crunch of expensive condos and bumper-to-bumper traffic here, but this beautiful, resortlike town tucked into the eastern shore of Lake Washington has avoided the Eastside's typical concrete-and-strip-mall syndrome. People stroll here among congenial eateries, art galleries, and boutique retailers. When the sun comes out, sidewalks fill with locals and tourists, as do **PETER KIRK PARK** (202 3rd St) and the **KIRKLAND MARINA** (25 Lake Shore Plaza). Catch an **ARGOSY** (206/623-1445 or 800/642-7816; www.argosycruises.com; Apr–Nov) boat for a lake cruise at Kirkland City Dock. The 402-seat **KIRKLAND PERFOR-MANCE CENTER** (350 Kirkland Ave; 425/893-9900; www.kpcenter.org) hosts a variety of shows. Even the obligatory mall, **KIRKLAND PARKPLACE** (6th St and Central Wy; 425/828-4468; www.kirklandparkplace.com), doesn't spoil the townscape—it's several blocks east of the waterfront. In addition to a cinema, there's a wonderful independent bookseller, **PARKPLACE BOOKS** (425/828-6546; www.parkplacebookskirkland.com), **RAVENNA GARDENS** (425/827-5501; www. ravennagardens.com) for flora-related gifts, and an outpost of **PURPLE CAFÉ AND WINE BAR** (323 Park Place Center; 425/828-3772; www.thepurplecafe.com).

For Italian eats, head to **PARADISO RISTORANTE** (120A Park Ln; 425/889-8601; www.ristoranteparadiso.com). **LYNN'S BISTRO** (214 Central Wy; 425/889-2808; www.lynnsbistro.com) serves French-inspired dishes in a charming, understated dining room. For more casual fare, try **RAGA CUISINE OF INDIA** (212 Central Wy; 425/827-3300), **CACTUS** (121 Park Ln; 425/893-9799; www. cactusrestaurants.com), or **WILDE ROVER IRISH PUB & RESTAURANT** (111 Central Wy; 425/822-8940; www.wilderover.com), serving hearty classics like shepherd's pie and Guinness lamb stew, plus pints of the dark stuff to go with it. Two stylish boutiques worth checking out are **MANHATTAN, SHOP IN THE CITY** (122 Lake St S; 425/576-1065; www.boutiquemanhattan.com) and **PROMESSE** (128 Central Wy; 425/828-4259; www.shoppromesse.com). An outpost of **SUR LA TABLE** (90 Central Wy; 425/827-1311; www.surlatable.com) has something for every home chef. Heading north to Juanita neighborhood, oenophiles should drop into **BRIX WINE CAFÉ** (9749 NE 119th Wy; 425/242-0280; www.brixwine cafe.com). For general information on Kirkland, visit www.ci.kirkland.wa.us or www.explorekirkland.com.

RESTAURANTS

Café Juanita / ★★★½

9702 NE 120TH PL, KIRKLAND; 425/823-1505

An unobtrusive exterior gives way to a serenely elegant interior space, where chef Holly Smith puts a magical twist on seasonal northern Italian classics, employing many Northwest and organic ingredients. Execution is precise and inspired, presentation flawless, and service nearly impeccable. Start with grilled octopus with fennel or pear salad with pine nuts, shaved Parmigiano-Reggiano, and white truffle oil. Rabbit *raviolini* with sage butter is offered in two sizes. The dessert list is formidable, with select cheeses or Valrhona chocolate-truffle cake with vanilla gelato, espresso sauce, and crisp almond wafer. Even the house-made cracker assortment that begins each meal is irresistible. Sit near the fireplace for optimum romance. *$$$–$$$$; AE, MC, V; no checks; dinner every day; full bar; reservations recommended; www.cafe juanita.com; at 97th Ave NE.* &

Third Floor Fish Café / ★★☆

205 LAKE ST S, STE 300, KIRKLAND; 425/822-3553

This tiered dining room—affording lake and marina views from nearly every table—could use an updating, but chef Greg Campbell's seafood is virtually flawless. Time and again, the kitchen produces perfectly cooked and balanced preparations like roasted king salmon, grilled sea scallops, rare ahi, and Atlantic monkfish with stir-fried pea vines. The dessert chef, too, is a real talent: if there's nothing on the menu featuring lemon, the honey tangerine *panna cotta* is light and refreshing. *$$$; AE, DC, DIS, MC, V; checks OK; dinner every day; full bar; reservations recommended; www.fishcafe.com; across from 2nd Ave S.* &

Trellis / ★★★★

220 KIRKLAND AVE, KIRKLAND; 425/284-5900

Most dishes on this modern but comfy restaurant's contemporary American menu are prepared with local, seasonal, organic, or naturally raised meats, dairy, and produce—including farmstead cheeses and handcrafted salami. And that includes those sourced from chef Brian Scheehser's 3-acre garden, coupled with efficient service and deliberate, refined cooking techniques. This is the kind of place you come to savor a meal, not rush through it. For starters, the *caprese* flatbread (a perfectly crisp thin-crust pizza) is a winner. The beet salad is as artfully presented as it is stunningly flavorful. Recent entrées included winter squash ravioli, flatiron steak, and a marvelous Pacific seafood soup. About 13 wines by the glass make pairing a snap, while the everchanging dessert menu offers several irresistible options. *$$; AE, DIS, MC, V; breakfast, lunch, dinner every day; full bar; reservations recommended; www. trellisrestaurant.net; at 3rd St.*

LODGINGS

The Heathman Hotel Kirkland / ★★★

220 KIRKLAND AVE, KIRKLAND; 425/284-5800

Kirkland is an offspring of the legendary Heathman Hotel Portland. Crisp and elegant without an iota of attitude, the Heathman is Kirkland's waterfront shopping district's only luxury hotel. Ninety-one guest rooms feature a blend of sophisticated textiles and decor accents contrasted with a warm color palette. All have desks, flat-screen TVs, complimentary wireless Internet access, French press coffee makers, MP3-compatible clock radios, and plush lounging robes. The hotel's exclusive bed menu lets you pick your room by preferred bed type, including Tempur-Pedic, European featherbed, or pillow-top. Bathrooms feature ultramodern Euro styling with pedestal sinks and Temple Spa soaps and shampoos. One of the Seattle area's best spas is on-site: Penterra Spa; Trellis Restaurant is next door. *$$$–$$$$; AE, DC, JCB, MC, V; checks OK; www.heathmankirkland.com; at 3rd St.*

The Woodmark Hotel, Yacht Club and Spa on Lake Washington / ★★★
1200 CARILLON PT, KIRKLAND; 425/822-3700 OR 800/822-3700
The only hotel on Lake Washington, this four-story brick building is just steps from a marina and a shoreline path popular with joggers. Elegant and traditional in decor, 100 rooms, about half with stunning lake views, offer a relaxing retreat and upscale baths, some with two-person jetted tubs. Complimentary extras include a late-night buffet and a cruise on the hotel's 28-foot 1956 Chris-Craft™. The hotel's wine-focused restaurant, bin vivant (425/803-5595), features a staggering 80 wines on the Enomatic wine preservation and dispensing system, with a food menu of predominantly small plates designed for wine pairing. The on-site spa, given a face-lift in 2008, is a must-visit. *$$$–$$$$; AE, DC, JCB, MC, V; checks OK; www.thewoodmark. com; at Lakeview Dr.* ⟟

Woodinville

Oenophiles and hops fanciers love this thriving Eastside town. **CHATEAU STE. MICHELLE** (14111 NE 145th St; 425/488-1133; www.chateaustemichelle.com), the state's largest winery, offers daily tastings and tours as well as a summer concert series, featuring big-name acts popular primarily with the 30-and-over set, on its lovely 87-acre estate. Across the street, **COLUMBIA WINERY** (14030 NE 145th St; 425/488-2776; www.columbiawinery.com) also has daily tastings and weekend tours. Both properties boast large, well-stocked shops. For a grain-based palate cleanser, wet your whistle at one of the state's first microbreweries, **RED-HOOK ALE BREWERY** (14300 NE 145th St; 425/483-3232; www.redhook.com), which, along with daily $1 tours (including a souvenir glass and plenty of samples), has a pub with tasty grub and live music on Saturday nights. In addition to Ste. Michelle and Columbia, Woodinville is home to more than 40 **WINERIES** (www.winesnw.com, www.woodinvillewinecountry.com, and www.gotastewine. com), many of which have tasting rooms ranging from bare-bones to elegant. **PURPLE CAFÉ AND WINE BAR** (14459 Woodinville-Redmond Rd NE; 425/483-7129; www.thepurplecafe.com) is good for a bite and a sip, particularly if you don't have time for a full-on winery tour.

RESTAURANTS

The Barking Frog / ★★★½
14582 NE 145TH ST, WOODINVILLE; 425/424-2999 OR 877/424-3930

Both the name and design of Barking Frog are inspired by Northwest Native culture; especially fine is the artwork found throughout the warm, wood-lined dining room. The seasonally shifting menu marries regional ingredients with classic preparations and technique, and results can be stunning: Grand Marnier prawns are a signature dish; the spiced sea scallops beignet could almost double as dessert; and if you're "game," the elk tenderloin with beluga lentils, a small black lentil type, and brussels sprouts is a marvel. The wine list pays particular homage to the restaurant's Woodinville neighbors. *$$$–$$$$; AE, DC, DIS, JCB, MC, V; no checks; breakfast every day, lunch Mon–Fri, dinner every day, brunch Sat–Sun; full bar; reservations recommended; www.willows lodge.com; between 148th Ave NE and Woodinville-Redmond Rd NE.* &

The Herbfarm / ★★★★

14590 NE 145TH ST, WOODINVILLE; 425/485-5300
This is a must-experience restaurant for anyone who loves gourmet dining and impeccable service. Executive chef Keith Luce is an inspired successor to renowned chef Jerry Traunfeld in his creation of seasonal menus featuring local produce and herbs—many grown in the Herbfarm's gardens. Over the course of four hours, your nine-course prix-fixe dinner (which can be paired with wines) in the lushly appointed dining room may include dishes like boletus and Dungeness crab "handkerchiefs" with chervil-chive butter, Oregon lamb loin on tongue-of-fire beans, and pear soufflé with orange thyme custard sauce. The wine cellar is world-class, particularly the Madeira collection. Book one of the Herbfarm's two lavishly appointed suites at Willows Lodge (see review) if you're too sated to drive home. *$$$$; AE, MC, V; checks OK; dinner Thurs–Sun; beer and wine; reservations required; www.theherbfarm. com; between 148th Ave NE and Woodinville-Redmond Rd NE.* &

Russell's Dining & Bar / ★★★

3305 MONTE VILLA PKWY, BOTHELL; 425/486-4072
North of Woodinville, housed in a huge 1927 barn that's been gorgeously renovated throughout with a soaring, cedar-lined vaulted ceiling in the private event space (formerly the hayloft—be sure to ask for a peek), this hard-to-find restaurant is worth the trip, particularly if you order chef-owner Russell Lowell's crispy duck breast, filet mignon with demi-glace bleu cheese butter, or rack of lamb. Pan-seared scallops with beurre blanc, either as a starter or main course, are eye-rollingly delicious. A select wine list complements the menu, and by all means, save room for a fresh, housemade dessert from the rotating list. Try the buttery bread pudding in a pool of caramel. *$$$; AE, MC, V; no checks; breakfast, lunch Mon–Fri, dinner Tues–Sat; full bar; reservations recommended; www.rdlcatering.com/russells; off 35th Ave SE.* &

LODGINGS

Willows Lodge / ★★★★

14580 NE 145TH ST, WOODINVILLE;
425/424-3900 OR 877/424-3930
Willows Lodge is a quintessential Northwest hotel, combining casual grace with an eco-friendly aesthetic. A 1,500-year-old cedar stands sentinel near the

entry, and 100-year-old reclaimed Douglas fir timbers form the soaring lobby. The 84 rooms and suites have balconies or patios, rock-lined fireplaces, and 40-inch HDTVs. Jetted tubs for two are particularly romantic. Other amenities include a full-service spa, an outdoor hot tub, and a Japanese garden. Willows is pet friendly; look for the unflappable basset hound in the lobby. Dine in grand style at the Herbfarm or the Barking Frog (see reviews), sip a local wine in Fireside Cellars, and take a few minutes to stroll the grounds. *$$$$; AE, DC, DIS, JCB, MC, V; no checks; www.willowslodge.com; between 148th Ave NE and Woodinville-Redmond Rd NE.* &

Issaquah

Though every so often a cougar shows up in this wealthy Cascade-foothills suburb 15 miles east of Seattle, Issaquah is pleasantly mild mannered. At the east end of the bustling shopping strip along NW Gilman Boulevard, composed largely of national chain stores, lies historic **GILMAN VILLAGE** (317 NW Gilman Blvd; 425/392-6802; www.gilmanvillage.com). A collection of refurbished farmhouses, the village offers an agreeable day of poking about in its 40 or so shops and eateries. The popular **VILLAGE THEATRE** (120 Front St N and 303 Front St N; 425/392-2202; www.villagetheatre.org), one of the top three professional theater companies in the region, entertains with mostly original, mainly musical productions. While you're there, try **FINS BISTRO SEAFOOD RESTAURANT** (301 Front St; 425/392-0109; www.finsbistro.com). Another fun spot is **XXX DRIVE-IN** (98 NE Gilman Blvd, Issaquah; 425/392-1266; www.triplexrootbeer.com), with burgers, shakes, and root beer; just look for the huge orange root beer barrel sign. Chocolate lovers should drop by **BOEHM'S** (255 NE Gilman Blvd; 425/392-6652; www.boehmscandies.com) for confections of all descriptions.

Seattleites cross the I-90 bridge in droves during summer weekends to scale the Issaquah Alps—Cougar, Squak, and Tiger mountains—which have miles of hiking trails from easy to challenging; the **ISSAQUAH ALPS TRAILS CLUB** (425/392-6660; www.issaquahalps.org) offers organized day hikes. Head over during the first full weekend of October for **ISSAQUAH SALMON DAYS** (425/392-7024; www.salmondays.org), a huge celebration—including food, crafts, music, and a parade—marking the return of the salmon that surge up Issaquah Creek. For more information on Issaquah, visit www.ci.issaquah.wa.us.

RESTAURANTS

Iris Grill / ★★☆

317 NW GILMAN BLVD, STE 28A, ISSAQUAH; 425/557-7899
Issaquah has plenty of casual eateries (including numerous fast-food chains), but Iris Grill is a great casual-chic place to take a date or visiting relations. They serve grown-up food, including steak tartar, a rarity on contemporary menus. For those who prefer their meats cooked, look for duck leg confit, filet mignon, and braised beef short ribs. Order Tim's Cheesecake for dessert, even

if it means taking half of it home for later. The bar, with a fine cocktail list, offers happy hour specials (both drinks and snacks) every day. *$$$; AE, MC, V; no checks; lunch Tues–Sat, dinner every day, brunch Sun; full bar; reservations recommended; www.theirisgrill.com; in Gilman Village.* &

SeaTac

SeaTac is bordered on three sides by I-5, SR 509, and SR 518. More than 25,000 people live in the 10-mile-square city, but like most airport environments, this one is dominated by hotels and chain restaurants.

LODGINGS

Doubletree Hotel Seattle Airport / ★★☆

18740 INTERNATIONAL BLVD, SEATAC; 206/246-8600 OR 800/222-8733
A resortlike facility spread across 25 acres, the Doubletree, recently given a $20 million face-lift, boasts 850 spacious guest rooms and suites. The Virtual Full Swing Golf simulator lets beginners and experienced golfers alike try their hand at the world's 50 finest courses. Amenities include heated outdoor pool, whirlpool, fitness room, business center, airport shuttle, lounge, restaurant, babysitting service, and 24-hour room service. (Complimentary chocolate chip cookies are a tummy-pleasing extra.) *$$–$$$; AE, DC, DIS, JCB, MC, V; checks OK; www.doubletree1.hilton.com; corner of S 188th St and Pacific Hwy S.* &

Hilton Seattle Airport Hotel / ★★☆

17620 INTERNATIONAL BLVD, SEATAC; 206/244-4800 OR 800/445-8667
A renovation doubled the size of this hotel—geared toward airport travelers and business types—to a total of 396 rooms (and 7 suites). Beds are so comfy, guests are in danger of missing early-morning flights. There's a pool, an outdoor Jacuzzi, a fitness room, a 24-hour business center, and a 40,000-square-foot conference center. The restaurant, Spencer's for Steaks and Chops (206/248-7153; www.spencersforsteaksandchops.com), serves all meals. Room service is 5am to midnight, and the complimentary airport shuttle is 24 hours. *$$–$$$; AE, DC, DIS, JCB, MC, V; checks OK; www.hilton.com; corner of S 176th St and Pacific Hwy S.* &

PUGET SOUND

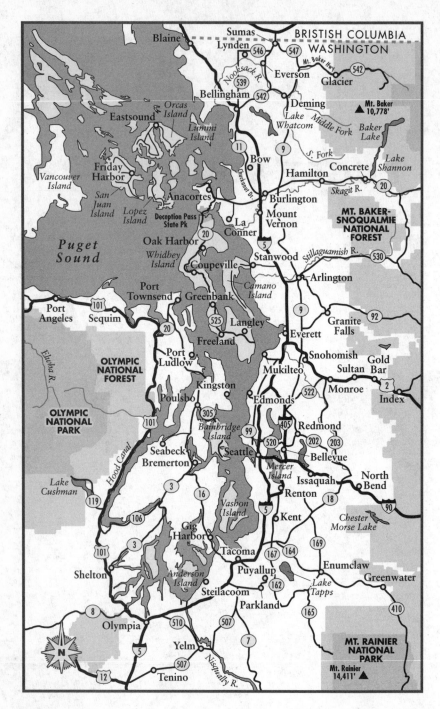

PUGET SOUND

The Puget Sound region, from the gardens in Blaine's Peace Arch Park at the Canadian border to the state's capital campus in Olympia, stands out among Washington's many idyllic areas. Each of the cities and towns along the Interstate 5 corridor, and each of the islands on the sound, has its own unique identity.

ACCESS AND INFORMATION

Fly into **SEATTLE-TACOMA INTERNATIONAL AIRPORT** (17801 Pacific Hwy S, SeaTac; 206/433-5388; www.portseattle.org/seatac)—13 miles south of Seattle and 16 miles north of Tacoma—and you have easy access to **INTERSTATE 5**. You'll need a car to best explore the region; most **CAR RENTAL** agencies have outlets at Sea-Tac Airport. **GRAY LINE** (206/626-6088 or 800/426-7532; www.seattlegrayline.com) runs the Seattle Downtown Airporter, an inexpensive shuttle service to downtown Seattle hotels.

Another transportation option is the **SOUNDER TRAIN** (206/398-5000 or 800/201-4900; www.soundtransit.org), which connects Tacoma, Seattle, and Everett with several stops in between during the work week. The ride is quiet and smooth, the scenery is interesting, and stops are located within walking distance from major attractions. **AMTRAK** (King Street Station, 303 S Jackson St, Seattle; 206/382-4125 or 800/USA-RAIL; www.amtrak.com) has daily runs between Portland, Oregon; Seattle; and Vancouver, British Columbia; stops include Olympia, Tacoma, Everett, and Bellingham.

WASHINGTON STATE FERRIES (Pier 52, Seattle; 206/464-6400 or 800/843-3779; www.wsdot.wa.gov/ferries) access the San Juan Islands, Whidbey, Vashon, and other islands in Puget Sound, as well as Tacoma on the mainland.

Edmonds

The quintessential seaside city, with a waterfront boardwalk and flower-lined streets, Edmonds is just 15 miles north of Seattle via I-5. City streets and neighborhoods burst into color every summer for the annual **EDMONDS IN BLOOM** (www.edmondsinbloom.com) competition. A stroll along the waterfront or in **BRACKETT'S LANDING PARK** (on both sides of ferry landing) offers clear views of the Olympic Mountains, Mount Baker, and the Cascades. The **TASTE OF EDMONDS** (www.edmondswa.com/events/taste; 2nd weekend in Aug) highlights the city's best restaurants and regional fare.

Arts are an integral element too, with a ballet, an orchestra, a symphony, and theater groups, all of which help host the **EDMONDS ARTS FESTIVAL** (www.edmondsartsfestival.com) each June. Antique lovers will find more than 200 shops at the somewhat dated **AURORA ANTIQUE PAVILION** (24111 SR 99, Ste 201; 425/744-0566), but for other great shopping, don't miss the quaint shops downtown near the ferry terminal.

A train station and nearby **EDMONDS HARBOR INN** (130 W Dayton; 425/771-5021 or 800/441-8033; www.nwcountryinns.com/edmonds) make this pleasant town an overnight destination as well. The **SHELL CREEK GRILL & WINE BAR** (526 Main St; 425/775-4566) specializes in Southwest cuisine, and **CHANTERELLE'S** (316 Main St; 425/774-0650; www.chanterellewa.com) is known for its addictive tomato bisque. Find information at the **EDMONDS CHAMBER OF COMMERCE** (121 5th Ave N; 425/670-1496; www.edmondswa.com).

Everett Area

Timber and fishing once supported Snohomish County, north of Seattle. Mansions along Everett's Grand and Rucker avenues are reminders of the days when timber barons ruled. Today, Naval Station Everett and the Port of Everett form the core of the growing economy in North Everett, which is bordered by the Snohomish River and Port Gardner Channel. Boeing's Paine Field facility occupies a major portion of the south end. From Everett, US Highway 2 heads east over the Cascades, and ferries run west from Mukilteo, just south of Everett. Information is available through **SNOHOMISH COUNTY TOURISM BUREAU** (909 SE Everett Mall Wy, Ste C300, Everett; 425/348-5802 or 888/338-0976; www.snohomish.org).

Mill Creek

Often called suburban nirvana, this tidy, country-club community northeast of Edmonds and south of Everett includes several **PARKS** (www.cityofmillcreek. com). One of the city's best-loved restaurants is nestled in Mill Creek Town Center, on State Route 527 east of exit 183 off I-5. **ZINNIA** (15130 Main St; 425/357-0512; www.zinniawa.com) offers lunch-goers generous salads and sandwiches, and evening diners can choose dishes ranging from vegetarian to wild game.

Mukilteo

Mukilteo, on the southwest edge of Everett via State Route 525 and State Route 526 west of I-5, is probably best known for the Mukilteo-Clinton ferry that gives access to Whidbey Island, Deception Pass, and the Olympic Peninsula. The restored 1906 lighthouse at **LIGHTHOUSE PARK** (follow signs from I-5; 425/513-9602; open Apr–Sept weekends and holidays) a block from the ferry dock is worth seeing. For a quick bite, dart into **IVAR'S** (710 Front St; 425/742-6180; www.ivars. net) next to the ferry terminal.

RESTAURANTS

Charles at Smugglers Cove / ★★

8340 53RD AVE W, MUKILTEO; 425/347-2700
A landmark building, a 1929 speakeasy high on a bluff above Possession Sound, houses this elegant French country–style restaurant. Diners enjoy the terrace overlooking the water. The classically French menu offers chicken,

seafood, lamb, and beef dishes. Save room for crepes suzette or Grand Marnier soufflé. *$$$; AE, MC, V; local checks only; lunch Tues–Fri, dinner Tues–Sat; full bar; reservations recommended; www.charlesatsmugglerscove. com; at SRs 525 and 526.*

LODGINGS

Silver Cloud Inn / ★★

718 FRONT ST, MUKILTEO; 425/423-8600 OR 800/311-1461
Adjacent to the Mukilteo ferry, this Silver Cloud Inn is built over the water. Many of its 70 rooms have spectacular views of Possession Sound, Whidbey Island, and the North Cascades. The location is ideal—fishing and crabbing from the beach in back, picnics at the park in front, restaurants down the street. Rooms include microwaves and refrigerators; some have jetted tubs and fireplaces. Eat your continental breakfast in the cozy sitting room off the lobby. *$$$–$$$$; AE, DC, DIS, JCB, MC, V; no checks; www.silvercloud. com/12home.htm; I-5 exit 189.* &

Snohomish

Rather than lamenting its urbanization, the town of Snohomish (on SR 9 south of Hwy 2 east of Everett) is living up to its moniker as the Antique Capital of the Northwest. Antique shops fill downtown. The **STAR CENTER MALL** (829 2nd St, Snohomish; 360/568-2131; www.myantiquemall.com/starcenter) is the largest, with nearly 200 dealers and a restaurant, **COLLECTOR'S CHOICE** (lower level; 360/568-1277; www.snohomish-restaurants.com). After you scour that mall, work your way up and down First Street around the corner. On the Snohomish River side of the street, **TODO MEXICO** (1101 1st St, Snohomish; 360/862-0210) is a good choice. For excellent fish-and-chips, flavorful smoked salmon, and a view of the Snohomish River, visit **CHUCK'S SEAFOOD GROTTO** (1229 1st St, Snohomish; 360/568-0782; www.csgp.net). For fine dining, **SEBASTIAN'S** (924 1st St, Snohomish; 360/568-3928) offers steaks, seafood, and pasta; **MARDINI'S** (101 Union Ave, Snohomish; 360/568-8080; www.mardinis.com) is all about Mediterranean food.

Everett

In Everett, at the junction of I-5 and Hwy 2, the impressive downtown **EVERETT EVENTS CENTER** (2000 Hewitt Ave; 866/332-8499; www.comcastarenaeverett. com), with a 10,000-seat capacity, is home to the **SILVERTIPS** (425/252-5100; www.everettsilvertips.com), Everett's Western Hockey League franchise team, and the **EVERETT HAWKS** (866/383-4295), a National Indoor Football League team. The **EVERETT AQUASOX** (3802 Broadway; 425/258-3673 or 800/GO-FROGS; www.aquasox.com) is a single-A, short-season farm team for the Seattle Mariners.

But there's more to Everett than sports. The **ARTS COUNCIL OF SNO-HOMISH COUNTY** (1507 Wall St; 425/257-8380; www.artscouncilofsnoco.org) features monthly exhibits. The **EVERETT PERFORMING ARTS CENTER** (2710 Wetmore Ave; 425/257-8600 box office; www.villagetheatre.org/epac) hosts events. The **FUTURE OF FLIGHT AVIATION CENTER & BOEING TOUR** (8415 Paine Field Blvd; 425/438-8100 or 888/467-4777; www.futureofflight.org; I-5 exit 189 to SR 526W and follow signs) offers a 60-minute tour of the plant where Boeing jets are assembled. Tours run every day and fill early; purchase tickets online.

For information, contact the **EVERETT CHAMBER OF COMMERCE** (2000 Hewitt Ave, Ste 205; 425/257-3222; www.everettchamber.com).

RESTAURANTS

Emory's on Silver Lake / ★

11830 19TH AVE SE, EVERETT; 425/337-7772
A former roadhouse on a country lake, Emory's sits in the middle of southeast suburban Everett, offering aged steaks and seafood—such as salmon, halibut, and cannelloni with Dungeness crab—as well as pasta, salads, and burgers. The Key lime cheesecake is worth the splurge. Emory's has an easygoing pub-style charm, lake views, and deck dining. After your meal, explore the dock. $$$; AE, DIS, MC, V; no checks; lunch Mon–Fri, dinner every day; full bar; reservations recommended; www.emorys.com; I-5 exit 186 north to SR 527. &

Pita King / ★★

2210 37TH ST, EVERETT; 425/258-4040
This Middle Eastern bakery is the only place in Western Washington where you can get fresh, hot *manakeesh*—Lebanese pizzas topped with *za'tar*, a blend of thyme, olive oil, sesame, and sumac. Also pick up fresh pita bread or spinach, cheese, or meat pies made to order, all in the authentic stone oven. The grocery portion of the bakery features treats like olives, feta cheese, halal (similar to kosher) meats, and baklava. A member of the gracious Alaeddine family will greet you with traditional Lebanese hospitality. $; MC, V; checks OK; breakfast, lunch every day; no alcohol; no reservations; www.pitakingbakery.com; I-5 exit 192. &

LODGINGS

The Inn at Port Gardner / ★★

1700 W MARINE VIEW DR, EVERETT; 425/252-6779 OR 888/252-6779
Talk about quiet. This place is truly that, and there's not much to do within walking distance except stroll along the marina or eat next door at Lombardi's Italian Restaurant. Yet the Inn at Port Gardner is nice. Thirty-three rooms are done up in neutral tones, some overlooking the water. Some rooms have sweeping mountain views, too. Suites are worth the price, and

all rooms include continental breakfast. The lobby's fireplace and art make it a nice place to lounge. *$$–$$$; AE, DC, DIS, MC, V; local checks only; www.innatportgardner.com; I-5 exit 193.* &

Stanwood

Pastoral Stanwood, west of I-5 on State Route 532, once was a thriving port on the Stillaguamish River, which you can easily imagine from the mural on the **STANWOOD CINEMAS** (6996 265th St NW; 360/629-0514; www.stanwood cinemas.com). Today this still largely agricultural community northwest of Everett is noted for **KAYAK POINT GOLF COURSE** (15711 Marine Dr NE; 360/652-9676; www.kayakpoint.com), consistently ranked one of America's Top 50 Public Golf Courses by *Golf Digest*. Grab a bite at the golf resort's **FIRE CREEK GRILL** (360/652-9676), or drive back to town for a sandwich at the **SCANDIA COFFEE HOUSE AND EATERY** (9808 SR 532; 360/629-2362; www.scandiacoffee.com) before you cross the bridge to Camano Island. For dinner, **MAXIME'S GLOBAL CUISINE** (10007 270th NW; 360/629-6002) is a local favorite.

Stanwood is also known for the 54-acre campus of internationally renowned **PILCHUCK GLASS SCHOOL** (1201 316th St NW; 360/445-3111; www.pilchuck. com), founded in 1971 by glass artist Dale Chihuly and others. Spring group tours (admission $30) and a summer open house (admission $20) give visitors a chance to see artists at work. Learn more from the **STANWOOD CHAMBER OF COMMERCE** (8725 271st St NW; 360/629-0562; www.stanwoodchamber.org).

Camano Island

Less than 2 miles west of Stanwood on SR 532 and an hour's drive north of Seattle, this 18-mile-long island still has that away-from-it-all feel. Beach access is plentiful at **CAMANO ISLAND STATE PARK** (southwest end of island; 360/387-3031), where the day-use area has picnic shelters; camping is also available. You can also comb beaches at two small county parks: **UTSALADY BAY** at the north end and **CAVALERO BEACH** on the southeast side of the island. Some of Washington's best bird-watching is here.

The island also boasts an 18-hole golf course, galleries, and restaurants, including the **CAMANO** (170 E Cross Island Rd, Camano Island; 360/387-9972) and **ISLANDERS ESPRESSO & EATERY** (848 N Sunrise Blvd, Bldg D, Camano Island). The 18-hole **CAMALOCH GOLF COURSE** (326 N East Camano Dr, Camano Island; 360/387-3084 or 800/628-1469; www.camalochgolf.com) also has a deli. Visit the island over Mother's Day weekend and take in the **CAMANO ARTS ASSOCIATION STUDIO TOUR** (360/631-0688; www.camanoarts.org). Find information at the **CAMANO ISLAND CHAMBER OF COMMERCE** (578 N Camano Dr, Camano Island; 360/629-7136; www.camanoisland.org).

LODGINGS

Camano Island Inn / ★★

> 1054 S WEST CAMANO DR, CAMANO ISLAND;
> 360/387-0783 OR 888/718-0783
> Each of the six rooms in this luxurious waterfront inn has a private deck
> and water view. It's not unusual to spot whales, seals, sea lions, and sea
> otters. Rooms have oversize showers; some have jetted tubs. Beds have
> down comforters and pillows. Curl up in front of the fireplace or take
> breakfast in bed. A paved path provides beach access; kayaks are available;
> massages can be arranged. *$$$; AE, DIS, MC, V; checks OK (in advance);
> www.camanoislandinn.com; I-5 exit 212, then SR 532 west.* &

Whidbey Island

The fifth-largest island in the contiguous United States, Whidbey has done some-
thing remarkable over the past 30 years: it has preserved its integrity as an island.
Old values and old growth have not been completely sacrificed to new growth.
Shoreline beauty is undisturbed for miles at a time. Prairies, pasture, meadows,
and woods can be roamed in peace and quiet. The citizenry has preserved **GREEN-
BANK FARM** (see Greenbank) and the 22-square-mile historic **EBEY'S LANDING
NATIONAL HISTORIC RESERVE** (162 Cemetery Rd, Coupeville; 360/678-6084;
www.nps.gov/ebla), as well as the small-town character of Coupeville and Langley. The town of Oak Harbor is kid friendly, with a waterfront park, a local
drive-in movie theater, a comic shop, and fast-food outlets. The five **STATE PARKS**
(www.parks.wa.gov) on Whidbey make for great family hikes and beach walks;
all but Joseph Whidbey State Park have camping.

The art scene here rivals Seattle in quality, and the literary arts are well represented, too. The **WHIDBEY WRITER'S CONFERENCE** (www.writeonwhidbey.org)
draws people nationwide. B and Bs also flourishing on Whidbey, ranging from
cozy rooms in a family home to over-the-top elegance, luxury, and privacy.

ACCESS AND INFORMATION

You can drive to the north end of Whidbey Island by taking I-5 north, turning west on **STATE ROUTE 20** to Anacortes, and following it south over the
Deception Pass bridge onto the island, where the highway continues south
to Keystone. The ferry to Clinton on the south end of the island leaves from
Mukilteo (see Everett Area section) approximately every half hour and takes
about 20 minutes; from the mainland, **SR 525** continues north on Whidbey
to SR 20. There's also a ferry between Keystone, about midway up the west
side of Whidbey, and Port Townsend on the Olympic Peninsula (where SR
20 continues south). The Keystone ferry's schedule is less frequent, the lines
can be long, and the ferry is sometimes waylaid by the tides and weather.
Best to check ahead with **WASHINGTON STATE FERRIES** (206/464-6400
or 888/808-7977; www.wsdot.wa.gov/ferries). Whether you're car-free on

purpose or by necessity, Whidbey has **ISLAND TRANSIT** (360/678-7771 or 360/321-6688; www.islandtransit.org), a fare-free bus system. Get more info at www.whidbeycamanoislands.com.

Clinton

This town is the gateway to Whidbey Island via ferry. Experienced kayaker or not, you'll find five locations to rent kayaks from **WHIDBEY ISLAND KAYAKING COMPANY** (360/321-4683 or 800/233-4319; www.whidbeyislandkayaking.com). If you're into leather, **ACE LEATHER GOODS, INC.** (221 2nd St, Ste 10, Clinton; 360/341-2699; www.aceleathergoods.com) has clothes and more.

RESTAURANTS

Trattoria Giuseppe / ★★

4141 E SR 525, CLINTON; 360/341-3454
This place is a surprise. The decor, in all its high-ceilinged and arched Tuscan taverna aplomb, is not exactly what you'd expect to see behind the Ken's Korner facade. The food is a surprise, too. The pollo Gorgonzola with penne pasta is a local favorite, and the seafood dishes get raves. Their standard Italian fare for dessert, Crema al Caramello, ranks way up there in creamy pleasure. Live classical and jazz piano Saturdays. *$$$; AE, MC, V; checks OK; lunch Mon–Fri, dinner every day; full bar; reservations recommended; www. trattoriagiuseppe.com; from Clinton ferry dock, 2 miles on SR 525, then turn right into Ken's Korner.* &

LODGINGS

The Chinook Retreat Center / ★★

6449 OLD PIETILA RD, CLINTON; 360/341-3404
The Chinook Retreat Center at the Whidbey Institute, on 70 lovely acres of forests and meadows, offers quiet cabins. Heron, Hermitage, Bag End, and Mushroom are smaller and don't have bathrooms or kitchens, which are in a separate building nearby. Each cabin has one bed and electricity, but that's about it. Bag End has a meditation loft and small woodstove. The Farmhouse, with seven bedrooms, and Granny's, with two bedrooms, offer more amenities. If you don't want to cook or eat out, chef Kristian Bentson presents buffet-style meals. *$$–$$$; AE, MC, V; checks OK; www.whidbeyinstitute.org; from Clinton ferry, 2 miles north on SR 525, then turn left at Cultus Bay Rd, go ½ mile to Campbell Rd, turn right, go 0.2 mile, look for sign on left.*

Langley

The Langley area was first established in 1880 when Jacob Anthes purchased 120 acres of forest to harvest cordwood for steamers. The town, on a side road north

WHIDBEY ISLAND THREE-DAY TOUR

DAY ONE: Approach Whidbey from the south via the Mukilteo-Clinton ferry, then grab a latte and bagel at **KIICHLI'S BAGEL BAKERY** (11600 SR 525, Clinton; 360/341-4302) once you're on the island by driving 2 miles north to Ken's Korner, the mini-mall with attitude and the largest shopping center plaza in Clinton. You can also stock up on sandwiches here, then visit **J. W. DESSERTS** (4400 Swan Rd, Clinton; 360/341-1827) for their flourless chocolate cake—these are your picnic rations for your south-end explorations. Drive west a few miles to get aired out at **SOUTH WHIDBEY STATE PARK**'s (www.parks.wa.gov) beach, then enjoy your picnic in the woods above. Spend the afternoon at the shops in **LANGLEY**. Afterward, find your B and B: If you love tall trees, head to the **EAGLES NEST INN** in Langley. If you love Italy, go west to **A TUSCAN LADY** in Freeland. If you love Northwest elegance, it's the **CLIFF HOUSE**, also in Freeland. After settling in, return to Clinton for dinner at **TRATTORIA GIUSEPPE**. For a nightcap, head to the **BEACHFIRE GRILL** (5023 Harbor Hill Dr, Freeland; 360/331-2363) a few miles north at Holmes Harbor, where you can play golf the next morning.

DAY TWO: After breakfast at your B and B, walk through meditative paths at the **EARTH SANCTUARY**, just outside Freeland, and linger in the labyrinth. Head to **BAYVIEW CORNER** and poke around the shops in the **CASH STORE BUILDING**,

of SR 525 just north of Clinton, was incorporated in 1913 and named after Seattle Judge J. W. Langley, who invested in the original woodcutting business. These days, it is the most sophisticated little town on Whidbey. Classy art galleries, fine cuisine, elegant accommodations, and intriguing shops abound. But Langley still preserves its small-town virtues. The much-loved 1930s **CLYDE THEATRE** (217 1st St; 360/221-5525; www.theclyde.net) has movies for $5. The **SOUTH WHIDBEY HISTORICAL MUSEUM** (321 2nd St; 360/221-2101; www.islandweb.org/swhs; open weekends) is inspiring. The views don't hurt either. And there's a pier, a waterfront park, and pocket beaches.

GREGOR RARE BOOKS (197A 2nd St; 360/221-8331; www.gregorbooks. com) provides an interesting afternoon's browse, and the **MOONRAKER** (209 1st St; 360/221-6962) showcases a collection of Northwest titles. Get cool clothes at the **COTTAGE** (210 1st St; 360/221-4747; www.thecottage210.com), **IN THE COUNTRY** (315 1st St; 360/221-8202), and **BIG SISTER** (208 1st St; 360/221-7056). Island time can be measured by a visit to Herb Helsel at **LANGLEY CLOCK AND GALLERY** (220 2nd St; 360/221-3422). He once had a motorcycle shop; now he fixes vintage clocks and is open "by chance and appointment." All things old and interesting, including Virginia, abound at **VIRGINIA'S ANTIQUES** (200 1st St; 360/221-7056). At the **GOOD CHEER THRIFT SHOP** (114 Anthes Ave; 360/221-6454; www.goodcheer.org), original art can be discovered amid castoffs.

then drive north a few miles to **GERRY'S KITCHEN** (1675 Main St, Freeland; 360/331-4818) for lunch. After lunch, visit **MEEKERK GARDENS** (3531 Meerkerk Ln, Greenbank; 360/678-1912) on the way to **GREENBANK FARM** to browse antique shops, sample fine cheeses, and have afternoon tea and loganberry pie at **WHIDBEY PIES CAFE** (765 Wonn Rd, Greenbank; 360/678-1288). Check in to your night's lodgings: If you love log cabins in the woods, it's the **GUEST HOUSE LOG COTTAGES** in Greenbank. If you like historical flavor near the water, it's the **FORT CASEY INN** near Coupeville. Then head into **COUPEVILLE** and spend the afternoon with some good shopping, or play pool at **TOBY'S TAVERN**. Eat dinner at the **OYSTERCATCHER**, then watch the sunset from **FORT CASEY STATE PARK**'s (3 miles south of Coupeville) beaches before calling it a night.

DAY THREE: Return to Coupeville for breakfast at **GREAT TIMES WATERFRONT COFFEE HOUSE**, then visit **EBEY'S LANDING NATIONAL HISTORIC RESERVE** and **FORT EBEY STATE PARK** (395 Fort Ebey Rd, Whidbey Island; 360/678-4636). Head north to Oak Harbor for lunch at **FLYERS RESTAURANT AND BREWERY**, or grab picnic fixings at **SEABOLTS SMOKEHOUSE**, then head out to **JOSEPH WHIDBEY STATE PARK** for the afternoon before returning to Oak Harbor for dinner at **KASTEEL FRANSSEN**. To end your tour, stay at the welcoming **COMPASS ROSE** B and B in Coupeville.

Lithographs and antique prints are found at **LOWRY-JAMES RARE PRINTS** (101 Anthes Ave; 360/221-0477; www.lowryjames.com).

At last count, there were 10 galleries in town, including **KARLSON/GRAY** (302 1st St; 360/221-2978; www.karlsongraygallery.com), where the sculpture of Georgia Gerber is on display. When you need a break, stroll **SEAWALL PARK** (below 1st St), where you'll encounter Gerber's sculpture of a boy and a dog. Her life-size bronze pig is a famous landmark in Seattle's Pike Place Market. The handblown glass in Langley is distinctive. George Springer, a glass artist for more than 30 years, can be found at his **HELLEBORE GLASS STUDIO** (308 1st St; 360/221-2067; www.helleboreglass.com). **MUSEO PICCOLO GALLERY** (215 1st St; 360/221-7737; www.museo.cc) also features glass art. The **ARTIST'S GALLERY COOPERATIVE** (117 Anthes Ave; 360/221-7675; www.whidbeyartists.com) includes everything from the sublime to the ridiculous. **ART WALKS** (www.artguide.com) are on the first Saturday of each month.

Everything chocolate can be had at the **CHOCOLATE FLOWER FARM AND THE GARDEN SHED** (5040 Saratoga Rd [farm]; 224 1st St [shop]; 360/221-4464; www.chocolateflowerfarm.com). Wines are offered at the Osenbach family–operated **WHIDBEY ISLAND WINERY** (5237 S Langley Rd; 360/221-2040; www.whidbeyislandwinery.com). There are too many good places to eat in this little town, including **DIMARTINI'S BAKERY** (221 2nd St; 360/221-3525), where the locals rave about the pesto pizza and the three-milk cake—which actually translates into cream in all its manifestations. Before or after a movie at the Clyde, stop in at **MIKE'S PLACE COFFEEHOUSE AND CREAMERY** (219 1st St; 360/221-6575), complete with a restaurant in back. The locals love **VILLAGE PIZZERIA** (106 1st St; 360/221-3363)—one East Coast transplant is rapturous about their meatball sandwich. A north island resident drives down to eat banana-bread French toast at the **BRAEBURN** (197D 2nd St; 360/221-3211).

Langley has **MYSTERY WEEKEND** in February, a **COFFEE FEST** in April, the **CHOOCHOKAM ARTS FESTIVAL** in July, and **DJANGOFEST** (www.djangofest. com/nw) in September. For information, contact the **SOUTH WHIDBEY CHAMBER OF COMMERCE** (208 Anthes Ave; 360/221-6765 or 888/232-2080; www. langleychamb.whidbey.com).

RESTAURANTS

Café Langley / ★★

113 1ST ST, LANGLEY; 360/221-3090
Since 1989 the brothers Garibyan have been holding court with the tastiest Mediterranean fare in the region. This storefront café has cuisine sparkling with creativity, from marinated-eggplant sandwiches to tasty lamb shish kebabs, in an atmosphere of comfy elegance. The hummus is creamy beyond delicious; the Northwest salmon and halibut are beautifully prepared; the Mediterranean seafood stew is rich with mussels, shrimp, salmon, and scallops. Russian cream with raspberry sauce is a signature dessert. *$$–$$$; AE, MC, V; checks OK; dinner every day (Tues–Sun winter); full bar; reservations recommended; www.cafelangley.com; downtown.*

The Edgecliff / ★★

510 CASCADE AVE, LANGLEY; 360/221-8899 OR 866/825-3640
Located on the bluff overlooking the Langley Marina, the first thing that gets your attention in this restaurant is the views of Puget Sound and the Cascades. The inside is elegant, too. And then, the food: mouth-watering steaks, seafood and creative fresh salads and pastas. The butternut-squash ravioli, for example, comes with a brown butter–brandy sauce, caramelized walnuts, roasted garlic, and fresh sage. Northwest wines and handcrafted desserts add to the appeal. *$$–$$$; AE, DIS, MC, V; checks OK; lunch, dinner every day; full bar; reservations recommended; on cliff near north end of 1st St.* ৬

LODGINGS

Inn at Langley / ★★★★

400 1ST ST, LANGLEY; 360/221-3033
This inn is tops in good taste, so if you want to stay at the "best of the best," go for it. Twenty-six luxurious rooms and cottages all have views, fireplaces, and original art. Spa services are available. Superb dinners are served only on weekends (which can start on Thursdays in the summer). Chef Matt Costello, once a culinary star in Seattle, sources excellent local ingredients and introduces each dish to diners. *$$$$; AE, MC, V; no checks; www.innatlangley.com; downtown.* ৬

Saratoga Inn / ★★★

201 CASCADE AVE, LANGLEY; 360/221-5801 OR 800/698-2910
A Cape Cod inn with a Puget Sound view, the Saratoga is elegant and trendy with its big wraparound porch, fireplaces in its 15 rooms, most with views, and careful detail in wood and stone. Teddy bears (for adoption) on the beds and the big cookie jar in the lobby cozy up the place. There's gourmet breakfast in the dining room and afternoon hors d'oeuvres in the parlor. *$$$–$$$$; AE, DC, DIS, MC, V; no checks; www.saratogainnwhidbeyisland.com; 2-minute walk from downtown.* &

Bayview Corner

In 1999 Nancy Nordhoff (a National Women's History Project award winner in 2006) invested in 22 acres of commercial land at historic Bayview Corner, just off SR 525, about halfway between Clinton and Freeland. Since 1924, the **CASH STORE BUILDING** has been a general store, a gas station, a feed store, a food co-op, an art store, and a pet laundry. It's now home to eclectic shops and restaurants, all celebrating local and environmental sensibilities guided by the **GOOSEFOOT COMMUNITY FUND** (www.goosefoot.org). **BAYVIEW ARTS** (360/321-8414; www.bayviewarts.org), under the eye of Mary Ann Mansfield, has impressive art. You can rent bikes at the **HALF LINK BICYCLE SHOP** (360/331-7980). The longest-running **FARMERS MARKET** on the island is at Bayview every Saturday March through September (www.bayviewfarmersmarket.com).

Freeland

Old Freeland is as funky and friendly as ever. The same family of feisty females runs the **FREELAND CAFÉ** (1642 E Main St, Freeland; 360/331-9945; www.whidbey.com/freelandcafe), where you can get breakfast all day as well as Virina's famous teriyaki sauce. This really is a local, no-frills joint. The **ISLAND TEA COMPANY** (1664 Main St, Freeland; 360/331-6080; www.islandteacompany.com) is a cottage tea shop.

Just outside Freeland, off Newman Road, is the **EARTH SANCTUARY** (6144 Wahl Rd, Freeland; 360/321-5465; www.earthsanctuary.org), where eco-artist Chuck Pettis has transformed sacred inspiration into 75 acres of earthy delight. The prayer wheels, stones, and meditative paths are calming. A $7 donation lets you walk a labyrinth, stand with sacred stones, or spin a high-tech Tibetan prayer wheel containing 1.3 trillion prayers. There's also a small retreat house.

Right across the street from the road to the Earth Sanctuary is **ISLAND GLASS** (2062 E Newman Rd, Freeland; 360/321-4439; 10am–5pm Sat–Sun), where Robert Adamson retreated after many years of jetting around the world teaching the art of glass-blowing, and now sells affordable handblown glass art.

LODGINGS

Cliff House / ★★

727 WINDMILL RD, FREELAND; 360/331-1566 OR 800/297-4118

Twenty-five years ago, Peggy Moore knew just what she was doing when she had Arne Bystrom design the exquisite Cliff House, with its central atrium, sunken living room, stone fireplace, spa tubs, and breathtaking views of sea, sky, and mountains. It's still a luxury to experience a private getaway in this unique A-frame with its original art, Native rugs, and rare Indian baskets. There's a trail down to miles of beach. The quaint and cozy Seacliff Cottage is less expensive and more playfully decorated, with a deck overlooking the water and a kitchenette. Peggy, who lives in a house on the premises, sets a beautiful breakfast table in each of the houses. Very pricey; very worth it. $$$$; *no credit cards; checks required (in advance); www.cliffhouse.net; Bush Pt Rd to Windmill Rd.*

A Tuscan Lady / ★★★

619 DOLPHIN DR, FREELAND; 360/331-5057

It's hard to be fully prepared for this opulent place. The extraordinary attention to detail inside and out makes A Tuscan Lady a complete getaway, even if you don't make it to the nearby beach. The gardens and the rooms are full of color and design. Artist-owner Darla Duchessa has poured her creative heart into this Italian holiday experience. The separate villa, which sleeps six, comes complete with a light-filled cathedral loft, with beds in each corner in honor of Darlene's four daughters, who always want to sleep in the same room together. The big, private bedroom is a romantic hideaway in the heart of the villa. *$$–$$$; MC, V; checks OK; www.atuscanlady.com; call for directions.*

Greenbank

When **GREENBANK FARM** (765 E Wonn Rd, Greenbank; 360/678-7700; www. greenbankfarm.com) suddenly seemed doomed to become a 700-home development, the locals took action. Within weeks, private and public money, and a common passion, combined to save the 522-acre farm. Once the largest loganberry farm in the country, Greenbank Farm is now home to everything from the Greenbank Car Show to the Burning Word Poetry Festival to the Loganberry Festival, as well as galleries, a cheese shop, and a weekly **FARMERS MARKET** on Sunday May through September.

LODGINGS

Guest House Log Cottages / ★★

24371 SR 525, GREENBANK; 360/678-3115 OR 800/997-3115

These log cabins in the woods are furnished with such care that you feel like you've come home to some long-lost memory. The five cabins, each with all the conveniences of a small house, are loaded with personal charm, comfy furnishings, warm fireplaces, and antiques. The large, private lodge overlooking the pond boasts a 24-foot-tall stone fireplace. It's your own personal dream home where you can meditate alone in the jetted tub in a solarium or play in the Jacuzzi for two with a view. There's a swimming pool in summer for all the guests. $$$–$$$$; DIS, MC, V; checks OK; www.guesthouselogcottages. com; 1 mile south of Greenbank Store.

Coupeville

Like any old town worth its history, Coupeville wages a war with itself over visitors—which is a good thing. Visually, historical preservation prevails, even if galleries and shops are shiny and new. Coupeville fills up on festival occasions, some of which involve kites, art, and water, so plan ahead.

It's **GRAY WHALE** country around here for a few months each year. Mid-March to May, they can be seen from the island's east shore on Saratoga Passage. Penn Cove mussels are harvested from here for good cause. In March the **PENN COVE MUSSEL FESTIVAL** (360/678-5434; www.thepenncovemusselfestival.com) offers bluegrass music, mussel-shell jewelry, cheap good beer, and bowls of mussels. In mid-May, watch tribal canoe races and admire Native arts and crafts during the **PENN COVE WATER FESTIVAL** (www.penncovewaterfestival.com). And yes, the **ISLAND COUNTY HISTORICAL SOCIETY MUSEUM** (908 NW Alexander St, Coupeville; 360/678-3310; www.islandhistory.org) really does have the largest collection of woolly-mammoth bones in the Puget Sound area.

For refreshments, stop at the patio at **GREAT TIMES WATERFRONT COFFEE HOUSE** (12 NW Front St, Coupeville; 360/678-5368) or at **KNEAD & FEED** (4 NW Front St, Coupeville; 360/678-5431; www.kneadandfeed.com). **CHRISTOPHER'S** (103 Coveland St, Coupeville; 360/678-5480; www.christophersonwhidbey.com) is also a local favorite for seafood and steaks. **TOBY'S TAVERN** (8 NW Front St, Coupeville; 360/678-4222; www.tobysuds.com) helps keep the town well supplied with good brews and pub grub.

Get information from the **CENTRAL WHIDBEY CHAMBER OF COMMERCE** (107 S Main St, Bldg E, Coupeville; 360/678-5434; www.centralwhidbeychamber. com), as well as two other Web sites (www.coupevillelodging.com, www.come tocoupeville.com).

RESTAURANTS

Oystercatcher / ★★★

901 GRACE ST, COUPEVILLE; 360/678-0683
This intimate—only eight tables—bistro commands a pretty setting on Penn Cove and serves high-quality yet simply prepared meals made with local, sustainable, Whidbey Island products. The chef, Susan Vanderbeek, shows off the skills she gained working under Alice Waters (of Chez Panisse fame): classic dishes mostly in the French tradition, expertly executed. The small space displays an open kitchen, so it can be quite noisy. The menu typically lists five appetizers, four entrées (fowl, pork, venison, and other meats, plus

a vegetarian item), a fish of the day, a few seasonal sides, and a number of house-crafted desserts, like honey ice cream—a must-try. *$$$; MC, V; checks OK; dinner Wed–Sun; beer and wine; reservations recommended; www. oystercatcherwhidbey.com; behind Coupeville Examiner office.*

LODGINGS

The Anchorage Inn / ★

807 N MAIN ST, COUPEVILLE; 360/678-5581 OR 877/230-1313

Owners-innkeepers Dave and Dianne Binder love what they are doing so much that they teach the art of innkeeping as well as practice it at the Anchorage Inn. Dave even folds the breakfast napkins into unique origami shapes reflecting the theme or mood of the day. Yes, it's fun here. This new "old" Victorian has seven lavishly appointed guest rooms, most with water views, all with cheery charm and private baths. Savor Dianne's hearty breakfast—and don't forget to ask Dave about his giant pumpkins. *$$; DIS, MC, V; checks OK; www.anchorage-inn.com; 1 block from waterfront.*

Captain Whidbey Inn / ★★

2072 W CAPTAIN WHIDBEY INN RD, COUPEVILLE;
360/678-4097 OR 800/366-4097

This log inn dates back to 1907. It's good if you like rustic knotty pine, bohemian ambience, and a bar where Hemingway would be happy to be reincarnated. Twelve rooms in the main lodge have shared bathrooms. Fear not: 4 cottages have fireplaces and baths, and 13 lagoon rooms—the best choices—have private baths and verandas. Avoid the rooms above the bar. Try an afternoon or extended sail on the *Cutty Sark. $$–$$$; AE, DIS, MC, V; no checks; www.captainwhidbey.com; off Madrona Wy on Penn Cove.*

Fort Casey Inn / ★

1124 S ENGLE RD, COUPEVILLE; 360/678-5050 OR 866/661-6604

Overlooking Puget Sound and Crockett Lake (a bird sanctuary), Fort Casey Inn is right next door to Fort Casey State Park, with its bunkers, beaches, lighthouse, and cannons that were fired only in practice. Each of the row of nine homes is fully restored in Georgian Revival–era style as a two-bedroom duplex B and B with a full bath; breakfast is stocked in each kitchen. The inn's history is reflected in the decor, which ranges from tied-rag rugs to old military photographs. *$$–$$$; MC, V; checks OK; www.fortcaseyinn.com; 2 miles west of Coupeville.*

Oak Harbor

This Navy town, with its transient military population, takes a lot of heat from the more "granola"-minded (in Oak Harbor–speak) islanders to the south. The truth is, along with the town's fast-food joints, big-box stores, traffic jams, and high decibels from low-flying naval planes, the nearby base preserves open space, provides jobs, and adds diversity. The Navy base's friendly, low-fee golf course with a view is even open to the public. Besides, if you're taking the kids along, they like the planes, burgers, and family-friendly accommodations.

CITY BEACH PARK, along the bay at the south end of town, has playground equipment, a saltwater lagoon to swim in, and ice cream at the windmill. Eat burgers at **FLYERS RESTAURANT AND BREWERY** (32295 SR 20; 360/675-5858; www.eatatflyers.com), then head off to the **BLUE FOX DRIVE-IN THEATRE** and **BRATTLAND GO-KARTS** (1403 Monroe Landing Rd; 360/675-5667; www.blue foxdrivein.com) for fun and nostalgia. There's a great video arcade here, too.

Oak Harbor is working hard to restore the historic qualities of its old town. On Pioneer Way, close to the harbor, there are three antique shops within two blocks, including **SHADY LADIES ANTIQUES** (Old Town Mall, 830 SE Pioneer Wy; 360/679-1902), which specializes in everything from fine and funky furniture to costume and estate jewelry. Check out **WHIDBEY WILD BIRD** (Old Town Mall, 860 SE Pioneer Wy; 360/279-2572), the **WIND & TIDE BOOKSHOP** (790 SE Pioneer Wy; 360/675-1342), and **EILEEN'S CREATIVE KITCHENWARE** (670 SE Pioneer Wy; 360/675-6894).

The locals swear by the Greek food at **ZORBAS** (841 SE Pioneer Wy; 360/279-8322), the tasty multiethnic dishes at **SWEET RICE THAI CUISINE** (885 SE Pioneer Wy; 360/679-8268), and the salmon and chowder at **SEABOLTS SMOKEHOUSE** (31640 SR 20, Ste 3; 360/675-1105 or 800/574-1120; www.seabolts.com).

Three miles west of Oak Harbor is **JOSEPH WHIDBEY STATE PARK** (888/226-7688; day-use only, open Apr–Oct), with a great beach. **DECEPTION PASS STATE PARK** (888/226-7688; camping year-round) is only 9 miles north. Even though it's the most-visited park in the state, with more than 4,000 acres, 15 miles of saltwater shoreline, and 38 miles of trails, solitude is only a hike away. Don't forget the trails on the north side of the much-photographed bridge that connects Whidbey to Fidalgo Island.

RESTAURANTS

Kasteel Franssen / ★

33575 SR 20 (AULD HOLLAND INN), OAK HARBOR;
360/675-2288 OR 800/228-0148

The trademark windmill, as well as the European fare and the local following, still prevail at this iconic Oak Harbor restaurant. Chef and co-owner Scott Fraser of Vancouver, British Columbia, was trained in French cooking and includes caribou and pheasant along with the favorite sautéed beef tenderloin served with brandy dijonnaise cream sauce. Adjacent to the restaurant, the Auld Holland Inn has 34 rooms with antiques, some with hot tubs; rates include continental breakfast. $$; AE, DIS, MC, V; checks OK; lunch, dinner every day; full bar; reservations recommended; www.auldhollandinn.com; ½ mile north of town.

LODGINGS

The Coachman Inn / ★

32959 SR 20, OAK HARBOR; 360/675-0727

The Coachman Inn at the north end of town makes a great base for a family weekend of exploring on Whidbey. Although it's on the main road and has a motel look to its various buildings, the inn has quiet rooms in the back with a mountain view, minikitchens, a pool, private entrances, and great rates. On the free-breakfast menu, there's sausage and gravy as well as cereals. *$$; AE, MC, V; no checks; www.thecoachmaninn.com; at Midway Blvd.* ⅃

The Skagit Valley

As you travel north of Everett on I-5, the expanse of the Skagit Valley is always a bit of a visual surprise: you drop rapidly off the ridge at Starbird Road and plummet quickly down to the valley floor (be aware that the Washington State Patrol loves this spot for catching speeders). Come March, and lasting roughly into mid-June, the fields are transformed into sheets of wondrous color when daffodils, tulips, and irises take the stage. The countryside is ideal for bicyclists, but beware the throngs of visitors during the annual **TULIP FESTIVAL** (100 E Montgomery St, Mount Vernon; 360/428-5959; www.tulipfestival.org; Apr). Contact the **MOUNT VERNON CHAMBER OF COMMERCE** (105 E Kincaid St, Mount Vernon; 360/428-8547; www.mountvernonchamber.com) for information.

Conway

RESTAURANTS

Conway Pub & Eatery / ★★

18611 MAIN ST, CONWAY; 360/445-4733

The menu here is classic Northwest tavern fare. The decor is rustic saloon. The atmosphere is one big, happy family. And the sign over the door reads, "Peace, love & joy to all who enter here." That sums up all you need to know about this legendary establishment, and a trip to the Skagit Valley is not complete without a stop here, even if it's just to buy a souvenir T-shirt. If you're planning on grazing your way through La Conner, at least try "the best oysters this side of the Mississippi." *$; AE, DIS, MC, V; checks OK; lunch, dinner every day; full bar; no reservations; I-5 exit 221.*

La Conner

La Conner was founded in 1867 by John Conner, a trading-post operator who named the town after his wife, Louisa A. Conner. Over the years, the town became a haven for nonconformists, always with a smattering of artists and writers, including Mark Tobey, Morris Graves, Guy Anderson, and Tom Robbins. This free-spirited attitude contributes to the harmony that exists between the Swinomish Nation on the Fidalgo Island side of the channel and the Skagit-side community, creating a cultural richness exceptional for a town the size of La Conner. Merchants have crafted a unique American bazaar here. **HELLAMS VINEYARD** (109 N 1st St, Ste 101; 360/466-1758; www.hellamsvineyard.com), La Conner's only specialty wine and beer shop, fits right into the bohemian atmosphere with tastings and dinner cruises through nearby Deception Pass.

Partake of tasty wood-fired pizzas and fine ales at **LA CONNER BREWING COMPANY** (117 S 1st St; 360/466-1415). Sample Spanish-Mediterranean fare at the **DULCE PLATE** (508 Morris St; 360/466-1630; www.dulceplate.com). Enjoy ambience and nostalgia at **SEEDS: A BISTRO & BAR** (623 Morris St; 360/466-3280) in the historic Tillinghast Seed Company building. **KERSTIN'S** (505 S 1st St; 360/466-9111) does marvelous European-style dishes. For rustic charm, organic food, and artisan breads, give **NELL THORN RESTAURANT & PUB** (205 Washington St; 360/466-4261) a visit.

GACHES MANSION (703 S 2nd St; 360/466-4288; www.laconnerquilts.com), home of the not-to-be-missed **QUILT AND TEXTILE MUSEUM**, is a wonderful example of American Victorian architecture, with period furnishings and a widow's walk that looks out on the entire Skagit Valley. The **MUSEUM OF NORTHWEST ART** (121 S 1st St; 360/466-4446; www.museumofnwart.org; Tues–Sun) is a regional gem. Each November, the community hosts the **ARTS ALIVE** festival (360/466-4778 or 888/642-9284; www.laconnerchamber.com).

RESTAURANTS

Calico Cupboard / ★★☆

720 S 1ST ST, LA CONNER (AND BRANCHES); 360/466-4451

The Calico Cupboard is a specialty café with a tradition of hearty breakfasts and soup-and-salad lunches. But don't stop there: the pastries earned the Calico "Best Bakery in Skagit County" awards for many years. Expect standing-room-only crowds on Tulip Festival weekends in March and April. Buy your goodies from the take-out counter and find a sunny bench by the water. *$; MC, V; checks OK; breakfast, lunch every day; beer and wine; no reservations; www.calicocupboardcafe.com; on main drag downtown.* &

Palmer's on the Waterfront / ★★★☆

512 S 1ST ST, LA CONNER; 360/466-3147

With sage green walls and high-gloss ivory woodwork, the spacious digs of La Conner's only waterfront fine-dining restaurant are enhanced by expansive views of the Swinomish Channel; there's also a deck. Dinner reflects a flair for French continental cuisine (à la the Northwest), with an emphasis on the art of sauté. Begin with the Wicked Escargot appetizer and the Crunchy Montrachet Salad while you deliberate on entrées ranging from the classic (roasted London broil) to the exotic (spicy calamari penne). Martinis are a specialty. *$$$; AE, MC, V; local checks only; lunch, dinner every day; full bar; reservations recommended; www.nwcuisine.com; left off Morris St at 1st St.* &

LODGINGS

The Heron Inn & Watergrass Day Spa / ★★

117 MAPLE AVE, LA CONNER; 360/466-4626 OR 877/883-8899

Welcome to one of the prettiest hostelries in town, with 11 jewel-box guest rooms. Relax on one of three outside decks with mountain views, or slip into the garden hot tub. Splurge on Room 32, with a gas fireplace, a spacious sitting area, and a wonderful view of the Skagit Valley and Cascades. The day spa has two treatment rooms. *$$–$$$; MC, V; checks OK; www.theheron. com; east edge of town.*

Hotel Planter / ★☆

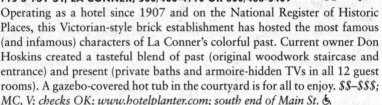

715 S 1ST ST, LA CONNER; 360/466-4710 OR 800/488-5409

Operating as a hotel since 1907 and on the National Register of Historic Places, this Victorian-style brick establishment has hosted the most famous (and infamous) characters of La Conner's colorful past. Current owner Don Hoskins created a tasteful blend of past (original woodwork staircase and entrance) and present (private baths and armoire-hidden TVs in all 12 guest rooms). A gazebo-covered hot tub in the courtyard is for all to enjoy. *$$–$$$; MC, V; checks OK; www.hotelplanter.com; south end of Main St.* &

Skagit Bay Hideaway / ★★☆

17430 GOLDENVIEW AVE, LA CONNER;
360/466-2262 OR 888/466-2262

This luxury waterfront hideaway features a Northwest shingle-style cottage divided into two identical suites. Watch the sun setting over Skagit Bay from your rooftop spa, or enjoy the view from your living room, complete with fireplace. In the morning, a full gourmet breakfast is served en suite. Bathroom showers are, literally, a blast, with double heads and multiple body sprays that will make you feel as if you just stepped into a waterfall. *$$$$; MC, V; checks OK; www.skagitbay.com; 1½ miles west of La Conner across Rainbow Bridge on Fidalgo Island.*

Wild Iris Inn / ★★

121 MAPLE AVE, LA CONNER; 360/466-1400 OR 800/477-1400

This 18-room inn with spacious suites feels a bit "country." Located at the entrance to La Conner, the inn is a short walk to downtown restaurants and shops. New owners took over in 2005 and made significant updates to the property. Twelve rooms are deluxe suites featuring gas fireplaces, oversize jetted tubs, flat-screen TVs, and panoramic Cascade and farmland views from decks or balconies. Most standard rooms, however, face the parking lot and seem a bit cramped. A complimentary two-course breakfast served in the private dining room is included with your stay. *$$$; AE, MC, V; checks OK; www.wildiris.com; east edge of town.* &

Mount Vernon

Mount Vernon is the "big city" of surrounding Skagit and Island counties. Like many of the small cities sprinkled throughout the Puget Sound basin, it is experiencing growth as Seattle's urban sprawl inches closer and closer. Still, Mount Vernon maintains its small-town flavor.

Pick up some goodies from the **SKAGIT VALLEY FOOD CO-OP** (202 S 1st St; 360/336-9777; www.skagitcoop.com). Or drop into the **SKAGIT RIVER BREWING COMPANY** (404 S 3rd St; 360/336-2884; www.skagitbrew.com) for pub grub. There's also a **CALICO CUPBOARD** (121-B Freeway Dr; 360/336-3107). Check out the burgeoning crop of retail merchants along Main Street. **IL GRANAIO** (100 E Montgomery St, Ste 110; 360/419-0674; www.granaio.com), Mount Vernon's answer to authentic Italian cuisine, is a great place to wind down.

RESTAURANTS

The Porterhouse / ★

416 W GATES, MOUNT VERNON; 360/336-9989
Silas and Elise Reynolds have created the warm environment of a British Isle public house through a sophisticated pub menu and their signature rotating beer selection. Make this your stop for a casual meal, a game of darts, a pint of porter, and a dose of genuine small-town hospitality. *$–$$; DIS, MC, V; checks OK; lunch, dinner every day; beer and wine; no reservations; just off corner of Main St.* &

The San Juan Islands

The San Juan Islands, an archipelago of more than 450 islands, are breathtakingly beautiful. The islands are a hiker's, kayaker's, wildlife lover's, and bird-watcher's year-round paradise: more than 275 species of birds have been sighted, and 50 pairs of eagles nest here. Orca whale pods frequent the area, and sometimes the aurora borealis is visible at night.

Only four islands are accessible by Washington State ferry (see Access and Information): Lopez, Orcas, San Juan, and Shaw. To best serve yourself, the place, and the community, savor the San Juans off-season. Don't worry about the weather because the islands see more than 200 days of sun a year, so the typical Northwest gloom does not take hold. Rarely is there an entire day without sun. Fall lasts nicely through October, and spring can begin in February. Even the winter is lovely, with low light spreading silver across sea and sky, and the quiet has deep appeal.

With ferry-fare increases and seasonal surcharges, it's pricey in the summer, plus the ferry lines are long and lodgings booked full. There's one exception, however: there's a great summer day trip to be had by walking on the ferry to Friday Harbor, getting a $15 day pass for the seasonal **SAN JUAN TRANSIT** (www. sanjuantransit.com; May–Sept), and spending the day exploring San Juan Island stop by stop. You can get to Lime Kiln State Park, Pelindaba Lavender Farm, the

---

SAN JUAN ISLANDS THREE-DAY TOUR

DAY ONE: Grab fixings at **CALICO CUPBOARD** in **ANACORTES** for a picnic breakfast on an early morning ferry to **FRIDAY HARBOR** on **SAN JUAN ISLAND**, and head out to **ROCHE HARBOR VILLAGE** (10 miles north) to stroll the village artists' booths and the **WESTCOTT BAY RESERVE SCULPTURE PARK** before having lunch at the **LIME KILN CAFÉ** or out on the deck at the **MADRONA BAR AND GRILL**. After lunch, take the five-minute drive along West Valley Road to the **SAN JUAN ISLAND NATIONAL HISTORIC PARK'S ENGLISH CAMP**. Then take Mitchell Bay Road to the scenic Westside Road where, during summer, orca whales can often be seen feeding. Stop at **LIME KILN POINT STATE PARK** for a whale update at the lighthouse. On your way south, take a left on Wold Road and drive a quarter mile to **PELINDABA LAVENDER FARM**, particularly lovely in summer. (The farm's products are also for sale at their shop in downtown Friday Harbor, so do a quick drive-by for a look at lavender and opt time-wise for whales if they're in local waters.) Continue south down Bailer Hill Road to False Bay Road, turn right, and find your way to Cattle Point Road. Turn right again and go about a mile to Old Farm Road. Turn right and then go left on Starlight Way to **OLYMPIC LIGHTS** B and B. Check in, relax, then take the short 10-minute drive back to **FRIDAY HARBOR**

---

alpaca farm, English Camp, and Roche Harbor. Arrive early enough in the day to make the most of the hourly pickups at each place.

ACCESS AND INFORMATION

The San Juan Islands are served year-round by the **WASHINGTON STATE FERRIES** (206/464-6400 or 800/843-3779; www.wsdot.wa.gov/ferries) from Anacortes (see Anacortes section). In the summer, getting your car on a ferry out of Anacortes can mean a three-hour-plus wait. Cars pay only westbound, so if you plan to visit more than one island, arrange to go to the farthest (San Juan) first and explore your way east.

Summer options for those who don't want to drive I-5 to Anacortes include the high-speed **VICTORIA CLIPPER** (2701 Alaskan Wy, Seattle; 206/448-5000 or 800/888-2535; www.clippervacations.com), which travels daily in season from downtown Seattle to Friday Harbor. **KENMORE AIR** (425/486-1257 or 866/435-9524; www.kenmoreair.com) has floatplane flights to the islands from Lake Union north of downtown Seattle and from north Lake Washington in Kenmore. **SAN JUAN AIRLINES** (800/874-4434; www.sanjuanairlines. com) offers flights from Boeing Field, Bellingham, and Anacortes.

The **AIRPORTER SHUTTLE** (866/235-5247; www.airporter.com) gets you from Sea-Tac Airport to ferry terminals in Anacortes, Bellingham, and

for pasta at **VINNY'S** before turning in for the night.

DAY TWO: Wake up to breakfast at the inn and then walk to neighboring **AMERICAN CAMP**. Stop at the visitor center and explore some of the trails along the shore or up on the hillside before heading to **FRIDAY HARBOR** and an afternoon ferry to **ORCAS ISLAND**. (No fare required for eastbound ferries.) Park your car in line early and save time for lunch at the **BACKDOOR KITCHEN** and a shopping stroll through town before the ferry leaves. On Orcas Island, check in to the **OUTLOOK INN** in Eastsound for the night. Stroll the shops and galleries in town and eat dinner at the **INN AT SHIP BAY RESTAURANT**. If there's time, check out the movie at the **SEA VIEW THEATRE** (A St, Eastsound; 360/376-5724).

DAY THREE: After breakfast with the locals at **VERN'S** (246 Main St, Eastsound; 360/376-2231), overlooking the water, take a drive up Mount Constitution in **MORAN STATE PARK** for the view and, if there's time, a short hike. (Get trail info at park headquarters.) Follow the morning's excursion with lunch at **CAFÉ OLGA**, with a fine art gallery as well as fine food. Get a late afternoon ferry to **LOPEZ ISLAND** and check in to the **MACKAYE HARBOR INN**. Go for a bike ride (compliments of the inn) or rent a kayak and paddle the shore, then head out for dinner at the **BAY CAFÉ**. Stroll the inn's gardens to end your final day in the islands.

Renton. The **ISLAND AIRPORTER** (360/378-7438; www.islandairporter.com) offers direct service between San Juan Islands and Sea-Tac Airport.

EMILY'S GUIDE & MAPS (360/378-2750; www.emilysguides.com) are a great resource. The **SAN JUAN ISLANDS VISITORS BUREAU** (888/468-3701; www.guidetosanjuans.com) Web site is excellent. For news, there's another Web site (www.sanjuanislander.com) to check out.

Anacortes

Anacortes, the gateway to the San Juans, is itself on an island: Fidalgo. Though most travelers rush through town on their way to the ferry, there are lots of reasons, especially the great parks, to stick around. The 2,800-acre **ANACORTES COMMUNITY FOREST LANDS** (360/293-3725; www.friendsoftheacfl.org), with 50 miles of trails, is exceptional. **WASHINGTON PARK** (360/293-1927 for campsite availability), less than a mile west of the ferry terminal, is another treasure. For Anacortes culture, **ART WALKS** (www.anacortesart.com) are the first Friday of each month. Historic **MURALS** deck the walls throughout town. **FESTIVALS** (www.anacortes.org) range from quilts to cars to jazz.

Seafaring folks should poke around **MARINE SUPPLY AND HARDWARE** (202 Commercial Ave; 360/293-3014; www.marinesupplyandhardware.com); established in 1913, it's packed with marine items as well as reclining ceramic frogs in polka-dot bikinis. For the other kind of yarn, **ANA CROSS STITCH** (719 Commercial Ave; 360/299-9010 or 877/358-KNIT; www.annacrossstitch.com) is a favorite. History buffs can visit the **ANACORTES HISTORY MUSEUM** (1305 8th St; 360/293-1915; www.museum.cityofanacortes.org). If kayaking is your passion, **ISLAND OUTFITTERS** (2515 Commercial Ave; 360/299-2300 or 866/445-7506; www.seakayakshop.com) offers tours out of **CAP SANTE MARINA** (360/293-0694; www.portofanacortes.com). Take a kayak lesson or rent one for a San Juan weekend; reservations required.

Casual eateries abound. A local favorite for breakfast, burgers, and fish-and-chips is **SAN JUAN LANES STORK'S RESTAURANT** (2821 Commercial Ave; 360/293-5185), at the local bowling alley. **GERE-A-DELI** (502 Commercial Ave; 360/293-7383) is a friendly hangout with good homemade food. **CALICO CUP-BOARD** (901 Commercial Ave; 360/293-7315; www.calicocupboardcafe.com) is an offshoot of the popular café-bakery in La Conner. You'll find artisan breads and more at **LA VIE EN ROSE FRENCH BAKERY AND PASTRY SHOP** (418 Commercial Ave; 360/299-9546; www.laviebakery.com) and decadent doughnuts at the **DONUT HOUSE** (2719 Commercial Ave; 360/293-4053), open all day every day for any 3am cravings. The bakery at the **STORE** (919 37th St; 360/293-2851) specializes in huge muffins; there's also a deli.

For local brews, try the **ROCKFISH GRILL AND ANACORTES BREWERY** (320 Commercial Ave; 360/588-1720; www.anacortesrockfish.com). Nearly next door, the **STAR BAR CAFÉ** (416½ Commercial Ave; 360/299-2120; www.starbaranacortes.com) is the healthy-fare hangout. The **GREEK ISLANDS** (2001 Commercial Ave; 360/293-6911), **ESTEBAN'S MEXICAN RESTAURANT** (1506 Commercial Ave; 360/299-1060), and **TOYKO JAPANESE RESTAURANT** (818 Commercial Ave; 360/293-9898) bring international fare to life.

If you're aiming for an early ferry, a good and reasonable overnight choice is the **SHIP HARBOR INN** (5316 Ferry Terminal Rd; 360/293-5177 or 800/852-8568; www.shipharborinn.com), right next to the terminal. It has a comfortable mix of refurbished and spotless motel-style rooms and cabins-with-a-view. Consider staying in Anacortes and day-tripping to the San Juans and Whidbey Island.

RESTAURANTS

Flounder Bay Café / ★

2201 SKYLINE WY, ANACORTES; 360/293-3680
This waterside café in Skyline Marina has boldly colored sails hanging from the ceiling and fresh, seasonal seafood on the plate. The Sunset Suppers are favorites with locals. There's live jazz on Sunday evenings and warm-season dinner cruises. *$$; AE, MC, V; no checks; lunch Mon–Sat, dinner every day; full bar; reservations recommended; www.flounderbaycafe.com; west of town.* &

Il Posto / ★★★

2120 COMMERCIAL AVE, ANACORTES; 360/293-7600

Il Posto is the new Italian restaurant in town, and thanks to chef Marcello Giuffrida, it's the real thing. But don't just stop for a quick bite on the way to the ferry. A long evening's dalliance with the food and wine—starting out with the *carpaccio di melanzine* (grilled eggplant with goat cheese, honey mustard, carmelized onions, pine nuts, and balsamic glaze) and ending with any dessert on the menu—is worth staying overnight for. *$$–$$$; AE, MC, V; checks OK; dinner Wed–Mon; full bar; reservations recommended; www. ilposto.com; at 21st St on way into town.* ⅃

LODGINGS

Majestic Inn & Spa / ★★★

419 COMMERCIAL AVE, ANACORTES; 360/299-1400

A few years ago, a fire ravaged the newly renovated beauty of this grand, historic 1889 hotel, but, phoenixlike, it keeps on rising from the ashes. The hotel architecture is meticulously restored turn-of-the-19th-century. The rooms, with their flat-screen TVs, crisp contemporary furniture, and polished bathrooms, make for a great relaxation zone after a trip to the spa. Try the Cocoon, a hydrothermal capsule body treatment, followed, perhaps, by amaretto biscotti torte with caramel sauce from the restaurant. *$$$; AE, DIS, MC, V; no checks; www.majesticinnandspa.com; in old town.* ⅃

Lopez Island

Lopez Island, the flat and friendly isle famous for drivers who wave, is also bike-friendly. Its 30-mile circuit is fairly level and suitable for the whole family. The **TOUR DE LOPEZ** (360/468-4664 or 877/433-2789; www.lopezisland.com/tour. html; late Apr) is typically Lopezian: low-key and noncompetitive. The only time this island gets competitive is on the Fourth of July, when they pride themselves on one of the largest private fireworks shows in the state.

You can rent a bike from **LOPEZ BICYCLE WORKS** (2847 Fisherman Bay Rd; 360/468-2847; www.lopezbicycleworks.com); you can also rent kayaks from **LOPEZ KAYAK** (www.lopezkayaks.com; May–Oct). Rent kayaks and take guided tours through **CASCADIA KAYAK TOURS** (360/468-3008; www.cascadiakayak tours.com). Agate Beach, Shark Reef Park, and Otis Perkins Park give great beach access; you can camp at 80-acre **ODLIN COUNTY PARK** (on right, about 1 mile south of ferry dock; 360/378-8420) or 130-acre **SPENCER SPIT STATE PARK** (on left, about 5 miles south of ferry dock; 888/226-7688; www.parks.wa.gov).

Lopez Village, 4 miles south of the ferry dock on the west shore near Fisherman Bay, has **CHIMERA** (Lopez Village; 360/468-3265; www.chimeragallery. com), with island glass, pottery, and paintings. **ISLANDS MARINE CENTER** (2793 Fisherman Bay Rd; 360/468-3377; www.islandsmarinecenter.com) is a full-service marina with 100 slips. This is also where you buy fishing and crabbing licenses.

LOPEZ ISLANDER RESORT (2864 Fisherman Bay Rd; 360/468-3382 or 800/736-3434; www.lopezislander.com), next door to the marina, is great for families.

A favorite food stop is **HOLLY B'S BAKERY** (Lopez Village; 360/468-2133; Apr–Nov), famous for her cinnamon rolls. The **LOVE DOG CAFÉ** (1 Village Center, Lopez Village; 360/468-2150) features Italian food, pizza, and a view. **VITA'S WILDLY DELICIOUS** (Lopez Village; 360/468-4268) is precisely that: gourmet to go—wine, too. **BUCKY'S** (Lopez Village; 360/468-2595) serves steaks as well as seafood; **CAFFE LA BOHEME** (Lopez Village; 360/468-2294) has Ruth Reichl's favorite coffee, Graffeo; and **ISABEL'S ESPRESSO** (Lopez Village; 360/468-4114), on the grassy knoll, serves organic coffee. The **GALLEY RESTAURANT AND LOUNGE** (3365 Fisherman Bay Rd; 360/468-2713; www.galleylopez.com) used to be the local beer joint; with its inventive menu and reasonable prices, it's the best family-friendly, year-round restaurant on Lopez.

RESTAURANTS

The Bay Café / ★★★

9 OLD POST RD, LOPEZ VILLAGE; 360/468-3700
After all these years, the Bay Café still has its great reputation as well as its great view. Its spacious, modern digs are close to the beach, but it still retains its eclectic flair. The Bay Café is a come-as-you-are kind of place. The food, however, is always well dressed. The oft-changing menu might include steamed mussels, Oregon bay-shrimp cakes, or grilled tofu with chickpea-potato cakes. *$$; AE, DIS, MC, V; checks OK; dinner every day (Thurs–Sun winter); full bar; reservations recommended; www.bay-cafe.com; junction of Lopez Rd S and Lopez Rd N.* &

LODGINGS

Inn at Swifts Bay / ★★

**856 PORT STANLEY RD, LOPEZ ISLAND;
360/468-3636 OR 800/903-9536**
A Tudor retreat on laid-back Lopez? Yup, complete with wing chairs and tons of books and movies. The flora and fauna and saltwater vistas make going outside nice, too. Five beautiful guest rooms, including three suites, have queen-size beds with down comforters. There's a secluded hot tub down a stone path at the edge of the forest. Breakfast might be hazelnut waffles with fresh berries and crème fraîche, crab cakes, or orange-cinnamon bread-pudding French toast with cinnamon-custard sauce. Innkeepers will arrange a ride from the ferry. *$$–$$$; AE, DIS, MC, V; checks OK; www.swiftsbay.com; 2 miles south of ferry landing.*

Lopez Farm Cottages and Tent Camping / ★

**555 FISHERMAN BAY RD, LOPEZ ISLAND;
360/468-3555 OR 800/440-3556**
Enjoy upscale camping with no RVs, dogs, or electronic music at this lovely, private farmland site, complete with a bathhouse, Adirondack chairs, a table, a hammock, and a flat spot for your tent. Something about this place

feels just right. The cottages are a cheerful Northwest Scandinavian style. Cottage guests (minimum age 14) enjoy the Jacuzzi and get breakfast delivered in a basket. *$$–$$$; MC, V; no checks; www.lopezfarmcottages.com; about 3 miles from ferry, 1 mile from village.* ⅋

MacKaye Harbor Inn / ★★

949 MACKAYE HARBOR RD, LOPEZ ISLAND; 360/468-2253 OR 888/314-6140
This tall white Victorian, built in 1927, was the first house on Lopez to boast electricity. The Harbor Suite is a good choice, with fireplace, private bath, and enclosed sitting area facing the beach. The wide veranda looking out over beach grasses and bay is appealing. Rent a kayak or borrow a mountain bike, head off, and return to fresh cookies. If you bike from the ferry, be warned: the closest restaurant is 6 miles back in town (although the Islandale Store is but a mile away). Four acres of gardens add to the charm. *$$$; MC, V; checks OK; www.mackayeharborinn.com; 12 miles south of ferry landing.*

Orcas Island

On Orcas, named after Spanish explorer Revilla Gigedo de Orcasitas, you can't miss 2,407-foot Mount Constitution, the centerpiece of **MORAN STATE PARK** (13 miles northeast of ferry landing; 360/902-8600; www.parks.wa.gov). It was Washington's first state park. From the old stone tower at the summit, which was built by the Civilian Conservation Corps in 1936, you can see from Vancouver to Mount Rainier and everything between. Get a campsite through a **CENTRAL RESERVATION SERVICE** (888/226-7688; www.parks.wa.gov).

The man for whom the park is named was shipbuilding tycoon Robert Moran. His old mansion was the focal point of Rosario Resort & Spa (scheduled to close at press time), just west of the park. The mansion, decked out in period memorabilia, is worth a stop. Its enormous pipe organ is still used for performances.

There are bikes for rent from **DOLPHIN BAY BICYCLES** (at ferry landing; 360/376-4157; www.rockisland.com/~dolphin) or **WILD LIFE CYCLES** (350 N Beach Rd, Eastsound; 360/376-4708; www.wildlifecycles.com). A new service is the seasonal **ORCAS SHUTTLE** (360/376-RIDE; www.orcasislandshuttle.com), offering regular bus service around the island as well as taxi and car rental. The $10-per-day bus pass is a great deal. Walk-ons stay at the **ORCAS HOTEL** (at ferry landing; 360/376-4300 or 888/672-2792; www.orcashotel.com) and do day trips.

The village of Eastsound is on the water's edge on the bridge of land between the two horseshoe halves of Orcas. It's a good 8 miles from the ferry, so unlike Friday Harbor on San Juan Island, which gets a lot of ferry foot traffic, Eastsound is quieter. On Saturdays, the **ORCAS FARMERS MARKET** (North Beach Rd, Eastsound; www.orcasislandfarmersmarket.org; May–Oct) has everything from tarot readings to organic beef. Walkable Eastsound's shops and galleries are distinctive. **TRES FABU** (238 North Beach Rd, Eastsound; 360/376-7673; www.tresfabu.com) has chic, funky clothes. **DARVILL'S BOOK STORE** (296 Main St, Eastsound; 360/376-2135; www.darvillsbookstore.com) also has lattes with a view; next door, **DARVILL'S RARE**

PRINT SHOP (360/376-2351; www.darvillsrareprints.com) has antique prints. The **ORCAS THEATER AND COMMUNITY CENTER** (917 Mount Baker Rd, Eastsound; 360/376-2281; www.orcascenter.org) offers music and theater entertainment.

ROSES BAKERY & RESTAURANT (382 Prune Alley, Eastsound; 360/376-5805) has gourmet groceries. Locals eat at **CHIMAYO'S** (Our House Mall, North Beach Rd, Eastsound; 360/376-6394) for affordable flavors of New Mexico. They go to **ORCAS HOME GROWN** (138 North Beach Rd, Eastsound; 360/376-2009) for fair-trade coffee and veggie juices or to **PORTOFINO PIZZERIA** (274 A St, Eastsound; 360/376-2085) for pizza.

In town, the historic **OUTLOOK INN** (171 Main St, Eastsound; 360/376-2200 or 888/688-5665; www.outlookinn.com) has everything from European-style rooms with shared baths to luxury suites with Jacuzzis; the **NEW LEAF CAFÉ** is on-site. For family gatherings, retreats, and reunions, a few minute's walk from Eastsound is **HEARTWOOD HOUSE** (360/317-8220; www.heartwoodhouse. com). Check out **BEACH HAVEN RESORT** (684 Beach Haven Rd, Orcas Island; 360/376-2288; www.beach-haven.com) and **WEST BEACH RESORT** (West Beach, Orcas Island; 360/376-2240 or 877/WEST-BCH; www.westbeachresort.com) for family-friendly cabins on the beach.

RESTAURANTS

Café Olga / ★

11 PT LAWRENCE RD, OLGA; 360/376-5098

It's a bit of a drive to Olga Junction but worth the experience, which includes the Orcas Island Artworks, a gallery that shares this renovated barn with the café. It's all local work, and artists take turns behind the counter. The popular café features home-style cooking, including fish of the day and local oysters, sandwiches, and huge salads. For dessert, try the terrific blackberry pie or the tiramisu. $$; MC, V; local checks only; breakfast, lunch every day, dinner Sat–Wed (Thurs–Tues off-season; closed Jan–early Feb); beer and wine; reservations recommended; at Olga Junction. &

Inn at Ship Bay Restaurant / ★★★

326 OLGA RD, EASTSOUND; 360/376-5886 OR 877/276-7296

On a site originally homesteaded in the 1860s that was a cornerstone of local agriculture, the orchard farmhouse is now home to the inn's dining room. Productive apple, pear, and plum orchards still surround the inn. Geddes Martin, the chef and co-owner of the inn, makes ice cream and serves it atop delicious flourless chocolate cake. His other specialties include handcrafted foods in the tradition of the slow foods movement with an emphasis on locally sourced and organic ingredients. Recent menu offerings included grass-fed beef filet in a potato puree with spring vegetables and black currant red wine sauce; and halibut with local potatoes and autumn vegetables in an apple syrup reduction. At the inn, 11 deluxe guest rooms have comfortable pillow-top beds and bay views. $$$; MC, V; no checks; dinner Tues–Sat (closed Dec–Jan); beer and wine; reservations recommended; www.innatshipbay.com; east of Eastsound. &

LODGINGS

Deer Harbor Inn and Restaurant / ★★

33 INN LN, DEER HARBOR; 360/376-4110 OR 877/377-4110
Over the years, owners Pam and Craig Carpenter have shored up this rustic old lodge, built in 1915 in an apple orchard overlooking Deer Harbor on the lovely southwest side of the island. Lodge rooms are small, with peeled-log furniture. The newer cabins are cozy, with log furniture, knotty pine walls, woodstoves or fireplaces, and private hot tubs. The Pond Cottage is our favorite, with two bedrooms, two bathrooms, and a kitchen. Dinners are served nightly in the lodge's rustic dining room. *$$$–$$$$; AE, MC, V; checks OK; www.deer harborinn.com; from ferry landing, follow signs past West Sound.* &

Doe Bay Resort & Retreat / ★★

107 DOE BAY RD, ORCAS ISLAND; 360/376-2291
Doe Bay, long an island destination of hippies and other eccentrics, is making yet another comeback. The resort—on 33 acres of waterfront—is a nature lover's paradise, complete with a private beach, hiking trails, meadows with deer, a small river with waterfalls, and hundreds of trees. After a six-year restoration, it's back in full stride with retreat programs, fine meals, and an eclectic array of reasonable accommodations. Whether staying in a hostel room, a rustic-style cabin or lodge, a trailer cabin, a tent or a yurt, you're free to partake of yoga classes, massage or acupuncture treatments, sea kayaking, hiking, whale watching, or soaking in one of three clothing-optional hot tubs and a sauna. Chef Janay Destello draws on local organic and seasonal products to create dinners for a wide range of palates. *$$–$$$$; MC, V; checks OK; www.doebay.com; about 40 minutes from ferry, 3 miles past Olga.* &

The Inn on Orcas Island / ★★★

114 CHANNEL RD, DEER HARBOR; 360/376-5227 OR 888/886-1661
Part Nantucket cottage, part English manor house, this stunning inn at the edge of Deer Harbor is a labor of love for owners Jeremy Trumble and John Gibbs. The two former Southern California art-gallery owners showcase collections of English paintings, needlepoint, and china. The art alone is worth a visit; the six manor rooms, all with water views, are worth at least six visits, and the 6 acres are worth year-round exploration. There's also a carriage house and a waterside cottage. Borrow the canoe or a bicycle for fun. *$$$–$$$$; AE, MC, V; checks OK; www.theinnonorcasisland.com; from ferry landing, follow signs past West Sound.*

Spring Bay Inn / ★★★

464 SPRING BAY TRAIL, OLGA; 360/376-5531
Sandy Playa and Carl Burger are youthful retired state park rangers, and their love of natural places graces this inn with a taste of the real Northwest. On 57 wooded seafront acres adjacent to Obstruction Pass State Park, Spring Bay Inn offers a big dose of the great outdoors. Wildlife abounds, and so

do creature comforts. Of the four guest rooms, all with private baths and fireplaces, the light-filled Treetop room is one of the most uplifting spaces around. Coffee, muffins, and fruit are delivered to each door in the morning— sustenance for a free kayak tour guided by your hosts. Soak under the stars in the bay-side hot tub. *$$$$; DIS, MC, V; checks OK; www.springbayinn.com; Obstruction Pass Rd to Trailhead Rd, left onto Spring Bay Trail.*

Turtleback Farm Inn / ★★★

1981 CROW VALLEY RD, EASTSOUND; 360/376-4914 OR 800/376-4914
At Turtleback Farm, amid trees and ponds, you get the feeling that not much has changed here in a long, long time. It seemed things might change, when the Turtleback Mountain site went up for sale a few years ago, but a collective effort preserved it. The inn continues to be one of the best B and Bs around. Bill and Susan Fletcher love Crow Valley and love what they do, and it shows. There are seven guest rooms, with views, in the Farmhouse. The four expansive suites with vistas in the Orchard House feature fir floors, trim, and doors; Vermont Casting woodstoves; and spacious baths with large claw-foot tubs and showers. *$$$–$$$$; AE, DIS, MC, V; checks OK; www.turtlebackinn. com; 6 miles from ferry.* &

San Juan Island

Arriving on San Juan Island means floating into **FRIDAY HARBOR**, which is the good news *and* the bad news. It's good because you have immediate access to food and lodgings. It's bad because you have to find your way past real estate offices and trinket traders to find the island's heart.

Historically, the island was summer home to Native Americans who fished and gathered food in the sheltering islands. Europeans then brought sheep farming, followed by orchards, agriculture, and commercial fishing.

San Juan Island also had a contested history that saw joint occupation by both British and American troops. The acrimony started in 1859 when an American farmer shot a British farmer's pig. The dispute was eventually settled in 1872 by Kaiser Wilhelm. The Pig War that never actually happened became history and eventually resulted in **SAN JUAN ISLAND NATIONAL HISTORIC PARK** (www.nps. gov/sajh), covering more than 1,700 acres at two distinct sites, **AMERICAN CAMP** (6 miles southeast of Friday Harbor along Cattle Point Rd) at the southern end of the island and **ENGLISH CAMP** (9 miles northwest of Friday Harbor on West Valley Rd) to the north.

From May through September the endangered orca whales cruise waters on the island's west side. Watching them from shore is worth the wait. They pass near **LIME KILN POINT STATE PARK** (www.parks.wa.gov) where there are trails, picnic spots, and a lighthouse usually staffed with a whale researcher in the summer. The **WHALE MUSEUM** in Friday Harbor (62 1st St N, Friday Harbor; 360/378-4710 or 800/946-7227; www.whalemuseum.org) is wonderful.

A short walk uptown is the **SAN JUAN ISLAND HISTORICAL MUSEUM** (405 Price St, Friday Harbor; 360/378-3949; www.sjmuseum.org). For an end-of-the-day respite, sip wine at **SAN JUAN VINEYARDS** (3136 Roche Harbor Rd, Friday Harbor; 360/378-9463; www.sanjuanvineyards.com). **WESTCOTT BAY SCULPTURE PARK** (near Roche Harbor Resort; 360/370-5050; www.westcottbay.org) has acres of art on the island's north end. If you visit in the summer, **ISLAND STAGE LEFT** (1062 Wold Rd, Roche Harbor; www.islandstageleft.org) has excellent outdoor Shakespeare productions, and it's free (donations accepted).

The **COUNTY FAIR** (360/378-4310; www.sanjuancountyfair.org) during the third weekend in August is one of the most eclectic fairs in the state. The **FARMERS MARKET** sets up on Saturdays May to mid-October at the county courthouse parking lot in Friday Harbor. **PELINDABA LAVENDER FARM** (33 Hawthorne Ln, San Juan Island; 206/264-0232 or 866/819-8946; www.pelindaba.com) has a festival in July and an eating and gathering place in town. For a few hours of scenic quiet, ride the interisland ferry circuit (free to walk-ons).

A side benefit to an off-season visit is the blues music scene. At the local Italian restaurant **BELLA LUNA** (175 1st St, Friday Harbor; 360/378-4118), blues musicians show up on Wednesday. Some are old pros, and the place rocks. In true island style, however, it's early to bed: the music ends at 9pm. There's a similar gathering of jazz musicians on Sunday. In the summer, there's live music at the Port of Friday Harbor, on the grounds of the historical museum, and at Roche Harbor, where there's an ongoing art fair.

ISLANDS STUDIOS (270 Spring St, Friday Harbor; 360/378-6550; www.islandstudios.com) features local artists. **WATERWORKS GALLERY** (315 Spring St, Friday Harbor; 360/378-3060; www.waterworksgallery.com) represents some of the finest artists in the San Juan Islands. **COTTON COTTON COTTON** (165 1st St, Friday Harbor; 360/378-3531; www.cottoncottoncottononline.com) has original designs, locally made jewelry, and comfortable clothing. **DAN LEVIN** (50 1st St, Friday Harbor; 360/378-2051) is renowned for his fine gold and silver craftsmanship. There are four bookstores in town, including **SERENDIPITY** (223 A St, Friday Harbor; 360/378-2665), in a historic old house.

You can rent bicycles year-round at **ISLAND BICYCLES** (380 Argyle St, Friday Harbor; 360/378-4941; www.islandbicycles.com) and kayaks from **CRYSTAL SEAS KAYAKING** (877/732-7877 or 360/378-4223; www.crystalseas.com). There are car rentals at **M&W** (725 Spring St, Friday Harbor; 800/323-6037; www.sanjuanauto.com), and in the summer, great bus service and tours with **SAN JUAN TRANSIT** (at Cannery Landing at ferry terminal, Friday Harbor; 360/378-8887 or 800/887-8387; www.sanjuantransit.com).

There's no shortage of food in Friday Harbor: breakfast at the **BLUE DOLPHIN** (185 1st St, Friday Harbor; 360/378-6116); dinner or lunch—usually with onion rings—on the deck at **DOWNRIGGERS** (10 Front St, Friday Harbor; 360/378-2700; www.downriggerssanjuan.com); good local brews at the **FRONT STREET ALEHOUSE** (1 Front St, Friday Harbor; 360/378-BEER; www.sanjuanbrewing.com); and fish-and-chips at the **HUNGRY CLAM** (205 A St, Friday Harbor; 360/378-3474). **HERB'S** (80 1st St, Friday Harbor; 360/378-7076) is the local tavern for good basic burgers, pool, and karaoke on Wednesday nights. **STEPS WINE**

BAR AND CAFÉ (140A 1st St, Friday Harbor; 360/370-5959; www.stepswine barandcafe.com) offers a touch of trendy. **MARILYN'S GARDEN PATH CAFÉ** (135 2nd St, Friday Harbor; 360/378-6255) is where locals go for lunch. The **BACK-DOOR KITCHEN** (400B A St, Friday Harbor; 360/378-9540; www.backdoor kitchen.com) is a local secret for both lunch and dinner tucked away in a nursery garden behind a warehouse at the end of Web Street. Finding it is half the fun.

At **ROCHE HARBOR VILLAGE** (248 Reuben Memorial Dr, Roche Harbor; 360/378-5757; www.rocheharbor.com), chef Bill Shaw keeps the menus lively and consistently good at all three restaurants: the **LIME KILN CAFÉ** is open year-round (for breakfast and lunch only in winter). Fine dining at **MCMILLAN'S** is available all year (Thurs–Sun in winter). In the summer, the **MADRONA BAR AND GRILL** has lively deck dining.

There's a range of places to stay in Friday Harbor. **WAYFARER'S REST BACK-PACKER'S HOSTEL** (35 Malcolm St, Friday Harbor; 360/378-6428; www.rock island.com/~wayfarersrest) is rustic and friendly. The motelish **ORCA INN** (770 Mullis St, Friday Harbor; 360/378-6184 or 877/541-ORCA; www.orcainnwa. com) is reasonable, has kitchens, and often has rooms available in the summer. On the other end of the historic spectrum, the 1898 **TUCKER HOUSE** (260 B St, Friday Harbor; 360/378-2783 or 800/965-0123; www.tuckerhouse.com), a block from the ferry dock, is family- and pet-friendly and comfortable. So is the **ELEMENTS** (410 Spring St, Friday Harbor; 360/378-4000 or 800/793-4765; www.hotel elements.com), where kids can swim in the pool and parents can get a massage at **LAVENDERA DAY SPA** (440 Spring St, Friday Harbor; 360/378-3637 or 800/369-0337; www.lavenderadayspa.com). For an independent stay in a downtown Friday Harbor suite, complete with Annie Howell Adams original art, antiques, bedrooms, and a kitchen, check out **NICHOLS STREET SUITES** (85 Nichols St, Friday Harbor; 866/374-4272; www.lodging-fridayharbor.com).

For camping, there's **LAKEDALE RESORT AT THREE LAKES** (4313 Roche Harbor Rd, Friday Harbor; 360/378-2350 or 800/617-2267; www.lakedale.com), which has everything from tent sites to a luxury lodge. Camping is also available at **SAN JUAN COUNTY PARK** (50 San Juan Park Dr, San Juan Island; 360/378-8420; www.co.san-juan.wa.us); at **SNUG HARBOR MARINA RESORT** (1997 Mitchell Bay Rd, San Juan Island; 360/378-4762; www.snugresort.com), and right next door at **MITCHELL BAY LANDING** (2101 Mitchell Bay Rd, San Juan Island; 360/378-9296; www.mitchellbaylanding.com), where you can rent kayaks.

RESTAURANTS

Duck Soup Inn / ★★☆

50 DUCK SOUP LN, FRIDAY HARBOR; 360/378-4878
For more than 30 years, Gretchen Allison has served special food in this serene setting with its rustic cottage, gardens, fireplace, and pond views. The focus of the ambitious menu is on seafood; specialties include applewood-smoked oysters and grilled fish. House-baked bread, a bowl of perfectly seasoned soup, and a large salad accompany ample portions. Leave room for white chocolate–banana cream pie. $$$; DIS, MC, V; checks OK; dinner

Tues–Sun (closed Nov–Mar); beer and wine; reservations recommended; www. ducksoupinn.com; 5 miles northwest of Friday Harbor.

The Place Bar & Grill / ★★★

1 SPRING ST, FRIDAY HARBOR; 360/378-8707
The soothing waterside view, friendly atmosphere, and splendid menu make for a memorable experience. This is a family affair: in summer, up to five Andersons are working. Chef-owner Steven Anderson prepares a rotating menu of dishes made with locally sourced ingredients. Try the mushroom sauté appetizer with artichoke hearts and warm goat cheese. Entrées include seafood, steaks, and lamp chops with unfussy sides. *$$$; MC, V; local checks only; dinner every day (Tues–Sat winter); full bar; reservations recommended; www.theplacesanjuan.com; at foot of Spring St.*

Vinny's / ★★

165 WEST ST, FRIDAY HARBOR; 360/378-1934
Vinny's is an upbeat, sophisticated, Tuscan-style eatery offering Italian classics and daily fresh seafood specials. The pasta dishes are generous; for a "hot" meal experience, split a caesar salad and an order of the "Pasta from Hell," a combo of garlic, pine nuts, raisins, and bell peppers in a spicy cream sauce. There's an island-style laid-back feel and a harbor view. *$$–$$$; AE, MC, V; checks OK; dinner every day; full bar; reservations recommended; downtown off 1st St.* ঊ

LODGINGS

Bird Rock Hotel / ★★

35 1ST ST, FRIDAY HARBOR; 360/378-5848 OR 800/352-2632
This elegantly renovated historic 1891 building is an oasis in the center of town. Of the 15 rooms, the best is the Eagle Cove, a third-floor, water-view perch with a deck, kitchen, double shower, and Jacuzzi. Some (economy) rooms share baths. All are graciously furnished. Heated bathroom floors and fresh-baked cookies in the afternoon are just two thoughtful touches. There are no grounds here, yet you can retreat to the outdoor deck and patio. *$$$–$$$$; MC, V; checks OK; www.birdrockhotel.com; 2 blocks from ferry.* ঊ

Friday Harbor House / ★★★

130 WEST ST, FRIDAY HARBOR; 360/378-8455 OR 866/722-7356
The plain architecture of Friday Harbor House belies its posh interior. It's serene: 23 guest rooms are decorated in muted, modern tones and have gas fireplaces and huge jetted tubs positioned to absorb both the fire's warmth and the harbor view. Some rooms have tiny balconies; not all offer full waterfront views. The view dining room (open to the public for dinner) maintains the inn's quixotic cool—which warms considerably when you take your first bite of pumpkin-and-goat-cheese ravioli or pan-seared sea scallops served with ancho-chile cream and fig-balsamic reduction as well as a wilted arugula salad. *$$$$; AE, DC, DIS, MC, V; checks OK; www.fridayharborhouse.com; from ferry, left on Spring St, right on 1st St, right on West St.* ঊ

Juniper Lane Guesthouse / ★

**1312 BEAVERTON VALLEY RD, FRIDAY HARBOR;
360/378-7761 OR 888-397-2597**

This guest house combines local chic, global sensibilities, avant-garde decor, and a pastoral landscape. There are practical backpacker bunk rooms, elegant private rooms, a kitchen, a common room, do-it-yourself breakfast, outdoor patios, and a fire pit, all within walking distance of town. Young owner-manager Juniper Maas was born and raised on the island, traveled the world, and returned to refurbish her dream guest house. She has created a truly unique environment for travelers of every age and inclination. *$$–$$$; MC, V; checks OK; www.juniperlaneguesthouse.com; on the edge of Friday Harbor, 1 mile from ferry.* ⅖

Lakedale Resort at Three Lakes / ★★★

**4313 ROCHE HARBOR RD, SAN JUAN ISLAND;
360/378-2350 OR 800/617-2267**

There are several surprising things about Lakedale Resort: it's right in the middle of the island rather than on the water; it works as both a campground and a luxury lodge; and its peace and beauty make you want to stay put, especially in the quiet off-season when the 82 acres of lakes and forests cast their meditative spell. For romance, the lodge is grand; the 10 rooms have slate fireplaces, balconies, and lake views. For families, the log cabins, with two bedrooms, two bathrooms, and kitchens, make a great getaway. The campground includes group sites as well as hiker- or bicycle-only sites. *$–$$$; AE, DIS, MC, V; checks OK; www.lakedale.com; 4.5 miles from ferry landing.* ⅖

Roche Harbor Resort / ★★★

**248 REUBEN MEMORIAL DR, ROCHE HARBOR;
360/378-2155 OR 800/451-8910**

Few places in the region take you back in time like a visit to Roche Harbor Resort. The centerpiece, the ivy-clad Hotel de Haro, was built in 1886. History buffs relish the piecework wallpaper and period furnishings; the creaky, uneven floorboards; and the thought that Teddy Roosevelt was once a guest. The view from the entry takes in the flower garden, cobblestone waterfront, and bay. The hotel offers 20 rooms; only four have private bathrooms. A fine-dining restaurant, café, and casual eatery are on the grounds (see section introduction). The newest addition, Quarryman Hall, has luxury suites, a spa, and several retail shops. During summer, village artist booths are open every day with local artists presenting and selling their pieces and wares. *$$–$$$$; AE, MC, V; checks OK; www.rocheharbor.com; on waterfront at northwest end of island.* ⅖

Sakya Kachod Choling / ★★

BOX 3191, AT HANNAH RD, SAN JUAN ISLAND; 360/378-4059

This Tibetan Buddhist retreat center was designed to blend the architecture of both Tibet and the Northwest. Inside, master Tibetan craftsmen painted the shrine-room walls with murals of museum quality. There are two single-bed retreat rooms and a kitchen and bathroom to share. The trees, mossy knolls, Mount Baker vista, and peace and quiet invite reflection and meditation. You don't have to be a Buddhist to come. Meals are an additional cost. *$; MC, V; checks OK; www.sakya-retreat.net; 8 miles west of Friday Harbor.*

Bellingham and Area

Bellingham is the metropolitan hub of northwestern Washington, on the shores of Bellingham Bay, flanked by the foothills of majestic Mount Baker. Numerous small towns dot the transition zone from the Skagit Valley to this thriving city on the Nooksack River.

Chuckanut Drive

This famous 17 miles (State Route 11) between Burlington in the Skagit Valley and Bellingham on the bay is one of the prettiest drives in the state. On a gorgeous, long summer evening, it may be the prettiest. It winds through lush farmlands, then clings to Chuckanut and Blanchard mountains with westerly views over Samish Bay. If you're in the driver's seat, however, keep both hands on the wheel and your eyes on the narrow, winding road. Take advantage of the numerous turn-outs so you can linger a bit longer over the magnificent vistas—and get impatient locals off your bumper. Watch out for cyclists, who use Chuckanut as a training ride. Access **CHUCKANUT DRIVE** (www.chuckanutdrive.com) either northbound (I-5 exit 231, Burlington) or do it in reverse, southbound (I-5 exit 250 to Fairhaven Pkwy, Bellingham)—take Fairhaven Parkway to 12th Street and turn left.

As you buzz along the mostly straight, flat stretch northbound between Burlington and Bow, it's hard to believe I-5 is only minutes away to the east. Removed from traffic, you'll discover orchards, oyster beds, slow-moving tractors, and migratory birds. As if by design, art galleries and antique shops are at convenient intervals. On the drive's south end is **CHUCKANUT GARDENS** (3533 Chuckanut Dr, Bow; 360/766-6716), with its serene Japanese garden, art gallery, tearoom, bamboo nursery, and antique shop. For a fascinating detour, visit the **PADILLA BAY NATIONAL ESTUARINE RESEARCH RESERVE** and the newly remodeled **BREAZEALE INTERPRETIVE CENTER** (1043 Bayview-Edison Rd, west of Chuckanut Dr; 360/428-1558; www.padillabay.gov; 10am–5pm Wed–Sun) Nearby **BAYVIEW STATE PARK** (360/757-0227; www.parks.wa.gov) has overnight camping, rustic cabins, and beachfront picnic sites.

BLAU OYSTER COMPANY on Samish Island (11321 Blue Heron Rd, 7 miles west of Edison via Bayview-Edison Rd and Samish Island Rd; 360/766-6171; www.blauoyster.com; Mon–Sat 8am–5pm) has been selling oysters since 1935; follow signs to the shucking plant. You'll also find oysters at **TAYLOR SHELLFISH FARMS** (2182 Chuckanut Dr, Bow; 360/426-6178; www.taylorshellfish.com), open every day in summer.

LARRABEE STATE PARK (off Chuckanut Dr, 7 miles south of Bellingham; www.parks.wa.gov) was one of Washington's first state parks. The Interurban Trail, once the electric rail route from Bellingham to Mount Vernon, is now a 5-mile trail connecting three parks on Chuckanut Drive: Larrabee State Park to Arroyo Park to Fairhaven Park in Bellingham. The **CHUCKANUT BAY GALLERY AND SCULPTURE GARDEN** (700 Chuckanut Dr, Bellingham; 360/734-4885 or 877/734-4885) on the drive's north end has a nice sculpture garden.

Bow

RESTAURANTS

The Oyster Bar on Chuckanut Drive / ★★★

2578 CHUCKANUT DR, BOW; 360/766-6185
Having come far from humble origins as a roadside oyster-vending shack in the Great Depression, this restaurant now fails to disappoint even the most discerning diner. The view is nothing short of spectacular, the fare is gourmet, and the wine cellar maintains its award-winning collection. Entrées might be a generous cedar-planked fillet of wild salmon or a perfectly cooked filet mignon. *$$$; AE, MC, V; local checks only; lunch, dinner every day; beer and wine; reservations recommended; www.theoysterbaronchuckanutdrive.com; closer to Bellingham end of Chuckanut Dr.* &

The Rhododendron Café / ★★

5521 CHUCKANUT DR, BOW; 360/766-6667
The Rhododendron Café can be the start of or the end to a delightful afternoon on Chuckanut Drive. It may not have the view of other eateries, but the commitment to quality and creativity here makes this a worthy stop. Once the site of the Red Crown Service Station in the early 1900s, the Rhody now serves homemade soup (chowder is excellent) and a tasty portobello burger. Lightly breaded and pan-fried Samish Bay oysters—the specialty of the area—are delicious. A nightly seafood stew has an ethnic or seasonal theme. Seating is intimate and tables fill up fast, so call ahead. *$$; AE, MC, V; checks OK; lunch, dinner Wed–Sun, brunch Sat–Sun (closed late Nov–Jan); beer and wine; reservations recommended; www.rhodycafe.com; at Bow-Edison junction.* &

LODGINGS

Benson Farmstead Bed & Breakfast / ★☆

10113 AVON-ALLEN RD, BOW; 360/757-0578 OR 800/441-9814
This 17-room restored 1914 farmhouse surrounded by gardens is filled with antiques and Scandinavian memorabilia. Four upstairs rooms (all with private baths) have antique beds and quilts. A cottage-style family suite is out back; there's also a suite by the waterfall garden. Jerry and Sharon Benson cook a country breakfast and sometimes serve desserts in the evening. Don't be surprised to hear music in the air; the Benson family are talented singers,

pianists, and violinists. (If you prefer accommodations closer to La Conner, the Bensons have a beach-front log home on Skagit Bay for rent too.) *$$; MC, V; checks OK; www.bbhost.com/bensonbnb; I-5 exit 232 west.*

Bellingham

Western Washington University is here, so Bellingham is definitely a college town, but not all of its identity is wrapped up in higher ed. The Bellwether on the Bay development on Squalicum Harbor—which includes the mini–grand hotel (see review)—will soon be joined by an even more ambitious plan as the Georgia-Pacific property is slowly dismantled and cleaned up, paving the way for much-needed waterfront places.

Opened in May 2006, the Depot Market Square provides a home for the beloved **BELLINGHAM FARMERS MARKET** (www.bellinghamfarmers.org; Apr–Dec) on the site of the historic railroad depot. The **WHATCOM MUSEUM OF HISTORY AND ART** (121 Prospect St; 360/778-8930; www.whatcommuseum.org) has at its centerpiece a massive 1892 Romanesque structure used as a city hall until 1940. Check out the **SYRE EDUCATION CENTER** (201 Prospect St; 360/778-8950) down the block and the **WHATCOM CHILDREN'S MUSEUM** (227 Prospect St; 360/778-8970) a few doors north. A short walk away is the **AMERICAN MUSEUM OF RADIO & ELECTRICITY** (1318 Bay St; 360/738-3886; www.americanradiomuseum.org).

The summer **BELLINGHAM FESTIVAL OF MUSIC** (360/201-6621; www.bellinghamfestival.org; July) is an institution, featuring more than two weeks of orchestral, chamber, and jazz performances. The **MOUNT BAKER THEATRE** (104 N Commercial St, Bellingham; 360/734-6080; www.mountbakertheatre.com), built in 1927 and renovated in 1995, is home to the **WHATCOM SYMPHONY ORCHESTRA** (www.whatcomsymphony.com; Oct–May) and hosts other events. The **SKI-TO-SEA RACE** (360/734-1330; www.skitosea.org) attracts teams from all over the world to an annual seven-event relay on Memorial Day weekend.

Outdoors, downtown Bellingham and Fairhaven are completely linked by trail. **SEHOME HILL ARBORETUM** (Bellingham Parks and Recreation, 360/676-6985; www.ac.wwu.edu/~sha), adjacent to the WWU campus, sports more than 5 miles of trails with prime views. **WHATCOM FALLS PARK** (1401 Electric Ave; 360/756-1445) has several miles of trails overlooking waterfalls. **BIG ROCK GARDEN PARK** (2900 Sylvan St, near Lake Whatcom; 360/676-6985; Apr–Oct) is a woodland of garden art and sculpture.

Bellingham's restaurant scene has picked up over the years. For spendy and swanky, there's **NIMBUS** (119 N Commercial St; 360/676-1307; www.nimbusrestaurant.com), aptly named for its location at the top of the Towers, or **GIUSEPPE'S ITALIAN RESTAURANT** (see review). **BOUNDARY BAY BREW-ERY** (1107 Railroad St; 360/647-5593; www.bbaybrewery.com) downtown is a popular hangout that serves a delicious lamb burger. Ethnic favorites are **BUSARA THAI CUISINE** (404 36th St, in Sehome Village; 360/734-8088), **TACO LOBO** (117 W Magnolia St; 360/756-0711) for Mexican, **OSAKA** (3207 Northwest Ave; 360/676-6268) for its superb sushi, and **LUCKY PANDA** (2311 James St;

360/738-2888; www.luckypandarestaurant.com) for exceptional Chinese. **CAL-LALOO CARIBBEAN KITCHEN** (1212 N State St; 360/676-5375) is a fresh breeze with a quirky menu and whimsical interior. Stop in at **MEDITERRANEAN SPECIAL-TIES** (505 32nd St, in Viking Plaza; 360/738-6895) for fantastic Greek, Italian, and Middle Eastern foods.

Once a separate town that was the result of a short-lived railroad boom in 1889, the **FAIRHAVEN HISTORIC DISTRICT** (www.fairhaven.com) retains its old-time charm and offers plenty of exploring. Today, the area is awash with new construction. The **MARKETPLACE** (Harris and 12th sts) houses shops in refurbished splendor. Crafts, galleries, coffeehouses, bistros and bars, trendy boutiques, bookstores, a charming garden, and a lively evening scene are all contained within several blocks. **VILLAGE BOOKS** (1200 11th St; 360/671-2626; www.villagebooks. com) is Northwest Washington's largest independent bookstore, also housing the popular **COLOPHON CAFÉ** (1208 11th St; 360/647-0092; www.colophoncafe. com), **PAPER DREAMS** (1206 11th Ave; 360/676-8676), and **BOOK FARE** (1200 11th Ave; 360/734-3434), a quiet coffee spot.

The cruise terminal at the end of Harris Street houses the southern terminus of the **ALASKA MARINE HIGHWAY SYSTEM** (355 Harris Ave; 360/676-8445 or 800/642-0066; www.dot.state.ak.us/amhs); here, travelers begin the three-day coastal journey through the famed Inside Passage. Between May and September, the **SAN JUAN ISLAND COMMUTER** (360/738-8099 or 800/443-4552; www. whales.com) operates daily between Bellingham, Orcas Island, and San Juan Island. **VICTORIA SAN JUAN CRUISES** (360/738-8099 or 800/443-4552; www. whales.com) offers overnight cruise and whale-watching packages to Victoria. The **AMTRAK** station (401 Harris Ave; 360/734-8851 or 800/USA-RAIL; www. amtrakcascades.com) is next door.

RESTAURANTS

Du Jour Bistro and the Vines Wine Shop / ★★

1319 CORNWALL AVE, BELLINGHAM; 360/714-1161
The merger of two businesses is usually not as convenient as it turned out for owners Mike Peterson and Becki Lawson. A wall came down, and voila! Du Jour Bistro was born. It partners with the Vines Wine Shop, where your meal can be accompanied by a bottle off the rack next to your table (with a modest corkage fee). The menu is French, with such delights as beef tenderloin with a port–mission fig demi-glace or duck breast with honey-lavender glaze. *$$–$$$; MC, V; checks OK; lunch, dinner Mon–Sat; beer and wine; reservations recommended; www.thevinesdujour.com; heart of downtown.* &

Giuseppe's Italian Restaurant / ★★

1414 CORNWALL AVE, BELLINGHAM; 360/714-8412
Warmly lit, elegantly appointed, this restaurant is in a charming historical building. Locals were jubilant when Giuseppe's reopened in its new location. Chef-owner Giuseppe Mauro enforces the motto "food is the essence of life" with his menu. Traditional Italian pasta, chicken, and steak dishes

are reasonably priced, and the ambience comes free. *$$; AE, MC, V; checks OK; lunch Mon–Fri, dinner every day; full bar; no reservations; www. giuseppesitalian.com; heart of downtown.*

Pepper Sisters / ★★

1055 N STATE ST, BELLINGHAM; 360/671-3414

Innovative Southwestern fare is served here. Cheerful service, a great location in a vintage brick building, and a wide-awake kitchen have made Pepper Sisters an institution. The grilled king salmon taco in a soft blue-corn tortilla with accents of kalamata olives, garlic, chipotle aioli, and fresh arugula is a wildly popular regular blackboard special. *$$; MC, V; checks OK; dinner Tues–Sun; beer and wine; no reservations; south of downtown.* &

LODGINGS

The Chrysalis Inn & Spa / ★★★

804 10TH ST, BELLINGHAM; 360/756-1005 OR 888/808-0005

Commanding prime waterfront real estate north of Fairhaven, the Chrysalis Inn & Spa keeps quietly racking up the accolades. Designed in an Asian-Northwest motif, the Chrysalis has 43 rooms (9 of which are luxury suites), each with oversize tub, window seat, fireplace, and water view. The spa provides numerous ways to be pampered. Fino's, their sophisticated wine bar-restaurant, is a terrific afternoon spot that also serves a free breakfast buffet for inn guests. *$$$$; AE, DIS, MC, V; checks OK; www.thechrysalisinn.com; I-5 exit at Fairhaven Pkwy.* &

Fairhaven Village Inn / ★★

1200 10TH ST, BELLINGHAM; 360/733-1311 OR 877/733-1100

This small boutique hotel offers the only overnight accommodations in the Fairhaven Historic District, with walkable access to the unique dining, shopping, and entertainment options in this popular Bellingham destination. Of the 22 rooms, 11 have bay views and 11 have park views. All come with a robe, a fireplace, and a balcony. *$$–$$$; AE, MC, V; checks OK; www. fairhavenvillageinn.com; I-5 exit 250, follow Old Fairhaven Pkwy.* &

Hotel Bellwether / ★★★★

1 BELLWETHER WY, BELLINGHAM; 360/392-3100 OR 877/411-1200

Bellingham's own small "grand" hotel is located on the waterfront near downtown overlooking Bellingham Bay, with terrific sunset views from most of the 68 rooms. Gas fireplaces, soaking tubs (also with views), and a rich decor of imported Italian furniture further enhance the Bellwether's splendor. At day's end, enjoy turn-down service with fine chocolates atop your Hungarian down pillow and Austrian bed linens. For the ultimate in seclusion, rent the dramatic three-story Lighthouse Suite, complete with champagne and caviar. *$$$–$$$$; AE, DIS, MC, V; local checks only; www.hotelbellwether.com; I-5 exit 256, turn right on Squalicum Wy, which becomes Roeder Ave.* &

Lummi Island

Sentinel to the entrance of Bellingham Bay, Lummi is an often-overlooked island of the San Juans. It's serviced by a tiny **FERRY** (360/676-6730; www.co.whatcom. wa.us/publicworks/ferry) that leaves Gooseberry Point at 10 minutes past the hour on weekends, more frequently on weekdays. It's cheap and quick. The ferry returns from Lummi on the hour on weekends, every 20 to 40 minutes on weekdays.

LODGINGS

The Willows Inn / ★★★

> **2579 WEST SHORE DR, LUMMI ISLAND;**
> **360/758-2620 OR 888/294-2620**
> Owners Judy Olsen and Riley Starks keep things interesting at this old favorite inn–turned–foodie destination resort. The main house has four guest rooms with private baths; two have private entrances. Several fully appointed off-site homes that accommodate three to six guests are also available. One of these—the Beach House—sleeps three, has terrific views of the bay, and is just steps from the ferry. Weekend dinners, served year-round, emphasize local and organic ingredients, and a slow food aesthetic; the owners grow much of it on their nearby Nettle's Farm. Meals are served in an intimate candlelit dining room with a picture-perfect view of the water. The Taproot pub is a local hot spot in the afternoons. *$$$; AE, MC, V; checks OK; www. willows-inn.com; north on Nugent Rd 3½ miles.* &

Ferndale

Tiny Ferndale (population 9,000) started as a voting precinct in the mid-1800s, blossomed briefly as a potential Whatcom County seat in the latter part of the 19th century, and endured the failings of an overzealous civic promoter. Today Ferndale is a pleasant community proud of its historical contributions. Notable attractions include **PIONEER PARK** (2004 Cherry St, Ferndale; 360/384-4302) with its log structure exhibits, living-farm **HOVANDER HOMESTEAD PARK** (5299 Nielsen Ave, Ferndale; 360/384-3444), and **TENNANT LAKE NATURAL HISTORY INTERPRETIVE CENTER** (5236 Nielsen Ave, Ferndale; 360/384-3064), a spectacular sanctuary.

　　CEDAR'S RESTAURANT & LOUNGE (2019 Main St, Ferndale, 503/384-2847) is the main place in town for sit-down lunch or dinner service, with a menu ranging from salads to burgers to steaks.

　　Contact the **FERNDALE CHAMBER OF COMMERCE** (5683 2nd Ave, Ferndale; 360/384-3042; www.ferndale-chamber.com) for information.

Lynden

This community, noted for its immaculate yards and colorful gardens, adopted a Dutch theme in tribute to its early settlers. To sample it, visit the **DUTCH**

BAKERY (421 Front St, Lynden; 360/354-3911), in Lynden's unusual shopping mall—there's a stream running through it. The **EASTSIDE MARKET & DELI** (1011 E Grover St, Lynden; 360/354-2246) specializes in Dutch foods, and the **DUTCH VILLAGE INN** (655 Front St, Lynden; 360/354-4440) is a bed-and-breakfast with lodging in a windmill; the six guest rooms are named after Dutch provinces.

Blaine

The northernmost city along the I-5 corridor, Blaine is the state's most popular and beautiful border crossing into British Columbia. Home to the grand International Peace Arch Monument, which spans the U.S.-Canadian border, the surrounding park borders on two bays: Semiahmoo on the U.S. side, Boundary on the Canadian side. The park is filled with gardens and sculptures. Each June, there's a Peace Arch celebration.

In Blaine itself, there aren't many places to stay, though one is pretty famous: **SEMIAHMOO RESORT-GOLF-SPA** (see review). East of town, **SMUGGLER'S INN B&B** (9910 Canada View Dr, Blaine; 360/332-1749; www.smugglersinnblaine. com) is a rambling replica Victorian gem on the border with expansive views.

LODGINGS

Semiahmoo Resort-Golf-Spa / ★★★

9565 SEMIAHMOO PKWY, BLAINE; 360/318-2000 OR 800/770-7992
On Semiahmoo Spit near a 1,100-acre wildlife preserve, Semiahmoo Resort offers golf, acres of wooded trails, and waterfront with views west to the sea and the San Juans and east to Drayton Harbor. Long a favorite of escapists from Seattle and Vancouver, the resort has a spa, a fitness center, a pool, and racquetball and tennis courts. The 198 rooms have classy earth-toned furnishings, and most have water views and fireplaces. Guests enjoy the five restaurants, café, and two award-winning golf courses. *$$$–$$$$; AE, DIS, MC, V; checks OK; www.semiahmoo.com; I-5 exit 270.*

Tacoma, Olympia, and the South Sound

Heading south from Seattle, I-5 takes you to the state's third-largest city, Tacoma, which has become a destination for museum and art lovers. Thirty miles farther to the south is the state's picturesque bay-side capital of Olympia. Scattered between these metropolises are intriguing small communities along Puget Sound.

Vashon Island

It almost feels accidental to find an idyllic island like this where locals still tell time by the tides, where shops and restaurants are mostly family owned. The lack of neon and billboards is refreshing on this hilly island with plentiful art, agriculture, and alpacas. Most restaurants and stores are in Vashon Center, the halfway point on this 12-mile-long island, but art galleries are peppered throughout its length. Beach access can be a challenge, but when you find it, you'll probably catch a glimpse of marine mammals skirting the shore.

Island arts are displayed at the **BLUE HERON ART CENTER** (19704 Vashon Hwy SW, Vashon; 206/463-5131; www.vashonalliedarts.com), managed by the Vashon Allied Arts, and at **SILVERWOOD GALLERY** (23927 Vashon Hwy SW, Vashon; 206/463-1722; www.silverwoodgallery.com). Gardeners like **DIG FLORAL & GARDEN** (19028 Vashon Hwy SW, Vashon; 206/463-5096; www.dignursery.com). Rent sea kayaks and receive instruction or guided trips at **PUGET SOUND KAYAK** (Jensen Point Boathouse at Quartermaster Harbor, Vashon; 206/463-9257; www.pugetsoundkayak.com). Walkers enjoy the garden shows, gallery walks, and celebrations like the Strawberry Festival in July. **MACRINA BAKERY AND CAFÉ** (19603 Vashon Hwy SW, Vashon; 206/567-4133) has goodies for breakfast and lunch.

Access Vashon via **WASHINGTON STATE FERRIES** (206/464-6400 or 800/843-3779; www.wsdot.wa.gov/ferries), which reach the north end from downtown Seattle (foot passengers only) or West Seattle (Fauntleroy ferry) or the south end from Tacoma via the Tahlequah ferry at Point Defiance. You can ferry to one end, drive to the other, then ferry from there to connect Seattle and Tacoma with nary a moment on I-5. Find more information at the **VASHON CHAMBER OF COMMERCE** (19021 Vashon Hwy SW, Vashon; 206/463-6217; www.vashonchamber.com).

RESTAURANTS

The Hardware Store / ★

17601 VASHON HWY SW, VASHON CENTER; 206/463-1800

This 1890s-era building has served many uses, but the one most people remember is its incarnation as a hardware store, so it made sense to keep the name. The shell of the building is original; almost everything else is updated and a little hip. The restaurant provides gallery space, hand-mixed drinks, and food prepared at an exhibition grill. The packed house confirms the wisdom of offering old favorites (meat loaf and mashed potatoes) and new ventures (Penn Cove mussels seared with bacon, shallots, and apple). *$$; AE, DIS, MC, V; local checks only; breakfast Sun, lunch Mon–Sat, dinner every day; full bar; reservations recommended; www.thsrestaurant.com; at Bank Rd downtown.* &

Tacoma

The City of Destiny has the country's seventh-busiest port and one of the nation's largest city parks: Point Defiance. Tacoma also is home to three universities, two military installations, and a world-class zoo. Yet increasingly this city is noticed for the revitalization of its downtown core and its emergence as a cultural destination. The transformation of Tacoma has been described as a renaissance, but "restoration" seems a more fitting adjective. Several historic buildings in the downtown warehouse district have been converted from industrial use to hip residential and commercial functions, such as the University of Washington's Tacoma campus. Today you'll find museums, theaters, art galleries, boutiques, and many fine restaurants.

The $63 million **MUSEUM OF GLASS** (1801 Dock St; 253/284-4750 or 866/468-7386; www.museumofglass.org) displays cutting-edge glass art and shows how it's made in the 180-seat amphitheater Hot Shop nestled into a 90-foot-tall steel cone. Amble across the **CHIHULY BRIDGE OF GLASS** to the Antoine Predock–designed **TACOMA ART MUSEUM** (1701 Pacific Ave; 253/272-4258; www.tacomaartmuseum.org). TAM makes art accessible through hands-on activities, lectures, and interpretations of exhibits. **UNTITLED**, the museum café, offers an excellent assortment of Northwest-inspired cuisine, as well as beer and wine, to museum visitors and passersby. The **WASHINGTON STATE HISTORY MUSEUM** (1911 Pacific Ave; 888/238-4373; www.wshs.org) occupies the arched brick building created to complement the old train station, **UNION STATION** (17th St and Pacific Ave), which now houses the **FEDERAL COURTHOUSE** and a spectacular public display of Dale Chihuly glass art. **JOB CARR'S CABIN** (2350 N 30th St; 253/627-5405; www.jobcarrmuseum.org) is a tiny Old Town museum that marks the city's birthplace. The **WORKING WATERFRONT MUSEUM** (705 Dock St; 253/272-2750; www.wwfrontmuseum.org) is a work in progress that has boats on display and hosts **TALL SHIPS** (www.tallshipstacoma.com; early July), a display of large working sailing ships in the Thea Foss Waterway. The free **KARPELES MANUSCRIPT MUSEUM** (407 S G St; 253/383-2575; www.rain. org), with changing exhibits of famous documents complemented by local art, is across from **WRIGHT PARK** (Division and I sts; www.metroparks.org). In Wright Park, a must-see is the **W. W. SEYMOUR BOTANICAL CONSERVATORY** (316 S G St; 253/591-5330), a 1908 glass, steel, and wood structure where flowers are always in bloom.

Three theaters downtown comprise the **BROADWAY CENTER FOR THE PERFORMING ARTS** (901 Broadway Plaza; 253/591-5890; www.broadwaycenter. org): the restored 1,100-seat **PANTAGES THEATER** (901 Broadway Plaza); the **RIALTO THEATER** (310 S 9th St), a former old movie house; and the contemporary and colorful **THEATER IN THE SQUARE** (915 Broadway). The **UNIVERSITY OF WASHINGTON TACOMA** branch campus (1900 Commerce St; 253/692-4000 or 800/736-7750; www.tacoma.washington.edu) is an excellent example of the use of reconditioned historic buildings. Stately homes and cobblestone streets in the north end are often used as sets by Hollywood moviemakers. One example is **STADIUM HIGH SCHOOL** (111 N E St; 253/571-3100), a turreted chateau originally built to be a luxury hotel.

Tacomans love the outdoors, and there are several ways to get your share of fresh air. **RUSTON WAY WATERFRONT** (between N 49th and N 54th sts) is a popular 2-mile seawall-sidewalk dotted with restaurants. **POINT DEFIANCE PARK** (5400 N Pearl St; 253/305-1000; www.metroparks.org), located on the northwest tip of Tacoma that reaches into **COMMENCEMENT BAY**, is a 700-acre largely old-growth forest. Children enjoy **CAMP 6**, a railroad village with a working steam engine, and **FORT NISQUALLY**, a reconstruction of the original Hudson Bay Company fort built in 1833. But the jewel in the crown of this park is **POINT DEFIANCE ZOO & AQUARIUM** (5400 N Pearl St; 253/591-5335; www.pdza.org).

This Pacific Rim–themed facility features creatures from countries bordered by the Pacific Ocean, a pleasure for the whole family. For a quick lunch or a romantic dinner, visit **ANTHONY'S AT POINT DEFIANCE** (5910 N Waterfront Dr; 253/752-9700) and enjoy looking out over Puget Sound.

The **TACOMA DOME** (2727 E D St; 253/572-3663; www.tacomadome.org), one of the world's largest wooden domes, is regularly booked for trade fairs, concerts, and sports shows. **CHENEY STADIUM** is a first-class ballpark best known as the home of the **TACOMA RAINIERS** (2502 S Tyler St; 253/752-7707; www.tacomarainiers.com), the triple-A affiliate of the Seattle Mariners.

Tacoma offers many restaurants and cafés, but a few favorites downtown include **HOTEL MURANO RESTAURANT AND BAR** (see Lodgings), with Italian cuisine; **PACIFIC GRILL** (1502 Pacific Ave; 253/627-3535; www.pacificgrilltacoma.com) for a dressy night on the town; and **RAVENOUS** (785 Broadway; 253/572-6374), where every dish pleases. Two notable pubs are the **HARMON** brew pub (1938 Pacific Ave; 253/383-2739) and the **SWISS PUB** (1904 S Jefferson Ave; 253/572-2821), where you can choose from 36 drafts.

Besides the **HOTEL MURANO** (see review) and **COURTYARD BY MARRIOTT** (1515 Commerce St; 253/591-9100; www.marriott.com/seatd) downtown—and the **SILVER CLOUD INN** (2317 N Ruston Wy, Tacoma) on the waterfront—Tacoma offers several quality B and Bs and inns. Learn more at the **TACOMA REGIONAL CONVENTION AND VISITOR BUREAU** (1119 Pacific Ave, 5th floor, Tacoma; 253/627-2836 or 800/272-2662; www.traveltacoma.com).

RESTAURANTS

Asado / ★★☆

2810 6TH AVE, TACOMA; 253/272-7770
Cowhide-backed booths, enormous longhorns, and the aroma of mesquite wood set the tone for experiencing *cucina* Argentina—a savory combination of French, Italian, and Spanish flavors. *Asado* means "roasted meat," and Black Angus beef is prized here, but seafood, pork, and chicken are also grilled to perfection. Many of the entrées are accented with delectable sauces and salsas such as *chimichurri*. The staff is competent and confident; trust their recommendations. $$–$$$; AE, DIS, JCB, MC, V; checks OK; dinner every day; full bar; reservations recommended; www.asadotacoma.com; between Pine and Anderson sts. &

El Gaucho / ★★★

2119 PACIFIC AVE, TACOMA; 253/272-1510
The dramatic entrance to this glamorous steak house promises a perfect evening, and the El Gaucho team delivers. Tableside-tossed caesar salad, chateaubriand for two, and bananas Foster are trademark items on the pricey menu. Tables in the sunken dining room are closer to the red tufted bar, grand piano, and open grill, but a table on the mezzanine lets you enjoy a view of it all. $$$$; AE, DIS, MC, V; no checks; dinner every day; full bar; reservations recommended; www.elgaucho.com; in museum district. &

Gateway to India / ★★

2603 6TH AVE, TACOMA; 253/552-5022
This friendly restaurant is a favorite for locals. Three cheerful siblings, C. J. and Surinder Singh and Kuljinder Kour, provide soothing decor, comfortable booths, and competent staff. Oh, and yes, the food is delicious. Delicately spiced dhal soup accompanies every entrée. Some traditional favorites are *ghosht korma*, *saag paneer*, and tandoori chicken, which arrives sizzling on a bed of onions. Try the lightly sweetened chai. Finish your meal with brilliant mango custard. *$$; DIS, MC, V; checks OK; lunch, dinner Tues–Sun; beer and wine; no reservations; www.gatewaytoindia.4t.com; at N Fife.*

Indochine / ★★

1924 PACIFIC AVE, TACOMA; 253/272-8200
Half a block before you reach the ornate doors of this exotic Southeast Asian restaurant, you'll smell basil, curry, and jasmine. On your first visit, sit at one of the Brazilian cherrywood tables beside the reflecting pond. The menu is overwhelming, so zero in on the house specialties: the best Thai, Vietnamese, and Chinese recipes combined to create treasures like the Black Sea—a mound of seafood tossed with nutty *kala masala* and coconut milk over black rice. A second, smaller, dressed-down location (2045 Mildred St W, Fircrest; 253/564-9409) is also reliable. *$$; AE, MC, V; no checks; lunch, dinner Mon–Sat; full bar; reservations recommended; www.indochinedowntown.com; just before 21st St, near the University of Washington Tacoma campus.* ᚼ

Parkway Tavern / ★★

313 N I ST, TACOMA; 253/383-8748
Tucked into a quiet north Tacoma neighborhood not far from Wright Park, the Parkway's Craftsman-like exterior, large windows, and lofty ceiling welcome you to one of the happiest bars in town. A splendid array of microbrews changes weekly, and the burgers are excellent. Try the mushroom-swiss. On weekends, pop in for a late breakfast of biscuits and homemade gravy—and a pint to wash it down. *$$; MC, V; no checks; breakfast Sat–Sun, lunch, dinner Mon–Sun; beer and wine; no reservations; north of Wright Park.*

Sea Grill / ★★★

1498 PACIFIC AVE, STE 300, TACOMA; 253/272-5656
Sea Grill is owned by the same folks who own El Gaucho and the Waterfront Seafood Grill in Seattle. Glass walls and copper-leaved chandeliers adorn the spacious dining room that flows into a circular bar. Come here for seafood and steaks: the all-out indulgence is Seafood Bacchanalia. Steaks are prepared on an open-pit charcoal grill in the exhibition kitchen. Stay long enough for someone to order the Mount Rainier Volcano: this version of baked Alaska, complete with chocolate lava, is flambéed tableside. *$$$–$$$$; AE, MC, V; no checks; dinner every day; full bar; reservations recommended; www.the-seagrill.com; at 15th St.* ᚼ

TACOMA THREE-DAY TOUR

DAY ONE: Start with breakfast at the **HOTEL MURANO RESTAURANT AND BAR** on the fourth floor of the **HOTEL MURANO**. Plan to be at the **WASHINGTON STATE HISTORY MUSEUM** as soon as it opens so you can spend the morning browsing its three floors. Head north on Pacific Avenue and up Ninth Avenue to Broadway for lunch at **RAVENOUS**. Go back down the hill to marvel at the **TACOMA ART MUSEUM** and be amazed at the possibilities of glass at the **MUSEUM OF GLASS**. Check in at the **HOTEL MURANO** and catch your breath with a glass of wine in the Lobby Atrium. Feast downtown at **SEA GRILL**.

DAY TWO: Enjoy a latte or cappucino and pastry at the **BLACKWATER CAFE** (747 S Fawcett; 253/404-0000; www.blackwatertacoma.com), where local hipsters, artists, and music lovers go to wake up. Continue on to the nearby **KARPELES MANUSCRIPT MUSEUM**. Cross the street and visit the **SEYMOUR BOTANICAL CONSERVATORY** in **WRIGHT PARK**. Drive back down the hill to the **WORKING WATERFRONT MUSEUM**, then drive up Schuster Parkway and follow 30th to 26th for a romantic lunch with wine at the **ROSEWOOD CAFE** (3323 N 26th; 253/752-7999; www.rosewoodcafe.com). Make arrangements in advance for the guided tour, then drive less than 13 miles to **LEMAY: AMERICA'S CAR MUSEUM** (325 152nd St E; 253/536-2885; www.lemaymuseum.com), where 400 vintage vehicles await. Return to north Tacoma to check in to the **CHINABERRY HILL BED AND BREAKFAST** (302 Tacoma Ave N; 253/272/1282; www.chinaberryhill.com), then return downtown to the **AVANTI SPA** (1506 Pacific Ave; 253/682-2005) before dinner at **INDOCHINE**. Consider taking in a show at one of three downtown theaters at **BROADWAY CENTER FOR THE PERFORMING ARTS**.

DAY THREE: Enjoy breakfast at your B and B, then visit **POINT DEFIANCE ZOO & AQUARIUM**. Have lunch at the **LOBSTER SHOP** (4015 Ruston Wy; 253/759-2165; www.lobstershop.com), then walk the 2-mile **RUSTON WAY WATERFRONT** promenade. Return to the Chinaberry for a relaxing bath before enjoying a burger and microbrew at the **PARKWAY TAVERN**.

LODGINGS

Hotel Murano / ★★★

1320 BROADWAY PLAZA, TACOMA; 253/572-3200 OR 877/986-8083
Designed to celebrate the city's growing art reputation—particularly art glass, thanks to Dale Chihuly—this downtown boutique hotel is an experience unto itself. A world-class art collection, including more than 45 pieces of international glass art, greets you as you enter the lobby as well as on every floor as you

step off the elevator. Even the rooms display sketches of the artists' inspirations. The entire space is enveloped in a chic, ultra-modern design, though creature comforts are not missed in any of the 320 rooms. Amenities include iPod docking stations, flat panel television, and premium bedding with high thread counts. Even the phone's "Help Me" button responds to any whim. Pet-friendly rooms are available. Bite, the hotel's dining room, features a luminescent glass counter and its own stunning collection of art, though the restaurant hasn't quite yet found its own creative groove. *$$$–$$$; AE, DC, E, MC, V; checks OK, www. hotelmuranotacoma.com; between Broadway and Commerce St.*

Thornewood Castle B&B / ★★★

8601 N THORNE LN, LAKEWOOD; 253/584-4393

You'll feel like royalty in this enormous Gothic-Tudor manor where richly paneled guest rooms are furnished with leather sofas, antique chests, and portraits of aristocrats. This mansion on 4 acres was the setting for the mini-series *Rose Red* by Stephen King. Eight of the 22 bedrooms are now used as guest rooms. Most have stained-glass windows, some have fireplaces, others have soaking tubs. The half-acre Olmstead-designed English garden is lovely. *$$$$; AE, DIS, MC, V; checks OK (in advance); www.thornewoodcastle.com; I-5 exit 123 to Thorne Ln.*

Gig Harbor

The tranquility of this picture-perfect fishing village north of Tacoma hasn't been disturbed by the addition of a second Tacoma Narrows bridge. While not many motorists leave State Route 16 to venture into downtown Gig Harbor, boat traffic remains as busy as ever. Good anchorage and various moorage docks continue to attract gunwale-to-gunwale pleasure craft. The harbor is still the life of the town, and you'll find bookstores, boutiques, bakeries, and a wild-birdfeed store along Harborview Drive, which almost encircles the bay.

Gig Harbor is a good place for celebrations. A maritime festival in June, an arts festival in mid-July, and a Scandinavian Fest in October are main events, but check the events calendar at the **GIG HARBOR CHAMBER OF COMMERCE** (3311 Harborview Dr; 253/851-6865 or 800/359-8804; www.gigharborchamber. com) for others. The Saturday **GIG HARBOR FARMERS MARKET** (www.gigharbor farmersmarket.com; mid-Apr–Sept) is located in the **SKANSIE BROTHERS PARK** (3270 Harborview Dr), where you can stroll along the waterfront.

KIMBALL ESPRESSO (6950 Kimball Dr; 253/858-2625) is a nice place for a snack, and it doubles as a gallery. Several restaurants along the harbor offer quick bites and sit-down dinners. Locals love **BRIX 25** (7707 Pioneer Wy; 253/858-6626; www.harborbrix.com), **EL PUEBLITO** (3226 Harborview Dr; 253/858-9077), and **JUDSON STREET CAFÉ** (3114 Judson St; 253/858-1176; www.judsonstcafe.com). The **MARITIME INN** (3212 Harborview Dr; 253/858-1818; ww.maritimeinn.com) is in the heart of downtown but can be noisy. The **BEST WESTERN WESLEY INN** (6575 Kimball Dr; 253/858-9690 or 888/462-0002; www.wesleyinn.com) up the hill has a pool.

PENINSULA GARDENS NURSERY (5503 Wollochet Dr NW, Gig Harbor; 253/851-8115; www.peninsulagardens.com) southwest of town is fun to explore. Just outside Gig Harbor, three parks have beaches where clam digging is sometimes allowed: **KOPACHUCK STATE PARK** (follow signs from SR 16; 253/265-3606), **PENROSE POINT STATE PARK**, and **JOEMMA STATE PARK**, the latter two on the Key Peninsula (south of SR 302, west of SR 16 at Purdy). You can also easily reach the beach at the Purdy Spit.

RESTAURANTS

The Green Turtle / ★★

2905 HARBORVIEW DR, GIG HARBOR; 253/851-3167
This unassuming, fun, and funky little restaurant is still considered one of Gig Harbor's finest. Asian, French, and Northwest combinations like Dungeness crab–stuffed mahi mahi and ginger- and wasabi-topped yellowfin ahi are our favorites. You wouldn't guess from the humble parking lot that the view from the deck, and even inside the dining room, is the best in the harbor. *$$–$$$; AE, DIS, MC, V; checks OK; lunch Tues–Fri, dinner Tues–Sun; beer and wine; reservations recommended; www.thegreenturtle.com; past Tides Tavern away from downtown.* &

LODGINGS

The Inn at Gig Harbor / ★★

3211 56TH ST NW, GIG HARBOR; 253/858-1111 OR 800/795-9980
This serene Craftsman-style inn with 64 rooms and suites is just 2 miles from the Narrows bridge, but it feels miles away from the fray. Eight types of rooms are available, including king suites with Jacuzzis, queen suites with fireplaces, and kitchenette units. Views of Mount Rainier are a bonus in the back, but it's quieter in front. Spend a few minutes looking at the historic black-and-white photos of Gig Harbor on the walls of each level. The theme flows into the Heritage Inn Restaurant, where you should have a bowl of the award-winning clam chowder. *$$$; AE, DIS, MC, V; no checks; www.innatgigharbor. com; 2 miles west of Narrows bridge, exit 10, left above overpass, right at Pt Fosdick Dr, 1 mile up on right.* &

Puyallup

This farm town southeast of Tacoma is best known as the place where you "Do the Puyallup." Few would argue that the Western Washington Fair has brought fame and fortune to this rapidly growing town, but an unfortunate by-product is traffic congestion. State Route 161 to the south is frenetic, so head east up the valley to Sumner and the White River (SR 410) or to Orting, Wilkeson, and Carbonado (SRs 162 and 165). If your destination is Mount Rainier through this gateway, State Route 410 leads to Chinook Pass, and State Routes 162 and 165 lead to the Carbon River and Mowich Lake entrances.

The **EZRA MEEKER MANSION** (321 Pioneer Wy, Puyallup; 253/838-1770; www.meekermansion.org; 12pm–4pm Wed–Sun) is the finest original pioneer mansion left in Washington. Its builder and first occupant, Ezra Meeker, introduced hops to the Puyallup Valley. His lavish 17-room Italianate house (circa 1890) has been beautifully restored.

Puyallup is big on old-time seasonal celebrations, and it hosts two of the Northwest's largest: April's **DAFFODIL FESTIVAL AND PARADE** (253/863-9524; www.daffodilfestival.net) and September's Western Washington Fair—better known as the **PUYALLUP FAIR** (110 9th Ave SW, Puyallup; 253/841-5045; www.thefair.com)—one of the nation's biggest fairs, with food, games, rides, and premier touring bands. The **PUYALLUP DOWNTOWN FARMERS MARKET** (www.puyallup mainstreet.com) is held Saturday mornings at **PIONEER PARK** (corner of Pioneer and Meridian sts, Puyallup) and runs through the growing season (usually late May–Sept).

Learn more at the **PUYALLUP/SUMNER CHAMBER OF COMMERCE** (47 E Pioneer St, Puyallup; 253/845-6755; www.puyallupchamber.com).

Steilacoom and Anderson Island

Steilacoom, a little community at the edge of Puget Sound southwest of Tacoma, was once a Native American village, then became Washington Territory's first incorporated town in 1854. Steilacoom prides itself on its heritage and encourages walking tours of its historic homes. Many of the houses include placards that list the construction date and original owners' names. The **STEILACOOM TRIBAL MUSEUM** (1515 Lafayette St, Steilacoom; 253/584-6308) is a turn-of-the-19th-century church overlooking the South Sound islands and the Olympic range. Midsummer's **SALMON BAKE** (last Sun in July), with canoe and kayak races, and October's **APPLE SQUEEZE FESTIVAL** (first Sun in Oct) are good reasons to pay a visit (www.steilacoom.org/museum for both). **PIERCE COUNTY FERRIES** (253/798-2766 recording; www.co.pierce.wa.us) run from here to Anderson Island. Reach Steilacoom via I-5 exit 128 to Steilacoom Boulevard. Visitor information is at **CITY HALL** (1717 Lafayette St, Steilacoom; 253/851-1900; www.townofsteilacoom.org).

LODGINGS

Anderson House on Oro Bay / ★★

12024 ECKENSTAM-JOHNSON RD, ANDERSON ISLAND; 253/884-4088
A visit to this country inn has all the hallmarks of a trip to grandma's house: hardwood floors, patchwork quilts, a breezy porch, and the smell of fresh-baked bread. Four guest rooms, all with private baths, are available in this farmhouse. For decompressing, there's the garden, the pasture, and the 200 acres of woods. You can fish, comb the beach, bicycle, or play nine holes at the nearby Riviera Community Club. Call for a pickup at the ferry landing, or use the dock if you're arriving by water. *$$$; MC, V; checks OK; www.non. com/anderson/house; call for directions.*

Olympia

This tidy and unpretentious capital city is an undiscovered gem. Walkers love the paths around the grounds of the capital campus and Capitol Lake, along the Puget Sound waterfront, and through downtown. Excellent restaurants, a thriving arts community, and the renowned Evergreen State College contribute to Olympia's appeal. Surrounding communities of Lacey and Tumwater enlarge the urban area.

The state capital's centerpiece—visible from the freeway—is the classic dome of the **WASHINGTON STATE LEGISLATURE BUILDING** (416 14th Ave, Olympia; 360/902-8880). This striking Romanesque structure houses the office of the governor and other executives. Hour-long guided tours are offered every day; maps are provided for self-guided tours; tours of the red-brick **GOVERNOR'S MANSION** are on Wednesday afternoons (360/902-8880; reservations required). The **STATE CAPITAL MUSEUM** (211 W 21st Ave, Olympia; 360/753-2580; www.wshs. org/wscm) houses a permanent exhibit documenting the state's political past. The **WASHINGTON STATE LIBRARY** (6880 Capitol Blvd S, Tumwater; 360/704-5200; www.statelib.wa.gov) is open to the public during business hours. Downtown, on Seventh Avenue between Washington and Franklin streets, you'll find the restored **OLD CAPITOL**, with pointed towers and high-arched windows.

The **WASHINGTON CENTER FOR THE PERFORMING ARTS** (512 Washington St, Olympia; 360/753-8586; www.washingtoncenter.org) is home to more than a dozen performance groups. Across Fifth Avenue, the **CAPITOL THEATER** (206 E 5th Ave, Olympia; 360/754-3635; www.olyfilm.org) provides a forum for the active **OLYMPIA FILM SOCIETY** (360/754-6670; www.olyfilm.org) and locally produced plays and musicals.

A few blocks from the heart of downtown, **CAPITOL LAKE** offers picturesque vantage points of the capitol and grassy areas for picnics and play, as well as a trail that encircles most of the lake. After a walk, treat yourself to award-winning peach cobbler at the **SOUTHERN KITCHEN RESTAURANT** (621 Capitol Wy S, Olympia; 360/352-7700) in the Ramada Inn, fitted between the lake and **HERITAGE PARK** in the town square.

Toward the harbor, the colorful **OLYMPIA FARMERS MARKET** (near Percival Landing; 360/352-9096; www.olympiafarmersmarket.com; Thurs–Sun Apr–Oct, Sat–Sun Nov–Dec up to Christmas) displays produce, flowers, and crafts from all over the South Sound. The waterfront park at **PERCIVAL LANDING** (700 N Capitol Wy, Olympia) is the site of several harbor festivals. In another part of downtown, adjacent to City Hall, is the serene **YASHIRO JAPANESE GARDEN** (1010 Plum St SE, Olympia; 360/753-8380), honoring one of Olympia's sister cities. The historic heart of the three-town area is **TUMWATER FALLS** (I-5 exit 103), where the Deschutes River flows into Capitol Lake. A nice walk along the river takes you past waterfalls.

The **EVERGREEN STATE COLLEGE** (2700 Evergreen Pkwy NW, Olympia; 360/867-6000; www.evergreen.edu), west of Olympia on Cooper Point, offers a regular schedule of plays, films, experimental theater, and special events. The library and pool are open to the public. The Nisqually Delta, at the outlet of the

Nisqually River (which springs from the foot of a Mount Rainier glacier), is the area's finest nature preserve. It enters Puget Sound just north of Olympia at the **NISQUALLY NATIONAL WILDLIFE REFUGE** (I-5 exit 114, follow signs; 360/753-9467; www.fws.gov/nisqually). A 5-mile hiking trail follows an old dike around the delta. More information is at the **OLYMPIA-LACEY-TUMWATER VISITOR AND CONVENTION BUREAU** (809 Legion Wy SE, Olympia; 360/704-7544 or 877/704-7500; www.visitolympia.com).

RESTAURANTS

Cielo Blu / ★★

515 CAPITOL WY S, OLYMPIA; 360/352-8007
When the owners of the former Capitale Restaurant opened Cielo Blu, legislators (and others) acquired a new favorite. The coppery-orange and green decor is a nice complement to the intense Asian, Italian, and Spanish creations like black bean ravioli topped with chipotle-lime cream, tomatillo salsa, and cilantro crème. Another spicy treasure is the cilantro-crusted grilled prawns with capellini and a creamy chile vinaigrette. Many of the sauces and garnishes are spicy. *$$; AE, DIS, MC, V; checks OK; dinner Mon–Sat; full bar; reservations recommended; www.cieloblufusion.com; near 5th Ave.* &

The Mark / ★★★

407 COLUMBIA ST, OLYMPIA; 360/754-4414
Red velvet draperies, black leather booths, and leopard-print upholstery give this chic restaurant and nightclub attitude and style. This is the kind of place writers love during the day. Businesspeople come for lunch, and at night, all types enjoy the live music inside and a DJ outside. The food, which emphasizes French and Spanish cheeses, olives, and breads, is the draw for those who appreciate sophisticated fare. The handmade pastas are excellent; pappardelle with artichoke is a favorite. *$$–$$$; AE, MC, V; local checks only; lunch, dinner Thurs–Sat; full bar; reservations recommended; www.the markolympia.com; between 4th and 5th aves.* &

Ristorante Basilico / ★★

507 CAPITOL WY S, OLYMPIA; 360/570-8777
The affection Olympia has for the two Italian men who own and operate this restaurant is mutual, evidenced by the exchange of hearty hugs patrons give and receive. Word-of-mouth recommendations are spreading like wildfire as visitors to this warm, friendly ristorante discover how simply elegant northern Italian cuisine can be. Filet mignon, seasoned only with truffle salt, is tender. Hand-rolled pasta offerings include *maltagliati all'antica con pesto*, with only a hint of garlic. *$$–$$$; AE, DIS, MC, V; checks OK; lunch, dinner Mon–Sat; full bar; reservations recommended; www.ristorantebasilico.com; between 5th Ave and Legion Wy.*

Trinacria / ★★

113 CAPITOL WY S, OLYMPIA; 360/352-8892

You can easily imagine Lady and the Tramp taking a table nearby to enjoy their plate of spaghetti in this sweet restaurant. Eugenio Aliotta, the Sicilian owner of this pizzeria, has been a legend in Olympia since 1989, but few outsiders know about his light hand with pizza and pasta. The favorite is his Sicilian pizza, folded over like a large calzone. The traditional ragù and Parmesan is simple and delicious. The Italian music near the kitchen is loud, so sit near the front. *$–$$; no credit cards; checks OK; lunch, dinner Tues–Sat; beer and wine; reservations recommended; at 4th Ave.* &

LODGINGS

Fertile Ground Guesthouse / ★★

311 9TH AVE SE, OLYMPIA; 360/352-2428

This three-room B and B makes its mark as an excellent example of green lodgings. New in 2008 were two satellite accommodations: the Atomic Ranch House, located in the woods two miles east of downtown, which features two bedrooms, and an extended-stay two-bedroom downtown Olympia apartment. Innkeepers Gail and Michael Di Marzo offer organic cotton linens on futons, organic soaps and shampoos, and an all-organic breakfast. Take time to explore their enormous herbicide- and pesticide-free garden, where they'll harvest ingredients for breakfast: waffles with fruit, huevos rancheros, or omelets with eggs from their free-range chickens—and free-trade coffee, of course. *$$; MC, V; checks OK; www.fertileground.org; between Adams and Franklin sts across from library.*

Yelm and Tenino

Yelm is home to the **OUTBACK BOUTIQUE** (207 1st St S, Yelm; 877/458-4618; www.outbackboutique.com), an oasis of antiques, linens, gifts, clothes, and personal indulgences displayed in dozens of creative settings under one large roof, easily identifiable by the purple and white striped awning. If you're on your way to Mount Rainier, **ARNOLD'S COUNTRY INN** (717 Yelm Ave E, Yelm; 360/458-3977) serves breakfast, lunch, and dinner. This still rural but steadily growing area south of Olympia on State Route 507 is known for **WOLF HAVEN** (3111 Offut Lake Rd, Tenino; 360/264-4695; www.wolfhaven.org), a sanctuary for captive-born wolves that offers public tours. Tenino is also known for the country-dining destination **ALICE'S RESTAURANT** (19248 Johnson Creek Rd SE, Tenino; 360/264-2887; www.alicesdinners.com).

OLYMPIC AND
KITSAP PENINSULAS

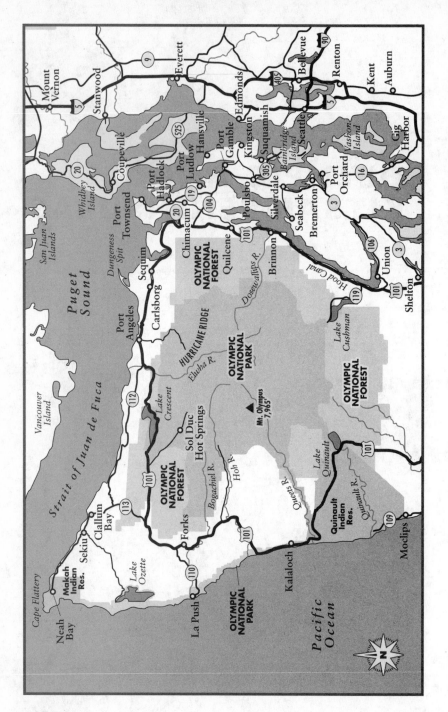

OLYMPIC AND KITSAP PENINSULAS

Five thousand square miles of diverse scenery and natural splendor surround the convivial small towns of this area.

In Kitsap County, Bremerton is well into a major revitalization. Over in Poulsbo, the Scandinavian atmosphere continues to draw visitors; and in Port Gamble the burg's historic dollhouse homes are the winning attraction. Across the Hood Canal Bridge into the farmlands, towns, and shores surrounding the Olympic Peninsula, the majestic mountains beckon. The area surrounding Ports Townsend and Angeles are ideal for savoring the calm of bucolic country inns and pampering the soul with solitude at historic oceanside and forest-edge lodges. These two towns, like Bremerton, offer the traveler a little bit more of a "city" experience with their burgeoning arts and restaurant scenes.

On the Olympic Peninsula, US Highway 101 wraps snugly around an empire built and ruled by Mother Nature. In the center, Olympic National Park is home to 1,200 plant species, 300 bird species, and 70 different kinds of mammals. The park's mountainous terrain descends to beaches, seascapes, and temperate rain forest: it seems to be three parks rolled into one. Every year more than 5 million people come to soak in the hot springs, wander through the rain forests, stroll the pristine beaches, and admire the stunning variety of plants and animals.

ACCESS AND INFORMATION

From the east shores of Puget Sound, the best route to the Kitsap and Olympic peninsulas is the **WASHINGTON STATE FERRIES** (206/464-6400 or 800/843-3779; www.wsdot.wa.gov/ferries), which regularly run between downtown Seattle and Bremerton, on the Kitsap Peninsula, or Bainbridge Island, gateway to both peninsulas. Ferries also dock in Port Townsend (from Keystone on Whidbey Island) on the Olympic Peninsula, in Kingston (from Edmonds) on the Kitsap Peninsula, and in Southworth (from Fauntleroy in West Seattle), near Port Orchard on the Kitsap Peninsula.

You can also drive around Puget Sound on **INTERSTATE 5** through Tacoma to reach the Kitsap Peninsula via the Narrows Bridge, or go through Olympia and Shelton to reach the Olympic Peninsula on **US HWY 101**, which circles the peninsula.

You can also reach Port Angeles on the Olympic Peninsula via Victoria, British Columbia. The MV *Coho*, operated by **BLACK BALL TRANSPORT** (360/457-4491; www.cohoferry.com), runs daily with a 1½-hour crossing; the much quicker **VICTORIA EXPRESS** (360/452-8088 or 800/633-1589; www.victoriaexpress.com) is a foot-passenger ferry that runs daily, late May to September.

Public bus transportation between communities is available through **KITSAP TRANSIT** (360/373-2877 or 800/501-RIDE; www.kitsaptransit. org), **JEFFERSON COUNTY TRANSIT** and **WEST JEFFERSON TRANSIT** (360/385-4777 or 800/371-0497; www.jeffersontransit.com), **CLALLAM**

TRANSIT SYSTEM (360/452-4511 or 800/858-3747; www.clallamtransit. com), and **MASON COUNTY TRANSPORTATION AUTHORITY** (360/426-9434 or 800/281-9434).

Small planes land at airports in Bremerton, Jefferson County, Shelton, Sequim, and Port Angeles. **KENMORE AIR** (425/486-1257 or 866/435-9524; www.kenmoreair.com), which lands at Fairchild International Airport in Port Angeles, is the largest airline to serve the peninsula.

For information, contact the **PORT TOWNSEND CHAMBER OF COMMERCE VISITOR INFORMATION CENTER** (2437 E Sims Wy, Port Townsend; 360/385-2722 or 888/ENJOY-PT; www.ptchamber.org) or the **NORTH OLYMPIC PENINSULA VISITOR & CONVENTION BUREAU** (360/452-8552 or 800/942-4042; www.olympicpeninsula.org) in Port Angeles.

Bainbridge Island

Some people consider Bainbridge an extension of Seattle—it's just a 30-minute ferry ride away. Once a major logging port, it's now a haven for city professionals, writers, and artists. It makes a pleasant tour by car or bike: you can see some farms, waterfront homes, and spectacular cityscapes—especially from **FAY BAINBRIDGE STATE PARK** (Sunrise Dr NE; 888/226-7688) on the northeast corner of the island. The wooded and waterfront trails in **FORT WARD STATE PARK** (along Rich Passage, 6 miles from ferry terminal; 888/226-7688), on the south end of the island, make a nice afternoon stroll. **BLOEDEL RESERVE** (7571 NE Dolphin Dr; 206/842-7631; www.bloedelreserve.org) encompasses 150 acres of gardens, woods, meadows, and ponds. Plants from all over the world make the grounds interesting any time of the year.

For a low-key day tour, ride the ferry and bike to the **BAINBRIDGE ISLAND VINEYARDS AND WINERY** (8989 Day Rd E; 206/842-9463; www.bainbridge vineyards.com), then head back downtown, take in the shops, have coffee at **PEGASUS COFFEE HOUSE** (8040 NE Day Rd; 206/842-3113; www.pegasus coffeehouse.org), and float back to Seattle.

RESTAURANTS

Four Swallows / ★★★

481 MADISON AVE N, BAINBRIDGE ISLAND; 206/842-3397

A favorite of locals and visitors alike, this welcoming restaurant in a converted 1889 farmhouse garners nothing but high praise. Their blend of Italian and inspired Pacific Northwest cuisine would make choosing a dinner easy—if it wasn't so tempting to try it all, all at once. Fresh, well-prepared seafood conspires against scrumptious beef, pasta, and pizza; sophisticated appetizers and salads all seem to clamor for attention; the world-class wine list has tasty and interesting selections that will cozy up to whatever main course you choose. The informed and decorous staff won't disappoint. Tasty desserts live up to expectations. Dine under the shade trees on the deck in summer, or in one of the warm, comfortable booths inside. *$$$–$$$$; AE, MC, V; no checks; dinner Tues–Sat; full bar; reservations recommended; www.fourswallows.com; SR 305 to Winslow Wy west, then north on Madison Ave.*

Madoka / ★★★½

241 WINSLOW WY W, WINSLOW; 206/842-2448

This pan-Pacific restaurant on a quiet street is an elegant tearoom during lunch hours. The chef departed Seattle for a more laid-back lifestyle and found it here. Try a small plate with savory delicacies such as Penn Cove mussels steamed with green curry, coconut milk, and basil, or tuck into more formidable entrées like sake-braised Oregon lamb shank, pan-seared weather-vane scallops, or chile-cured pork tenderloin. *$$$; AE, DIS, MC, V; no checks; dinner Wed–Sun; full bar; reservations recommended; www.madokaonbainbridge.com; downtown.* &

Kitsap Peninsula

Kitsap Peninsula, between the larger Olympic Peninsula and the mainland, is bordered by Puget Sound (with Bainbridge and Vashon islands) on the east and Hood Canal on the west. A thin waist of land at the southeastern tip of Hood Canal connects the Kitsap and Olympic peninsulas, as does the Hood Canal Bridge in the north. The Tacoma Narrows Bridge connects southeastern Kitsap Peninsula to the mainland.

Belfair

This small, vibrant town thrives at the tip of Hood Canal's "hook," on State Route 3 between Shelton and Port Orchard. From here, travelers on the Kitsap Peninsula can drive northeast to Bremerton and the Seattle ferries, north to the Hood Canal Bridge, or southeast to the Narrows Bridge (via State Routes 302 and 16).

LODGINGS

Selah Inn / ★★

NE 130 DULALIP LANDING, BELFAIR; 360/275-0916 OR 877-232-7941

Selah Inn is an ideal spot for couples, families, and special occasions. Set on the serene north shore of Hood Canal, the inn is within a 10-mile radius of four golf courses. Just south is Belfair State Park, a 63-acre park noted for its saltwater tide flats, wetlands with windblown beach grasses—perfect for beach walking and saltwater swimming on warm days. On rainy days, park yourself by the stone fireplace and enjoy a book from the inn's library. Full breakfasts are served in the dining room and sunroom. Gourmet dinners are available by reservation. *$$–$$$; MC, V; checks OK; www.selahinn.com; southeast end of Hood Canal.*

Port Orchard

A busy marina and a quaint waterfront make this small town on **SINCLAIR INLET** particularly intriguing to travelers. The main boardwalk on Bay Street is lined with antique shops, restaurants, and art galleries. **SIDNEY ART GALLERY** (202 Sidney Ave; 360/876-3693; www.sidneymuseumandarts.com) and **BETHEL AVENUE BOOK COMPANY** (1037 Bethel Ave; 360/876-7500; www.bethelavebook.com) are two good stops. The **PORT ORCHARD FARMERS MARKET** (Marina Park, 1 block from Bay St; 360/275-7105; www.pofarmersmarket.org; Sat late Apr–Oct) grows each year.

To reach the peninsula and **PORT ORCHARD** via ferry, take the **FAUNTLEROY FERRY** from West Seattle to Southworth, then drive SR 160 west. Or drive north on SR 3 from Shelton or north on SR 16 from Tacoma.

RESTAURANTS

Cosmos Ristorante & Delicatessen / ★★

1821 LUND AVE, PORT ORCHARD; 360/895-3138
This Italian restaurant may be located next door to an office supply store in a bright pink building, but that's easily overlooked once you taste Cosmos' rustic Italian food—with recipes from the co-owner's Italian mom—in the front of the building or order from the well-stocked gourmet deli (closed Sun) in back. Portions are huge and delicious, and the atmosphere is cozy. *$$; AE, MC, V; checks OK; lunch, dinner Mon–Sat; full bar; reservations recommended; www.cosmosdeli.com; south side of town.* &

LODGINGS

Reflections Bed and Breakfast Inn / ★★

3878 REFLECTION LN E, PORT ORCHARD; 360/871-5582
Overlooking Sinclair Inlet, this inn's gardens are alive with visiting birds. Enjoy views of Bainbridge Island and Port Orchard Passage from the hot tub on the deck. Heirloom quilts grace the beds, and the house is filled with colonial antiques. Two guest rooms offer private baths; two others share a bath. A variety of breakfast entrées is offered in the formal dining room. *$$; MC, V; no checks; www.reflectionsbnb.com; east of town off Beach Dr.* &

Bremerton

This quintessential Navy town continues to evolve. Bremerton is hopping with transplants looking for metropolitan comforts minus the traffic and smog. The once dead downtown has perked up. Luxurious waterfront condominiums have replaced parking lots and industrial slums. Bremerton now boasts a convention center, a waterfront hotel, and a six-story city government center. A new marina opened in 2008. In his second term, Mayor Cary Bozeman has helped keep businesses pouring in and revitalization on track.

The boardwalk offers views of the **USS TURNER JOY** (300 Washington Beach Ave, Bremerton; 360/792-2457; www.ussturnerjoy.org), while the **BREMERTON NAVAL MUSEUM** (402 Pacific Ave, Bremerton; 360/479-7447) depicts the region's shipbuilding history. See the first Revolutionary War submarine at the **NAVAL UNDERSEA MUSEUM** (1 Garnet Wy, Keyport; 360/396-4148; www.keyport museum.cnrnw.navy.mil; SR 3 north of town to SR 308 east).

For information on the **FIRST FRIDAY ART WALK** (downtown Bremerton), contact the **MADE IN BREMERTON STORE** (408 Pacific Ave, Bremerton; 360/782-1500). The **ADMIRAL THEATRE** (515 Pacific Ave, Bremerton; 360/373-6743; www.admiraltheatre.org), a movie house built in 1942, is the place to catch live shows. Both classy and casual, the **BOAT SHED** (101 Shore Dr, Bremerton; 360/377-2600; www.theboatshedrestaurant.com), a restaurant at the end of the Manette Bridge, offers a family-friendly menu along with excellent views of the waterfront.

Reach Bremerton by **FERRY** from downtown Seattle's Pier 52. If you're driving from Poulsbo or Shelton, take **SR 3**. From Tacoma or Seattle, take I-5 to **SR 16**, then cross the Tacoma Narrows Bridge and drive north.

RESTAURANTS

Anthony's Home Port Bremerton / ★★★

20 WASHINGTON AVE, BREMERTON; 360/377-5004
It's one of a multirestaurant chain, but the fresh seafood is a winner on par with the stunning view of Sinclair Inlet. Order up wild king salmon, local oysters, and Dungeness crab. Sit outside if the sun is shining. Complimentary guest moorage is available in front of the restaurant. *$$$; AE, DIS, MC, V; no checks; lunch, dinner every day; full bar; reservations recommended; www. anthonys.com; right off ferry dock.* &

La Fermata / ★★★

2204 E 11TH ST, BREMERTON; 360/373-5927
Dark wood, warm candlelight, and a formidable wine list increase this restaurant's romantic quotient, as do the fireplace, bar, and fresh flowers adorning the tables. Along with ambience, La Fermata delivers flavor—northern Italian with a Northwest twist. The balsamic-glazed duck wins rave reviews, and the seafood is extraordinarily fresh. The menu changes often and never disappoints. An extensive selection of wines from around the world and a customary pre-order taste makes finding the perfect pairing a snap. Think big-city quality transported to a small town. *$$$; AE, MC, V; checks OK; dinner Tues–Sat; beer and wine; reservations recommended; across Manette Bridge.* &

LODGINGS

Illahee Manor / ★★★

6680 ILLAHEE RD NE, BREMERTON; 360/698-7555 OR 800/693-6680
Russian immigrants built this wonderful manor in 1926. Five large guest rooms, each with a soaking tub and one with a sauna, grace the main house.

OLYMPIC PENINSULA THREE-DAY TOUR

DAY ONE: Begin in **PORT TOWNSEND**. First, stop by the **VISITORS CENTER** on SR 20 and pick up maps of the vicinity, including a local tour map. Fuel up at **TYLER STREET COFFEE HOUSE** with a hand-twisted cinnamon braid and a cup of coffee. Check out the shops along **WATER STREET**, especially the **ANCESTRAL SPIRITS GALLERY** for authentic aboriginal and tribal arts and crafts. Next, take the local driving tour, detailing 72 notable Victorian-era buildings and homes in town. Grab gourmet picnic food at **PROVISIONS** (939 Kearney St, Port Townsend; 360/385-4541; www.provisionspt.com) and head to **FORT WORDEN STATE PARK**. Before your beach picnic, visit the **MARINE SCIENCE CENTER** to interact with marine life in the touch tanks. Then head for the beach on foot and, after your picnic, explore the old gun batteries of the fort. Point yourself back toward downtown to catch an early movie at the **ROSE THEATRE**, a refurbished architectural gem with undeniably the best popcorn anywhere. Enjoy dinner at the **WILD COHO**, where dishes feature the in-season bounty of the Northwest. Spend the night at the impeccably furnished **JAMES HOUSE**.

DAY TWO: After breakfast at the B and B, stop by **SWEET LAURETTE CAFÉ & BISTRO** for French pastries to enjoy on the road. Take SR 20 to US Hwy 101 west toward Sequim. Follow the Sequim Avenue exit into downtown Sequim and head to **MIKE'S BIKES** (150 W Sequim Bay Rd, Sequim; 360/681-3868). Rent a mountain bike or city cruiser and hit the trails. Mike's is adjacent to the **OLYMPIC**

Six or 10 people can sleep comfortably in the two vacation homes. Outside, a cascade burbles past the small orchards and gardens, where you'll see grazing llamas, fallow deer, and many birds. Follow a grassy roadway to the shell-strewn private beach after you savor the three-course breakfast prepared by a French-trained chef. *$$$; AE, MC, V; checks OK; www.illaheemanor.com; across Manette Bridge in east Bremerton.*

Silverdale

Ranked by *Money Magazine* as one of the top 100 best places to live, this tiny community north of Bremerton is mostly a shopping-mall city with a suburban feel. Located just off SR 3, Silverdale has grown in part because of the Navy's decision to build a base for Trident nuclear submarines at Bangor, just minutes north of the town. Local attractions include the marina and Waterfront Park, along Dyes Inlet. The scenic Clear Creek Trail winds through Silverdale's urban areas.

DISCOVERY TRAIL (360/683-7180; www.peninsulatrailcoalition.com), one of the most popular trails in the area for recreational cycling. The car-free trail, much of it built on old railroad grade, stretches for 22 miles to Port Angeles through farmland and forests. On your ride, check out an impressive local bird exhibit and get information on the flora and fauna of the Olympic Peninsula at the **DUNGENESS RIVER AUDUBON CENTER** at **RAILROAD BRIDGE PARK** (2151 W Hendrickson Rd, Sequim; 360/681-4076; www.dungenessrivercenter.org). Stop at **SUNNY FARMS COUNTRY STORE**, the spot for picnic food, only a short detour from the trail about halfway between Sequim and Port Angeles. After a picnic and a full day of biking, return to Sequim and check in at **COLETTE'S BED AND BREAKFAST** for true Northwest luxury, then drive to Port Angeles and go to dinner at **BELLA ITALIA**.

DAY THREE: After your breakfast at Colette's, continue west on Hwy 101 past **LAKE CRESCENT** toward Forks. Stop in at **SOL DUC HOT SPRINGS** for a relaxing soak, and grab a bite for lunch in **SOL DUC HOT SPRINGS RESORT**'s restaurant before you leave. Keep heading west on Hwy 101 to **FORKS** and take SR 110 toward La Push. Stop for a short hike to **THIRD BEACH**, which weaves 1.4 miles through dense forest to the Pacific. Tote a camera, as you are likely to spot seals, deer, eagles, otters, and, at the right time of year, whales. After your hike, drive back to Hwy 101 and continue south to **KALALOCH LODGE**. Check in to a cozy cabin, then enjoy the magnificent view from the dining room with your dinner.

RESTAURANTS

Bahn Thai / ★★

9811 MICKELBERRY RD, SILVERDALE; 360/698-3663
Customers here remove their shoes, cross their legs to sit on the traditional Thai-style cushions, and tuck into exotic dishes. Bahn Thai serves authentic Thai flavors—bamboo strips, basil, lemongrass, galangal, and kaffir lime leaves. Choose from many vegetarian options and six different curries. *$; AE, MC, V; local checks only; lunch Mon–Fri, dinner every day; beer and wine; no reservations; ½ block north of Bucklin Hill Rd.* &

Breezy Hill Bistro / ★★

3611 NW BUCKLIN HILL RD, SILVERDALE; 360/698-7197
Rich French flavors predominate—filet mignon, for example, with red onion marmalade, woodland mushrooms, Roquefort gratin, and sauce bordelaise. The only thing lacking is ambience: the dining room in a converted house with office carpet and vinyl benches just doesn't quite do it. *$$$;*

AE, DIS, MC, V; no checks; lunch Tues–Fri, dinner Tues–Sat; beer and wine; reservations recommended; www.breezyhillbistro.com; in west Silverdale off Silverdale Wy. &

Waterfront Park Bakery & Café / ★★

3472 NW BYRON ST, SILVERDALE; 360/698-2991

Many locals admit to making this a twice-a-day destination. Waterfront Park Bakery and Café claims to be "the center of the known universe for coffee and comfort," and it's true enough. Everything here is made from scratch with organic and locally sourced ingredients when feasible. The menu includes fresh-baked pastries, crab-asparagus quiche, wraps, soups, sandwiches, and cookies. The owners are committed to sustainability and a small footprint: food waste is composted, and everything possible is recycled. *$; MC, V; no checks; breakfast, lunch Mon–Sat; no alcohol; no reservations; www. waterfrontbakery.com; old town.* &

LODGINGS

Silverdale Beach Hotel / ★★★

**3073 NW BUCKLIN HILL RD, SILVERDALE;
360/698-1000 OR 800/544-9799**

Many of this hotel's rooms have outstanding views of the waterfront. All offer straightforward comfort with just the right touch of luxury. Family fun includes a large indoor pool (with walls of windows looking out to Puget Sound), a game room, a fitness center, a whirlpool spa, and tennis courts. *$$–$$$; AE, DIS, MC, V; no checks; www.silverdalebeachhotel.com; right off Silverdale Wy.*

Suquamish

Suquamish is located on the Port Madison Indian Reservation, home of the Suquamish Tribe, reached via State Route 305 from either Bainbridge Island (follow signs past Agate Passage) or Poulsbo. To learn more about this historic area, visit the **SUQUAMISH MUSEUM** (in the Tribal Center, 15838 Sandy Hook Rd NE, Suquamish; 360/598-3311), which is devoted to Puget Sound Salish Indian culture.

One of the most influential Native American leaders of the Northwest—**CHIEF SEALTH** (also known as Seattle, and for whom the city is named, born 1786 and died June 7, 1866)—lived here and is buried nearby in a small tribal cemetery behind St. Peter's Catholic Church on South Street, about a block from downtown. Every third week in August, the Suquamish Tribe honors Chief Seattle at **CHIEF SEATTLE DAYS**. A mile or so from Chief Seattle's grave is the site of **OLD MAN HOUSE**, a Suquamish longhouse that stretched 900 feet along a sandy beach. It was a home to Suquamish families, a place for tribal ceremonies, and a stronghold. Long ago torched by the U.S. government, the site is now **OLD MAN HOUSE STATE PARK** (360/598-3311; www.stateparks.com), a beach-fronted, block-square spot with trees, grass, and an outdoor display describing the longhouse history.

Suquamish's location provides the perfect vantage point for taking in sweeping views of the Kitsap Peninsula. Look across Puget Sound to the city of Seattle and the peaks of the Cascade Range, including Mount Rainier.

Poulsbo

Poulsbo's history is still apparent. Known as "little Norway," the town has architecture that is modeled after the fjord villages of Norway; signs reading "Velkommen til Poulsbo" line Front Street, the main drag (SR 305). Downtown on the waterfront, **LIBERTY BAY PARK** is a great place to picnic. Rent a kayak from **OLYMPIC OUTDOOR CENTER** (18971 Front St; 360/697-6095 or 800/592-5983; www.olympicoutdoorcenter.com).

Pick up a book at **LIBERTY BAY BOOKS** (18881D Front St; 360/779-5909; www.libertybaybooks.com) and head to **POULSBOHEMIAN COFFEEHOUSE** (19003 Front St; 360/779-9199; www.poulsbohemian.com) to hang out in comfy living-room chairs. Stop by **CASA LUNA OF POULSBO** (18830 Front St; 360/779-7676) and get a mammoth burrito to go; appease your sweet tooth at **BOEHMS CHOCOLATE** (18864 Front St; 360/697-3318) or **SLUYS BAKERY** (18924 Front St; 360/779-2798).

RESTAURANTS

Molly Ward Gardens / ★★★

27462 BIG VALLEY RD, POULSBO; 360/779-4471
Housed on the outskirts of Poulsbo in a converted barn surrounded by organic gardens, this restaurant lives up to its motto: "the very best ingredients, simply prepared." An eclectic collection of chandeliers and well-placed antiques gives every table its own unique character. The menu—organic greens and fruits from the gardens, local seafood, natural meats—is on a rolling whiteboard that changes daily. Patio seating is available in summer. *$$$; MC, V; checks OK; lunch Wed–Sat, dinner Tues–Sun, brunch Sun; full bar; reservations recommended; www.mollywardgardens.com; approximately 3 miles south of Hood Canal Bridge off SR 3.* &

Mor Mor Bistro Bar / ★★★

18820 FRONT ST NE, POULSBO; 360/697-3449
Mor Mor, which means "grandmother" in Norwegian, is run by a husband-and-wife team; black-and-white photos of the young couple's grandmothers in their youth hang on the walls. The atmosphere is sophisticated yet comfortable. Flavors and presentation are excellent, and the dinner menu changes daily. Try the grilled Oregon natural cheeseburger served on Sluys Poulsbo Bread, fresh three-cheese ravioli, organic greens, and Quinault Bay razor clams. Head upstairs and check out the Far Mor ("grandfather") Wine Studio. *$$$; AE, DIS, MC, V; local checks only; lunch, dinner every day; full bar; reservations recommended; www.mormorbistro.com; west end of Front St.* &

LODGINGS

The Green Cat Guest House / ★★

25819 TYTLER RD NE, POULSBO; 360/779-7569

With the Olympic Mountains as a backdrop, each of the three guest rooms in this lovely four-story retreat has a queen-size bed, a sitting area, a coffee-maker, a fireplace or woodstove, wi-fi, TV/DVD, and a private deck or patio with a view of the mountain, 3 acres of cedar forest, and gardens. You also have access to a washer and dryer, a hot tub, and an herb-scented sauna. Breakfast (included) is made-to-order: traditional, vegetarian, or vegan with local and organic ingredients. Or whip up your own meals in the fully equipped guest kitchen. *$$–$$$; MC, V; no checks; www.thegreencatbb.com; Tytler Rd following Grantham signs for ¾ mile.*

Port Gamble

Built in the mid-19th century by the Pope & Talbot timber company, this picture-postcard town on State Route 104 between Kingston and Hood Canal is well worth a look. More than a dozen Victorian houses line the main street (Rainier Avenue), and a nice collection of shops encourage visitors to amble around.

PORT GAMBLE MUSEUM (32400 Rainier Ave, in back of Port Gamble General Store; 360/297-8074) provides an in-depth history of the town. **PORT GAMBLE GENERAL STORE** (32400 NE Rainier Ave, Port Gamble; 360/297-7636) is packed with camping and fishing supplies; beer, wine, and a café are in back. The **TEA ROOM** at Port Gamble (32279 Rainier Ave, Port Gamble; 360/297-4225) is a nice place to relax.

Hansville

A couple of the prettiest, most accessible, and least-explored beaches on the Kitsap Peninsula are near Hansville, at the north end of Hansville Road NE via SR 104 near Kingston. You should definitely make a point to visit **POINT NO POINT**. A sandy spit that juts a quarter mile into Puget Sound, its lighthouse is one of the oldest in Puget Sound, beginning service in 1879 with a kerosene lantern as a beacon for ships. The point owes its name to Lieutenant Charles Wilkes, who explored Puget Sound by ship in 1841. Wilkes thought it looked like a big point of land but as he sailed closer, he found it was a very small point, and thus it got its name.

Follow the road from Hansville to the west to reach **FOULWEATHER BLUFF PRESERVE** (via NE Twin Spits Rd). The short trail through the woods can be tough to find, so look for the Nature Conservancy sign on the south side of the road.

Hood Canal and Northeast Olympic Peninsula

Along the west side of Hood Canal, Hwy 101 goes through tiny towns with names like Lilliwaup, Duckabush, and Union; vacation homes line the miles of scenic shoreline. Sample a variety of wines at **HOODSPORT WINERY** (N 23501 Hwy 101, Hoodsport; 360/877-9894 or 800/580-9894; www.hoodsport.com).

Shelton

These days Shelton, a former logging community, is reinventing itself as a tourist destination. On the shore of Oakland Bay, off Hwy 101 between Olympia and Hood Canal, Shelton rises from a far southwestern reach of Puget Sound.

Popular hangout **LYNCH CREEK FLORAL** (331 W Railroad Ave; 360/426-8615; www.lynchcreekfloral.com) is a café and home decor store rolled into one. **SAGE BOOK STORE** (116 W Railroad Ave; 360/426-6011; www.sagebookstore.com) has a fireplace, making it a cozy spot to browse. **LA FACTOR DAY SPA** (117 N 8th St; 360/427-3189; www.thelafactor.com), a full-service spa, is an unexpected indulgence in Shelton.

North of Shelton along Hwy 101, there is access to several recreational areas in the **OLYMPIC NATIONAL FOREST**, including **CAMP CUSHMAN** (7211 N Lake Cushman Rd, Hoodsport; www.lakecushman.com).

RESTAURANTS

Travaglione's Ristorante Italiano / ★★

825 FRANKLIN ST, SHELTON; 360/427-3844
Homemade ravioli and other fresh country Italian pasta from family recipes make Travaglione's a must-visit destination on the Olympic Peninsula. Housed in a renovated 1930s Craftsman bungalow, the restaurant is bright in daytime and intimate at night with an outstanding wine list. A drive-up window provides deli sandwiches, soups, and beverages for take-and-eat diners; a retail shop sells heat-and-serve meals, bottled wine, and fresh-frozen house-crafted ravioli. *$$; AE, DIS, MC, V; checks OK; lunch, dinner every day; beer and wine; reservations recommended; www.travagliones.com; downtown west Shelton on Franklin St. &*

Xinh's Clam & Oyster House / ★★★

221 W RAILROAD AVE, STE D, SHELTON; 360/427-8709
Chef Xinh Dwelley, a five-time West Coast oyster-shucking champion, makes happiness in her kitchen. This is one of the best little clam and oyster houses on the Olympic Peninsula. Diners come from afar, eager for some of the region's freshest seafood, enlivened with Vietnamese flavors; the mussels in curry sauce are outstanding. *$$; AE, MC, V; checks OK; dinner Mon–Sat; beer and wine; reservations recommended; www.taylorshellfishfarms.com; downtown. &*

Union

A resort town north of Shelton on State Route 106, Union is on the south shore of Hood Canal's "hook," between Belfair and Hwy 101.

RESTAURANTS

Robin Hood / ★★

E 6790 SR 106, UNION; 360/898-4400

Since the mid-1930s, this stone and log establishment has been a dance hall and tavern, a drugstore, and a B and B. Now it's a popular spot for good food. A restaurant fronts the building; you can sip cocktails or beer out back in the cavelike pub. High-beamed ceilings and a fireplace in the dining room add charm, while large windows overlooking a wooded creek provide peaceful views. Seafood, steak, lamb, pork, and poultry are aptly prepared. The pub menu includes gourmet hamburgers, fish-and-chips, and old-fashioned potpie are pub menu specialties. *$–$$$; AE, DIS, MC, V; checks OK; dinner Wed–Sun; full bar; reservations recommended; www.therobinhood.com; ¼ mile west of Alderbrook Resort.* &

LODGINGS

Alderbrook Resort and Spa / ★★★★

10 E ALDERBROOK DR, UNION; 360/898-2200 OR 800/622-9370

Established in 1913, the resort has been renovated to harmonize full-scale modern-day luxury with the original rustic spirit. Guest rooms offer soothing views of native gardens and a wooded creek or inspiring vistas of the Olympic Mountains and Hood Canal. All have soaking tubs and window-box daybeds. Each of the one- and two-bedroom beachfront cottages has its own fireplace. In addition to a full-service spa, there's a fitness center, a saline swimming pool enclosed in glass, and a first-class restaurant. *$$$$; AE, MC, V; no checks; www.alderbrookresort.com; south end of Hood Canal.*

Quilcene

Quilcene, on Hwy 101 between Shelton and Sequim, overlooks Dabob Bay on Hood Canal, south of the Hood Canal Bridge and SR 104. Every summer weekend at the **OLYMPIC MUSIC FESTIVAL** (11 miles west of Hood Canal Bridge on SR 104, then 1 mile south of Quilcene exit on Center Rd; 360/732-4800; www.olympic musicfestival.org), this popular eastern access point to the Olympic Mountains hosts concerts by the internationally acclaimed Seattle-based Philadelphia String Quartet and other world-class artists. Just south of Quilcene, **MOUNT WALKER** (5 miles past Hood Canal Ranger Station, 295142 Hwy 101 S; 360/765-2200), a 6-mile hike or drive, offers some of the best views of Puget Sound.

Port Ludlow

In the late 1800s, this port was a mill town known for shipbuilding. Just north of the Hood Canal Bridge and SR 104 and east of SR 19, the port town overlooks the mouth of Hood Canal at Admiralty Inlet in Puget Sound.

LODGINGS

The Resort at Port Ludlow / ★★☆

1 HERON RD, PORT LUDLOW; 360/437-7000 OR 877/805-0868

A majestic New England–style resort, this destination sparkles on scenic Ludlow Bay, near the mouth of Hood Canal. The resort has a marina, hiking trails, and a uniquely designated Audubon Cooperative Sanctuary golf course. Guest rooms and condo lodgings feature amazing Olympic Mountain and Hood Canal views. Two restaurants, the Fireside and Harbormaster, serve outstanding cuisine. *$$$–$$$$; AE, MC, V; checks OK; www.portludlowresort. com; 6 miles north of Hood Canal Bridge on west side of canal.*

Port Hadlock

The back road to Port Hadlock from Port Ludlow follows the shoreline of Oak Bay. Port Hadlock is on SR 116, a more direct route east of SR 19 between SR 104 and Port Townsend, at the south end of Port Townsend Bay.

Faux-front, old west–style buildings in Port Hadlock sport bright colors. **VILLAGE BAKER** (10644 Rhody Dr, Port Hadlock; 360/379-5310) specializes in artisan breads and pastries. Local events include **HADLOCK DAYS** in July and musical performances throughout summer at nearby Fort Flagler State Park (see Marrowstone Island section).

RESTAURANTS

Ajax Café / ★☆

21 N WATER ST, PORT HADLOCK; 360/385-3450

Get a hat on—literally—at the charming Galster House, built in the late 1800s and once the home of Samuel Hadlock, the town's founder. It's located on the waterfront in the historic district of (lower) Port Hadlock. The host or servers hand out whimsical hats to wear while you wait. And it's all worth waiting for: a menu of fresh local seafood and produce, including wild berries and mushrooms, plus live music on weekends and a staff ready to put it all together in the best possible way. *$$; MC, V; local checks only; dinner every day (Tues–Sun winter; closed Jan); beer and wine; reservations recommended; www.ajaxcafe.com; on waterfront, off Oak Bay Rd.*

Marrowstone Island

Long ago, Marrowstone Island's enterprise was turkey farming. Things went from fowl to seafood—specifically, oyster farming and clam harvesting. Twenty minutes southeast of Port Townsend via SR 116 east of Port Hadlock and Indian Island, Marrowstone moves at a slower pace.

FORT FLAGLER STATE PARK (10541 Flagler Rd, Marrowstone Island; 360/385-1259) is an old coastal fortification, and a seal and gull hang out at the end of the sand spit, across Admiralty Inlet from Whidbey Island. Pick up a bag of oysters at the historic **NORDLAND GENERAL STORE** (7180 Flagler Rd, Marrowstone Island; 360/385-0777), or rent a boat and paddle around at **MYSTERY BAY STATE PARK** (west side of Marrowstone Island; 360/902-8844).

LODGINGS

Beach Cottages on Marrowstone / ★

10 BEACH DR, NORDLAND; 360/385-3077 OR 800/871-3077
Choose from eight cabins on 10 acres bordering a tidal estuary—each offering excellent views of the Olympics and Mount Rainier. The place fits like a glove with its surroundings. Naturalized landscaping meshes with the adjacent salt marsh and provides access to 2 miles of beach. Cabins are equipped with kitchens, Tempur-Pedic beds, and woodstoves for heat (wood, kindling, and newspaper provided). Bring a good book, a pair of binoculars, and, in summer, your bathing suit. *$$–$$$; MC, V; checks OK; www.ecologicplace. com; off SR 116, right at "Welcome to Marrowstone" sign.*

Port Townsend

The residents—about 8,300—of this Victorian town have done a great job of preserving its history. Settlers in the mid-1800s built more than 200 ornate Victorian homes. Foreign consuls brought a cosmopolitan flavor to the city, and that, along with speculation that the city would be the largest harbor on the West Coast—wealthy and prosperous—helped Port Townsend earn its City of Dreams moniker. The elite investors left when an expected railroad extension from Tacoma failed. By the late 1880s, Port Townsend became a land of dashed dreams and vacant mansions, leaving it in an architectural time warp.

By the 1970s, the area's cheap houses and relatively remote location began to draw new, younger residents. Homes that were affordable in the '70s are now multimillion-dollar babies that regularly go on the market. As a result, many of the town's Victorian bed-and-breakfast inns closed as buyers who could afford the massive homes weren't interested in slinging hash for boarders. They live in them, and at least the magnificent buildings and views remain, as does the quirky entrepreneurial and artistic spirit of the community—and the thousands of tourists who come to visit. Fortunately, a few stellar B and Bs remain, along with vintage hotels and other unique accommodations.

It is also home to an abundance of cultural and artistic events and offers some of the finest dining on the Olympic Peninsula. The area's scenic mountains, sparkling waters, beaches, trails, parks, and nearby forests all add up to Northwest paradise.

ACCESS AND INFORMATION

Port Townsend sits at the north end of the **QUIMPER PENINSULA** on SR 20, which continues east of here on Whidbey Island and southwest of here to its terminus at Hwy 101 on Discovery Bay. You can also reach the town by the **KEYSTONE FERRY** (206/464-6400 or 888/808-7977; www.wsdot.wa.gov/ferries) from Whidbey Island, though departures may be disrupted by wind and tides in stormy weather.

The town is generally divided into two quadrants: downtown and uptown. In reality, the town is so small the uptown and downtown designations don't matter, but locals make the distinction when you ask for directions. Get a map at the **VISITORS CENTER** (2437 E Sims Wy; 360/385-2722).

MAJOR ATTRACTIONS

Apart from some unavoidable suburban sprawl on the outskirts of town, the streets and buildings are much the same as they were a century ago. The Visitors Center map has a driving tour of 74 historical points, including many of the ornate homes and buildings. Other architectural gems include the Carnegie Library, US Post Office, and Jefferson County Courthouse. The **ROTHSCHILD HOUSE** (corner of Franklin and Taylor sts; 360/385-1003; www.jchsmuseum. org) also happens to be Washington's smallest state park, measuring 50 by 200 feet. The Greek Revival–style house with a garden is open seasonally for tours.

Other architectural points of interest include **MANRESA CASTLE** (7th and Sheridan sts; 360/385-5750 or 800/732-1281; www.manresacastle.com), built in 1892 for Charles and Kate Eisenbeis, prominent members of the early Port Townsend business community. Its design is similar to some of the castles in the Eisenbeis's native Prussia. Today the castle is a hotel and restaurant. **HALLER FOUNTAIN** (Washington and Taylor sts) is where Galatea, Port Townsend's brazen 1906 goddess, lives. Visit the **JEFFERSON COUNTY HISTORICAL SOCIETY** (540 Water St; 360/385-1003; www.jchsmuseum.org) for a fascinating museum in the original city hall.

One of several parks, **CHETZEMOKA PARK** (Jackson and Blaine sts) is a memorial to the S'Klallam Indian chief who became friends with the first white settlers. It has an inviting gazebo, picnic tables, tall Douglas firs, and a grassy slope down to the beach.

FORT WORDEN STATE PARK (200 Battery Wy; 360/344-4434; www.parks.wa.gov/fortworden) offers everything from beach walks to lodging to cultural events. Along with sister forts on Marrowstone and Whidbey islands, it was part of the defense system established to protect Puget Sound more than a century ago. The 434-acre complex overlooking Admiralty Inlet now incorporates turn-of-the-20th-century officers' quarters—where you can stay

FUN IN PORT TOWNSEND

Time it right, and your visit to this lively town is sure to coincide with at least one of its well-known events or outings. Contact the **VISITORS CENTER** (2437 E Sims Wy, Port Townsend; 360/385-2722; www.ptguide.com) for dates.

FIRST NIGHT (360/385-1003; www.jchsmuseum.org), focusing on heritage and the arts with music, games, and other fun, is held on New Year's Eve. The **VICTORIAN FESTIVAL** (360/379-0668; www.victorianfestival.org) arrives in March with a focus on Victorian fashion and many other events. The **RHODY FESTIVAL GRAND PARADE** (www.rhodyfestival.org) is in May. The **SECRET GARDEN TOUR** is in June, as is the opening of the **FARMERS MARKET** (360/379-9098; www.ptfarmersmarket.org; Wed and Sat through Oct). The **FESTIVAL OF AMERICAN FIDDLE TUNES** and the **JAZZ PORT TOWNSEND FESTIVAL** (360/385-3102; www.centrum.org) are held in July. The **PORT TOWNSEND COUNTRY BLUES FESTIVAL CONCERT** (360/385-3102; www.centrum.org) is in August. In September, it's time for the annual **WOODEN BOAT FESTIVAL** (360/385-3628; www.woodenboat.org), the **WEST COAST SEA KAYAK SYMPOSIUM** (800/755-5528; www.wcsks.org), the **PORT TOWNSEND FILM FESTIVAL** (www.ptfilmfest.com), and the **HISTORIC FALL HOMES TOUR** (www.ptguide.com/homes tour). Every October, the city hosts the **KINETIC SCULPTURE RACE** (www.ptkineticrace.org); creatively designed human-powered vehicles complete a course that includes city streets, the waters of Puget Sound, sand, and the stretch of bay and patch of mud called the Dismal Bog.

—James Eric Lawson

overnight (see Lodgings)—campgrounds, gardens, a theater, and a concert hall. The setting may look familiar to those who saw the movie filmed here: *An Officer and a Gentleman*. Within the park is the **MARINE SCIENCE CENTER** (360/385-5582 or 800/566-3932; www.ptmsc.org), where you can touch sea animals and later catch a cruise to nearby **PROTECTION ISLAND NATIONAL WILDLIFE REFUGE** (at mouth of Discovery Bay), the region's largest seabird rookery. The park is also home to **CENTRUM** (360/385-3102; www.centrum.org), a gathering place for all types of artists. They sponsor concerts, workshops, and festivals throughout the year (see "Fun in Port Townsend").

Take in a movie at the restored 1907 **ROSE THEATRE** (235 Taylor St; 360/385-1089; www.rosetheatre.com). Two local wineries offer tastings: **FAIR WINDS WINERY** (1984 Hastings Ave W; 360/385-6899; www.fairwindswinery.com) and **SORENSEN CELLARS LTD.** (274 Otto St, Ste S; 360/379-6416; www.sorensencellars.com).

Active travelers find dozens of options for beachcombing, hiking, kayaking, biking, whale watching, or golfing.

SHOPPING

You can pick up all the usual tourist T-shirts and shot glasses, but the town also has an eclectic variety of galleries featuring fine art, crafts, and Native arts. Stores carry kitchenware, antiques, and gifts, and there are some unusual indie shops.

Among the colorful places that line **WATER STREET**, you'll find some standouts, including the **WINE SELLER** (940 Water St; 360/385-7673; www.ptwineseller.com), which stocks wines, microbrews, and cigars. **WILLIAM'S GALLERY** (914 Water St; 360/385-3630; www.williams-gallery.com) carries water fountains, copper and ceramic fish, watercolors, jewelry, and functional pottery.

On the west side of Water Street is **ANCESTRAL SPIRITS GALLERY** (701 Water St; 360/385-0078; www.ancestralspirits.com) with artifacts and art created by aboriginal people. Music lovers covet **QUIMPER SOUND** (230 Taylor St; 360/385-2454; www.quimpersound.com), an old-school record shop.

Not all shopping is on Water Street. The best place for vintage and antique finds is the **TOWNSEND ANTIQUE MALL** (802 Washington St; 360/379-8069). **DOLCE LA BELLE** (842 Washington St; 360/385-2969; www.dolcelabelle.com) offers a refreshing collection of Northwest indie designs, including skirts, vintage hand-dyed lingerie, and silk-covered journals. **WASTE NOT WANT NOT** (1532 W Sims Wy; 360/379-6838) deals in decades of discards, from old-fashioned farmhouse sinks to salvaged windows.

RESTAURANTS

Fins Coastal Cuisine / ★★☆

1019 WATER ST, PORT TOWNSEND; 360/379-3474

White tablecloths, open-beamed ceilings, and beautiful views of Port Townsend Bay are supporting actors for the star here: seafood. Starters include chilled Hood Canal oysters on the half shell, clam chowder, sea scallops, and crab cakes. Don't miss the house specialties, like salmon with garlic cream chive sauce and lingcod with mushroom marsala sauce. Lunch includes organic buffalo pepperjack cheeseburgers, salmon BLTs, and shrimp grinders. *$$$; AE, DIS, MC, V; local checks only; lunch, dinner every day; full bar; reservations recommended; www.finscoastalcuisine.com; between Tyler and Polk sts.*

Fountain Café / ★★☆

920 WASHINGTON ST, PORT TOWNSEND; 360/385-1364

Locals like to think this diminutive restaurant with its European bistro ambience is a secret, but it's not. Patrons can't keep from spreading the word. The space has nine tables and four seats at the old wooden counter. Try warm salads with potatoes, prosciutto, and sautéed veggies topped with pesto dressing and pine nuts. For dinner, the roasted walnut and Gorgonzola penne is divine, as is the Zuppa Pesce, a fresh fish soup with mussels, clams, prawns, and vegetables in a savory saffron wine broth. *$$; MC, V; checks OK; lunch, dinner every day; beer and wine; reservations recommended; between Tyler and Taylor sts.*

Hanazono Asian Noodle / ★★

225 TAYLOR ST, PORT TOWNSEND; 360/385-7622

Gyotaku prints by a local artist grace the walls of this small open-kitchen restaurant. It's a good spot for tasty noodle dishes and culinary entertainment. Sit at the large *jatoba* wood counter and watch owner Kaori Hull throw soft egg noodles, vegetables, and pork into big pans of splattering oil for yakisoba. The *champon* soup is filling and delicious, stocked with noodles, seafood, pork, and vegetables in a spicy broth. Teriyaki chicken is a favorite standby. Sake is de rigueur. *$; MC, V; local checks only; lunch, dinner Tues–Sat; beer and wine; reservations recommended; corner of Washington St.* &

Lanza's Ristorante / ★★

1020 LAWRENCE ST, PORT TOWNSEND; 360/379-1900

This Italian restaurant makes you feel like part of the family. Friendly service, classic dishes, and generous portions add up to a homey atmosphere. Start with the heaping antipasto platter. Traditionalists love the spaghetti with the famous family meatballs or sausage. The Seafood Lorraine is loaded with, well, seafood. Pizzas are made to order with crusts ranging from thin and crispy to thick. Canines can visit the back door, where Lori Lanza hands out special meatballs. Save room for Grandma Glory's Italian wedding cake, an angel food with rich frosting and a hint of almond and coconut. *$$; MC, V; local checks only; dinner Tues–Sat; beer and wine; reservations recommended; between Polk and Tyler sts.*

The Salal Café / ★★

634 WATER ST, PORT TOWNSEND; 360/385-6532

Late risers needn't worry about missing out on this café's hearty breakfast—it's served until 2pm! On weekend mornings, patrons spill out onto the sidewalk to gain entrance to the dining room. With more than 50 breakfast items, the choice can be difficult. Homemade biscuits and gravy are always good, as are the crispy-thin blueberry crepes topped with whipped cream. Choose the salmon crepe or one of the generous salads for lunch. *$; MC, V; checks OK; breakfast, lunch every day; beer and wine; reservations recommended; between Madison and Quincy sts.*

Sweet Laurette Café & Bistro / ★★★

1029 LAWRENCE ST, PORT TOWNSEND; 360/385-4886

Floor-to-ceiling windows, lemony-lime-colored walls, and bright floral and candy-striped café curtains give this place a Provençal charm. Alfresco dining on the garden patio enhances each meal's perfection. For breakfast, try fruit-stuffed pancakes, fluffy omelets, or Frenchman's Toast. For lunch, the roast–pork loin sandwich perfectly blends flavors of caramelized onions, Gorgonzola, and green apples. *$$–$$$; MC, V; local checks only; breakfast, lunch Thurs–Mon; beer and wine; reservations recommended; www.sweetlaurette. com; between Polk and Tyler sts.* &

Tyler Street Coffee House / ★★★

215 TYLER ST, PORT TOWNSEND; 360/379-4185
Everything here tastes fresh and luxurious, with dough handmade from scratch. As a result, the place is usually packed. If you try nothing else, indulge in one of the cinnamon twists made from croissant dough sandwiched with almond butter, sprinkled with cinnamon sugar, double twisted, baked, and glazed. For lunch, the New England clam chowder and the fantastic pulled-pork barbecue sandwich are good bets. *$; no credit cards; local checks only; breakfast, lunch Tues–Sat; no alcohol; no reservations; at Water St.*

The Wild Coho / ★★★

1044 LAWRENCE ST, PORT TOWNSEND; 360/379-1030
Painted in earthy colors, this intimate restaurant is for gourmands serious about Northwest cuisine. Local, organic ingredients are used whenever possible. Jay Payne, a former Seattle chef, is tremendously creative with wild coho salmon, duck, oysters, Dungeness crab, and meats. The menu changes frequently, but one always outstanding staple is wild coho salmon with sweet-potato crust, chive butter, and spiced tomato relish. Thursday is small plates night ($5–$7 each); it's the best way to taste the bounty. *$$$; MC, V; checks OK; dinner Tues–Sat; full bar; reservations recommended; www.thewildcoho. com; between Polk and Tyler sts.* &

LODGINGS

The Bishop Victorian Hotel and Gardens / ★★½

714 WASHINGTON ST, PORT TOWNSEND; 360/385-6122 OR 800/824-4738
Victorian character, great service, and a fine location make this the best of the vintage hotels in town. More than a century old, it retains its classic grandeur but has been improved with many comforts. Just one block off the busy Water Street strip, it has lovely manicured gardens, an ornate reception area with a fireplace, Victorian antiques, and period lighting throughout. Town and water views are available from 15 of the 16 guest rooms. Your room key also gives you access to an athletic club. *$$–$$$; AE, DIS, MC, V; checks OK; www.bishopvictorian.com; between Adams and Quincy sts.* &

Chevy Chase Beach Cabins / ★★

3710 S DISCOVERY RD, PORT TOWNSEND; 360/385-1270
Named after the Cheviot Hills in England where the family of Mary Chase, the resort's developer, originated, this resort first opened in 1913 to serve Seattle's "smart set." These beachfront cabins are about 8 miles from downtown Port Townsend. The property has views of Discovery Bay and Vancouver Island, miles of private beach front (including a sand-dollar bed yielding thousands in the summer), and a swimming pool circa 1951. Cabins, most with fully equipped kitchens, range from cozy studios to the roomy three-bedroom Homestead House. Cabin No. 4 has the best view. No food is available, so bring your own. *$$–$$$$; MC, V; checks OK; www.chevychasebeachcabins. com; at Cape George Rd.*

Commander's Beach House / ★★

400 HUDSON ST, PORT TOWNSEND; 360/385-1778 OR 888/385-1778
Location, location, location—Commander's Beach House has it in spades. Situated just steps from the Admiralty Inlet beach, it offers a stunning water view with the Cascades as backdrop, best enjoyed from the porch or on the Adirondack chairs on the lawn. Originally a residence for Navy commanding officers, this charming colonial home has four cozy rooms, two of which enjoy the mighty view. Breakfast is included with your stay. *$$–$$$; MC, V; checks OK; www.commandersbeachhouse.com; 4 blocks NE of downtown.*

Fort Worden State Park / ★

200 BATTERY WY, PORT TOWNSEND; 360/344-4400
Within Fort Worden State Park are 33 former officers' quarters dating back to 1904. These spacious two-story houses come with complete kitchens. The most coveted one-bedroom house is Bliss Vista, perched on the bluff, with a fireplace and romantic appeal. Alexander's Castle, a miniature monument with a three-story turret, is charming in its antiquity, sequestered away from the officers' houses. RV and tent sites are also on-site, near the beach or tucked into the woods. Make summer reservations well in advance. The Commons houses a coffee shop and café, open daily. *$$; MC, V; checks OK; www.fortworden.org; 1 mile north of downtown.*

The James House / ★★★½

1238 WASHINGTON ST, PORT TOWNSEND; 800/385-1238
This gorgeous 1889 Victorian perched on a bluff overlooking Puget Sound is truly the best of the local B and B bunch. The welcoming owner, Carol McGough, has managed to spare the chintz and so has not spoiled the elegant house. Each of the 10 guest rooms has a view, a private bathroom, and charming period antiques. Chef Donna Kuhn has been delighting guests for more than a decade with full breakfasts that include such delicacies as baked spiced pears and cranberry and white chocolate-chip scones. For more privacy and contemporary furnishings, stay at one of the two separate bungalows. *$$–$$$$; AE, MC, V; checks OK; www.jameshouse.com; between Fillmore and Harrison sts.*

Sequim and the Dungeness Valley

If you desire sunshine, Sequim (pronounced "skwim"), popular with retirees and young families, is the place to be on the Olympic Peninsula. The sun is out about 306 days a year, and annual rainfall averages only 16 inches. Ironically, that is because Sequim sits in the middle of the rain shadow cast by the Olympic Mountains. The downtown area, off Hwy 101 above Sequim Bay, is busy and full of hip shops.

On the bay near Blyn, a few miles east of Sequim, the S'Klallam Indians operate the unique **NORTHWEST NATIVE EXPRESSIONS ART GALLERY** (1033 Old Blyn

Hwy, Sequim; 360/681-4640). Across the highway stands the **SEVEN CEDARS** (270756 Hwy 101, Sequim; 360/683-7777 or 800/4LUCKY7; www.7cedarscasino. com), a mammoth gambling casino with valet parking.

For Olympic Mountain ice cream made on the peninsula, great coffee, and local artwork, visit the **BUZZ** (128 N Sequim Ave, Sequim; 360/683-2503; www.the buzzbeedazzled.com). **CEDARBROOK HERB FARM** (1345 S Sequim Ave, Sequim; 360/683-7733 or 800/470-8423; www.cedarbrooklavendar.com), Washington's oldest herb farm, has a large variety of plants and a gift shop. **SUNNY FARMS COUNTRY STORE** (261461 Hwy 101 W, Sequim; 360/683-8003), halfway between Sequim and Port Angeles, sells organic produce, deli food, and hanging plants.

The **JULY LAVENDER FESTIVAL** (877/681-3035; www.lavenderfestival.com) has put Sequim on the map as the lavender capital of North America—more than 35,000 people attend. **DUNGENESS NATIONAL WILDLIFE REFUGE** (6 miles northwest of Sequim; 360/457-8451), one of the world's longest natural sand spits, has a bird refuge near its start. A walk down the narrow 5½-mile beach leads to a remote lighthouse; marine mammals and aquatic wildlife are often seen. For information, contact the **OLYMPIC PENINSULA VISITOR BUREAU** (800/942-4042; www.northwestsecretplaces.com) or **DESTINATION SEQUIM** (800/737-8162; www.visitsun.com).

RESTAURANTS

Alder Wood Bistro / ★★★

139 W ALDER ST, SEQUIM; 360/683-4321
Elegant, wood-fired dishes are mostly prepared with locally grown, organic ingredients. The menu changes seasonally, but it's always fun—and tasty. For lunch, get creative and try the pumpkin pie pizza. The salads are masterpieces of elaborate simplicity. Dinner includes traditional favorites such as alder-planked fish and meat loaf, as well as more creative dishes: portobello mushroom–based Tower or another vegetarian concoction. End it all with a glass of fine port, crème brûlée, or carrot cake. *$$–$$$; AE, DIS, MC, V; local checks only; lunch, dinner Tues–Sat; beer and wine; reservations recommended; www.alderwoodbistro.com; at Sequim Ave.* &

Old Mill Café / ★★★

721 CARLSBORG RD, SEQUIM; 360/582-1583
Elk antlers and 10-foot crosscut saws hang on the walls. In the 1920s, this spot was the local tavern frequented by workers from the mill across the street. Recently renovated and reopened, this always-packed café is known for its homemade food, huge portions, and down-home feel. Logger burgers, house-smoked ribs, Dungeness crab cakes, organic greens, and free-range eggs are served here. On Sunday, breakfast is served all day. *$–$$; AE, MC, V; checks OK; breakfast, lunch Tues–Sun, dinner Wed–Sun; full bar; no reservations; corner of Spath Rd.* &

LODGINGS

Colette's Bed and Breakfast / ★★★

339 FINN HALL RD, PORT ANGELES; 360/457-9197 OR 877/457-9777

The great room and dining area of this eco-conscious and yet very luxurious B and B has panoramic windows filled with a view of the Strait of Juan de Fuca. Don't be surprised if you see bald eagles flying outside or sea lions swimming in the strait. Two suites in the Forest House and three in the main inn all come with jetted tubs in the private baths, plus gas fireplaces and views of the strait. Bed linens are 400 thread count. Hosts Lynda and Peter Clark serve a five-course gourmet breakfast. *$$$–$$$$; MC, V; checks OK; www. colettes.com; ½ mile NW of Port Angeles.*

Lost Mountain Lodge / ★★★

303 SUNNY VIEW DR, SEQUIM; 360/683-2431 OR 888/683-2431

This lodge leaves no luxury stone unturned. The main lodge has three private suites with wide-screen TVs, crème de la crème of toiletries, and 400-thread-count sheets on the king-size beds. Nearby, three upscale cottages with full kitchens are ideal for families. A tray of wine and hors d'oeuvres is served upon arrival, and homemade lattes are frothed upon request. An outdoor hydrotherapy spa overlooks a pretty pond. The gourmet breakfast includes a pleasing array of choices: frittata, fruit, yogurt, sweet bread. *$$$–$$$$; AE, MC, V; no checks; www.lostmountainlodge.com; 3 miles west of Sequim.*

Port Angeles and the Strait of Juan de Fuca

Hwy 101 parallels the Strait of Juan de Fuca beyond Sequim through Port Angeles and along Lake Crescent to Sappho, where the highway turns south toward Forks. State Route 112, however, hugs the shoreline more closely, extending west through tiny communities including Clallam Bay, Sekiu, and Neah Bay.

Port Angeles

Port Angeles, the largest natural deep-water harbor north of San Francisco, is a launch spot to Victoria, British Columbia (see Access and Information at beginning of this chapter), and the northern gateway to **OLYMPIC NATIONAL PARK** (360/565-3130; www.nps.gov/olym). The park, as big as Rhode Island, with a buffer zone of national forest surrounding it, has the largest remaining herd of Roosevelt elk, which occasionally create "elk jams" along the highway. **OLYMPIC RAFT AND KAYAK SERVICE** (360/452-1443 or 888/452-1443) offers trips down the Elwha and Hoh rivers.

In downtown Port Angeles, stop by **PORT BOOK AND NEWS** (104 E 1st St; 360/452-6367; www.portbookandnews.com). Browse **SWAIN'S GENERAL STORE**

(602 E 1st St; 360/452-2357; www.swainsinc.com) for everything else. **ITTY BITTY BUZZ** (110 E 1st St; 360/565-8080) is a great coffee stop.

In and around Port Angeles, small and notable wineries dot the map: **CAMARA-DERIE CELLARS** (334 Benson Rd; 360/417-3564; www.camaraderiecellars.com), **LOST MOUNTAIN WINERY** (3174 Lost Mountain Rd; 360/683-5229 or 888/683-529; www.lostmountain.com), **BLACK DIAMOND WINERY** (2976 Black Diamond Rd; 360/457-0748; www.blackdiamondwinery.com), and **OLYMPIC CELLARS WINERY** (255410 US Hwy 101; 360/452-0160; www.olympiccellars.com).

The October **DUNGENESS CRAB & SEAFOOD FESTIVAL** (360/452-6300; www. crabfestival.org) showcases the foods and traditions of the Olympic Peninsula. **PORT ANGELES VISITORS CENTER** (360/452-2363; www.portangeles.org) is the best source for information.

RESTAURANTS

Bella Italia / ★★★

118 E 1ST ST, PORT ANGELES; 360/457-5442
Bella Italia is a culinary gem on the Olympic Peninsula. Renowned for its wine list (more than 500 selections), fresh seafood, and local organic produce, this is where the natives go for dinner. The restaurant is warmly lit, and dining tables and booths are intimate and comfortable. "Olympic coast cuisine," their daily specials sheet, has fresh-catch options that come from different parts of the peninsula, such as Quilcene oysters and Neah Bay salmon. *$$$; AE, DIS, MC, V; checks OK; dinner every day; beer and wine; reservations recommended; www.bellaitaliapa.com; between Laurel and Lincoln sts.* &

Joy's Wine Bistro / ★★★

1135 E FRONT ST, PORT ANGELES; 360/452-9449
Joy's, owned by the Siemion family, is a new hot spot in Port Angeles. It's bright: glowing orange walls, bright red chairs, hand-painted tabletops. Joy Siemion, a New York–trained chef, has worked in restaurants on both the East and West coasts. Mom Barbara Gooding grinds the wheat berries for the bread. The roasted-chicken sandwich has smoked mozzarella, roasted tomatoes, Cajun mayo, and chicken pulled from the bone. *$$$; MC, V; checks OK; lunch Mon–Fri, dinner Tues–Sun; beer and wine; no reservations; www. joyswinebistro.com; east side of town.* &

LODGINGS

Five SeaSuns / ★

1006 S LINCOLN ST, PORT ANGELES; 360/452-8248 OR 800/708-0777
This B and B, a 1926 Dutch Colonial house, is centrally located, wireless, and classy but comfortable. Guests are greeted with fresh cookies baked daily in the afternoon. The main house has four guest rooms with private baths—each decorated to evoke a season. The Carriage House, a separate house with a kitchenette, is the fifth season (Indian summer). After the 7:30am wake-up

knock, you have exactly an hour before sitting down to a homemade breakfast. Just as well—the location is very noisy. Parking, particularly because it's on-street, can also be difficult to find. *$$–$$$; AE, DIS, MC, V; checks OK; www.seasuns.com; corner of E 10th St.*

Lake Crescent

Crystal-clear Lake Crescent, part of Olympic National Park, is home to rainbow trout and steelhead, Beardslee trout, and the famous Crescenti trout. Hwy 101 follows the south shore of this 600-foot-deep lake—so closely that drivers can see jumping fish. East Beach is on a road off the highway; 10 miles away, Fairholm Store and boat launch are on the far west end of the lake. Rental boats are available. Ask about the easy 1-mile hike to 90-foot Marymere Falls.

LODGINGS

Lake Crescent Lodge / ★

416 LAKE CRESCENT RD, PORT ANGELES; 360/928-3211

Once known as Singer's Tavern, this lodge was built in 1916. In 1937, Franklin D. Roosevelt stayed here while he studied the proposal that would create Olympic National Park in 1938. A grand veranda on the main building overlooks the deep lake waters. Inside, a restaurant and a relaxed bar encourage visitors to rest after traveling. Five rooms upstairs share a bathroom; rooms in the separate one- and two-story buildings are the best buy. A cluster of tiny, basic cabins, each with porch and fireplace, offer a bit more seclusion. *$$–$$$; AE, MC, V; no checks; partially closed mid-Oct–Apr; www.lakecrescentlodge. com; 20 miles west of Port Angeles.* &

Sol Duc Hot Springs

The Quileute Indians called the area Sol Duc—"sparkling water." In the early 1900s, **SOL DUC HOT SPRINGS** (Sol Duc Rd, 28 miles west of Port Angeles; 360/327-3583 or 866/476-5382; open every day mid-Mar–Oct) became a Mecca for affluent travelers. Today part of Olympic National Park, the pools are a popular spot for achy hikers and those in search of relaxation in the naturally enriched mineral water. The concrete pools are rather tired looking, but the surrounding old-growth trees make up for the basic facilities. One-hour massages are also available.

LODGINGS

Sol Duc Hot Springs Resort / ★★

12076 SOL DUC HOT SPRINGS RD, PORT ANGELES;
360/327-3583 OR 866/476-5382

The 32 small, carpeted cabins have private baths and two double or queen beds. Some have kitchens. As many as five guests may share the cabins; the three-bedroom River Suite sleeps 10. Favorite cabins have river-facing porches. Camping and RV sites are also available. The Springs Restaurant serves breakfast and dinner in summer (limited hours spring and fall); a poolside deli is open midday through the season. *$$$; AE, DIS, MC, V; checks OK; closed Nov–Feb; www.visitsolduc.com; off Hwy 101 west of Lake Crescent.* &

Clallam Bay and Sekiu

If fishing and whale watching are on your list, head to Clallam Bay and nearby Sekiu, on SR 112 along the Strait of Juan de Fuca. **CHITO BEACH RESORT** (7639 SR 112, Clallam; 360/963-2581; www.chitobeach.com) offers cabins on the beach, a communal bonfire, and an edible herb garden. **STRAITSIDE RESORT** (241 Front St, Sekiu; 360/963-2100; www.straightsideresort.com) is a hideaway ideal for families.

Twenty-one miles south of Sekiu is Lake Ozette, the largest natural body of freshwater in the state, part of Olympic National Park. At the north end of the lake is the **OZETTE RANGER STATION** (end of Hoko-Ozette Rd, Lake Ozette; 360/963-2725), a campground, and trailheads. The **CAPE ALAVA TRAIL** and the **SAND POINT TRAIL** each lead 3 miles to beaches, Cape Alava, the tiny Ozette Indian Reservation, the Indian Village Trail, ancient Indian petroglyphs, and views of Flattery Rocks National Wildlife Refuge offshore. At Cape Alava, you can see the coastal cliffs where a tidal erosion in the 1960s exposed a 500-year-old Native American village—once covered by a mud slide—with homes perfectly preserved. The archaeological dig was closed in 1981 after 11 years of excavation. Artifacts are on display in Neah Bay.

Neah Bay

This is the end of the road, literally: SR 112 ends at this small waterside town on the northern edge of the **MAKAH INDIAN RESERVATION**. A road leads to **CAPE FLATTERY**. The Makah graciously allow public access across their ancestral lands—a half-mile walk on a new boardwalk to land's end: 60-foot sheer cliffs with flying eagles overhead. You can often spot gray whales along the coast in April and May. Outlooks offer views of **TATOOSH ISLAND** and the entrance to the Strait of Juan de Fuca. Sandy Hobuck Beach is open for picnics and surfing.

The **MAKAH CULTURAL AND RESEARCH CENTER** (1880 Bay View Ave, Neah Bay; 360/645-2711; www.makah.com/mcrchome.htm) has wonderful exhibits, including artifacts from the Ozette digs (see Clallam Bay and Sekiu section). **HOBUCK BEACH RESORT** (360/645-2339; www.makah.com) has campsites and cabins. Farther on, you'll find access to Tsoo-Yas Beach (pronounced "sooes"); pay the landowners a parking fee. **PORT ANGELES VISITORS CENTER** (360/452-2363; www.portangeles.org) has information.

Forks and the Hoh River Valley

With average annual rainfall of 133.58 inches, the Hoh Rain Forest in Olympic National Park is the wettest spot in the contiguous United States. More than 3,000 species of plant life flourish here—including a giant Sitka spruce more than 500 years old and nearly 300 feet tall. **HOH VISITORS CENTER** (on Hoh River Rd; 360/374-6925) and campground are 30 miles southeast of Forks. For an incredible hiking trip, take a one- to three-day trip up the Hoh River Trail. The best time to take the longer trip to Glacier Meadows or to Mount Olympus is in mid-July to October. Stop in at **PEAK 6 ADVENTURE STORE** (4883 Upper Hoh Rd, Forks; 360/374-5254) for all your gear needs.

Forks

This little town and very independent community on Hwy 101 on the west end of the Olympic Peninsula is a salt-of-the-earth and end-of-the-earth kind of place. It is also the gateway to Olympic National Park adventures. Four rivers flow near Forks, making it a hot fishing destination. The staff at **OLYMPIC SPORTING GOODS** (190 S Forks Ave; 360/374-6330) can recommend fishing guides and provide licensing information. Check out the **FIVE-DAY TRIPS GUIDE** (800/443-6757; www.forkswa.com/23.html) for the west side of the peninsula.

The **TIMBER MUSEUM** (1421 S Forks Ave; 360/374-9663) tells the story of the West End's logging heritage. **FORKS VISITORS CENTER** (1411 S Forks Ave; 360/374-2531 or 800/44-FORKS; www.forks-web.com/fg/visitorscenter.htm) has information and free wireless Internet access 24 hours a day. For lodging, head to **QUILLAYUTE RIVER RESORT** (473 Mora Rd; 360/374-7447) where you will enjoy splendid beaches and a verdant rain forest for the family to explore.

La Push and Pacific Ocean Beaches

The Dickey, Quillayute, Calawah, and Sol Duc rivers merge and enter the ocean near La Push. Miles of protected wilderness coastline (part of Olympic National Park)—the last stretch remaining in the United States outside of Alaska—extend to the north and south. La Push, at the end of State Route 110 west of Hwy 101, is home to the Quileute Indians, a small community that maintains its subsistence fishing heritage. **QUILEUTE OCEANSIDE RESORT** (320 Ocean Dr, La Push; 360/374-5267 or 800/487-1267; www.quileuteoceanside.com), one of the only nearby lodgings, is the place to go to watch whales. It's on First Beach, part of the Quileute Indian Reservation.

Other nearby beaches that are a part of **OLYMPIC NATIONAL PARK** (800/833-6388; www.nps.gov/olym) include **SECOND BEACH** (0.8-mile hike off SR 110; visit at low tide) and **THIRD BEACH** (1.4-mile hike off SR 110). The latter is more crowded with surfers and whale watchers. From this beach, though, hikers can continue south to a trailhead near the Hoh River. **RIALTO BEACH** (north of La

Push off Mora Rd) is a 0.1-mile walk from the parking area on a paved trail; from here, hikers can continue north to trailheads at Lake Ozette.

About 25 miles south of Forks, Hwy 101 reaches the Pacific shoreline at **RUBY BEACH** (400 yards off Hwy 101), offering ocean glimpses and easier beach access for a 10-mile stretch. Ruby Beach has excellent views of **DESTRUCTION ISLAND**; nearby, a trail leads to the world's largest western red cedar.

WARNING: All ocean beaches can be extremely dangerous due to fluctuating tides and unfordable creeks during periods of heavy rain.

LODGINGS

Kalaloch Lodge / ★★

157151 HWY 101, FORKS; 866/525-2562

On a bluff with incredible views of the rugged Olympic National Park coastline but only steps from the beach, Kalaloch Lodge has campgrounds and more than 60 lodging options, including cabins, rooms, and suites. Franklin fireplaces warm the cozy stacked-log cabins. The lodge restaurant serves Northwest cuisine with gorgeous ocean views. *$$–$$$; AE, DIS, MC, V; checks OK; www.visitkalaloch.com; 35 miles south of Forks.*

Lake Quinault

Lake Quinault, at the inland apex of the **QUINAULT INDIAN RESERVATION**, is usually either the first or the last stop on Hwy 101's scenic loop around the Olympic Peninsula. Firs and part of Olympic National Park surround the north shore of the lake; Olympic National Forest surrounds the south shore. The fishing is memorable. A gravel road and bridge over the Quinault River connect the north shore and south shore, making for a wonderful drive past campgrounds and trailheads.

RAIN FOREST RESORT VILLAGE (516 South Shore Rd, Quinault; 360/288-2535 or 800/255-6936; www.rainforestresort.com) on Lake Quinault has lodgings; the adjoining **SALMON HOUSE RESTAURANT**, open to the public, is a nice choice for dinner. **QUINAULT RANGER STATION** (South Shore Rd, Quinault; 360/288-2525) just east of the majestic **LAKE QUINAULT LODGE** (345 South Shore Rd, Quinault; 360/288-2900 or 800/562-6672 in WA and OR only) provides information.

NORTH CASCADES

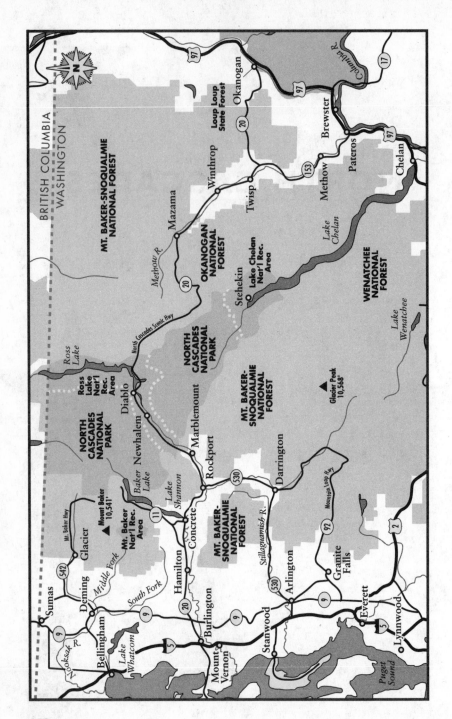

NORTH CASCADES

Jagged, rocky mountains, big lakes, vast forests, few roads—the North Cascades have it all. Upon these mountains, sometimes called the North American Alps, the most jaded visitor and longtime residents equally cannot help but gaze in awe. Here wilderness enfolds towns and dwellings, from the alpine glory of the Mount Baker and Shuksan peaks in the northwest, east across the rugged Cascade crest to the sagebrush hills above the Columbia River, and south to the long, cold waters of Lake Chelan.

ACCESS AND INFORMATION

Mount Baker and Mount Shuksan are east on **MOUNT BAKER HIGHWAY, STATE ROUTE 542**, from I-5 in Bellingham. To get to the **NORTH CASCADES SCENIC HIGHWAY, STATE ROUTE 20**, take Interstate 5 to Sedro-Wooley, 65 miles north of Seattle. To get there from US Highway 2, take US Highways 97A and 97 north up the Columbia River to Lake Chelan and, beyond, the confluence with the Methow River at Pateros, then take State Route 153 north up the Methow Valley to the junction with SR 20 south of Twisp.

Snow closes the North Cascades Highway every winter, typically from Mazama in the east to Diablo in the west. This stretch is usually blocked from mid-November to mid-April. During that interval, visitors from the Puget Sound area reach Lake Chelan and the Methow Valley by crossing the Cascades via the more southerly routes of Hwy 2 or Interstate 90.

No airports or train stations are available in the region. For more information, contact **MOUNT BAKER FOOTHILLS CHAMBER OF COMMERCE** (7802 Silver Lake Rd, Maple Falls; 360/599-1518; www.mtbakerchamber.org), **NORTH CASCADES NATIONAL PARK** (810 SR 20, Sedro-Woolley; 360/854-7200; www.nps.gov/noca), or the **LAKE CHELAN CHAMBER OF COMMERCE AND VISITOR INFORMATION CENTER** (102 E Johnson Ave, Chelan; 509/682-3503 or 800/4-CHELAN; www.lakechelan.com).

Mount Baker

Not far from its beginning in Bellingham, **MOUNT BAKER HIGHWAY** (SR 542) reaches the cheerful Nooksack River, then follows it east up onto Mount Baker through tall forests and small towns such as Deming, Maple Falls, and Glacier. At the end of the highway, Heather Meadows, Picture Lake, and Artist Point offer stunning vistas of two of the state's most impressive sights: 10,778-foot Mount Baker and 9,131-foot Mount Shuksan.

MOUNT BAKER SKI AREA (end of SR 542; 360/734-6771; www.mtbaker.us), 56 miles east of Bellingham, is coveted by extreme skiers and snowboarders from all over the world. The mountain has the highest average annual snowfall—595 inches—in North America, with a record-breaking snowfall of 1,140 inches in the 1998–99 season. A range of lodgings are available, including cabins through **MOUNT BAKER LODGING** (7463 Mount Baker Hwy, Maple Falls; 800/709-7669

NORTH CASCADES THREE-DAY TOUR

DAY ONE: Start your day in the Puget Sound area with breakfast at the **FARM-HOUSE RESTAURANT** (13724 La Conner Whitney Rd, Mount Vernon; 360/466-4411) and then head eastbound on the **NORTH CASCADES SCENIC HIGHWAY** for a daylong drive. Pack a lunch or grab a burger at the **MARBLEMOUNT DRIVE INN** (59924 SR 20, Marblemount; 360/873-9309) before stopping at the **NORTH CASCADES VISITOR CENTER** in Newhalem. Peruse the center's exhibits, then take a short, easy hike to view the Picket Range. Back in your vehicle, begin driving across the mountains, allowing at least two hours with intermittent stops. The overlooks at **DIABLO LAKE** and **WASHINGTON PASS** offer sweeping, panoramic views. Continue driving into the Methow Valley for dinner at the **MAZAMA COUNTRY INN** before calling it a night.

DAY TWO: After your complimentary breakfast at the inn, drive into **WIN-THROP** and take the morning to explore its western-themed ambience. For a historical overview of the area, stop at **SHAFER MUSEUM**. Stroll the main street's old-west storefronts, antique stores, and blacksmith shop. Lunch at the nearby

---

or 360/599-2453; www.mtbakerlodging.com) and dormitory-style housing at the Mountaineers' **MOUNT BAKER LODGE** (SR 542 at Picture Lake; 206/284-8484 or 800/573-8484; www.mountaineers.org/lodge/baker).

During the second week of June, a festival celebrating the Northwest logging tradition is held on the **DEMING LOGGING SHOW GROUNDS** (360/592-3051; www.demingloggingshow.com). The museum and outdoor exhibits make a stop worthwhile anytime. Just north of Maple Falls, the **BLACK MOUNTAIN FORESTRY CENTER** (on SR 542; 360/599-2623; www.blackmountainforestry.com) is run by a nonprofit organization dedicated to forestry education. The center features photographs, antique tools, and an adjacent working sawmill.

Deming

Deming is a tiny outpost on the Mount Baker Highway. Pick up last-minute snacks and camping goods at **EVERYBODY'S STORE** (5465 Potter Rd; 360/592-229). The Nooksack Valley has a long, mild growing season, perfect for growing the types of grapes favored by **MOUNT BAKER VINEYARDS** (4298 Mount Baker Hwy; 360-592-2300), open daily for tastings and serene views of Mount Baker from the picnic area. The **NOOKSACK RIVER CASINO** (5048 Mount Baker Hwy; 360/592-5472) is also located nearby.

TOPO CAFÉ, where you'll enjoy healthy Asian cuisine. In the early afternoon, unwind at **PEARRYGIN LAKE STATE PARK**, where you can take a swim, rent a boat, or relax with a book under the shady pines. Spend the night at **SUN MOUNTAIN LODGE** and enjoy an indulgent dinner at its exquisite dining room.

DAY THREE: For breakfast, head to Winthrop's **DUCK BRAND HOTEL & CANTINA**, where they serve huevos rancheros and fluffy omelets. Then start your drive to Chelan. The 56-mile trip takes a surprising 1½ hours, but allow time to stop in Twisp to pick up snacks at **TWISP RIVER PUB** or **CINNAMON TWISP** bakery and a visit to the **CONFLUENCE GALLERY & ART CENTER**. In Chelan, check in to **CAMPBELL'S RESORT ON LAKE CHELAN** and settle into a lakeside lawn chair on the lodge's sandy beach or, better yet, indulge in a spa treatment. If you still have some energy after getting your trigger points freed, explore the downtown area before heading to dinner at the **CAMPBELL HOUSE CAFÉ**. Walk off dessert with an evening stroll through **RIVERWALK PARK** (downtown, between two city bridges).

NOTE: Portions of the North Cascades Highway are closed in winter.

RESTAURANTS

The North Fork / ★

6186 MOUNT BAKER HWY, DEMING; 360/599-2337

Billing itself as a brewery, pizzeria, wedding chapel, and beer shrine, the North Fork's thin-crust pizza is especially good—hand-tossed and inexpensive. Build your own, and choose from an ample selection of microbrews on tap. For those wishing to tie the knot, an on-site minister is available—really. Nearly a century's worth of empty bottles and cans make up the beer shrine. *$; MC, V; local checks only; lunch Sat–Sun, dinner every day; beer and wine; no reservations; www.northforkbrewery.com; milepost 21 on SR 542.* &

Glacier

RESTAURANTS

Milano's Restaurant and Deli / ★★

9990 MOUNT BAKER HWY, GLACIER; 360/599-2863

On your way home from Mount Baker, Milano's is the best bet around for Italian food. Tasty raviolis are stuffed with spinach, smoked salmon, or porcini mushrooms; the *linguine vongole* is clam-packed. Desserts include chocolate truffles, Mount Baker apple pie, tiramisu, and cappuccino chocolate torte. If you're in a rush, grab a take-out sandwich. *$$; MC, V; local checks only; breakfast, lunch, dinner every day; beer and wine; reservations recommended; www.milanorestaurant.us; on SR 542.*

LODGINGS

Inn at Mount Baker / ★★★

8174 MOUNT BAKER HWY, GLACIER; 360/599-1776

Everything about this classy chalet is elegant. Trimmed in fir with vaulted ceilings, all five guest rooms of the Inn at Mount Baker offer spectacular views of Mount Baker and Nooksack River Valley. Amenities include feather beds, down duvets, extra-deep tubs, plush robes, and fresh flowers. A massage therapist is also on hand to work out those road-weary or recreation-strained muscles. Enjoy the view from the large outdoor hot tub, as well as Bill's famous potato pancakes for breakfast. *$$$; AE, DIS, JCB, MC, V; no checks; www.theinnatmtbaker.com; just before milepost 28 on SR 542.*

North Cascades Scenic Highway

One of the nation's prettiest drives, the **NORTH CASCADES SCENIC HIGHWAY** (SR 20) takes you past waterfalls and alpine meadows, mountain lakes and pine woods. Don't miss the spectacular vistas of turquoise-colored Diablo and Ross lakes, created by Seattle City Light's hydroelectric dam projects. Watch for mountain goats and black bears among the rocky crags beside the road.

The highway, the most northerly cross-state route, connects the damper west side of the Cascades and the semiarid and sunnier eastern portion of the state. Nearly a three-hour drive from Sedro-Wooley to Twisp, the road meanders and climbs east along the Skagit River from peaceful farmland through lush, thick evergreens to rugged mountains and immense glaciers. There the road bumps through **RAINY PASS** and **WASHINGTON PASS**, then glides down into the wide-open, pastoral **METHOW RIVER** valley, where grassy meadowlands give way to desert steppes, orchards, and farmland.

Winter snowfall and frequent avalanches close a 36-mile stretch of this 140-mile road every year—usually between mid-November and mid-April. It's a good idea to check **MOUNTAIN PASS REPORTS** (800/695-ROAD; wsdot.wa.gov/traffic/passes) before heading across any time near winter. For more information about the highway, contact the **CASCADE LOOP ASSOCIATION** (509/662-3888; www.cascadeloop.com) or **NORTH CASCADES VISITOR CENTER** (SR 20 near milepost 120, Newhalem; 206/386-4495 ext 11).

Marblemount

Every year, from December through February, bald eagles convene along the Skagit River near Marblemount. A careful eye and good set of binoculars reveal hundreds of the raptors feasting on spawned-out salmon. They're often easily viewable from

SR 20 between Marblemount and Rockport. Some of the best viewing is from the river via float tours. For information, contact **CHINOOK EXPEDITIONS** (800/241-3451; www.chinookexpeditions.com), **WILDWATER RIVER TOURS** (253/939-2151 or 800/522-WILD; www.wildwater-river.com), or the **MOUNT BAKER RANGER DISTRICT** (810 SR 20, Sedro-Woolley; 360/856-5700).

North Cascades National Park

The North Cascades possess extraordinary grandeur along with majestic scenery that make them a worldwide attraction. In 1968, 505,000 acres of mountainous wilderness immediately south of the U.S.-Canadian border was set aside as a national park. It's largely a landscape of jagged peaks draped in ice and glaciers—318 of them. Part of the Cascade Range, the peaks are not tall—the highest hover around 9,000 feet—but their vertical rise takes them from almost sea level into the clouds, making them steep-walled, exhilarating to view, and, in many places, inaccessible.

Although the North Cascades Highway bisects the wilderness area and provides dramatic views, the range's interior contains no roads, no lodges, and no visitor centers. Fortunately, the adventurous have more than 386 miles of maintained trails to explore—and the rest can take solace in the scenic drive. About a three-hour drive from Seattle via I-5, the North Cascades Scenic Highway (SR 20) leads east into the park.

The main highway provides access to dozens of trails, including the **PACIFIC CREST NATIONAL SCENIC TRAIL**. Backpackers also hike into the park from Stehekin, at the northern end of Lake Chelan. Hiking usually starts in June; snow commonly melts off by July. Summer storms are frequent; be prepared with rain gear. Hope for glimpses—however fleeting—of wildlife (bears, deer, mountain goats, and marmots) in the backcountry.

Backcountry camping requires a free permit, available at the **NORTH CASCADES NATIONAL PARK HEADQUARTERS** (810 SR 20, Sedro-Woolley; 360/854-7200; www.nps.gov/noca) or the **WILDERNESS INFORMATION CENTER** (7280 Ranger Station Rd, Marblemount; 360/854-7245). Both offices have park information.

Diablo and Ross Lakes

Ancient forests, abundant wildlife, and waterfalls abound in the Diablo and Ross lakes areas. Enjoy the **DIABLO LAKE ADVENTURE TOURS** for panoramic views; visit the **NEWHALEM SKAGIT TOURS OFFICE** (500 Newhalem St, Rockport; 206/684-3030; June–Sept) for more information. Also of interest is the nonprofit North Cascades Institute's recently opened **ENVIRONMENTAL LEARNING CENTER** (360/856-5700 ext 209), including a dining hall and an amphitheater.

The Methow Valley

East of the Cascade crest, SR 20 descends through pine forests into the lush, meadowy bottomlands and arid sagebrush ridges along the Methow (pronounced "MET-how") River. The Methow Valley harkens to the days of the old west, from Winthrop's authentic western storefronts to the valley's working ranches and farms. In summer, white-water rafting trips and fly-fishing draw visitors; during winter, it's a haven for cross-country skiers and snowshoeing enthusiasts.

Mazama

Thirteen miles north of Winthrop on SR 20 is tiny Mazama (pronounced "ma-ZAH-ma"). Here you'll find a quintessential backcountry store, the **MAZAMA STORE** (50 Lost River Rd; 509/996-2855), as well as a picnic area and the only gas pump for 70 miles, if you're traveling west over the mountains. The town also hosts the annual summertime **METHOW MUSIC FESTIVAL** (509/996-6000; www.methowmusicfestival.org), a classical music series.

RESTAURANTS

Freestone Restaurant at Wilson Ranch / ★★★

31 EARLY WINTERS DR, MAZAMA; 509/996-3906 OR 800/639-3809
This classy restaurant offers candlelit tables and an ever-changing menu. Breakfast includes cast-iron-skillet prime-rib hash, eggs provençal, and the Wilson Ranch country breakfast. At dinner, try the grilled Dungeness crab cakes, double-cut lamb chops, pan-seared New York steak, homemade fettuccine, or brook trout. Desserts are equally satiating, including apple–white cheddar crisp or burnt lemon custard tart. The inn also offers lodging. *$$$; AE, MC, V; local checks only; breakfast every day, dinner Tues–Sun; beer and wine; reservations recommended; www.freestoneinn.com; 1½ miles west of town.* &

LODGINGS

Mazama Country Inn / ★★

15 COUNTRY RD, MAZAMA; 509/996-2681 OR 800/843-7951
Tucked into the Methow Valley, this comfortable inn offers tremendous views and luxurious amenities near some of the most rugged mountain wilderness in the Northwest. After a long day of hiking, mountain biking, or cross-country skiing, you can steam out the kinks in the sauna or soak them smooth in the outdoor hot tub. Want something a little less rigorous than outdoor pursuits? Simply enjoy the pool and tennis and squash courts. Despite the designation of "inn," each of the 18 spacious rooms has a private bath and at least one queen- or king-size bed. The inn also rents nearby privately owned vacation homes and cabins. The restaurant—a local favorite—serves breakfast, lunch, and dinner in summer; family-style breakfasts and dinners are served in winter. *$$–$$$; MC, V; checks OK; mazamacountryinn.com; ¼ mile from SR 20.* &

Winthrop

Sun-baked (or snow-covered) hills and wide-open sky are a natural setting for the western motif of this mountain town. False-front stores and boardwalks may remind you of Tombstone, the famous Arizona gunslinging town. As in Tombstone, there's a bit more behind the facades here than you expect. Several hold galleries featuring local and regional art; another is home to the **SHAFER MUSEUM** (285 Castle Ave; 509/996-2712; www.winthropwashington.com/winthrop/shafer). This is the beating heart of tourism in the Methow Valley.

After a big day outside, sip a beer at the **WINTHROP BREWING COMPANY** (155 Riverside Ave; 509/996-3183), in an old schoolhouse on the main street. **WINTHROP MOUNTAIN SPORTS** (257 Riverside Ave; 509/996-2886 or 800/719-3826; www.winthropmountainsports.com) sells outdoor-activity equipment and supplies and rents bikes, skies, snowshoes, and ice skates. The **TENDERFOOT GENERAL STORE** (177 Riverside Ave; 509/996-2288) has anything else you might need. The 100-year-old **WINTHROP PALACE** (149 Riverside Ave; 509/996-2245 or 509/996-2103), a steak and seafood restaurant-lounge, is one of the town's oldest landmarks. If a quiet afternoon tasting exceptional regional wines suits you, don't miss the **LOST RIVER WINERY** (26 SR 20; 509/996-2888; www.lostriverwinery.com).

PEARRYGIN LAKE STATE PARK (509/996-2370) is a good swimming hole 5 miles north of town. The **WINTHROP R&B FESTIVAL** (800/422-3048; www.winthrop bluesfestival.com) in mid-July, and similar events throughout the year, can be booked through **CENTRAL RESERVATIONS** (509/996-2148 or 800/422-3048; www.lodgingcentral.net). For more details, there's also the valley's **VISITOR INFORMATION SOURCE** (114 Riverside Ave; 509/996-2022; www.methownet.com).

RESTAURANTS

Duck Brand Hotel & Cantina / ★

248 RIVERSIDE AVE, WINTHROP; 509/996-2192 OR 800/996-2192
Since opening 27 years ago, this funky Winthrop restaurant has been called "the Duck" by locals. Its menu has evolved over the years, from Mexican and Italian dishes to an ever-changing, quirky selection that might include eggs McDuck for breakfast, a Fallbrooker BLT for lunch, or filet mignon for dinner. Literally on top of a delicious bakery, the Duck Brand Hotel (upstairs) has six inexpensive and sparsely furnished rooms. $–$$; AE, DC, DIS, MC, V; local checks only; breakfast, lunch, dinner every day; full bar; no reservations; www.methownet.com/duck; on main street.

Sun Mountain Lodge Dining Room / ★★★

604 PATTERSON LAKE RD, WINTHROP;
509/996-2211 OR 800/572-0493
The first thing you notice when entering the Sun Mountain Lodge Dining Room is the spectacular scenery. Every seat has a view from the nearly 3,000-foot elevation. The menu includes beef tenderloin, mushrooms foraged from the Cascades, and vegetables from the Sunny M Farm. You'll pay

for the experience, but it's worth it. *$$$; AE, DC, MC, V; local checks only; breakfast, lunch, dinner every day; full bar; reservations recommended; www. sunmountainlodge.com; 9.6 miles southwest of town.* &

LODGINGS

Hotel Rio Vista / ★

285 RIVERSIDE AVE, WINTHROP; 509/996-3535 OR 800/398-0911
Stand on the private deck of any of the 29 rooms overlooking the confluence of the Chewuch and Methow rivers, and you quickly understand the hotel's name: it means "river view" in Spanish. The setting is just part of the appeal of this western-themed hotel a little south of downtown—rooms are nicer than you'd expect of a hotel in the area. They also rent a lofted cabin that sleeps six, 10 minutes west of Winthrop. *$$; MC, V; checks OK; www.hotelriovista. com; on main road.*

Sun Mountain Lodge / ★★★½

604 PATTERSON LAKE RD, WINTHROP;
509/996-2211 OR 800/572-0493
Sun Mountain Lodge is a luxury resort surrounded by 360 degrees of stunning scenery, which is its hallmark. Perched on a hill 3,000 feet above the valley, this place is an outdoor enthusiast's Nirvana. It was the first destination cross-country ski resort in the Northwest; it is now the largest. All rooms are fabulous, but the Mount Robinson rooms are the newest, and they're dazzling; sit in your whirlpool bath and gaze at the mountains. *$$$–$$$$; AE, DC, MC, V; checks OK; www.sunmountainlodge.com; 9.6 miles southwest of town.* &

WolfRidge Resort / ★★

412B WOLF CREEK RD, WINTHROP; 509/996-2828 OR 800/237-2388
Located about 5 miles from the highway, this collection 19 beautifully crafted one- and two-bedroom log townhouses, studios, and hotel-style rooms vie for your selection. The one-bedroom suite in the fourplex building, for example, has a queen bed and single daybed, log-beam cathedral ceiling, fully equipped kitchen, and sliding glass doors opening onto a view balcony. Enjoy the outdoor pool and hot tub in a river-rock setting. Venture off with skis or bikes on the trails that run right outside your door. *$$–$$$; AE, MC, V; checks OK; www.wolfridgeresort.com; up Twin Lakes Rd 1½ miles, right on Wolf Creek Rd, 4 miles to entrance on right.*

Twisp

A few miles south of Winthrop you'll find Twisp, the state's sunflower capital. It's worth a stop. Stroll along Glover Street, a block off the highway, where several vibrant businesses prosper, including **ANTLER'S SALOON & CAFÉ** (132 Glover St; 509/997-5693).

CROSS-COUNTRY SKIING THE METHOW

Bright winter sunshine, dry powder snow, jaw-dropping views of mountain peaks—add almost 125 miles of well-groomed trails, and you have one of the nation's premier cross-country ski destinations. The **METHOW VALLEY SPORT TRAILS ASSOCIATION** (MVSTA, 209 Castle Ave, Winthrop; 509/996-3287 or 800/682-5787; www.mvsta.com) maintains this vast network of trails, the second largest in the country. The system has three linked sections, and many of the trails go directly past the valley's lodgings, so you can ski from your door. Special trails have also been set aside for snowshoeing.

The largest section surrounds **SUN MOUNTAIN LODGE** in Winthrop, where more than 40 miles of trail cut through rolling hills. Below it, the Community Trail section snakes past farms and through bottomland as it meanders from Winthrop to Mazama. Mazama's flat terrain and open meadows are ideal for novices.

The remaining section, called Rendevous, connects the **RENDEZVOUS HUTS** (Rendezvous Outfitters; 509/996-8100; www.methownet.com/huts/index.html) and is recommended for intermediate to expert skiers only. Set above the valley at 3,500 feet, trails pass through rugged forestland, where five huts are available for overnight stays. Each hut bunks up to eight people.

Trail passes are required for skiing on MVSTA trails. The passes are available at ski shops and some lodgings in the valley during the ski season, which typically begins in early December and continues through March.

—Nick Gallo

Other Twisp notables include the **METHOW VALLEY FARMERS MARKET** (Methow Valley Community Center; Sat Apr 15–Oct 15) and the **CONFLUENCE GALLERY & ART CENTER** (104 Glover St; 509/997-ARTS; www.confluence gallery.com). The **MERC PLAYHOUSE** (101 Glover St; 509/997-7529; www.merc playhouse.org) offers local productions. Find amazing sweet treats, including fresh baked breads and other locally sourced and organic goodies, at the **CINNA-MON TWISP** (116 Glover St; 509/997-5030; www.cinnamontwisp.com). For more information, contact the **TWISP CHAMBER OF COMMERCE VISITOR INFORMA-TION CENTER** (509/997-2926; www.twispinfo.com).

RESTAURANTS

Twisp River Pub / ★★

201 SR 20, TWISP; 509/997-6822 OR 888/220-3360
Above-standard pub fare, fresh seafood, and a kids' menu, along with a riverside deck and beer garden in summer, make the Twisp River Pub a favorite for all. The pub, home of the Methow Brewing Company, has handcrafted

brews that are sterling examples of the art; guest beers from other Northwest brewers ensure fresh choices. Try a pull of cask-conditioned ale from the traditional beer engine for a special treat. High sound levels permeate on weekend evenings, with live music, as well as an open mike most Saturday nights. *$$; AE, DIS, MC, V; checks OK; lunch, dinner every day (Wed–Sun winter); full bar; no reservations; www.twispriverpub.com; on highway.*

Pateros

Here at the confluence of the Columbia and Methow rivers, lodgings are booked solid in summer. Popular with boaters, white-water rafters, and other water-sports enthusiasts, the town offers an enticing waterfront park for picnics, a public boat launch on the Columbia River, and a friendly welcome to all. Fun events include the more than 60-year-old **APPLE PIE JAMBOREE** held on the third weekend in July and **HYDROPLANE RACES** on the fourth weekend in August. For more details, contact the **PATEROS CHAMBER OF COMMERCE** (kiosk in city hall, 113 Lakeshore Dr, Pateros; 509/923-2200 ext 101; www.pateros.com).

RESTAURANTS

Rivers Restaurant / ★

245 LAKESHORE DR, PATEROS; 509/923-2200

Disguised as a gas station quick stop, this restaurant has solarium dining overlooking the confluence of the Columbia and Methow rivers that is a pleasant surprise. The views are splendid; the food is worthy. Try the great steaks; local grain-fed cows from the Double R Ranch turn out mighty tasty. *$; MC, V; no checks; breakfast, lunch, dinner every day; no alcohol; no reservations; www. paterossuperstop.com; on river side of Hwy 97, near confluence.* &

LODGINGS

Lake Pateros Motor Inn / ★

115 S LAKESHORE DR, PATEROS; 509/923-2203 OR 866/444-1985

It seems as if everything in Pateros is on the waterfront—but not every place has a boat dock and waterfront park right outside, as the Lake Pateros Motor Inn does. Comfortable, if plain, rooms offer especially relaxing views. Book well in advance, especially during July and August. *$$; MC, V; no checks; www.lakepaterosinn.com; on river side of Hwy 97 near confluence.*

Lake Chelan

Lake Chelan is where it seems like everyone in Washington goes on vacation. The mix of vacationers who come for the more than 300 annual days of sunshine include college kids, young families, and comfortable retirees. New condos and homes continue to pop up around the southern end of the lake near the town of Chelan, but development hasn't discouraged the masses of visitors.

For peace and quiet, hop on a boat or a plane for a 55-mile ride to the northern tip of the lake and the laid-back settlement of Stehekin. Two passenger vessels ply the waters of Lake Chelan from end to end. The **LADY OF THE LAKE** (1418 W Woodin Ave, Chelan; 509/682-4584; www.ladyofthelake.com) features year-round tours. The **INNAMORATA** (at Lakeshore Marina on Lake Chelan, Chelan; 509/682-9500), a 56-foot yacht that was owned by the late great Dean Martin, offers nightly dinner cruises. **CHELAN AIRWAYS** (1328 W Woodin Ave, Chelan; 509/682-5555; www.chelanairways.com) flies direct 30-minute flights to Stehekin from Chelan.

The lake also has 16 boat-in campgrounds up lake from Chelan. Permits are required: obtain them at the **CHELAN RANGER STATION** (428 W Woodin Ave, Chelan; 509/682-2576) and elsewhere. Some campgrounds are accessible by road: **LAKE CHELAN STATE PARK** (888/226-7688 for reservations) and **TWENTY-FIVE MILE CREEK CAMPGROUND** (19 miles west of Chelan; 360/902-8844; closed Oct–Apr).

Chelan

Chelan and environs, at the southern tip of Lake Chelan, has everything you might want from a town by a lake in an outdoor paradise. Families enjoy the city's **LAKESIDE PARK,** a 10-acre retreat, and nearly everybody loves **SLIDEWATERS** (102 Waterslide Dr, Chelan; 509/682-5751; www.slidewaters.com; off Hwy 97). Try the 420-foot, completely darkened tunnel called Purple Haze. The park also has a 60-person hot tub, a swimming pool, and a toddlers' aqua park. Lake Chelan provides a 55-mile stretch of beautiful water for boating and water-skiing. Take your pick of the **RENTAL SHOPS** situated in and around the town (www. cometothelake.com).

For accommodations, try **CHELAN QUALITY VACATION PROPERTIES** (509/682-9782 or 888/977-1748; www.lakechelanvacationrentals.com). **WAPATO POINT ON LAKE CHELAN** (1 Wapato Pt Wy, Manson; 509/687-9511 or 888/768-9511; www.wapatopoint.com) offers a full-fledged resort in the neighboring town of Manson.

Overlooking Lake Chelan is the newest glint in the landscape: the 6,000-acre Bear Mountain Ranch, a newer development with home sites at Bandera and Hawk's Meadow. For golfers, though, the prize attraction is **BEAR MOUNTAIN RANCH GOLF COURSE** (509/682-8200 or 877/917-8200; www.bearmt.com).

If you're interested in Chelan's back story, visit the **LAKE CHELAN HISTORICAL SOCIETY MUSEUM** (204 E Woodin Ave, Chelan; 509/682-5644). The **LAKE CHELAN CHAMBER OF COMMERCE** (509/682-3503 or 800/4-CHELAN; www. lakechelan.com) is a good resource. The **CHELAN RANGER STATION** (428 W Woodin Ave, Chelan; 509/682-2576) is open year-round.

RESTAURANTS

Campbell House Café / ★★

104 W WOODIN AVE, CHELAN; 509/682-4250

Chelan may be a long way from the coast, but you can still find the town's freshest seafood at Campbell's. They also offer dependable steaks and acceptable pastas. Breakfast is very popular. Upstairs, the Second Floor Pub and Veranda is more casual. Order burgers and brews, then people watch on a warm summer evening. *$$$; AE, MC, V; checks OK; breakfast, lunch, dinner every day; full bar; reservations recommended (café), no reservations (pub); www.campbellsresort.com; downtown facing main street near lake.* &

LODGINGS

Best Western Lakeside Lodge & Suites / ★

2312 W WOODIN AVE, CHELAN; 509/682-4396 OR 800/468-2781

This iconic inn, nestled among the fragrant pines on the lake, holds 95 rooms, with vaulted ceilings in the top-floor units. Besides the awesome location, next to Lakeside Park with its sandy public beach and views of the North Cascades, the lodge also has heated indoor and outdoor pools, two outdoor spas, and free continental breakfast. *$$$; AE, DC, DIS, MC, V; checks OK; on Hwy 97, 2 miles south of town.* &

Campbell's Resort on Lake Chelan / ★★★

104 W WOODIN AVE, CHELAN; 509/682-2561 OR 800/553-8225

Campbell's, the city's landmark family-owned resort hotel built in 1901, is located on 1,200 feet of sandy beach at the warm, shallow end of the lake in the town of Chelan. Over the years, the original hotel sustained two serious fires and a half dozen renovations. The latest one, completed in May 2008, included updating rooms with a sophisticated, style-conscious decor. Each room features direct access to the beach, custom textiles, and unique furnishings that highlight Campbell's multigenerational appeal and beautiful lakeside setting. The 170-room resort complex is set on 8 acres with two pools, two all-season hot tubs, boat moorage, a boardwalk, outdoor barbecues and picnic tables, a poolside beach bar, a restaurant, a bar, a full-service spa, and a fitness center. *$$-$$$; AE, MC, V; checks OK; www.campbellsresort.com; on lake at end of main street near downtown.*

Kelly's Resort / ★★

12800 LAKESHORE RD, CHELAN; 509/687-3220 OR 800/561-8978

Fourteen miles up lake on the south shore of Lake Chelan, Kelly's has been a family getaway for six decades. Eleven well-spaced cottages feature pine-paneled living rooms, one or two baths, full kitchens, one or two bedrooms, fireplaces, and air conditioning. The heated pool is surrounded by forest. The five lakeside units have full kitchens, living rooms, one or two bedrooms, and decks. A sandy beach and boat moorage fronts the lake. A small store, fireplace room, deck, and coffee bar are in the main building. *$$$–$$$$; MC, V; checks OK; www.kellysresort.com; 14 miles west of town.*

Stehekin

This tiny hamlet at the northern tip of Lake Chelan is reminiscent of a bygone era. Come by Chelan Airways' floatplane, on foot via hiking trails, or by boat. No matter how you travel here, you'll notice an immediate drop in blood pressure and stress the minute you arrive. Stock up on baked goods at the **PASTRY COMPANY** (2 miles up Stehekin Valley Rd from boat landing; 800/536-0745), and don't miss the cinnamon rolls. A primary gateway into the interior wilderness, Stehekin is a point of access for trails in North Cascades National Park. **MOUNTAIN TRANSPORTER** (509/996-8294; mid-May–mid-Oct) provides transportation from Stehekin to trailheads. **STEHEKIN LANDING RESORT** (509/682-4494; www.stehekinlanding.com)—a year-round lodge featuring 28 rooms, a restaurant, a store, and a rental shop for bikes, boats, skis, and snowshoes—is part of the national park complex.

The **STEHEKIN VALLEY RANCH** (509/682-4677 or 800/536-0745; www.courtneycountry.com) has served as a mainstay for visitors for years. It's a great place to use as a base camp. Open during summer, the ranch rents 12 units; 7 are rustic tent-cabins. Prices include three hearty meals a day. **CASCADE CORRALS** (509/682-7742; www.cascadecorrals.com) arranges horseback rides and mountain pack trips. A newer addition is **RAINBOW FALLS LODGE** (66 Rainbow Ln, Stehekin; 206/508-1025; www.rainbowfallslodge.com), at the base of 312-foot Rainbow Falls. The house, offering suites and surrounding cabins, is built in plain sight of the falls.

LODGINGS

Silver Bay Inn Resort / ★★

10 SILVER BAY RD, STEHEKIN; 800/555-7781
Kathy and Randall Dinwiddie, former Seattle-area teachers, are now the innkeepers at Silver Bay Inn Resort, a regular in these pages since 1986. The four waterfront cabins feature kitchens and spectacular views. Other amenities include complimentary bikes, canoes, and rowboats and a hot tub with a 360-degree view of the lake and surrounding mountains. *$$$–$$$$; MC, V; checks OK; closed Nov–Mar; www.silverbayinn.com; 1½ miles up Stehekin Valley Rd from boat landing.*

CENTRAL CASCADES

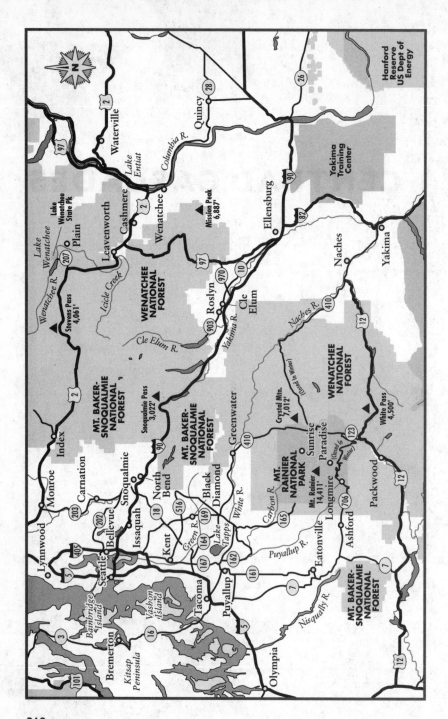

CENTRAL CASCADES

The Cascade Range dominates the landscape of Western Washington, but it is Mount Rainier—fondly referred to by locals as "the Mountain"—that is harder to miss. The state's highest peak is protected within the boundaries of one of the nation's greatest natural treasures—Mount Rainier National Park—and serves as an omnipresent icon of the grandeur of the Pacific Northwest.

The Cascades once formed a geological barrier between Eastern and Western Washington. Today the main cross-state routes of Interstate 90 (Snoqualmie Pass) and US Highways 2 (Stevens Pass) and 12 (White Pass) provide year-around access, though occasionally they get so choked with snow that intermittent road closures are inevitable. These essential routes link the west side to a vital agriculture region in the east and act as a gateway to outdoor adventures and scenic byways.

On the east side of Stevens Pass, the Bavarian-style village of Leavenworth and the tiny village of Plain to the north provide year-round diversions, offering travelers a bevy of sightseeing and recreational opportunities. On the east side of Snoqualmie Pass, the small towns of Cle Elum and Roslyn showcase their working-class roots next to their new neighbor: high-end Suncadia with its Arnold Palmer–designed golf course and 3,000-plus new homes being built.

From late spring to early fall, many Northwesterners head to "the Mountain" to picnic in Paradise. Mount Rainier's trailheads are an easy day trip from the Puget Sound area, but a diversity of overnight lodging are readily available throughout the area.

ACCESS AND INFORMATION

The scenic 400-mile **CASCADE LOOP** follows US Hwy 2 east from Everett, crosses Stevens Pass to Leavenworth and Wenatchee, then heads north (see North Cascades chapter) to Lake Chelan, Winthrop, and the North Cascades Scenic Highway (State Route 20). The route can be accessed from I-90 at Cle Elum by taking US Hwy 970 north to US Hwy 97, which continues north. It joins US Hwy 2 just east of Leavenworth. A brochure is available from the **CASCADE LOOP ASSOCIATION** (509/662-3888; www.cascadeloop.com).

The most popular east-west route across Washington, I-90 connects I-5 at Seattle with Ellensburg, Moses Lake, and Spokane (and beyond). A map of this multilane freeway is available from the **MOUNTAINS TO SOUND GREENWAY TRUST** (206/382-5565; www.mtsgreenway.org).

Lesser-known **US HIGHWAY 12** is an exceptionally scenic two-lane highway. Access Mount Rainier from the south by taking Hwy 12 to SR 7, then north from Morton to Ashford and the Nisqually entrance. Or take Skate Creek Road north from Packwood on Hwy 12 to the Ohanapecosh entrance (closed in winter). Continue east on Hwy 12 to White Pass Ski Resort, Yakima, and beyond.

It's a good idea to check **MOUNTAIN PASS REPORTS** (800/695-ROAD; www. wsdot.wa.gov/traffic/passes) before heading over the mountains in winter.

CENTRAL CASCADES THREE-DAY TOUR

DAY ONE: From Seattle, head north on I-5, then east on US Hwy 2 toward Sultan. Stop in at the **SULTAN BAKERY** (711 Stevens Ave, Sultan; 360/793-7996) to fuel up with some late-morning breakfast or pastries. Continue east over **STEVENS PASS** into **LEAVENWORTH**, a reproduction Bavarian village offering unique gift, wine, and cheese shops, as well as galleries and restaurants. Have lunch at **MUNCHEN HAUS BAVARIAN GRILL AND BEER GARDEN** when you've "done" the village. After checking in at **SLEEPING LADY MOUNTAIN RETREAT**, admire the inn's collection of Chihuly *Icicles* and Beyer *Shaman Salmon* sculptures. In the evening, indulge in a traditional Viennese-style dinner at **CAFÉ MOZART**. Travelers with children head to the **ICICLE VILLAGE RESORT**. After a game of minigolf or a splash in the pool, enjoy dinner at the family-friendly **VISCONTI'S RISTORANTE ITALIANO**, then drive to **LEAVENWORTH SUMMER THEATER AT SKI HILL AMPHITHEATER** (Ski Hill Dr, Leavenworth; 509/548-2000; www.leavenworthsummertheater.org) to see *The Sound of Music* under the stars (make reservations in advance; it frequently sells out).

DAY TWO: After breakfast at the Sleeping Lady's Kingfisher Dining Lodge, head east on US Hwy 2 to **SMALLWOOD'S HARVEST** (509/548-4196; www.smallwoodsharvest.com), a huge country mercantile with a petting farm for the kids. Next stop is **CASHMERE**. Visit **PIONEER VILLAGE AND MUSEUM** for a historical snapshot

US Highway 2 and Stevens Pass

Hwy 2 heads east-west across the state, from I-5 at Everett to Spokane (and farther east), winding up to Stevens Pass along the Skykomish River. **STEVENS PASS SKI AREA** (on Hwy 2, 65 miles east of I-5; 206/812-4510; www.stevenspass.com; late Nov–early Apr) is a favorite of Seattle-area skiers, offering downhill and cross-country skiing as well as snowshoeing; the **NORDIC CENTER** is located 5 miles east of the summit. Day lodges at the summit include a half-dozen casual eateries. From the pass, Hwy 2 drops down to the Wenatchee River. Along the way, the towns of Leavenworth, Cashmere, and Wenatchee give travelers reason to stop. Across the Columbia, the highway continues east through Waterville and beyond.

Leavenworth

With the Cascades as a backdrop, this former timber and rail town reinvented itself in the 1960s as a Bavarian village. In winter, the snowy village ups its thematic ante of alp horns, traditional dancing, and yodeling with a 250,000-holiday-light display, earning it distinction from the A&E Channel as the "Ultimate Holiday Town

of the late 1800s and the **LIBERTY ORCHARDS** factory store for Aplets and Cotlets. Order sandwiches at the **ANJOU BAKERY** (898 Old Monitor Rd, Cashmere; 509/782-4360) and continue on to **WENATCHEE**. Amble around **OHME GARDENS**, following its mile-long trail of steps and stones. Drive north to the small town of **WATERVILLE** and check in to the **WATERVILLE HISTORIC HOTEL**; then walk to dinner at **KNEMEYER'S** (115 W Locust, Waterville; 509/745-8348).

DAY THREE: Start your day with fresh-baked cinnamon rolls at **COYOTE PASS CAFÉ** (Box 308, Waterville; 509/745-9999), and then head back west on Hwy 2 and south past Wenatchee and Cashmere, hooking back onto Hwys 97 and 970 south to **CLE ELUM**. Refuel with fresh-baked pastries and coffee at **CLE ELUM BAKERY** or at **PIONEER COFFEE ROASTING COMPANY** (121 Pennsylvania Ave, Cle Elum; 509/674-4100). Drive on to **ROSLYN**, a city that retains vestiges of its rough-and-tumble mining heyday and is well known as the location for the TV series *Northern Exposure*. Stroll through the **ROSLYN HISTORICAL CEMETERY** for a unique historical perspective. Stop by the **ROSLYN CAFÉ** for a burger before heading over to **SUNCADIA RESORT**, a four-season resort and golf community. In summer, rent bikes and hit the trails, or play a twilight round of golf on Prospector Golf Course. In winter, hit the golf course's snowshoe or cross-country ski trails. Enjoy cozy fireside dinners of fresh, innovative, Northwest-focused cuisine at the **INN AT SUNCADIA'S GAS LAMP GRILLE**.

USA." Twice ABC's *Good Morning America* "Lights Up the Holidays" has showed up to flip the switch at the annual Christmas Lighting Festival.

Bavarian festivals, food, architecture, art, and music are the fabric of life here. Excellent lodging is plentiful, most with touches of Bavarian style. In addition to its hugely popular Christmas Lighting Festival, Leavenworth also is known for throwing other perennially favorite celebrations, including the Spring Bird Fest, the Washington State Autumn Leaf Festival, and Oktoberfest. Contact the Leavenworth Chamber of Commerce for information.

Explore the shops along Front Street. Stops include **DIE MUSIK BOX** (933 Front St; 509/548-6152 or 800/288-5883; www.musicboxshop.com); the **BAVARIAN CLOTHING COMPANY** (933 Front St; 509/548-2442), where you can custom order genuine lederhosen or buy dirndls and capes; and **KRIS KRINGL** (907 Front St; 509/548-6867 or 888/KKRINGL; www.kkringl.com) for year-round Christmas shopping.

Cultural offerings are numerous. **ICICLE ARTS** (509/668-4663; www.iciclearts. org) organizes arts events. The **ARTIST GUILD OF LEAVENWORTH** (509/668-4663; www.artistguildofleavenworth.org) presents work ranging from wrought-iron sculptures to wearable art. During warmer months, you can take a sunny stroll through the **VILLAGE ART IN THE PARK** (509/548-5809; www.villageart inthepark.org; weekends May–Oct).

In town, seek out the **UPPER VALLEY MUSEUM**, colocated with the **BARN BEACH RESERVE** at the former Haus Lorelei B&B (347 Division St; 509/548-0728; www.uppervalleymuseum.org). Keep in step with the Bavarian theme by visiting the **LEAVENWORTH NUTCRACKER MUSEUM** to view more than 5,000 nutcrackers (735 Front St; 509/548-4573 or 800/892-3989; www.nutcracker museum.com; afternoons May–Oct, weekends Nov–Apr).

Great music sounds even better in the stunning alpine setting. **MUSIK-KAPELLE LEAVENWORTH** (567/456-7890; www.musikkapelleleavenworth.com), a town band that sounds pleasingly like the best Bavarian village bands, plays at all major festivals and events. Concerts at **ICICLE CREEK MUSIC CENTER** (7409 Icicle Rd; 509/548-6347 or 877/265-6026; www.icicle.org) highlight a range of styles. The **MARLIN HANDBELL RINGERS** (509/548-5138 or 509/548-4319; www. marlinhandbells.com) perform seasonal and special-occasion concerts.

Boutique wineries continue to crop up (see "Columbia Cascade Wine Region: Touring and Tasting"). For a picnic, pair wine with cheese from the **CHEESEMON-GER'S SHOP** (633 Front St, Ste F; 509/548-9011; www.cheesemongersshop.com). Complement your cheese with a bottle of award-winning wine from **KESTREL VINTNERS TASTING ROOM** (843 Front St; 509/548-7348; www.kestrelwines. com). For a more casual experience of German cuisine (apple-cider kraut, sausages, finely crafted beers), stop by the family- and pet-friendly **MUNCHEN HAUS BAVARIAN GRILL AND BEER GARDEN** (709 Front St; 509/548-1158; www. munchenhaus.com), offering outdoor dining.

Leavenworth also serves as a gateway to outdoor adventure, with hundreds of miles of accessible walking, hiking, cross-country skiing, and backpacking trails, most within the nearby Wenatchee National Forest. The closest walking and hiking trails are in Waterfront Park, paralleling 2 miles of the Wenatchee River. For backcountry adventures, check with the **LEAVENWORTH RANGER STATION** (600 Sherbourne St; 509/548-6977; just off Hwy 2 on eastern edge of town) or the **LEAVENWORTH CHAMBER OF COMMERCE** (940 Hwy 2; 509/548-5807; www. leavenworth.org) for information.

RESTAURANTS

Café Mozart / ★★★

829 FRONT ST (UPSTAIRS), LEAVENWORTH; 509/548-0600

Nibble on schnitzel or sauerbraten in this elegant family-run dining retreat overlooking Front Street. Or splurge on the chateaubriand for two, a whopping 20-ounce Black Angus steak, served with grilled vegetables. For a sampler of Bavarian specialties, order the Hofbrauhaus Platter for two. Don't miss the hot apple strudel with ice cream. The extensive "wine attic" can be viewed from the dining area, and live harp music and elegant decor add a romantic touch. *$$$; AE, DIS, MC, V; local checks only; lunch, dinner every day (lunch Fri–Sun winter); full bar; reservations recommended; www.cafe mozartrestaurant.com; across from park.*

Visconti's Ristorante Italiano / ★★

636 FRONT ST, LEAVENWORTH; 509/548-1213

Italian food is served up in a lively fine-dining atmosphere in the upper levels of Leavenworth's former brewery. Pizza and entrées—including savory clams—come out of the wood-fired ovens. The homemade gelato shop Viadolce! opens at 6am. Leavenworth Visconti's has a shorter menu than the one in Wenatchee, but both are popular and frequently packed, and both offer a kids menu. *$$; AE, DIS, MC, V; local checks only; lunch, dinner every day; beer and wine; reservations recommended; www.viscontis.com; across from park.* &

LODGINGS

Abendblume Pension / ★★★

12570 RANGER RD, LEAVENWORTH; 509/548-4059 OR 800/669-7634

This Austrian-style chalet is perennially popular by the minute. And no wonder: it's one of the most elegant, sophisticated inns in town, run by a gracious host. A sweeping staircase leads upstairs to the two best rooms, which have fireplaces, Italian marble bathrooms with two-person whirlpool tubs and his-and-hers sinks, and window seats with views. Outside is a patio hot tub. Breakfast is at your own pace in the pine-trimmed morning room; *abelskivers* (a pancake) are a specialty. *$$$; AE, DIS, MC, V; checks OK; www. abendblume.com; north on Ski Hill Dr at west end of town.*

Icicle Village Resort / ★★★

505 HWY 2, LEAVENWORTH; 509/548-8225 OR 800/961-0162

Fun, kid-friendly places aren't easy to come by in Leavenworth, but here's one that tries hard. This large Best Western has more than 90 rooms, yet it doesn't feel like a chain hotel. Each of the Aspen Suites condos can sleep six, with two bathrooms and a kitchen. The outdoor pool is open year-round (under a bubble in winter); there's also minigolf, a video arcade, and a movie theater. Check out the Coca Cola Soda Fountain and JJ Hills train-themed restaurant. *$$$; AE, DIS, MC, V; checks OK; www.iciclevillage.com; near Icicle Rd.*

Mountain Home Lodge / ★★★

8201 MOUNTAIN HOME RD, LEAVENWORTH;
509/548-7077 OR 800/414-2378

A contemporary mountainside lodge offering a secluded escape-to-nature experience, the motto here is "children are seldom seen but often created." Most of the 10 themed rooms are on the small yet cozy side; for more space, splurge on a cabin. Room themes echo the region's nature and wildlife, including the Moose, Mountain Trout, Robin's Nest, and Timberline rooms. Hearty breakfasts and gourmet dinners ensure that guests stay energized for exploring their passions—indoor and out. *$$$$; DIS, MC, V; checks OK; www.mthome.com; off E Leavenworth Rd and Hwy 2.*

Natapoc Lodging / ★★★

12348 BRETZ RD, LEAVENWORTH;
509/763-3313 OR 888/NATAPOC

Natapoc offers an idyllic, classic "cabin in the woods" experience. Choose from seven small or spacious log houses along the Wenatchee River. All have gas grills, TV/DVDs, and kitchens. You can fish, cross-country ski, or shop in Leavenworth. Or just sit on the deck and listen to the river, or gaze at the stars as you slip into your hot tub. The larger lodges sleep up to 18, with home-away-from-home amenities that make them popular for families. *$$$$; AE, MC, V; checks OK; www.natapoc.com; 14 miles northwest of Leavenworth, then 2 miles north of Plain.*

Sleeping Lady Mountain Retreat / ★★★

7375 ICICLE RD, LEAVENWORTH; 509/548-6344 OR 800/574-2123

This one-of-a-kind place is a quintessential Northwest retreat built to blend with nature. The former Civilian Conservation Corps camp has 58 rustic but elegant units, clustered in groups of 10 surrounding courtyards. Each unit has its own bath, woodstove, coffee maker—with complimentary, free-trade organic coffee—and log beds, but no phones, minifridges, or TVs. A bunkhouse sleeps eight, and there's a luxury cabin with a whirlpool. A variety of notable art is showcased throughout the property; an old chapel is now a theater. The boulder-lined swimming pool is open 24 hours seasonally; the hot pool year-round. Breakfast, lunch, and dinner are served at the inn's Kingfisher Dining Lodge and are prepared with regional ingredients and organic produce from the garden. Casual foods—deli sandwiches and salads—can be purchased at O'Grady's Pantry, located at the entrance to the retreat. *$$$–$$$$; AE, DIS, MC, V; checks OK; www.sleepinglady.com; 2 miles southwest of town.*

Cashmere

This little orchard town gives cross-mountain travelers who aren't in a Bavarian mood an alternative to Leavenworth. Western-style stores line the low-key main street; the Wenatchee River and a railroad border the town. Cashmere's **PIONEER VILLAGE AND MUSEUM** (600 Cottage Ave; 509/782-3230; www.visitcashmere.com) are worth a stop.

Cashmere is particularly famous for its Aplets and Cotlets, or "Confection of the Fairies," a favorite American fruit and nut confection since the 1930s. Tour the plant at **LIBERTY ORCHARDS** (117 Mission Ave; 509/782-2191 or 800/888-5696; www.aplets.com). In an orchard off Hwy 2, 1 mile east of Cashmere, is **ANJOU BAKERY** (3898 Old Monitor Hwy; 509/782-4360; www.anjoubakery.com), serving artisan breads, sandwiches, European-style pastries, and premium-roast coffee.

COLUMBIA CASCADE WINE REGION: TOURING AND TASTING

Bordered by the Cascade Mountains to the west and sagebrush-covered hills to the east, the north-central region of Washington is the fastest-growing wine area in the state. Grape growing and winemaking have helped farmers weather the economic ups and downs of growing increasingly less prosperous fruit.

The **COLUMBIA CASCADE WINERY ASSOCIATION** (301 Angier Ave, Cashmere; 509/782-0708; www.columbiacascadewines.com) was formed to promote the region's growing roster of more than a half dozen wineries, including ones as far north as Oroville and Mazama and south to Quincy. Extensive outdoor recreation opportunities put this area on the map, but now wineries have added to its panache as a distinguished tourist destination.

In Leavenworth, two annual festivals focus on wine—a wine walk in early June and wine tasting in August—and 10 tasting rooms are open year-round. The Leavenworth area has six well-established wineries, including **BERGHOF KELLER** (11695 Duncan Rd, Leavenworth; 509/548-5605; www.berghofkeller.com), which, appropriately, creates German-style wines. At **ICICLE RIDGE WINERY** (8977 North Rd, Leavenworth; 509/548-7019; www.icicleridgewinery.com), the Wagoner family welcomes visitors to their log home and tasting room; in the summer, jazz concerts are held on-site.

Head east to Cashmere to visit the **COLUMBIA CASCADE WINE EXPERIENCE** in **APPLE ANNIE'S ANTIQUE GALLERY** (Eel Rd and Hwy 2/97, Cashmere; 509/782-9463; 10am–6pm every day), a wine-tasting and sales facility operated by the Columbia Cascade Winery Association.

—James Lawson

Wenatchee

A visit to Wenatchee, very near the geographic center of Washington, also puts you in the heart of apple country, with the Apple Blossom Festival at the end of April. **OHME GARDENS** (3327 Ohme Rd; 509/662-5785; www.ohmegardens.com), just north of town on Hwy 97A, is a 9-acre alpine retreat with cool glades and water features. It sits on a promontory 600 feet above the Columbia River, offering splendid views.

The **APPLE CAPITAL LOOP TRAIL** on the banks of the Columbia makes for a pleasant evening stroll or an easy bike ride; the 11-mile loop traverses both sides of the river and crosses two bridges from Wenatchee to East Wenatchee. The best place to join the trail is via a pedestrian overpass at the east end of First Street. The **WENATCHEE VALLEY MUSEUM AND CULTURAL CENTER** (127 S Mission St; 509/888-6240;

www.wenatcheevalleymuseum.com; 10am–4pm Tues–Sat) has permanent and rotating exhibits covering the region's geological, industrial, and artistic development.

MISSION RIDGE SKI & BOARD RESORT (on Squilchuck Rd, 13 miles southwest of town; 509/663-6543; www.missionridge.com) hoards so much winter sun, it owns boasting rights to the driest and lightest snow in the Northwest. In addition to the region's best powder, Mission Ridge offers 36 runs served by four chair lifts (including a quad lift), as well as a terrain park and half-pipe for snowboarders. Visit in mid-April to watch athletes compete in six grueling events in the **RIDGE-TO-RIVER RELAY** (509/662-8799; www.r2r.org).

The **WENATCHEE VALLEY CONVENTION & VISITORS BUREAU** (25 N Wenatchee Ave, Ste C111; 800/572-7753; www.wenatcheevalley.org) is a good source for local information.

RESTAURANTS

Shakti's / ★★★

218 N MISSION ST, WENATCHEE; 509/662-3321 OR 888/662-3321
Former ballet dancer–turned-chef Shakti Lanphere and her mother, Renee, partnered to create this wonderful oasis with linen tablecloths and soft lighting. The food focus is northern Italian with a local seasonal twist. Fresh seafood, hand-cut dried aged meats, and inventive pastas are the highlights, but you also can get a great steak or Kobe beef burger. Service is friendly and informed. *$$$; AE, MC, V; checks OK; dinner every day; full bar; reservations recommended; www.shaktisfinedining.com; in Mission Square, downtown.*

Visconti's Ristorante Italiano / ★★

1737 N WENATCHEE AVE, WENATCHEE; 509/662-5013
Italian food is served up in a lively fine-dining atmosphere in a fancy roadhouse on the main drag. Pizza and entrées—including savory clams—come out of the wood-fired ovens. The homemade gelato shop Viadolce! opens at 6am. This is the original Visconti's, popular and frequently packed; notably with a kids menu. *$$; AE, DIS, MC, V; local checks only; lunch Mon–Fri, dinner every day; beer and wine; reservations recommended; www.viscontis.com; Hwy 2 where it becomes Wenatchee Ave.* &

The Windmill / ★★

1501 N WENATCHEE AVE, WENATCHEE; 509/665-9529
This restaurant has seen several incarnations since its debut in 1931, including life as a former roadhouse, speakeasy, and steak house. With its knotty pine interior and built-in wooden booths, it evokes a bygone era while retaining a simple charm. Meals are western American classics like handcut steaks, slow-roasted prime rib, seafood, and house-crafted desserts. But why mess with tradition? Stick with the meat. If the barbecued pork ribs are on the menu, indulge—they're worth it. *$$; MC, V; checks OK; dinner every day; beer and wine; no reservations; www.thewindmillrestaurant.com; Hwy 2 Wenatchee exit, then 1½ miles south.*

LODGINGS

Coast Wenatchee Center Hotel / ★

201 N WENATCHEE AVE, WENATCHEE; 509/662-1234 OR 800/716-6199
This is the nicest hotel on the strip (a very plain strip, mind you, with numerous motels), with a city and river view. Connected to Wenatchee's convention center, it's especially popular with business travelers. The nine-story hotel has classic rooms with contemporary accents, upgraded in 2007. The Wenatchee Roaster and Ale House, on the top floor, features a DJ. Swimmers enjoy outdoor and indoor pools. *$$; AE, DC, DIS, MC, V; checks OK; www.coasthotels. com or www.wenatcheecenter.com; center of town.*

Waterville

Head 25 miles north of Wenatchee on Hwy 2 to reach the highest incorporated town in Washington. Waterville has several buildings and a downtown district listed in the National Register of Historic Places. Learn about farming history and see a huge rock collection at the **DOUGLAS COUNTY HISTORICAL MUSEUM** (124 W Walnut St; 509/745-8435; Tues–Sun late-May–mid-Oct).

LODGINGS

Waterville Historic Hotel / ★★

102 E PARK ST, WATERVILLE; 509/745-8695 OR 888/509-8180
Step back in time at this gracious hotel that first opened its doors in 1903. Owner Dave Lundgren has been painstakingly restoring it since the late 1990s. Rooms are decorated with period furnishings and have vintage-style radio shells containing cassette players. Tapes of old radio shows are provided. Two larger suites are great for families. Evenings, chat with other guests in the comfy lobby or on the spacious front porch. *$–$$; AE, DIS, MC, V; checks OK; www. watervillehotel.com; closed Nov–Mar; downtown on Hwy 2.*

Interstate 90 and Snoqualmie Pass

Carnation

Carnation is a verdant stretch of cow country nestled in the Snoqualmie Valley along bucolic State Route 203 (which connects I-90 to Hwy 2 at Monroe). At **TOLT MACDONALD PARK AND CAMPGROUND** (Fall City Rd and NE 40th St; 206/205-7532; www.metrokc.gov/parks), trails and a suspension bridge provide a great picnic setting; campsites and recently added yurts are available year-round.

Snoqualmie Valley farms produce great fruit and veggies. Go to the source at **REMLINGER FARMS** (off SR 203, on NE 32nd St; 425/333-4135; www.remlinger farms.com), for u-pick south of town. It's also a happening place for agri-entertainment, with the Country Fair Family Fun Park in summer; in October, kids love the farm's October Fall Harvest Festival with a u-pick pumpkin patch, wagon rides, and a flashlight maze.

Snoqualmie

The lovely Snoqualmie Valley is best known for its waterfalls and scenery. The 268-foot **SNOQUALMIE FALLS**, just up State Route 202 from I-90 (parking lot next to Salish Lodge & Spa; see review), is stunning. Use the observation deck or take a lightweight picnic down the 1-mile trail to the base.

The **NORTHWEST RAILWAY MUSEUM** (38625 SE King St; 425/888-3030; www.trainmuseum.org; every day year-round) runs a tour to the Snoqualmie Falls gorge from the towns of Snoqualmie and North Bend (most Sat–Sun Apr–Oct).

RESTAURANTS

The Dining Room at Salish Lodge & Spa / ★★★☆

**6501 RAILROAD AVE SE, SNOQUALMIE;
425/888-2556 OR 800/272-5474**

The views are breathtaking, but it's the food that really rocks. Literally. Don't miss the Snoqualmie River Hot Rocks, an appetizer of different fish cooked on sizzling stones. Even if you don't like fish, it's fun to watch. In fact, this place is all about the watching. Nearly everything is mixed in front of you, creating a unique fine-dining experience. Reserve the best table, a private room that juts out, providing a 180-degree view of the falls. The regionally focused menu and legendary wine list—some 1,700 labels—offer an astonishing culinary experience worth every extravagant dollar you'll pay for it. *$$$–$$$$; AE, DIS, MC, V; checks OK; breakfast every day, dinner Tues–Sun; full bar; reservations recommended; www.salishlodge.com; I-90 exit 25.* &

LODGINGS

Salish Lodge & Spa / ★★★☆

**6501 RAILROAD AVE SE, SNOQUALMIE;
425/888-2556 OR 800/272-5474**

Rustic lodge meets upscale elegance at this luxurious inn built in 1988 atop Snoqualmie Falls. Salish replaced Snoqualmie Lodge, which was built in 1916 and served as a logging route stopover. The exquisite spa, regularly updated, and the sights and sounds of the extraordinary waterfall make return trips not only desirable but also inevitable. The rooms are spacious, with thoughtful details and a swinging window that separate the bedroom from the romantic Jacuzzi tub or the spectacular view. Couples will find the romantic, side-by-side, heated river-rock massage at the spa a very worthwhile indulgence. The lodge also arranges kayaking, climbing, hiking, and rafting trips from your door. *$$$; AE, DIS, MC, V; checks OK; www.salishlodge.com; I-90 exit 25.*

North Bend

Zipping along I-90 eastbound, exit 31 at North Bend looks like just a pit stop with gas stations, fast-food outlets, the last Starbucks before Snoqualmie Pass, and a plain outlet mall. But take the time to drive less than a mile north via Bendigo Boulevard into town, and you'll find some fascinating shops, restaurants, and diversions. **ROBERTIELLO'S** (101 W North Bend Wy; 425/888-1803) serves excellent Italian food in the restored 1922 McGrath Hotel.

LODGINGS

Roaring River B&B / ★★

46715 SE 129TH ST, NORTH BEND; 425/888-4834 OR 877/627-4647

It's quite the find to discover such a secluded place less than an hour from city life, with reasonable rates to boot. Rhododendrons frame pathways at this retreat situated high above the Snoqualmie River, with views to match. The original home has one suite with a sauna; two other suites have whirlpool tubs and fireplaces. Herb's Place is a remodeled hunting cabin; crooked floors add to its charm. A warm breakfast basket is left at your doorstep. *$$$; AE, DIS, MC, V; checks OK; www.theroaringriver.com; I-90 exit 31, about 4 miles northeast via North Bend Wy and Mt Si Rd.*

Snoqualmie Pass

The **SUMMIT AT SNOQUALMIE** (on I-90, 52 miles east of Seattle; 425/434-7669; www.summitatsnoqualmie.com) includes four associated ski areas: **ALPENTAL, SUMMIT WEST, SUMMIT CENTRAL,** and **SUMMIT EAST**. They offer the closest skiing to Seattle. A free shuttle runs between the four areas on weekends, serving the largest night-skiing program in the Northwest. Alpental is the most challenging; Summit West, with one of the largest ski schools in the United States, has excellent instruction for all levels; Summit Central provides demanding bump runs and a great tubing hill; and the smallest, Summit East, is favored by cross-country skiers.

In summer, the transmountain pass is a good starting point for many hikes. Contact the **NORTH BEND RANGER STATION** (42404 SE North Bend Wy, North Bend; 425/888-1421) for information. The **SUMMIT LODGE AT SNOQUALMIE PASS** (603 SR 906, Snoqualmie Pass; 425/434-6300 or 800/557-STAY; www.snoqualmie summitlodge.com) is your only choice for year-round lodging at the pass.

Roslyn

Modest turn-of-the-20th-century homes in this formerly rough-and-tumble coal-mining town have become weekend places for city folk. But Roslyn's main intersection still offers a cross section of the town's character. The **BRICK** (100 W Pennsylvania Ave; 509/649-2643), once the set for the TV series *Northern Exposure*, is a recognizable old stone tavern. Also familiar is the **ROSLYN CAFÉ** (201 W Pennsylvania Ave; 509/649-2763), popular for its American fare. The small **ROSLYN BREWING COMPANY** (208 W Pennsylvania Ave; 509/649-2232; Sat–Sun year-round, Fri–Sun summer) is worth a visit to sample their excellent German-style lagers.

At the **ROSLYN THEATRE** (101 Dakota Ave; 509/649-3155), in a former mortuary, you can bring your dog. Down the road, behind the junkyard, you'll find **CAREK'S CUSTOM MARKET** (510 S A St; 509/649-2930), one of the state's better purveyors of fine specialty meats and sausages; try the beef jerky. The **ROSLYN HISTORICAL CEMETERY**, separated by lodge (Elks, IOOF, etc.) and country of origin (Slovak, Polish, Italian, etc.), pays homage to the fraternal memberships and ethnic diversity of the miners who settled here.

LODGINGS

Suncadia Resort / ★★★

3600 SUNCADIA TRAIL, ROSLYN; 866/904-6300

A mile from the working-class town of Roslyn, a high-end mountain resort development is underway. When it's finished, there will be more than 3,000 homes and condos on the 6,000-plus acres. First to open were the Inn at Suncadia and its restaurant, the Gas Lamp Grille, plus the Prospector Golf Course. The small inn has sumptuous furnishings and a Northwest lodge design. The 14 rooms and 4 suites have stocked bookshelves, bathrooms with soaking tubs, and decks with rocking chairs. A pool and fitness facility opened in summer 2007. More than 200 condos, many available for rental, opened in 2008. A village of shops and restaurants is growing year by year. $$$$; AE, DC, DIS, MC, V; checks OK; www.suncadia.com; I-90 exit 80, then follow signs.

Cle Elum

This small mining town of about 2,000 parallels and is divided by I-90 just east of Roslyn, with Cle Elum on one side of the freeway and South Cle Elum on the other. Freeway access at either end of town leads to First Street, Cle Elum's main thoroughfare, which makes the town a handy in-and-out stop. **CLE ELUM BAKERY** (501 E 1st; 509/674-2233) is a longtime local institution popular with travelers. From one of the last brick ovens in the Northwest come baked goods such as *torchetti* (an Italian butter pastry rolled in sugar). Try **OWENS MEATS** (502 E 1st St; 509/674-2530) and **MAMA VALLONE'S STEAK HOUSE** (302 W 1st St; 509/674-5174). The latter offers cozy Italian dishes in a pleasant country-style home on the main street.

LODGINGS

Iron Horse B&B / ★

526 MARIE AVE, SOUTH CLE ELUM; 509/674-5939 OR 800/228-9246

Iron Horse B&B is housed in a 1909 building originally for railroad employees. Listed on the National Register of Historic Places, the bunkhouse, with seven rooms including a honeymoon suite, is furnished with reproduction antiques. The four caboose car suites are fun for all. Railroad memorabilia is on display. Owners Mary and Doug Pittis are restoring the South Cle Elum Train Depot in nearby Iron Horse State Park. *$$; MC, V; checks OK; www. ironhorseinnbb.com; adjacent to Iron Horse State Park Trail.*

Mount Rainier National Park

Iconic Mount Rainier's perennially snowcapped block-style summit is one of the world's most visually interesting peaks. On clear days, you can see the mountain from Portland, Oregon, and Vancouver, BC. A subtly active stratovolcano, its cone rises 14,411 feet above sea level, several thousand feet higher than any other Cascade Range summit and with more glaciers than any other mountain in the Lower 48 states. Singularly created in 1899 to preserve the prized peak, **MOUNT RAINIER NATIONAL PARK** (55210 238th Ave E, Ashford; 360/569-2211; www.nps.gov/ mora; entrance fee $15 per automobile, $5 per person on foot, bicycle, horseback, or motorcycle) receives more than 2 million visitors annually. The best way to appreciate Rainier is to explore its flanks: 260 miles of backcountry trails lead to forests, glaciers, waterfalls, and meadows. Get required backcountry-use permits for overnight stays from the ranger stations at park entrances. Of the five entrance stations, the three most popular are described here; the northwest entrances—Carbon River and Mowich Lake—via long, unpaved roads aren't great for visitors. The Carbon River Road remains closed to motor vehicles due to flood damage in 2006.

State Route 410 heads east from Sumner through Enumclaw to the **WHITE RIVER ENTRANCE** (northeast corner) and **SUNRISE VISITOR CENTER** (Jul–Oct), continuing on to Chinook Pass and connecting with either Cayuse Pass (SR 123) or Hwy 12 near Naches. SR 410 beyond the Crystal Mountain spur road is closed in winter, with no access to Sunrise and Cayuse and Chinook passes; take the loop trip via the passes, or the road to Sunrise, late May through October.

State Routes 7 and 706 connect Tacoma and I-5 with the main **NISQUALLY ENTRANCE** (southwest corner) at **LONGMIRE**; the road continues east to SR 123 between Cayuse Pass and White Pass. The road remains open during daylight hours in winter only from Longmire to Paradise; carry tire chains and a shovel, and **CHECK CONDITIONS** by calling a 24-hour service (360/569-2211).

The **STEVENS CANYON ENTRANCE** (southeast corner) on SR 123, connecting SR 410 and Hwy 12 via Cayuse Pass, is closed in winter. In summer, **OHANAPECOSH** is a favorite stop.

Black Diamond

Located along State Route 169 in Maple Valley, this quiet, former coal-mining town is 10 miles north of Enumclaw. The historic **BLACK DIAMOND BAKERY** (32805 Railroad Ave, Black Diamond; 360/886-2235)—built in 1902—is worth a stop. The last wood-fired brick oven in the area, the bakery offers 26 different types of bread. The associated café serves tasty American standards at breakfast and lunch.

Greenwater

A tiny blink-and-you-miss-it community as you head east on SR 410 to Crystal Mountain Ski Resort or Chinook Pass, Greenwater is a good place to stop for gas. And check out the fun ski clothing store, **WAPITI WOOLIES** (58414 SR 410 E, Greenwater; 360/663-2268).

LODGINGS

Alta Crystal Resort / ★★

68317 SR 410 E, GREENWATER; 360/663-2500 OR 800/277-6475
This intimate mountain retreat has a cozy setting in the forest, yet is convenient to both Crystal Mountain Ski Resort (10 miles east) and the northeast entrance to Mount Rainier National Park. The 24 one- and two-bedroom lodgings are condo-style with kitchens, and the pool and hot tub are open year-round. The Honeymoon Cabin is popular with couples. The bonfires, games, and other activities give the place a fun summer-camp flavor. *$$$–$$$$; MC, V; checks OK; www.altacrystalresort.com; about 12 miles east of Greenwater.*

Crystal Mountain

CRYSTAL MOUNTAIN SKI RESORT (off SR 410 west of Chinook Pass, on northeast edge of Mount Rainier National Park; 360/663-2265; www.skicrystal.com), southeast of Enumclaw, is the state's best ski area, with panoramic views at the top. There are runs for beginners and experts, plus fine backcountry skiing. And yes, there are even things to do here in summer. Besides the usual, try sunset dining at the state's highest restaurant, the **SUMMIT HOUSE** (360/663-3085). Rent on-mountain condos from **CRYSTAL MOUNTAIN LODGING** (360/663-2558 or 888/668-4368; www.crystalmountainlodging.com) or hotel rooms from **CRYSTAL MOUNTAIN HOTELS** (360/663-2262 or 888/SKI-6400; www.crystalhotels.com).

Sunrise

Open early July through early October, **SUNRISE** (6,400 feet) is the closest you can drive to Rainier's peak. The old lodge has no overnight accommodations but offers a **VISITOR CENTER** (northeast corner of park, 31 miles north of Ohanapecosh; 360/663-2425; www.nps.gov/mora/planyourvisit/sunrise.htm), a snack bar, and mountain exhibits. Many hiking trails begin here, such as the short one to a magnificent view of **EMMONS GLACIER**, the largest in the Lower 48 states.

Eatonville

At **EATONVILLE,** just east of US Highway 7 on State Route 161, 17 miles south of Puyallup, the big draw is **NORTHWEST TREK** (just off of Meridian Ave/SR 161 on Trek Dr E; 360/832-6117; www.nwtrek.org; every day mid-Feb–Oct, weekends and holidays Nov–mid-Feb; group rates available). Here, visitors board small open-air trams for hour-long tours of the 435-acre grounds for views of elk, moose, deer, bighorn sheep, and bison—the herd steals the show.

Ashford

If Ashford is the gateway to Paradise, then **WHITTAKER'S BUNKHOUSE** (30205 SR 706 E, Ashford; 360/569-2439; www.whittakersbunkhouse.com) is the place to stop on the way to the very top—of Mount Rainier, that is. Rooms are basic (bunks available in summer) but plush compared to camping. There's an espresso café, and Vinyasa Flow yoga is offered (Mon, Wed, and Sat). Mount Tahoma Ski Huts, run by the **MOUNT TAHOMA TRAILS ASSOCIATION** (360/569-2451; www.skimtta.com), is Western Washington's first hut-to-hut ski trail system. It offers 50 miles of trails (20 groomed), three huts, and one yurt. For expert advice, stop by the **MOUNT RAINIER VISITORS ASSOCIATION** booth (877/617-9950; www.mt-rainier.com; every day year-round), inside **WHITTAKER MOUNTAINEERING'S OFFICE** (30027 SR 706 E, Ashford; 800/238-5756).

You'll find a few small restaurants in and near Ashford, including the **COPPER CREEK INN AND RESTAURANT** (35707 SR 706E, Ashford; 360/569-2326; www.coppercreekinn.com) and the **HIGHLANDER STEAK HOUSE** (30319 SR 706E, Ashford; 360/569-2953). For the most unusual art around, don't miss Dan Klennert's **EX-NIHILO** (a Latin word meaning "from nothing") sculpture park (22410 SR 706E, Elbe; 360/569-2280; May–Oct). His *Recycled Spirits of Iron* are lively sculptures.

LODGINGS

Altimeter Cabin / ★★★

34509 SR 706E, ASHFORD; 360/569-2140 OR 866/267-6814
Built around 1900, this cabin offers a taste of mountaineering history from life as "the Guest House" on the property of famed mountaineer Lou Whittaker. The home and cabin housed mountain guides for years. Local couple Andrea Brannon and Ray Morford bought it from Whittaker a few years ago. They live in the main house and have restored the cabin with unique touches—Andrea is a glass artist, and her talents are evident throughout. The cozy cabin sleeps two in the loft and up to two more on the futon. It has a claw-foot tub, kitchen, flat-screen TV with DVD and XBox, woodstove, and wi-fi, but no phone. Outdoors, there's a campfire space, a putting green, and a hot tub. $$$; DIS, MC, V; checks OK; www.altimetercabin.com; on north side of hwy just east of Skate Creek Rd.

Stormking Spa and Cabins / ★★

37311 SR 706E, ASHFORD; 360/569-2964
In recent years, the owners turned their B and B, a historic 1890 homestead, into a pampering spa. Four secluded cabins are nestled in gorgeous forest settings. The Wolf and Raven cedar cabins are yurt-shaped, with skylights

and decks. The Eagle features a two-person "greenhouse" shower; the Raven and Wolf have river-rock rain showers; the Heron has a two-person overhead sunflower shower with four body sprays. All have gas fireplaces, outdoor hot tubs, and rustic elegance. These very private cabins include terry cloth robes and slippers, and continental breakfasts are left in their refrigerators for morning comfort. *$$$; MC, V; checks OK; www.stormkingspa.com; 4½ miles east of town.*

Longmire and Paradise

A few miles inside the southwestern park border, the village of **LONGMIRE** has the 25-room **NATIONAL PARK INN** (360/569-2275; www.rainier.guestservices.com/rainier), with tasteful, hickory-style furnishings; 19 rooms have private baths. A small **MUSEUM** with wildlife exhibits, a **HIKING INFORMATION CENTER** (360/569-2211; Apr–Sept), and snowshoe and cross-country ski **RENTALS** (360/569-2411) are nearby.

At 5,400 feet, **PARADISE** is the most popular destination on Rainier. You'll catch views of Narada Falls and Nisqually Glacier on the way to the parking lot and the **HENRY M. JACKSON MEMORIAL VISITOR CENTER** (just before Paradise; 360/569-6036; every day May–Oct, weekends and holidays Nov–Apr). The center, housed in a flying saucer–like building, has a standard cafeteria and gift shop, nature exhibits and films, and a view from its observation deck. Notable guests at **PARADISE INN** (just past the newly upgraded visitor center) include President Harry Truman, Cecil B. DeMille, the crown prince of Norway, Shirley Temple, Sonja Henie, and Tyrone Power. The massive inn built of silver fir opened in 1917 and closed in 2005 for renovations and a seismic retrofit after serving several generations of park visitors. It reopened in May 2008. Depending on the season, you can picnic at Paradise (best to bring your own fixings) among the wildflowers, explore the hiking trails (rangers offer guided walks), let the kids slide on inner tubes in the snow-play area, try a little cross-country skiing, or even take a guided snowshoe tromp.

White Pass

WHITE PASS SKI AREA (on Hwy 12, 12 miles southeast of Mount Rainier National Park; 509/672-3101; www.skiwhitepass.com) is an off-the-beaten-path ski destination offering downhill (with a high-speed quad lift) and cross-country skiing. Its base is the highest on the Cascade crest, at 4,500 feet. A Nordic center near the day lodge serves cross-country skiers with about 11 miles of trails. Summer hiking can be found in adjacent William O. Douglas and Goat Rocks wilderness areas. Lodging is available slope-side at the **VILLAGE INN CONDOMINIUMS** (509/672-3131; www.whitepassvillageinn.com). The nearby town of Packwood has several motels; try **MOUNTAIN VIEW LODGE** (13163 Hwy 12, Packwood; 877/277-7192; www.mtvlodge.com) for comfy rooms—some with fireplaces—hot tub, and seasonal outdoor pool.

SOUTHWEST WASHINGTON

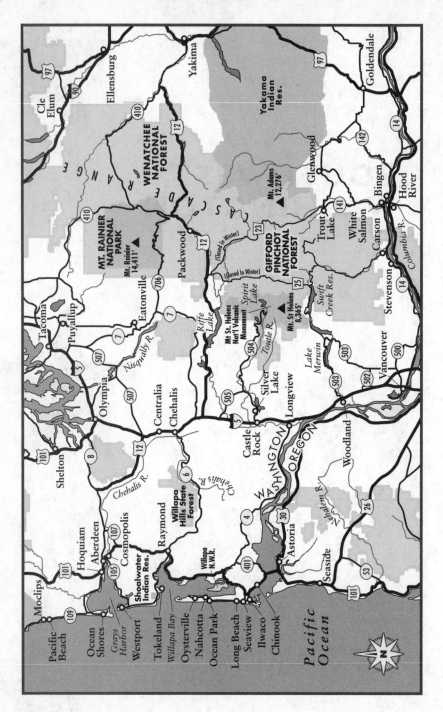

SOUTHWEST WASHINGTON

The muscular Chehalis River in the north, and west the vast Pacific Ocean; the majestic Columbia River Gorge to the south, and snow-topped Mounts St. Helens and Adams in the north and east: these surround the tree-covered hills and low peaks of the Coast Range in Southwest Washington's interior, where fertile green pastures and fields lie in wide valleys along plump brown rivers.

Locals and visitors alike flock to estuaries and beaches along the coast to fish, boat, fly kites, gather shellfish, bask in nature, contemplate history, and sample local wines and maritime cuisine. Along the lower Columbia River, oceangoing vessels make their way up and down the deep-water channel, to and from ports at Longview, Kalama, Woodland, and Vancouver on the Washington side, Portland and St. Helens on the Oregon side. Farther upriver, in the Columbia Gorge, world-class athletes windsurf and kiteboard in internationally renowned waters while spectators admire their acrobatic feats. Private fishing and pleasure boats wind their way through the windsurfers and kiteboarders, and massive barges churn past, carrying diesel fuel and other commodities upriver, returning downriver loaded with grain, lumber, and other agricultural products.

Inland, gigantic tree farms and commercial forests blanket the Coast Range and the western foothills of the Cascades. Pastoral farms line the dark-earthed river valleys. To the north and east, mountain streams tumble and froth down the slopes of the Cascade mountains, where hiking, camping, fishing, hunting, and volcano gazing are the most popular pastimes. Along the western foothills of the Cascades, trucks, buses, and private autos follow Interstate 5 between the urban attractions of Vancouver in the south and the more rural charms of Centralia and Chehalis in the north.

ACCESS AND INFORMATION

INTERSTATE 5 runs north-south through Southwest Washington, east of the Cascades, but the more scenic drives are on the east-west Columbia Gorge **STATE ROUTE 14** between Vancouver, Bingen, and US Highway 97; on the north-south Long Beach Peninsula **STATE ROUTE 103** between Ilwaco and Oysterville; on the north-south coastal **US HIGHWAY 101**, and on the coastal **STATE ROUTES 105 AND 109** near Grays Harbor. From I-5 to the coast, **STATE ROUTE 4** runs between Longview and Hwy 101, **STATE ROUTE 6** runs between Chehalis and Raymond–South Bend, and **US HIGHWAY 12** north of Centralia runs to Aberdeen, Hoquiam, and Ocean Shores.

AMTRAK (800/USA-RAIL; www.amtrak.com) rail service stops in **CEN-TRALIA** (210 Railroad Ave; 360/736-8653), **KELSO-LONGVIEW** (501 S 1st Ave; 360/578-1870), and **VANCOUVER** (1301 W 11th St; 360/694-7307) on the *Coast Starlight* route. **GREYHOUND** (800/231-222; www.greyhound.com) bus service is available to Centralia, Kelso-Longview, and Vancouver.

Grays Harbor and Ocean Shores

A water wonderland for birds, people, and shellfish alike, Grays Harbor is at the mouth of the Chehalis River. The coastal area north of the harbor, from Ocean Shores to Moclips, is known as North Beach; the coastal area south of the harbor, from Westport through Grayland and North Cove—18 miles of beach—to Tokeland is known as South Beach. **BOWERMAN PENINSULA** in **GRAYS HARBOR NATIONAL WILDLIFE REFUGE** (SR 109, 1½ miles west of Hoquiam; 360/753-9467; www.fws.gov/graysharbor), and **DAMON POINT STATE PARK** (on Point Brown Ave, Ocean Shores) are great bird-watching areas. The new **OCEAN SHORES CONVENTION CENTER** (120 W Chance a la Mer Ave, Ocean Shores; 800/874-6737; www.oceanshoresconventioncenter.com) is home to the area's **VISITOR CENTER**.

Elma

This little burg is at the junction of Hwy 12 and State Route 8, about 20 miles east of Aberdeen. Elma started life as a trading center for homesteaders settling the Chehalis valley before 1860. In 1888 the town was incorporated. Timber and agriculture drove the local economy then, just as they do now.

RESTAURANTS

Saginaw's / ★

301 W MAIN ST, ELMA; 360/482-8747
Husband-and-wife team Scott and LouAnne Kendall created this cozy deli-diner as a way to share their passion for food with others. The place is often filled with locals eating salads, soups, and sandwiches at lunch or pastas and meats at dinner. Never pass up their seafood cioppino when it's the special. Don't forget to have one of LouAnne's homemade bar cookies. *$$; AE, DIS, MC, V; local checks only; lunch Mon–Sat, dinner Tues–Sat; full bar; reservations recommended; www.saginaws.com; at S 3rd St.* &

Aberdeen and Hoquiam

An inconspicuous street is the border between Hoquiam (pronounced "HO-kwe-um") and Aberdeen, towns at the mouths of the Chehalis, Wishkah, and Hoquiam rivers on Grays Harbor. Old Victorian homes grace the hillsides, and the shared logging and maritime history of the towns is evident from the area's mills and fishing boats. When it's docked in its home port, don't miss visiting the reproduction of **ROBERT GRAY**'s *Lady Washington* (www.ladywashington. org). More-permanent structures are the **OLYMPIC STADIUM** (2811 Cherry St, Hoquiam) and the **SEVENTH STREET THEATRE** (313 7th St, Hoquiam; 360/537-7400; www.7thstreettheatre.com). Built in 1937, the stadium is one of the few all-wooden ones remaining in the country. Go to **GRAYS HARBOR CHAMBER OF COMMERCE** (506 Duffy St, Aberdeen; 360/532-1924; www.graysharbor.org) for more information.

RESTAURANTS

Gabelli's Parma / ★★★

116 W HERON ST, ABERDEEN; 360/533-6100
Aberdeen's beloved Pierre Gabelli, a Swiss-trained chef, cooked northern Italian dishes for 12 years at his popular restaurant, Parma. Now he offers a lower-cost menu of the same incredible food at this location. The warm lighting and rich colors create an intimate space reminiscent of a quaint European café. A profusion of pasta entrées make ordering a challenge, but the offerings won't disappoint. The olive oil–garlic mixture is powerful, and Pierre's mom's *canoneini* (a puff pastry) is a must-have. *$$; AE, DIS, MC, V; local checks only; dinner Tues–Sat; beer and wine; reservations recommended; www.gabellis parma.com; downtown between S K and S Broadway sts.* &

Mallard's Bistro & Grill / ★

118 E WISHKAH ST, ABERDEEN; 360/532-0731
Ask chef-owner Niels Tiedt how the tremendous duck collection started, and he'll point to one particular poster. Ask him about the success of his 10-year-old restaurant, and he'll tell you about his 50-year love affair with food. This place, known for its large portions and more than 25 entrées, is always packed. Special occasions are celebrated with the venerable duck call. *$$; MC, V; local checks only; dinner Tues–Sat; beer and wine; reservations recommended; between S I and S Broadway sts.* &

LODGINGS

A Harbor View Inn Bed & Breakfast / UNRATED

111 W 11TH ST, ABERDEEN; 877/533-7996
Each of the five guest rooms in this antique-filled 1905 Colonial Revival house has a view of the harbor. Eat a full breakfast served on a porch overlooking the harbor before setting out for a day of whale watching, birding, beachcombing, or deep-sea fishing. The central location is ideal for exploring both the North Beach and South Beach areas. In the evening, stroll among the historic Broadway Hill homes nearby. *$$$–$$$$; AE, MC, V; checks OK; www.aharborview.com; off Hwy 101 via Broadway to 11th.*

Hoquiam Castle Bed & Breakfast / ★★

515 CHENAULT AVE, HOQUIAM; 360/533-2005
After staying a night in this 1897 mansion, you'll feel as grand as the bed you slept in. The four royalty-themed and -decorated rooms are over-the-top opulent. The King's Suite is ideal for that special romantic getaway. Sisters Pat and Kathy have retained most of the home's original furnishings. Breakfast

is served with fine china, and the vanilla ice cream French toast is delicious. Formal teas and afternoon tours are available for nonguests. *$$$; MC, V; no checks; www.hoquiamcastle.com; west on Emerson Ave, right on Garfield St, uphill to Chenault Ave.*

Ocean Shores

Crooner Pat Boone, who played golf here in the late 1960s, hoped to turn this coastal community into a destination resort town. It didn't happen. However, since the late 1990s there's been quite a buzz stirring up business and property values. The new **OCEAN SHORES CONVENTION CENTER** (see this section's introduction) will attract crowds as large as those seen at the **QUINAULT BEACH RESORT AND CASINO** (see Lodgings).

But there's more on this 6,000-acre peninsula than golf and gambling. Visit the home of the 2005 and 2006 World Sport Kite Championship winners, **CUTTING EDGE KITES** (676 Ocean Shores Blvd NW; 360/289-0667 or 800/379-3109; www.cuttingedgekites.com) and pick up a good-looking wind toy and great kite-flying tips. **B J'S FAMILY FUN CENTER** (752 Pt Brown Ave NE; 360/289-2702; www.bjsfuncenter.com) and **PACIFIC PARADISE FAMILY FUN CENTER** (767 Minard Ave NW; 360/289-9537) offer bumper boats for kids and adults. Horse riding is a popular pastime; **CHENOIS CREEK HORSE RENTALS** (360/289-5591) and **NAN-SEA STABLES** (2551 SR 115; 360/289-0194; www.horseplanet.com) offer rides on the beach.

Go shopping at **FUSIONS** (834 Pt Brown Ave NE; 360/289-2811; www.introspectivevision.com), a gallery representing more than 70 Pacific Northwest artists, and at **JOAN OF ARTE** (740 Pt Brown Ave NE, Ste A; 360/289-2554; www.joanofarte.com), which has unique candles and self-help books. Also stop by **FLYING CATS** (114 E Chance a la Mer NE; 360/289-2287; www.flyingcats.com) for body-care products; sample fruit curds, then sip Irish tea next door at **MCCURDY'S CELTIC MARKETPLACE** (360/289-3955).

A **TRAVEL AND TOURISM WEB SITE** (www.oceanshores.com) has information.

RESTAURANTS

Palm's Restaurant at Floating Feather Inn / ★★

982 PT BROWN AVE SE, OCEAN SHORES;
360/289-2490 OR 888/257-0894

The only canal-front restaurant in Ocean Shores, Palm's is an intimate, softly lit space with just six tables and very limited hours. Try Thai chicken curry puffs with a cucumber-cilantro relish, or an artichoke–crab dip appetizer. The pan-seared rib-eye steak with grape tomato–balsamic salsa is tasty. Sit outside on the private dock in summer. *$$; AE, DIS, MC, V; local checks only; breakfast Sat–Sun (by reservation only), dinner Fri–Sat (more days in summer); beer and wine, champagne cocktails; reservations recommended; www.floating featherinn.com; 3½ miles south of town's stone gate entrance.* &

LODGINGS

Floating Feather Inn / ★★★

982 PT BROWN AVE SE, OCEAN SHORES; 360/289-2490 OR 888/247-0894
After 35 years in the travel industry, co-owner Nancy Milliman knows what it takes to run a first-rate B and B. From the moment you walk in, she and her husband, Roger, will make you feel at home. Located at the quiet end of town, the inn's four comfy guest rooms (stay in one of the two that overlook the canal rather than the street) have feather beds and down comforters. Breakfast scones are toothsome, and Ghirardelli chocolates and free movies ice the cake. *$$–$$$; AE, DIS, MC, V; local checks only; www.floating featherinn.com; 3½ miles south of town's stone gate entrance.* &

Quinault Beach Resort & Casino / ★★

78 SR 115, OCEAN SHORES; 360/289-9466 OR 888/461-2214
Don't let the frightening bright-purple foyer scare you away. Walk into the hotel's lobby, and you'll be rewarded with more-hospitable colors and classy decor. The 150 rooms are tastefully furnished and reasonably sized, but some have oddly placed gas fireplaces in the middle of the room that separates the bed from the sitting area. Three restaurants are onsite, there's 16,000 square feet of casino to play in, and you can beachcomb out the front door. *$$–$$$$; AE, DIS, MC, V; checks OK; www.quinaultbeachresort.com; on the beach on west side of hwy.* &

Copalis

LODGINGS

Iron Springs Resort / ★

3707 SR 109, COPALIS BEACH; 360/276-4230
Families flock to this very rustic resort for the impressive ocean views and great clam digging; they stay—and return to stay again—because they want to live more with less for a while. Without television reception (movies are available) or phones, you'll enjoy more time on the beach and wooded trails just outside your door. Furnishings are minimal and funky, but the river-rock fireplaces make it all seem grand. Cabins 22–25 are best, since they're the newest. The steamy indoor pool will help you relax; homemade cinnamon rolls greet you when you wake up. *$$$; AE, DIS, MC, V; checks OK; www. ironspringresort.com; 3 miles north of Copalis Beach.* &

Pacific Beach and Moclips

These two quiet towns along the northern end of SR 109 have a smattering of cliff-hugging, antiquated hotels, a restaurant with a priceless view, and a noteworthy museum. One of the best options if you plan to spend at least a few days in the area is **SEABROOK** (SR 109; 360/276-0099; www.seabrookwa.com; 1 mile south of Pacific Beach), a planned community designed with a new-urbanism aesthetic by Laurence Qamar. It offers affordable vacation homes and beach cottages with all the modern amenities you can think of and can be rented by the weekend, week, or month. The **SANDPIPER RESORT** (4471 SR 109, Pacific Beach; 360/276-4580; www.sandpiper-resort.com) and **OCEAN CREST RESORT AND HOTEL** (4651 SR 109, Moclips; 800/684-8439) offer decent lodgings, and the latter also offers fine dining. A more reasonably priced eatery along this stretch of coastline is **PACIFIC TANGO** (61 Main St, Pacific Beach; 360/276-0102). The **MUSEUM OF NORTH BEACH** (4658 SR 109, Moclips; 360/276-4441; www.moclips.org) has an impressive collection. Contact the **WASHINGTON COAST CHAMBER OF COM-MERCE** (2616-A SR 109, Ocean City; 360/289-4552 or 800/286-4552; www. washingtoncostchamber.org) for more information.

Westport and Grayland

These South Beach towns on an 18-mile stretch of beach may be known for their charter fishing, cranberry bogs, and world-class surfing, but the area is quickly becoming something else: the hottest tourist destination on Washington's coast.

With new restaurants, oceanfront and marina condominiums, and a planned links-style 18-hole golf course, Westport is on its way to becoming the perfect getaway. Places not to miss include the **WESTPORT MARITIME MUSEUM** (2201 Westhaven Dr, Westport; 360/268-0078; www.westport.wa/museum), which offers tours of the **GRAYS HARBOR LIGHTHOUSE** (2201 Westhaven Dr, Westport). **WINDS OF WESTPORT** (320 Dock St, Westport; 360/268-1760; www.windsof westport.com) rents electric and pedal-powered boats. One of the many charter fishing companies is **OCEAN CHARTERS** (2315 Westhaven Dr, Float 6, Westport; 360/268-9114 or 800/562-0105).

GRAYLAND BEACH STATE PARK (925 Cranberry Rd, Grayland; 360/267-4301) has excellent beachcombing and well-maintained yurts and camping sites. Two good shops are **POMEGRANATE** (1752 SR 105, Grayland; 360/267-0701) and the **ROSE COTTAGE** (1794 SR 105, Grayland; 360/267-0205), both offering unique gifts and home furnishings.

Check the **WESTPORT-GRAYLAND CHAMBER OF COMMERCE** (2985 S Montesano St, Westport; 360/268-9422 or 800/345-6223; www.westportgrayland-chamber.org), **GRAYS HARBOR COUNTY TOURISM AGENCY** (800/621-9625; www.graysharbor tourism.com), and a good **WEB SITE** (www.westportwa.com) for information.

RESTAURANTS

Anthony's Restaurant / ★★★⯪

**421 E NEDDIE ROSE DR (ISLANDER RESORT),
WESTPORT; 360/268-9166 OR 800/322-1740**
Chef Mark Potovsky has spent more than 20 years working in the finest Pacific Northwest restaurants. An archway leads to an intimate dining area with white-linen tablecloths and handsomely dressed servers. Grilled pear,

blue cheese, and prosciutto salad may be a meal's perfect beginning. Apricot-glazed chicken and cranberry polenta will do nothing to dispel the perfection. *$$–$$$; AE, DIS, MC, V; local checks only; dinner every day; full bar; reservations recommended; www.westport-islander.com; off SR 105, follow Montesano St approx 4 miles, left on Westhaven Dr, follow to its end.* ♿

Half Moon Bay Bar & Grill / ★★★

421 E NEDDIE ROSE DR (ISLANDER RESORT), WESTPORT; 360/268-9166 OR 800/322-1740

In this superb dining spot by the sea, overlooking the marina, fresh fish is their forte—and no wonder: much of it is caught just outside. A combination of cozy booths and tables, warm earth tones, and Moroccan-style lanterns create a comfortable atmosphere. The Surf's Up caesar salad and Jetty Surf Melt will have you savoring every bite. Light jazz on weekends, live music on the deck in the summer, and a monthly Winemaker's Dinner keep the place abuzz. *$$–$$$; AE, DIS, MC, V; local checks only; breakfast, lunch, dinner every day; full bar; no reservations; www.westport-islander.com; off SR 105, follow Montesano St approx 4 miles, left on Westhaven Dr, follow to its end.* ♿

LODGINGS

Vacations by the Sea / ★★½

1600 W OCEAN AVE, WESTPORT; 360/268-1119 OR 877/332-0090

These oceanfront condominiums have plush interiors with all the comforts of home. One- and two-bedroom rentals are so well maintained you might feel terrible tracking in sand. Views are lovely, and the ocean is just a few steps from your front door, down the trail through the beach grass. Rock hunting is a blast here: beautiful orange-colored agates are abundant. Access to the recreation center is included. *$$$–$$$$; AE, DIS, MC, V; checks OK; www.vacationbythesea.com; off Montesano St, left on Ocean Ave.* ♿

Tokeland

Named after an Indian chief, this quiet community on the north shore of Willapa Bay south of Grayland hosts an extravagant Fourth of July celebration. A public pier and boat launch at the small marina access great fishing, crabbing, and bird-watching. The nearby **SHOALWATER BAY CASINO** (on SR 105 at Tokeland turn-off; 888/332-2048; www.shoalwaterbaycasino.com) is a hot spot.

LODGINGS

Tokeland Hotel / ★★

100 HOTEL RD, TOKELAND; 360/267-7006

This century-old inn teetered on the edge of collapse until husband and wife Scott and Katherine White restored it. Despite its creaky floors and shared bathrooms, the antique furnishings and serene setting warm the heart. Get one of the four rooms with a view of Willapa Bay if you can. The living room is a comfy place to settle in with a good book and a cup of tea. An in-house restaurant serves decent, home-cooked food at good prices. *$; AE, DIS, MC, V; checks OK; www.tokelandhotel.com; SR 105 Tokeland exit, then follow Hotel Rd 2 miles.* &

Long Beach Peninsula and Willapa Bay

The slender finger of land between Willapa Bay and the Pacific, Long Beach Peninsula is famous for its 37-mile-long flat stretch of public beach, gentle marine climate, kite flying, clamming, and rhododendrons. Out in the bay, Long Island, reachable only by boat, is the site of a huge old-growth cedar grove. Some trees are more than 200 feet tall. The island is part of the **WILLAPA NATIONAL WILDLIFE REFUGE** (3888 SR 1, Ilwaco; 360/484-3482), with headquarters on Hwy 101, 10 miles north of Seaview. The **LONG BEACH PENINSULA VISITORS BUREAU** (3914 Pacific Hwy, Seaview; 360/642-2400 or 800/451-2542; www.funbeach.com) has an excellent Web site; the **WILLAPA CHAMBER OF COMMERCE** (360/942-5419; www.visit.willapabay.org) may also be helpful.

Skamokawa

Founded in 1844, Skamokawa (meaning "smoke on the water") was originally called Little Venice, a daily stop for sternwheel steamboats running between Portland and Astoria. The **RIVER LIFE INTERPRETIVE CENTER** in Redmen Hall, a well-restored 1894 Queen Anne–style schoolhouse, is worth a look. A block south of town, **SKAMOKAWA VISTA PARK** lies on the site of a village occupied 2,300 years ago. Lewis and Clark passed through more recently, in 1805.

LODGINGS

Inn at Lucky Mud / ★★½

44 OLD CHESTNUT DR, SKAMOKAWA; 360/482-8747 OR 800/806-7131
The inn is in the middle of nowhere, and that's the point. Four spacious guest rooms with private baths and porches overlook the pond—and an occasional herd of elk. You'll fall asleep to frog lullabies and wake to the smell of good breakfast and strong coffee. Explore the trails in the 40 acres of woods and pastures, or check out the 18-hole disc golf course. Jessica's chocolate mud puffs are an extra treat. *$$; MC, V; checks OK; www.luckymud.com; north off SR 4 on Skamokawa Valley Rd to E Valley Rd, left ¼ mile past mile marker 6, first house on right.*

Chinook

From primeval times to the present, fish and fishing have loomed large in Chinook, southeast of the Long Beach Peninsula on Hwy 101. The site of the first salmon hatchery in Washington is east of town. A bit farther east on Scarborough Hill, **FORT COLUMBIA STATE PARK** (on Hwy 101, 2 miles west of Astoria Bridge; every day) hosts a collection of restored turn-of-the-20th-century wooden buildings that once housed soldiers guarding the river mouth. The former commander's house is now a **MILITARY MUSEUM** (mid-May–Sept). Rent the fully furnished two-bedroom **STEWARD'S HOUSE** or five-bedroom **SCARBOROUGH HOUSE** (888/226-7688); advance reservation is required. **ST. MARY'S CATHOLIC CHURCH** (on Hwy 101 at milepost 2, just east of Chinook), which sits along the Columbia River, is worth a visit.

Ilwaco

Known as a salmon-fishing and -processing port and not much else a decade ago, Ilwaco's harbor pulsates with new energy, particularly at **ILWACO HARBOR VILLAGE**, an array of galleries, restaurants, and shops. **SHOALWATER COVE GALLERY** (177 Howerton Wy SE; 360/642-4040 or 877/665-4382; www.shoalwatercove.com) features local artist Marie Powell's watercolors. Chow down on chicken-basil sausage hoagies at the **CANOE ROOM CAFE** (161 Howerton Wy SE; 360/642-4899). **OLE BOB'S SEAFOOD MARKET** (151 Howerton Wy; 360/642-4332 or 888/748-8156; www.olebobs.com) is good for fresh oysters and crab, the **WADE GALLERY** (223 Howerton Wy; 360/642-2291; www.thewadegallery.com) for photography, and **NAUTICAL BRASS** (139 Howerton Wy; 360/642-5092; www.nauticalbrass.com) for gifts. A seasonal **SATURDAY MARKET** (May–Sept) also happens here.

Ilwaco is still a charter-fishing hot spot. Two popular operators are **COHO CHARTERS** (237 Howerton Wy SE; 800/339-2646; www.cohocharters.com) and **SEA BREEZE CHARTERS** (185 Howerton Wy SE; 360/642-2300 or 800/204-9125; www.seabreezecharters.net). Many charter operators also offer eco-tours. The **COLUMBIA PACIFIC HERITAGE MUSEUM** (115 SE Lake St; 360/642-3446; www.ilwaco-heritagemuseum.org) features a good Lewis and Clark exhibit.

Nearby **CAPE DISAPPOINTMENT STATE PARK** (off Hwy 101, 2 miles southwest of Ilwaco; 360/642-3078) is one of Washington's most popular attractions, with almost 2,000 acres stretching from **NORTH HEAD LIGHTHOUSE** to **CAPE DISAPPOINTMENT**, where another sentinel illuminates the Columbia River's mouth; both lighthouses are approachable by trail. Open all year, the park has yurts for comfortable winter stays and is home to the **LEWIS AND CLARK INTERPRETIVE CENTER** (360/642-3078; www.parks.wa.gov/lcinterpctr.asp), which offers a retelling of the explorers' journey. But the biggest draw here is the incredible view.

RESTAURANTS

Port Bistro Restaurant / ★★☆

235 HOWERTON WY, ILWACO; 360/642-8447

Chef Larry Piaskowy assumed the reins in 2006. After a meal here, you won't be sorry he did. His motto—"craft first, then art"—explains the solid menu and consistently well-made, not to mention luscious, fare. The custom-made copper bar, open kitchen, and imaginative art combine to make the entire experience satisfying. *$$; AE, MC, V; checks OK; lunch, dinner Thurs–Tues; beer and wine; reservations recommended; www.theportbistro.com; waterfront along the port.* &

LODGINGS

China Beach Retreat / ★★★

222 CAPTAIN ROBERT GRAY DR, ILWACO; 360/642-5660
This lovely hideaway by the bay is an ideal place to romance your sweetie. Three guest rooms harmonize with the beauty that surrounds this water wonderland. Upstairs rooms provide the best views; all have private baths, and the downstairs suite offers a two-person jetted tub. Stained-glass windows and handmade tiles in the tubs are displays of art. The owners have added the Audubon Cottage, perfect for more privacy. Elaborate gourmet breakfasts you won't soon forget are served 5 miles away at the charming Shelburne Inn (see review). *$$$$; AE, MC, V; checks OK; www.chinabeachretreat.com; ½ mile west of downtown.*

Seaview

Touted as an ocean retreat for Portlanders early in the 20th century, with visitors arriving in Ilwaco via river steamer, then transferring to the "Clamshell Railroad" to reach Seaview, the town now basks in the legacy of stately older beach homes along a pretty beachfront and some of the best dining and lodging on the Long Beach Peninsula. Nearly every road heading west reaches the ocean, and you can park your car and stroll the dunes. Don't miss the **WILD MUSHROOM FESTIVAL** in October.

RESTAURANTS

The Depot Restaurant / ★★★

1208 38TH PL, SEAVIEW; 360/642-7880
The former Seaview train station on the long-defunct Ilwaco-Nahcotta line is now a fine-dining experience. Michael Lalewicz's Italian-French influences, coupled with local ingredients, turn out mouth-watering combinations. The CrabMac appetizer is outstanding, as is the Depot House Greens salad. "Dine at the source" by choosing the special seafood entrée caught that day, or savor one of the land foods— from Northwest quail to pork rib sugo to Moroccan chicken. An open kitchen allows patrons to observe the magic. *$$$; MC, V; local checks only; dinner Wed–Sun; beer and wine; reservations recommended; www.depotrestaurantdining.com; off SR 103 on 38th Pl Seaview Beach approach.* &

42nd Street Café / ★★★

4201 PACIFIC WY, SEAVIEW; 360/624-2323

When you enter this cozy roadside café, its friendly atmosphere will remind you of a festive family holiday. Chef Cheri Walker, along with her husband, Blaine, have made fine dining in a down-home place a reality. Service is prompt and pleasant. Decor is bright and cheery. Delectable sauces marry with equally delicious entrées. Take home a jar of their dandy marionberry jam. *$$; AE, MC, V; checks OK; breakfast, lunch, dinner every day; beer and wine; reservations recommended; www.42ndstreetcafe.com; at 42nd St.* ♿

LODGINGS

The Shelburne Inn / ★★★

4415 PACIFIC WY, SEAVIEW; 360/642-2442 OR 800/466-1896

It's no surprise that when you enter this nationally recognized inn with 103 years of continuous operation, you'll feel immediately welcome. Lovingly crafted and maintained, the inn has 15 guest rooms full of exquisite antiques and old-world charm. Two suites offer fresh-baked cookies and in-room breakfast service if desired. You'll be talking about the five-course breakfast long afterward. *$$$; AE, MC, V; checks OK; www.theshelburneinn.com; on SR 103 at N 45th.* ♿

Long Beach

The epicenter of peninsula tourist activity, Long Beach hosts throngs of summer visitors who browse the gift shops and arcades and wander the beach **BOARDWALK**—a pedestrian-only half-mile stroll with night lighting (wheelchairs and baby strollers welcome). Those looking for a longer walk take the 8-mile **DISCOVERY TRAIL**, which retraces the route of **CAPTAIN WILLIAM CLARK** between Long Beach and Ilwaco.

A big draw is August's weeklong **WASHINGTON STATE INTERNATIONAL KITE FESTIVAL** (www.kitefestival.com), when the town swells to more than 50,000. Visit the **WORLD KITE MUSEUM AND HALL OF FAME** (303 Sid Snyder Dr; 360/642-4020; www.worldkitemuseum.com); get in on the fun yourself by shopping at **LONG BEACH KITES** (115 Pacific Ave N; 360/642-2202 or 800/234-1033) or **OCEAN KITES** (511 Pacific Ave S; 360/642-2229).

For a tastier museum visit, check out the **CRANBERRY MUSEUM AND GIFT SHOP** (2907 Pioneer Rd; 360/642-5553; www.cranberrymuseum.com; every day Apr–Dec) and take a self-guided tour of the bogs. **ANNA LENA'S PANTRY** (111 Bolstad Ave E; 360/642-8585) has 20 or so varieties of fudge; it's also a quilters' destination. Grab a sandwich or a pizza to go at **SURFER SANDS** (1113 Pacific Hwy S; 360/642-7873).

CAMPICHE STUDIOS (101 S Pacific Ave; 360/642-2264; www.campiche studios.net) exhibits watercolors, pottery, and photos. Kitschy and fun, **MARSH'S FREE MUSEUM** (409 S Pacific Ave; 360/642-2188; www.marshsfreemuseum.com)

LONG BEACH PENINSULA THREE-DAY TOUR

DAY ONE: Begin your day with breakfast at the **42ND STREET CAFÉ** in Seaview. Drive south through Ilwaco to **CAPE DISAPPOINTMENT STATE PARK** and hike one of the coastal trails. Tour the **NORTH HEAD LIGHTHOUSE** or go for a dip at **WAKIKI BEACH**, the only swim-safe beach on the peninsula. Return inland to Ilwaco to view the boats while lunching at the **PORT BISTRO RESTAURANT**. Check in at the Audubon Cottage at **CHINA BEACH RETREAT** and watch nature on the beach for the rest of the afternoon. Have dinner at the **PELICANO RESTAURANT** (177 Howerton Wy SE, Ilwaco; 360/642-4034; www.pelicanorestaurant.com).

DAY TWO: After a huge breakfast at the **SHELBURNE INN** (included with your stay at the Audubon Cottage), drive north to Long Beach. Go kite flying after visiting the **WORLD KITE MUSEUM AND HALL OF FAME**, or swing your club for a while at the **PENINSULA GOLF COURSE** (9604 Pacific Hwy, Long Beach; 360/642-2828). Have lunch at the **CRAB POT** (1917 Pacific Hwy S, Long Beach; 360/642-8870). Browse **SHOPS** along Pacific Highway, or stroll the boardwalk. Buy a T-shirt at **FRANTIC FRED'S** (310 Pacific Ave S, Long Beach;

---

features nationally famous Jake the Alligator Man, a mummified half-man, half-alligator who inspired a line of "Believe It Or Not"–style sportswear.

LODGINGS

Boreas Bed & Breakfast / ★★★

607 N OCEAN BEACH BLVD, LONG BEACH; 360/642-8069 OR 800/642-8069
When you meet owners Susie Goldsmith and Bill Verner, you'll understand why their B and B garners glowing accolades. Five generously sized guest rooms, each with a private bath, are colorful and artsy. Plush robes, signature dark chocolates, upscale bath products, and fresh flowers add to the satisfaction. An impressive, three-course gourmet breakfast is served midmorning. *$$$; AE, DIS, MC, V; checks OK; www.boreasinn.com; 1 block west of SR 103.*

Inn at Discovery Coast / ★★★

421 11TH ST SW, LONG BEACH; 360/642-5265 OR 866-843/5782
This boutique hotel is the epitome of luxury when it comes to oceanfront accommodations on the Long Beach Peninsula. The ultramodern three-story inn has nine guest rooms, all with pine floors, neutral colors, and sleek furnishings. Some rooms have two-person jetted tubs, while others have two-headed showers. You'll appreciate the down bedding and fine bath products, as well as the basket of breakfast goodies delivered to your door. *$$$; AE,*

360/642-3838), and indulge at **SCOOPER'S ICE CREAM** (101 N Pacific Ave, Long Beach; 360/642-8388). Leave crowds behind and check in to your evenings accommodations at the **BOREAS BED & BREAKFAST**. Relax before freshening up for dinner back in Seaview at the **DEPOT RESTAURANT**.

DAY THREE: Your morning meal at your B and B will get you started for the day. As you drive from Long Beach toward the northern tip of the peninsula, stop in Ocean Park at **WEIR STUDIOS** (2217 Bay Ave, Ocean Park; 360/665-6821; www.weirstudios.com) for fused-glass pendants and at **WIEGARDT STUDIO GALLERY** (2607 Bay Ave, Ocean Park; 360/665-5976; www.ericwiegardt.com) for watercolor paintings. Take the west-shore road to **LEADBETTER POINT STATE PARK** and spend the late morning bird-watching, beachcombing, and clam digging. Drive south through Oysterville and sit in the lovely **OYSTERVILLE CHURCH** (along Territory Rd, Oysterville; www. oysterville.org/church.html) for a moment or two before going to Nahcotta for lunch at **BAILEY'S BAKERY AND CAFÉ**. Return to Ocean Park and check in to **DOVESHIRE BED AND BREAKFAST** before dinner at **LUIGI'S** (1201 Bay Ave; Ocean Park; 360/665-3174).

DIS, MC, V; no checks; www.innatdiscoverycoast.com; left at Sid Snyder Dr, go 4 blocks, left on Shoreview Dr, right on 11th St. &

Ocean Park, Nahcotta, and Oysterville

Just because these three communities are on the quiet northern end of the Long Beach Peninsula doesn't mean they're dull. Check with the **OCEAN PARK CHAMBER OF COMMERCE** (360/665-4448 or 888/751-9354; www.opwa.com) for local happenings. This area is great for clamming, beachcombing, golfing, and oyster eating. The **NORTHWEST GARLIC FESTIVAL** in June and the **ROD RUN** in September are two events not to be missed in Ocean Park.

Visit the **WILLAPA BAY INTERPRETIVE CENTER** in Nahcotta (360/942-5419; www.visit.willapabay.org; open Sat–Sun in summer) to learn about the oyster industry. Stroll through Oysterville and imagine the slower pace of life 100 years ago. Head out to **LEADBETTER POINT STATE PARK** (from SR 101, north on SR 103 19 miles to Stackpole Rd) and bird-watch.

RESTAURANTS

Bailey's Bakery and Café / ★

26910 SANDRIDGE RD, NAHCOTTA; 360/665-4449
Owner Jayne Bailey's breakfast goodies are well worth the journey you'll make to her cheery roadside café at the northernmost end of the Long Beach

Peninsula. The local following favors fresh scones loaded with tart cherries or blueberries. On Sundays, the "Thunder Buns" go fast—come early for these currant-pecan sticky buns. A daily soup special and a nice selection of sandwiches and salads round out the lunch fare. *$; no credit cards; checks OK; breakfast, lunch Thurs–Mon; no alcohol; no reservations; www.baileysbakery cafe.com; adjacent to Nahcotta Post Office.* &

LODGINGS

Charles Nelson Guest House / ★

26205 SANDRIDGE RD, OCEAN PARK; 360/665-3016 OR 888/862-9756
While you stay at this 1920s Craftsman house, offering three guest rooms with sunny country decor, you might want to take a watercolor lesson from internationally renowned artist Eric Wiegardt (360/665-5976; www.eric weigardt.com). It's a short walk to his studio, and a short distance of another kind from there to inspiration. Or try kiting, kayaking, birding, fishing, whale-watching, or clamming instead—after the wonderful big breakfast, many activities may seem necessary that didn't before. *$$$; AE, MC, V; checks OK; www.charlesnelsonbandb.com; right off SR 103 onto Bay Ave, left on Sandridge Rd.*

Moby Dick Hotel & Oyster Farm / ★★

25814 SANDRIDGE RD, NAHCOTTA; 360/665-4543
This nine-room hotel is as eclectic as its name. The exterior orange stucco walls are a pleasant prelude to what awaits inside: brightly painted rooms adorned with art and throw rugs. The heated-floor yurt and dry-heat sauna are nice. Most rooms have shared baths. Room 2 is our favorite, with its own soaking tub and sitting deck. Multicourse breakfasts in their restaurant (dinner Thurs–Mon; full bar; reservations recommended) often include oysters from the farm. *$$–$$$; AE, DIS, MC, V; checks OK; www.mobydickhotel. com; south of Bay Ave.* &

Centralia and Chehalis

Near each other on the I-5 corridor south of Olympia, these two towns are close to SR 6 west to Raymond and South Bend, and Hwy 12 east to White Pass, with access to Mount Rainier National Park and Mount St. Helens National Volcanic Monument. Take a walking tour through historic Centralia, shop for antiques, or catch a **STEAM TRAIN RIDE** (1101 Sylvenus St, Chehalis; 360/748-9593; www. steamtrainride.com). Visit the **LEWIS COUNTY CONVENTION AND VISITOR BUREAU** (1401 W Mellen St, Centralia; 800/525-3323; www.tourlewiscounty. com) for more information. For reliable dining, the **MCMENAMINS OLYMPIC CLUB HOTEL, PUB AND THEATER** (112 N Tower Ave, Centralia; 360/736-5164; www.mcmenamins.com) offers food, beer, and lodging similar to what you'll find at McMenamins throughout Oregon.

RESTAURANTS

The Shire Bar & Bistro / ★

465 NW CHEHALIS AVE, CHEHALIS; 360/748-3720

The "eat, drink, and be merry" spirit still infuses this former men's club and tavern. Owner Joel Wall put together a restaurant with fine food, live entertainment, and old-world charm. The bar, crafted in France in the late 1800s, glows with rich, dark wood tones. The chicken and crab Savoy, Voodoo shrimp, and cornmeal catfish are top menu picks. *$–$$; MC, V; local checks only; lunch Tues–Fri, dinner Tues–Sat; full bar; reservations recommended; www.theshirebarandbistro.com; at NW Pacific Ave.* &

LODGINGS

Great Wolf Lodge / ★★★

20500 OLD HWY 99SW, CENTRALIA; 360/273-7718 OR 800/640-WOLF

You have to see this resort to believe it. It's truly a spectacle, but a wonderful one. Best for families with children or for spirited 20-something couples, the resort's key attraction is its amazing, balmy 84°F, 56,000-square-foot indoor water park, offering six waterslides, three pools, and a four-story treehouse water fort; it's the first of its kind in the region. Accommodations include 400 Northwoods-themed suites, many offering in-room forts with bunk beds. Special suites feature fireplaces, lofts, balconies, and whirlpool tubs; all have microwaves and refrigerators. The resort also has a children's craft-activity center, a teen tech center, and an arcade with more than 100 video games. MagiQuest, a live-action fantasy adventure game, keeps kids moving and absorbed for hours. Guests have several dining options on-site, including two restaurants. *$$$–$$$$; AE, DIS, MC, V; no checks; www.greatwolf.com; intersection of I-5 and Hwy 12.*

Mount St. Helens National Volcanic Monument

May 18, 1980, remains a vivid memory for many people in the Pacific Northwest: one of the Cascade Range's most active volcanoes, Mount St. Helens, erupted. People as far away as British Columbia heard the explosion, and ash blew hundreds of miles. After being relatively quiet for 25 years, the mountain began to emit ash and steam in September 2005. **JOHNSTON RIDGE OBSERVATORY** (on SR 504 at milepost 52; 360/274-2140), with its impressive views of the crater, is one of the most visited sites in Washington. The easiest way to reach the mountain is by taking the Castle Rock exit off I-5 and traveling east on SR 504. Known as the **SPIRIT LAKE MEMORIAL HIGHWAY**, this 52-mile-long road has five visitor centers en route to the mountain. Don't miss stopping at the **MOUNT ST. HELENS VISITOR CENTER** (3029 Spirit Lake Hwy, Castle Rock; 360/274-0962) for more information about the 1980 eruption and the mountain's current volcanic activity.

Vancouver and Camas

Downtown Vancouver has seen extensive urban revitalization in recent years. The epicenter of the changes is **ESTHER SHORT PARK** (8th and W Columbia sts), founded in 1853, the oldest public park in Washington. New businesses and living spaces also continue to flood **UPTOWN VILLAGE** (on Main St between Mill Plain and Fourth Plain Blvd), where the new and old blend nicely.

The **VANCOUVER NATIONAL HISTORIC RESERVE TRUST** (750 Anderson St; 360/992-1800; www.vnhrt.org) represents historic sites in the oldest and fourth-largest city of Washington. **FORT VANCOUVER** (612 E Reserve St; 360/816-6230; www.nps.gov/fova), **OFFICERS ROW** (E Evergreen Blvd, between I-5 and E Reserve St), and **PEARSON AIR MUSEUM** (1115 E 5th St; 360/694-7026; www.pearson airmuseum.org) are noteworthy places.

The **WATERFRONT RENAISSANCE TRAIL** (Columbia Wy between I-5 and SE Topper Dr) along the Columbia River is an ideal place to run, take a stroll, or ride a bike. **VANCOUVER LAKE PARK** (6801 NW Lower River Rd, Vancouver; 360/619-1111) and **LACAMAS LAKE** (2700 SE Everett Rd, just north of downtown Camas; 360/619-1111) are popular for water sports.

Annual festivals celebrate music, art, and food in the summer. The **FOURTH OF JULY** fireworks display entertains thousands. The **SOUTHWEST WASHINGTON CONVENTION AND VISITORS BUREAU** (101 E 8th St, Vancouver; 360/750-1553 or 877/600-0800; www.southwestwashington.com) offers information.

RESTAURANTS

Bortolami's Pizzeria / ★★☆

9901 NE 7TH AVE, VANCOUVER; 360/574-2598
This family-owned restaurant showcases two of Italy's greatest contributions: pizza and bicycles. While you dine on slices of your favorite pizza, delight in the eye-catching cycling paraphernalia on the walls. The Rainbow Jersey (Canadian ham and pineapple with marinara) is flavorful. Or try the Domestique, which has chicken, roasted red peppers, and feta cheese. Children and parents alike appreciate the fortlike play area for kids. *$$; AE, MC, V; checks OK; lunch, dinner every day; beer and wine; no reservations; www.bortolami. com; I-5 exit at 99th St, go 1 block west.* &

Hudson's Bar & Grill / ★★★☆

17805 GREENWOOD DR (HEATHMAN LODGE), VANCOUVER; 360/816-6100 OR 888/475-6101
Chef Ray Delgado has stepped into media darling chef Marc Hosack's shoes. Following the example of his mentor, he uses the freshest Northwest ingredients to craft exciting dinner combinations like lobster ravioli and pepper-crusted New York steak. Lofty ceilings, an open kitchen, and a huge fireplace create a comfortable space. *$$$; AE, DIS, MC, V; checks OK; breakfast, lunch, dinner every day; full bar; no reservations; www.hudsonsbarandgrill.com; left on NE Greenwood Dr off NE Parkway.* &

Roots Restaurant / ★★★

19215 SE 34TH AVE, CAMAS; 360/260-3001
Don't let the unassuming storefront in a strip mall–like place prevent you from coming here. Roots has extraordinary dishes at reasonable prices. The mushroom-stuffed chicken breast has a lot going for it, and the dark chocolate mousse cake is addicting. An open kitchen, an intimate bar, and a square dining area create a sociable atmosphere, but the humble decor makes the space appear a little cold. You'll praise the attentive waitstaff and cheer the dark-colored curtains that obscure the dismal parking-lot view. *$$$; AE, MC, V; no checks; lunch, dinner every day; full bar; reservations recommended; www.rootsrestaurantandbar.com; Riverstone Marketplace Shopping Center.* &

Tommy O's / ★

801 WASHINGTON ST, VANCOUVER; 360/694-5107
For more than a decade, Tommy Owens has brought a touch of the Hawaiian Islands to downtown Vancouver. Formerly the Aloha Café, the bistro offers up Pacific Rim cuisine with panache. Fresh halibut rolled in sweet macadamia nuts stays moist and delicious. The seafood appetizers are tastier than the chicken or beef options. Surfing paraphernalia, Hawaiian music, and tropical tablecloths (white linens at dinner) add to the island charm. *$–$$$; AE, MC, V; local checks only; breakfast, lunch, dinner every day; full bar; reservations recommended; www.tommyosaloha.com; at 8th St.* &

Vinotopia / ★★★

11700 SE 7TH ST, VANCOUVER; 360/213-2800 OR 877/608-2800
Here you can eat dinner while watching a big-screen movie. Vinotopia lives in Cinetopia, probably the country's most luxurious high-tech movie theater. Owner Rudyard Coltman's love of cinema inspired the ultimate movie experience. Leather seats, incredible sound technology, and 50-foot screens will leave you awestruck. And that's just the theater. Art, live entertainment, a wine bar, and Vinotopia provide the rest. The only downside? Mediocre tapas-style small plates. *$$; AE, MC, V; checks OK; lunch, dinner every day; beer and wine; reservations recommended (restaurant); www.cinetopiatheaters. com; I-5 exit 28 at Mill Plain, go 2 blocks east, right on SE 117th Ave.* &

LODGINGS

The Fairgate Inn / ★★★★

2213 NW 23RD AVE, CAMAS; 360/834-0861
A 15-year love affair with B and Bs and an amazing talent for design and decor helped Chris and Jack Foyt build this exquisite colonial mansion. Along with being an incredible place to stay, the inn hosts hundreds of weddings, meetings, and retreats. The foyer's grand Brazilian-cherry staircase leads to eight beautifully furnished, luxurious guest rooms, each with a private bath and fireplace. Gorgeous hardwood furniture, high thread-count linens, and

COLUMBIA GORGE THREE-DAY TOUR

DAY ONE: Have breakfast at **TOMMY O'S** in Vancouver and grab some picnic fixings at the **FARMERS MARKET** (at W 8th and Esther sts, Vancouver; 360/737-8298; www.vancouverfarmersmarket.com; Apr–Oct) before beginning your scenic, winding drive east on SR 14. Stop at **BEACON ROCK STATE PARK** (on SR 14E at milepost 35; 509/427-8265; www.parks.wa.gov; 10 miles west of Stevenson) and carefully walk the short, steep trail to the incredible river views at the top, then refuel with a picnic. Continue east to watch salmon and steelhead move up the fish ladder at **BONNEVILLE LOCK AND DAM** (off SR 14 at milepost 40; 509/427-4281). Return west a short way to North Bonneville and check in to the **BONNEVILLE HOT SPRINGS RESORT AND SPA** (1252 E Cascade Dr, North Bonneville; 509/427-7767 or 866/459-1678), swim in their therapeutic mineral pool, and then spend the rest of the afternoon in their spa. Venture just a few miles east and north to Skamania Lodge's Cascade Room in Stevenson for dinner.

DAY TWO: Head east and check out the **COLUMBIA GORGE INTERPRETIVE CENTER MUSEUM** before stopping at **BAHMA COFFEE BAR** in Stevenson for breakfast. Walk to **BOB'S BEACH** (along Cascade Ave, ½ block west of the city's

a savory gourmet breakfast leave long-lasting impressions. *$$$; AE, MC, V; checks OK; www.fairgateinn.com; SR 14 exit 192, right on Brady, right on 16th, right on 18th, left on Astor, right on 23rd.* &

Heathman Lodge / ★★★☆

7801 GREENWOOD DR, VANCOUVER; 360/254-3100 OR 888/475-3100
Despite being next to a busy shopping mall, this is the nicest place to stay on the east side of Vancouver. It really is an odd place for this beautiful, rustic hotel, but for the corporate traveler or for others wanting the illusion of a mountain getaway in the city, it works. Northwest Native American decor and design appear in the 121 guest rooms, 21 suites, and elsewhere throughout the property. A business center and an indoor heated pool with sauna and fitness room are some of the amenities. Great meals aren't far away: highly acclaimed Hudson's Bar & Grill (see review) is on-site. *$$–$$$$; AE, DC, DIS, MC, V; checks OK; www.heathmanlodge.com; SR 500 exit at Thurston.* &

Hilton Vancouver / ★★★

301 W 6TH AVE, VANCOUVER; 360/993-4500 OR 800/321-3232
The latest luxury hotel in Vancouver feels more like a boutique than a corporate behemoth. Part of the new convention center, it's not just smaller than the average Hilton, it's sexier. All 226 rooms offer Crabtree & Evelyn

dock, Stevenson) and marvel at windsurfers and kiteboarders along the Columbia River before driving east to White Salmon to do some serious retail shopping. Stop to have lunch or coffee at **GROUND ESPRESSO BAR & CAFE** (166 E Jewett Blvd, White Salmon; 509/493-1340; www.groundespressobarandcafe.com), where you'll find home-baked goods, soups, and sandwiches. Head down the hill to Bingen to sample Washington vintages at **GORGE WINE MERCHANTS**, then go next door and have dinner at **VIENTO BURGER & STEAK BAR**. Travel north up SR 141 and head east to Glenwood, where you'll stay in the **MOUNT ADAMS LODGE AT FLYING L RANCH**.

DAY THREE: After a huge homemade breakfast at the ranch, drive the winding canyon roads southeast, parallel to the Klickitat River, before connecting to SR 142. Head east to Goldendale and visit **GOLDENDALE OBSERVATORY STATE PARK** before stopping for Greek food and pastries for lunch at **ST. JOHN'S BAKERY, COFFEE & GIFTS**. Take US Hwy 97 south to SR 14 and make stops at the **STONEHENGE** replica, **MARYHILL MUSEUM OF ART**, and **MARYHILL WINERY** before heading west to Lyle to check in to the **LYLE HOTEL** for the night. During the winter months, have dinner in the **HOTEL'S RESTAURANT** next to the woodstove. In the summer, enjoy your meal on their patio.

bath products and have specially made alarm clocks that play programmed music of your choice. Paintings by Northwest artists accent the contemporary design and furniture. A lofty entrance, beautifully colored carpets, and exquisite lighting add up to grand style. *$$–$$$; AE, MC, V; checks OK; www.vancouverwashington.hilton.com; corner of Columbia and W 6th sts.* &

Columbia River Gorge and Mount Adams

The **COLUMBIA GORGE INTERPRETIVE CENTER MUSEUM** (990 SW Rock Creek Dr, Stevenson; 509/427-8211 or 800/991-2338; www.columbiagorge.org), on SR 14 just west of Stevenson, displays numerous exhibits, including such marvels as a 37-foot-high replica of a 19th-century fishwheel, the world's largest collection of rosaries, and multimedia presentations detailing the gorge's natural history.

Mount Adams and its surroundings, 30 miles north of the Columbia via State Route 141, offer natural splendor largely overlooked by visitors, who seldom venture north from the gorge. Along with climbing to the summit of the 12,276-foot mountain—greater in mass than any of the five other major volcanic peaks in the Northwest—you can explore miles of trails in the **MOUNT ADAMS WILDERNESS AREA** and **GIFFORD PINCHOT NATIONAL FOREST**. Contact the **MOUNT ADAMS RANGER STATION** (2455 SR 141, Trout Lake; 509/395-3400) for information.

Stevenson

Thanks to the city of **STEVENSON** (www.cityofstevenson.com), the Wi-Fi Project provides free wireless Internet access downtown. Browse through women's clothing and gifts at **DUCK SOUP** (350 SW SR 14; 509/427-5136) and visit the **RIVER HOUSE ART GALLERY AND STUDIO** (115 NW 2nd St; 509/427-5930; www.riverhouseartgallery.com) to view the work of well-known watercolorist Marilyn Wood Bolles. **WALKING MAN BREWERY** (240 SW 1st St; 509/427-5520; www.walkingmanbrewing.com) and **BIG RIVER GRILL** (192 SW 2nd St; 509/427-4888; www.bigrivergrill.us) are ideal for a beer and a good meal. Two music festivals— **BLUES, BREWS, AND BARBEQUE** in June and the **BLUEGRASS FESTIVAL** in July— are hits. Stop by the **SKAMANIA COUNTY CHAMBER OF COMMERCE** (167 NW 2nd Ave; 509/427-8911 or 800/989-9178; www.skamania.org) to learn more.

RESTAURANTS

Bahma Coffee Bar / ★★☆

256 2ND ST, STEVENSON; 509/427-8700
Bahma, Hebrew for "place of comfort," is Stevenson's first and finest coffeehouse. Well-worn couches and lushly painted walls give a bohemian-renaissance feel to the space. The owners serve up more than a good cup of joe. Yummy breakfast and lunch items like scones, croissant sandwiches, quiche, soups, salads, and fruit smoothies are available. Check for live music on the weekends. *$; MC, V; checks OK; breakfast, lunch every day; beer and wine; no reservations; www.bahmacoffeebar.com; on SR 14, across street from AJ Market.* &

The Cascade Room / ★★★

1131 SW SKAMANIA LODGE WY (SKAMANIA LODGE), STEVENSON; 509/427-7700 OR 800/221-7117
Aside from the view of the Columbia River, the Cascade Room will afford you out-of-this-world traditional fish and meat dishes, salmon chowder, a luscious cheese tart, and heavenly desserts—among other tasty delights. Friday-night buffets and Sunday brunches are feasts fit for royalty. *$$$; MC, V; no checks; breakfast, lunch, dinner every day, brunch Sun; full bar; reservations recommended; www.skamania.com; just west of town, turn north onto Rock Creek Dr, left onto Skamania Lodge Wy.* &

LODGINGS

Skamania Lodge / ★★★

1131 SKAMANIA LODGE WY, STEVENSON; 509/427-7700 OR 800/221-7117
Skamania is a destination resort in the middle of the Washington side of the Columbia Gorge. The views from the lodge, situated on a bluff overlooking a valley and the river, are spectacular. A playground for sports enthusiasts, Skamania includes a golf course, an indoor pool, tennis courts, and bikes.

Native American and Pacific Northwest themes dominate in the 254 rooms, the meeting spaces, and elsewhere throughout the property. *$$$–$$$$; AE, DIS, MC, V; checks OK; www.skamania.com; just west of town, turn north onto Rock Creek Dr.* &

Carson

LODGINGS

Carson Mineral Hot Springs Resort / ★★

372 ST MARTIN RD, CARSON; 509/427-8292 OR 800/607-3678
The funk factor of this 100-year-old resort has faded from its glory days. Gone are the cabins on the hillside. In their place is an imposing two-story structure with 28 simple rooms. Come prepared for serenity, and not only while relaxing in the spa: the rooms have no telephones or televisions. A golf course and restaurant opened in 2007. *$; MC, V; checks OK; www.carson hotsprings.upcsites.org; off SR 14, left at Carson Junction, 1 mile to 4-way stop, right onto Hot Springs Rd, left onto St Martin Rd.* &

Carson Ridge Cabins / ★★★☆

1261 WIND RIVER RD, CARSON; 509/427-7777 OR 877/816-7908
Seven colorful cabins, nestled into the foothills of the Cascades, offer privacy and seclusion. Lie in one of the huge log beds, or sit in a comfortable leather chair in front of the gas fireplace. Take a bath in the jetted tub. Nibble on the goodies in your welcome basket. Watch satellite TV. Breakfasts are served in a separate building. *$$$$; AE, DIS, MC, V; no checks; www.carsonridgecabins. com; off SR 14, left onto Carson Junction, 1.2 miles on left.* &

White Salmon and Bingen

High on a bluff overlooking the Columbia River, the towns of White Salmon and Bingen are the retail centers of Klickitat County. They're also in the heart of the **COLUMBIA RIVER GORGE NATIONAL SCENIC AREA** (902 Wasco St, Ste 200, Hood River; 541/308-1700). The **WHITE SALMON RIVER** is one of the state's most popular rafting and kayaking destinations, April through October. Two of the best outfitters are **ZOLLER'S OUTDOOR ODYSSEYS** (1248 SR 141, BZ Corner; 509/493-2641 or 800/366-2004; www.zooraft.com; north of White Salmon) and **WET PLANET** (860 SR 141, north of White Salmon; 509/493-8989 or 877/390-9445; www.wetplanetwhitewater.com; on right side of hwy just before crossing river at Husum Falls).

At **RAY KLEBBA'S WHITE SALMON BOAT WORKS** (230 E Jewett Blvd, White Salmon; 509/493-4766; www.raysdreamboats.com), the staff can teach you how to make your own woodstrip-construction sea kayak or canoe. **NORTHWESTERN LAKE RIDING STABLES** (126 Little Buck Creek Rd, White Salmon; 509/493-4965;

www.nwstables.com) offers backcountry horseback-riding packages ranging from one hour to overnight.

If a less strenuous outing is in order, visit **WIND RIVER CELLARS** (196 Spring Creek Rd, Husum; 509/493-2324; www.windrivercellars.com) or **GORGE WINE MERCHANTS** (218 W Steuben St, Bingen; 509/493-5333; www.gorgewine merchants.com). Jewett Boulevard in White Salmon has several shops worth checking out, including **WHITE SALMON GLASSWORKS** (105 E Jewett Blvd, White Salmon; 509/493-8400; www.whitesalmonglass.com), **COLLAGE OF THE GORGE** (111 E Jewett Blvd, White Salmon; 509/493-4483), and **NAYLOR ART** (157 Jewett St, White Salmon; 509/493-4567; www.naylorart.com).

The **MOUNT ADAMS CHAMBER OF COMMERCE** (1 Heritage Plaza, White Salmon; 509/493-3630 or 866/493-3630; www.mtadamschamber.com; SR 14 at milepost 65) has information.

RESTAURANTS

Viento Burger & Steak Bar / UNRATED

216 W STEUBEN ST, BINGEN; 509/493-0049

Mandy Ross purchased the former Viento's in 2008 and changed the focus. Now it's a counter-service casual dining restaurant, and everything is made in-house. American comfort food in this case includes three kinds of fries: potato, sweet potato, and chickpea. It also includes better-than-competent burgers and steaks, local microbrews, and Columbia Gorge wines. Viento is a rare gem in a small town, located between two main windsurfing launches, with a menu that is an active traveler's dream come true. *$; MC, V; no checks; lunch, dinner Tues–Sun; beer and wine; no reservations; www.vientokitchen. com; on SR 14 at Alder St.* &

LODGINGS

Inn of the White Salmon / ★

172 W JEWETT BLVD, WHITE SALMON; 509/493-2335 OR 800/972-5226

Since 1990, owners Roger and Janet Holden have retained their inn's old-time charm. Although the antique furnishings and photographs are fascinating and the 15 guest rooms, including the eight-bed hostel room, are bright, the dark hallways give it a cloistered feel. It's not the best place for a romantic evening, but it's good for adventure seekers who want a homey place to stay while exploring the gorge. An outdoor hot tub, a computer for guest use, and wi-fi Internet access are pluses. Breakfast is included for the private rooms. *$–$$$; MC, V; checks OK; www.innofthewhitesalmon.com; left off SR 14, 1½ miles uphill.*

Trout Lake

LODGINGS

Serenity's / ★★☆

2291 SR 141, TROUT LAKE; 509/395-2500 OR 800/276-7993
Situated in a serene setting in the woods, these four sweet chalet cabins are nonsmoking and offer a gas-log fireplace as well as a small refrigerator, a microwave, and a coffee maker. Music and movies can be had, but you'll appreciate the fact that there are no phones—the tranquil surroundings work wonders. Windows in each cabin have lovely views of Mount Adams. Fresh flowers and chocolates are nice touches. Marcy Nordwall and Carmella DePersia are gracious hosts who have created a magical and memorable haven. *$$; MC, V; checks OK; www.serenitys.com; off SR 141, 23 miles north of White Salmon.* ⅃

Glenwood

LODGINGS

Mount Adams Lodge at Flying L Ranch / ★★☆

25 FLYING L LN, GLENWOOD; 509/364-3488
This sprawling mountain ranch east of Trout Lake is a homey haven. When TVs and phones are absent, your family feels closer. Seven guest rooms populate the main lodge building, five are in the guesthouse, and four cabins complete the roster. Most rooms have their own baths, and a full-size kitchen is in the lodge. Bird-watching, mountain gazing, berry picking, bike riding, and hot tubbing are the main draws, but you could also play volleyball or badminton, or take a walk on a loop trail around the property. Big breakfasts are likely to include huckleberry pancakes served in the cozy kitchen house. Meadow and mountain views are gorgeous. *$$–$$$; AE, MC, V; checks OK; www.mt-adams.com; east through Glenwood about ¼ mile toward Goldendale, turn north, proceed ½ mile to driveway on right.*

Lyle

Little more than a town to whiz past on your way through the Columbia Gorge, Lyle also serves as a gateway into the Gifford Pinchot National Forest.

LODGINGS

Lyle Hotel / ★★

100 7TH ST, LYLE; 509/365-5953 OR 800/447-6310
In the middle of seemingly nowhere, on SR 14 east of White Salmon, the Lyle Hotel provides Columbia Gorge adventure seekers an affordable resting

place. This quaint, 100-year-old hotel has been seeing some wonderful changes. Antique furniture and colorful quilts adorn the 10 rooms. You'll share bathrooms, but you can make up for it by asking for a room with a river view. The outdoor patio and restaurant (dinner Wed–Sun; beer and wine; reservations recommended) are sweet spots to enjoy a good meal and glass of wine. *$$; AE, DIS, MC, V; checks OK; www.lylehotel.com; 2 blocks south of SR 14.*

Goldendale

Though Goldendale, on Hwy 97 10½ miles north of SR 14, is the seat of Klickitat County, it's not a case of bright lights, big city. This makes it the perfect location for **GOLDENDALE OBSERVATORY STATE PARK** (602 Observatory Dr, Goldendale; 509/773-3141; www.parks.wa.gov; Wed–Sun in summer, Sat–Sun by appointment in winter).

On your way to the nearby **MARYHILL MUSEUM OF ART** (35 Maryhill Museum Dr, Goldendale; 509/773-3733; www.maryhillmuseum.org; Mar–Nov), stop at the **MARYHILL WINERY** (877/627-9445; www.maryhillwinery.com) next door. Both are near the junction of SR 14 and Hwy 97. About 2 miles east of the Maryhill Museum on SR 14 is a life-size replica of England's neolithic **STONEHENGE**, built to honor fallen World War I soldiers from Klickitat County and as an antiwar memorial.

RESTAURANTS

St. John's Bakery, Coffee & Gifts / ★★★

2378 HWY 97, GOLDENDALE; 509/773-6650

Stop at this little café and gift shop for the best Greek food you've ever had. Greek Orthodox nuns, who live at the monastery behind the café, spend their days praying and baking authentic delicacies like eggplant lasagne, spanakopita, and baklava. They also sell religious items like icons and their homemade soaps, lotions, and candles. You'll know your money goes toward a good cause: the 18 nuns and novices at St. John's Monastery support themselves solely by their handiwork and donations. They practice the traditional arts of the Orthodox church, including writing Byzantine icons, knotting prayer ropes, making incense, and dipping beeswax candles. They also mount icon prints, make natural soap and lotion, and bake traditional Greek food and sweets for their bakery and gift shop. *$; MC, V; local checks only; breakfast, lunch Mon–Sat; no alcohol; no reservations; www.stjohn monastery.org/store.html; between mileposts 23 and 24.*

SOUTHEAST WASHINGTON

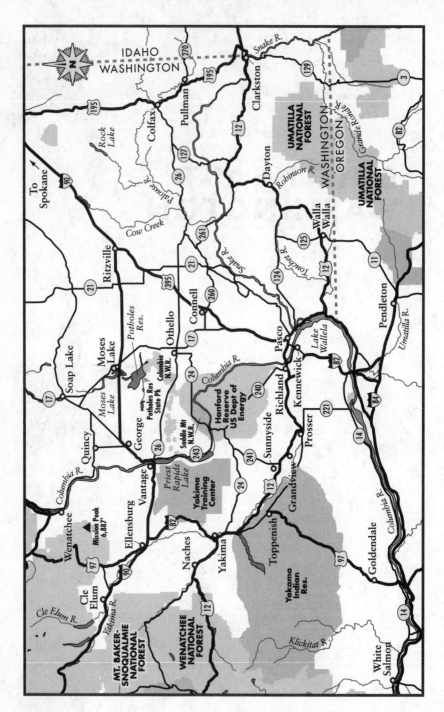

SOUTHEAST WASHINGTON

Southeast Washington, home to most of the state's wineries and two major universities, stretches from the upper reaches of the Naches (pronounced "na-CHEESE") River in the northwest, east to Ellensburg, Vantage, and George, and across the Palouse hills to Pullman, south to include the northernmost part of the Blue Mountains, west through Walla Walla and the Tri-Cities (Pasco, Kennewick, and Richland) to the eastern end of the Columbia Gorge, and north up the Yakima Valley.

Three large rivers, the Yakima, the Snake, and the Walla Walla, join the Columbia River near the Tri-Cities. Huge pumping stations move water from these rivers through a system of canals and center-pivot sprinklers to irrigate crops throughout central Washington. Locks and dams completed in the 1970s on the Columbia and Snake rivers allow tugs to push barges carrying diesel fuel and other commodities upriver as far as Clarkston, returning downriver with wood chips, lumber, grain, and other agricultural products.

Dramatic basalt cliffs and stately bluffs tower above the rivers; wine grapes, orchard fruits, and numerous other crops thrive in the rich soil under the sunny skies. Long-established wheat and lentil fields in the deep soil on the rolling hills of the Palouse give way to more-recently planted vineyards and orchards in the shallower soil near Walla Walla, the Tri-Cities, and Yakima. Whoever comes here, whether to visit or to stay, cannot help but embrace the landscape, linger over the soft, long vistas, and savor the fruits of the sun and the earth.

ACCESS AND INFORMATION

Most people drive to Southeast Washington. Even if you fly, you'll probably need a car. **INTERSTATE 90** is the most practical route from Seattle, connecting at Ellensburg with **INTERSTATE 82**, which descends through the Yakima Valley to the Tri-Cities at the junction with **US HIGHWAY 395**. From there, Walla Walla is an easy trip via Interstate 82 and **US HIGHWAY 12**.

From Portland, **INTERSTATE 84** or the two-lane **STATE ROUTE 14** on the Washington side leads to Eastern Washington. If you're heading to Ellensburg or Yakima, turn north on **US HIGHWAY 97**. If your destination is the Tri-Cities, take Interstate 82/Hwy 395. It snows a lot in Central Washington, so carry tire chains and food between November and April.

The **TRI-CITIES AIRPORT** (3601 N 20th Ave, Pasco; 509/547-6352; www. portofpasco.org/aphome.htm) is served by Horizon Air, Delta Connection, United Express, and Allegiant Air. **HORIZON AIR** (800/547-9308; www. horizonair.com) also serves the region's smaller airports, including Walla Walla and Yakima.

Most major car rental companies operate out of the Tri-Cities Airport. The **PASCO TRAIN STATION** (535 N 1st Ave, Pasco) serves **AMTRAK** (800/USA-RAIL; www.amtrak.com) and **GREYHOUND** (509/547-3151 or 800/231-2222; www.greyhound.com). The local public transit company is **BEN FRANKLIN TRANSIT** (509/735-5100; www.bft.org). The **TRI-CITIES VISITOR AND CONVENTION BUREAU** (6951 W Grandridge Blvd, Kennewick; 509/735-8186 or 800/254-5824; www.visittri-cities.com) has information.

Columbia Plateau

The Columbia Plateau (also called the Columbia Basin) is a flood-basalt plateau between the Cascades and the northern Rocky Mountains. In Washington, the plateau is primarily rich agricultural land irrigated by the Columbia River via more than 2,000 miles of canals to a million acres of fields.

Vantage and George

Sitting on a scenic stretch west of the Columbia just north of I-90, Vantage offers a gorgeous view of the river. Have a picnic at the nearby **GINKGO PETRIFIED FOREST STATE PARK** (I-90 exit 136; 509/856-2700; www.parks.wa.gov), a dinosaur-inspired interpretive center that's open every day during the summer.

A small town named after the country's first president, George is just off I-90 on the eastern bluffs above the Columbia. The area boasts the naturally terraced **GORGE AMPHITHEATER** (754 Silica Rd NW, George; www.livenation.com) with a view overlooking the Columbia Gorge. Big names of all musical genres play here; arrive early to avoid traffic jams. Other caveats should be noted: restrooms are scarce, and locals have reached the end of their patience with rowdy concertgoers. **TICKETMASTER** (206/628-0888; www.ticketmaster.com) has tickets. George is a three-hour drive from Seattle and two hours from Spokane. For those wanting to stay the night, two options are available: the **GORGE CAMPGROUND** (509/785-2267), which charges $35 per car per night, or the new **CAVE B INN AT SAGECLIFFE** (see review).

LODGINGS

Cave B Inn at SageCliffe / ★★★

344 SILICA RD NW, QUINCY; 509/785-2283 OR 888/785-2283
Inside, a rock fireplace 30 feet high anchors the main lobby. Outside, vineyards and orchards surround a main lodge that echoes the shapes, textures, and colors of the bluffs and river in the view west. Each of the 12 cavelike guest rooms, one of the three suites, and another 15 separate houses offer panoramic views west through floor-to-ceiling windows. Two suites have views of the vineyards. An on-site restaurant serves regional fare with produce from the SageCliffe organic gardens. The inn also offers a wine-tasting bar and culinary demonstration kitchen. $$$$; AE, MC, V; no checks; www.cavebinn.com; I-90 exit 143. &. (2 rooms)

Ellensburg and Yakima Valleys

The Ellensburg and Yakima valleys descend through the eastern foothills of the Cascades to the Columbia River. This region produces cattle, hay, and more fruit trees than any other region in the country. Look for apples, mint, winter pears, and hops. Attractions here reflect this bounty, including the **AMERICAN HOP MUSEUM** (22 S B St, Toppenish; 509/865-4677; www.americanhopmuseum. org) and the **CENTRAL WASHINGTON AGRICULTURAL MUSEUM** (4508 Main St, Yakima; 509/457-8735; www.centralwaagmuseum.org). The agriculture industry has drawn many migrant workers, resulting in a large Hispanic population and a culturally rich community. Visit the **YAKIMA VALLEY VISITORS AND CONVENTION BUREAU** (10 N 8th St, Yakima; 800/221-0751; www.visityakima.com).

Ellensburg

In its early years, Ellensburg almost became the state capital. In 1890 the city lobbied for this honor until a fire hit its downtown, then Olympia won the honor. Today hay and cowboys dominate this small town in the Kittitas Valley. For culture, look no farther than **CENTRAL WASHINGTON UNIVERSITY** (400 E University Wy; 509/963-1262 or 866/298-4968; www.cwu.edu), where you'll find the serene Japanese Garden and the **SARAH SPURGEON GALLERY** (Randall Hall; 509/963-2665; www.cwu.edu/~art/gallery.html), which holds art exhibits yearround. Another must-visit is the **CHIMPANZEE AND HUMAN COMMUNICATIONS INSTITUTE** (400 E University Wy; 509/963-2244; www.cwu.edu/~cwuchci), where humans and chimps communicate through American Sign Language.

Art can be found in Ellensburg off-campus as well. The **CLYMER MUSEUM OF ART** (416 N Pearl St; 509/962-6416; www.clymermuseum.com) honors John Clymer, Ellensburg's chronicler of the western frontier whose work appeared in the *Saturday Evening Post*. **GALLERY ONE** (408 N Pearl St; 509/925-2670; www. gallery-one.org) sells regional crafts and displays contemporary art.

Locals recommend the **TAV** (117 W 4th Ave; 509/925-3939) for its attractive crew of servers and reasonably priced burgers, or try the funky **D&M COFFEE** (215 W 3rd Ave; 509/925-5313).

Annual events include the **WESTERN ART SHOW** in May, **JAZZ IN THE VALLEY** in late July, and the **ELLENSBURG RODEO** each Labor Day weekend. Ellensburg is also popular for skiing, rafting, hiking, and fly-fishing for trout. Contact the **ELLENSBURG CHAMBER OF COMMERCE** (609 N Main St; 509/925-2002 or 888/925-2204; www.ellensburg-chamber.com) for details.

RESTAURANTS

Pearl's on Pearl Wine Bar & Bistro / ★★

311 N PEARL ST; ELLENSBURG; 509/962-8899
Locals appreciate the variety of Pearl's ever-changing menu. You might start with a sun-dried tomato tart, spicy lemon shrimp, or farfalle pasta with smoked salmon and sautéed veggies in champagne cream sauce, then move on to an entrée featuring catfish, venison, or crab legs. After dinner, nibble some cheesecake, or luxuriate at the bar. *$$; AE, MC, V; local checks only; dinner every day (June–Sept; Mon–Sat winter); full bar; no reservations; www. pearlsonpearl.com; between 3rd and 4th aves.* &

SOUTHEAST WASHINGTON THREE-DAY TOUR

DAY ONE: Start your morning with breakfast at Ellensburg's **DAKOTA CAFÉ** (417 N Pearl St; 509/925-4783; www.dakotacafe.net), followed by a stroll through downtown's shops. Head to **CENTRAL WASHINGTON UNIVERSITY** and watch a **CHIMPOSIUM**. Next, drive 30 miles to Yakima via the Yakima River **CANYON ROAD**, stopping along the way to enjoy the scenery. Have a leisurely lunch at the **DEPOT RESTAURANT AND LOUNGE** in Yakima's **NORTH FRONT STREET HISTORICAL DISTRICT**. Then take the **YAKIMA TROLLEY** (S 3rd Ave at Pine St, Yakima; 509/249-5656; www.yakimavalleytrolleys.org) to Selah and back in the summer. Listed on the National Register of Historic Places, it's one of the last turn-of-the-20th-century interurban railroads left in the United States. Drive to the **WINE SHOP OF YAKIMA** (5110 Tieton Dr, Ste 260, Yakima; 509/972-2811) for an overview of the area's wine industry. Finally, drive east a short way and check in to **BIRCHFIELD MANOR COUNTRY INN** for the evening and enjoy dinner there.

DAY TWO: Begin your day with a stroll along the 10-mile Yakima **GREENWAY**, a great walking and running path paralleling the Yakima River. For a yummy pastry and hot cup of coffee, visit **ESSENCIA ARTISAN BAKERY & CHOCOLATERIE** in downtown Yakima, then jump in your car and head south on I-82 about

The Valley Café / ★★

105 W 3RD AVE, ELLENSBURG; 509/925-3050
Valley Café's fine 1930s art deco interior design complements the dining, while candlelit mahogany booths and back bar supply rich accents. For lunch, try the sandwiches and salads—the lemon tahini dressing is marvelous—or the specialty quiche. Dinner could be fresh seafood or Ellensburg lamb. Afterward, crème brûlée and fresh fruit pies present major temptations. Owner Greg Beach also owns a wine and takeout shop next door, so the length of the café's wine list is no surprise. *$$; AE, DIS, MC, V, checks OK; lunch, dinner every day; beer and wine; no reservations; www.valleycafe.org; ½ block east of Main St.*

Yellow Church Café / ★

111 S PEARL ST; ELLENSBURG; 509/933-2233
Despite meals that sound religious—St. Benedict's Eggs, the Last Supper—a secular experience awaits you at the Yellow Church Café. This picturesque church was built for German Lutherans in 1923 but has since served the community in many ways: it's been an office, a home, and an art gallery. Preachers' kids now own the restaurant, so the place's history seems fitting. Scratch cooking and baking underlie a menu that encompasses steaks, seafood, chicken, and pasta. High on the wall, a quote may remind you of where you

15 miles. Detour through Toppenish to view some of the 64 **MURALS** adorning city buildings, then head to the **YAKAMA NATION CULTURAL HERITAGE CENTER** and visit the museum. It's one of the few in the state run by Native Americans. Keep heading south and drive another 15 miles through Sunnyside, where you can visit **DARIGOLD'S DAIRY FAIR** and tour the cheese factory. Continue east about 35 miles and end your drive by checking in to the **COURTYARD RICHLAND COLUMBIA POINT**, overlooking the river. Before you turn in, have dinner at nearby **KATYA'S BISTRO & WINE BAR**.

DAY THREE: Take another morning stroll, this time along the **WATERFRONT TRAIL** right outside your hotel. After stopping at **GLORIA'S LA DOLCE VITA** (743 the Pkwy, Richland; 509/943-7400) for breakfast, head to the **COLUMBIA RIVER EXHIBITION OF HISTORY, SCIENCE & TECHNOLOGY**. Next, head east about 50 miles on Hwy 12 to Walla Walla. En route, stop at the **WHITMAN MISSION NATIONAL HISTORIC SITE**, where 19th-century missionaries and Native Americans clashed. Lunch in downtown Walla Walla at **MERCHANTS DELICATESSEN**, then visit the historic buildings of **FORT WALLA WALLA**. Check in to the restored 1928 **MARCUS WHITMAN HOTEL**, and finish your day with dinner at **CREEK TOWN CAFÉ**.

are and what might happen next: "In an ordinary day, there are a thousand miracles." *$; AE, MC, V; local checks only; breakfast Sat–Sun, lunch, dinner every day; beer and wine; reservations recommended; www.yellowchurchcafe. com; at E 1st Ave.* &

LODGINGS

The Inn at Goose Creek / ★

1720 CANYON RD, ELLENSBURG; 509/962-8030 OR 800/533-0822
Despite being next to I-90 between a motel and a gas station, the Inn at Goose Creek makes guests welcome and comfortable. With 10 themed guest rooms, one will suit your mood: the I Love Christmas room cheers with yuletide spirit, including the music, year-round; the Ellensburg Rodeo room whoops it up with a cowboy motif; the All-Star Sports Fan room plays to win. The Victorian Honeymoon room inspires romance with lace and a canopied bed. People don't stay here for the view but, rather, for the whimsy. *$$; AE, DC, MC, V; checks OK; www.innatgoosecreek.com; I-90 exit 109, then north.* &

Yakima

When approaching Yakima via I-82 from the north, you're greeted by a sign that reads "Yakima, the Palm Springs of Washington." Though the folks in Palm Springs haven't reciprocated that sentiment, Yakima still enjoys more than 300 days of sunshine annually. For first-time visitors, stop at exit 33, where you'll see the **NORTH FRONT STREET HISTORICAL DISTRICT** and several classy restaurants and shops. At the **DEPOT RESTAURANT AND LOUNGE** (32 N Front St; 509/949-4233; www.depotrestaurantandlounge.com), in the renovated **1910 YAKIMA TRAIN STATION,** you'll find great food. Next door at Yakima Avenue and East B Street is a 22-car train that houses more restaurants and shops. The **YAKIMA VALLEY MUSEUM** (2105 Tieton Dr; 509/248-0747; www.yakimavalleymuseum. org) features pioneer equipment, costumes, a children's underground museum, and an old-fashioned soda fountain.

The **GREENWAY** (509/453-8280; www.yakimagreenway.org) is a 10-mile-long paved path for walkers, runners, and cyclists that stretches along the Naches and Yakima rivers from Selah Gap to Union Gap. The Greenway offers excellent views of wildlife, including bald eagles. Entrance points are at **SARG HUBBARD PARK** (111 S 18th St), **SHERMAN PARK** (E Nob Hill Blvd), **ROTARY LAKE** (on R St), and **HARLAN LANDING** (west side of I-82 between Selah and Yakima).

Yakima has many places to stay; one of the nicest is the **HOLIDAY INN EXPRESS** (1001 E A St; 509/249-1000).

RESTAURANTS

Barrel House / ★★

22 N FIRST ST, YAKIMA; 509/453-3769

Built in 1906, the historic structure housing this restaurant first held a saloon and hotel. Traces of the structure's history remain: the stamped-tin ceiling, the cowboy gun safe . . . and what may be Washington's largest urinal. Now a swanky little restaurant, the Barrel House appeals to the urbane with a whole lot of class. The cheese course includes three cheeses—a soft, a veined, and a hard—served individually or all together, base the cheese course; appetizers might be portobello pear sauté, bruschetta, or smoked salmon. The daily soups are tasty, as are the chipotle cobb and seared-scallop spinach salads. Entrées range from flatiron steak to pork shank with Creole risotto and sweet chile chicken to scallops Florentine. *$$; MC, V; no checks; lunch, dinner Mon–Sat; beer and wine; no reservations; www.thebarrelhouse.net; near Yakima Ave.* ♿

Birchfield Manor Country Inn / ★★

2018 BIRCHFIELD RD, YAKIMA; 509/452-1960 OR 800/375-3420

Birchfield Manor's antiques-packed dining room also fills with the solid aromas of French-country cuisine featuring Northwest ingredients and influences. Choose from a seasonally changing menu of multi-course dinners featuring steak, fish, foul, and lamb entrées. Each meal also includes a basket of

TRAVELING BACK IN TIME

Immortalized in photos by Ansel Adams, the **YAKIMA RIVER CANYON ROAD** is one of several Washington state scenic byways. This 25-mile stretch of breathtaking scenery along SR 821 parallels the Yakima River, connecting the towns of Ellensburg and Yakima. Before I-82 was built, this was the main route, and its winding, narrow roadway still slows you down today. Enjoy taking your time: if you look sharp, you might see eagles, bighorn sheep, nesting hawks, falcons, deer, and elk.

Four primitive **CAMPING SITES** run by the Bureau of Land Management (915 N Walla Walla Ave, Wenatchee; 509/665-2100) are great places to stop and soak in the scenery, watch rafters float by, or join the local fly fishers. The area is known as a blue-ribbon catch-and-release trout stream.

Each year, thousands of people visit the Yakima River Canyon to see the immense basalt cliffs, some rising more than 2,000 feet above the river. Depending on the season and the time of day, the colors of the steep rock change, enhanced by shadows, sun, clouds, and your own point of view.

Get really close by renting a rubber raft and floating part of the Yakima River. Stop at **RED'S FLY SHOP** (on Canyon Rd near mile marker 15, Ellensburg; 509/929-1802; www.redsflyshop.com) for equipment rentals and details. You'll be floating on a class I river—so easy, it's almost like sitting in your bathtub. Besides camping, Red's also offers a few small cabins for rent. During the summer, human armadas can be seen floating the river.

Mother Nature's work doesn't get much better.

—Rick Stedman

house-crafted bread and butter, an appetizer *du jour*, a specialty salad, a fresh vegetable side, and hand-dipped chocolates for dessert (in addition to more elaborate sweets). The Inn offers five B and B rooms above the restaurant and six cottage rooms in a separate building. Fireplaces warm some rooms; some have two-person whirlpool tubs. Guests also have access to an outdoor pool. *$$$$; AE, DIS, MC, V; checks OK; dinner Thurs–Sat; beer and wine; reservations recommended; www.birchfieldmanor.com; I-82 exit 34 onto SR 24, then 2 miles east of town.* &

Café Melange / ★★

7 N FRONT ST, YAKIMA; 509/453-0571

Café Melange brings an intimate yet casual Mediterranean influence to Yakima's North Front Street Historical District. Ed's Cheap Dates—dates stuffed with walnuts and goat cheese, then baked in a bacon wrap—will certainly whet your appetite for main courses such as shiitake tenderloin, aioli-baked salmon, and wild mushroom meat loaf. After dinner and a made-from-scratch dessert, stroll the historical promenade outside. *$$; AE, DIS, MC, V; checks OK; lunch, dinner Mon–Sat; full bar; reservations recommended; www.cafe melangeyakima.com; I-82 exit 33B, then 1 mile west.* &

Essencia Artisan Bakery & Chocolaterie / ★★

4 N 3RD ST, YAKIMA; 509/575-5570

Long fermentation complicates the flavor of the dough; the enjoyment of it remains simple. That's the essence of fine baking. To prove the syllogism, Essencia's breads and pastries are baked by artisans in their stone-and-steam oven, using fresh local ingredients whenever possible. Savor a hot or cold drink concocted from the intense, house-made chocolate essence with your bread or pastry. It'll be a while before you eat as well again. *$; MC, V; no checks; breakfast, lunch Mon–Fri; no alcohol; no reservations; www.essenciabakery. com; downtown.* &

Greystone Restaurant / ★★★

5 N FRONT ST, YAKIMA; 509/248-9801

At Greystone, mahogany trim, 19th-century furniture, and soft lighting contribute to the ambience in a building that dates back to 1899. The crab cakes have been a specialty for years, but that needn't keep you from rack of lamb, pan-seared salmon, or filet mignon. Don't leave without trying the hot Yakima apple cake: served with hot rum caramel sauce and vanilla ice cream, it sets a new standard for desserts. *$$–$$$; DIS, MC, V; local checks only; lunch Mon–Fri, dinner Mon–Sat; full bar; reservations recommended; www. greystonedining.com; at Yakima Ave.*

LODGINGS

Orchard Inn Bed & Breakfast / ★★

1207 PECKS CANYON RD, YAKIMA; 509/966-1283 OR 866/966-1283

This productive cherry orchard makes an intriguing setting for a B and B. Serenely quiet guest rooms, with private baths and jetted tubs, are just minutes west of downtown Yakima. The separate B and B entrance leads to a cozy living room with a library of books on travel, wine, cuisine, fishing, and music. This is a perfect four-season destination. The German innkeepers also offer cherry-related products like chocolate-covered cherries and cherry jam for sale. *$$; MC, V, checks OK; www.orchardinnbb.com; Hwy 12 exit at 40th St, then ¾ mile to Powerhouse Rd.*

A Touch of Europe B&B / ★★★

220 N 16TH AVE, YAKIMA; 509/454-9775 OR 888/438-7073

This Queen Anne Victorian mansion was built in 1889. In 1995 Jim and Erika Cenci opened it as a B and B. Three antique-filled guest rooms have private baths and air-conditioning; the Prince Victorian Mahogany Room has a gas fireplace. Erika, an internationally renowned chef who was raised in Germany, has written several cookbooks. Her sumptuous multicourse breakfasts are served in the dining room or privately in the turret by candlelight. Erica also prepares luncheons, traditional high teas, and three- to seven-course dinners by prior arrangement. *$$$; AE, MC, V; checks OK; www.winesnw. com/toucheuropeb&b.htm; I-82 exit 31, then west on Hwy 12.*

Naches

For information on hiking trails and other outdoor activities, stop at the **NACHES RANGER DISTRICT** (10237 Hwy 12; 509/653-1400), where they provide maps and more on the Okanogan and Wenatchee national forests.

LODGINGS

Whistlin' Jack Lodge / ★★

20800 SR 410, CHINOOK PASS; 509/658-2433 OR 800/827-2299
This 1931 mountain hideaway has been Whistlin' Jack Lodge since 1957. Come for the nearby hiking, alpine and cross-country skiing, and fishing, or just to escape civilization. Weekend rates vary by room type: cottage, bungalow, or motel unit. Cottages, which have full kitchens and hot tubs, are close to the river and make great private retreats. Guests who want to dine out opt for motel rooms or bungalows. Whistlin' Jack's restaurant serves a specialty panfried trout, with live music on weekends. The lodge also has a convenience store and a 24-hour gas pump. *$$; AE, DIS, MC, V; local checks only; www.whistlinjacklodge.com; 27 miles west of Yakima via Hwy 12 then SR 410.*

Toppenish

The town's best-known native son, western artist Fred Oldfield, has turned Toppenish's streets into an art gallery with more than 60 historical murals. These efforts by the **TOPPENISH MURAL SOCIETY** (5A Toppenish Ave; 509/865-3262) complement stores selling western gear, antiques, and art, making this a nice place for a walking tour and giving an authentic feel to summer rodeos.

The **YAKAMA NATION CULTURAL HERITAGE CENTER** (100 Spiel-yi Loop; 509/865-2800; www.yakamamuseum.com; off Hwy 97 and Buster Rd) includes a Native American museum and restaurant, reference library, gift shop, theater, and the 76-foot-tall Winter Lodge for banquets. Nearby is the tribe-run **LEGENDS CASINO** (580 Fort Rd; 509/865-8800 or 877/7COME11; www.yakamalegends. com). **FORT SIMCOE STATE PARK** (May–Sept), a frontier military post built in 1865, stands in desolate grandeur 30 miles west of Toppenish on the Yakama Indian Reservation. Off Hwy 97 in Toppenish (north- or southbound), take Fort Road west. Drive about 20 miles to the city of White Swan. In White Swan, keep an eye out for signs to the park.

Yakima Valley Wine Country

The Yakima Valley wine country is a sub-appellation of the Columbia Valley Appellation (APA)—a viticulture region or wine-producing region with a distinct growing climate—which stretches southwest from Yakima to the Tri-Cities and encompasses Zillah, Sunnyside, Grandview, Prosser, and Benton City. Washington boasts more than 500 wineries, with most of them along the Yakima River. **WINE YAKIMA VALLEY**'s (800/258-7270; www.wineyakimavalley.org) excellent Web site lists details (see "Southeast Washington Three-Day Wine Tour" for recommendations). Most valley wineries are family-owned and run.

Zillah

RESTAURANTS

El Porton / UNRATED

905 VINTAGE VALLEY PKWY, ZILLAH; 509/829-6226

The locals throng this brightly painted restaurant in Zillah. Fabulous giant *taquitos* bring in some diners; the splendid mole and really hot salsa bring more. In an area where authentic Mexican cuisine is common, the food here is uncommonly good. *$; MC, V; local checks only; lunch, dinner Mon–Sat; full bar; no reservations; I-82 exit 52, then north.* &

Outlook, Sunnyside, and Grandview

This is true farm country, with sights and aromas to match. If you need a snack, stop at **DARIGOLD'S DAIRY FAIR** (400 Alexander Rd, Sunnyside; 509/837-4321; every day) for sandwiches, old-fashioned ice cream, free cheese samplings, and self-guided tours of the factory.

RESTAURANTS

Dykstra House Restaurant / ★

114 BIRCH AVE, GRANDVIEW; 509/882-2082

Dykstra House, a 1914 Craftsman formerly owned by a Grandview mayor, is listed in the National Register of Historic Places. Owner Linda Hartshorn makes bread from hand-ground whole wheat harvested in the surrounding hills. Her entrées take advantage of other local in-season produce, such as asparagus. Dessert favorites include apple caramel pecan torte and Dykstra House chocolate pie, which has been on the menu since she opened the place in 1984. *$$; AE, DC, DIS, MC, V; checks OK; lunch Tues–Sat, dinner Fri–Sat; beer and wine; reservations recommended; I-82 exit 75.*

La Fogata Mexican Restaurant / ★

1204 YAKIMA VALLEY HWY, SUNNYSIDE; 509/839-9019
This small, simple Mexican taqueria is rich with coral walls—and Michoacan specialties such as posole, a stew of pork back and feet plus hominy. Less adventurous diners won't go wrong with the excellent tacos and burritos. *$; MC, V; checks OK; breakfast, lunch, dinner Wed–Mon; full bar; no reservations; middle of town.*

Snipes Mountain Microbrewery & Restaurant / ★

905 YAKIMA VALLEY HWY, SUNNYSIDE; 509/837-2739
Snipes is expansive from every angle. A huge stone fireplace and exposed rafters lend a mountain-lodge feel to the brew-pub reality. Terry Butler, head brewer, brews small batches of handcrafted beers on-site, and the food takes good steak-house fare a step beyond itself. Meals can be as fancy as you choose, ranging from wood-fired pizza to hazelnut-crusted rack of lamb with mustard demi-glace. *$–$$; AE, DIS, MC, V; checks OK; lunch, dinner every day; beer and wine; no reservations; www.snipesmountain.com; I-82 exit 63 or 69.* ♿

LODGINGS

Cozy Rose Private Country Suites / ★

1220 FORSELL RD, GRANDVIEW; 509/822-4669 OR 800/575-8381
Owners Mark and Jennie Jackson offer four suites, each with a private entrance, bathroom, fireplace, cable TV, and stereo. Splurge and get the separate two-bedroom Irish House cottage, with its private outdoor hot tub and deck. Breakfast in your room might be French toast, omelets, or pecan pancakes. The Jacksons grow their own strawberries, herbs, and apples. After breakfast, visit the llamas. Later, take a romantic walk in the nearby vineyard, or slip off to tour others of the 40 wineries and vineyards within 30 miles of the inn. *$$$–$$$$; MC, V; checks OK; www.cozyroseinn.com; I-82 exit 69.*

Prosser

Who could resist a quick stop in Prosser, the "pleasant place with pleasant people"? Wine-tasting rooms are east and north of town in scenic vineyards. Sample world-class wines at **SNOQUALAMIE VINEYARDS** (660 Frontier Rd; 509/786-5558 or 800/852-0885), **OLSEN ESTATES** (500 Merlot Dr; 509/786-7007) and **HOGUE CELLARS** (2800 Lee Rd; 509/786-4557), among some 25 others. In June and July, don't miss the tasting room at **CHUKAR CHERRIES** (320 Wine Country Rd; 800/624-9544; www.chukar.com) for samples of the heavenly local Bing and Rainier cherries. You'll find a tasty menu (breakfast, lunch, and dinner) of iconic American foods at **BLUE GOOSE** (306 7th St; 509/786-1774; NE corner of Wine Country Rd and 7th St). Stop by the Prosser Chamber of Commerce Depot (1230 Bennett Ave; 509/786-3177 or 800/408-1517; downtown) for wine maps and more information.

SOUTHEAST WASHINGTON THREE-DAY WINE TOUR

When driving along I-82 toward Washington wine country, you know you've arrived when you see the first huge sign just before exit 33: "Welcome to Washington Wine Country." Although the **SPRING BARREL TASTING** (last weekend in Apr) and **THANKSGIVING IN WINE COUNTRY** are two of the largest draws, any weekend during late spring and summer is good, especially if you want to avoid crowds. One of the best ways to visit a sampling of the 40-plus wineries is by limousine. Several limo companies offer four-hour trips. Some favorites include **MOONLIT RIDE LIMOUSINE** (3908 River Rd, Yakima; 509/575-6846; www.moonlitride.com) and **PACIFIC LIMOUSINE** (Tri-Cities; 509/585-7717; www.limo01.com).

When devising an itinerary on your own, here are some great places to visit:

DAY ONE: Start in downtown Yakima at **ESSENCIA ARTISAN BAKERY & CHOCOLATERIE** with a cup of espresso and a croissant (grab a baguette to-go while you're at it), then head to the tasting room at **KANA WINERY** (10 S 2nd St, Yakima; 509/453-6611; www.kanawinery.com). Next, head south on I-82 for about 9 miles and take exit 40 to visit **SAGELANDS VINEYARD** (71 Gangl Rd, Wapato; 800/967-8115; www.sagelandsvineyard.com), with spectacular views of the Yakima Valley and Mount Adams. Have a picnic lunch there. Stay on Yakima Valley Hwy and drive up the hill to **WINDY POINT VINEYARDS** (420 Windy Pt Rd, Wapato; 509/877-6824; www.windypointvineyards.com). One winery you can't miss is **PIETY FLATS** (2560 Donald-Wapato Rd, Wapato; 509/877-3115; www.pietyflatswinery.com). Their tasting room is in the 1911 Donald Fruit Mercantile Building, which feels like an old country store. After dinner in Sunnyside at **LA FOGATA MEXICAN RESTAURANT**, drive toward Grandview to spend the night at the **COZY ROSE PRIVATE COUNTRY SUITES**.

DAY TWO: After a hearty breakfast in your room, head south and stop at nearby **TUCKER CELLARS WINERY** (70 Ray Rd, Sunnyside; 509/837-8701;

LODGINGS

The Vintner's Inn at Hinzerling Winery / ★

1524 SHERIDAN AVE, PROSSER; 509/786-2163 OR 800/727-6702
If you'd like an insider's view of life in wine country, the Vintner's Inn is the place. The winery is one of the region's oldest, and this 1907 Victorian-style home exudes decades-old charm. Quaint and comfortable, the three bedrooms upstairs come with private bathrooms. Downstairs, dinner is served Fridays and Saturdays by reservation only. The owner grows most of the

www.tuckercellars.com), one of the states's oldest wineries. Your next stop is about 10 miles south, in Prosser, at **SNOQUALMIE VINEYARDS** (660 Frontier Rd, Prosser; 509/786-5558 or 800/852-0885; www.snoqualmie.com), then head to **BLUE GOOSE** (306 7th St, Prosser; 509/786-1774) for salads, sandwiches, or burgers. After lunch, taste more obscure, boldly flavored wine at **HINZERLING WINERY** (1520 Sheridan Ave, Prosser; 509/786-2163 or 800/727-6702; www. hinzerling.com). Then continue east 15 miles to Benton City for **SETH RYAN WINERY** (35306 Sunset Rd, Benton City; 509/588-6780; www.sethryan.com) and **KIONA VINEYARDS** (44612 N Sunset Rd, Benton City; 509/588-6716; www.kionawine.com). Continue east some 20 miles to Pasco and check in at the **RED LION HOTEL PASCO**, then go back across the river for dinner in Richland at **TAGARIS WINERY** (844 Tulip Ln, Richland; 877/862-7999). The stylish tavern features a bistro and wine bar and serves gourmet pizzas and Pacific Northwest fare.

DAY THREE: After breakfast in the hotel, cross the river again to taste a few varieties at **BARNARD GRIFFIN WINERY** (878 Tulip Ln, Richland; 509/627-0266; www.barnardgriffin.com) before leaving the Tri-Cities. Drive about 50 miles south and east to Walla Walla, stopping at the bright yellow storefront of **CAYUSE VINEYARDS** (17 E Main St, Walla Walla; 509/526-0686; www.cayusevineyards. com) for some more sampling. Enjoy lunch across the street at **MERCHANTS DELICATESSEN**. Afterward, take a short drive south of town to visit **BASEL CELLARS ESTATE WINERY** (2901 Old Milton Hwy, Walla Walla; 509/522-0200 or 888/259-9463; www.baselcellars.com; tastings 10am–4pm every day), then return to downtown and stop at **CANOE RIDGE VINEYARD** (1102 W Cherry St, Walla Walla; 509/527-0885; www.canoeridgevineyard.com), which specializes in classic merlot. After a stroll down Main Street, head a short way east and check in to the cozy **INN AT BLACKBERRY CREEK**. To round out your evening and three-day journey, return to downtown and dine in elegance at **26 BRIX** before calling it a day.

herbs and vegetables used in the kitchen. *$$; DIS, MC, V; checks OK; www. hinzerling.com; just off Wine Country Rd.*

The Tri-Cities

The Tri-Cities' main attractions are its wineries, rivers, and golf courses. Its vineyards overlap the Red Mountain, Horse Heaven Hill, Rattlesnake Hills, Walla Walla, and Yakima Valley sub-appellations of the Columbia Valley APA, with tasting rooms throughout the area. Two notable ones include **BARNARD GRIFFIN**

(878 Tulip Ln, Richland; 509/627-0266) and **BADGER MOUNTAIN/POWERS WIN-ERY** (1106 S Jurupa St, Kennewick; 800/643-9463), Washington State's first certified organic winery. Three major rivers converge on the Tri-Cities, including the Yakima, the Snake, and the mighty Columbia. The area boasts seven golf courses and two championship putting ranges. But more intriguing, perhaps, is the area's history—from Lewis and Clark's stop at what is now **SACAJAWEA STATE PARK** (see Pasco) to Kennewick's annual hydroplane races to Richland's role in ending World War II with top-secret atomic research at Hanford. The region is made up of three cities—Pasco, Kennewick, and Richland—and two counties (Benton and Walla Walla), but the **TRI-CITIES VISITOR AND CONVEN-TION BUREAU** (6951 W Grandridge Blvd, Kennewick; 509/735-8486 or 800/254-5824; www.visittri-cities.com) pulls them together.

Richland

Richland was once a secret city, hidden away while atomic-bomb workers did research in the 1940s. The **COLUMBIA RIVER EXHIBITION OF HISTORY, SCIENCE & TECHNOLOGY** (95 Lee Blvd; 509/943-9000 or 877/789-9935; www.crehst.org) explains how the Tri-Cities area emerged during World War II when Hanford was created. **COLUMBIA RIVER JOURNEYS** (1229 Columbia Park Trail; 509/734-9941 or 888/486-9119; www.columbiariverjourneys.com; May–Oct) offers jet-boat tours through Hanford Reach, a preserved section of the Columbia River.

ALLIED ARTS GALLERY (89 Lee Blvd; 509/943-9815; www.alliedartsrichland. org) displays local artists' work and sponsors an annual July arts festival. Dining opportunities here include not just Mexican cuisine but also an excellent Thai restaurant, the **EMERALD OF SIAM** (1314 Jadwin Ave; 509/946-9328; www. emeraldofsiam.com).

RESTAURANTS

Atomic Ale Brewpub & Eatery / ★

1015 LEE BLVD, RICHLAND; 509/946-5465
The Atomic Ale Brewpub & Eatery holds the distinction of being the Tri-Cities' first brew pub. Standard pub fare gets a boost from specialties like wood-fired artisan pizzas and Atomic Ale red potato soup. As the name suggests, the Atomic Ale Brewpub capitalizes on the area's nuclear history, with many historical photos adorning its walls. Beers get radioactive names like Atomic Amber, Plutonium Porter, and Half-Life Hefeweizen. Everyone walks out glowing. *$; AE, DIS, MC, V; checks OK; lunch, dinner Mon–Sat; beer and wine; no reservations; I-82 exit at George Washington Wy.* &

Katya's Bistro & Wine Bar / ★★

430 GEORGE WASHINGTON WY, RICHLAND; 509/946-7777
Dishes are rooted in classic Italian, with French influences that play up fresh ingredients. Proprietor Stephen Hartley uses only certified Angus beef for the

impressive list of entrées: beef tenderloin, New York strip, rib-eye steak, steak Oscar, Three City flatiron steak. The Chilean sea bass and rack of lamb don't play second fiddle to the beef. The Ukrainian borscht, a house specialty, is no slouch either. Start with a spinach artichoke dip accompanied by warm kalamata olive bread. *$$$; AE, DIS, MC, V; local checks only; dinner Mon–Sat; beer and wine; reservations recommended; www.katyasbistro.com; between Davenport and Falley sts.*

LODGINGS

Courtyard Richland Columbia Point / ★

480 COLUMBIA PT DR, RICHLAND; 509/942-9400 OR 800/618-7723
This beautiful hotel perched on the Columbia River is located right across the street from the river—where residents walk, run, and bike the Waterfront Trail—and only a half mile from golf links. Convenience and low-key comfort are the real attraction at this easy-going hotel. An indoor pool, fitness center, and comfortable lounge are staple amenities, but some rooms also come with fireplaces. A complimentary breakfast buffet is served every day, and includes toast, bagels, yogurt, fresh fruit, scrambled eggs, and waffles, as well as juice and coffee. *$$$; AE, DIS, MC, V; checks OK; www.richlandmarriott.com; Hwy 12 W exit at George Washington Wy.* ⅊

Kennewick

Kennewick is the largest of the Tri-Cities, sharing a border with Richland and the magnificent Cable Bridge (lighted at night) with Pasco. Its many malls include Columbia Center, which draws shoppers from smaller towns, ranches, orchards, and vineyards throughout the area, who come to stock up and for the occasional entertainment of it all. Nearby **COLUMBIA PARK** (between SR 240 and Columbia River; 509/585-4293) also offers plenty of recreation and diversions, especially when you have kids in tow. At the park's east end, volunteers built the wooden castle-like **PLAYGROUND OF DREAMS** (near Hwy 395 blue bridge), with climbing structures and twisty slides. It's next to the **FAMILY FISHING POND**, where adults can teach children to catch and release. The park also is the site of July's **WATER FOLLIES** and **COLUMBIA CUP** (509/783-4675; www.waterfollies.com) featuring unlimited hydroplane races. Winter sports fans focus on the **TRI-CITY AMERICANS** hockey team (509/736-0606; www.amshockey.com), which plays at the **COLISEUM** (7000 W Grandridge Blvd; 509/783-9999).

RESTAURANTS

El Chapala / ★

107 E COLUMBIA DR, KENNEWICK; 509/586-4224
At El Chapala, in the east end of Kennewick, they like things big: they put the place in the *Guinness Book of World Records* in 1999 by making the world's largest burrito. Their margaritas come in two sizes: *grande* and *mucho grande.*

The food is authentic Mexican, with a kids' menu and several low-fat options. *$; AE, DIS, MC, V; checks OK; lunch, dinner every day; full bar; no reservations; www.casachapala.com; just off Columbia Center Blvd (Belfair Pl), east of N Washington St (Columbia Dr).*

Pasco

Pasco has the most diverse population of the Tri-Cities, with an economy based on light manufacturing and food processing. Historically a railroad town, Pasco is home to the **WASHINGTON STATE RAILROADS HISTORICAL SOCIETY MUSEUM** (122 N Tacoma Ave; 509/543-4159 or 800/465-5430; www.wsrhs.org; Sat May–Sept), which features old motorcars, railcars, and steam locomotives, including the state's oldest, the *Blue Mountain*, circa 1877.

Downtown is the **PASCO FARMERS MARKET** (4th Ave and Columbia St; 509/545-0738; www.pascofarmersmarket.org; May–Oct), one of the state's largest open-air produce markets. **SACAJAWEA STATE PARK** (off Hwy 12) honors the remarkable Native American woman who accompanied Lewis and Clark's Corps of Discovery.

LODGINGS

Red Lion Hotel Pasco / ★

2525 N 20TH AVE, PASCO; 509/547-0701 OR 800/RED-LION
Four blocks from the Tri-Cities Airport, the Red Lion Hotel Pasco is also right next to Sun Willows Golf Course and Columbia Basin College. It's the region's largest hotel, with 279 standard rooms, a huge ballroom, two outdoor pools, and an exercise room. The hotel's Bin No. 20 Steak & Seafood restaurant showcases vintages from Washington wineries. The Grizzly Bar is a perennially hot night spot. *$$; AE, DC, DIS, MC, V; checks OK; www.redlion.rdln.com; I-82/Hwy 395 exit 12.* &

Walla Walla and the Blue Mountains

The Walla Walla Valley is hot, not only because of its weather but also its nationally known wines and sweet onions. Tourists in the know clamor for Columbia River and Walla Walla Valley merlot and cabernet sauvignon; the climate is ideal for growing the grapes needed to make merlot, a hard-to-get-right wine. The northerly latitude extends the growing season with long, sunny days balanced by cool nights, limited rain, and intricate soil—all things that lead to wine with better flavor and complexity. In addition to some of the best merlot in the country, winemakers are bottling varietals that are otherwise largely unprecedented in the United States, with stunning results: among others, malbec, barbera, viognier, tempranillo, and Sangiovese.

And Walla Walla is also an important historical area. In the early 1800s, the Lewis and Clark Expedition passed through, fur trappers set up Fort Walla Walla, and Dr. Marcus Whitman built a mission. Then smallpox hit area tribes, and a group of Cayuse men killed the missionaries in what's now known as the Whitman Massacre. The interpretive center at the **WHITMAN MISSION NATIONAL HISTORIC SITE** (along Hwy 12, 7 miles west of town; 509/522-6357 or 509/529-2761; www.nps.gov/whmi) fleshes out the story. The **WALLA WALLA VALLEY CHAMBER OF COMMERCE** (29 E Sumac St, Walla Walla; 509/525-0850 or 877/998-4748; www.wwvchamber.com) has information.

Walla Walla

"The town so nice, people say it twice" is an insider's play on the town's name. About a decade ago, Walla Walla was the place for some of the best wines in the country—but not for food. All that has changed, profoundly. The city is emerging as a culinary destination.

Downtown bustles. The arts are big here, and the **WALLA WALLA SYMPHONY** (26 E Main St; 509/529-8020; www.wwsymphony.com) is the oldest symphony orchestra west of the Mississippi. Performances are held in **CORDINER HALL** (345 Boyer Ave; www.whitman.edu/cordiner) on the grounds of private **WHITMAN COLLEGE** (509/527-5176; www.whitman.edu). The **WALLA WALLA FOUNDRY** (405 Woodland Ave; 509/522-2114; www.wallawallafoundry.com) is a hub of art activity, where famous artists have come to cast sculptures. **FORT WALLA WALLA** (755 Myra Rd; 509/525-7703; www.fortwallawallamuseum.org) has a museum featuring 14 historic buildings and a collection of pioneer artifacts.

RESTAURANTS

Creek Town Café / ★★

1129 S 2ND AVE, WALLA WALLA; 509/522-4777
Creek Town Café has quickly become one of Walla Walla's favorites, so expect a wait on weekends. A rock half-wall divides the room in two, and dark wood wainscoting complements framed historic photos. Dinner menus reflect the seasons: expect well-prepared seafood, meat, and pasta dishes any time of year. Save some appetite for bread pudding or coconut cream pie. *$$$; AE, DIS, MC, V; checks OK; lunch, dinner Tues–Sat; beer and wine; reservations recommended; www.creektowncafe.com; at E Morton St.* &

Merchants Delicatessen / ★★

21 E MAIN ST, WALLA WALLA; 509/525-0900
Merchants has been a mainstay—especially for liberal-arts college students who come for the Wednesday-only spaghetti dinners—since 1976. The huge space across three storefronts serves healthy morning and midday meals. A full in-house bakery makes treats such as chocolate croissants and pizzas, while a well-stocked deli case serves picnic needs. Look for international groceries, gourmet foodstuffs, organic coffee beans, and wines. *$; AE, DIS, MC, V; checks OK; breakfast, lunch Mon–Sat, dinner Wed; beer and wine; no reservations; www.merchantsdeli.com; Hwy 12 exit at 2nd St.* &

26 brix / ★

207 W MAIN ST, WALLA WALLA; 509/526-4075

The chef from the glamorous Salish Lodge near Seattle left to open 26 brix, a fine-dining restaurant where nearly every dish stars local products. Chef Mike Davis uses the area's famous sweet onions to make caramelized sweet-onion consommé with onion ravioli, or he places asparagus from nearby Locati farms alongside a salmon dish. The pleasing wine list focuses strongly on local vineyards with enough worldly picks thrown in to make for excellent taste comparisons and food pairings. Unfortunately, the uneven food and service, of late, is not on par with the wine list. *$$$; DIS, MC, V; local checks only; breakfast, lunch Sun, dinner Thur–Mon; full bar; reservations recommended; www.twentysixbrix.com; downtown.*

Whitehouse-Crawford / ★★★

55 W CHERRY ST, WALLA WALLA; 509/525-2222

Here's another Walla Walla place with a notable chef who once worked in Seattle: Jamie Guerin from Seattle's Campagne. The restaurant is in a restored 1905 former planing mill. Tasty appetizers—try spicy calamari with ginger—pair well with local wines. Entrées have fun, unexpected twists, such as Southwest-style salmon with black beans, corn, and squash in a piquant tomato sauce, or pork smoked and served with grilled fresh figs, shallots, and spaetzle. Desserts are divine, including refined treats like lemon verbena crème brûlée and twice-baked chocolate cake. *$$$; AE, MC, V; checks OK; dinner Wed–Mon; full bar; reservations recommended; www.whitehouse crawford.com; downtown at 3rd Ave.* &

LODGINGS

Green Gables Inn / ★★

922 BONSELLA ST, WALLA WALLA; 509/525-5501 OR 888/525-5501

The title character from L. M. Montgomery's *Anne of Green Gables* series loved staying in guest rooms. That spirit lives on in five rooms named for topics in the popular books, such as Idlewild, with a fireplace and Jacuzzi, and Dryad's Bubble, with a small balcony. The Carriage House is good for families; separate from the main house; it gives kids more room to run around. An exceptional full breakfast comes on fine china by candlelight. A wraparound porch and air-conditioning make for pleasant summer evenings. *$$$; AE, DIS, MC, V; no checks; www.greengablesinn.com; Hwy 12 to Clinton St.*

Inn at Abeja / ★★★

2014 MILL CREEK RD, WALLA WALLA; 509/522-1234

More than 100 years old, this 22-acre farmstead doubles as a working winery and luxurious retreat east of town. Surrounded by the rolling Palouse hills and the Blue Mountains, visitors experience country tranquility with unobtrusive modern conveniences. The Chicken House Cottage has vaulted ceilings, a slate-tiled walk-in shower for two, and an airy full kitchen. Best is the two-story Summer Kitchen Cottage, with a deck overlooking the vineyards, a sky-lit bathroom, a king-size bed, a claw-foot tub, and full kitchen and living room. *$$$$; MC, V; checks OK; closed Tues–Wed and Dec–Feb; www.abeja. net/inn; on Hwy 12, 1.6 miles east of town.* &

Inn at Blackberry Creek / ★★

1126 PLEASANT ST, WALLA WALLA; 509/522-5233 OR 877/522-5233

Just around the corner from Pioneer Park and Whitman College is a charming 1912 farmhouse. Innkeeper Barbara Knudson restored the farmhouse and now runs the inn with a fine attention to important details. Fresh cookies in the evening, not to mention three flawlessly decorated guest rooms, make for a pleasant stay. All rooms afford views of the serene, tree-lined property. The light-filled common area overlooking the lawns is an inviting place to play chess, thumb through magazines, or read in comfortable chairs. *$$$; MC, V; checks OK; www.innatblackberrycreek.com; 4 blocks southeast of Pioneer Park.*

Marcus Whitman Hotel / ★★

6 W ROSE ST, WALLA WALLA; 509/525-2200 OR 866/826-9422

Owner Kyle Mussman has restored the elegant and historic Marcus Whitman, one of the largest structures in downtown Walla Walla. Numerous dignitaries and entertainers, Dwight Eisenhower and Shirley Temple among them, have enjoyed a stay here. The best of the 91 comfortable rooms are suites in the original tower—the West Wing was added in the 1960s. Decorated in handsome, almost masculine colors, standard rooms don't have the same city views. *$–$$$; AE, MC, V; checks OK; www.marcuswhitmanhotel. com; at 2nd Ave.* &

Dayton

Dayton, a small farming town northeast of Walla Walla, is one of the state's first communities. Small wonder it's full of almost 90 Victorian-era buildings. The **DAYTON HISTORIC DEPOT** (222 E Commercial St; 509/382-2026; tours Wed–Sat), built in 1881, is the state's oldest surviving railroad station and is now a museum. Stop by the **DAYTON CHAMBER OF COMMERCE** (166 E Main St; 800/882-6299; www.historicdayton.com) for details.

Don't miss the **MONTEILLET FROMAGERIE** (109 Ward Rd, Dayton; 509/382-1917; www.monteilletcheese.com; 1½ miles west of town), where you can sample fresh goat and sheep cheese. Dayton is also known for easy access to **BLUEWOOD SKI RESORT** (off Hwy 12, 22 miles south of Dayton; 509/382-4725; www. bluewood.com) in Umatilla National Forest in the Blue Mountains. The resort has frequent clear skies, dry powder, and the second-highest base elevation (4,545 feet) in the state.

RESTAURANTS

Patit Creek Restaurant / ★★★

725 E DAYTON AVE, DAYTON; 509/382-2625

Patit Creek is a classic off-the-beaten-path discovery and a classy place to end a day of valley wine touring or skiing at Bluewood. Bruce and Heather Hiebert turned a 1920s service station into a 10-table restaurant famous for fillets in green peppercorn sauce, chèvre-stuffed dates wrapped in bacon, fresh vegetables, and huckleberry pie. *$$$; MC, V; local checks only; lunch Wed–Fri, dinner Wed–Sat; beer and wine; reservations recommended; north end of town.* &

LODGINGS

The Purple House B&B Inn / ★

415 E CLAY ST, DAYTON; 509/382-3159 OR 800/486-2574

The 1882 Queen Anne mansion housing this B and B really is purple. What with the color, and the graceful touches of exterior gingerbread, even seeing the place may make you smile a little. If you go inside for a stay, your smile will broaden. Four guest rooms with modern amenities include air-conditioning. Two have private baths. Your full breakfast might include strudel or crepes—the innkeeper, Christine Williscroft, a native of southern Germany, loves to cook; you'll love it that she does. *$$–$$$; MC, V; checks OK; www.purplehousebnb.com; 1 block off Hwy 12.* &

The Weinhard Hotel / ★

235 E MAIN ST, DAYTON; 509/382-4032

This is a favorite place in the Walla Walla Valley. Fresh flowers and fruit greet guests in each room. Owners Dan and Ginny Butler restored the old Weinhard building, which originally housed a saloon and lodge hall in the late 1800s, and filled it with elegant Victorian antiques collected from across the country. The 15 rooms have antique dressers, desks, and canopied beds. The Signature Room has a jetted tub. Inside the hotel is the Weinhard Café, with tasty, inventive fare. *$$–$$$; AE, MC, V; checks OK; www.weinhard. com; downtown.* &

Pullman and the Palouse

Washington's golden Palouse region, next to Idaho and north of the Blue Mountains, is an area of rolling hills covered with wheat, lentils, and other crops. **KAMIAK BUTTE COUNTY PARK** (on SR 27, 13 miles north of Pullman) is a good place for a picnic with a view of the hills. **STEPTOE BUTTE STATE PARK** (on US Hwy 195, about 30 miles north of Pullman) is great for a panoramic view.

At **PALOUSE FALLS STATE PARK** (2 miles off SR 261 between Washtucna and Tucannon; 800/233-0321), the Palouse River roars over a basalt cliff higher than Niagara Falls, dropping 198 feet into a steep-walled basin on its way to the Snake River. A hiking trail leads to an overlook above the falls, most spectacular during spring runoff. Camping and canoeing are allowed in **LYONS FERRY STATE PARK** (on SR 261, 7 miles north of Starbuck; 800/233-0321), at the confluence of the Palouse and Snake rivers; the park also has a public boat launch.

Pullman

The heart of the Palouse beats in Pullman, at the junction of US Highway 195 and State Route 27 near the Idaho border, and that heart is **WASHINGTON STATE UNIVERSITY** (visitor center: 225 N Grand Ave; 509/335-8633; www. wsu.edu/visitor). Established in 1892, WSU is where 17,000 die-hard Cougars live during the academic year. Your trip wouldn't be complete without sampling the ice cream or Cougar Gold cheese made at the WSU creamery, **FERDINAND'S** (Agriculture Science Bldg; 509/335-4014; Mon–Fri). The $39 million Student Recreation Center, open to the public for a small fee, includes a large spa as part of the swimming complex. The Student Book Corp., affectionately called the **BOOKIE** (700 NE Thatuna St; 509/332-2537; www.wsubookie.net), is a great place to browse or pick up Cougar paraphernalia. This place is jammed on home football weekends in the fall. There's also a second store: the **BOOKIE, TOO** (405 Stadium Wy; 509/334-3661).

If you visit one restaurant while in town, make it the **COUGAR COTTAGE** (900 NE Colorado St; 509/332-1265), aka the Coug. This is a Pullman institution since 1932, and every frat boy and football player has done his penance there. For just hanging out, the **DAILY GRIND** (230 Main St; 509/334-9171 or 800/59-DAILY; www.dailygrindespresso.com) is a great place to grab coffee or a sandwich.

Pullman is also known for its historical buildings, with brick masonry and early 1900s classical and Georgian architecture. Its cultural offerings are increasing with the addition of the **THEATRE OF THE PALOUSE** (165 NE Kamiaken; 509/334-0750; www.rtoptheatre.org), which produces such classics as the *Wizard of Oz*. Find more information at the **PULLMAN CHAMBER OF COMMERCE** (415 N Grand Ave; 509/334-3565 or 800/365-6948; www.pullmanchamber.com).

RESTAURANTS

Hilltop Restaurant / UNRATED

920 NW OLSEN ST, PULLMAN; 509/334-2555

A 58-year institution, this steak house has an incredible view of the university and surrounding hills. Crisp linens and attentive service complement the romantic vista. Red meat, from prime rib and steaks to Sunday's midday roast-beef family dinner, is prominent on the menu. A wide variety of pasta and seafood dishes share the limelight. Homemade desserts include cheesecakes, mud pie, and chocolate truffles. Hilltop is connected to the three-story, 59-room Hawthorne Inn & Suites (928 NW Olsen St, Pullman; 509/332-0928), where it provides room service. *$$; AE, DIS, MC, V; checks OK; lunch Mon–Fri, dinner every day; full bar; reservations recommended; www.hilltoprestaurant. com; on Davis Wy.*

Swilly's Restaurant / ★★

200 NE KAMIAKEN ST, PULLMAN; 509/334-3395

Come here to sit creekside or to escape the student crowds. Local artwork covers the exposed-brick walls. The menu defines eclectic: Moroccan lamb, Thai shrimp, and grilled tenderloin are all served here. Or just stick with the good homemade soups, salads, sandwiches, burgers, and pastas. *$$; AE, MC, V; checks OK; lunch Mon–Fri, dinner Mon–Sat; beer and wine; no reservations; www.swillys.com; at NW Olson St.* &

SPOKANE AND NORTHEASTERN WASHINGTON

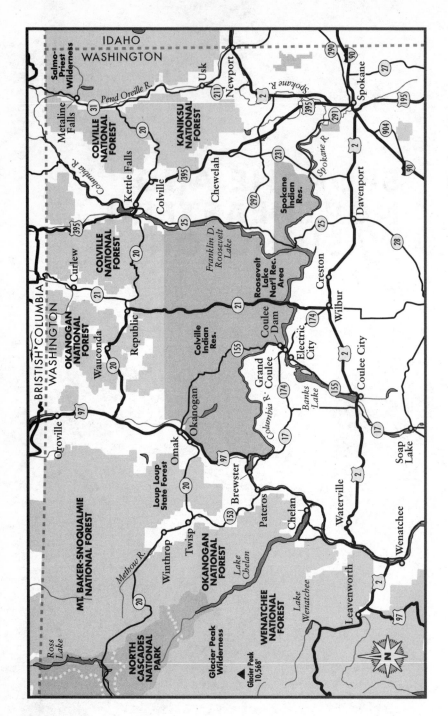

SPOKANE AND NORTHEASTERN WASHINGTON

Forested mountain ranges, gorgeous countryside, and vast farmlands on the Columbia Plateau form the fabric of Northeastern Washington. Rivers lace through that fabric like glittering seams; chief among them are the Columbia, Spokane, and Pend Oreille rivers. Lakes, natural and man-made, shine from pockets in the land: Franklin D. Roosevelt Lake is the largest, stretching 150 miles behind Grand Coulee Dam on the Columbia River; Banks Lake, the next largest, is itself pumped from the waters of Roosevelt Lake. On the shores of the lakes and rivers, in among the farms and forests, towns and cities thrive. Of them, Spokane, the biggest city and the cultural hot spot of the inland Pacific Northwest, glows brightest.

Along with Spokane's urban attractions, the mountains, rivers, and lakes draw many visitors to Northeastern Washington. Three north-south mountain ranges—the Okanogan Range of the eastern Cascades, the Kettle River and Selkirk ranges of the western Rockies—dominate the land in the northern part of the area. On those ranges, a variety of wildlife, comfortingly beautiful views, and charming trails abound in three national forests: the Okanogan, Colville, and Kaniksu.

In the southern part of the region, where the mountain ranges gentle down onto the basalt-based, channeled scablands of the Columbia Plateau, Lake Roosevelt National Recreation Area and the spacious lakes in Grand Coulee afford seemingly endless opportunities for water-based recreation amid spectacular scenery. Natural and man-made wonders astound visitors, who marvel at the present-day evidence of vast ancient floods at Dry Falls, gape at the mountain of concrete that is Grand Coulee Dam, and blink at the mere idea of the grandiose irrigation system supported by the massive generators, pumps, and pipes that create and sustain Banks Lake.

ACCESS AND INFORMATION

The fastest, most direct surface route to Spokane from Seattle is **INTERSTATE 90**; **US HIGHWAY 2** and the more-northerly, less-traveled **STATE ROUTE 20** are other east-west routes to points in Northeastern Washington. The three principal north-south routes through the region are **US HIGHWAY 97** on the eastern slope of the Cascades; **STATE ROUTE 21**, which crosses the Columbia River on historic **KELLERS FERRY** in the central part of the region; and **US HIGHWAY 395**, which runs through Spokane and Colville.

Ten passenger airlines—Alaska, Delta, ExpressJet, Frontier, Horizon, Northwest, Skywest, Southwest, United, and US Airways—serve **SPOKANE INTERNATIONAL AIRPORT** (9000 W Airport Dr, Spokane; 509/455-6455; www.spokaneairports.net), a 10-minute drive west of downtown. For train and bus traffic, Spokane's **INTERMODAL CENTER** (221 W 1st Ave, Spokane) is the depot stop for **AMTRAK**'s (800/USA-RAIL; www.amtrak.com) *Empire Builder* between Seattle and Chicago, as well as **NORTHWESTERN TRAILWAYS** (4611 S Ben Franklin Ln, Spokane; 509/838-4029 or

---

SPOKANE THREE-DAY TOUR

DAY ONE: Kick your day off with a cone and a latte at South Hill's **ROCK-WOOD BAKERY** (315 E 18th Ave, Spokane; 509/747-8691; www.rockwood bakery.com) before walking to **MANITO PARK**, a few blocks away. Spend the morning strolling through the park's European, Japanese, and rose gardens. Take a spin along Cliff Drive Parkway to gaze at the old mansions and lovely views west as you head back downtown for a late lunch at **MIZUNA**. Explore the upscale shops at **RIVER PARK SQUARE** and browse the shelves of Spokane's favorite bookstore, **AUNTIE'S** (402 W Main Ave, Spokane; 509/838-0206; www.auntiesbooks.net), celebrating 30 years of independence in 2008. For a light dinner, if you're still full from lunch, stop at the **BLUEFISH** for some spicy tuna rolls, or if you're famished, try **MOXIE** next door. Gaze at the silent movies playing outside your window on the side of the Fox Theater as you nod off to sleep in style at the **MONTVALE HOTEL**.

DAY TWO: Grab breakfast at the Palm Court Grill in the **DAVENPORT HOTEL**. Explore the historic mansions in the nearby **BROWNE'S ADDITION** neighborhood before popping by the **NORTHWEST MUSEUM OF ARTS AND CULTURE** in the late morning. Nab a porch seat at the **ELK PUBLIC HOUSE** and enjoy a

---

800/366-3830; www.trailways.com) and **GREYHOUND** (221 W 1st Ave, Spokane; 509/624-5251 or 800/231-2222; www.greyhound.com) buses. **SPOKANE TRANSIT AUTHORITY** (509/328-7433; www.spokanetransit.com) provides bus service to Cheney, Spokane Valley, and other nearby towns.

The **SPOKANE REGIONAL CONVENTION AND VISITORS CENTER** (201 W Main Ave, Spokane; 509/747-3230 or 888/SPOKANE; www.visit spokane.com) is a good source of information. For more information on **LAKE ROOSEVELT NATIONAL RECREATION AREA** (1008 Crest Dr, Coulee Dam; 509/633-9441; www.nps.gov/laro), stop by the **FORT SPOKANE VISITOR CENTER** (off SR 25 north of Davenport; 509/725-2715 ext 43 summer or 509/633-9441 ext 130 fall–spring) or the **KETTLE FALLS INFORMATION CENTER** (near junction of Hwy 395 and SR 25; 509/684-7000).

Spokane

Always the bridesmaid and never the bride, Spokane, the second-largest city in the state, seems to live forever in the shadow of Seattle's cosmopolitan city lights. For those who know firsthand, though, the notion that Spokane is inferior doesn't always ring true. Whether the measure is of art, history, shopping, neighborhood cachet, outdoor activities, or other attractions, Spokane has its own grand charms and unique advantages.

hearty lunch. Rent a bike or skates at the downtown **RIVERFRONT PARK** and explore the **CENTENNIAL TRAIL** up the Spokane River. Before sunset, take a drive west and dip your toes in the historic waters of **MEDICAL LAKE**. Head over to nearby Cheney for plate upon plate of Italian food at **LENNY'S AMERICAN & ITALIAN**. On your way back into Spokane, enjoy a nightcap at Cavallino Lounge, on the first floor of **HOTEL LUSSO**, where you'll stay for the night.

DAY THREE: Enjoy a classic breakfast at **FRANK'S DINER** before heading north to explore the beauty of **RIVERSIDE STATE PARK** and hike around the Bowl and Pitcher lava formations. Then head back downtown and grab a burrito (we recommend the Veggie Thai) at **NEATO BURRITO** (827 W 1st Ave, Spokane; 509/847-1234). Spend the afternoon strolling around the **GONZAGA UNIVERSITY** campus and check out the original Dale Chihuly artwork at the school's **JUNDT ART MUSEUM**. Head to the South Hill for dinner at **GORDY'S SICHUAN CAFÉ**, then venture into town for a play at **CENTERSTAGE** (1017 W 1st Ave, Spokane; 509/747-8243; www.spokanecenterstage.com) or a concert at the **MET** (901 W Sprague Ave, Spokane; 509/227-7638; www.mettheater.com). Sip a Peacock Punch at the **DAVENPORT'S HOTEL**'s Peacock Room before heading upstairs to your luxurious pad.

Art is nearly everywhere in the Lilac City. Visual art is at its prime at the modern **NORTHWEST MUSEUM OF ARTS AND CULTURE** (2316 W 1st Ave; 509/456-3931; www.northwestmuseum.org) and the small **LORINDA KNIGHT GALLERY** (523 W Sprague Ave; 509/838-3740; www.lorindaknight.com). Gonzaga University's **JUNDT ART MUSEUM** (202 E Cataldo Ave; 509/323-6611; www.gonzaga.edu) is worth a long look, with its cutting-edge art exhibits and original Dale Chihuly hanging glass chandelier. Elsewhere, at large in the city, stunning public art graces the downtown tunnels, park lawns, and building faces.

The rich history of Spokane remains very much a part of everyday life. Many of the homes of the city's forefathers still stand, from the towering **GLOVER MANSION** (321 W 8th Ave; 509/459-0000; www.glovermansion.com), which serves today as a popular event facility, to the Victorian-era homes of the **BROWNE'S ADDITION** neighborhood. A reminder of the more playful side of history, the wonderful and painstakingly preserved **SPOKANE 1909 LOOF CARROUSEL** (Riverfront Park; 800/336-7275; www.spokanecarrousel.org) continues to operate daily.

Spokane centers on the powerful Spokane River, the majestic Spokane Falls, and **RIVERFRONT PARK** (downtown Spokane; 509/652-6632 or 800/336-PARK; www.spokaneriverfrontpark.com), which was built on the banks of the river for Expo '74. The urban green space is home to an amusement park, the IMAX theater, and a breathtaking gondola ride. For the best view of the raging falls, a short ride on the gondola on a sunny day is well worth the small admission price.

The park is also home to a 26-ton, 12-foot-high Radio Flyer wagon sculpture, a favorite of Spokane youngsters.

Riverfront Park provides access to the 37-mile **CENTENNIAL TRAIL**, which links downtown Spokane, the **GONZAGA UNIVERSITY** campus (502 E Boone Ave; 800/986-9585; www.gonzaga.edu), and points east before it finally ends on Higgins Point beyond Coeur d'Alene, Idaho. **COEUR D'ALENE**, just 32 miles east of Spokane on the banks of scenic Lake Coeur d'Alene, hosts festivals throughout the year; contact the **COEUR D'ALENE CHAMBER OF COMMERCE** (877/782-9232; www.coeurdalene.org) for details.

Downtown Spokane, also known as the **RIVERSIDE DISTRICT**, is home to the high-end shops of **RIVER PARK SQUARE** (808 W Main Ave; 509/363-0304; www. riverparksquare.com) and some of the city's finest hotels and restaurants. Other popular shopping areas include **NORTHTOWN MALL** (4750 N Division; 509/482-0209; www.northtownmall.com) and **GARLAND VILLAGE**, a business center within the North Hill neighborhood, 2 miles north of downtown. Just northwest of downtown, one of the largest urban development projects in the country, **KENDALL YARDS** (110 N Post St; 208/665-2005 or 866/239-6750; www.kendallyards. com), will soon be a new neighborhood on the north shore of the Spokane River, overlooking the Centennial Trail; the development will include hundreds of town-homes, condominiums, and apartments as well as retail shops and offices.

A drive through the tree-canopied neighborhoods of Spokane's South Hill is pleasant day or night; be sure to stop at **MANITO** (1702 S Grand Blvd; 509/625-6622; www.manitopark.org) and **CANNON HILL PARKS** (S Lincoln St and W 18th Ave) for a picnic. The **SOUTH PERRY DISTRICT** (www.southperry.com), one of the South Hill's most up-and-coming neighborhoods, is anchored by the **SHOP** (924 S Perry St; 509/534-1647; www.theshop.bz), a cozy coffee joint in a refurbished gas station. It's known for acoustic music shows and delicious espresso. In summer, the owners open the nearby ice creamery, the **SCOOP** (1001 W 25th Ave; 509/535-7171) and show free movies in the Shop's parking lot.

Spokane is a short drive from some of the region's best skiing. **MOUNT SPOKANE** (29500 N Mount Spokane Park Dr; 509/238-2220; www.mtspokane.com) is only an hour's drive north of downtown. Hiking, biking, horseback riding, and camping during the warm months are just west of downtown in **RIVERSIDE STATE PARK** (9711 W Charles Rd, Nine Mile Falls; 509/465-5064; www.riverside statepark.org). Evening strolls, apple groves, fruit festivals, and endless pumpkin patches make for country fun at **GREEN BLUFF** (Day–Mount Spokane Rd and Green Bluff Rd; www.greenbluffgrowers.com), a community of family farms open during monthly festivals.

The first Saturday in May, Spokane kicks into high gear with the annual **BLOOMSDAY RUN** (1610 W Riverside Ave; 509/838-1579; www.bloomsday. org). More than 50,000 runners take part in the event. Not long after, the week-long **LILAC FESTIVAL** (3021 S Regal, Ste 105; 509/535-4554; www.lilacfestival. org) builds up to a grand torchlight parade on the third Saturday in May. Come June, the amazing **SPOKANE HOOPFEST** (509/624-2414 or 888/880-HOOP; www.spokanehoopfest.net), a citywide three-on-three basketball tournament, holds court—or, more precisely, holds 400 courts with more than 140,000 players.

RESTAURANTS

Bittersweet Bakery and Bistro / ★★

1220 S GRAND BLVD, SPOKANE; 509/455-8658
Now a persistent favorite in Spokane, Bittersweet Bistro appeals to all palates. Savory crepes and other goodies are served in a warm pastel setting. Although the crepes may seem a bit pricey, fresh local ingredients and gourmet cheeses make them worth the bucks. Admire the view of the nearby architectural delight: St. John's Cathedral. *$; AE, MC, V; checks OK; breakfast, lunch Tues–Sat; full bar; no reservations; at 12th Ave.* &

Bluefish / ★★

830 W SPRAGUE AVE, SPOKANE; 509/747-2111
Stylish sushi, seafood, and steaks are served among hues of blue and tanks of sea life. Sushi here creatively blends simple elements to please aficionados and dilettantes alike. Nearly everybody likes blue, and that's true here too. *$$$; AE, DIS, MC, V; no checks; lunch Mon–Fri, dinner Mon–Sat; full bar; reservations recommended; www.bluefishspokane.com; at N Lincoln St.* &

Chicken-n-More / ★★★

414½ W SPRAGUE AVE, SPOKANE; 509/838-5071
Spokane's place for Southern soul food, Chicken-n-More is informal, counter-order dining. Don't let the style throw you. It gets jammed at lunchtime, but the grub is worth the fuss. Fried chicken? Catfish sandwich? Beef brisket? Pulled pork? Tasty sides? Sweet potato pie? Oh yes, all! Nice, friendly people sweeten the pie. *$; AE, DIS, MC, V; local checks only; lunch, dinner Mon–Sat; beer and wine; no reservations; across from Ridpath Hotel.* &

The Elk Public House / ★

1931 W PACIFIC AVE, SPOKANE; 509/363-1973
A summer meal at the Elk, known for a kicked-back atmosphere and not-so-average pub fare, perfects a long day. The burgers gush caramelized onions, and the chicken sandwiches melt in honey cream cheese. Opt for corn pasta salad as a side. When you can, have a drink at the bar and wait for a porch seat—you'll be glad you did. *$; AE, DIS, MC, V; checks OK; lunch, dinner every day; full bar; no reservations; www.wedonthaveone. com; at S Cannon St.* &

Frank's Diner / ★★

1516 W 2ND AVE, SPOKANE; 509/747-8798
10929 N NEWPORT HWY, SPOKANE; 509/465-2464
That classy train car you saw from the freeway in downtown Spokane or the north end? That's no derailment—those are diners. Grab a stool at the counter and watch as the hilarious cooking staff carefully craft your eggs, hash browns, and huckleberry pancakes. Add a thick, whip-topped milk shake,

and feel no regrets. *$; DIS, MC, V; local checks only; breakfast, lunch, dinner every day; beer and wine; no reservations; www.franksdiners.com; downtown at S Walnut St; north end, just past Northpoint Shopping Center.* &

Gordy's Sichuan Café / ★★

501 E 30TH AVE, SPOKANE; 509/747-1170

Gordy's puts Spokane on the ethnic cuisine map. The bite-sized strip-mall storefront is a no–Web site, no–e-mail, no-reservation kind of place, with a yes-everything menu. Scarf Gan Pung chicken, savory tofu, or cashew prawn stir-fry. Pay attention to the specials chalkboard—that's often where Gordon Crafts' understanding of Sichuan cuisine shines. If it's on the board, try the soup. Save room for dessert: ginger-orange ice cream is worth loosening your belt a notch if need be. *$$; AE, MC, V; checks OK; lunch Tues–Fri, dinner Mon–Sat; beer and wine; no reservations; off Grand Blvd.* &

Lenny's American & Italian / ★

1204 1ST ST, CHENEY; 509/235-6126

Sure, the name sounds strip-mall-ish, and the drive may seem a little far, but rest assured: Lenny's is the real deal. Italian owner and chef John Maticchio runs this simple, checkered-tablecloths place. The menu boasts every popular Italian dish: pasta, eggplant Parmesan, lasagne, fettuccine Alfredo, Italian sandwiches, and a few burgers, for good measure. *$$; MC, V; checks OK; dinner Tues–Sat; beer and wine; no reservations; I-90 exit at Cheney–Four Lakes, to downtown Cheney.* &

Luna / ★★★

5620 S PERRY ST, SPOKANE; 509/448-2383

Buried in the unlikeliest of Spokane's South Hill neighborhoods, Luna is easy to miss, but you'll never forget it after eating there. Food, wine, and service are at their very best in the candlelit atmosphere. Revel in the complexities of Luna's menu (such as charred lamb rack with juniper berry glace and eggplant risotto), but don't feel guilty sampling what's familiar: applewood-oven pizzas, coconut curry prawns, or the simple pasta dishes that hold tenure here. *$$$; AE, DIS, MC, V; checks OK; lunch, dinner every day, brunch Sun; full bar; reservations recommended; www.lunaspokane.com; on 57th Ave.* &

Mizuna / ★★★

214 N HOWARD ST, SPOKANE; 509/747-2004

Meat lovers and veggie heads unite here over plates of savory cuisine in the coziest restaurant in town. Mizuna boasts a gorgeous candlelit dining room and a polished, fun waitstaff. A wine bar dominates half the space. Go light with the Vermont cheddar and apple salad, or stuff yourself with the vegetarian "meat loaf" sandwich. Mizuna used to be all vegetarian, and dishes can still be made veg-friendly. Save plenty of room for tasty desserts. *$$$; AE, DIS, MC, V; checks OK; lunch Mon–Fri, dinner every day; full bar; reservations recommended; www.mizuna.com; at Spokane Falls Blvd.* &

Moxie / ★★★⯪

816 W SPRAGUE AVE, SPOKANE; 509/456-3594
On a date at Moxie? Get a seat with a view of the tsunami mural. Chef Ian Wingate painted the mural, and he interprets traditional dishes with similar style: charbroiled chipotle-glazed meat loaf, seared prosciutto-wrapped scallops, and more. *$$$; AE, DIS, MC, V; checks OK; lunch Mon–Fri, dinner Mon–Sat; full bar; reservations recommended; www.moxiemoxie.com; at Lincoln St.* &

Thai on 1st / ★★

411 W 1ST AVE, SPOKANE; 509/455-4288
Thai on 1st is a lustrous gem in the city's drabbest area. It's the best Thai in Spokane—good and familiar. Decor is sparse, but the family that runs it makes you feel at home. Service and efficiency, along with consistent, delicious food, are what recommend this place. Plates of phad thai or the tongue-scalding curries satisfy a range of palates. *$; MC, V; no checks; lunch Mon–Fri, dinner Mon–Sat; beer and wine; no reservations; at Washington St.* &

LODGINGS

The Davenport Hotel / ★★★
10 S POST ST, SPOKANE; 509/455-8888 OR 800/899-1482
The Davenport bathes any visitor in luxury, from the grand lobby and ballrooms to the decadent guest rooms and suites. Rooms range from standard suites to wet-bar-and-sitting-room spaces. The Palm Court Grill is overpriced; opt for the surrounding restaurants. Davenport cuisine stands on the Sunday brunch—a larger-than-life meal. The Peacock Room, a stunning stained-glass lounge, and Spa Paradiso are citywide favorites. *$$$$; AE, DC, DIS, MC, V; checks OK; www.thedavenporthotel.com; at Sprague Ave.* &

E. J. Roberts Mansion Bed and Breakfast / ★★

1923 W 1ST AVE, SPOKANE; 509/456-8839 OR 866/456-8839
After 23 years of meticulous restoration, this grand 1889 Queen Anne–style Victorian mansion is now replete with the quiet elegance of a bygone era. Four suites and a cottage are offered, each more charming than the last; expect high ceilings, stained-glass windows, opulent drapes, shining wood floors, discreet scroll and lattice work, private baths . . . the inexorable result is a profound sense of contentment. Enjoy a visit with friends in the parlor, a good read in the library, or a relaxed game on the mahogany table in the billiards room. *$$$; MC, V; checks OK; www.ejrobertsmansion.com; at Cannon St.*

Hotel Lusso / ★★★

1 N POST ST, SPOKANE; 509/747-9750
Step into an intimate, romantic stay at Hotel Lusso—a pint-size hotel within walking distance of shopping, restaurants, and Riverfront Park. Oversize windows in the 48 high-ceilinged rooms offer downtown views. Italian

marble bathrooms pamper guests, as do the complimentary breakfast and hors d'oeuvres at the hotel's restaurant, Fugazzi. *$$$–$$$$; AE, DC, DIS, MC, V; checks OK; www.hotellusso.com; at Sprague Ave.* &

The Montvale Hotel / ★★★

1005 W 1ST AVE, SPOKANE; 509/747-1919 OR 866/668-8253
Contemporary and bursting with character, the Montvale provides some of the best lodging in the city. Built in 1899, the hotel was recently renovated; it now boasts 36 luxurious rooms. And we do mean luxurious: pillowy mattresses, flat-screen televisions, waterfall showerheads, and views of Spokane's Davenport arts district. Book a room overlooking the Fox Theater; at night you can catch silent movies projected onto the theater's exterior. The Catacombs Pub—a German *bierhaus*-style place—is in the basement. *$$$; AE, DIS, MC, V; checks OK; www.montvalehotel.com; at Monroe St.* &

Pend Oreille and Colville River Valleys

The Pend Oreille valley somehow stays relatively undiscovered, and that's just fine with those who come here to enjoy the solitude, wild terrain, wildlife, and the region's wide river, the Pend Oreille (pronounced "pon-der-RAY"). The river flows north to Canada, where it meets the Columbia River just north of the border. One drainage west, the sparsely populated Colville River valley, home to tiny farming and logging communities, also provides a haven for outdoor recreation, from fishing and boating to hiking, hunting, and skiing.

The Pend Oreille

This northernmost corner of the state is generally considered a place to drive through on the way to Canada. In fact, it's nicknamed "the forgotten corner." But don't overlook this delightful region along the Washington leg of the only International Scenic Byway, the **INTERNATIONAL SELKIRK LOOP** (888/823-2626; www.selkirkloop.com). Take SR 20 down the **PEND OREILLE RIVER**, north from Hwy 2 at Newport, then continue down the river along SR 31 past where SR 20 heads west to Colville. East of Metaline Falls, grizzly bears, black bears, woodland caribou, bighorn sheep, gray wolves, and other wildlife call the **SALMO-PRIEST WILDERNESS AREA** home. More than 38 miles of hiking trails traverse the flanks of 7,318-foot Gypsy Peak, the highest peak in Eastern Washington. North of Metaline, stop by the **FLUME CREEK MOUNTAIN GOAT VIEWING AREA** on Forest Service Road 2975; not only is this one of the most reliable places to see mountain goats in Washington, but also the surrounding forests and high meadows support a greater variety of breeding songbirds than anywhere else in the state. Continue on FR 2975 to Crawford State Park for a tour of **GARDNER CAVE**.

SPOKANE'S HAUNTED HISTORY

Spokane is a city long on memory, which is understandable considering nearly every street has a backstory. Even today, longtime residents talk about the good old days of Expo '74, double features at the Fox Theater, and hamburgers and fries at Dick's, which still stands at the corner of Division Street and Third Avenue. Where there's history, there are sure to be ghost stories—and Spokane possesses both.

Start your ghost tour in Browne's Addition, where towering mansions beckon with windows and high, towerlike roofs. Rumors of a ghost in the **PATSY CLARK MANSION** (2208 W 2nd Ave; 509/747-0101; www.patsyclarks.com), which now houses a law firm, ran rampant when a full-scale restaurant operated in the space. Ghosts supposedly haunted the wine cellar and were said to have thrown wine bottles across the cellar to protest unsatisfactory varietals.

Ghost hunting in Spokane must include a stop at Gonzaga University's **MONAGHAN MANSION** (217 E Boone Ave), otherwise known as the school's music building. Built in 1898 for James Monaghan, the massive building is home to Spokane's creepiest tales. For years, students at Gonzaga reported stories of pianos playing without pianists, eerie tunes echoing throughout the rooms, and doors slamming on their own. After a series of incidents, an exorcism was performed on the mansion in 1975—but students today claim that a presence still lurks there.

Like any burial ground, the **GREENWOOD CEMETERY** (19911 W Coulee Hite Rd) near Spokane Falls Community College is the subject of a popular haunted story. A staircase in the cemetery, nicknamed 1,000 Steps, is feared by the superstitious and ghost hunters alike. Tales say that no one can scale the entire flight of stairs without colliding with a sudden, unbearable sense of fear.

Everyone here has one spooky tale or another to share. Stories fly about haunting spirits in the corridors of the **DAVENPORT HOTEL** and mysterious noises in the **SPOKANE COUNTY COURTHOUSE** (1116 W Broadway). Whether you believe it or not, it's hard to say that Spokane's soot-covered downtown buildings, soaring mansions, and midtown alleyways don't at least feel a little haunted.

—Leah Sottile

Colville and Kettle Falls Area

In the Colville River valley, the working-class feel of the lumber-and-ranch town is alive and well. Chewelah, Colville, and Kettle Falls are tight-knit blue-collar communities where you might spot "Cream of Spotted Owl" bumper stickers on the logging trucks chugging down the roads. **CHEWELAH**, between Spokane and Colville on Hwy 395, is home to a challenging (and inexpensive) 18-hole course at the **GOLF AND COUNTRY CLUB** (2537 E Sand Canyon Rd, Chewelah; 509/935-6807; www.chewelahgolf.com). East of Chewelah on the pleasingly monickered Flowery Trail Road, the tiny but friendly **49 DEGREES NORTH** ski area (3311 Flowery Trail Rd, Chewalah; 509/935-6649 or 866/376-4949; www.ski49n.com) offers free beginner lessons.

Farther north, visit the exhibits, including a quaint Main Street of period shops, at Colville's **STEVENS COUNTY HISTORICAL MUSEUM** (700 N Wynne St, Colville; 509/684-5968; www.stevenscountyhistoricalsociety.org). Not far beyond Colville is the town of **KETTLE FALLS**, by Lake Roosevelt. **CHINA BEND WINERY** (3751 Vineyard Wy, Kettle Falls; 509/732-6123 or 800/700-6123; www.chinabend.com), north of Kettle Falls, grows organic grapes in the northernmost vineyards of the state. The owners run a bed-and-breakfast at the winery; their breakfasts and dinners feature organic foods.

West of Kettle Falls, across the Columbia, hikers can trek to the Kettle Crest, one of the best hikes in the region. You might see black bears, deer, coyotes, and birds on the 42-mile trip. The Colville branch of the **U.S. FOREST SERVICE** (765 S Main St, Colville; 509/684-7000) maintains some shorter loop trails that access the crest; their summer guided wildflower tours have become so popular that reservations are recommended.

Grand Coulee Area

This wonderful area is grand indeed, from the columnar basalt cliffs to the colossal Grand Coulee Dam containing the **COLUMBIA RIVER**, which slices through Northeastern Washington with a huge quiet power, water rushing through enormous chasms. In prehistoric times, glacial melting created a river with the largest flow of water ever known. Today it's the second-largest river in the nation, traversing a basalt plateau of equally staggering scale.

Some 15 miles upstream of Grand Coulee Dam, the tiny **KELLER FERRY** (on SR 21; 800/695-7623 ext 511) shuttles across the Columbia dozens of times a day at no charge; the *Martha S* holds just a dozen cars. The crossing takes 15 minutes to traverse the waterborne section of SR 21, the link between the Colville Indian Reservation north of the river and the Columbia Plateau south. On the Grand Coulee side is a small store run by the Colville Tribe that sells fishing licenses and some groceries and also rents boats.

For many years **LAKE ROOSEVELT**, the massive 150-mile-long reservoir created by Grand Coulee Dam, was untapped by the RV-on-pontoon fleets. Now several companies offer part-week or weekly houseboat rentals. Some of these vessels have deluxe features such as on-deck hot tubs, stereo systems, gourmet kitchens, and outdoor rinse-off showers. For rates and reservations, contact **ROOSEVELT RECREATIONAL ENTERPRISES** (800/648-LAKE; www.rrehousboats.com) or **LAKE ROOSEVELT RESORT & MARINA** (800/635-7585; www.lakeroosevelt.com).

Grand Coulee Dam

GRAND COULEE DAM (509/633-9265; www.usbr.gov/pn/grandcoulee) itself is a marvel of engineering that harkens back to a time when man-made dams were the cutting edge of industrial design. Sometimes referred to as the eighth wonder of the world, the dam was conceived as part of an irrigation project that now supplies water to more than 600,000 acres of farmland. World War II gave it a new purpose: generating power for the production of plutonium at Hanford and aluminum for aircraft. As tall as a 46-story building and the length of a dozen city blocks, the dam was completed in 1942.

Clustered around Grand Coulee Dam are the towns of Grand Coulee, Coulee Dam, and Electric City. The **VISITOR CENTER** (509/633-9265; every day) features movies and exhibits; during summer months (end of May–Aug), the laser light show is a spectacular treat. Visit the **GRAND COULEE DAM AREA CHAMBER OF COMMERCE** (319 Midway Ave, Grand Coulee; 800/268-5332; www.grand couleedam.org) for more information. If you're feeling lucky, stop in at the Colville Tribe's **COULEE DAM CASINO** (515 Birch St, Coulee Dam; 509/633-0766 or 800/556-7492; www.colvillecasinos.com).

RESTAURANTS

La Presa / ★

515 E GRAND COULEE AVE, GRAND COULEE; 509/633-3173
Head here for authentic Mexican food from a menu offering around 100 different dishes. Offerings include the standard Mexican plates, combos, steaks, and seafood—and even chicken teriyaki. You won't go wrong with traditional favorites such as enchilada verde, made with fresh tomatillos. La Presa, which means "the dam," has a south-of-the-border feel, with velvet paintings and wool blankets hanging on the walls. *$; DIS, MC, V; checks OK; lunch, dinner every day; full bar; reservations recommended; www.grandcouleedam. com/lapresa/html_files/index.html; on SR 21, just up from dam.* &

Soap Lake

The town of Soap Lake earns its name on windy days, when frothy whitecaps dot the surface of the nearby lake. Many believe the lake, known for its high content of soft minerals, has healing properties. Contact the **SOAP LAKE CHAMBER OF COMMERCE** (300 N Daisy St; 509/246-1821; www.soaplakecoc.org) for information on renting canoes and sailboats.

DRY FALLS, north of Soap Lake in Sun Lakes State Park, shows the power of ice—but not dry ice. When glacial Lake Missoula overflowed its ice-age dams some 12,000 years ago, torrential floods pounded west to the Pacific. The force of the water carved out what is now this ancient waterfall, 3½ miles wide and 400 feet high (by comparison, Niagara Falls is 1 mile wide and 165 feet high). The **DRY FALLS INTERPRETIVE CENTER** (on SR 17, 4 miles southwest of Coulee

City; 509/632-5583; 10am–6pm every day May–Sept), at the top of the canyon, is a half mile from the scenic overlook. **SUN LAKES STATE PARK** (509/632-5583; www.parks.wa.gov) also offers campsites, shore fishing, boat ramps and rentals, 15 miles of hiking trails, horseshoe pits, and a nine-hole golf course.

LODGINGS

Notaras Lodge / ★★

236 E MAIN, SOAP LAKE; 509/246-0462

Notaras has 15 rooms in four huge log cabins, right on Soap Lake. In fact, the lake's mineral waters are on tap in the bathrooms, several of which have in-room whirlpools. Six rooms have lake views; snag one of those if you can. Each room has a quirky theme: Luck of the Draw, for example, has a slot-machine pull handle at the entrance. The owners run Don's Restaurant (14 Canna St, Soap Lake; 509/246-1217; lunch Sun–Fri, dinner every day), which specializes in steak, seafood, and Greek entrées. *$$–$$$; MC, V; checks OK; www.notaraslodge.com; SR 28 at Soap Lake exit, to Canna St.* க்

Omak

To reach downtown Omak—a town of 4,000, 50 miles north of Grand Coulee on State Route 155—exit the highway from either direction on the business loop; the town isn't even visible from Hwy 97.

Perhaps Omak's best-known draw, the **OMAK STAMPEDE** (509/826-1002 or 800/933-6625; www.omakstampede.org), a popular four-day rodeo, climaxes with the infamous and brutal Suicide Race; riders race their horses 210 feet downhill at a 62-degree angle, plow through the Okanogan River, and cross 500 feet of Colville Indian land. The race routinely injures horses and their riders. During the stampede, Omak's population balloons to 30,000.

While you're downtown, try **GRANDMA'S ATTIC** (12 N Main St; 509/826-4765) and **SISTERS** (13 N Main St; 509/826-1968), both cute gift shops. Besides knickknacks, Grandma's Attic has a mini–soda fountain. If you're looking for lunch or dinner, try the **BREADLINE CAFÉ** (102 S Ash; 509/826-5836; www.breadlinecafe.com); they also operate a bakery and a market selling the work of local artists and artisans.

VANCOUVER
AND ENVIRONS

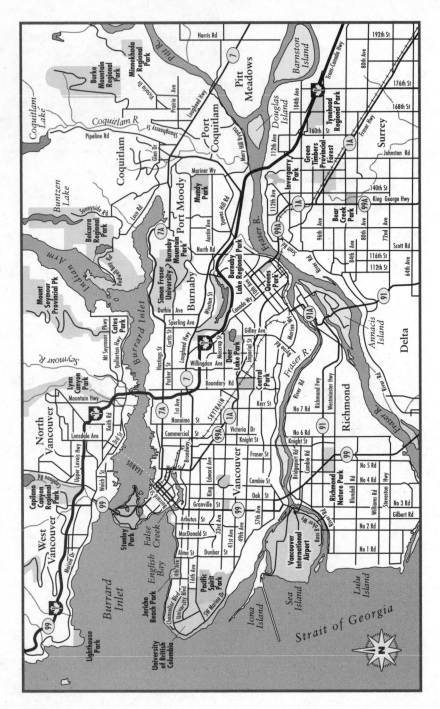

VANCOUVER AND ENVIRONS

Rated as one of the world's most livable cities (recently ranked first and second by two major awarding bodies), Vancouver, British Columbia, is both cosmopolitan and outdoorsy. An ethnically diverse community, a bustling business port and downtown core, and a growing reputation as a foodie and film-production destination—it's been dubbed Hollywood North—combine with a striking natural setting between mountains and sea to give the city and its metropolitan area world-class appeal. These elements also make it an ideal host city for the 2010 Winter Olympic Games.

As the city and its surroundings (including the top-ranked ski-and-snowboard resort of Whistler) gear up to host the ultimate international event, the region is in a frenzy of preparations. New construction is everywhere, from sports arenas to condo towers to a rapid-transit line linking the airport with downtown. Six new hotels are set to open in the downtown core alone, which will help lodge visitors coming for the pre-Olympics festivities, including top-quality theater, dance, and art.

Also on the horizon is the 38th annual JUNO awards, Canada's largest music awards show, which has chosen Vancouver as its next host city. Popular events like the Songwriters' Circle, Juno Cup, and Junofest will kick off in March 2009.

Vancouver may be preparing to welcome the world, but in recent decades immigrants, primarily from Asia, have helped transform the city into a vibrant gateway to the Pacific Rim. More than 30 percent of Vancouver's population is of Asian descent, and the city is home to some of the best Asian restaurants in North America, from simple noodle shops to spectacular Hong Kong–style banquet rooms. Whether you crave freshly steamed dumplings, some of the best sushi on the continent, or bubble tea in a mind-bending array of flavors, you can find it all here.

ACCESS AND INFORMATION

VANCOUVER INTERNATIONAL AIRPORT (3211 Grant McConachie Wy, Richmond; 604/207-7077; www.yvr.ca; 9 miles/15 km south of downtown on Sea Island) is a major international airport with daily flights to every continent. Look for **FIRST NATIONS** artwork throughout the terminals. For advice and basic directions, newcomers can turn to an army of about **250 GREEN COATS**, volunteer goodwill ambassadors for the airport authority. Several car rental agencies are located on the ground floor of the three-level parking structure.

Weathered but still graceful, **PACIFIC CENTRAL STATION** (1150 Station St, Vancouver) is the local terminus of several bus and rail services. **GREYHOUND CANADA** (604/661-0328 or 800/661-8747; www.greyhound.ca) operates five buses daily between Vancouver and Seattle, with connections in Seattle to other U.S. points. **VIA RAIL** (888/842-7245; www.viarail.ca) is Canada's national passenger rail service. **AMTRAK** (800/872-7245; www.amtrak.com) trains make daily runs between Seattle and Vancouver. The **WHISTLER MOUNTAINEER** (604/606-8460 or 888/687-7245; www.whistlermountaineer.com) train runs to Whistler from North Vancouver, with a shuttle connection from downtown Vancouver hotels.

BC FERRIES (250/386-3431 or 888/223-3779; www.bcferries.bc.ca) serves the Vancouver area with boats to Victoria, the Gulf Islands, the Sunshine Coast, and points north. The ferry terminals are south of the city at Tsawwassen or northwest of town at Horseshoe Bay. **PACIFIC COACH LINES** (604/662-7575 or 800/661-1725; www.pacificcoach.com) operates a convenient bus-ferry-bus service between Vancouver's **PACIFIC CENTRAL STATION** and downtown Victoria.

If you are driving, choose between two major highways. **HIGHWAY 99**, the main north-south highway connecting Vancouver to Seattle, leads south from the city across the fertile delta at the mouth of the Fraser River and connects with Washington State's **INTERSTATE 5**. Hwy 99, also known as the **SEA TO SKY HIGHWAY**, also connects Vancouver to the ski resort town of Whistler, about two hours north. **TRANSCONTINENTAL HIGHWAY 1**, the main east-west highway, arrives from the east through the lower BC mainland and terminates in Vancouver; it runs along the south shore of the Fraser River. Another route is **HIGHWAY 7**, which runs east-west along the river's north shore.

Vancouver's weather is the mildest in Canada, thanks to ocean currents and weather patterns that bring warm, moist air in from the Pacific year-round. Spring comes early (by mid-March, usually); July and August are warmest; late summer and autumn days (through October) tend to be warm and sunny, with the occasional shower. Winter is rainy season—roughly November through March—but rain usually falls as intermittent all-day showers or soft drizzles. Heavy continuous downpours are rare, as are thunderstorms and strong winds.

Vancouver

Vancouver is one of the few cities in the world where you can go snowboarding and golfing—or snowshoeing and sailing—on the same day. It's a relaxed, outdoorsy city, its walking paths and sidewalk cafés jam-packed at the first glimmer of sunshine. Along **ROBSON STREET** (see Shopping), the city's fashionable downtown shopping strip, a seemingly endless parade of shoppers includes locals and international visitors. Yet glance away from the opulence of the shops as you saunter along Robson, and you'll see, at the end of a side street, the peaceful waters of Burrard Inlet lapping at the shore. On the horizon north of the city, the snowy crest of Grouse Mountain shimmers for half the year.

Vancouver is one of North America's most demographically diverse cities, and half of all British Columbians live in Vancouver and its environs. The city is composed of an amalgam of neighborhoods, each area possessing a unique character or culture.

In **YALETOWN**, you'll find brick warehouses transformed into loft apartments, offices, chic shops, and trendy restaurants, while row after row of glittering condo towers line the shores of False Creek.

Home to one of North America's largest urban redevelopment projects, the **FALSE CREEK** Basin is centered around the bustling—and must-see—market area and arts community on **GRANVILLE ISLAND**. Dynamic alternative cultures flourish in **KITSILANO** (known as "Kits"), formerly a low-rent hippie haven that has been gentrified by an influx of baby boomers and young families, and the **WEST END**, home to Canada's most densely populated neighborhood and western Canada's largest gay and lesbian community. The West End is just south of Stanley Park; Kits is west across False Creek.

In **GASTOWN**, the city's oldest neighborhood, souvenir shops, galleries specializing in First Nations art, and avant-garde boutiques fill renovated spaces in century-old brick buildings. Vancouver's favorite Eastside neighborhood is **MAIN STREET**, located on the east-west boundary and best known for hip cafés, eclectic restaurants, and small boutiques. **COMMERCIAL DRIVE**, farther east, is a diverse bohemian strip, where the multipierced and tattooed younger generation sips espresso alongside graying oldsters outside the many cafés.

The city's public transit system is an efficient way to get around town. **TRANS-LINK** (604/953-3333; www.translink.bc.ca) runs buses that travel throughout the metropolitan area: the **SKYTRAIN** that operates between downtown, the Eastside, and the city's eastern suburbs and the **SEABUS** that crosses the harbor between downtown and North Vancouver. A new rapid-transit line, currently under construction, is scheduled to connect the airport with downtown by 2009. More information is available from the **VANCOUVER TOURIST INFO CENTRE** (200 Burrard St; 604/683-2000; www.tourismvancouver.com). Or check the route planner on the Translink Web site for transit information and schedules.

MUSEUMS AND GALLERIES

Downtown's **VANCOUVER ART GALLERY** (750 Hornby St; 604/662-4719; www.vanartgallery.bc.ca) is in what was formerly an elegant old courthouse designed by Francis Mawson Rattenbury, a British architect who was both noted and somewhat notorious. The gallery holds major exhibitions, and its permanent collection emphasizes regional artists, including more than 200 works by Emily Carr, a Victorian-era First Nation–inspired painter from British Columbia who studied in San Francisco, London, and Paris. There are also a few supersized photographs from a native son, the photographer Jeff Wall. On selected Fridays, the gallery hosts FUSE, a popular performance art and music gathering, from 6pm to 12am.

If you're interested in Pacific Northwest art and culture, don't miss the **MUSEUM OF ANTHROPOLOGY** at the University of British Columbia (6393 NW Marine Dr; 604/822-3825; www.moa.ubc.ca). This stellar museum has an extensive collection of artifacts from coastal British Columbia Native cultures, including an impressive display of totem poles and a complex of Haida houses. Look for the sculpture *The Raven and the First Men* by noted Haida artist Bill Reid.

Many of the city's commercial galleries are located across the water from downtown on the dozen blocks just south of the Granville Bridge, on and around Granville Street between 6th and 16th Avenues. Art galleries here, including the **MONTE CLARK GALLERY** (2339 Granville St; 604/730-5000; www.monteclarkgallery.com) and the **BAU-XI GALLERY** (3045 Granville St;

VANCOUVER THREE-DAY TOUR

DAY ONE: Start your day at the **GRANVILLE ISLAND PUBLIC MARKET**, which opens at 9am. It's a good place to turn breakfast into a progressive meal: a chai at the **GRANVILLE ISLAND TEA COMPANY** (1117-1689 Johnston St; 604/683-7491), apple focaccia from **TERRA BREADS**, candied salmon from **SEAFOOD CITY** (143-1689 Johnston St; 604/688-1818). After exploring the shops, studios, and galleries, hop on the **SEABUS** for a seaside lunch at sophisticated seafood purveyor **C RESTAURANT** or the eclectic, contemporary **NU**. Then continue on to Yaletown and check in to the oh-so-hip **OPUS HOTEL** or the budget-friendly **YWCA HOTEL**. Next stop: **CHINATOWN**, for a guided tour through the **DR. SUN YAT-SEN CLASSICAL CHINESE GARDEN**, before walking the frenzied streets looking for jade treasures or tasting steamed buns from one of the many bakeries. Return to your room and change for a run along the **STANLEY PARK SEAWALL** or a sunset stroll along **ENGLISH BAY BEACH** before heading to dinner at the **RAINCITY GRILL**, **CHAMBAR**, or **RARE**, which all showcase Vancouver's finest ingredients.

DAY TWO: Stroll to one of the city's intriguing cafés, perhaps **CHOCOLATL** (1127 Mainland St; 604/676-9977) for Mexican-style hot chocolate, or fuel up at the **ELBOW ROOM** (560 Davie St; 604/685-3628), a quirky local diner. Next, head to the **UNIVERSITY OF BRITISH COLUMBIA** and the **MUSEUM OF ANTHROPOLOGY** to see impressive First Nations artifacts and the UBC **BOTANICAL GARDEN**, the oldest and one of the finest gardens in Canada. At lunch, stop for

604/733-7011; www.bau-xi.com), represent internationally renowned painters and photographers.

Granville Island, site of the **EMILY CARR INSTITUTE OF ART AND DESIGN** (1399 Johnston St; 604/844-3800; www.eciad.ca), has many pottery and craft studios. Work by local and regional artists is on display at the **GALLERY OF BC CERAMICS** (1359 Cartwright St; 604/669-3606; www.bcpotters.com) and at **CRAFTHOUSE** (1386 Cartwright St; 604/687-7270; www.cabc.net), run by the **CRAFTS ASSOCIATION OF BRITISH COLUMBIA**.

Vancouver's very small **CONTEMPORARY ART GALLERY** (555 Nelson St, at Richards; 604/681-2700; www.contemporaryartgallery.ca) downtown is worth a look if you're interested in avant-garde work. On a rough-around-the-edges block on the perimeter of Chinatown, check out a show at the promising **CENTRE A** (2 W Hastings St; 604/683-8326; www.centrea.org), Vancouver's **INTERNATIONAL CENTRE FOR CONTEMPORARY ASIAN ART**.

Several Gastown galleries showcase First Nations artwork, including **INUIT GALLERY** (206 Cambie St; 604/688-7323; www.inuit.com) and **MARION SCOTT GALLERY** (308 Water St; 604/685-1934; www.marionscottgallery.

Malaysian food at **BANANA LEAF MALAYSIAN CUISINE** or fiery Chinese fare at **GOLDEN SZECHUAN**. Then go back downtown to stroll **ROBSON STREET**, a trendy boulevard of prêt-à-porter boutiques and swank eateries, or head for up-and-coming South Main Street (**SOMA**) to check out what the local designers are offering. Check out evening shows at the half-price booth at **TICKETS TONIGHT**; afterward, treat yourself to a late supper of "tapatizers" at **BIN 941 TAPAS PARLOUR**. Or skip the show in favor of a leisurely dinner featuring more local flavors at **BISHOP'S, AURORA BISTRO,** or **CRU** before returning to your hotel.

DAY THREE: Start the morning with coffee and pastries at **BREAD GARDEN BAKERY & CAFE RICHMOND** (020-11660 Steveston Hwy, Richmond; 604/271-5642). Afterward, head over to the Asian malls or go back toward downtown Vancouver, stopping to take in the views and trails at **QUEEN ELIZABETH PARK** or to check out the aviary in the park's **BLOEDEL CONSERVATORY**. Go to **YALE-TOWN** for a bowl of chowder and a beer at **RODNEY'S OYSTER HOUSE**, or nosh and sip on sushi and sake at **BLUE WATER CAFE + RAW BAR** before browsing the upscale boutiques and visiting the **VANCOUVER ART GALLERY**, which showcases the city's international reputation for photography and conceptual art. If the sun is shining and you want to explore nature near the city, head over to the North Shore and do an easy hike in West Vancouver's **LIGHTHOUSE PARK** with its stunning city view. For dinner later, go all out with a four-star meal at **WEST** (2881 Granville St, Vancouver; 604/738-8938; www.westrestaurant.com), **LUMIÈRE,** or **YEW RESTAURANT + BAR** before returning to your hotel.

com). In Yaletown, the **COASTAL PEOPLES FINE ARTS GALLERY** (1024 Mainland St; 604/685-9298; www.coastalpeoples.com) has a particularly striking First Nations collection.

PARKS AND GARDENS

With its temperate climate, Vancouver is green throughout the year and especially pretty in spring and summer when flowers and trees are in bloom. Take a walk through the quiet rain forest in **STANLEY PARK** (via Lions Gate Bridge, Georgia St, Robson or Nelson sts, or Beach Ave; 604/257-8400). This 1,000-acre/400-hectare park is within walking distance of downtown but feels worlds away. Walk, jog, or bike along the **SEAWALL** that orbits the park's perimeter; relax at **SECOND BEACH** or **THIRD BEACH** (on west side of park—especially nice right before sunset); stroll in the formal rose gardens; take the kids to the **VANCOUVER AQUARIUM** (604/659-3474; www.vanaqua.org); stop in at one of several restaurants; admire the totem poles; and hike numerous wilderness trails. Nearby, **ENGLISH BAY BEACH** (Beach Ave, at foot of Denman St) is a see-and-be-seen strip of sand that hums even when the sky is gray.

At **QUEEN ELIZABETH PARK**, the highest point in Vancouver proper, dramatic winding paths, sunken gardens, and waterfalls skirt the **BLOEDEL CONSERVATORY** (Cambie St and 33rd Ave; 604/257-8570), a domed structure that houses a variety of tropical flowers and birds; the brilliant floral displays will perk you up on any dreary-sky day. Near Queen Elizabeth Park, **VANDUSEN BOTANICAL GARDEN** (5251 Oak St; 604/878-9274; www. vandusengarden.org) encompasses 55 acres/22 hectares of botanical enticements. Their online "bloom calendar" provides current blooming alerts.

In Chinatown, the **DR. SUN YAT-SEN CLASSICAL CHINESE GARDEN** (578 Carrall St; 604/662-3207; www.vancouverchinesegarden.com) re-creates a spectacular Chinese scholar's garden, complete with pavilions and water walkways; the one-hour tour offering insight into the garden's design is particularly worthwhile.

The **UNIVERSITY OF BRITISH COLUMBIA** boasts several superb gardens: the **BOTANICAL GARDEN** (UBC campus, 6804 SW Marine Dr; 604/822-9666; www.ubcbotanicalgarden.org), the **NITOBE MEMORIAL GARDEN** (a serene Japanese garden), and the **PHYSIC GARDEN**, which showcases traditional medicinal plants.

KITSILANO BEACH (Cornwall Ave and Arbutus St, bordering English Bay) is a year-round haven for joggers, dog walkers, and evening strollers, while farther west, **JERICHO BEACH** (off Pt Grey Rd at Wallace St, or off NW Marine Dr at Discovery St), **LOCARNO BEACH** (NW Marine Dr), and **SPANISH BANKS BEACH** (NW Marine Dr) are local favorites for picnicking, strolling, and sunning.

SHOPPING

In **YALETOWN** (bordered by Pacific Blvd and Nelson, Cambie, and Seymour sts), former warehouses shelter ultrahip clothing stores, including **BABE BELANGERE BOUTIQUE** (1059 Mainland St; 604/806-4010), **GLOBAL ATOMIC DESIGNS** (1006 Mainland St; 604/806-6223; www.globalatomic. com), and **VASANJI** (1012 Mainland St; 604/669-0882).

Weekends are especially crowded along **ROBSON STREET** (between Beatty St and Stanley Park), when urbanites and visitors alike stroll the many boutiques and restaurants. There's much to see and experience, from art books, jewelry, and gifts by local artists at the Gallery Shop in the **VANCOUVER ART GALLERY** (see Museums and Galleries) to a string of international chains to local clothing stores. The yoga-inspired streetwear at **LULULEMON ATHLETICA** (1148 Robson St; 604/681-3118; www.lululemon.com) is popular with everyone from teens to parents, while the young and hip buy casual clothes at **ARITZIA** (1110 Robson St; 604/684-3251; www.aritzia.com). Inside the main branch of the **VANCOUVER PUBLIC LIBRARY** (at Robson and Homer sts; 604/331-3603; www.vpl.ca), designed by renowned architect Moshe Safdie, **BOOKMARK** (604/331-4040) sells fascinating literary gifts.

PACIFIC CENTRE (700 W Georgia St to 777 Dunsmuir St; 604/688-7235; www.pacificcentre.ca) is downtown's biggest mall, with more than 140 outlets, including high-end department store HOLT RENFREW (604/681-3121; www.holtrenfrew.com). Also downtown is the SINCLAIR CENTRE (757 W Hastings St; 604/660-6000; www.sinclaircentre.com), a restored heritage building. Inside you'll find the designer department store LEONE (604/683-1133; www.leone.ca) as well as an assortment of upscale boutiques.

Emerging local designers have set up shop in GASTOWN, particularly along the 300 block of W Cordova Street and along the surrounding streets.

Across False Creek from downtown, SOUTH GRANVILLE, along Granville Street from about 6th to 16th avenues, is home to art galleries, antique stores, and trendy designer clothing and housewares shops. Under the Granville Street Bridge on Granville Island, warehouses and factories have been transformed into a public market and craft shops. Some fine local designers are located in the NET LOFT BUILDING, and several intriguing studios are located along RAILSPUR ALLEY, including NORTHWEST BUNGALOW (1333 Railspur Alley; 604/633-1351; www.nwbungalow.ca), a sliver of a shop where owner Fritz Muntean designs and builds beautiful Arts and Crafts–style furniture. At the GRANVILLE ISLAND PUBLIC MARKET (1689 Johnston St; 604/666-5784; www.granvilleisland.bc.ca), shop for local goods from fresh wild salmon to fresh local produce. This is also where you'll find the best charcuterie in town—it's worth waiting in line for the high-quality pâtés and cured meats at OYAMA SAUSAGE (126-1689 Johnston St; 604/327-7407), which you can pair with a crusty baguette from TERRA BREADS (107-1689 Johnson St; 604/685-3102).

Foodies should detour just west of Granville Island to the city's best cheese shop, LES AMIS DU FROMAGE (1752 W 2nd Ave, near Burrard; 604/732-4218; www.buycheese.com) to sample the 400 to 500 varieties in stock and take in the staff's gracious and highly knowledgeable advice. On the same block, BARBARA JO'S BOOKS TO COOKS (1740 W 2nd Ave; 604/688-6755; www.bookstocooks.com) has an amazing selection of cookbooks, including many by Canadian chefs; check the Web site for a schedule of food-related events.

Locals refer to KITSILANO—located just west of Granville Island—as Kitifornia, supposedly because it reminds them of what a California beach town is supposed to be like. The boutiques in this area, along W Fourth Avenue between Burrard and Vine streets, offer some of the city's most whimsical and eclectic shopping. Look for GRAVITY POPE (2205 W 4th Ave; 604/731-7673; www.gravitypope.com), with its designer shoes, and its new sister store, GRAVITY POPE TAILORED GOODS (2203 W 4th Ave; 604/731-7647) for hot fashion. And stop in at DUTHIE'S BOOKS (2239 W 4th Ave; 604/732-5344; www.duthiebooks.com), a small but well-stocked independent bookstore.

South Main—or SOMA, as locals call the area around Main Street, from about 7th Avenue south to around 30th Avenue—has become Vancouver's hottest shopping district, home to a clutch of alternative shops and designers. It's hard to believe this was once an area way down on its luck. Before you hit the streets shopping, fuel up on lattes at one of the many independent coffee shops. Try **SOMA CAFÉ** (151 E 8th Ave; 603/630-7502; www.soma vancouver.com) just west of Main Street. For one-of-a-kind clothing, steer toward the blocks between 20th and 23rd avenues. **EUGENE CHOO** (3683 Main St; 604/873-8874; www.eugenechoo.com) is the latest "it" boutique, selling Canadian designer labels and a few international labels, as well as a rotating selection of seasonal gifts, books, and accessories. **TWIGG & HOTTIE** (3617 Main St; 604/879-8595; www.twiggandhottie.com) sells creations made solely by local designers. **NARCISSIST DESIGN CO.** (3659 Main St; 604/877-1555; www.narcissist.com), a contemporary women's clothing label known for its body-conscious fit, sells separates and dresses designed and manufactured in Canada. Visit the **BAREFOOT CONTESSA** (3715 Main St; 604/879-1137; www.thebarefootcontessa.com) for the perfect mix of quirky clothing, gifts, and unique trinkets.

CHINATOWN (off Main St, on Pender and Keefer sts) is the oldest and biggest of Vancouver's ethnic communities. During summer, check out the weekend open-air night market (6pm–midnight) at Main and Keefer streets. Don't look for happy hour at **PEKING LOUNGE** (83 E Pender St; 604/844-1559; www.pekinglounge.com) unless you're into furniture; they stock antique armoires, tables, and textiles from China. **MING WO** (23 E Pender St; 604/683-7268; www.mingwo.com) sells dishes and kitchenware.

Vancouver's large East Indian immigrant community's shopping area, called the **PUNJABI MARKET** (at 49th and Main sts, in south Vancouver), is equally tantalizing. Bargain for a custom-fit sari or Rajasthani jewelry, and get the latest Bollywood blockbuster on DVD.

PERFORMING ARTS

TICKETMASTER (604/280-4444; www.ticketmaster.ca) has information about events. **TICKETS TONIGHT** (200 Burrard St; 604/684-2787; www.ticketstonight.ca), in the Vancouver Tourist Information Centre, sells half-price day-of-show theater tickets.

Theater and Dance

The **CENTRE IN VANCOUVER FOR PERFORMING ARTS** (777 Homer St; 604/602-0616; www.centreinvancouver.com), another Moshe Safdie design (who also designed Library Square), showcases touring musical shows, the occasional Chinese acrobatic troupe or dance company, and corporate events. The well-regarded **VANCOUVER PLAYHOUSE THEATRE COMPANY** (Hamilton and Dunsmuir sts; 604/873-3311; www.vancouverplayhouse.com) presents spectacular contemporary and classical productions.

The **ARTSCLUB THEATRE COMPANY** (604/687-1644; www.artsclub.com) also performs a mix of works on two stages: the 650-seat art deco–style **STANLEY INDUSTRIAL ALLIANCE STAGE** (2750 Granville St) and the 450-seat **GRANVILLE ISLAND STAGE** (1585 Johnston St). Next door, the **REVUE STAGE** (1585 Johnston St) is home to the improvisational **VANCOUVER THEATRESPORTS LEAGUE** (604/738-7013; www.vtsl.com), which runs several shows, including the NC-17-rated **EXTREME IMPROV** weekends at 11:45pm.

Every summer, **BARD ON THE BEACH** (Kits Point at foot of Whyte Ave; 604/739-0559; www.bardonthebeach.org) performs Shakespeare's works in tents at Vanier Park. Book in advance for any hope of securing tickets to this popular event.

For more avant-garde theater and dance, head to the Eastside and the **VANCOUVER EAST CULTURAL CENTRE** (1895 E Venables St, at Victoria Dr; 604/251-1363; www.vecc.bc.ca), known as the Cultch. They also offer popular kids' programming that presents family-friendly entertainment throughout the year.

BALLET BRITISH COLUMBIA (604/732-5003; www.balletbc.com), directed by John Alleyne, performs striking contemporary dance at the elegant **QUEEN ELIZABETH THEATRE** (Hamilton and W Georgia sts; 604/665-3050; www.city.vancouver.bc.ca/theatres). Check with the **SCOTIABANK DANCE CENTRE** (677 Davie St; 604/606-6400; www.thedancecentre.ca) for year-round dance shows and festivals.

Music

Under the leadership of music director Bramwell Tovey, the 73-member **VANCOUVER SYMPHONY ORCHESTRA** (604/876-3434; www.vancouver symphony.ca) performs at several locations, including the 1927 **ORPHEUM THEATRE** (601 Smithe St) downtown. The **VANCOUVER OPERA** (Hamilton at W Georgia St; 604/683-0222; www.vancouveropera.ca) presents four to five productions a year at the Queen Elizabeth Theatre.

On the UBC campus, international, national, and local musicians—from classical to world music—take the stage at the modern **CHAN CENTRE FOR THE PERFORMING ARTS** (6265 Crescent Rd; 604/822-9197; www.chan centre.com). Check the calendar at the **ROUNDHOUSE COMMUNITY ARTS & RECREATION CENTRE** (181 Roundhouse Mews, at Davie and Pacific sts; 604/713-1800; www.roundhouse.ca) in Yaletown, which presents an offbeat mix of music, dance, and literary offerings.

Big names play the **VANCOUVER INTERNATIONAL JAZZ FESTIVAL** (604/872-5200; www.coastaljazz.ca) each June, and the annual **VANCOU-VER FOLK MUSIC FESTIVAL** (604/602-9798; www.thefestival.bc.ca) brings toe-tapping crowds to Jericho Beach in July.

One of Vancouver's biggest summer events is the **HSBC CELEBRATION OF LIGHT** (www.celebration-of-light.com), a series of spectacular (and free) fireworks displays, with music simulcast on radio station 101.1 FM; it takes place on four nights in late July and early August. The center of the fireworks action is along the West End's English Bay beaches, but you can also see the show from Kitsilano Beach, Vanier Park, Jericho Beach, and many other spots around town.

FOOD AND WINE

Vancouver Island has become a rapidly growing international gastronomic tourism destination with a well-deserved reputation. The thriving urban restaurant scene is driven by chefs who bring multicultural influences to their craft and a new breed of sustainable fishers, farmers, wild forest harvesters, and winemakers, who provide local and regional treasures from the sea, farms, forests, and vineyards. **TOURISM VANCOUVER** (www.tourismvancouver.com) lists participating restaurants. The annual **VANCOUVER PLAYHOUSE INTER-NATIONAL WINE FESTIVAL** (604/872-6622; www.playhousewinefest.com) attracts 25,000 people each spring to sip samples from more than 175 wineries from at least 15 countries at tastings, dinners, and wine-related events.

Food channel–loving gastronomes will want to sign up with **EDIBLE BRITISH COLUMBIA** (604/812-9660 or 888/812-9660; www.edible-british columbia.com) for food-oriented tours of the Granville Island Public Market, Chinatown, or Commercial Drive, or other foodie events.

NIGHTLIFE

Evenings out in Vancouver are exciting. The club scene is much like that found in many big cities, running the gamut from an old-time rock 'n' roll bender to a no-holds-barred cabaret to an all-night rave in a factory warehouse. Live pop, rock, and world-music concerts lure aficionados to the **COMMODORE BALLROOM** (868 Granville St; 604/739-7469; www.livenation.com), a 1929 downtown theater. Hit the **CELLAR JAZZ CLUB** (3611 W Broadway; 604/738-1959; www.cellarjazz.com) in Kitsilano to get your groove on.

The unpretentious **RAILWAY CLUB** (579 Dunsmuir St; 604/681-1625; www.therailwayclub.com) downtown hosts a variety of local musicians and bands, or sip a cocktail while enjoying open mike happenings in the **CHILL LOUNGE**, the club's beautiful no-smoking back bar. Blues fans crowd the long-standing **YALE HOTEL** (1300 Granville St; 604/681-9253; www.theyale. ca), particularly for the popular jam sessions on Saturday and Sunday afternoons. **MONA'S** (see review) offers Middle Eastern music, belly dancing, and a hookah lounge on Friday and Saturday nights. On the Eastside, **RIME** (1130 Commercial Dr; 604/215-1130; www.rime.ca), a Japanese restaurant and music club in a sleek, modern space, spotlights a diverse mix of local performers and a comedy night alongside a high-caliber menu of Japanese cuisine, including sushi, sashimi, and nigiri-sushi.

At the clubby **BACCHUS PIANO LOUNGE** (845 Hornby St, in Wedgewood Hotel; 604/608-5319), a piano player serenades imbibers, who slink back in red velvet banquettes, with everything from soft rock to old standards. Yaletown's **OPUS BAR** (350 Davie St, in Opus Hotel; 604/642-0557) is equally upscale but as trendy as Bacchus is traditional. With Vancouver rapidly emerging as a film and TV production center, Opus is one of the key hot spots attracting film crews and urbanites alike.

Vancouverites are a microbrew-loving lot, supporting a bevy of brew pubs where several top-notch labels are brewed. Try **YALETOWN BREW-ING COMPANY** (1111 Mainland St; 604/681-2739; www.drinkfreshbeer. com), **STEAMWORKS** (375 Water St; 604/689-2739; www.steamworks.com), or **DOCKSIDE BREWING COMPANY** (1253 Johnston St, Granville Island; 604/685-7070; www.docksidebrewing.com), where you quench your thirst with a waterfront view on the patio.

To get a weekly snapshot of Vancouver's music scene and schedule, check out the alternative weekly **GEORGIA STRAIGHT** (www.straight.com), published on Thursday, and the Thursday Westcoast Life section of the **VANCOUVER SUN** (www.vancouversun.com), the city's major daily newspaper.

SPORTS AND RECREATION

A quick scan of city streets and parks demonstrates just how popular outdoors sports are in Vancouver. A good in-city route for runners or in-line skaters is along the 5.5-mile/8.85-km **STANLEY PARK SEAWALL**. Cycling maps are available from the **CITY OF VANCOUVER** (www.city.vancouver.bc.ca). **ECOMARINE** (888/425-2925; www.ecomarine.com) rents kayaks from three locations. The **GRANVILLE ISLAND SHOP** (1668 Duranleau St; 604/689-7575) is open year-round; the **JERICHO BEACH LOCATION** (1500 Discovery St, at Jericho Sailing Centre; 604/689-7575) opens late April; and the **ENGLISH BAY BEACH SHOP** (1700 Beach Ave; 604/689-7575) opens from June through September.

The NHL's **VANCOUVER CANUCKS** play at **GENERAL MOTORS PLACE** (800 Griffiths Wy; 604/899-7400; www.canucks.com). The local devotion to this team makes getting tickets a challenge. The Canadian Football League's **BC LIONS** play at **BC PLACE STADIUM** (777 Pacific Blvd; 604/589-7627; www.bclions.com).

The **VANCOUVER WHITECAPS** (604/669-9283; www.whitecapsfc.com)—professional men's and women's soccer teams—play at **SWANGARD STADIUM** (intersection of Boundary Rd and Kingsway, Burnaby; 604/435-7121). The family-friendly games have won them legions of fans among Vancouver's soccer-playing youth and their parents.

Thoroughbreds race at **HASTINGS PARK** (Hastings and Renfrew sts, Vancouver; 604/254-1631; www.hastingspark.com; mid-Apr–Nov), at the **PACIFIC NATIONAL EXHIBITION** grounds.

Tickets for most events are at the gates or **TICKETMASTER** (604/280-4444; www.ticketmaster.ca).

RESTAURANTS

Aurora Bistro / ★★★

2420 MAIN ST, VANCOUVER; 604/873-9944
In this minimalist modern storefront, an anchor in the redeveloping Main Street area, chef-owner Jeff Van Geest serves a casual but trendy crowd creative dishes emphasizing Pacific Northwest ingredients. Look for intriguing dishes like bison carpaccio, mushroom risotto in ginger sauce, and local Queen Charlotte halibut with potato and mushroom hash. At brunch, locals line up for the five-spice doughnuts. *$$$; AE, MC, V; no checks; lunch Mon–Fri, dinner every day, brunch Sat–Sun; full bar; reservations recommended; www.aurorabistro.ca; at E 8th Ave.* &

Bacchus Restaurant & Lounge / ★★★

**845 HORNBY ST (WEDGEWOOD HOTEL),
VANCOUVER; 604/608-5319**

Located in one of the city's best hotels, this elegant retreat serves local busi-nesspeople by day, but in the evening when the lights go low, its swanky bur-gundy velvet benches, soft piano music, and servers who cater to your every whim transform it into a beautifully nuanced setting that has earned it kudos as the "most romantic restaurant in Vancouver." The seasonally changing menu includes fresh salads, Nova Scotia lobster, tortellini of smoked organic chicken, or roasted duck breast. *$$$$; AE, DC, MC, V; no checks; breakfast, lunch, dinner every day, brunch Sat–Sun; full bar; reservations recommended; www.wedgewoodhotel.com; between Robson and Smithe sts.* &

Banana Leaf Malaysian Cuisine / ★★

**820 W BROADWAY, VANCOUVER; 604/731-6333
1096 DENMAN ST, VANCOUVER; 604/683-3333
3005 W BROADWAY, VANCOUVER; 604/734-3005**

A dinner in one of these three brightly decorated, laid-back Malaysian restau-rants is like a tropical vacation. Settle under the vibrant batik wall hangings and tuck into the *roti canai*, a fluffy crepe with a curry dipping sauce. With seafood among the house specialties, chile-fried Dungeness crab or prawns in black peppercorn butter are top picks. Many dishes can be ordered and prepared meatless, but don't miss the piquant *sambal* green beans for an excellent side. A wide temperature range of spice options is available. *$$; AE, MC, V; no checks; lunch, dinner every day; full bar; no reservations (Den-man location); www.bananaleaf-vancouver.com; between Laurel and Willow sts (820 W Broadway), between Pendrell and Comox sts (1096 Denman St), at Carnarvon St (3005 W Broadway).*

Bin 941 Tapas Parlour / ★★★
Bin 942 Tapas Parlour / ★★★

**941 DAVIE ST, VANCOUVER; 604/683-1246
1521 W BROADWAY, VANCOUVER; 604/734-9421**

To snag a table at these funky shoebox-sized tapas bars, visit as early in the evening as possible. By 9pm lines run into the street, and you can be sure the party has begun. Best bets: order a glass of "bingria" (sangria with apricot brandy) and several "tapatizers" for two. Nosh on crab cakes with burnt orange chipotle sauce, mussels steamed in habaneros and kaffir lime leaf, flank steak with a maple-chipotle glaze and shoestring fries, or olive hummus paired with Navajo fry bread. Sit at the bar and watch the frenetic kitchen action. *$$; MC, V; no checks; dinner every day; beer, wine, and liqueurs; no reservations; www.bin941.com; between Burrard and Howe sts (Bin 941), between Fir and Granville sts (Bin 942).* &

Bishop's / ★★★★

2183 W 4TH AVE, VANCOUVER; 604/738-2025

One of Vancouver's first restaurants to offer a menu featuring local, seasonal ingredients, Bishop's strives to serve only 100 percent organic cuisine. A consummate host, owner John Bishop warmly greets his guests and visits each table, serving, pouring, and discussing. The dishes are light, with subtly complex flavors. Dungeness crab is matched with pear-cranberry chutney, and wild sockeye salmon is perfectly grilled—while in season, of course. Pan-roasted sablefish and Fraser Valley lamb are top picks from the compelling menu. *$$$$; AE, DC, MC, V; no checks; dinner every day (closed 2 weeks in Jan); full bar; reservations recommended; www.bishopsonline.com; between Yew and Arbutus sts.*

Bistro Pastis / ★★★

2153 W 4TH AVE, VANCOUVER; 604/731-5020

With hardwood floors, bold and bright banquettes, mirrors reflecting well-dressed diners, and a trendy Kitsilano location, this bistro is stylish, appealing, and affordable. The staff makes everyone feel equally at home—whether you're dining with a business associate, a date, or your grandmother. The kitchen puts a modern twist on French bistro classics, including onion soup gratiné, cassoulet with duck confit and *merguez* sausage, or steak with *pommes frites* and your choice of béarnaise or peppercorn sauce. *$$$; AE, MC, V; no checks; lunch Tues–Fri, dinner Tues–Sun, brunch Sat–Sun; full bar; reservations recommended; www.bistropastis.com; just west of Arbutus St.*

Blue Water Cafe + Raw Bar / ★★★

1095 HAMILTON ST, VANCOUVER; 604/688-8078

Spend an evening "bar-hopping" in this converted Yaletown warehouse turned posh seafood restaurant. First stop: the main bar, to slurp Cortes Island oysters and sip British Columbia's Blue Mountain Brut. Next stop: the raw bar, for elaborate sushi rolls with chilled sake. Finally, settle into a plush banquette for the formidable seafood tower, followed by the soy- and sake-glazed sablefish, lobster in jalapeño sauce, or whole Dungeness crab. *$$$$; AE, DC, E, MC, V; no checks; dinner every day; full bar; reservations recommended; www.bluewatercafe.net; at Helmcken St.* &

C Restaurant / ★★★

1600 HOWE ST, VANCOUVER; 604/681-1164

Praised by foodies as one of the best in Vancouver, this restaurant, led by seafood master chef Rob Clark, is an unparalleled culinary experience. In the Zen-like dining room with a stellar view of False Creek and Granville Island, Clark prepares sustainable seafood dishes that are as intriguing to the palate as they are dramatic on the plate. Starters include Asian-flavored scallops; tuna carpaccio with white chocolate, grapefruit, and black truffle essence; and lobster knuckles "Waldorf" salad with walnut dressing. Among the main dishes, look for pan-roasted sablefish with creamy hollandaise sauce, or butter poached lobster and a handful of gnocchi. Try for a seat on the water-side patio, particularly around sunset, for views that are as exquisite as the food. *$$$$; AE, DC, E, MC, V; no checks; lunch Mon–Fri, dinner every day; full bar; reservations recommended; www.crestaurant.com; at Beach Ave.* &

The Cannery Seafood House / ★★★

2205 COMMISSIONER ST, VANCOUVER; 604/254-9606
For fresh, straightforward seafood, this relatively remote east-end dockside location is worth seeking out. Due to port security, access from downtown is via Clark Drive and through a security checkpoint. The restaurant looks modest, but the interior boasts expansive water and mountain views. Salmon Wellington has reigned as the house specialty since 1971. It's still a winner, but the Alaskan black cod with British Columbia wild mushrooms in a lemon but-ter sauce is simply amazing. *$$$; AE, DC, MC, V; no checks; lunch Mon–Fri, dinner every day; full bar; reservations recommended; www.canneryseafood. com; off Clark Dr, north of E Hastings St.*

Century / ★★★

432 RICHARDS ST, VANCOUVER; 604/633-2700
Mixing the elegance of a former bank—marble floors and soaring gilt-beam ceilings—with murals of cowboys and Cuban revolutionaries, this eclectic space has one of the most distinctive settings in the city. Cash to burn? Book a private party in the vault. Not everything that comes out of the *nuevo* Latino kitchen works as well as the offbeat decor, but the Dungeness crab fritters, with hints of ginger and lime, and mango-infused mayo are well worth sam-pling. Head upstairs to the Heist Lounge after dinner to dance the night away, or book it for a large private party. *$$–$$$; AE, MC, V; no checks; lunch, dinner Tues–Fri; full bar; reservations recommended; www.centuryhouse.ca; between Dunsmuir and Pender sts.*

Chambar Belgian Restaurant / ★★

562 BEATTY ST, VANCOUVER; 604/879-7119
Chef-owner Nico Schuermans cooked at Michelin-starred restaurants in Bel-gium before he and his wife, Karri, opened this hot spot interestingly located between the Queen Elizabeth Theatre and Chinatown. The cooking is top qual-ity without a hint of stuffiness. Nico's Belgian background shows up in several incarnations of *moules frites* (mussels and French fries), but don't overlook his more creative preparations: arctic char served with risotto and an olive vinaigrette or North African–influenced lamb *tagine*. The long, lean space gets packed and loud; bring the gang and savor some of the most entertaining food in town. *$$$; AE, MC, V; no checks; dinner every day; full bar; reservations recommended; www.chambar.com; between Dunsmuir and Pender sts.* &

CinCin Ristorante & Bar / ★★★

1154 ROBSON ST, VANCOUVER; 604/688-7338

From the Mediterranean-inspired decor to the wood-fired open kitchen, this bustling restaurant exudes warmth. The crowd-pleasing menu combines Italian influences with West Coast flavors. Try the antipasto platter, then tuck into a pasta dish, or try the seared scallops from Qualicum Bay with aged risotto or braised rabbit with veggies and potato gnocchi. Other options include sablefish with a smoked squid and chickpea purée, or a wood-fired pizza topped with wild mushrooms, peppercorn pecorino, and caramelized onions. Enjoy a cocktail at the bar, have a light meal in the lounge (till midnight), or dine on the heated terrace overlooking Robson Street. *$$$; AE, DC, MC, V; no checks; dinner every day; full bar; reservations recommended; www. cincin.net; between Bute and Thurlow sts.*

Cioppino's Mediterranean Grill & Enoteca / ★★

1133 HAMILTON ST, VANCOUVER; 604/688-7466

Pino Posteraro's Mediterranean creations—grilled calamari with mushrooms and black olives, linguine with lobster, and spit-roasted duck breast and leg confit—have earned him a loyal following in this side-by-side pair of Yaletown restaurants. For dessert, try Gelato Affogato, a take on the Italian classic with espresso custard and whiskey cream cascading onto ice cream, or *limoncello* cheesecake. Next door, the Enoteca is a low-key wine bar with a rotisserie. *$$$$; AE, DC, MC, V; no checks; lunch Mon–Fri summer, dinner Mon–Sat; full bar; reservations recommended; www.cioppinosyaletown.com; between Helmcken and Davie sts.* &

Circolo / ★★★

1116 MAINLAND ST, VANCOUVER; 604/687-1116

Umberto Menghi, one of Canada's best-known restaurateurs, set out to capture the moods of his favorite cities, easily evoking several of them at this chic eatery. You could be in a bustling oyster bar in Manhattan, a romantic bistro in Paris, or a classic restaurant in Florence. Settle into a curvy banquette and order some fresh oysters or escargots. Move on to the *bistecca fiorentina* for two: 32 ounces of grilled porterhouse, complemented by a bottle of Tuscan Bambolo. *$$$–$$$$; AE, DC, E, MC, V; no checks; dinner Mon–Sat; full bar; reservations recommended; www.umberto.com/redo/circolo. htm; between Helmcken and Davie sts.* &

Cru / ★★★

1459 W BROADWAY, VANCOUVER; 604/677-4111

This inviting storefront restaurant, done in warm coffee and butterscotch hues, is especially appealing to oenophiles. Each item on the imaginative menu is color-coded to match the wines (all sold, amazingly, by the glass). Try the three-course prix-fixe meal or, even better, taste your way through the excellent small plates. The caesar salad and the best duck confit get deserved raves from regulars. Another good choice is the bruschetta trio: with fig and

415

walnut tapenade; marinated peppers, fennel, and pine nuts; and white beans with sage. *$$; AE, MC, V; no checks; dinner every day; full bar; reservations recommended; www.cru.ca; between Granville and Hemlock sts.* ঙ

Diva at the Met / ★★★

645 HOWE ST (METROPOLITAN HOTEL), VANCOUVER; 604/602-7788
The tantalizing appetizer of roasted purple garlic velouté in a scallion purée with crispy rice is just one of the standouts at this sleek, multitiered, contemporary dining room offering lunch and dinner menus a step up from the usual hotel fare. There's a business buzz midday when financial types meet over lamb panini or crispy calamari. In the evenings, it's more sedate. Desserts are particularly memorable—chocoholics will want to try pastry chef Thomas Haas's signature chocolate bar: a rich ganache with caramel crunch. *$$$–$$$$; AE, DC, JCB, MC, V; no checks; breakfast, lunch Mon–Fri, dinner every day, brunch Sat–Sun; full bar; reservations recommended; www. metropolitan.com/diva; between Dunsmuir and W Georgia sts.* ঙ

The Fish House at Stanley Park / ★★

8901 STANLEY PARK DR, VANCOUVER; 604/681-7275 OR 877/681-7275
Sure, it's touristy—but you'll still want to belly up to the Oyster Bar with the best of them and slurp a few raw and so fresh you'll feel like you're seaside. If table service is more your style, try for fireside tables, or enjoy the gorgeous park surroundings from the patio. This fish house constantly reinvents its fresh sheet, with items like Pacific swordfish or naturally smoked Alaskan black cod, served with lemon butter of course. Otherwise, order up the excellent seafood bowl stuffed with grilled prawns, Manila clams, mussels, and seasonal fresh fish in tomato white wine broth and traditional aioli. *$$$; AE, DC, DIS, JCB, MC, V; no checks; lunch Mon–Sat, afternoon tea, dinner every day, brunch Sun; full bar; reservations required for 6 or more; www.fishhousestanleypark.com; at Lagoon Dr.* ঙ

Go Fish! / ★

1505 W 1ST AVE, VANCOUVER; 604/730-5040
Gord Martin, chef-owner of Bin 941 and Bin 942 (see review), opened this fish shack on False Creek a short stroll from Granville Island, and fish-and-chips has never been the same. The menu is simple: a few fresh fish dishes, paired with a tangy Asian-style slaw or fries. Only a handful of outside tables are available, so consider taking your meal to go. It's primarily a lunch venue, and closing times here vary; call to confirm. *$; MC, V; no checks; lunch Tues–Sun; no alcohol; no reservations; at False Creek Fisherman's Wharf.*

Golden Szechuan / ★★

1788 W BROADWAY, VANCOUVER; 604/738-3648
Authentic Szechuan fare is the draw at this no-frills Westside eatery. It's popular with Asian families and groups of young people. Choices include rich and meaty double-cooked smoked pork, hot and sour tofu, an assortment of

dumplings, and whatever seasonal Chinese vegetable is available (ask for it garlic-fried). Spice hounds should request an off-the-menu special: fiery free-range whole chicken, poached and served cold. *$$; MC, V; no checks; lunch, dinner every day; full bar; no reservations; at Burrard St.*

Gotham Steakhouse & Cocktail Bar / ★★

615 SEYMOUR ST, VANCOUVER; 604/605-8282
Meat is the main course in this downtown power dining room, where the steaks may be even more beautiful than the people are. From the New York strip to the splendid 24-ounce porterhouse, it's a cattle drive for the taste buds. Vegetables are à la carte, so you order sides of mashed potatoes, creamed spinach, or crispy French fries. For sheer entertainment value, take a seat at the bar and enjoy some of the best people watching in all of Vancouver. Beware: This place prices under the assumption that everyone has a Swiss bank account. *$$$$; AE, DC, MC, V; no checks; dinner every day; full bar; reservations recommended; www.gothamsteakhouse.com; at Dunsmuir St.* &

Imperial Chinese Seafood Restaurant / ★★★

355 BURRARD ST, VANCOUVER; 604/688-8191
The Imperial feels like a grand ballroom of eras past: a central staircase leads to the mezzanine, and windows look out onto Burrard Inlet and the North Shore mountains. Chinese classics can be equally polished—sautéed lobster and crab with ginger and green onions; honey and garlic sauce soaked through pan-fried beef; and a superb pan-smoked black cod. Dim sum is popular with local businesspeople, perhaps because service is courteous and informative. *$$$; DC, MC, V; no checks; lunch, dinner every day; full bar; reservations recommended; www.imperialrest.com; between Cordova and Hastings sts.*

Kitanoya Guu / ★★
Kitanoya Guu with Garlic / ★★
Kitanoya Guu with Otokomae / ★★

838 THURLOW ST, VANCOUVER; 604/685-8817
1698 ROBSON ST, VANCOUVER; 604/685-8678
105-375 WATER ST, VANCOUVER; 604/685-8682
Izakayas—casual Japanese bars serving small plates—have sprouted up all over Vancouver, and this friendly trio offers an opportunity to sample this tapas-with-sake trend. The Thurlow Street location is handy for a lunchtime shopping break, while the Water Street branch "with Otokomae" (in a converted Gastown warehouse) is the most stylish. Locals flock to the tiny storefront "with Garlic" on Robson, though, for the best food. Don't miss the kimchee udon (noodles with cod roe and cabbage), the kabocha *karokke* (an egg coated with pumpkin, then fried), or the grilled cod with mushrooms and garlic-spinach sauce. *$; AE, MC, V; no checks; lunch Mon–Fri (Kitanoya Guu), dinner every day; beer, wine, and sake; reservations recommended; www.guu-izakaya.com; at Robson St (Kitanoya Guu), at Bidwell St (Guu with Garlic), at W Cordova St (Guu with Otokomae).*

VANCOUVER'S BEST GOURMET MARKETS

As Vancouver's foodie reputation grows, so do the number and variety of specialty food shops. Before heading off to hike **GROUSE MOUNTAIN** in **NORTH VANCOUVER** or to picnic in **STANLEY PARK**, you'll want to hit the markets in advance. Just off the seawall in downtown's stylish Yaletown neighborhood, **URBAN FARE** (177 Davie St; 604/975-7550; www.urbanfare.com) offers gourmet antipasto, custom mixed salads, imported cold cuts, sandwiches, breads, and pastries. Nab a sidewalk table for some of the best people watching in the city.

MINERVA'S MEDITERRANEAN DELI (3207 W Broadway; 604/733-3954) in Kitsilano features an olive and feta bar, with dozens of varieties of each, and a truly authentic Greek salad. Pick up all things organic at **CAPERS COMMUNITY MARKETS** (2285 W 4th Ave; 604/739-6676), where bohemian values meet sophisticated taste. The custom-built sandwiches and homemade soups are perfect for takeout, or eat in the café area that overlooks Kitsilano's bustling Fourth Avenue. Capers have other locations **DOWNTOWN** (1675 Robson St; 604/687-5288) and **ON CAMBIE** (3277 Cambie St; 604/909-2988).

The food hall at the **GRANVILLE ISLAND PUBLIC MARKET** is a smorgasbord of delights, featuring everything from farm-fresh local produce to specialty

La Terrazza / ★★
1088 CAMBIE ST, VANCOUVER; 604/899-4449
Specializing in traditional Italian cuisine with a creative modern twist, this eatery has managed to combine fresh ingredients with the classic dishes diners know and love. Opulent silk-weave works grace the 30-foot ceiling; the comfortable dining room is intriguingly decorated with furnishings that evoke an exquisite Italian villa. Dig into the delicious *ravioli caserecci* made fresh in-house every day, and don't miss the *torta d'amore*, a silky, rich chocolate cake filled with luscious cream. An extensive and varied wine list and in-the-know servers makes for the most perfect pairing possible. You will not be disappointed. *$$$; AE, MC, V; no checks; dinner every day; full bar; reservations recommended; www.laterrazza.ca; at Pacific Blvd.* &

Le Crocodile / ★★★
100-909 BURRARD ST, VANCOUVER; 604/669-4298
Classic, elegant, and ever so francophone, French-born chef-owner Michel Jacob's graceful downtown restaurant is a culinary escape. Everyone orders Jacob's savory onion tart and his Dover sole in a beurre blanc, but other classics, such as garlic-sautéed frogs' legs, double-cut veal chop, and sweetbreads with tarragon, all pay their respects to tradition. The professional service and European atmosphere make a meal at Le Crocodile an event. *$$$–$$$$;*

teas. Try the **STOCK MARKET** for homemade soups and salad dressings. **TERRA BREADS** sells the city's best focaccia, baguettes, and specialty breads, while nearby **OYAMA SAUSAGE COMPANY** sells the finest cheeses and charcuterie. On the South Granville Rise, **MEINHARDT** (3002 Granville St; 604/732-4405; www.meinhardt.com) dishes up curry chicken-breast salad and roasted vegetables, plus old-fashioned favorites like berry trifle and man-sized chocolate-chip cookies. **PICNIC**, Meinhardt's eat-in café next door, offers dining at one long marble community table.

QUINCE (1780 W 3rd Ave; 604/731-4645; www.quince.ca) is foodie Nirvana. Pick up gourmet all-natural, vacuum-packed food to go and hearty lunch fare like air-dried salami on country bread or shrimp and chervil salad, you also take away tips for perfecting your own cooking skills. At **CUPCAKES** (1116 Denman St; 604/974-1300; 2887 W Broadway; 604/974-1302; www.cupcakesonline.com), locals covet the Mint Condition (chocolate cake topped with green butter cream) and the Koo Koo cakes (cream cheese frosting and shredded coconut slathered on coconut cake)—confections that come in bite-size minis, too. Definitely, grab a six-pack to go.

—Lori Henry

AE, DC, MC, V; no checks; lunch Mon–Fri, dinner Mon–Sat; full bar; reservations recommended; www.lecrocodilerestaurant.com; at Smithe St. &

Lumière with Daniel Boulud / UNRATED

2551 W BROADWAY, VANCOUVER; 604/739-8185
Celebrating foodies will want to put this contemporary Kitsilano dining room on their "A" list. A European feel and contemporary French menu make for a very tasteful Lumière, which has offered arguably the city's best food. Choose from several seasonal tasting menus, including the 12-course "Signature" selection, designed to make you swoon. From the Queen Charlotte Island lingcod crusted in chorizo to roasted duck breast with veggies and Madeira sauce to salted butter caramel *cremeaux*—it is true food exaltation. *$$$$; AE, DC, MC, V; no checks; dinner Tues–Sun; full bar; reservations recommended; www.lumiere.ca; between Trafalgar and Larch sts. &*

Mistral French Bistro / ★★

2585 W BROADWAY, VANCOUVER; 604/733-0046
Even one small bite of the pissaladière (a thin-crusted tart of onions, olives, and anchovies) at this sunny Kitsilano neighborhood bistro is like a round-trip ticket to the south of France. Chef-owner Jean-Yves Benoit prepares a menu of Provençal classics, while his wife, Minna, adds her own sunshine to the small dining room. Duck lovers can share the platter of rillettes, pâté, and

smoked duck breast, and the hearty cassoulet is comfort food, rain or shine. The dark chocolate mousse, the lemon tart, or the Brie with pears makes a suitably classic ending. *$$$; AE, MC, V; no checks; lunch, dinner Tues–Sat; full bar; reservations recommended; www.mistralbistro.ca; at Trafalgar St.*

Mona's / Mona's Beirut Express / ★★

1328 HORNBY ST, VANCOUVER; 604/689-4050
806 W BROADWAY, VANCOUVER; 604/874-2121
1183 DAVIE ST, VANCOUVER; 604/642-4297

A recent diner at Mona's described her experience there as "My Big Fat Lebanese Wedding." Even if you miss the film reference, chef-owner Mona Chaaban's grown kids, Ibrahim and Wassan, will greet and serve you. Husband Khalil is behind the scenes (his paintings, though, are all over the walls). The festive feeling is amped up on Friday and Saturday nights, when an Arabic band gets everyone dancing. But it's the food that is the real star. You'll find plenty of traditional Middle-Eastern favorites like baba gannoujh, hummus, and tabbouleh, as well as a menu of Lebanese dishes, including baked *kafta*, eggplant casserole, and spinach stew. The downtown restaurant features a *nargila* ("hookah") room, a waterfall, an outside patio, and traditional belly dancing on Fridays and Saturdays. If you're in a hurry, head to the West Broadway or Davie Street locations for quick takeout. *$$–$$$; AE, MC, V; no checks; lunch every day (Mona's Beirut Express), dinner Tues–Sun (Mona's); full bar; reservations recommended; www.lebanesecuisine.shawbiz. ca; between Drake and Pacific sts (Mona's), at Willow and Bute sts (Mona's Beirut Express).* &

Montri's Thai Restaurant / ★

3629 W BROADWAY, VANCOUVER; 604/738-9888

Near the University of British Columbia, this pretty and always busy dining room serves first-rate traditional Thai fare. The salads are excellent, particularly the *som tum* (a spicy mix of shredded green papaya, lime, and fish sauce) and the *yum pla-muk* (squid jumbled up with lime juice, spices, tomato, onions, and mint leaves). Other favorites include the simple *lard nar* (fried rice noodles with broccoli in a soy gravy), the garlic pork, or the British Columbia salmon in a red curry sauce. Cool off with Thailand's Singha beer. *$$; MC, V; no checks; dinner Tues–Sun; full bar; reservations recommended; www.montri-thai.com; near Alma St.* &

Nat's New York Pizzeria / ★

2684 W BROADWAY, VANCOUVER; 604/737-0707
1080 DENMAN ST, VANCOUVER; 604/642-0777

Nat and Franco Bastone learned how to create Naples-style pizza at their uncle's pie parlor in Yonkers, New York, and, along with their wisecracking staff, now serve some of the best thin-crust pizza around. Pull up a chair under the Big Apple memorabilia and sink your teeth into a slice loaded with chorizo and mushrooms or artichokes and pesto. Kids and teens love it here; the West

Broadway location gets jammed at noon with students from nearby Kitsilano High, where Nat himself went to school. Check the hours if you're heading to the Denman location, as they change seasonally. *$; MC, V; no checks; lunch, dinner every day; no alcohol; no reservations; www.natspizza.com; between Stephens and Trafalgar sts (Broadway), at Helmcken St (Denman).*

Nu / ★★★

1661 GRANVILLE ST, VANCOUVER; 604/646-4668

Funky midcentury modern—oversize mohair chairs and neon lighting—meets *The Jetsons* in this stylish restaurant located on the water overlooking False Creek. Don't let the space-age ambience fool you. The kitchen puts out some earnest dishes. After settling into your quirky (albeit uncomfortable) bucket seat, taste your way through wildly creative small plates, like the shrimp and scallop mix with roasted mushrooms or a salad of albacore tuna, herbs, and soy chile dressing. Then move on to the wild salmon with orange fennel or the wild-shrimp risotto. *$$–$$$; AE, MC, V; no checks; lunch, dinner every day, brunch Sat–Sun; full bar; reservations recommended; www.whatisnu.com; at Beach Ave, under Granville Bridge.* &

Ouzeri / ★★

3189 W BROADWAY, VANCOUVER; 604/739-9378

While small-plate fever has gripped much of Vancouver in recent years, this lively little Greek restaurant located in Kitsilano's Greektown area has been serving *mezethes* ("dishes to share") long before the idea was trendy. Partake of all the usual specialties, from stuffed grape leaves to moussaka to char-grilled lamb chops. Friendly, casual, and reasonably priced, Ouzeri is especially pleasant in summer when its doors open onto the sidewalk and small patio. Pick up some tasty olives or baklava in the nearby markets and bakeries while you're in the area. *$$; AE, DC, MC, V; no checks; lunch Tues–Sat, dinner every day; full bar; no reservations; www.ouzeri.ca; at Trutch St.* &

Parkside / ★★★

1906 HARO ST, VANCOUVER; 604/683-6912

This sophisticated garden-level restaurant in Vancouver's West End— decorated in deep browns and creamy beiges—holds a stylish yet cozy dining space. The Mediterranean- and French-influenced menu offers an innovative mix of fresh and seasonal, classically grounded dishes, available individually or as a three-course prix-fixe menu ($65). The seasonally changing menu might include starters of mushroom soup with truffle cream sauce or a gem lettuce salad with grilled asparagus and crisp serrano ham finished with a *gribiche* vinaigrette and shaved manchego. For your entrée, try the grilled swordfish surrounded by garbanzos, tomato fondue, and anchovies, or the Polderside Farms organic chicken, truffled noodles, leeks, and wild mushrooms, all perfectly infused with roast chicken *jus. $$$; MC, V; no checks; dinner Wed–Sun; full bar; reservations recommended; www. parksiderestaurant.ca; 2 blocks north of Denman St.*

Quattro on Fourth / ★★★

2611 W 4TH AVE, VANCOUVER; 604/734-4444

With its crimson walls and glowing wrought-iron chandeliers, this comfortable Italian trattoria radiates romance. Start with grilled bocconcini wrapped in prosciutto and radicchio, or *carpaccio senape*, beef carpaccio with aioli, capers, and Asiago. Kudos for the oven-roasted beef tenderloin in aged balsamic syrup, the grilled Cornish game hen, and the Spaghetti Quattro ("for Italians only"), a well-seasoned sauce of chicken, chiles, black beans, and plenty of garlic. The Corsi family, who own Quattro, also own restaurants in North Vancouver and Whistler. *$$$–$$$$; AE, DC, MC, V; no checks; dinner every day; full bar; reservations recommended; www.quattrorestaurants.com; at Trafalgar St.* &

Raincity Grill / ★★

1193 DENMAN ST, VANCOUVER; 604/685-7337

This contemporary West End restaurant dazzles diners with views of English Bay and creative regional cuisine. Chef Peter Robertson takes "all things local" seriously, sourcing ingredients from the province and confident that the wild salmon is fished especially for his restaurant. Menus change seasonally, but you might start with the warming butternut squash and hazelnut soup or pasta with confit duck leg, walnuts, and currants. Tuck into wild salmon paired with braised leeks, parsnips, and applewood-smoked bacon sauce. *$$$; AE, DC, MC, V; no checks; dinner every day, brunch Sat–Sun; full bar; reservations recommended; www.raincitygrill.com; at Davie St.* &

Rare / ★★★

1355 HORNBY ST, VANCOUVER; 604/669-1256

The chefs at this Vancouver star aren't afraid to experiment, and the results, while not always perfect, range from admirable to breathtaking. Start with the interesting beet caviar, topped with a puff of horseradish foam and sprinkled with chives; the duck breast surpasses the ordinary as it's combined with rhubarb, green onion, and smoked almond risotto. Even the more conventional dishes—beef tenderloin, Dungeness crab—are made with first-rate ingredients. *$$$–$$$$; AE, MC, V; no checks; dinner every day; full bar; reservations recommended; www.rarevancouver.com; between Pacific and Drake sts.*

Rodney's Oyster House / ★★

1228 HAMILTON ST, VANCOUVER; 604/609-0080

All oysters, all the time—that's the reason to visit this unpretentious fish house and bar. While the slogan here is "The lemon, the oyster, and your lips are all that's required," you can choose one of several sauces instead of taking your oysters straight. Also offered are creamy chowders, steamed mussels and clams, and local Dungeness crab. A few tables are available upstairs, but the main-floor bar is where the action is. Prices are moderate, especially given its location in trendy Yaletown. *$$–$$$; AE, E, MC, V; no* *checks; lunch Mon–Sat, dinner every day; beer, wine, cider, Scotch, and Caesars (Canadian Bloody Marys); no reservations; www.rodneysoysterhouse.com; between Davie and Drake sts.*

Stella's Tap and Tapas Bar / ★

1191 COMMERCIAL DR, VANCOUVER; 604/254-2437

Belgian beer on tap and funky small plates make this upbeat Eastside eatery a welcome addition to Commercial Drive. Like Vancouver itself, Stella's eclectic kitchen looks to Asia for inspiration, from the peanut- and curry-coated pork wontons to the grilled fish and jumbo shrimp with Thai spices and aioli. But it maintains its European roots with caesar salad, *moules frites*, and, of course, its beer. It's the sort of place every neighborhood needs, where you can come by yourself or with the gang, wearing whatever you happen to have on, to drink and graze. *$–$$; MC, V; no checks; lunch, dinner every day, brunch Sat–Sun; full bar; no reservations; www.stellasbeer.com; at Napier St.*

Sun Sui Wah Seafood Restaurant / ★★

3888 MAIN ST, VANCOUVER; 604/872-8822 OR 866/872-8822

Simon Chan brought the proven track record and signature dishes of this successful Hong Kong restaurant group to Vancouver, where fans have been savoring its Cantonese masterpieces since the mid-1980s. Recommended dishes include the crispy roasted squab; Alaskan king crab steamed with garlic; scallops on silky bean curd; chicken with broccoli, black mushrooms, and ham; and meaty geoduck clams. Or just ask the staff to suggest whatever seafood and vegetables are freshest. Traditional dim sum, with carts circling the bustling room, is deservedly popular. Sun Sui Wah has another branch in Richmond (4940 No. 3 Rd; 604/273-8208). *$$; AE, DC, MC, V; no checks; lunch, dinner every day; full bar; reservations recommended; www.sunsuiwah. com; at E 23rd Ave.* &

Tequila Kitchen / UNRATED

1043 MAINLAND ST, VANCOUVER; 604/681-2120

One of the rare traditional Mexican restaurants in the city, this newbie has taken root in trendy Yaletown. Step inside and leave the pretense behind in this simply adorned but authentic-feeling eatery. Start with the traditional *botanas*, eaten as appetizers or tapas: an assortment of seafood with a kick, delicious black bean soup, or homemade *quesadillitas*. Dinner offers the opportunity to taste an authentic Aztec- and Mayan-style cuisine that can't be found anywhere else in the city, serving spicy pork ribs, sweet roasted duck, and a "drunken" lamb dish. A full tequila bar pumps out creative margaritas, *mojitos*, Caesars, and even a tequila Cosmo. The creations will abolish the stereotype of tequila in a shot glass and a cruel hangover in the morning. On some evenings, the restaurant showcases live music and also extends hours during the summer. *$$; MC, V; no checks; lunch, dinner, brunch Tues–Sun; full bar; no reservations; www.tequilakitchen.ca; between Helmcken and Nelson sts.*

Tojo's / ★★★

1133 W BROADWAY, VANCOUVER; 604/872-8050

Hidekazu Tojo is Vancouver's best-known sushi maestro. A loyal clientele fills his spacious upstairs restaurant; most want to sit at the 10-seat sushi bar, sip sake, and order *omakase*: "chef's choice." Tojo-san will create a parade of courses till you cry uncle. Although the *omakase* experience starts at $50 per person and goes up rapidly from there, it's worth putting yourself in Tojo-san's hands if your budget will bear it; he's endlessly innovative. He created the BC roll (barbecued salmon skin, green onions, cucumber, and daikon), now found in almost every Japanese restaurant in Vancouver. *$$$$; AE, DC, JCB, MC, V; no checks; dinner Mon–Sat; full bar; reservations recommended; www.tojos.com; between Heather and Willow sts.* &

Vij's / ★★⯪

1480 W 11TH AVE, VANCOUVER; 604/736-6664

Gregarious owner Vikram Vij serves imaginative Indian fare that is as far from run-of-the-mill curries as Vancouver is from his native Mumbai. His signature dish is the lamb "popsicles": dainty racks of charbroiled lamb in a creamy fenugreek-scented curry. Other items on the seasonally changing menu might include spicy masala sauce covering green beans and mushrooms, pork tenderloin with roasted cashews, or the hook and line–caught lingcod smothered in buttermilk and saffron broth. Arrive early, or be prepared to wait an hour or more. If you want to avoid lines or are dining midday, stop in to Rangoli next door, which serves more casual versions of Vij's food for lunch, as well as tea, and offers gourmet takeout. *$$–$$$; AE, DC, MC, V; no checks; dinner every day; beer and wine; no reservations; www.vijs.ca; between Granville and Hemlock sts.* &

West / ★★★★

2881 GRANVILLE ST, VANCOUVER; 604/738-8938

An eye-catching cherry-wood and marble bar with a temperature-controlled, floor-to-ceiling "wall of wine" dominates this restaurant's sleek interior. The kitchen maintains continuity with this modern dining space and a menu of contemporary regional cuisines prepared with premium, locally sourced, seasonally changing ingredients. Order seared weathervane scallops with butternut squash, fillets of sturgeon served with fennel marmalade and artichokes, or roast loin of rabbit with ravioli of confit shoulder with green olive tapenade and braised artichoke chicken. Stellar tasting menus (including a vegetarian version) are available, as well as a prix-fixe dinner from 5:30pm to 6pm nightly. Desserts are equally compelling. The kitchen offers two "chef's tables" for an insider's view on the culinary action. If you can dine before 6pm, the early prix-fixe meal is a decent value. *$$$$; AE, DC, E, MC, V; no checks; lunch Mon–Fri, dinner every day; full bar; reservations recommended; www.westrestaurant.com; at W 13th Ave.* &

YEW Restaurant + Bar / ★★

791 W GEORGIA ST (FOUR SEASONS), VANCOUVER; 604/689-9333

This new restaurant housed in the Four Seasons Hotel highlights the natural beauty of western British Columbia. Gorgeous hardwoods grace the soaring 40-foot ceilings along with a huge, elegant rock fireplace. Nibble grilled octopus with a hint of chile at the raw bar or dig into the broiled bass in lime broth as one of the delicious plates for two. Sip a pour from one of the 150 selections of wine by the glass, and you'll be easily persuaded to bring your friends next time to use the communal dining table that accommodates 14. *$$$$; AE, DC, JCB, MC, V; no checks; breakfast every day, lunch Mon–Sat, dinner every day, brunch Sun; full bar; reservations recommended; www. fourseasons.com; at Howe St.* &

Yoshi Japanese Restaurant / ★★

689 DENMAN ST, VANCOUVER; 604/738-8226

For authentic Japanese, head downtown to this dining room located in an airy second-floor space near Stanley Park. Choose from a huge selection of always-fresh sushi and sashimi, any of the grilled dishes from the *robata*, as well as classics like tempura, teriyaki, and soba. The pretty patio is tempting, but beware of the traffic noise from busy Georgia Street below. Solo diners will feel welcome at the sushi bar. *$$–$$$; AE, DC, MC, V; no checks; lunch Mon–Fri, dinner every day; full bar; reservations recommended; www. yoshijapaneserestaurant.com; at W Georgia St.* &

LODGINGS

Fairmont Hotel Vancouver / ★★★

900 W GEORGIA ST, VANCOUVER; 604/684-3131 OR 800/441-1414

One of the grand chateau-style hotels built by the Canadian Pacific Railway, this stately hotel downtown dates to 1887. The 556 spacious rooms retain their elegance with dark-wood furnishings and comfortable seating areas (ask for a room high above the street noise). There's a health club with a lap pool beneath skylights, and on the lower level, the Absolute Spa pampers (try the chocolate body wrap or the rose facial). Unwind over drinks in the 900 West Lounge, with live jazz every night. *$$$$; AE, DC, E, JCB, MC, V; checks OK; www.fairmont.com; at Burrard St.* &

Four Seasons / ★★★★

791 W GEORGIA ST, VANCOUVER; 604/689-9333 OR 800/819-5053

Guests get the full-on luxury treatment at this sumptuous hotel in a modern tower connected to the Pacific Centre Mall. Despite the city-center location, many rooms offer appealing downtown views as well as peeks at the harbor. Relax in the indoor-outdoor pool or work out at the health club, then head to dinner at the brand-new YEW Restaurant + Bar (see review). Kids are welcomed not only with milk and cookies but also with kid-sized bathrobes and toys. *$$$$; AE, DC, JCB, MC, V; no checks; www.fourseasons.com; at Howe St.* &

Hotel le Soleil / ★★☆

567 HORNBY ST, VANCOUVER; 604/632-3000 OR 877/632-3030

It's easy to walk right by the bland facade of this downtown boutique hotel, but inside, the lavish decor demands attention. The high-ceilinged lobby, a study in gilded opulence, features original oil paintings, a grand fireplace, and a cozy sitting area. The 112 guest suites are on the small side, but their layout is efficient, and they're decorated in regal reds and golds. If you grow weary of cocooning, you can use the state-of-the-art YWCA Fitness Centre next door. *$$$$; AE, DC, MC, V; no checks; www.lesoleilhotel.com; between Dunsmuir and Pender sts.* ♿

"O Canada" House / ★★

1114 BARCLAY ST, VANCOUVER; 604/688-0555 OR 877/688-1114

This lavishly restored 1897 Victorian home in the West End is where the national anthem, "O Canada," was written in 1909. The front parlor with its welcoming fireplace and large, comfy chairs harkens back to gentler times; complimentary sherry is served in the evenings. A wraparound porch looks out onto the English-style garden. The late-Victorian decor continues into the six guest rooms. The huge Penthouse Suite offers two gabled sitting areas, skylights, and a downtown view. A small separate guest cottage has a gas fireplace and private patio. *$$$; MC, V; no checks; www.ocanadahouse.com; at Thurlow St, 1½ blocks south of Robson St.*

Opus Hotel / ★★★

322 DAVIE ST, VANCOUVER; 604/642-6787 OR 866/642-6787

Fun-loving romantics won't want to leave this sexy boutique hotel in Yaletown. Each room is decorated in one of five bold design themes, from "Modern & Minimalist" to "Artful & Eclectic" to "Daring & Dramatic." All rooms feature spa bathrooms with oversize vanities, luxurious European toiletries, and Frette robes, while the penthouse suites boast double-sided fireplaces, plasma-screen TVs, and deep soaker tubs. If you're feeling voyeuristic, request a room overlooking the street; the bathroom has floor-to-ceiling windows and two sets of blinds—one allows you to see out but blocks the view in, and the other gives you complete privacy. *$$$; AE, DC, JCB, MC, V; no checks; www.opushotel.com; at Hamilton St.* ♿

Pacific Palisades Hotel / ★

1277 ROBSON ST, VANCOUVER; 604/688-0461 OR 800/663-1815

Located in the heart of the downtown shopping district, this contemporary boutique hotel encompasses two former apartment towers just off busy Robson Street. Not for everyone, the Miami-style rooms feature übermodern furnishings and refreshingly cool colors. For the best views, request a room above the 10th floor. Added perks include the large indoor pool and the nightly wine hour in the hotel art gallery. *$$$; AE, DC, MC, V; no checks; www.pacificpalisadeshotel.com; at Jervis St.* ♿

Pan Pacific Hotel / ★★★

300-999 CANADA PL, VANCOUVER; 604/662-8111 OR 800/663-1515 (U.S.)
No hotel in Vancouver has a more stunning location or architectural presence. The Pan Pacific's five famous giant white sails (which are actually the roof of the adjacent convention center) jut out into Vancouver's inner harbor. Many of the 504 rooms showcase spectacular water and mountain views; rooms feature muted colors, down-filled duvets, and marble bathrooms. Ask for a corner room (with views from your tub). Sip cocktails in the Cascades Lounge with its dramatic wall of windows, or claim a window table in the Five Sails restaurant (604/844-2855; dinner only) overlooking the harbor and North Shore mountains. *$$$$; AE, DC, E, JCB, MC, V; no checks; www. panpacific.com/vancouver; at foot of Burrard St.* ♿

The Sutton Place Hotel / ★★★★

845 BURRARD ST, VANCOUVER; 604/682-5511 OR 866/378-5513
When Hollywood stars show up in Vancouver, this residential-style hotel is often where they stay. With its plush interior, Sutton Place would rank as a top hotel in any European capital. Each of the 350 soundproof guest rooms and suites has all the amenities one could want. The beds are king-size; the furnishings are quality reproductions of European antiques. The bellhops snap to attention when you arrive. The Fleuri restaurant (604/642-2900; breakfast, lunch, dinner) serves elegant meals, a civilized afternoon tea, and a decadent chocolate buffet. *$$$$; AE, DC, DIS, E, JCB, MC, V; no checks; www.vancouver.suttonplace.com; between Robson and Smithe sts.* ♿

Victorian Hotel / ★

514 HOMER ST, VANCOUVER; 604/681-6369 OR 877/681-6369
You get plenty of character for your money at this friendly 40-room inn in a restored 1898 building between downtown and Gastown. It's not fancy, but all the rooms have wood floors, puffy duvets, and high ceilings. The best are the "deluxe" rooms on the second floor, which are furnished with a brass or sleigh bed and a handful of antiques; rooms 205, 206, and 207 have peekaboo mountain views. Even the 20 inexpensive shared-bath rooms are comfortable (ask for one with a bay window). A continental breakfast is served in the small but graceful lobby. *$$; DIS, MC, V; no checks; www.victorianhotel. ca; between W Pender and Dunsmuir sts.*

Wedgewood Hotel / ★★★

845 HORNBY ST, VANCOUVER; 604/689-7777 OR 800/663-0666
From its ideal downtown location just off Robson Street to its renowned Bacchus Restaurant (see review), this 83-room hotel is all that a small urban luxury hotel should be—and then some. The finely appointed rooms—surprisingly large and decorated with vibrant colors and English antiques—have the feel of a grand home, full of old-world charm. Though its views are lost to taller buildings in the neighborhood, this is the place to spend your

honeymoon—and many do. *$$$; AE, DC, DIS, E, JCB, MC, V; no checks; www.wedgewoodhotel.com; between Robson and Smithe sts.* &

West End Guest House Bed & Breakfast / ★★

1362 HARO ST, VANCOUVER; 604/681-2889 OR 888/546-3327

Don't be put off by the blazing-pink exterior of this 1906 Victorian home. Owner Evan Penner runs a fine eight-room B and B. Rooms are generally small but well furnished; all have feather beds; and there are antiques—as well as wireless Internet access—throughout the house. Sherry or iced tea is offered on the deck overlooking the verdant garden or in the parlor, and breakfast is a three-course affair. Penner also rents a two-bedroom suite next door—a better choice for families with children. *$$$; AE, DIS, MC, V; no checks; www. westendguesthouse.com; at Broughton St, 1 block off Robson St.*

YWCA Hotel / ★

733 BEATTY ST, VANCOUVER; 604/895-5830 OR 800/663-1424

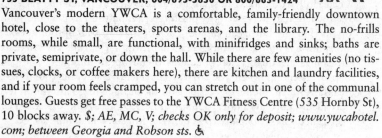

Vancouver's modern YWCA is a comfortable, family-friendly downtown hotel, close to the theaters, sports arenas, and the library. The no-frills rooms, while small, are functional, with minifridges and sinks; baths are private, semiprivate, or down the hall. While there are few amenities (no tissues, clocks, or coffee makers here), there are kitchen and laundry facilities, and if your room feels cramped, you can stretch out in one of the communal lounges. Guests get free passes to the YWCA Fitness Centre (535 Hornby St), 10 blocks away. *$; AE, MC, V; checks OK only for deposit; www.ywcahotel. com; between Georgia and Robson sts.* &

Around Vancouver

Richmond

This Vancouver suburb south of the city, where the airport is located, is becoming known as "Asia West." Richmond has developed a food and shopping scene to cater to its significant Asian population, including many well-to-do immigrants from Hong Kong and Taiwan. The city houses an increasing number of outstanding Chinese restaurants as well as several postmodern shopping complexes where Asian pop culture meets the western strip mall. You'll find convincing iterations of life in Tokyo at **YAOHAN CENTRE** (3700 No. 3 Rd; 604/231-0601), in Taipei at **PRESIDENT PLAZA** (8181 Cambie Rd; 604/270-8677), or in Hong Kong at **ABERDEEN CENTRE** (4151 Hazelbridge Wy; 604/270-1234) and at **PARKER PLACE SHOPPING CENTRE** (4380 No. 3 Rd; 604/273-0276). From Taipei tank tops to calligraphy of Shanghai to Hong Kong–style steamed buns, the wares of Asia are on sale. Bargain hunters could spend hours in the **DAISO STORE** (Aberdeen Centre; 604/295-6601), the North America flagship of a Japanese megachain, where every product sells for $2.

In the summer, join the crowds at the **RICHMOND NIGHT MARKET** (12631 Vulcan Wy; 604/244-8448; www.richmondnightmarket.com; 7pm–midnight Fri–Sat, 7–11pm Sun, mid-May–Oct), and you might think you've stumbled into a market in China. Its food stalls sell everything from fiery noodles to tofu varieties, and its vendors offer T-shirts, socks, acupressure massage, whiz-bang vacuum cleaners, and pretty much anything else you can imagine. Bargaining is de rigueur. To get here, take Bridgeport Road to Sweden Way, past the Home Depot.

The Richmond village of **STEVESTON** on the south edge of town showcases a different culture. This former fishing community is home to the **GULF OF GEORGIA CANNERY** (12138 4th Ave, Steveston; 604/664-9009), a national historic site. You can explore the life of the cannery workers by trying your hand on the packing line and learn more about the area's fishing industry and marine life. Afterward, pick up fish-and-chips to go from one of the nearby shops and stroll along the riverfront boardwalk.

RESTAURANTS

Shiang Garden / ★★

4540 NO. 3 RD, RICHMOND; 604/273-8858
No visit to Richmond is complete without a stop for dim sum, and this Hong Kong–style seafood palace serves some of the best. It's unlikely you'd stumble on it, set back from No. 3 Road amid rows of strip malls, but it's worth seeking out. There are no carts of buns or dumplings in these ornate, high-ceilinged dining rooms; order off the menu (or point at whatever looks good at the neighboring tables), and the staff will whisk your selection from the kitchen piping hot. Although they serve commendable Cantonese fare in the evenings, dim sum is the star here. *$$; AE, MC, V; no checks; lunch, dinner every day; full bar; no reservations; at Leslie Rd.* &

Zen Fine Chinese Cuisine / ★★★

2015-8580 ALEXANDRA RD, RICHMOND; 604/233-0077
Those who know about this place are regulars, and those who don't might never notice its unlikely location, but the critics have been paying close attention to young Chef Lau since his restaurant was given the status "world's greatest Chinese restaurant outside of China" by a *New York Times* reporter in 2008. The modern Chinese cuisine with western presentation went from a fruitless idea to the city's best-kept secret in all of one week. Dishes must be ordered from one of the four eight-course taster menus, which include delicious samples like steamed live crab in garlic sauce, black bean spareribs on bamboo rice, and shark's fin soup in coconut. All diners at the table must order from the same set menu, so make sure you're not eating with someone whose palate is opposite to yours. *$$–$$$; AE , MC, V; checks OK; dinner Wed–Mon; full bar; reservations recommended; www.zencuisine.ca; just off Garden City Rd.* &

LODGINGS

Fairmont Vancouver Airport / ★★★

3111 GRANT MCCONACHIE WY, RICHMOND; 604/207-5200 OR 800/676-8922
While most airport hotels simply cater to harried business travelers, this technologically advanced lodging is an oasis of tranquility at Vancouver International Airport. A lobby waterfall and soundproof glass on all floors eliminate outside noise. The room heat turns on when you check in; lights turn on when you insert your key and turn off when you leave; illuminating the "do not disturb" sign routes calls to voice mail. Even if you're not a guest, you can while away preboarding time by the large fireplaces, at the bar, or in the workout facilities, or you can dine in the contemporary Globe@YVR (604/207-5200; breakfast, lunch, dinner), which focuses on regional ingredients. *$$$$; AE, DC, E, MC, V; checks OK; www.fairmont.com/vancouverairport; on departure level of airport.* ♿

North and West Vancouver

A trip to Vancouver isn't complete without a closer look at the natural setting that makes it such a beautiful city. As you head to North or West Vancouver, the ride across **LIONS GATE BRIDGE** offers picture-postcard views of the **NORTH SHORE**, **STANLEY PARK**, and **BURRARD INLET**.

In West Vancouver, **LIGHTHOUSE PARK** (on Marine Dr, West Vancouver; 604/925-7200) is a pleasant place for a rain-forest stroll and stellar city views. Skiers and 'boarders take to the slopes on **CYPRESS MOUNTAIN** (Cypress Provincial Park, Hwy 1 exit 8 to Cypress Bowl Rd; 604/926-5612; www.cypressmountain. com), the largest of the North Shore peaks. West Vancouver is also home to Canada's first shopping mall, the sprawling **PARK ROYAL** complex (Marine Dr at Taylor Wy, West Vancouver; 604/925-9576).

In North Vancouver, on the way up Capilano Road is **CAPILANO REGIONAL PARK**, home to a fish hatchery, the huge **CLEVELAND DAM**, and the 450-foot/137-m **CAPILANO SUSPENSION BRIDGE** (3735 Capilano Rd, North Vancouver; 604/985-7474; www.capbridge.com), a dizzying span across the most picturesque canyon inside any major city. Farther up the road, you can make the 3,600-foot/1,100-m ascent of **GROUSE MOUNTAIN** aboard the **SKYRIDE GONDOLA** (604/984-0661; www.grousemountain.com) to ski, mountain bike, or simply take in the views. Another route to the top is the challenging 1.8-mile/2.9-km **GROUSE GRIND HIKING TRAIL** that gains 2,880 feet/880 m in elevation. Either way, at the top on a clear day you'll enjoy a superb vista of Vancouver and the Lower Mainland. You can have a meal or a drink in the casual **ALTITUDES BISTRO** (604/984-0661).

Back closer to sea level, the public market at **LONSDALE QUAY** (123 Carrie Cates Ct, North Vancouver; 604/985-6261; www.lonsdalequay.com), adjacent to the SeaBus terminal, has two levels of shops and produce stands, selling everything from crafts to smoked salmon, chowder, and smoothies.

North Vancouver is home to a large Iranian population, and its attendant marketplace offers trinkets, market goods, bakery goods, and restaurants. Inside the **YAAS BAZAAR** (1860 Lonsdale Ave, at 19th Ave, North Vancouver; 604/990-9006), a small grocery selling nuts, spices, produce, and breads, a no-frills lunch counter serves excellent and inexpensive kebab plates. Walk down the street to the **GOLESTAN BAKERY** (1554 Lonsdale Ave, North Vancouver; 604/990-7767) to pick up some bite-size baklava or other Persian pastries.

Still looking for something sweet? Visit **THOMAS HAAS PÂTISSERIE** (128-998 Harbourside Dr, North Vancouver; 604/924-1847), where this noted pastry chef (see Diva at the Met review) offers elegantly crafted chocolates, pastries, and cookies in a tiny shop adjacent to his factory. From Marine Drive, drive south on Fell Avenue and turn right onto Harbourside Drive into an industrial park. The patisserie is on the right at the end of the road.

RESTAURANTS

Gusto di Quattro / ★★

1 LONSDALE AVE, NORTH VANCOUVER; 604/924-4444

Take a short cruise across the harbor on the SeaBus for a sumptuous meal at Gusto. At lunch, choices range from salads or grilled sandwiches to wild spring salmon with Dungeness crab risotto and arugula pesto. In the evening, start with the generous antipasto platter. Among the more intriguing pastas are *spaghetti con polpette*—housemade Sicilian meatballs and ricotta salata—and *rotolo farcito*, a pasta roll with various cheeses and a roasted garlic cream tomato sauce. Try the pistachio-crusted cod in a sweet pepper sauce, Cornish game hen, or lamb chops—all amazingly prepared. *$$–$$$; AE, DC, MC, V; no checks; lunch Mon–Fri, dinner every day; full bar; reservations recommended; www.quattrorestaurants.com; across from Lonsdale Quay Market.* &

La Régalade / ★★

2232 MARINE DR, WEST VANCOUVER; 604/921-2228

This bistro is as near to France as you can get—at least this side of the Lions Gate Bridge—from the rustic French cuisine to the homey decor to the chalkboard menus. Not to be missed: the escargots, with plenty of garlic butter, and the *terrine maison*—thick slices of country-style pâté with cornichons. Slow-food aficionados will appreciate the beef bourguignon or other simmering stews that generally comprise several of the daily specials. Finish with the exceptional cheese selection or one of the classic desserts. *$$$; MC, V; no checks; lunch Tues–Fri, dinner Tues–Sat; full bar; reservations recommended; www.laregalade.com; at 22nd St.* &

LODGINGS

Thistledown House / ★★★

3910 CAPILANO RD, NORTH VANCOUVER; 604/986-7173 OR 888/633-7173
Set amid a half acre of lush gardens, this white 1920 Craftsman-style home offers five luxuriously furnished guest rooms; antiques and period pieces intermingle with eclectic international art. The romantic Under the Apple Tree room has a two-person jetted tub and a private patio, while Sweet Tibby's is furnished with a queen-size sleigh bed and gorgeous stained-glass windows. The sumptuous multicourse breakfast includes items like homemade granola, breads and jams, nectarines in red wine, and a hearty dish such as pork on puff pastry. Genial owners Rex Davidson and Ruth Crameri also offer afternoon tea by the fireplace or on the porch. *$$$; AE, DC, E, MC, V; no checks; closed mid-Dec–Jan; www.thistle-down.com; north of Capilano Suspension Bridge.*

LOWER MAINLAND
BRITISH COLUMBIA

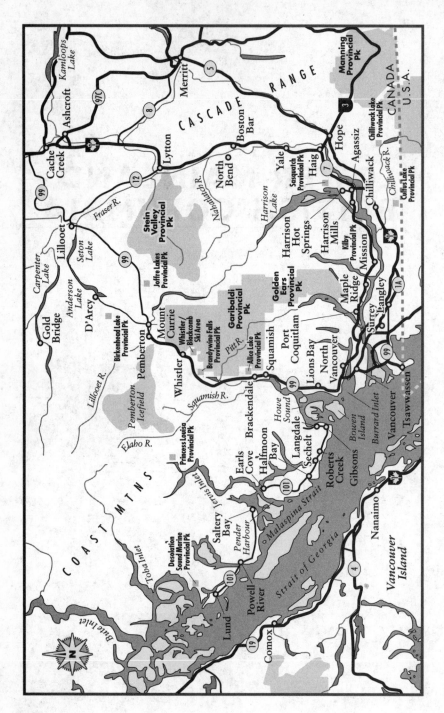

LOWER MAINLAND BRITISH COLUMBIA

The Lower Mainland—a name commonly applied to the region surrounding the city of Vancouver—has become a metropolitan area in its own right, a place where people can, and do, live and work or commute to Vancouver from as far as Abbotsford, Bowen Island, and Squamish. Despite its transformation into a megalopolis, the Lower Mainland holds much for travelers, aside from the obvious appeal of Whistler, in the north. The eastern end of the lower Fraser Valley is an agricultural paradise. The Sunshine Coast offers a multitude of charming inns and lodging. Squamish, in particular, has become a world-renowned recreation center.

ACCESS AND INFORMATION

Border crossings link Washington state and the Lower Mainland at four locations. The busiest are the crossings at Blaine, Washington, where Interstate 5 turns into **HIGHWAY 99** at the Peace Arch, and at Douglas, linking with British Columbia's **HIGHWAY 15**. The others are located just south of Aldergrove on **HIGHWAY 13** and at Sumas just south of Abbotsford, which is on **HIGHWAY 1**. (The latter is the "secret" crossing seasoned travelers use for access to interior British Columbia and much of the lower Fraser Valley.) Hwy 1 (the Trans-Canada Highway) runs east-west, linking the south Fraser Valley with Vancouver. **HIGHWAY 17** links the **BC FERRIES** (www.bcferries. com) Tsawwassen terminal with Hwy 99. The North Shore is reached by traveling west on Hwy 1 across the Ironworkers Memorial Second Narrows Bridge or via the Lions Gate Bridge from downtown Vancouver on Hwy 99A. **HIGHWAY 1/99A** (or the Upper Levels Highway, as it is called on the North Shore) crosses North and West Vancouver to Horseshoe Bay, site of the BC Ferries terminal connecting to Nanaimo on Vancouver Island, Langdale (and Highway 101) on the Sunshine Coast, and nearby Bowen Island. From Horseshoe Bay, Hwy 99 (the Sea to Sky Highway) links the North Shore with Squamish, Whistler, Pemberton, and Lillooet. Travelers on Hwy 99 should be aware that intensive upgrading of the road is readying it for the 2010 Winter Olympics—delays are common, and shutdowns occasionally take place.

The nearest major airport is **VANCOUVER INTERNATIONAL AIRPORT** (3211 Grant McConachie Wy, Richmond; 604/207-7077; www.yvr.ca). The Fraser Valley is also served by **ABBOTSFORD INTERNATIONAL AIRPORT** (30440 Liberator Ave, Abbotsford; 604/855-1001; www.abbotsfordairport. ca). Many Americans fly into **SEATTLE-TACOMA INTERNATIONAL AIRPORT** (17801 International Blvd, SeaTac; 206/433-5388; www.portseattle. org/seatac) and rent a car for the journey into British Columbia; it's about three hours from Sea-Tac to the U.S.-Canadian border.

GREYHOUND CANADA (604/898-3914 in Squamish, 604/932-5031 in Whistler, 800/661-8747 in Vancouver; www.greyhound.ca) offers frequent daily bus service between Vancouver, Squamish, Whistler, Pemberton, and Mount Currie. **WHISTLER AIR** (604/932-6615 or 888/806-2299;

www.whistlerair.ca; May–Sept) offers floatplane service between Vancouver and Whistler.

The **VANCOUVER, COAST & MOUNTAINS TOURISM REGION** (600-210 W Broadway, Vancouver; 604/739-9011 or 800/667-3306; www.vcmbc.com) is a font of information.

Sea to Sky Highway (Highway 99)

The scenic Sea to Sky Highway crosses paths with two historic routes—the Pemberton Trail and the Gold Rush Trail—that linked the coast with the interior before there were cars. Now vehicles can cover the entire 142-mile/236-km Sea to Sky route between Horseshoe Bay and Lillooet in about five hours, making the transit from downtown Vancouver to Whistler in three hours.

Squamish

"Squish," as it is playfully known, is far smaller (population 15,000) and funkier than better-known Whistler. Located between water and mountains, Squamish is a gateway to outdoor pursuits. It has so many things going for it—location, geography, wildlife, weather—that tourism and recreation have assumed almost equal importance to the forest products industry, which has substantially declined due to resource depletion and new environmental laws. Not surprisingly, the town crowned itself the outdoor recreation capital of Canada in 2002. Nearby **STAWA-MUS CHIEF PROVINCIAL PARK** encompasses the area around the Chief, a 2,296-foot massive granite wall that overlooks the southern entrance to Squamish on the scenic Sea to Sky Highway. The 1,248-acre/506-hectare park is famous for its world-class rock climbing, waterfalls, and hiking trails.

Not all is 21st-century recreation here, though: right along Hwy 99, 5 miles/8 km south of Squamish proper, is the **BC MUSEUM OF MINING** (on Hwy 99, Britannia Beach; 604/896-2233 or 800/896-4044; www.bcmuseumofmining. org), which occupies what was once the world's largest copper mine. For area information, contact the **SQUAMISH VISITOR INFORMATION CENTRE** (102-38551 Loggers Ln, Squamish; 604/815-4994 or 866/333-2010; www.tourism squamish.com).

RESTAURANTS

Howe Sound BrewPub / ★★☆

37801 CLEVELAND AVE (HOWE SOUND INN),
SQUAMISH; 604/892-2603 OR 800/919-2537
Rated one of the best pubs for food and beer in the Lower Mainland, this cozy hangout for locals and visitors alike features floor-to-ceiling windows and rustic post-and-beam construction that spotlights the natural beauty of the area. Pull up a chair to a wooden table, or settle down beside the fireplace and enjoy planked salmon or one of their various fresh pastas and pizzas. $$;

AE, MC, V; no checks; breakfast summer only, lunch, dinner every day; full bar; reservations required for 6 or more; www.howesound.com; downtown. ♿

LODGINGS

Howe Sound Inn & Brewing Company / ★★

37801 CLEVELAND AVE, SQUAMISH; 604/892-2603 OR 800/919-2537

This 20-room inn with a massive chimney (the exterior of which doubles as a climbing wall) is part pub, part restaurant, part hotel. Owner Dave Fenn fashioned his gathering place with outdoor enthusiasts in mind. Take in mountain views and stay in rooms 13 to 20, on the quiet side of the inn not above the pub. Rooms are compact. *$$; AE, MC, V; no checks; www.howesound.com; downtown.* ♿

SunWolf Outdoor Centre / ★☆

70002 SQUAMISH VALLEY RD, BRACKENDALE; 604/898-1537 OR 877/806-8046

SunWolf's 10 homey and elegant rustic cabins sit at the confluence of two rivers and the 5½-acre/2.2-hectare center makes an ideal base for exploring. Each of the cabins (some with kitchenettes) comes with a fireplace, fir floors, pine furnishings, and both a single and a double bed. Get light meals from the café before hitting the rivers for white-water rafting and eagle-viewing float trips, two specialties here. *$$; MC, V; no checks; www.sunwolf.net; 2½miles/4 km west of Hwy 99.*

Whistler

Things have changed in Whistler—and more change is to come as the town gears up for the 2010 Winter Olympics. What was once a quirky half-hippie, half-family ski area has transformed into one of the highest-profile resort towns on earth. Regularly ranked near the top in global popularity, Whistler draws the glitz-and-glamour crowd in droves, their members competing with hard-core 'boarders mindful of the mountain's extravagant statistics: 1 mile/1.6 km of vertical, huge experts-only bowls and glaciers, and skiing well into summer.

The Resort Municipality of Whistler (permanent population 9,500) nestles in a narrow valley below Blackcomb and Whistler mountains. No other valley in the Sea to Sky region enjoys such a wealth of small and medium-sized lakes. Remnants of the most recent ice age persist in glaciers on the highest peaks in **GARIBALDI PARK** (www.env.gov.bc.ca/bcparks), to the south of Whistler. Above all, no other ski area offers quite what Whistler does: two massive gondola-served mountains, reliable snow, and an almost-eternal season, with midsummer skiing on **BLACKCOMB GLACIER**. This resort, where the average house price now tops $1 million, is expensive, but you can generally count on outstanding value in return.

The town of Whistler consists of neighborhoods linked to the hotels and restaurants in the village core by roads and the pedestrian-friendly **VALLEY TRAIL**. Hop

---

WATCHING EAGLES SOAR

Although bald eagles are the United States' national symbol, they're ironically more common in British Columbia than anywhere else except Alaska; in neither place were the birds endangered as they were in the Lower 48. These majestic raptors are an iconic Pacific Northwest sight, soaring high in thermals over waters or forests. Each winter they migrate to lowland rivers that have late salmon runs, one of which is the **SQUAMISH RIVER** along the Sea-to-Sky Highway. (The other is the Skagit River in Washington state.)

Every year hundreds, and sometimes more than 1,000, eagles come to roost in the tall cottonwoods that line the Squamish in the Brackendale area. And as wildlife watching has grown, thousands of humans congregate in Brackendale to watch. The phenomenon led to creation of the **BRACKENDALE BALD EAGLE SANCTUARY** in 1996, which protects the habitat and imposes rules.

Peak viewing is December through February, when visitors can sometimes spot dozens of birds in the trees. Patient observation often rewards with the sight of a

---

on one of the **WAVE** (Whistler and Valley Express) buses (604/932-4020; www. busonline.ca), which connect with all Whistler neighborhoods, from Function Junction to Emerald Estates, as well as the nearby towns of Pemberton and Mount Currie. WAVE operates a free village shuttle with stops at Whistler Village, Village North, Upper Village, and the Benchlands. All buses are equipped with racks for skis and snowboards in winter and bikes in summer.

WHISTLER MOUNTAIN, elevation 7,160 feet/2,182 m, and **BLACKCOMB MOUNTAIN**, elevation 7,494 feet/2,284 m, were rivals for two decades before merging under the Intrawest corporate umbrella in 1997, an event that fans of Whistler, the older mountain, viewed with some trepidation but have since accepted. You can just as easily explore one as the other; each offers a complementary perspective on its companion and has a loyal following. Whistler is usually considered the more family-friendly mountain; Blackcomb, the locale for experts, 'boarders, and serious skiers. Either is reached from the Whistler Village base—via gondolas that depart just yards from each other—and Intrawest is proposing a mind-boggling peak-to-peak gondola that will link the upper areas of the two mountains.

Whistler and Blackcomb have developed trails covering more than 8,100 acres/3, 277 hectares, and these trails have been shaped to hold snow in winter and provide downhill cycling in summer in **WHISTLER MOUNTAIN BIKE PARK**. For information, contact **WHISTLER-BLACKCOMB GUEST RELATIONS** (604/904-8134 or 866/218-9690; www.whistler-blackcomb.com).

Whistler Village's **LOST LAKE PARK** (604/905-0071; www.crosscountry connection.bc.ca) features a 20-mile/32-km network of packed and tracked trails for cross-country skiers, snowshoers, and, in summer, mountain bikers. Skiing around the lake takes 60–90 minutes. Trails are marked for beginners to experts;

bird feasting on a spawned-out salmon that has washed up on a gravel bar. Best viewing is in early morning, before crowds gather and drive the birds to more distant trees.

The **BRACKENDALE ART GALLERY** (604/898-3333; www.brackendaleart gallery.com) has created a January festival and bird count to honor the phenomenon and offers guided walks to observe. **SUNWOLF OUTDOOR CENTRE** (www.sunwolf.net) and **CANADIAN OUTBACK ADVENTURES** (www.canadian outback.com) offer guided float trips to watch. Bring warm waterproof clothing and binoculars, and please observe the eagle-protection code: be quiet, don't try to get too near the birds, and don't ever land on a gravel bar where an eagle is feeding.

It's a wildlife spectacle rarely matched, an opportunity to experience the renewal of a timeless natural cycle. As the salmon give birth to a new generation and die, they enable the eagles to survive the rigors of winter and carry their kind on into generations beyond.

—Eric P. Lucas

the 2-mile/4-km **LOST LAKE LOOP TRAIL** is lit for night skiing. A designated cross-country ski trail in winter and a hiking, cycling, and in-line skating loop in summer, the 12-mile/20-km **VALLEY TRAIL**'s access points include the Whistler Golf Course on Hwy 99 in Whistler Village, the Meadow Park Sports Centre on Hwy 99 in Alpine Meadows, and Rainbow Park on Alta Lake Road.

Snowmobiling is big at Whistler: check out **CANADIAN SNOWMOBILE ADVEN-TURES** (604/938-1616; www.canadiansnowmobile.com) and **COUGAR MOUN-TAIN WILDERNESS ADVENTURES** (604/932-4086 or 888/297-2222; www.cougarmountain.ca), which also offers dogsledding, horseback riding, snowshoeing, fishing, and mountain bike tours.

Heli-skiing or -boarding at Whistler can be arranged with **WHISTLER HELI-SKIING** (102-4154 Village Green; 604/932-4105 or 888/435-4754; www.whistlerheliskiing.com), **COAST RANGE HELISKIING** (604/894-1144 or 800/701-8744; www.coastrangeheliskiing.com), and **BLACKCOMB HELICOPTERS** (9960 Heliport; 604/938-1700 or 800/330-4354; www.blackcombhelicopters.com).

Some of the most inviting snowshoe trails in Whistler are those in the forest surrounding Olympic Station on Whistler Mountain. **OUTDOOR ADVENTURES AT WHISTLER** (218-4293 Mountain Square; 604/932-0647; www.adventureswhistler.com) offers rentals and guided tours, including evening outings on Blackcomb.

For summer visitors, golf choices include the scenic Arnold Palmer–designed **WHISTLER GOLF CLUB** (4001 Whistler Wy; 604/932-3280 or 800/376-1777; www.whistlergolf.com) and the equally esteemed Robert Trent Jones Jr. **LINK COURSE** at Chateau Whistler (4612 Blackcomb Wy; 604/938-2092 or 877/938-2092). There is also **NICKLAUS NORTH** (8080 Nicklaus N Blvd; 604/938-9898 or 800/386-9898), a Jack Nicklaus–designed course in the Green Lake area.

TOURISM WHISTLER'S ACTIVITY AND INFORMATION CENTRE's two locations (4010 Whistler Wy; 604/938-2769 or 877/991-9988; 4230 Gateway Dr; 604/935-3357; www.tourismwhistler.com) provide advice on local happenings. With the area receiving more than 2 million ski visits alone each winter, advance reservations are recommended for all lodging and restaurants. Many rooms in the area, as well as condos, are owned by individuals and investment companies but are managed by rental combines or the hotel operator whose buildings they occupy.

RESTAURANTS

Araxi Restaurant & Bar / ★★★½

4222 VILLAGE SQUARE (BLACKCOMB LODGE), WHISTLER; 604/932-4540

Whistler's culinary cornerstone anchors the Village Square's patio scene. The restaurant's glittering ambience can be experienced either at the mahogany-topped bar or at one of the white-linen tables in the main dining room. With its emphasis on fresh, locally sourced fare prepared with French and Italian influences, Araxi's menu—just like its artwork—undergoes a complete makeover every six months. $$$; AE, DC, MC, V; no checks; lunch (summer), dinner every day; full bar; reservations recommended; www.araxi.com. &

Bearfoot Bistro / ★★★★

4121 VILLAGE GREEN, WHISTLER; 604/932-3433

Though Bearfoot hews to the catalog of Pacific fish and hearty meat dishes that are so prevalent in Whistler, execution and imagination of these distinguish this fairly inconspicuous restaurant that some critics have called one of the best in the world—yes, the *world*. Diners select three courses for the nightly prix fixe ($98) or choose the chef's daily five-course menu ($148). Add in the sommelier's five-course wine pairing, and you're looking at well over $250. Breathtaking prices, indeed, but the result is worth it. Stuffed silly, many diners repair to Bearfoot's cigar bar after dinner, one of the few indoor smoking venues in the province. $$$$; AE, DC, MC, V; no checks; lunch, dinner every day; full bar; reservations required; www.bearfootbistro.com; 1 block east of Whistler Wy. &

Caramba! / ★★½

4314 MAIN ST TOWN PLAZA, WHISTLER; 604/938-1879

Caramba! proves dining out in Whistler doesn't have to break the bank. This fun, boisterous, Mediterranean-influenced restaurant holds down a corner of the Town Plaza on one of Village North's busiest walkways. High-energy service twins with big, soul-satisfying portions of pasta, pizza, and roasts. The open kitchen, zinc countertops, alder-fired pizza ovens, and sizzling rotisseries lend a warm, casual tone to the room. $; AE, MC, V; no checks; lunch (in season), dinner every day; full bar; reservations recommended; www.caramba-restaurante.com; at Town Plaza Square. &

La Rúa Restaurante / ★★★★

4557 BLACKCOMB WY (CHAMOIS HOTEL), WHISTLER; 604/932-5011
Longtime Whistler restaurateur Mario Enero's stylish restaurant is tucked away in the Chamois hotel, one of Whistler's snazziest lodgings. Superb dishes created by R. D. Stewart, one of Whistler's top-ranked chefs, are served in portions that will satisfy the most discriminating palate. The menu has been simplified a bit, but the basics remain the same: highly flavored presentations of regional foods with a slight Mediterranean twist. Start with a pyramid of bocconcini cheese or ravioli and scallops. No one prepares lamb better. *$$$; AE, DC, MC, V; no checks; dinner every day; full bar; reservations recommended; www.larua-restaurante.com; Upper Village, at Lorimer Rd.* &

Quattro at Whistler / ★★★

**4319 MAIN ST (PINNACLE INTERNATIONAL HOTEL),
WHISTLER; 604/905-4844**
Quattro is upbeat, vibrant, and innovative. *La cucina leggera*, or "the healthy kitchen," is the motto here. Fungi fanciers love the carpaccio featuring sliced portobello mushrooms. Kudos also for the grilled scallops and prawns, served with a Dungeness crab risotto inside a phyllo roll. Pasta dishes are equally inspired. Portions are generous, and desserts are stunning. *$$$; AE, MC, V; no checks; dinner every day; full bar; reservations recommended; www. quattrorestaurants.com; Village North, at Library Square.* &

Rim Rock Café / ★★

**2117 WHISTLER RD (HIGHLAND LODGE),
WHISTLER; 604/932-5565 OR 877/932-5589**
Chef Rolf Gunther dishes up superb food in this cozy, woody café with its centerpiece stone fireplace. It's filled to the open rafters with locals who consistently rate this Creekside cornerstone, little known to tourists, is their favorite. A daily fresh sheet features fish and game. Along with the café's reputation for superb seafood, the service here is ranked the best in town. *$$$; AE, MC, V; no checks; dinner every day (closed mid-Oct–mid-Nov); full bar; reservations recommended; www.rimrockwhistler.com; 2 miles/3.5 km south of main Whistler Village entrance.*

Splitz Grill / ★

4369 MAIN ST (ALPENGLOW), WHISTLER; 604/938-9300
You'll be hard-pressed to find a hamburger this thick, juicy, and tantalizing anywhere else. In fact, Splitz tops the polls as Whistler's best burger joint. Burgers on crusty buns are elevated to new heights with your choice of umpteen toppings. A meal is less than $10, half that for kids, whose selections come with house-cut fries and a soft drink. Sweet temptations include a caramelized banana split. *$; MC, V; no checks; lunch, dinner every day; beer and wine; no reservations; www.splitzgrill.com; Village North, across from 7-Eleven.* &

WHISTLER THREE-DAY TOUR

DAY ONE: Check in to the spectacularly renovated (to be completed Fall 2009) **WESTIN WHISTLER**, just a three-minute walk from the gondola base in Whistler Village. Get a hearty breakfast at Chef Bernard's **CIAO-THYME BISTRO** (4573 Chateau Blvd; 604/932-7051; www.ciaothymebistro.com), then grab your gear from the ski valet and head to **WHISTLER-BLACKCOMB GUEST RELATIONS**, the all-encompassing ticket and information source for the two mountains; a three-day pass is the best bargain. Hop on the **WHISTLER VILLAGE GONDOLA** to ride to the top, warming up with a run or two down the slopes under the Emerald Express quad chair. Then hop the Peak Chair for its mind-boggling ride up over the cliffs of **WHISTLER MOUNTAIN** to the area's pinnacle at 7,160 feet/ 2,182 m. Stop to admire the view of the Coast Range, then glide down to the Saddle to ski through this gap that was blasted in the rock to open up the vast bowl for intermediate skiers. Head on down to the **CHIC PEA** (top of Garbanzo Express Chair; 604/932-3434) for lunch, then all the way down to the bottom to get on the **EXCALIBUR GONDOLA** to whisk you up **BLACKCOMB MOUNTAIN**. Spend the afternoon exploring the vast intermediate terrain in **7TH HEAVEN** or the experts-only mecca on the **BLACKCOMB GLACIER**. After a rest in your room, walk five minutes to dinner at **BEARFOOT BISTRO**.

DAY TWO: Have breakfast and coffee at **MOGULS BAKERY** (4202 Village

---

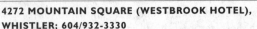

Sushi Village / ★★

**4272 MOUNTAIN SQUARE (WESTBROOK HOTEL),
WHISTLER; 604/932-3330**

A mainstay for years in Whistler, Sushi Village is one of those popular local hangouts the parking valets will tell you about. Even though it's perched on the second floor of the Westbrook Hotel, people patiently wait in line. It's worth it. Extremely fresh sushi, sashimi, and *maki* platters, as well as combinations served in wooden sushi boats, are prepared by animated experts at the counter. Simple Japanese-style decor allows for privacy. *$$; AE, DC, MC, V; no checks; lunch Fri–Sun, dinner every day; full bar; reservations recommended; www.sushivillage.com; Whistler Village, at Sundial Crescent.* &

LODGINGS

Adara Hotel / ★★★

4122 VILLAGE GREEN, WHISTLER; 604/905-4009 OR 866/502-3272

Deliberately designed to be the antithesis of the usual Whistler lodging, the Adara succeeds admirably at its mission—and at offering a splendid place to stay in the heart of the village. With candles and sculptures in the lobby and

Square; 604/932-4845), then head back up to the top of Whistler Mountain to spend the morning skiing the wide expanses of the **FLUTE BOWL**. Lunch at **BEET ROOT CAFÉ** (4340 Lorimer Rd; 604/932-1163), a great soup-and-sandwich place. Then it's back over to the **EXCALIBUR GONDOLA**, this time for a short ride up to the **TUBE PARK**. Spend a few hours with a gaggle of delirious parents and kids bombing down the tube runs—when the attendants at the top of the hill ask how fast you want to go, say "as fast as you can." Don't forget to ask them for a spin run. Reserve a table at **ARAXI RESTAURANT & BAR**, one of the best restaurants in British Columbia, and in the evening put on your go-to-dinner clothes.

DAY THREE: Start with coffee and muffins at **HOT BUNS** (4324 Sunrise Alley; 604/932-2112), then hike over to **LOST LAKE PARK** to pick up Nordic equipment for a 5K jaunt along the **VALLEY TRAIL**. Hop a shuttle to **GREEN LAKE** for a few hours of skating on this 3-mile/4.8-km "rink" where residents carve out hockey layouts. Back at Whistler Village, have a late lunch at **SUSHI VILLAGE**, then head back up the gondola for one last run from the peak. Afterward, for a change of pace, check in to the hip **ADARA HOTEL** and stroll through the village for window shopping. Have burgers-as-you-like at **SPLITZ GRILL**, then cap off your Whistler visit with homemade ice cream at **LA RÚA RESTAURANTE**. (If you want to extend your ski vacation, add two days in the pristine wilderness at **CALLAGHAN LODGE** in an alpine valley southwest of Whistler.)

fake furs, molded plastic chairs, and zebra-wood furnishings in the rooms, it's hip. Exotic amenities range from bedside white-noise machines to personal oxygen devices in the bathrooms. *$$$$; AE, MC, V; no checks; www.adara hotel.com; Whistler Village.* &

Brew Creek Lodge / ★★

1 BREW CREEK RD, WHISTLER; 604/932-7210
This sparkling hideaway sits at the foot of Brandywine Mountain south of Whistler. A sheltering forest buffers all sounds from the steady stream of nearby traffic on Hwy 99. Brew Creek, the lodge's crowning feature, flows through the 12-acre/4.8-hectare property past a massive main lodge with six guest rooms. Nearby are two suites that share the Guest House; also on-site are the Trappers Cabin and the romantic Treehouse. No TVs or phones intrude on the calm, which is best appreciated from the creekside hot tub. *$$–$$$; AE, MC, V; checks OK; www.brewcreeklodge.com; 0.6 mile/1 km west of Hwy 99, 12 miles/16 km south of Whistler.* &

Callaghan Lodge / ★★

CALLAGHAN VALLEY, WHISTLER; 604/938-0616 OR 877/938-0616

It's hard to imagine a more sensational setting for a winter sports lodge. Perched on a small hill in the middle of an alpine valley at 6,000 feet/1.8 m, Callaghan Lodge overlooks a snowy wilderness. The lodge has comfy guest rooms, plus a two-level family suite. Packages include meals and access to cross-country trails. The valley below the lodge will be the site for Nordic events in the 2010 Winter Olympics; for now, peace and quiet reign. Access is by snowmobile or snowcat only; the ride takes an hour from the Hwy 99 pickup point. *$$$$; AE, MC, V; no checks; www.callaghancountry.com; off Hwy 99, accessible only by snowmobile, snowshoes, or skis in winter and helicopter or hike-in in summer.*

Durlacher Hof Alpine Country Inn / ★★★

7055 NESTERS RD, WHISTLER; 604/932-1924 OR 877/932-1924

This farmhouse is a traditional country inn, right down to hut slippers that await guests' feet. Hand-carved furniture and fixtures adorn all eight guest rooms, plus the piano bar and cozy kitchen with its *kachenelofen*—an old-fashioned fireplace oven. For simple overnight stays, book one of the Sunshine rooms with mountain views. The Library Room is fully wheelchair accessible, with a roll-in shower. Attention to detail is evident everywhere, such as in the cozy après-ski area where afternoon tea is served. *$$$$; MC, V; checks OK; www.durlacherhof.com; Nesters neighborhood.* &

Fairmont Chateau Whistler Resort / ★★★★

4599 CHATEAU BLVD, WHISTLER; 604/938-8000 OR 866/540-4424

In keeping with the cachet its sister chateaus enjoy in Banff and Lake Louise, the 12-story, 563-room Chateau Whistler is among Whistler's signature accommodations. Anchoring the Upper Village neighborhood, it offers sweeping views of the mountains, an indoor-outdoor pool, and a spa. As at every upscale hotel, pampering is provided here. Given the grand impression of the foyer, however, standard rooms—particularly junior suites—are only adequately sized. The chateau's public areas are some of the most inviting in Whistler, deserving of a look even if you're staying elsewhere. *$$$$; AE, DC, DIS, MC, V; checks OK; www.fairmont.com; at foot of Blackcomb.* &

Four Seasons / ★★★★

4591 BLACKCOMB WY, WHISTLER; 604/935-3400 OR 800/819-5053

Canada's signature four-star hotel chain is ably represented in Whistler by this massive complex with 273 rooms, a separate building of 37 private residences, and a 15-room spa. The entry is quintessential Four Seasons: a sweeping driveway that leads to a discreetly elegant hallway with exquisite West Coast art and a hushed, professional atmosphere. The prevailing decor themes are earthy fabrics and woods in browns and tans. *$$$$; AE, DC, MC, V; checks OK (call for policy); www.fourseasons.com/whistler; at far eastern end of Upper Village.* &

Pan Pacific Village Centre / ★★★

4299 BLACKCOMB WY, WHISTLER; 604/966-5500 OR 888/966-5575

Of the two Pan Pacific properties in Whistler, this is the newest, smallest, and nicest. With just 83 guest rooms (all of them suites), it offers an intimate atmosphere not possible at its bigger (121-room) sister property. The setting affords expansive views. The three penthouse suites are among the best-situated in Whistler, with sensational views of both mountains, if you're in the four-figures-per-night bracket. *$$$$; AE, DC, MC, V; no checks; www. panpacific.com; off Blackcomb Wy.* &

Westin Whistler / ★★★★☆

4090 WHISTLER WY, WHISTLER; 604/905-5000 OR 888/634-5577

One of Whistler Village's largest new hotels is also one of its best. With 419 suites—many undergoing renovations scheduled to be completed by fall 2009—designed to emphasize home comfort and convenience, guests enjoy fireplaces, modern furnishings, inviting soaker tubs, and windows that open to fresh mountain air. Rooms include junior studios, one- and two-bedroom suites (with quality-appointed kitchens), and 1,500 square-foot Penthouse Mountain Suites for those looking for the ultimate in luxury. But what really makes this hotel appealing is the hotel staff: an obviously well-trained crew—friendly, knowledgeable, and remarkably competent, even in the face of the daunting crowds. Need help with a Rim Rock Café reservation? Not one, not two, but three workers staff the concierge desk. *$$$; AE, DC, MC, V; no checks; www.westinwhistler.com; off Blackcomb Wy.* &

Pemberton and Mount Currie

In the decades before Hwy 99 was pushed through to Pemberton, this farming community that's evolving into a Whistler suburb existed in isolation from the rest of the Lower Mainland. Public transit now connects Pemberton and nearby Mount Currie, which is 3.7 miles/6 km east of Pemberton, with Whistler 22 miles/35 km to the south. For a schedule, contact **WAVE** (604/932-4020; www. busonline.ca).

Today this valley is experiencing growth in both visitors and new residents, many of whom work in Whistler. To get the feel, attend the annual **CANADA DAY CELEBRATION** the last week in June. There won't be a potato in sight (though Pemberton—or Spud Valley—is renowned for the quality of its seed potatoes), but you can try other specialties. By then there will be produce at **NORTH ARM FARMS** (1888 Sea to Sky Hwy; 604/894-5379; www.northarmfarm.com; midway between Pemberton and Mount Currie).

This is also the territory of the Lil'wat people: Mount Currie and D'Arcy, 23½ miles/38 km north of Mount Currie. Everyone is welcome at First Nation events, such as the **LILLOOET LAKE RODEO**, held each May in Mount Currie, and August's **D'ARCY SALMON FESTIVAL**.

The quaint **PEMBERTON HERITAGE MUSEUM** (Camus and Prospect sts, Pemberton; June–Sept) offers a glimpse of pioneer life. **BIKE CO. PEMBERTON** (1392 Portage Rd, Pemberton; 604/894-6625) rents bikes. **PEMBERTON STABLES** (Pemberton Valley, north of town; 604/894-6615) sends guests out on pleasant rides.

In this area, small cafés such as **GRIMM'S GOURMET & DELI** (7433 Frontier Ave, Pemberton; 604/894-5303) are the standard for dining. **WICKED WHEEL PIZZA** (2021 Portage Rd, Mount Currie; 604/894-6622) is packed on all-you-can-eat nights.

The **PEMBERTON VISITOR INFO CENTRE** (Hwy 99 and Portage Rd, Pemberton; 604/894-6175; www.pemberton.net; May 15–Sept) provides details.

Lillooet

As the Sea to Sky Hwy winds 62 miles/100 km east and north from Mount Currie to Lillooet, it passes through an ever-changing landscape, some of the most picturesque and notably varied terrain of its entire length. This steep-sided section of Hwy 99 is also called the Duffey Lake Road. Cayoosh Creek runs east from Duffey Lake and accompanies the highway almost to Lillooet. Stop at one of the numerous pull-offs along the way and admire the snowcapped 10,000-foot/3,048 meter peaks above you.

Just before Lillooet, BC Hydro's recreation area at **SETON LAKE** offers a beach, salmon spawning channels, and a campground with an abandoned Chinese baking oven, a relic from the Cariboo Gold Rush era. In the late 1850s, Lillooet (population 2,779) was the staging ground for an estimated 50,000 stampeders as they headed north to Clinton and beyond (see the Central British Columbia chapter). Lillooet, where summer temperatures are among the hottest in Canada, is the gateway to the stunning **SOUTH CHILCOTINS BACKCOUNTRY**.

While in town, check out the superb **LILLOOET BAKERY** (719 Main St; 250/256-4889). The **4 PINES MOTEL** (108 8th Ave; 250/256-4247 or 800/753-2576; www.4pinesmotel.com) is a good overnight option in town. The **LILLOOET INFO CENTRE** (790 Main St; 250/256-4308; www.lillooetbc.com; May–Oct) is located in an A-frame former church, which it shares with the town museum.

RESTAURANTS

Dina's Restaurant / ★

690 MAIN ST, LILLOOET; 250/256-4264

A whitewashed Greek restaurant suits Lillooet's summer days. Dina's patio is the place to be in early evening. Zesty panfried *saganaki* with goat cheese speaks to the Pulolos family's roots in northern Greece. Twenty-six kinds of pizza keep one wood-fired oven busy; halibut steaks and calamari are must-try recommendations. *$$; MC, V; no checks; lunch Mon–Sat, dinner every day; full bar; no reservations; on east side of Main St.* &

LODGINGS

Tyax Mountain Lake Resort / ★★★

**TYAUGHTON LAKE RD, GOLD BRIDGE;
250/238-2221 OR 877/918-8929**

At 34,000 square feet/10,364 sq m, this is the largest log structure on the West Coast. The lodge sits beside Tyaughton Lake, with a huge park nearby. There's a sauna, an outdoor Jacuzzi, games and work-out rooms, a 100-seat restaurant, and a western lounge. Affable owner Gus Abel welcomes guests to explore the lake. The 34-unit lodge has floatplanes that take anglers and their kids up to the Trophy Lakes. In winter, the lodge is home base for TLH Heli-skiing (www.tlhheliskiing.com), which flies guests into the snowfields of the South Chilcotin Mountains. *$$$; AE, MC, V; no checks; www.tyax. com; 56 miles/90 km west of Lillooet on Hwy 40, then 3 miles/5 km north on Tyaughton Lake Rd.* ♿

Fraser Valley

The wide, fertile Fraser Valley runs 93 miles/150 km inland from the Pacific to the small town of Hope, with the Fraser River—broad, deep, and muddy—flowing down the middle of the valley. Travelers can follow the north side (Hwy 7) or the south side (Hwy 1) of the river. Bridges are located at Abbotsford, Chilliwack, and Hope, and the free Albion Ferry takes vehicles and foot passengers between Fort Langley and Maple Ridge. A new major bridge between north Langley and Maple Ridge is due to open in 2009. While the Fraser Valley includes some of the fastest-growing communities in Canada, this still-rural area supports a blend of farming and forestry, with outdoor recreation high on everyone's list.

Fort Langley

Several historic 19th-century forts in British Columbia serve as reminders of the West's original European settlers. In Fort Langley (population 2,700), on the south side of the Fraser off Hwy 1, **FORT LANGLEY NATIONAL HISTORIC SITE** (23433 Mavis St; 604/513-4777) is a preserved and restored Hudson's Bay Company post. This is where British Columbia was proclaimed a crown colony in 1858, to fend off American designs after gold was discovered in the Cariboo. The **LANGLEY CENTENNIAL MUSEUM** (9135 King St; 604/888-3922; www.langleymuseum.org) houses a permanent collection of memorabilia. Glover Road, Fort Langley's main street, features shops, cafés, and restaurants, many in heritage buildings; the large community hall has been lovingly preserved. Archival photographs from Fort Langley's past line the walls of the **FORT PUB** (9273 Glover Rd; 604/888-6166; www.fortpub.com). Chocoholics shouldn't miss **EUPHORIA CHOCOLATES** (9103 Glover Rd; 604/888-9506; www.euphoriastore.ca), where you can sample truffles featuring local flavors such as cranberry wine, blueberry, and raspberry.

RESTAURANTS

Wendel's Bookstore and Café / ★

9233 GLOVER RD, FORT LANGLEY; 604/513-2238
Locals and visitors alike keep this little bistro at the river end of Fort Langley's main street buzzing. Light meals, snacks, coffees, and a selection of decadent desserts are the draw, along with sidewalk dining. Order the salmon burger and a slice of peanut butter pie for eating in or takeout, then browse the bookshelves while you wait. And keep your eyes open for famous faces; Fort Langley's historic buildings are popular with moviemakers, and the town is often dressed up for location shoots. *$; DC, MC, V; no checks; breakfast, lunch, dinner every day; full bar; no reservations; www.wendelsonline.com; north end of Glover Rd.*

Chilliwack

Odors in Chilliwack (population 70,000) are inescapably agricultural. Most travelers whizzing through on Hwy 1 travel too fast to get more than a pungent whiff as they pass big-box stores interspersed with the occasional barn. They're missing the best corn in Canada—from early August through October, farm stands offer what longtime British Columbia residents all know just as "Chilliwack corn." To get beyond the facade of fast-food outlets, supply stores, and junkyards, follow historic Yale Road from exit 116 east into the hidden heart of Chilliwack, where the original city hall, built in 1912, now houses the excellent **CHILLIWACK MUSEUM** (45820 Spadina Ave; 604/795-5210; www.chilliwack.museum.bc.ca). Designed in Classic Revival style, the museum looks like the U.S. White House. Year-round information is available from the **CHILLIWACK INFO CENTRE** (44150 Luckakuck Wy; 604/858-8121 or 800/567-9535; www.tourismchilliwack.com).

Harrison Lake

All of 12 miles/18 km long, the Harrison River, which drains south from Harrison Lake into the Fraser River, is among British Columbia's shortest yet most significant waterways. Throughout fall, major runs of spawning salmon make their way upstream into tributaries of the Harrison watershed. This quiet backwater is anchored by **KILBY PARK** (www.env.gov.bc.ca/bcparks) at the community of Harrison Mills on Hwy 7, on the north side of the Fraser. **KILBY HISTORIC STORE** (adjacent to Kilby Park, Harrison Mills; 604/796-9576; www.kilby.ca; Apr–Dec) has a wonderful pioneer history.

Bigfoot (called Sasquatch locally) is said to frequent the southern end of Harrison Lake—perhaps itching for a soak in the renowned waters of **HARRISON HOT SPRINGS** (224 Esplanade Ave, Harrison Hot Springs; 604/796-2244). The indoor public bathing pool is one of the most inviting places in this lakefront town (population 1,573). Harrison Lake is too cold for most swimmers, but a constructed lagoon at the south end of the lake is rimmed by sand and a small, quiet row of low buildings. In summer, rent sailboats or bikes or hike nearby trails. Annual events include the long-running **HARRISON FESTIVAL OF THE ARTS** in June (www.harrisonfestival.com), the **WORLD CHAMPIONSHIP SAND SCULPTURE COMPETITION** in September (www.harrisand.org), and the **BALD EAGLE FESTIVAL** in November (www.fraservalleybaldeaglefestival.ca). The **HARRISON HOT SPRINGS VISITOR INFO CENTRE** (499 Hot Springs Rd; 604/796-5581; www.harrison.ca) can also provide details.

LODGINGS

Harrison Beach Hotel / ★★

160 ESPLANADE AVE, HARRISON HOT SPRINGS;
604/796-1111 OR 866/338-8111

The newest accommodation in Harrison Hot Springs is a shiny four-story property facing the lake, with 42 guest rooms and suites and an excellent lakeside location. The suites are housekeeping units with spacious sitting areas and full kitchens. The earth-toned rooms all have balconies or patios, and those on the north side of the building enjoy sensational views of Harrison Lake and its surrounding mountains. The town's hot-springs pool is just a block away, but the hotel itself has no mineral pool. *$$–$$$; AE, MC, V; checks OK; www.harrisonbeachhotel.com; right in town.* &

The Harrison Hot Springs Hotel / ★★★

100 ESPLANADE AVE, HARRISON HOT SPRINGS;
604/796-2244 OR 888/818-2999

This legendary hotel on the south shore of Harrison Lake was built in 1926 to capitalize as much on its location as on the thermal springs nearby. The current establishment has 334 rooms and suites spread among the 100-room main building and two wings. Avoid the main building, where noise seeps between the walls. A maze of hot-springs pools is steps away from the newest wing, where each room has a view. The best rooms are the suites, which have been tastefully redone, replacing the old '60s and '70s chintz. The Copper Room is fun for big-band-style dancing. Over the past six years, the hotel has been undergoing a $16 million renovation to update rooms and add amenities. *$$–$$$; AE, DC, DIS, MC, V; checks OK; www.harrisonresort.com; west end of Esplanade Ave on lake.* &

Hope

Hope (population 6,667) is a pretty Fraser River town where the two main streets are lined with fast-food joints. Because Hope is located at an important highway junction, the heart of town is frequently overlooked. Spend a few minutes here, if for no other reason than to breathe the fresh air that characterizes Hope. Visit **HOPE MUSEUM** (south end of Water St; 604/869-7322; May–Sept) and **MANNING PROVINCIAL PARK** (16 miles/26 km east on Hwy 3; www.env.gov.bc.ca/bcparks), with the family-oriented **MANNING PARK LODGE** (on Hwy 3, Manning Provincial

Park; 250/840-8822 or 800/330-3321; www.manningpark.com; 37 miles/60 km east of Hope) and **PINEWOODS DINING ROOM** (250/840-8822). Check out the **HOPE VISITOR INFO CENTRE** (919 Water Ave; 604/869-2021) for details.

The Sunshine Coast

The Sunshine Coast is aptly named: bright days outnumber gloomy ones by a wide margin. Even though the Sunshine Coast occupies a fairly narrow bench of land at the toe of the Coast Mountains, much of it is naturally hidden. Side roads with colorful names like Red Roof and Porpoise Bay lead to places that don't announce themselves until you stumble upon them, such as **SMUGGLER COVE MARINE PARK** near Sechelt and **PALM BEACH PARK** (a serene oasis, though there are no palms) south of the town of Powell River.

The region is split by Jervis Inlet. The southern half, between the ferry slips at Langdale and Earls Cove, consists of mainland British Columbia and the Sechelt Peninsula; the northern half lies between the ferry slip at Saltery Bay and the little port of Lund, the latter on the Malaspina Peninsula. The world's longest highway, the **PAN-AMERICAN**—Hwys 1 and 101 in parts of the United States and Hwys 99 and 101 in Canada—stretches 9,312 miles/15,020 km from Chile to Lund on British Columbia's Sunshine Coast. The 87-mile/140-km stretch of Hwy 101 between Langdale and Lund leads to dozens of parks.

ACCESS AND INFORMATION

The Sunshine Coast is accessible from the rest of the Lower Mainland only by boat or floatplane. Travelers aboard **BC FERRIES** (250/386-3431 or 888/223-3779; www.bcferries.com) leave Horseshoe Bay in West Vancouver for a 40-minute ride to Langdale on the Sechelt Peninsula. During peak season (June–Sept), the extra investment ($15) in a reservation is well worth it. **HIGHWAY 101** links Langdale with Earls Cove, 50 miles/80 km north. Another ferry crosses Jervis Inlet to Saltery Bay, a 60-minute ride. Hwy 101 makes the second leg of its journey, extending 37 miles/60 km north through the town of Powell River to Lund. BC Ferries also connects Powell River with Comox on the east side of central Vancouver Island.

One of the best parts about enjoying the Sunshine Coast in the off-season (Sept–May)—particularly midweek—is catching ferries without experiencing interminable lines. You'll still have to allow four hours to reach Powell River from Horseshoe Bay, but you can do it without hurrying. Ferry connections are scheduled to allow adequate time to make the drive from one dock to the next. Those traveling up the entire coast or returning via Vancouver Island should ask at the Horseshoe Bay terminal about special fares (saving up to 30 percent) for the circle tour of four ferry rides.

MALASPINA BUS LINE (604/885-2217 or 877/227-8287; www.malaspina coach.com) runs daily scheduled service between Vancouver and Powell River, with stops on request anywhere in between. **PACIFIC COASTAL**

AIRLINES (604/273-8666 or 800/663-2872; www.pacific-coastal.com) flies daily between Vancouver and Powell River.

Get detailed **INFORMATION ON THE SUNSHINE COAST** (www.sun coastcentral.com) regarding current weather and transportation schedules before you go.

Gibsons

Gibsons (population 4,000), a colorfully low-key waterfront village 2½ miles/ 4 km west of the BC Ferries dock in Langdale, is famous among Canadians as the setting of a long-popular, long-ago CBC-TV show, *The Beachcombers*. Make the **GIBSONS VISITOR INFO CENTRE** (417 Marine Dr; 604/886-2374 or 866/222-3806; www.gibsonsbc.ca) your first stop in the heart of town to stock up on maps and brochures. Fans of *The Beachcombers* will want to visit **MOLLY'S REACH** (647 School Rd; 604/886-9710), one of the main locations used in the show and now home to a collection of memorabilia. Then head to the nearby government wharf, where there's often **FRESH SEAFOOD**. Take a walk along the harbor seawall that leads past homes and boat sheds with character. A cairn at **CHASTER REGIONAL PARK** (on Gower Point Rd) honors British Navy Captain George Vancouver, who camped here in June 1792.

LODGINGS

Bonniebrook Lodge / ★★★⯪

1532 OCEAN BEACH ESPLANADE, GIBSONS;
604/886-2887 OR 877/290-9916

This popular, stylishly renovated 1920s-era waterfront bed-and-breakfast has been recently updated with flat-screen TVs, iPod docks, and luxury linens by new owners. The lodge features four self-contained suites spread between two upper floors. Two one-bedroom ocean-view suites occupy the yellow clapboard house's second floor, with two smaller penthouse suites with private decks above. The best values are the three "romance" suites set back in the forest. Explore the stretch of private beach that leads to nearby Chaster Park. *$$$$; AE, MC, V; no checks; www.bonniebrook.com; follow Gower Point Rd from downtown.* ⅟

Roberts Creek

The free-spirited community of Roberts Creek (population 2,000) lies 4 miles/ 7 km northwest of Gibsons on **HIGHWAY 10**. Stop first at **MCFARLANE'S BEACH** (south end of Roberts Creek Rd), where, early in the 19th century, Harry Roberts operated a freight shed. On its side he painted "Sunshine Belt"—and visitors ever since have been referring to the area as the Sunshine Coast. From here, look north toward the beaches at **ROBERTS CREEK PARK** (on Hwy 101, 9 miles/14 km north of Gibsons; www.env.gov.bc.ca/bcparks), popular for summer picnics. A reward for braving ferry traffic on **BC DAY** (first weekend in Aug) is taking in the annual Gumboot parade and Mr. Roberts Creek contest. Bed-and-breakfast-style lodging is available at the lovely **COUNTRY COTTAGE B&B** (1183 Roberts Creek Rd, Roberts Creek; 604/885-7448; www.countrycottagebb.ca).

RESTAURANTS

Gumboot Garden Café / UNRATED

1057 ROBERTS CREEK RD, ROBERTS CREEK; 604/885-4218

As you drive down Roberts Creek's main drag, look for an old maroon house with a simple sign: café. Inside, a sun painted on the yellow wall radiates warmth, as do linoleum table mats. The menu of light fare shines with a Mexican influence. Popular entrées include Thai salad and homemade veggie burgers. On Friday evenings, locals come to hang out and listen to music. In keeping with the community and clientele, service is relaxed. A second location has opened across the parking lot. The two restaurants share a dedication to fresh, local ingredients; a kitchen garden supplies organic seasonal veggies, flowers, and herbal teas. As at the café, live music is frequently featured. *$; MC, V; local checks OK; every day (call for hours); beer and wine; reservations recommended; junction with Lower Rd.*

Sechelt

If it weren't for a small neck of land less than ½ mile/0.8 km wide, a large portion of the peninsula north of Sechelt would be an island. This wedge of sand backs ocean water, which flows in from the northwestern entrance to Sechelt Inlet near Egmont. Nestled on the wedge is Sechelt (population 9,224), one of the fastest-growing towns in Canada and home to the Sechelt First Nation, whose **HOUSE OF HEWHIWUS** (5555 Hwy 101; 604/885-8991)—"House of the Chiefs"—is both a cultural and an art center; ask for a tour. The **SECHELT VISITOR INFO CENTRE** (Seaside Centre, 5790 Teredo St; 604/885-1036 or 877/885-1036; www.sechelt visitorinfo.com) fills you in on the rest.

RESTAURANTS

Blue Heron Inn / ★★

5591 DELTA RD, SECHELT; 604/885-3847 OR 800/818-8977

The Blue Heron is one of the most consistently pleasant places to dine on the Sunshine Coast—partly for the waterfront views of Sechelt Inlet (complete with blue herons, of course). But the food is another draw: fresh clams, veal *limonie* with prawns, grilled wild salmon with fennel, smoked black cod with hollandaise, halibut fillet with red onion and strawberry salsa, creamy caesar salad, bouillabaisse. The romantic atmosphere—fresh flowers, candlelight, local art—is another plus. *$$$; MC, V; no checks; dinner Wed–Sun; full bar; reservations recommended; west of Hwy 101 on Wharf St, right along Porpoise Bay Rd 1 mile/1.6 km, sign on left side.* &

Georgia Strait / ★★

4349 SUNSHINE COAST HWY, WILSON CREEK; 604/885-1997

Housed in an old service station painted purple, this cheery bistro has brought gourmet dining to the Sechelt area, with an eclectic West Coast menu that ranges from the usual salmon, lamb, chicken, and crab to upscale deli items. The spacious interior is filled with light from large windows, and a southwest-facing deck basks in the sun. What distinguishes Georgia Strait above all else, though, is the best Reuben sandwich in British Columbia, perhaps the Northwest. *$$; MC, V; no checks; lunch every day, dinner every day (summer, Wed–Sat (winter), brunch Sat–Sun; full bar; reservations recommended; 4 miles/6.4 km north of Roberts Creek.*

LODGINGS

Rockwater Secret Cove Resort / ★★☆

**5356 OLE'S COVE RD, HALFMOON BAY;
604/885-7038 OR 877/296-4593**

Owner Kevin Toth has transformed a popular but aging property into a distinctive resort featuring modern furnishings and amenities with a rustic, almost Japanese Zen, ambience. The main building still overlooks one of the largest swimming pools on the Sunshine Coast—which itself overlooks the Strait of Georgia. The dining room, whose dinners feature good West Coast seafood, has a lavish Sunday brunch. The most spectacular feature, however, remains the waterfront bluffside location facing into the sunset. *$$$$; AE, MC, V; no checks; closed first two weeks of Jan; www.rockwater secretcoveresort.com; off Hwy 101, 28 miles/45 km from the ferry, 1 mile/ 1.6 km past Secret Cove.* &

Pender Harbour

At the north end of the Sechelt Peninsula—a puzzle-shaped piece of geography—it's hard to tell where freshwater lakes end and saltwater coves begin. Fingers of land separate the waters around Agamemnon Channel from a marvelous patch-work of small and medium-sized lakes. Three ocean-side communities—**MADEIRA PARK, GARDEN BAY**, and **IRVINES LANDING**—lie tucked along the shoreline. Together they comprise Pender Harbour, which has decided to market itself as "Venice of the North." In summer, stop by the **PENDER HARBOUR TOURIST/ VISITOR INFO BOOTH** (12911 Madeira Park Rd, Madeira Park; 604/883-2561; www.penderharbour.org). As you head north of Pender Harbour toward the BC Ferries terminal at **EARLS COVE**, Hwy 101 climbs around Ruby Lake, with views of the jewel-like setting. A splendid lodging worthy of a stay is **SUNSHINE COAST RESORT** (12695 Sunshine Coast Hwy, Madeira Park; 604/883-9177); it's tucked into a hillside and has a great harbor view.

LODGINGS

Ruby Lake Resort / ★

RUBY LAKE, MADEIRA PARK; 604/883-2269 OR 800/717-6611
An engaging family from Milan—the Cogrossis—operate Ruby Lake Resort, with its 10 cedar cottages, each rustically decorated, and safari-style tents for two or four campers. Two B and B suites, with private entrances—and no TVs—are housed in the Dream Catcher cottage. Rent one of the lodge's canoes and explore nearby Ruby Lake, which boasts some of the warmest waters in coastal BC and is dotted with tiny islets perfect for a private picnic. The family's restaurant draws accolades for its northern Italian cuisine and fresh seafood. *$$–$$$; MC, V; no checks; closed Dec–Feb; www.rubylakeresort.com; 6 miles/10 km south of Earls Cove.* ⅙

Egmont

An impressive natural show occurs twice daily in **SKOOKUMCHUK NARROWS PARK** (on Hwy 101; www.env.gov.bc.ca/bcparks) in the tiny district of Egmont, about 7 miles/12 km north of Ruby Lake. One of the largest saltwater rapids in Canada boils as water forces through Skookumchuk Narrows at the north end of Sechelt Inlet. A 2½-mile/4-km trail leads to viewing sites at North Point and nearby Roland Point. At low tide, the bays around both points display astonishingly colorful and varied forms of marine life. After your hike, stop in at the **GREEN ROSETTE CAFE** (at the trailhead) for some well-deserved refreshments.

LODGINGS

West Coast Wilderness Lodge / ★★

6649 MAPLE RD, EGMONT; 604/883-3667 OR 877/988-3838
Perched above island-specked Jervis Inlet, the 20-room lodge's name says it all. Opened in 1998 by Paul and Patti Hansen, the lodge's most endearing feature is a deck from which guests watch wildlife ranging from Pacific dolphins to swans. Inside, rattan chairs rescued from a Trader Vic's restaurant and comfy couches ring a fireplace that rises two floors above the inn's dining area and lounge. Guides work with guests to sharpen sea kayaking and paddling skills. An ocean-side sauna soothes sore muscles. *$$$; MC, V; checks OK; www.wcwl.com; 1 mile/1.6 km north of Egmont harbor.* ⅙

Powell River

Travelers looking to experience the leisurely pace of ferry sailings enjoy the journey between Earls Cove and Saltery Bay on Jervis Inlet. As you continue north by car on Hwy 101, Powell River (population 13,000) is a pleasant drive 19 miles/31 km north of the ferry terminal at Saltery Bay. This mill town on Malaspina Strait is the jumping-off point to Texada and Vancouver islands, as well as the 12-lake Powell Forest canoe route, a full-on 35-mile/57-km adventure. Powell River is also home to the **INTERNATIONAL CHORAL KATHAUMIXW FESTIVAL** (www.kathaumixw.org; early July) and the weeklong **BLACKBERRY FESTIVAL** each August. Contact the **POWELL RIVER VISITOR INFO CENTRE** (4871 Joyce Ave; 604/485-4701 or 877/817-8669; www.discoverpowellriver.com) for information. Nearby is **ROCKY MOUNTAIN PIZZA & BAKERY** (4471 Marine Ave; 604/485-9111), where you can eat and people watch.

RESTAURANTS

jitterbug café / ★

4463 MARINE AVE, POWELL RIVER; 604/485-7797

One of Powell River's most enduring eateries, the jitterbug café shares a stylishly renovated 1920s coastal home with the Wind Spirit Gallery. Art animates the walls of the brightly lit dining room. From a window table, take in sweeping views of islands. Better yet, enjoy a glass of sangria on the back deck. The eclectic menu includes sandwiches, salads, pastas, and tortas at lunch; steak, chicken, prawns, and salmon for dinner. All meals are prepared with fresh, local ingredients. True to its name, the café features music on Friday and Saturday evenings. *$$; AE, MC, V; no checks; lunch, dinner Tues–Sat; full bar; reservations recommended; www.windspirit.com; downtown.* &

Lund

Little ports don't come better hidden than Lund, at the north end of the Sunshine Coast where the Malaspina Peninsula narrows to a thin finger of land wedged between Malaspina Strait and Okeover Arm. More boaters than vehicles make their way here. Lund retains much of the wilderness charm that drew settlers here from Finland. The historic 1918 **LUND HOTEL** (1436 Hwy 101; 604/414-0474 or 877/569-3999; www.lundhotel.com) has 31 guest rooms to suit a variety of budgets. **FLO'S STARBOARD CAFÉ** (on Lund harbor) serves espresso in a little bistro. The **RAGGEDY ANNE** (604/483-9749), a red water taxi, ferries passengers to nearby Savary Island. **OKEOVER ARM PARK** (off Hwy 101, 3 miles/5 km east of Lund; www.env.gov.bc.ca/bcparks) is the kayakers' choice.

RESTAURANTS

The Laughing Oyster Restaurant / ★★

10052 MALASPINA RD, LUND; 604/483-9775

Though the view overlooking Okeover Arm is sensational—and tables on the deck are premium—the food remains the draw at Laughing Oyster. And while the menu is wide-ranging, seafood is the mainstay. There's nothing memorably inventive, but they make unfailingly excellent fish entrées that hew a bit toward old-fashioned chophouse standards; the popular "seafood harvest" platter for two is a great deal. *$$$; AE, MC, V; no checks; lunch, dinner every* *day, brunch Sun (Wed–Sun Oct–Mar); full bar; reservations required; www. laughingoyster.ca; 20 minutes north of Powell River.* ⅙

Nancy's Bakery / ★★

1431 HWY 101, LUND; 604/483-4180

Housed in an impressive new post-and-beam structure on the shoreline, Nancy's has certainly grown past its muffin-and-scones roots in a nearby shack. Today, it's one of the best bakeries in British Columbia. Besides a wide selection of bakery goods, a café menu offers soups, salads, pastas, and hearty sandwiches—get a pastrami sandwich, and you'll be enjoying the bakery's handcrafted bread as well as meat smoked on-site. Snag a table outside to scan the harbor for wildlife while savoring your meal. *$; MC, V; no checks; breakfast, lunch every day; beer and wine; no reservations; end of Hwy 101.*

LODGINGS

Desolation Resort / ★★★

2694 DAWSON RD, LUND; 604/483-3592 OR 800/399-3592

The way the afternoon sun slants through the forest that embraces this resort's wood cabins makes the place seem like a movie set. Perched on 7 acres/2.83 hectares above quiet waters and almost literally at the end of the road, the resort has 10 units that offer splendid privacy, spaciousness, and comfort. The timber-frame fir and cedar interiors are warm, though not luxurious; two cottages (which the resort mysteriously calls chalets, though they're not) have their own hot tubs. Package deals include dinners at the Laughing Oyster Restaurant (see review) in nearby Lund and guided kayak trips; rental canoes and kayaks are also available. *$$; MC, V; no checks; www. desolationresort.com; 20 minutes north of Powell River.*

VICTORIA AND
VANCOUVER ISLAND

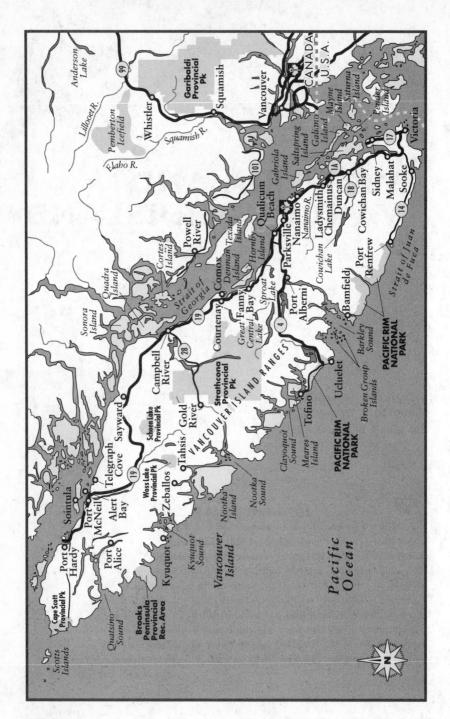

VICTORIA AND VANCOUVER ISLAND

Vancouver Island, British Columbia's maritime jewel, takes up the southwestern area of the province. Wildlife viewing, Native heritage, and friendly people are part of what makes this region so appealing. Visitors and residents alike partake of the many outdoors pursuits that make the island a boating, hiking, kayaking, storm-watching, and white-water rafting utopia.

The stunning capital, Victoria, is known for its British influence and culture, as well as its abundance of manicured gardens. Close proximity to the region's natural bounty has led to a plethora of farm-to-table dining options; executive chefs flock here to get creative with the wealth of seafood caught locally. Explore the rest of the island to discover wineries, organic farms, and established arts communities. Go even farther afield and cross into the cherished Gulf Islands, where the pace slows down, with populations much under 10,000 people. Each island has its own unique charm, where you'll find a paradise of artists, markets, and good old-fashioned hospitality.

ACCESS AND INFORMATION

You get to the biggest island in North America by boat or by plane. From Western Washington, you have four options by boat. From downtown Seattle, the **VICTORIA CLIPPER** (2701 Alaskan Wy, Pier 69, Seattle; 206/448-5000 in Seattle, 250/382-8100 in Victoria, or 800/888-2535 elsewhere; www.clippervacations.com) zips to downtown Victoria in two to three hours via a high-speed passenger-only catamaran. You can also cruise to Victoria via the scenic San Juan Islands on **WASHINGTON STATE FERRIES** (from Anacortes, two hours north of Seattle; 206/464-6400 or 888/808-7977; www.wsdot.wa.gov/ferries); a three-hour trip from Anacortes (follow prominent signage to ferry dock) runs to Sidney, British Columbia, 17 miles/27 km north of Victoria by highway. **BLACK BALL TRANSPORT** (360/457-4491 in Port Angeles or 250/386-2202 in Victoria; www.cohoferry.com) operates the MV *Coho* car-and-passenger ferry from Port Angeles (follow signage in downtown Port Angeles) on the Olympic Peninsula to downtown Victoria, a 90-minute trip across the Strait of Juan de Fuca. Even though there are four daily sailings of the *Coho* in summer, reservations are essential. **VICTORIA SAN JUAN CRUISES** (360/738-8099 or 800/443-4552; www.whales.com; mid-May–early Oct) makes a three-hour passenger-only cruise—including whale-watching and a salmon and chicken buffet—between Bellingham and Victoria's Inner Harbour.

From the British Columbia mainland, you have three options by boat. **BC FERRIES** (250/386-3431 or 888/223-3779; www.bcferries.com) runs car ferries from the Tsawwassen terminal (south of Vancouver) into Swartz Bay, 20 miles/32 km north of Victoria; from Horseshoe Bay north of Vancouver to Nanaimo; and from Departure Bay south of Nanaimo to Tsawwassen. Car reservations cost $17.50 in addition to the fare each way. Or hop on the bus with **PACIFIC COACH LINES** (1150 Pacific Central Station, Vancouver; 604/662-7575 or 800/661-1725; www.pacificcoach.com), which travels on the BC Ferries system.

The fastest way to travel is straight to Victoria's Inner Harbour by air. **KENMORE AIR** (6321 NE 175th St, Seattle; 425/486-1257 or 866/359-2842; www.kenmoreair.com) makes regular daily flights from Lake Union near downtown Seattle. From Sea-Tac International Airport, **HORIZON AIR** (800/547-9308; www.horizonair.com) flies into **VICTORIA INTERNATIONAL AIRPORT** (250/953-7500), 15 miles/25 km north of the city. From downtown Vancouver and Vancouver International Airport, **HELIJET INTERNATIONAL** (455 Waterfront Rd, Vancouver; 604/273-4688 or 800/665-4354; www.helijet.com) transports you to Victoria by helicopter. Carbon-neutral seaplanes for **HARBOUR AIR** (1075 W Waterfront Rd, Vancouver; 604/274-1277 or 800/665-0212; www.harbour-air.com) carry passengers from Vancouver. From Vancouver International Airport, fly with **AIR CANADA** (888/247-2262; www.aircanada.com).

In peak season—May through September and particularly July and August—crowds are greatest, prices are highest, and tourist services are best. Gardens and greenery are freshest in May and June; days are sunniest in July and August, except on the west coast, when fog is common. April and September are pleasant months for quieter, reduced-rate travel. Rates are often quite low November through April, except during holidays. **TOURISM VANCOUVER ISLAND** (250/754-3500; www.vancouverisland.travel) and **TOURISM VICTORIA** (250/953-2033 or 800/663-3883; www.tourismvictoria.com) have more information.

Victoria

Rudyard Kipling's hallowed turn-of-the-20th-century visit spurred Victoria to sell itself as a wee bit of Olde England. The fancy is an appealing one, conjuring red double-decker buses and high tea as keynote themes in the Garden City. Kilted bagpipers rub shoulders with Victoria's annual 3.63 million tourists, who come from all over the world to walk along the waterside causeway, sit for caricature portraits, and marvel at jugglers. In the harbor, celebrity yachts rest within hailing distance of an antique three-masted sailing ship. But for sophisticated travelers, the city has grown far past its bucolic Brit persona.

One terrific thing about Victoria—rated among the world's top 10 cities by numerous travel magazines—is that in the main central city, everything from the elegant Parliament buildings to old Chinatown is within walking distance. In recent years Victoria has seen an explosion of whale-watching tours, and outdoor enthusiasts can sea kayak or mountain bike from the city's doorsteps. Minutes from downtown, seaside Dallas Road and Beach Drive meander through the city's finest old residential districts, offering a view of the spectacular Olympic, Cascade, and Coast mountains south and east across the Straits of Juan de Fuca and Georgia.

ACCESS AND INFORMATION

A horse-drawn carriage ride with **VICTORIA CARRIAGE TOURS** (corner of Belleville and Menzies sts; 250/383-2207 or 877/663-2207; www.victoria carriage.com) is a romantic favorite; the larger **TALLY-HO CARRIAGES** (corner of Belleville and Menzies sts; 250/514-9257 or 866/383-5067; www. tallyhotours.com) offer rides at a family rate. The Inner Harbour is the departure point of numerous popular maritime excursions, like **VICTORIA HARBOUR FERRIES** (250/708-0201; www.victoriaharbourferry.com), which offers tours of local waterways. Perched on the Inner Harbour across from the Empress Hotel is **TOURISM VICTORIA**'s (812 Wharf St; 250/953-2033; www.tourismvictoria.com) visitor center.

MAJOR ATTRACTIONS

Stroll through the main-floor hallways and shops of the venerable **FAIRMONT EMPRESS HOTEL** (721 Government St; 250/384-8111 or 800/441-1414; www.fairmont.com/empress), a postcard doyenne since 1908. The elegant Rattenbury-designed 1898 provincial **PARLIAMENT BUILDINGS** (501 Belleville St; 250/387-3046 or 800/663-7867; www.legis.gov.bc.ca) can be seen via frequent tours. The **VICTORIA BUG ZOO** (631 Courtney St; 250/384-2847; www.bugzoo.bc.ca) fascinates children and adults alike, with features such as a surprisingly cute miniature apartment scaled to its cockroach denizens.

Opulent **CRAIGDARROCH CASTLE** (1050 Joan Crescent; 250/592-5323; www.craigdarrochcastle.com), once visited only by 19th-century socialites, is now open to the public to take in the parlors of Victoria's long-ago richest resident, coal baron Robert Dunsmuir. Heritage-home connoisseurs enjoy **POINT ELLICE HOUSE** (2616 Pleasant St; 250/380-6506; www.pointellice house.ca), an early Victoria residence in tasteful Italianate style, and **EMILY CARR HOUSE** (207 Government St; 250/383-5843; www.emilycarr.com), the birth home of the legendary Canadian artist and writer.

MUSEUMS AND GALLERIES

Across the street from the Fairmont Empress Hotel, the **ROYAL BRITISH COLUMBIA MUSEUM** (675 Belleville St; 250/356-7226; www.royalbc museum.bc.ca) delights with its extensive collection of Canadian indigenous art and the Old Town display, a reconstructed 19th-century streetscape. Kids are drawn to the Ocean Station exhibit, a simulated submarine ride, and the IMAX theater. The **ART GALLERY OF GREATER VICTORIA** (1040 Moss St; 250/384-4101; www.aggv.bc.ca) is notable for its Asian art; the courtyard garden is home to North America's only Shinto shrine.

PARKS AND GARDENS

On the southern edge of downtown, the city's beloved **BEACON HILL PARK** (between Douglas and Cook sts; www.beaconhillpark.ca) boasts 200 acres of manicured gardens and romantic bridges over ponds. The renowned **BUTCHART GARDENS** (800 Benvenuto Ave, Brentwood Bay; 250/652-4422

> ## VICTORIA THREE-DAY TOUR
>
> **DAY ONE:** Have breakfast at the **DELTA VICTORIA OCEAN POINT RESORT'S LURE SEAFOOD RESTAURANT AND BAR** (45 Songhees Rd, Victoria; 250/360-5873)—try the eggs Benedict with candied salmon—with seating overlooking the beautiful Inner Harbour. Then head out on a walking tour of downtown, strolling along **GOVERNMENT STREET** to **CHINATOWN**. Stop for dim sum for lunch at **DON MEE SEAFOOD RESTAURANT**. Return to the Inner Harbour promenade and flag down a horse-drawn **TALLY-HO CARRIAGE** for a tour of **BEACON HILL PARK**. Ask the driver to wait a few minutes while you grab an ice cream at **BEACON DRIVE-IN RESTAURANT**, then visit the **EMILY CARR HOUSE** to learn about Victoria's most famous native daughter. Afterward, check in to the Windsor Suite at **PRIOR HOUSE BED & BREAKFAST INN**. Return to the Inner Harbour to catch a **VICTORIA HARBOUR FERRY** to **SONGHEES PARK** on Songhees Road, then meander five minutes along the waterfront to **SPINNAKERS BREWPUB**, where you sample Mount Tolmie Darks and relax into a pub-food dinner.
>
> **DAY TWO:** After the lavish breakfast at Prior House, hop in your car to Mile

or 866/652-4422; www.butchartgardens.com) are 13 miles/21 km north on the Saanich Peninsula. This 1904 estate masterpiece, laid into an old stone quarry, is crowded with blossoms in the manicured precincts of the Italian Garden, Rose Garden, and delicate Japanese Garden. Take city bus No. 75 Central Saanich; it stops in downtown Victoria on Douglas Street in front of Crystal Gardens.

SHOPPING

For those seeking English goods, **GOVERNMENT STREET** north to Yates Street offers the best selection of tweeds and china. For men's suits and casual wear, **BRITISH IMPORTERS** (960 Yates St; 250/386-1496) will please, as will upscale **W & J WILSON** (1221 Government St; 250/383-7177 or 888/887-1188), featuring fine women's wear. Stop at **IRISH LINEN STORES** (1019 Government St; 250/383-6812 or 877/966-6868) and **MURCHIE'S TEA & COFFEE** (1110 Government St; 250/383-3112) for well-known Fair Isle specialties.

Other obvious stops include **ROGER'S CHOCOLATES** (913 Government St; 250/881-8771), **CHOCOLATES BY BERNARD CALLEBAUT** (621 Broughton St; 250/380-1515), **OLD MORRIS TOBACCONISTS** (1116 Government St; 250/382-4811 or 888/845-6111), and **MUNRO'S BOOKS** (1108 Government St; 250/382-2464 or 888/243-2464). **SASQUATCH TRADING** (1233 Government St; 250/386-9033) and **COWICHAN TRADING** (1328 Government St; 250/383-0321) both offer Canadian and West Coast arts, crafts, and

Zero of the **TRANS-CANADA HIGHWAY** at Dallas Road and Douglas Street and take the scenic drive out Dallas Road to Clover Point. Fly your kite on the windy embankment, as residents do, or just take a stroll along the water. Then follow the Scenic Marine Drive signs along Beach Drive, traversing the Uplands to gawk at million-dollar heritage homes, and travel north up Hwy 17 to **SIDNEY** for lunch at **DOCKSIDE GRILL**. Afterward, head across the Saanich Peninsula to **BUTCHART GARDENS** to wander these world-famous, immaculately kept floral displays. Then head back to the city to check in to **FAIRHOLME MANOR**, resting a while before dinner at **PAPRIKA BISTRO**.

DAY THREE: After breakfast at the manor, stroll over to **CRAIGDARROCH CASTLE** to admire the opulent home of Victoria's first tycoon, coal magnate Robert Dunsmuir. Then walk down Fort Street's **ANTIQUE ROW** to poke your head in oddments shops, heading to Government Street for lunch at **SAM'S DELI**. Afterward, wander over to the Royal BC Museum to experience the marvelous collection of First Nations art, particularly masks. Follow up with afternoon tea at the **FAIRMONT EMPRESS HOTEL**, then check in to a suite with a soaking tub (you'll need it) at **ABIGAIL'S HOTEL**. Return to Fort Street for dinner at **CAFÉ BRIO**.

memorabilia. Buy a kite at **KABOODLES TOY STORE** (1320 Government St; 250/383-0931).

BEACON DRIVE-IN RESTAURANT (126 Douglas St; 250/385-7521) has the city's best soft ice cream. At **DEMITASSE CAFÉ** (1320 Blanshard St; 250/386-4442), breakfast is the thing. Heaping sandwiches feed office workers at **SAM'S DELI** (805 Government St; 250/382-8424). Outdoor seating is popular at **TORREFAZIONE ITALIA** (1234 Government St; 250/920-7203). The **CANOE BREWPUB** (450 Swift St; 250/361-1940), near Chinatown, is a good spot for a waterfront microbrew.

Johnson Street (between Government and Wharf sts) has quirky stores, highlighted by the enclosure of historic **MARKET SQUARE** (Johnson St, between Government and Store sts). **VICTORIA'S CHINATOWN** (Fisgard St between Government and Store sts), the oldest in Canada, is worth visiting, especially to see narrow, shop-lined Fan Tan Alley. Outside Old Town, **ANTIQUE ROW** (Fort St east of downtown from Blanshard to Cook sts) beckons connoisseurs of 18th- to 20th-century goods.

PERFORMING ARTS

The **MCPHERSON PLAYHOUSE** (3 Centennial Square; 250/386-6121 or 888/717-6121; www.rmts.bc.ca) is Victoria's leading live-theater venue. The **ROYAL THEATRE** (805 Broughton St; 250/386-6121 or 888/717-6121) is home to a range of performances, from **PACIFIC OPERA VICTORIA** (1815 Blanshard St; 250/385-0222) to the **VICTORIA SYMPHONY ORCHESTRA**

(610-620 View St; 250/385-6515). One of the most-anticipated public events is the sunset Symphony Splash, an Inner Harbour concert held the first Sunday of August. The free weekly *Monday Magazine*, downtown in yellow boxes, has the best listings.

SPORTS AND RECREATION

For an ocean adventure in the Inner Harbour, you can rent a kayak at the **GORGE ROWING AND PADDLING CENTRE** (2940 Jutland Rd; 250/380-4668); **OCEAN RIVER SPORTS** (1824 Store St; 250/381-4233 or 800/909-4233) rents kayaks and canoes and also runs guided paddles. Those who want to see wildlife up close and personal can hop aboard one of **SPRING-TIDE CHARTERS & TOURS** (1207 Wharf St; 250/384-4444 or 800/470-3474; www.springtidecharters.com) to see marine life at its best. Land adventures are another way to experience Victoria, with **CYCLE BC RENTALS'** (950 Wharf St; 250/380-2453 or 866/380-2453; www.cyclebc.ca) bike, motorcycle, and scooter rentals.

RESTAURANTS

Brasserie L'Ecole / ★★

1715 GOVERNMENT ST, VICTORIA; 250/475-6260
At this little brasserie, oddly located at the edge of Chinatown, eat simple French-country cooking. Rich pomegranate walls are decked out with fin de siècle bistro posters, and a long bar makes a welcoming snacking spot. The menu is classic, too: mussels and *frites*, steak *frites*, and marinated olives; most of the meat and vegetables are organic, and the fish is wild-caught. Blackboards list the day's options for oysters, cheeses, and desserts. *$$–$$$; MC, V; no checks; dinner Tues–Sat; full bar; reservations recommended; www. lecole.ca; at Herald St.* ♿

Café Brio / ★★★

944 FORT ST, VICTORIA; 250/383-0009
This lively Antique Row restaurant glows with warmth, from the recycled fir in the weathered floor and cozy booths to the visual feast of nudes and still lifes on the gold walls. The café serves contemporary regional cuisine with Italian leanings. Appetizers might include local oysters or house-made charcuterie. Entrées range from red wine–braised duck legs from Cowichan Bay to the local farm feature of organic pork from Sloping Hills Farm. The 300-label wine list has one of the best selections of British Columbia wines in the province. *$$$; AE, MC, V; no checks; dinner every day; full bar; reservations recommended; www.cafe-brio.com; at Vancouver St.* ♿

Don Mee Seafood Restaurant / ★★

538 FISGARD ST, VICTORIA; 250/383-1032
Though Don Mee serves an extensive and sophisticated Cantonese and classical Mandarin menu, dim sum is the draw. Its version of this lunchtime-only

treat is among the most inventive in the Northwest, with particular emphasis on crab confections, such as the breaded and deep-fried crab claws. Reservations are a good idea during peak season, at lunch or dinner. *$–$$; AE, MC, V; no checks; lunch, dinner every day; beer and wine; reservations recommended; www.donmee.com; in Chinatown between Government and Wharf sts.* &

Il Terrazzo Ristorante / ★★

555 JOHNSON ST, VICTORIA; 250/361-0028

You'll find a true taste of Italy in this beautiful restaurant tucked away on Waddington Alley. Surrounded by six outdoor fireplaces, plants, and flowers, Il Terrazzo offers a haven of privacy for alfresco dining in busy Old Town. Classic carpaccio, flatbread sandwiches, wood-oven pizzas, pastas, and entrées such as *maiale* (pork) tenderloin scaloppine attest to the menu's diversity. *$$$; AE, DC, MC, V; no checks; lunch Mon–Sat (Mon–Fri in winter), dinner every day; full bar; reservations recommended; www.ilterrazzo.com; near Market Square.* &

Paprika Bistro / ★★★

2524 ESTEVAN AVE, VICTORIA; 250/592-7424

The sheer savor and diversity of chef George Szasz's food belies (not intentionally) the whole fussy British Victoria ethos. This neighborhood bistro makes fresh sausage (pork *merguez*) daily, offers goulash almost every night, and is famed for its roast duck in cherry and ginger sauce. If you're lucky, they'll have roasted a whole spring lamb, and individual diners can order platters. *$$; MC, V; no checks; dinner Tues–Sat; beer and wine; reservations recommended; www.paprika-bistro.com; between Vancouver and Cook sts.* &

Rebar Modern Food / ★★

50 BASTION SQUARE, VICTORIA; 250/361-9223

Victoria's original vegetarian health-food restaurant is packed at lunch and dinner. Sip one of the refreshing fresh-fruit drinks, such as the Atomic Glow (apple, strawberry, and ginger juices) or the Cootie Bug (strawberry, pineapple, and orange juices) while perusing the menu. Delicious enchiladas, curries, and almond burgers are specialties, along with pastas and salads. Breads are all homemade. Friendly, helpful service exemplifies Rebar's philosophy. *$–$$; AE, DC, MC, V; no checks; breakfast, lunch every day, dinner Mon–Sat, brunch Sun; beer and wine; reservations recommended (not accepted for brunch); www.rebarmodernfood.com; at Langley St.*

Spinnakers Brewpub & Guesthouse / ★★

308 CATHERINE ST, VICTORIA; 250/386-2739 OR 877/838-2739

One of the first brew pubs in Canada, Spinnakers has been around since 1984. On the waterfront west of the Inner Harbour, it has one of the best views in Victoria. Traditional pub fare—fish-and-chips (wild Pacific salmon or BC halibut), burgers, and pastas—is the order of the day. Try the seafood chowder or one of the dinner specials, such as braised rockfish or ale-braised lamb shanks. Nine rooms and suites, all delightfully decorated with art and antiques, are available nearby. *$$; AE, DC, MC, V; no checks; lunch, dinner every day; full bar; reservations recommended; www.spinnakers.com; across Johnson St Bridge from downtown.*

Temple Restaurant & Lounge / ★★

525 FORT ST, VICTORIA; 250/383-2313

The slogan here evinces its philosophical bent: dinner is the start of the night, not the end of the day—to prove it, they're open until 12am on weeknights, 2am on weekends. The look is cool and minimalist, but there's no hiding the enthusiasm of chef Sam Benedetto's devotion to organic cuisine. Most of the menu, from the wild BC salmon to the Gulf Island mussels, is Vancouver Island–caught or –raised; the style—light, with crisp, clean flavors and Asian touches—is also very West Coast. Feeling decadent? Book a table in the Velvet Room, where you lounge on low cushions and chairs. *$$$; AE, MC, V; no checks; dinner Mon–Sat; full bar; reservations recommended; www.thetemple. ca; at Langley St.* &

LODGINGS

Abigail's Hotel / ★★

906 MCCLURE ST, VICTORIA; 250/388-5363 OR 800/347-5054

The substantial, four-story Tudor facade of this elegant 23-room 1930 manor house promises grandeur, and the standard rooms, modernized and furnished with a mix of new and antique furniture, deliver. Top-floor suites, and those in the adjoining Coach House, display more elaborate furnishings and fixtures, such as wrought-iron bedsteads, vaulted ceilings, marble bathrooms, and double Jacuzzi tubs; some feature wood-burning fireplaces and claw-foot bathtubs for extra charm. Mornings bring a three-course breakfast. *$$$–$$$$; AE, MC, V; no checks; www.abigailshotel.com; at Quadra St, access from Vancouver St.*

Andersen House Bed & Breakfast / ★★

301 KINGSTON ST, VICTORIA; 250/388-4565 OR 877/264-9988

An exceptionally ornate and well-preserved home built in 1891 for a sea captain, Andersen House has only three guest rooms. Inside the Queen Anne–style structure, furnishings are a mix of antiques, Persian rugs, stained-glass windows, and contemporary art. The spacious Casablanca Room has a private balcony with steps to the garden. The even roomier two-bedroom Captain's Apartment can sleep five. All rooms feature jetted tubs and offer robes and romantic touches such as champagne goblets. The dining room's 12-foot ceilings are rendered homey by a communal breakfast table. *$$$–$$$$; MC, V; checks OK; www.andersenhouse.com; at Pendray St.*

Beaconsfield Inn / ★★

998 HUMBOLDT ST, VICTORIA; 250/384-4044 OR 888/884-4044

This Edwardian manor, built by businessman R. P. Rithet as a wedding gift for his daughter, is tastefully furnished in period antiques. In downstairs rooms, swirling art nouveau designs glimmer in rows of stained-glass windows. The Emily Carr and Duchess suite displays understated, jewel-toned elegance. Most of the nine guest rooms have fireplaces, and many have whirlpool tubs for two. The library, where full afternoon tea and sherry are served, harks back to the days of smoking jackets. Breakfast is served at intimate dining room tables or by the fountain in the conservatory. *$$$–$$$$; AE, JCB, MC, V; no checks; www.beaconsfieldinn.com; at Vancouver St.*

Delta Victoria Ocean Pointe Resort and Spa / ★★★

45 SONGHEES RD, VICTORIA; 250/360-2999 OR 800/667-4677

Dominating the Inner Harbour, along with the great monuments of the Empress Hotel and the Parliament buildings, the modern Ocean Pointe has sweeping views. Standard rooms, done in a rich sage and burgundy, have tall windows and views from the water side of the hotel. For luxury, splurge on a suite. Family parking spots, kids' check-in packs, and story time with cookies and milk each evening make this one of Victoria's most family-friendly hotels. *$$$$; AE, DC, JCB, MC, V; no checks; www.deltahotels.com; across Johnson St Bridge.* &

Fairmont Empress Hotel / ★★★

721 GOVERNMENT ST, VICTORIA; 250/384-8111 OR 800/441-1414

This is one of the most famous hotels in the world—one of Canada's key landmarks. The hotel was built in 1908 in the style of a French chateau, and the rooms are furnished in Edwardian style. Although some of the rooms are compact and unremarkable, the draw is the location, harbor view, and overall atmosphere. In the public areas, tourists gather to sip afternoon tea; a separate lobby for guests assures privacy. All the high-end facilities are here, including an indoor pool, a fitness center, and a spa. The Empress Room is the most visually impressive dining room in Victoria. The grand space retains the original carved beams in the ceiling, the tapestry-filled walls, and spacious tables. *$$$$; AE, DC, DIS, MC, V; no checks; www.fairmont.com/empress; between Humboldt and Belleville sts.* &

Haterleigh Heritage Inn / ★★

243 KINGSTON ST, VICTORIA; 250/384-9995 OR 866/234-2244

This turn-of-the-20th-century heritage home, which architect Thomas Hooper built for himself in 1901, is decorated throughout with mint-condition antiques under 12-foot ceilings. The original stained-glass windows are exceptional, and the guest rooms are bright, roomy, and romantic: the main-floor Day Dreams Suite has a separate sitting area with a double-jetted tub, a bed with a satin-finish scrollwork headboard, and a trio of full-length windows topped with stained-glass panels. As old-fashioned as the

467

atmosphere is, free wireless Internet access keeps guests connected. *$$$–$$$$; MC, V; no checks; www.haterleigh.com; at Pendray St.*

Magnolia Hotel & Spa / ★★★

623 COURTNEY ST, VICTORIA; 250/381-0999 OR 877/624-6654
The 63-room Magnolia styles itself after European boutique hotels, with attentive service, tastefully luxurious rooms and suites, and a full-service spa. The lobby is paneled in rich mahogany, and underfoot are limestone tiles. Many rooms have fireplaces, such as our favored seventh-floor "diamond level" corner suite. Sumptuous bathrooms have marble counters, with deep soaker baths. Downstairs, Hugo's Grill and Brewhouse is all dark wood and artful metal trellising; if quiet is important to you, book a room several floors above the pub. *$$$$; AE, DC, DIS, JCB, MC, V; no checks; www.magnoliahotel. com; at Gordon St.* &

Prior House Bed & Breakfast Inn / ★★★

620 ST. CHARLES ST, VICTORIA; 250/592-8847 OR 877/924-3300
Truly a queen among B and Bs, this large 1912 manor has dramatic stonework on its lower levels and Tudor styling above. Gardens are visible from most of the six guest rooms; some have balconies. More-private, ground-level garden suites have separate entrances, patio space, and one or two bedrooms. An in-house chef creates the elaborate breakfasts and afternoon teas served daily. *$$$–$$$$; MC, V; checks OK; www.priorhouse.com; between Fairfield and Rockland sts.*

Sooke to Port Renfrew

Forty minutes west of Victoria on **HIGHWAY 14**, Sooke is a friendly little town set in idyllic surroundings. Beyond Sooke, the road continues west past stellar beaches to Port Renfrew, southern trailhead for the famed West Coast Trail. **HATLEY PARK NATIONAL HISTORIC SITE** (2005 Sooke Rd, Victoria; 250/391-2666 or 866/241-0674), on the road to Sooke, is a grand former Dunsmuir family castle in medieval style; tours are available. In this area, the shallow, relatively warm waters of **WITTY'S LAGOON REGIONAL PARK** (west of Victoria via Hwy 14 and Metchosin Rd) are popular with local families. The swimming holes at **SOOKE POTHOLES PROVINCIAL PARK** (end of Sooke River Rd) are a treat on a hot day.

Locals pack the booths at the '50s-era **MOM'S CAFÉ** (2036 Shields Rd, Sooke; 250/642-3314) for hearty diner fare; traditional pub food warms travelers at the historic **17 MILE HOUSE** (5126 Sooke Rd, Sooke; 250/642-5942). Stop by the **SOOKE COUNTRY MARKET** (at Otter Pt and West Coast rds, Sooke; 250/642-7528; Sat mid-May–Sept). Hikers fuel up on mile-high cheesecakes and homemade pies at the **COUNTRY CUPBOARD CAFÉ**, 15 minutes west of Sooke (402 Sheringham Point Rd, Sooke; 250/646-2323).

The entire coast between Sooke and Port Renfrew has parks with trails down to beaches; **CHINA BEACH** (23 miles/37 km west of Sooke) is the start of the rigorous

Juan de Fuca Marine Trail. **SOMBRIO BEACH** (34 miles/57 km west of Sooke) is popular with local surfers. **BOTANICAL BEACH** (follow signs at end of paved road just west of Port Renfrew) has miles of tide pools that expose sea life. The **SOOKE VISITOR INFORMATION CENTRE**, in the **SOOKE REGION MUSEUM** (2070 Phillips Rd, Sooke; 250/642-6351 or 866/888-4748), has details.

RESTAURANTS

Markus' Wharfside Restaurant / ★★

1831 MAPLE AVE S, SOOKE; 250/642-3596
Housed in a former fisherman's cottage overlooking Sooke Harbour, this This restaurant's views of the water can be enjoyed from two little antique-furnished dining rooms (one with a cozy fire) or from the patio. Risotto, Tuscan seafood soup, and baked goat cheese with roasted garlic are mainstays; crab, when available, comes straight from the docks next door. *$$$; MC, V; no checks; dinner Tues–Sat, brunch Sun (check for winter closures); full bar; reservations recommended; www.markuswharfsiderestaurant.com; at foot of Maple Ave, off Hwy 14.* ♿

Point No Point Restaurant / ★★

10829 WEST COAST RD (POINT NO POINT RESORT), SOOKE; 250/646-2020
This little glass-enclosed restaurant, perched high on a bluff over the crashing waves, is known for its dramatic water and mountain views as well as the creative surf-and-turf menu. Tuck into starters of steamed local shellfish with white wine and spinach pesto or crispy confit of duck leg; seared wild salmon with fava beans, herb aioli, and creamy white beans or beef tenderloin with tarragon-anchovy sauce and spaetzle are excellent entrée picks. *$$$; AE, MC, V; no checks; lunch, afternoon tea every day, dinner Wed–Sun (Feb–Dec); beer and wine; reservations recommended; www.pointnopointresort.com; Hwy 14, 15 miles/24 km west of Sooke.*

Sooke Harbour House / ★★★☆

1528 WHIFFEN SPIT RD, SOOKE; 250/642-3421 OR 800/889-9688
Almost three decades after Frédérique and Sinclair Philip started setting Canadian cuisine on its ears, their globally famous restaurant remains ever-intriguing. Entrées range from sautéed rosethorn rockfish with a strawberry and begonia dressing to locally raised leg of lamb marinated in fenugreek, cumin, garlic, and golden rosemary. Thrill seekers can book ahead for the Gastronomic Adventure and enjoy seven to nine courses. The 600-label wine list, placed in the world's top 90 by *Wine Spectator* magazine, features excellent French vintages. The dining room, with its ocean views, fireplace, and roomy tables, is refreshingly informal. *$$$$; DC, JCB, MC, V; checks OK; dinner every day; full bar; reservations recommended; www.sookeharbour house.com; end of Whiffen Spit Rd, off Hwy 14.* ♿

LODGINGS

Markham House / ★★☆

1775 CONNIE RD, SOOKE; 250/642-7542 OR 888/256-6888

Guests choose Markham House for gentle pleasures: tea on the patio, country hospitality, feather beds, and fireside sherry before turning in. Immaculately groomed grounds include a hot tub in a gazebo, a small river, a trout pond, a putting green, and iris gardens. One of the three guest rooms has a double Jacuzzi overlooking the pond. The very private Honeysuckle Cottage makes an ideal romantic hideaway. *$$–$$$; AE, DC, DIS, JCB, MC, V; checks OK; www.markhamhouse.com; turn south off Hwy 14 east of Sooke.*

Point No Point Resort / ★★★

10829 WEST COAST RD, SOOKE; 250/646-2020

The Soderberg family owns a mile of beach and 40 acres of undeveloped coastline facing the Strait of Juan de Fuca. They rent 25 cabins among the trees near the cliff. Several newer, pricier cabins have hot tubs; in-room spa services are available. Wood is supplied, and each cabin has a fireplace and kitchen, though the restaurant (see review) serves excellent food. *$$$–$$$$; AE, MC, V; checks OK; www.pointnopointresort.com; Hwy 14, 15 miles/24 km west of Sooke.* &

Richview House / ★★

7031 RICHVIEW DR, SOOKE; 250/642-5520 OR 866/276-2480

Views of the Strait of Juan de Fuca and the Olympic Mountains from each room's private hot tub are just part of what keeps couples returning to this adult-oriented B and B on Sooke's waterfront. Each of the three guest rooms in François and Joan Gething's handcrafted, modern-with-a-touch-of-Tudor home has a private entrance, a deck or patio (with a hot tub), and a fireplace; the lower-floor room boasts a private steam room. Much of the lovely furniture and woodwork was crafted by François himself. *$$$; MC, V; no checks; www.bnbsooke.com; Whiffen Spit Rd off Hwy 14, turn right onto Richview Rd.*

Sooke Harbour House / ★★★★

1528 WHIFFEN SPIT RD, SOOKE; 250/642-3421 OR 800/889-9688

This bucolic waterside establishment is one of Canada's finest inns. Innkeepers Frédérique and Sinclair Philip's Northwest art collection—among the country's most extensive and intriguing—graces everything. The gardens, too, are works of art. Local craftspeople helped create distinctive themes for each of the 28 guest rooms. The Mermaid Room is lavished with mythic art; the Victor Newman Longhouse Room features museum-quality First Nations art. Most rooms have water and mountain views, fireplaces, and Japanese-style deep soaking tubs on their balconies. A lavish complimentary breakfast—hazelnut–maple syrup waffles with loganberry purée, for example—is delivered to your room. *$$$$; DC, JCB, MC, V; checks OK; www.sookeharbourhouse.com; end of road, off Hwy 14.* &

Sidney and the Saanich Peninsula

This pretty rural area, although increasingly subject to urban development, holds bucolic corners, particularly off West Saanich Road. En route to the floral splendor of **BUTCHART GARDENS** (see Victoria, Parks and Gardens), stop at **CHURCH & STATE WINES** (1445 Benvenuto Ave, Brentwood Bay; 250/652-2671) for a tasting or a meal on the wraparound veranda overlooking the vineyards. Bibliophiles like seaside **SIDNEY-BY-THE-SEA** (Saanich Peninsula), with 10 bookstores to browse through.

RESTAURANTS

Deep Cove Chalet / ★★★

11190 CHALET RD, SIDNEY; 250/656-3541
Chef-owner Pierre Koffel brings European formality to this rural seaside setting northwest of Sidney. The large windows of this 1913 wooden lodge overlook lawns and a splendid view of Saanich Inlet. Guests can dine in the garden under a grape arbor on fine days. Lobster bisque, rack of lamb, coq au vin, and beef Wellington are among the continental classics. Book a suite upstairs for a private dinner or an overnight stay. *$$$$; AE, MC, V; local checks only; lunch Wed–Sun, dinner Tues–Sun; full bar; reservations recommended; www. deepcovechalet.com; call for directions.* &

Dockside Grill / ★★

2320 HARBOUR RD, SIDNEY; 250/656-0828
One of the busiest spots in Sidney during the summer, this new (formerly Dock 503) Pacific Northwest eatery wins big. Blue-canvas blinds over marina-view windows create a low-key nautical air at this casual 55-seat spot, which is surrounded on three sides by water views and fancy yachts. Seafood is the key, with chef Josh Hall creating original takes on dishes like calamari, crab cakes, and chowder, using fresh local ingredients. The wine list is all about BC, so diners can sample wines from all over the province. If the weather's nice, get there early to grab a seat on the sun-drenched patio overlooking Tsehum Harbour and mountain views. *$$$; AE, DC, MC, V; no checks; lunch, dinner every day, brunch Sun; full bar; reservations recommended; www.dock503. vanislemarina.com/docksidegrill; at marina north of Sidney.* &

The Latch Inn & Restaurant / ★★★

2328 HARBOUR RD, SIDNEY; 250/656-4015
This offbeat 1925 mansion was designed by noted Victoria architect Samuel Maclure as a summer home for the lieutenant governor of British Columbia. The exterior is rustic British Columbian; inside is all old-world elegance. The menu's West Coast fare with an Italian infusion includes appetizers like steamed mussels or a rabbit roulade with arugula, Belgian endive, and prosciutto. Entrées range from rack of lamb to Cowichan Bay duck breast or a vegetarian stuffed portobello mushroom. The six guest rooms feature

VANCOUVER ISLAND THREE-DAY TOUR

DAY ONE: From Victoria, get a healthful breakfast at **REBAR MODERN FOOD**, then head north and hop aboard one of the Swartz Bay ferries to **SALT SPRING ISLAND**. Browse the **SATURDAY MARKET** in the heart of Ganges. Have lunch at **MOBY'S MARINE PUB** and drive up Cranberry Road to the top of **MOUNT MAXWELL** for a panoramic view. Check in to **HASTINGS HOUSE COUNTRY HOUSE HOTEL** and eat dinner at **RESTAURANT HOUSE PICCOLO**.

DAY TWO: After your delivered breakfast at Hastings House, zip out to Vesuvius Bay on the island's western side and catch the ferry to Crofton, on the mainland just south of Chemainus. From there, drive north on the Trans-Canada Hwy (Hwy 1). Just past **LADYSMITH**, take a side trip to Yellow Point to lunch at the **CROW AND GATE PUB**. At **NANAIMO**, continue north on the inland Hwy 19 to **PARKSVILLE**, then take Hwy 4A west to visit **COOMBS**; browse the **OLD COUNTRY MARKET**. Continue west, joining Hwy 4, and pause on the road to Port Alberni to admire the trees of Cathedral Grove in **MACMIL-LAN PROVINCIAL PARK**. Keep on driving to the west coast, then turn north to **TOFINO**. Check in to a room at the **MIDDLE BEACH LODGE** (400 MacKenzie Beach, Tofino; 250/725-2900; www.middlebeach.com) and dine by the surf at the **POINTE RESTAURANT** in the Wickaninnish Inn.

DAY THREE: After coffee and pastries at Middle Beach Lodge, head out for a morning of whale-watching or kayaking. Pack your swimsuit and stop for a plunge at **HOT SPRINGS COVE** en route. Lunch at **SOBO** in the **TOFINO BOTANICAL GARDENS**, then drive to the inimitable **LONG BEACH**. Spend the afternoon exploring the beach before checking in for the night at **TAUCA LEA RESORT & SPA** in Ucluelet and dine at its **BOAT BASIN** restaurant.

antique wood paneling hewn from local Douglas fir; one has the original 1925 10-headed shower. If rooms are full, check out Miraloma on the Cove (see review) beside the restaurant. *$$$; AE, DC, DIS, E, MC, V; no checks; dinner every day; full bar; reservations recommended; www.latchinn.ca; ½ mile/ 1 km north of Sidney.*

LODGINGS

Brentwood Bay Lodge & Spa / ★★★★

849 VERDIER AVE, BRENTWOOD BAY; 250/544-2079 OR 888/544-2079

Perched elegantly above its lovely namesake bay, this posh post-and-beam lodge is the best accommodation in the vicinity of Butchart Gardens. (In fact, guests can paddle a canoe to Butchart's back entrance or hop on a water shuttle.) Decorated in subdued earth tones with clear fir trim, the 33 suites all have water views plus fireside sitting areas, whirlpool tubs, and European linens. The swimming pool and spa are discreetly tucked into the garden level. The Arbutus Grille dining room, a dramatic space with 30-foot windows, takes a tapaslike approach to seafood, while the brand-new specialty wine liquor store makes a night in just a little more enticing. *$$$$; DC, JCB, MC, V; no checks; www.brentwoodbaylodge.com; right on Verdier Ave, follow signs to Mill Bay Ferry.* &

Miraloma on the Cove / ★★★

2326 HARBOUR RD, SIDNEY; 250/656-6622 OR 877/956-6622
Right at the end of Harbour Road, this comfortable waterfront resort feels like a home away from home. Most of the studios and one- and two-bedroom suites feature en suite laundry facilities, two-sided gas fireplaces, entertainment systems, and fully equipped kitchens. Other treats like wireless Internet access, continental breakfast, mountain bike usage, DVDs, hot chocolate, and freshly baked cookies all come at no charge. The 22 suites are all furnished in BC-style decor, with an emphasis on wood, stone, and unpretentious style. An outdoor hot tub is located in the private gardens. If you're not in the mood to cook in one of the gorgeous kitchens, ask the front desk staff to reserve you a spot at the neighboring Latch Inn & Restaurant (see review). *$$$–$$$$; DC, JCB, MC, V; no checks; www.miraloma.ca; left on Harbour Rd, follow .7 km to its end.*

Malahat

The Malahat is an ominous word among local drivers: it signals steep roads and winter fog and ice. But for leisurely drives, this section of the Trans-Canada Highway (Hwy 1) from Victoria to Mill Bay is one of the prettiest drives on the island. Lush Douglas fir forests hug the narrow-laned highway, past beloved **GOLD-STREAM PROVINCIAL PARK** (2930 Trans-Canada Hwy/Hwy 1, 8 miles northwest of Victoria; 250/478-9414; www.goldstreampark.com), where hundreds of bald eagles gather to feed on salmon mid-December through February. At the summit, northbound pullouts offer breathtaking views of Saanich Inlet clasped by surrounding hills.

RESTAURANTS

Bonelli Lounge / ★★½

600 EBEDORA LN (AERIE RESORT), MALAHAT; 250/743-7115 OR 800/518-1933
Bonelli (Italian for "eagle") is the Aerie Resort's (see review) more casual dining option. The Mediterranean-themed à la carte menu for both lunch and dinner offers soups, salads, sandwiches, and straightforward main dishes like lamb chops, beef strip loin, and free-range chicken breast with morel cream sauce—all from the same high-standard, made-from-scratch kitchen as the main dining room's. A plate of local artisan cheese or chocolate fondue for two are reason enough to linger. *$$$; AE, DC, MC, V;*

no checks; lunch, dinner every day; full bar; reservations recommended; www.aerie.bc.ca; 30 minutes from downtown Victoria, take Spectacle Lake turnoff from Trans-Canada Hwy.

Culinaire / ★★★

600 EBEDORA LN (AERIE RESORT), MALAHAT; 250/743-7115 OR 800/518-1933
Perched high on Malahat Mountain, the Aerie Resort (see review) dining room is as spectacular and inspiring as its view. Executive Chef Castro Boateng incorporates produce from nearby organic farms, local wild mushrooms, and other forest edibles into his multicourse tasting menus, creating such imaginative dishes as Cowichan Bay Farm duck leg with fig balsamic reduction or herb roasted root vegetable gnocchi with oyster mushrooms and truffles for the vegetarians. Choose from a custom four- or five-course tasting menu. *$$$$; AE, DC, MC, V; no checks; dinner every day; full bar; reservations recommended; www.aerie.bc.ca; 30 minutes from downtown Victoria, take Spectacle Lake turnoff from Trans-Canada Hwy.* &

Malahat Mountain Inn / ★★

265 TRANS-CANADA HWY, MALAHAT;
250/478-1979 OR 800/913-1944
Wrought-iron candelabras and local art punctuate the dramatic color scheme, booths offer intimacy, and a wide deck makes the most of the view over Finlayson Arm. The menu is big on seafood and pastas. At dinner, vegetarians dig into the grilled vegetable penne; meatier fare includes lamb sirloin with mint demi-glace or stuffed coho salmon. The Malahat Mountain Inn (250/478-1979 or 800/913-1944) operates 10 suites next door with soaker tubs, fireplaces, and, of course, views. *$$–$$$; AE, MC, V; no checks; breakfast, lunch, dinner every day; full bar; reservations recommended; www. malahatmountaininn.com; at top of Malahat Dr (Hwy 1).*

LODGINGS

The Aerie Resort / ★★★

600 EBEDORA LN, MALAHAT; 250/743-7115 OR 800/518-1933
The Aerie is quite simply over the top—too much so for some tastes—but its faux-Mediterranean-Empire decadence draws celebrities seeking indulgence high atop Malahat. The 35 creamy white terraced units were designed as a modern take on Mediterranean villages. Set in 85 acres of woods and gardens, it achieves an idyllic Isle-of-Capri mood. Most guest rooms feature whirlpool tubs, fireplaces, private decks, and Persian and Chinese silk carpets. Romantics seeking ultimate privacy (and views) opt for one of the six hilltop suites, several hundred feet up and away from the main building. *$$$$; AE, DC, MC, V; no checks; www.aerie.bc.ca; 30 minutes from downtown Victoria, take Spectacle Lake turnoff from Trans-Canada Hwy.*

The Gulf Islands

Dotting the azure Strait of Georgia are clusters of beautiful, bucolic islands, Canada's counterpart to the U.S. San Juans. Serene, remote, laid-back, artsy, and quirky, the Gulf Islands are divine places. Services can be sketchy on the smaller islands, so plan accordingly.

The Gulf Islands fall into three groups. The best known are the southern Gulf Islands; of these, **SALT SPRING**, **GALIANO**, **MAYNE**, **SATURNA**, and **PENDER** are accessible via the BC Ferries terminal at Swartz Bay outside Victoria (or from Tsawwassen outside Vancouver), while **GABRIOLA** is reached from Nanaimo. Visited several times a day by ferry, the southern Gulf Islands—particularly Salt Spring and Galiano—offer the widest selection of services. Farther north, **DENMAN** and **HORNBY ISLANDS**, with trails beloved by mountain bikers, are a short hop from Buckley Bay, 12 miles/20 km south of Courtenay. **QUADRA**, **CORTES**, and **SONORA** make up the closely linked Discovery Islands—fishing and boating meccas east of Campbell River.

ACCESS AND INFORMATION

BC FERRIES (250/386-3431 or 888/223-3779; www.bcferries.com) offers many trips daily, but plan ahead in summer for car traffic; popular runs fill fast. Island hopping is possible, but schedules are complex and times do not always mesh. If you are planning to island hop, ask BC Ferries about their **SAILPASS**—it may save you some money. Advance reservations are possible between the British Columbia mainland and the southern Gulf Islands at no extra charge. Less stressful—and less expensive—is leaving the car at home; most inns and B and Bs offer ferry pickup. Bring your own bike or rent one; the islands (with the exception of busy Salt Spring) are wonderful (if hilly) for cycling. **TOURISM VANCOUVER ISLAND** (335 Wesley St, Ste 203, Nanaimo; 250/754-3500; www.vancouverisland.travel) has information on touring the Gulf Islands.

Salt Spring Island

Salt Spring is the largest and most populous of the southern Gulf Islands (with over 10,000 residents) and has artisans' studios and pastoral farms. Non-Native settlement dates back to the mid-19th century, and early settlers included African Americans from San Francisco after the Civil War. The Kanakas, as the indigenous people of Hawaii were then called, also played a role in early settlement.

Today Salt Spring is a place where there are no fast-food chains (residents block proposals to build them) and dogs greet you everywhere. The landscape has a pioneer imprint of farms and forests, interspersed with lakes. From Victoria, ferries leave Swartz Bay and land 35 minutes later at Salt Spring's **FULFORD HARBOUR**, a small artists' village at the island's south end. Here you can fuel up at **TREEHOUSE SOUTH** (2921 Fulford-Ganges Rd, Salt Spring Island; 250/653-4833) or

MORNINGSIDE ORGANIC BAKERY AND CAFÉ (107 Morningside Rd, Salt Spring Island; 250/653-4414) for the 20-minute drive to Ganges.

MOUNT MAXWELL PROVINCIAL PARK (7 miles/11 km southwest of Ganges via Fulford-Ganges Rd and Cranberry Rd), on the west side of the island 2,000 feet/610 m above sea level, has a rewarding view. For walk-in camping and seaside walks, head for **RUCKLE PROVINCIAL PARK** (10 minutes from Fulford Harbour ferry dock, take right onto Beaver Rd; 250/539-2115 or 877/559-2115; www.env. gov.bc.ca/bcparks) on the island's east side. **ST. MARY LAKE** and **CUSHEON LAKE** are good spots for a dip; the ocean waters are clean but chilly.

GARRY OAKS WINERY (1880 Fulford-Ganges Rd, Salt Spring Island; 250/653-4687; www.garryoakswine.com) and **SALT SPRING VINEYARDS** (151 Lee Rd, Salt Spring Island; 250/653-9463; www.saltspringvineyards.com; off 1700 block of Fulford-Ganges Rd), which also has a B and B, is open for tastings March through September and weekends until December. Locals and tourists alike love the **SALT SPRING ISLAND SATURDAY MARKET**'s (Centennial Park, Ganges; 250/537-4448; www.saltspringmarket.com; Mar–Oct) cheeses, organic produce, pottery, hand-smoothed wooden bowls, and more. Similarly fine wares can be found at the **ARTCRAFT SALE** (250/537-0899; May–Sept) in Ganges's Mahon Hall. Dozens of arts and crafts studios throughout the island are open to the public. A Studio Tour map from the **SALT SPRING ISLAND VISITOR INFORMATION CENTRE** (121 Lower Ganges Rd, Ganges; 250/537-5252 or 866/216-2936; www.saltspring today.com) will show you the way.

The annual (since 1896) **SALT SPRING FALL FAIR** (Farmer's Institute, 351 Rainbow Rd; Sept) is a family favorite, with sheep shearing, crafts, animals, games for kids, baked goods, and more. Enjoy a snack and organic coffee at the vegetarian bakery and café **BARB'S BUNS** (1-121 McPhillips Ave, Ganges; 250/537-4491); views, hearty meals, and microbrews at **MOBY'S MARINE PUB** (124 Upper Ganges Rd, Ganges; 250/537-5559); live music and wholesome, made-from-scratch meals at the **TREEHOUSE CAFÉ** (106 Purvis Ln, Ganges, 250/537-5379); and wood-fired pizzas at the **RAVEN STREET MARKET CAFÉ** (321 Fernwood Rd, Salt Spring Island; 250/537-2273; north end of island).

RESTAURANTS

Hastings House Country House Hotel / ★★★

160 UPPER GANGES RD, GANGES; 250/537-2362 OR 800/661-9255

The dark-wood ambience of this well-known inn (see review) extends to its restaurant, where an enormous fireplace warms the foyer of a house built as a replica English country manor. The prix-fixe menu (choose three or five courses) changes daily, offering such appetizers as grilled sea scallop with parsnip chips and sweet pepper reduction or Pacific halibut paired with citrus salsa and cilantro oil. Entrées run from pan-seared Fraser Valley duck breast to oven baked sablefish with smoked bacon and soya emulsion. Local lamb is almost always available. *$$$$; AE, MC, V; no checks; breakfast, lunch by arrangement, dinner every day, brunch Sun (July–Aug, some holidays; closed* *mid-Nov–mid-Mar); full bar; reservations recommended; www.hastingshouse. com; just north of Ganges.*

Restaurant House Piccolo / ★★★★

108 HEREFORD AVE, GANGES; 250/537-1844
Chef Piccolo Lyytikainen, a member of the prestigious Chaîne des Rôtisseurs, brings upscale European cuisine to this intimate Ganges restaurant, widely regarded as among the finest in the region. Set in a tiny heritage house, Piccolo has a candlelit ambience that is island-style informal. Main dishes range from charbroiled fillet of beef with Gorgonzola sauce to roasted Muscovy duck breast and local lamb. Enjoy the baked-to-order warm chocolate cake. *$$$$; AE, DC, MC, V; local checks only; dinner every day; full bar; reservations recommended; www.housepiccolo.com; downtown at Lower Ganges Rd.*

LODGINGS

Bold Bluff Retreat / ★★

1 BOLD BLUFF, SALT SPRING ISLAND; 250/653-4377 OR 866/666-4377
This secluded retreat accessible only by private boat borders 2,600 acres of protected land. Salty's Cabin, which sleeps five, sits on a rocky outcropping where the tide rushes in and out right under the deck. The Garden Cottage, which sleeps six, is nestled in an old orchard. Singles and couples enjoy the single B and B room in the main house, a 1940 cedar lodge. The newest addition is a furnished tepee on the bluff's edge, with a deck, solar shower, and camp kitchen. Owner Tamar Griggs will gladly pick up guests for the 5-minute boat ride from Burgoyne Bay or the 10-minute jaunt from Maple Bay on Vancouver Island. Three-night minimum for cabins in July and August. *$–$$$; AE, MC, V; checks OK; Salty's Cabin closed Nov–Mar, B&B and tepee closed Oct–May; www.boldbluff.com; from Burgoyne Bay, 10 minutes northwest of Fulford Harbour, from Maple Bay on Vancouver Island.*

Hastings House Country House Hotel / ★★★

160 UPPER GANGES RD, GANGES; 250/537-2362 OR 800/661-9255
The English-country ambience at this 22-acre seaside estate is as genuine as it gets outside the United Kingdom. The farm was founded by an immigrant British farmer in the 19th century, and the six buildings have either been renovated or built to replicate the original property. The Farmhouse has two spacious, two-level suites overlooking the water. In the Manor House, two upstairs suites feature the same lovely views and Sussex-style charm. The Post is a compact cabin popular with honeymooners. Seven Hillside suites offer lofty ocean views in a modern board-and-batten building; these, however, get some road noise, lack the charm of the other units, and overlook the patio of the pub next door. *$$$$; AE, MC, V; no checks; closed mid-Nov–mid-Mar; www.hastingshouse.com; just north of Ganges.*

North and South Pender Islands

Pender "Island" is actually two islands united by a small bridge. Both are green and rural, though South Pender is the less developed of the two. The population here is decidedly residential, so don't expect many restaurants, lodgings, or shops. Beaches, however, abound: **MORTIMER SPIT** (western tip of South Pender) and **GOWLLAND POINT BEACH** (end of Gowlland Point Rd, South Pender) are among 30 public ocean-access points. Maps are available at the **PENDER ISLAND LIONS VISITOR INFORMATION CENTRE** (2332 Otter Bay Rd; 250/629-6541; www. penderisland.info; mid-May–Labor Day), near the Otter Bay ferry terminal on North Pender.

To take advantage of the fabled Gulf Island viewscape, the trails on **MOUNT NORMAN** (accessible from Ainslie Rd or Canal Rd, South Pender), part of the new Gulf Islands National Park Reserve, are steep but rewarding. The gentle terrain of South Pender is particularly appealing for cyclists; rent bikes at **OTTER BAY MARINA** (2311 MacKinnon Rd, North Pender; 250/629-3579) and then head to South Pender. While waiting for the ferry at **OTTER BAY** on North Pender, grab an excellent burger—try a venison, oyster, or ostrich variation—at the humble trailer called the **STAND** (Otter Bay ferry terminal, North Pender; 250/629-3292).

LODGINGS

Poets Cove Resort & Spa / ★★★

**9801 SPALDING RD, SOUTH PENDER ISLAND;
250/629-2100 OR 888/512-7638**

Known for years as Bedwell Harbour Resort, this new complex represents an almost complete revamp except for the sheltered cove and marina, backed by a wooded hillside, with stunning sunset views. The three-story lodge, with its stone detailing and pretty rounded gables, has 22 ocean-view, Arts and Crafts–style rooms with fireplaces and balconies. Cottages and villas have kitchens, fireplaces, and balconies; most have views of the cove, and some have private hot tubs. A water-sports center offers lessons. Aurora Restaurant, located in the lodge, serves wild salmon, Pender Island lamb, and other treats. *$$$$; AE, MC, V; no checks; www.poetscove.com; from Vancouver Island, take resort's water taxi from Sidney or BC Ferries from Swartz Bay to Otter Bay.*

Saturna Island

The remotest of the southern Gulf Islands—it takes two ferries to get here—Saturna has a scant 300 residents, two general stores, a café, and a pub overlooking the **LYALL HARBOUR** ferry stop. No camping is available on the island, but hiking abounds on **MOUNT WARBURTON PIKE**, the second-highest peak in the southern Gulf Islands. **WINTER COVE PARK** (1 mile/1.6 km from ferry dock, off East Point Rd) is an inviting place to beachcomb or picnic above the

Strait of Georgia. Or take the scenic ocean drive to the tidal pools and sculpted sandstone of remote **EAST POINT REGIONAL PARK** (eastern tip of island). **SATURNA ISLAND VINEYARDS** (8 Quarry Rd; 250/539-5139 or 877/918-3388; www.saturnavineyards.com) has merlot, chardonnay, pinot gris, pinot noir, and Gewürztraminer.

LODGINGS

Saturna Lodge and Restaurant / ★

130 PAYNE RD, SATURNA ISLAND; 250/539-2254 OR 888/539-2254

This lovely frame lodge sits high on a hill overlooking Boot Cove. Windows wrap around the dining room, and a fire beckons in the lower-floor lounge. Seven sunny guest rooms upstairs are contemporary in feel, with pleasant sitting areas and ocean or garden views. Five have private baths; the honeymoon suite has a soaker tub and private balcony. The menu at the restaurant (serving breakfast to guests, dinner to the public; reservations recommended) offers lamb and organic produce; the wine cellar features Saturna's own wines. *$$–$$$; MC, V; no checks; closed mid-Oct–mid-May; www.saturna. ca; follow signs from ferry.*

Mayne Island

During the Cariboo Gold Rush of the mid-1800s, Mayne was the southern Gulf Islands' commercial and social hub, a way station between Victoria and Vancouver. Today the pace of life is more serene. Rolling orchards and warm, rock-strewn beaches dominate this pocket-size island of 5 square miles/13 sq km. A complete bicycle tour of the island takes five hours; at **DINNER BAY PARK** (about ½ mile/1 km south of ferry terminal at Village Bay), a traditional Japanese garden commemorates the many Japanese families who settled on the island before World War II.

RESTAURANTS

Oceanwood Country Inn / ★★★

630 DINNER BAY RD, MAYNE ISLAND; 250/539-5074

Exquisitely prepared four-course dinners in the dining room overlooking Navy Channel highlight entrées such as rosemary-roasted Mayne Island lamb or salmon and squash steamed in cabbage. Appetizers are strikingly inventive: smoked-sablefish and beet terrine with stinging-nettle juice, for example. At dessert, a goat-cheese cake with walnut sabayon and rosemary-caramel–roasted apples might make an appearance. *$$$$; MC, V; Canadian checks only; dinner every day (closed mid-Oct–late-Mar); full bar; reservations required; www.oceanwood.com; right on Dalton Dr, right on Mariners St, immediate left onto Dinner Bay Rd, look for signs.*

LODGINGS

Oceanwood Country Inn / ★★

630 DINNER BAY RD, MAYNE ISLAND; 250/539-5074

The split-level, high-ceilinged Wisteria Room, the largest of the Oceanwood's 12 guest rooms, has striking views over Navy Channel. Fireplaces, deep soaker tubs, and ocean views are features of many rooms. Some, like the Lilac Room, are done in a floral theme; others, like the blue-hued Heron Room, come in more masculine tones. After kayaking, bird-watching, or cycling (the inn has bikes on hand), eat in the excellent dining room (see review). *$$$–$$$$; MC, V; Canadian checks only; check for winter hours; www.ocean wood.com; for directions, see review in Restaurants.*

Galiano Island

Residents here dismiss bustling Salt Spring as "towny," as well they might from their undeveloped, secluded island. Dedicated locals protect the natural features along the island's narrow 19 miles/30 km: cliffs, bluffs, meadows, and harbors. Despite being the closest of the southern Gulf Islands to Tsawwassen (one hour), Galiano has just over 1,000 residents and only a few services and shops, clustered at its south end at Sturdies Bay.

On Bodega Ridge, a clifftop walk rewards with views across the islands. From Bluffs Park and Mount Galiano, you can watch eagles, ferries, and sweeping tides on Active Pass. Most Galiano roads accommodate bicycles, but there's some steep going. Rent a bike at **GALIANO BICYCLE** (36 Burrill Rd; 250/539-9906). **MONTAGUE HARBOUR PROVINCIAL MARINE PARK** (5 miles/8 km west of ferry dock; 250/539-2115) is a sheltered bay with beaches and more. At Montague Harbour Marina, just east of the park, go kayaking with **GULF ISLANDS KAYAKING** (250/539-2442), rent from **GALIANO MOPEDS & BOAT RENTALS** (250/539-3443 or 877/303-3546), or stop for a barbecue on the deck of the **HARBOUR GRILL** (250/539-5733).

You'll find local color at the **HUMMINGBIRD PUB** (47 Sturdies Bay Rd; 250/539-5472) and, on weekends, four-course dinners at **LA BÉRENGERIE** (2806 Montague Rd; 250/539-5392), a cozy house in the woods.

While away time in the Sturdies Bay ferry line at **TRINCOMALI BAKERY, DELI & BISTRO** (2540 Sturdies Bay Rd; 250/539-2004) or the funky, diner-style **GRAND CENTRAL EMPORIUM** (2740 Sturdies Bay Rd; 250/539-9885). The **GALIANO CHAMBER OF COMMERCE** (Sturdies Bay Village Center; 250/539-2233; www. galianoisland.com) runs a small information center in summer.

RESTAURANTS

Atrevida Restaurant at the Galiano Inn / ★★★

134 MADRONA DR, GALIANO ISLAND; 250/539-3388 OR 877/530-3939

Named for a Spanish ship that once explored these waters, Atrevida has charred-look wood floors and First Nations art that combine Pacific Northwest and Spanish styles with grace. Entrées range from local salmon to free-range lamb. Under a lofty, open-beamed ceiling, every table in the curved atrium-style dining room has an expansive view of the seals, otters, and ferries plying Active Pass. The Oceanside Patio Grill offers a lighter lunch menu during the summer. *$$$; MC, V; no checks; lunch, dinner every day (no lunch Oct–Apr, except guests with packages); full bar; reservations recommended; www.galianoinn. com; uphill from ferry terminal, turn left on Madrona Dr.*

Woodstone Country Inn / ★★★

743 GEORGESON BAY RD, GALIANO ISLAND;
250/539-2022 OR 888/339-2022
The dining room at this inn (see review) ranks high: co-innkeeper and chef Gail Nielsen serves a fine four-course table d'hôte dinner that might include cioppino of fresh mussels, shrimp, and seafood or boneless duck breast with oranges, grilled yellowfin tuna aioli, and vegetable gratin. Locals are fiercely loyal to the bread pudding with rum sauce. Enjoy a neoclassical room (think Italianate columns) overlooking a serene field. *$$$; AE, MC, V; local checks only; dinner every day (closed Dec–Jan); full bar; reservations required; www. woodstoneinn.com; left off Sturdies Bay Rd onto Georgeson Bay Rd.* &

LODGINGS

The Bellhouse Inn / ★★★

29 FARMHOUSE RD, GALIANO ISLAND; 800/970-7464
Andrea Porter and David Birchall are consummate gentlefolk farmers, conversing with guests and feeding sheep with equal aplomb. This historic farmhouse, painted cream and barn red, contains six lovely guest rooms. All have balconies, duvets made with wool from the farm's own sheep, and private bathrooms (though one is across the hall). The Kingfisher room is the largest, with a Jacuzzi plus picture windows allowing an expansive view of Bellhouse Bay from bed. *$$–$$$; MC, V; Canadian checks only; www.bellhouseinn.com; uphill from ferry terminal, left on Burrill Rd, left on Jack Rd, right on Farmhouse Rd.*

Galiano Inn / ★★★

134 MADRONA DR, GALIANO ISLAND;
250/539-3388 OR 877/530-3939
This romantic oceanfront inn, with its mix of Mediterranean and Northwest styles, has 20 spacious, ocean-view guest rooms, each with a private deck or patio, sitting area, and wood-burning fireplace. Some rooms have jetted tubs (with a separate shower), and all have luxurious touches. The rooms' creams, yellows, and blues are just right for winding down after a soak in the hot tub or a massage at the on-site Madrona del Mar Spa. A full breakfast and afternoon tea are included, and the Atrevida Restaurant (see review) serves Pacific Northwest fare. Two-night minimum on weekends. *$$$$; MC, V; no checks; www.galianoinn.com; uphill from ferry terminal, left on Madrona Dr.* &

The Cowichan Valley and Southeast Shore

The farmland and forest of the Cowichan Valley stretches from the town of Shawnigan Lake north to Duncan, then west to Cowichan Lake; the microclimate lends itself to grape growing, making it Vancouver Island's best-known vineyard region. Try a pinot noir at **BLUE GROUSE VINEYARDS** (4365 Blue Grouse Rd, off Lakeside Rd, Duncan; 250/743-3834; www.bluegrousevineyards.com); also visit **CHERRY POINT VINEYARDS** (840 Cherry Point Rd, Cobble Hill; 250/743-1272; www.cherrypointvineyards.com) and **GLENTERRA VINEYARDS** (3897 Cobble Hill Rd, Cobble Hill; 250/743-2330; www.glenterravineyards.com). Time your lunch for a visit to **VIGNETI ZANATTA** (5039 Marshall Rd, Duncan; 250/748-2338; www.zanatta.ca), which has a restaurant in a 1903 farmhouse.

Or head to **MERRIDALE CIDER WORKS** (1230 Merridale Rd, Cobble Hill; 250/743-4293 or 800/998-9908; www.merridalecider.com), where you can enjoy a meal in the European-style bistro. Merridale, one of the Northwest's few cideries, makes cider in the English tradition; the best time to visit is mid-September through mid-October, when apples are running through the presses. If you're traveling directly to the valley from the Sidney or Swartz Bay ferry terminal, taking the **BRENTWOOD BAY–MILL BAY FERRY** (250/386-3431 or 888/223-3779; www.bcferries.com) saves you a drive into Victoria.

Cowichan Bay

This charming little seaside village off Hwy 1 is built on pilings over the water. Brightly painted stilt houses are home to restaurants and gift shops. The Wooden Boat Society displays and Native artisans' studio at the **COWICHAN BAY MARITIME CENTRE AND MUSEUM** (1761 Cowichan Bay Rd; 250/746-4955; www.classicboats.org) are worth a visit. The **ROCK COD CAFÉ** (1759 Cowichan Bay Rd; 250/746-1550) and the **UDDER GUYS ICE CREAM PARLOUR** (1759 Cowichan Bay Rd; 250/746-4300) can fulfill cravings for fish-n-chips and ice cream.

RESTAURANTS

The Masthead Restaurant / ★

1705 COWICHAN BAY RD, COWICHAN BAY; 250/748-3714
The Masthead, housed in the waterfront 1868 Columbia Hotel, hews to the overall island culinary bent: the salmon is wild, the vegetables come from local farms, and the cellar has the best selection of Vancouver Island wines anywhere. A favorite starter is the rich salmon and shrimp chowder. In summer the Masthead's seaside deck opens as the outdoor Chowder Café, serving a casual menu. *$$$; AE, MC, V; no checks; dinner every day (closed Oct–Apr); full bar; reservations recommended; www.themastheadrestaurant. com; at south end of village.*

LODGINGS

Dream Weaver Bed & Breakfast / ★

1682 BOTWOOD LN, COWICHAN BAY;
250/748-7688 OR 888/748-7689

This modern wood-shake home is modeled on gabled, multistoried, Victorian-era construction. The large Magnolia Suite, nestled in the top-floor gables, is done in flower prints, with a double Jacuzzi tub. Downstairs, the Rosewood Suite is Victorian and floral, with wallpaper borders and a wrought-iron bedstead, while the Primrose Suite has a more masculine look, with deep plum and green hues and a Jacuzzi tub in the bedroom. Only the Magnolia has a view, but all stays come with a full gourmet breakfast. *$$; MC, V; no checks; www.dreamweaverbedandbreakfast.com; at south end of village.*

Duncan

Forty-five minutes north of Victoria on the Trans-Canada Highway (Hwy 1), the City of Totems features modest **TOTEM POLES** sprinkled around the town's walkable core. Another claim to fame is the world's largest hockey stick, notably affixed to an arena. The **QUW'UTSUN' CULTURAL AND CONFERENCE CENTRE** (200 Cowichan Wy, Duncan; 250/746-8119 or 877/746-8119; www.quwutsun. ca) on Duncan's southern edge is excellent. In summer, dine at the center's **RIVERWALK CAFÉ** and watch as the region's renowned **COWICHAN SWEATERS** are made. The center also features an open-air carving shed, where carvers craft 12- to 20-foot totem poles.

In the old downtown, a good lunch can be had at the popular **ISLAND BAGEL COMPANY** (48 Station St; 250/748-1988) or at **BISTRO 161** (161 Kenneth St; 250/746-6466), which also serves Asian- and Mediterranean-inspired dinners and has a pretty patio.

RESTAURANTS

The Quamichan Inn / ★★

1478 MAPLE BAY RD, DUNCAN; 250/746-7028

Traditional fresh seafood dishes join inventions such as exotic game and fowl at this turn-of-the-20th-century Tudor-style country manor. Outside, the garden is profuse with flowers. The proprietors gladly pick up yachties and drop them off after dinner. Accommodations consist of four guest rooms; rates include an English hunt breakfast: fruit, eggs, bacon, sausage, and fried tomato. *$$$; AE, MC, V; local checks only; dinner Wed–Sun, brunch Sun; full bar; reservations recommended; www.thequamichaninn.com; just east of Duncan, follow signs to Maple Bay.*

LODGINGS

Fairburn Farm / ★★

3310 JACKSON RD, DUNCAN; 250/746-4637

This lovingly restored 1894 manor house overlooks a breathtaking 130-acre farm, where part of the charm is the chance to pitch in with chores. Anthea and Darrel Archer operate Canada's first water-buffalo dairy, although chef Mara Jernigan is the often-talked-about woman behind the restaurant. Breakfasts include farm-raised products. The three guest rooms are simply decorated; tall windows offer views across the gardens, fields, and forest. Some rooms have fireplaces and whirlpool tubs, and all are phone- and TV-free but have free wireless Internet access. A two-bedroom cottage with a kitchen overlooks the fields. *$$; MC, V; checks OK; closed mid-Oct–mid-Nov; www.fairburnfarm.bc.ca; 7 miles/11 km southwest of Duncan (call for directions—no signs to farm).*

Chemainus

Heralded as "the little town that did," seaside Chemainus bounced back from the closure of its logging mill and turned to tourism with flair. Buildings are painted with murals depicting the town's colorful history, an idea since borrowed by other towns, notably Toppenish, Washington (see the Southeast Washington chapter). The whole town has a theatrical feel, underlined by productions at the popular **CHEMAINUS THEATRE** (9737 Chemainus Rd; 250/246-9820 or 800/565-7738; www.chemainustheatrefestival.ca).

RESTAURANTS

The Waterford Restaurant / ★★

9875 MAPLE ST, CHEMAINUS; 250/246-1046

French cuisine gets a West Coast twist at the Waterford, a cozy nine-table bistro with a greenery-draped veranda ensconced in an old-town heritage building. Lunch prices are surprisingly low for the upscale cuisine: paupiette of sole, mushroom or seafood crepes, and seafood marinara. Dinner is slightly pricier: choices can include rack of lamb dijon, a traditional bouillabaisse, duck with blackberry port sauce, or local wild salmon. *$$; AE, MC, V; no checks; lunch, dinner Tues–Sat (lunch Wed–Sat, dinner Thurs–Sat Oct–Apr; call for hours in Jan); full bar; reservations recommended; waterfordrestaurant@ shaw.ca; a few blocks from downtown.* &

Nanaimo

Nanaimo, once the island's coal capital, is more than the strip mall it appears to be from the highway—Hwys 19 and 19A meet in Nanaimo. The **HUDSON'S BAY COMPANY BASTION** (at Bastion and Front sts; summer only), built in 1853, is one of the few forts of this type left in North America. It's part of the **NANAIMO DISTRICT MUSEUM** (100 Museum Wy; 250/753-1821; www.nanaimomuseum. ca), which also has a replica of a Chinatown street.

In Nanaimo's old town, cafés mix with shops. At **DELICADO'S** (358 Wesley St; 250/753-6524) eat wraps, or go for Mexican at **GINA'S** (47 Skinner St; 250/753-5411), a popular restaurant. In summer, hop a ferry to the **DINGHY DOCK** (No. 8 Pirates Ln; 250/753-2373 for pub or 250/753-8244 for ferry information), a nautical floating pub. Nanaimo is best known as a transportation hub, with frequent sailings to Vancouver on **BC FERRIES** (250/386-3431 or 888/223-3779; www.bcferries.com).

The island's second-largest city is also a good place to launch a scuba-diving holiday. Thrill seekers head for the **BUNGY ZONE** (15 minutes south of Nanaimo; 250/716-7874 or 800/668-7874) to experience North America's only legal bungee-jumping bridge, over the Nanaimo River. Check out the **BATHTUB RACE** on the third weekend of July.

The spit at **PIPER'S LAGOON** (northeast of downtown), extending into the Strait of Georgia, is great for bird-watching. **NEWCASTLE ISLAND PROVINCIAL MARINE PARK** is an auto-free wilderness reached by ferry from Nanaimo's inner harbor.

Golf courses with views proliferate from Nanaimo northward. Most noteworthy is the **NANAIMO GOLF CLUB** (2800 Highland Blvd; 250/758-6332; www.nanaimogolfclub.ca), an 18-hole championship course 2 miles/3 km north of the city. **PRYDE VISTA GOLF COURSE** (155 Pryde Ave; 250/753-6188), 1 mile/2 km northwest of Nanaimo, and **FAIRWINDS** (3730 Fairwinds Dr, Nanoose Bay; 250/468-7666 or 888/781-2777; www.fairwinds.ca) are alternative options. **TOURISM NANAIMO** (2290 Bowen Rd; 250/756-0106; www.tourismnanaimo. com) has information.

RESTAURANTS

The Mahle House / ★★★

2104 HEMER RD, CEDAR; 250/722-3621

Find this cozy 1904 home-turned-restaurant in Cedar, just minutes southeast of Nanaimo, and sample the inventive cuisine of chef/co-owner Maureen Loucks. Begin with "porcupine" prawns, quickly deep-fried in shredded phyllo, then taste chicken stuffed with Dungeness crab and drizzled with preserved-lemon sauce. On Wednesdays, diners can sample numerous different dishes—all surprises selected by the chef—and Thursdays are Tapas for Two night. $$$; AE, MC, V; no checks; dinner Wed–Sun; full bar; reservations recommended; www.mahlehouse.ca; 10 minutes south of Nanaimo. &

Parksville

Parksville and the surrounding area are renowned for sandy beaches, especially in lovely **RATHTREVOR BEACH PROVINCIAL PARK** (off Hwy 19A, 1 mile/2 km south of Parksville; 800/689-9025 for camping reservations;

www.env.gov.bc.ca/bcparks). Families love its lengthy shallows and relatively warm water, the camping, and August's annual sand-castle competition.

A little farther a field, picnic at thunderous **ENGLISHMAN RIVER FALLS PRO-VINCIAL PARK** (8 miles/12.8 km southwest of town; 800/689-9025 for camping reservations; www.env.gov.bc.ca/bcparks), then mosey along to shop in **COOMBS**, a tiny town on Hwy 4A that hovers near kitsch with its overblown pioneer theme. Stop for a sandwich at the popular **OLD COUNTRY MARKET** (on Hwy 4 in Coombs; 250/248-6272; www.oldcountrymarket.com; Apr–Nov), where goats graze on the roof. **MACMILLAN PROVINCIAL PARK** (on Hwy 4, 20 miles/32 km west of Parksville; www.env.gov.bc.ca/bcparks) contains Cathedral Grove, an impressive old-growth forest.

LODGINGS

Tigh-Na-Mara Resort, Spa & Conference Centre / ★★☆

1155 RESORT DR, PARKSVILLE; 250/248-2072 OR 800/663-7373
The grotto—a thermal mineral pool complete with waterfalls and cave effects—is the centerpiece of Tigh-Na-Mara's lavish three-story spa, which, combined with a wealth of supervised children's activities, makes this a great spot for parents in need of a little adult time. Log cottages, spread throughout 22 acres of wooded grounds, offer privacy, though the cottages are some-what dark. Oceanfront condominiums are newer and spiffier, with log-beam details; some have jetted tubs and kitchens. The upscale Forest Studios and Woodland Suites surround the spa facility but are farthest from the beach. The Cedar Room restaurant has Pacific Northwest fare. *$$–$$$; AE, DC, MC, V; local checks only; www.tigh-na-mara.com; 1¼ miles/2 km south of Parksville on Hwy 19A.*

Qualicum Beach

This little town 20 minutes north of Parksville on Hwy 19A has a pleasant beach-front promenade and a growing shopping district. For its size, it boasts a good selection of cafés—a favorite is funky spot **MURPHY'S COFFEE & TEA COMPANY** (177 W 2nd Ave; 250/752-6693). For more retro character, drive 10 minutes north for a burger at the **COLA DINER** (6060 W Island Hwy; 250/757-2029), a joyful ode to the classic 1950s burger joint. At **MILNER GARDENS AND WOOD-LAND** (2179 W Island Hwy; 250/752-8573), you can stroll through 10 acres of gardens and stop for tea in a 1930s seaside manor.

RESTAURANTS

Old Dutch Inn / ★

2690 W ISLAND HWY, QUALICUM BEACH; 250/752-6914
Waitresses in triple-peaked, starched lace caps serve breakfast platters with eggs Benedict or French-toast sandwiches. Have we wandered back in time? The Dutch theme is taken seriously, with turned oak chairs and Delft tiles. At

lunch you can join retirees and tourists for a *uitsmijter*, an open-faced sandwich with Dutch smoked ham and cheese, or Indonesian-inspired *loempia*, a 10-spice spring roll with pork and roasted peanuts. Expansive windows look out on Qualicum Bay. *$; AE, DC, DIS, MC, V; no checks; breakfast, lunch, dinner every day; full bar; reservations recommended; www.olddutchinn.com; on Hwy 19A.*

LODGINGS

Bahari / ★

5101 W ISLAND HWY, QUALICUM BEACH; 250/752-9278 OR 877/752-9278 The look here is 1980s West Coast with Asian touches, including a Japanese kimono hung in the two-story foyer. The two suites open onto a deck, one has a fireplace, and both have ocean views. Seven acres of lawn, gardens, and woods include a trail down to a pebbly beach; a private hot tub in the woods overlooks Georgia Strait and the northern Gulf Islands. *$$$–$$$$; AE, MC, V; no checks; closed Dec–Feb; www.baharibandb.com; 10 minutes north of town on Hwy 19A.*

Barkley Sound and Tofino

Most visitors pass through Port Alberni via Hwy 4 to Tofino or take the scenic boat trip on the **LADY ROSE** or **FRANCES BARKLEY** (250/723-8313 or 800/663-7192) from Port Alberni to Bamfield, Ucluelet, or the Broken Group Islands. Boats offer passenger day trips as well as freight service.

Port Alberni

Shops, galleries, and restaurants cluster at the Harbour Quay, where boats to Barkley Sound dock in this industrial logging and fishing town. A favored nosh stop is the **CLAM BUCKET** (4479 Victoria Quay; 250/723-1315).

Bamfield

This tiny fishing village of 200, home to a marine biology research station and known for the big salmon pulled from nearby waters, is reached by boat (see chapter introduction) or via logging roads from Port Alberni or Lake Cowichan. In Bamfield, the road extends only to the east side of the village. The west side, across Bamfield Inlet, has no vehicle access; **WATER TAXIS** ($30 per trip) link the two. Bamfield bustles when the West Coast Trail summer season hits—it's the end of the line for the world-famous, five- to seven-day, mettle-testing wilderness trail that's so popular, hikers have to make reservations. For information contact **HELLO BC** (250/387-1642 or 800/435-5622; www.hellobc.com). The **BAMFIELD CHAMBER OF COMMERCE** (250/728-3006; www.bamfieldchamber.com) also has information. **WOOD'S END LANDING** (380 Lombard St, Bamfield; 250/728-3383 or 877/828-3383; www.woodsend.travel.bc.ca) offers comfortable and unique accommodations.

Ucluelet

"Ukie" is still a little rough around the edges, as the economic staples of fishing and logging began to wane only a decade ago, but for many visitors, that's part of its charm. The town, with several fine B and Bs and lodges, aspires to tourism success like its sister town Tofino has enjoyed. A highlight is the **WILD PACIFIC TRAIL**, a two-part, 4-mile/6.5-km path through the old growth and within sight of the pounding surf. It's the jump-off point for Barkley Sound kayak adventures.

Budget B and B accommodations line the road into town, offering easy access to **PACIFIC RIM NATIONAL PARK RESERVE** (250/726-7721); stop by the visitor centre (at turnoff to Tofino on Hwy 4). The Broken Group Islands, accessible only by boat, attract intrepid kayakers and scuba divers. Visitors to Ucluelet have come to enjoy the expanse of awe-inspiring Long Beach. The park's lone campground, **GREEN POINT** (at park's midway point, well marked by signs; 800/689-9025; www.pc.gc.ca), is often full during peak times and is closed in winter.

Six miles/10 km north of Ucluelet, the **WICKANINNISH INTERPRETIVE CENTRE** (1 Wickaninnish Rd; 250/726-4701) has oceanic exhibits and an expansive view, shared by the on-site Wickaninnish Restaurant—not to be confused with the **WICKANINNISH INN** (see review in Tofino section).

During March and April, 20,000 gray whales migrating along the West Coast on their way to the Bering Sea can often be seen from shore; orcas and humpbacks cruise the waters much of the year. For close-up views, whale-watching tours leave from both Ucluelet and Tofino; tours are easy to arrange once you arrive. The **PACIFIC RIM WHALE FESTIVAL** (www.pacificrimwhalefestival.org; mid-Mar–early Apr) hosts events here and in Tofino.

RESTAURANTS

The Boat Basin / ★★

1971 HARBOUR DR (TAUCA LEA RESORT AND SPA), UCLUELET; 250/726-4625 OR 800/979-9303

The fresh wild seafood and great harbor views at Tauca Lea Resort's (see Lodgings) Boat Basin restaurant have significantly heightened dining in Ucluelet. The setting is airy and uncluttered; features include striking First Nations art and a deck overlooking the local fishing fleet. Start with steamed Salt Spring Island mussels, rice congee, and Thai-style chicken dumplings, or green coconut curry soup with prawns. Your main course could be *gnocchetti* with braised lamb, rare seared Pacific albacore tuna, or whatever is fresh at the docks that day. Their participation in the Ocean Wise program means the Vancouver Aquarium recommends them as an ocean-friendly seafood choice. $$$; AE, DC, MC, V; no checks; dinner every day; full bar;

reservations recommended; www.taucalearesort.com; from Hwy 4, turn left onto Seaplane Base Rd.

Matterson House / ★★

1682 PENINSULA RD, UCLUELET; 250/726-2200
Tofino residents happily make the half-hour drive to Ucluelet for the generous helpings and reasonable prices at casual Matterson House. Breakfast standards such as eggs Benedict and huevos rancheros make way for lunch's Matterson Monster Burger, fully loaded with bacon, cheese, mushrooms, and more. Look for caesar salads, chicken burgers, and homemade bread—and nothing deep-fried. Dinner sees hungry hikers and residents dig into prime rib, salmon phyllo, or veggie lasagne. *$$; MC, V; local checks only; breakfast, lunch, dinner every day; full bar; reservations recommended; on Hwy 4 on way into town.*

LODGINGS

Eagle Nook Ocean Wilderness Resort / ★★★

VERNON BAY, BARKLEY SOUND; 250/723-1000 OR 800/760-2777
This wilderness lodge, reached only by boat or floatplane, caters to the outdoors lover. Visitors enjoy hiking the trails lacing the resort's forested 70 acres/28 hectares or joining cruises to see harbor seals, bald eagles, and possibly whales. Back at the resort, guests feast on beautifully prepared West Coast or continental meals from window seats before a fire. All 23 rooms have ocean views; two one-bedroom cabins have water views and sitting areas, fireplaces, and kitchenettes. The resort's ocean-side deck features a hot tub and cedar-hut sauna. *$$$$; AE, MC, V; no checks; closed Oct–May; www.eaglenook.com; if driving to Vancouver Island, arrange to meet resort's water taxi in Ucluelet.*

A Snug Harbour Inn / ★★

460 MARINE DR, UCLUELET; 250/726-2686 OR 888/936-5222
The million-dollar view here encompasses the rugged coast and islands where harbor seals, whales, and eagles play. All six guest rooms have private balconies and stunning views from the 85-foot cliff. Honeymooners prefer the tiered Atlantis Room, which has a spectacular view, and the Sawadee Room, with its fireplace and jetted tub. Others favor the split-level Lighthouse Room, with round brass ships' portholes and picture windows. *$$$–$$$$; MC, V; no checks; www.awesomeview.com; through village and right on Marine Dr.*

Tauca Lea Resort & Spa / ★★★

1971 HARBOUR DR, UCLUELET; 250/726-4625 OR 800/979-9303
Set on its own little peninsula on the edge of Ucluelet, Tauca Lea's one- and two-bedroom apartment-sized suites have kitchens and water views. The spacious, light-filled suites are decorated with leather armchairs and handcrafted furniture; a few higher-end units have hot tubs. The resort's Boat Basin

restaurant (see review) is one of the best places to eat in the area. *$$$–$$$$;*
*AE, DC, MC, V; no checks; www.taucalearesort.com; from Hwy 4, turn left
onto Seaplane Base Rd.*

Tofino

At the end of Hwy 4 is the island's wild west coast, drawing surfers, kayakers,
storm watchers, and nature lovers from all over the world. Although it was once
an area visited almost exclusively in summer, now winter storms draw hordes of
visitors to watch the Pacific thrash the coast. A large number of international visi-
tors have resulted in a greater number of excellent hotels, B and Bs, and restau-
rants than one would expect from a town of fewer than 2,000 residents.

People arrive at Tofino primarily by car, via the winding mountainous route
of Hwy 4 (five hours from Victoria). **KENMORE AIR** (www.kenmoreair.com) flies
from Seattle and **HARBOUR AIR** (www.harbour-air.com) from Vancouver—but
you'll want a car here; try **BUDGET** (250/725-2060) for rentals.

You can explore the coast with one of numerous water-taxi or whale-watching
companies, by floatplane, or by kayak. **TOFINO SEA KAYAKING COMPANY** (320
Main; 250/725-4222 or 800/863-4664; www.tofino-kayaking.com) offers kayak
rentals or guided tours with experienced boaters and naturalists. **REMOTE PAS-
SAGES** (71 Wharf St; 250/725-3330 or 800/666-9833; www.remotepassages.com)
offers guided tours by kayak, Zodiac, or covered whale-watching boat. The
PACIFIC RIM WHALE FESTIVAL (www.pacificrimwhalefestival.org; mid-Mar–early
Apr) hosts events here and in Ucluelet. Retired Coast Guardsman Mike White of
BROWNING PASS CHARTERS (250/725-3435; www.browningpass.com) offers
thoughtful, low-impact wildlife-watching tours in Clayoquot Sound.

A number of boat and floatplane companies, including **TOFINO AIR** (50 1st St;
250/725-4454 or 866/486-3247; www.tofinoair.ca), offer day trips to the calming
pools of **HOT SPRINGS COVE**; you can overnight at the six-room **HOT SPRINGS
COVE LODGE** (250/670-1106 or 866/670-1106; www.hotspringcove.com). The
12-acre **TOFINO BOTANICAL GARDENS** (1084 Pacific Rim Hwy; 250/725-1220;
www.tbgf.org) features indigenous plant life in a scenic waterfront setting.

Gift shops and galleries are sprinkled throughout town. The longhouse of the
EAGLE AERIE GALLERY (350 Campbell St; 250/725-3235 or 800/663-0669) sells
art by **COAST TSIMSHIAN** artist **ROY HENRY VICKERS** (www.royhenryvickers.
com). **HOUSE OF HIMWITSA** (300 Main St; 250/725-2017 or 800/899-1947;
www.himwitsa.com) features First Nations masks, jewelry, and gifts.

Get organic coffee, baked treats, and counterculture news at the **COMMON
LOAF BAKE SHOP** (180 1st St; 250/725-3915), fresh sushi at the **INN AT TOUGH
CITY** (350 Main St; 250/725-2021 or 877/725-2021; www.toughcity.com), or
highly rated organic global takeout from **SOBO** (311 Neill St; 250/725-2341;
www.sobo.ca), a café in the Conradi Building. **CAFFE VINCENTE** (441 Campbell
St; 250/725-2599) offers great coffee and sensational baked goods. The **TOFINO
VISITORS INFO CENTRE** (1426 Pacific Rim Hwy; 250/725-3414) is on Hwy 4,
just south of town.

RESTAURANTS

The Pointe Restaurant / ★★☆

500 OSPREY LN (WICKANINNISH INN), TOFINO;
250/725-3100 OR 800/333-4604
"The Wick's" restaurant is perched over a rocky headland; waves crash just outside the windows that have 240-degree panoramic views, adding drama to your meal. The distinctively Northwest menu focuses on seafood ranging from oysters to seaweed and other artfully presented ingredients. An à la carte menu features Tofino Dungeness crab, smoked Wenzel duck breast, and a potlatch of local seafood, but many diners opt for one of the multicourse tasting menus. *$$$$; AE, DC, MC, V; no checks; breakfast, lunch, dinner every day; full bar; reservations required (dinner); www.wickinn.com; off Hwy 4, 3 miles/5 km south of town.* &

RainCoast Café / ★★☆

120 4TH ST, TOFINO; 250/725-2215
Husband-and-wife team Lisa Henderson and Larry Nicolay operate one of the best restaurants in Tofino. The decor of their intimate room (with an outdoor patio) is sleek and modern—as is the menu, which focuses on seafood, often with an Asian twist. Starters range from Thai hot and sour seafood soup, *edamame*, and a south Asian bread basket to fresh local oysters, clams, and mussels. Popular main dishes include halibut with sake, mango, and lime sauce, or phad thai with all the usual fixings. Dessert is a bit less cosmopolitan: chocolate-peanut butter pie. *$$$; AE, MC, V; local checks only; dinner every day; beer and wine; reservations recommended; www.raincoastcafe.com; near 4th St dock.* &

LODGINGS

Clayoquot Wilderness Resorts / ★★★

BEDWELL RIVER, TOFINO; 250/726-8235 OR 888/333-5405
This luxury resort's past main lodge, now a private residence that floats on a barge on the edge of Clayoquot Sound, helped inaugurate the wilderness lodge industry in British Columbia; it's now known for its safari-style tent camp at the inn's Wilderness Outpost on the banks of the Bedwell River. The outpost is accessible by floatplane from Vancouver, arranged by the resort. Accommodations at the wildly popular Wilderness Outpost put a whole new spin on camping: guests sleep in roomy cabin tents outfitted with Oriental rugs, propane heaters, handmade furniture, and private decks; they dine on seafood and wine on china and crystal. Relax in the sauna or in one of the wood-fired hot tubs. Three-night minimum. *$$$$; AE, MC, V; no checks; closed Oct–Apr; www.wildretreat.com.*

InnChanter / ★★★

HOTSPRINGS COVE, TOFINO; 250/670-1149

This unique, luxuriously refitted 1920s boat is moored in Hotsprings Cove near the hot springs, one of the most popular (and overcrowded) attractions on Vancouver Island. The InnChanter is accessible only by floatplane, whale-watching tour, or water taxi from Tofino. The elegant floating B and B features five staterooms, a salon with a wood-burning fireplace, and a sundeck. Host Shaun Shelongosky is a brilliant and quirky conversationalist, as well as an excellent chef who attends to all meals (included in the room rate). He specializes in vegetarian fare but uses a lot of fresh seafood as well—look for a salmon barbecue or halibut in Thai green coconut curry. *$$$; no credit cards; checks OK; www.innchanter.com; call for directions.*

Wickaninnish Inn / ★★★★

500 OSPREY LN, TOFINO; 250/725-3100 OR 800/333-4604

My, what Charles McDiarmid started when he built his lavish, upscale inn in little Tofino and announced he would promote winter travel to watch storms crash ashore. Skeptics scoffed—but now the Wick, as it's known, reaches its highest occupancy in January. Set dramatically on the edge of its rocky headland, the inn includes architectural details by master carver Henry Nolla. The 75 guest rooms and suites feature ocean views, private balconies, and double soaker tubs. Ancient Cedars Spa offers much pampering. *$$$$; AE, DC, MC, V; no checks; www.wickinn.com; off Hwy 4, 3 miles/5 km south of Tofino.* &

The Comox Valley

The Comox Valley, on the island's middle east coast, has skiing in winter, water sports in summer, and scenic access to Powell River on the mainland Sunshine Coast via **BC FERRIES** (250/386-3431 or 888/223-3779 in BC; www.bcferries. com). Skiers and, in summer, hikers and mountain bikers flock to **MOUNT WASHINGTON ALPINE RESORT** (13 miles/20 km west of Courtenay; 250/338-1386 or 888/231-1499; www.mountwashington.ca), where five chair lifts whisk alpine skiers and 'boarders to the top, and cross-country skiers enjoy 33 miles/ 55 km of track leading into **STRATHCONA PROVINCIAL PARK**. The **CROWN ISLE RESORT & GOLF COMMUNITY** (399 Clubhouse Dr, Courtenay; 250/703-5050 or 888/338-8439; www.crownisle.com) boasts the longest course on the island, an elaborate clubhouse, and chic condos.

Fanny Bay

Blink, and you'll miss this tiny hamlet. For a true roadhouse experience, stop at the **FANNY BAY INN** (7480 Island Hwy, Fanny Bay; 250/335-2323)—or the FBI, as it is more familiarly known. The mostly standard pub-fare menu features Fanny Bay oysters, panfried or in burgers. A couple miles north, the tiny **HARBOUR VIEW**

BISTRO (5575 S Island Hwy, Union Bay; 250/335-3277) has a loyal following; diners book months ahead for weekend dinners of duck à l'orange or poached wild salmon. The romantic **SHIPS POINT INN** (7584 Ships Pt Rd, Fanny Bay; 250/335-1004 or 877/742-1004; www.shipspointinn.com), located at the end of a quiet country road, offers four-course breakfasts served in the kitchen or on the wide deck with views.

Courtenay and Comox

These adjacent towns are the hub of the valley. Courtenay's in-town browsing ranges from antiques, kitchenware, and retro clothing shops to the thought-of-everything **TRAVELLER'S TALE SHOP** (526 Cliffe Ave, Courtenay; 250/703-0168; www.travellers-tale.com). Break for a delectable treat at **HOT CHOCOLATES** (368 5th St, Courtenay; 250/897-1297 or 866/468-2462; www.hotchocolates. ca). Locals recommend the eclectic eats at **ATLAS CAFÉ** (250 6th St, Courtenay; 250/338-9838). Dinosaur fossils found in the Comox Valley are on display at the **COURTENAY** and **DISTRICT MUSEUM AND PALAEONTOLOGY CENTRE** (207 4th St, Courtenay; 250/334-0686; www.courtenaymuseum.ca). The ferry to Denman Island leaves from **BUCKLEY BAY**, about 10 minutes south of Courtenay.

RESTAURANTS

Kingfisher Dining Room / ★★★

4330 S ISLAND HWY, COURTENAY; 250/338-1323 OR 800/663-7929
Executive chef Troy Fogarty takes an imaginative approach to West Coast seafood dishes at this nautical-decor restaurant in its namesake resort (see review). It's hard to find something truly unique on a Vancouver Island menu these days, but raw Fanny Bay oysters with cilantro-carrot sorbet as a garnish will do, as will porcini mushroom raviolis with tomato-chipotle coulis. The once-a-month Grand Seafood Buffet offers more than 50 (yes, 50) items, ranging from salmon-shrimp terrine to pumpkin cheesecake. *$$$; AE, DC, DIS, JCB, MC, V; no checks; breakfast, lunch, dinner ever day, brunch Sun; full bar; reservations recommended; www.kingfisherspa.com; 5 miles/8 km south of Courtenay off Hwy 19A.*

LODGINGS

Kingfisher Oceanside Resort and Spa / ★★★

4330 S ISLAND HWY, COURTENAY; 250/338-1323 OR 800/663-7929
Though Kingfisher's modern identity has been wrested from its previous incarnation as a seaside motel, the resort has been splendidly expanded, updated, and upgraded. The two dozen beachfront suites are the nicest accommodations. Ocean-view rooms, set back from the sea, are blander but a good value. The spa's centerpiece is the Pacific Mist Hydropath, where you spend an hour traveling through a grotto equipped with mineral pools and waterfall-like showers. A sauna, a steam room, a hot tub, tennis courts, and

an outdoor swimming pool with a mini-waterfall add to the ethos. *$$$–$$$$; AE, DC, DIS, JCB, MC, V; no checks; www.kingfisherspa.com; 5 miles/8 km south of Courtenay off Hwy 19A.*

Denman and Hornby Islands

Tranquil and pastoral, the sister islands of Denman and Hornby sit just off the east coast of central Vancouver Island. The larger, Denman—10 minutes by ferry from **BUCKLEY BAY** (12 miles/20 km south of Courtenay)—is known for farmlands and artisans. Most visitors skip right through to Hornby Island, but the beach at **FILLONGLEY PROVINCIAL PARK** (2 miles/3.2 km east of ferry landing; 800/689-9025; www.env.gov.bc.ca/bcparks) is great; the island's flat landscape makes it a natural for cyclists. Stop at the **DENMAN BAKERY AND PIZZERIA** (3646 Denman Rd, Denman Island; 250/335-1310; Mon–Sat). On weekends, the **BISTRO** (at Denman Island Guesthouse, 3806 Denman Rd; 250/335-2688) serves organic meals; rooms in the farmhouse are available every day. Home-cooked meals are served every day at the **DENMAN CAFÉ** (in General Store, Northwest Rd and Denman Rd, Denman Island; 250/335-2999).

Ten minutes from Denman by ferry, Hornby is a dream for mountain bikers. The center of life on Hornby is at the island-owned **HORNBY CO-OP** (Central and Shields rds, Hornby Island; 250/335-1121). Grab lunch at **JAN'S CAFÉ** (5875 Central Rd, Hornby Island; 250/335-1487). Hornby's **HELLIWELL PROVINCIAL PARK** (southeast corner of Hornby Island; 800/689-9025; www.env.gov.bc.ca/bcparks) has seaside cliffs, while beach lovers go to **TRIBUNE BAY PROVINCIAL PARK** (Tribune Bay Rd, Hornby Island; 800/689-9025; www.env.gov.bc.ca/bcparks).

LODGINGS

Outer Island R&R / ★★

4785 DEPAPE RD, HORNBY ISLAND; 250/335-2379
Karen Young's delightful farm (she calls her place an agri-villa) embraces 14 acres/5.6 hectares of pasture and orchard, with sheep, chickens, horses, and Dove, the miniature donkey, to greet kids. Not all is rustic—there's a pool for summer use. Stay in a lovely two-bedroom old farmhouse with eclectic country furnishings and kitchenette looking out on the orchard, or in a larger, equally eclectic, wood-trimmed rambler whose four bedrooms function as B and B rooms in summer. *$$$; MC, V; checks OK; www.outerisland.bc.ca; near Sandpiper Beach.*

Campbell River and North Vancouver Island

The north end of Vancouver Island has logging towns abutting wilderness, plus a unique attraction: snorkeling Campbell River to watch spawning salmon.

Campbell River the town, home base of famed writer Roderick Haig-Brown and once known almost solely as a fishing mecca, has developed a new identity as a retirement center and recreation hub.

Seattle's **KENMORE AIR** (800/435-9524; www.kenmoreair.com) flies directly to the area's fishing lodges. From Vancouver, **AIR CANADA** (888/247-2262; www. aircanada.ca) and **PACIFIC COASTAL AIR** (800/663-2872; www.pacificcoastal. com) serve Campbell River's airport.

The **MUSEUM AT CAMPBELL RIVER** (470 Island Hwy; 250/287-3103; www. crmuseum.ca) is one of the island's best. The **CAMPBELL RIVER MARITIME HERI-TAGE CENTRE** (621 Island Hwy; 250/286-3161; www.bcp45.org) is home to BCP45, the iconic fishing boat on the old Canadian five-dollar bill. For more art, the **WEI WAI KUM HOUSE OF TREASURES** (1370 Island Hwy; 250/286-1440) is set in a beautiful longhouse, incongruously tucked behind a shopping mall. Locals like the fresh pastas at **FUSILLI GRILL** (220 Dogwood S; 250/830-0090; www. fusilligrill.bc.ca).

STRATHCONA PROVINCIAL PARK (about 25 miles/40 km west of town on Hwy 28; 800/689-9025; www.env.gov.bc.ca/bcparks) is a place of superlatives. It contains Canada's highest waterfall as well as Vancouver Island's tallest mountain, 7,200-foot/2,195-m **GOLDEN HINDE**.

During August's **SALMON FESTIVAL**, this mall-rich town of 30,000 is abuzz with fisherfolk. The **VISITOR INFO CENTRE** (1235 Shoppers Row, Campbell River; 250/830-0411 ext 1 or 877/286-5705; www.visitorinfo.incampbellriver. com) has information.

RESTAURANTS

Koto Japanese Restaurant / ★★

80 10TH AVE, CAMPBELL RIVER; 250/286-1422

It makes sense: a very fresh sushi bar in the middle of fishing country. Chef Takeo (Tony) Maeda has single-handedly developed the locals' taste for nigiri-sushi. Teriyaki is a big seller too—beef, chicken, or salmon—but look for more-exotic food from the deep, such as freshwater eel, flying-fish roe, and local octopus. *$$; AE, DC, MC, V; no checks; lunch Tues–Fri, dinner Tues–Sat; full bar; reservations recommended; behind HSBC Bank bldg.*

LODGINGS

Painter's Lodge / ★★

1625 MCDONALD RD, CAMPBELL RIVER; 250/286-1102 OR 800/663-7090

Fishing is the raison d'être of this lodge run by the Oak Bay Marine Group of Victoria, but whale- and bear-watching tours, a pool, a hot tub, and tennis appeal to nonanglers, and the waterfront location is a plus. Strive to catch the big one here, and maybe your photo will join the row in the plush lobby. Fare in the Legends dining room is focused on local seafood, and the casual Tyee Pub is great for quaffing a brew while overlooking Discovery Passage. A free 10-minute water taxi runs to April Point Resort & Spa, Painter's sister resort on Quadra Island (see review in Discovery Islands section). *$$$–$$$$;*

AE, DC, MC, V; *no checks; closed late Oct–Mar;* www.painterslodge.com; *2½ miles/4 km north of Campbell River.*

Strathcona Park Lodge and Outdoor Education Centre / ★★

**EDGE OF STRATHCONA PROVINCIAL PARK,
CAMPBELL RIVER; 250/286-3122**

Strathcona Provincial Park, one of the oldest in Canada, is a wilderness recreation paradise, and its namesake lakeside lodge is for those who enjoy active living. The instructors gently guide even the most timid city slickers through outdoor pursuits. The ropes course isn't as scary as it looks. The 50 varied units in the lodge and lakefront cabins are modest but attractive; some of the newer suites are quite chic, and there are jaw-dropping views everywhere. *$$; MC, V; local checks only; limited facilities Dec–Feb;* www.strathcona.bc.ca; *28 miles/45 km west of Campbell River on Hwy 28.*

Discovery Islands

The closely linked Discovery Islands—fishing and boating meccas east of Campbell River—include **QUADRA, CORTES,** and **SONORA.** To visit the most accessible—Quadra and Cortes—take the 10-minute ferry ride from Campbell River to Quadra's Quathiaski Cove dock; from **HERIOT BAY** on Quadra, another 45-minute ferry takes you to Cortes. Other islands in the chain are accessible only by private boat, water taxi from Campbell River, or floatplane.

LODGINGS

April Point Resort & Spa / ★★

900 APRIL PT RD, QUATHIASKI COVE; 250/285-2222 OR 800/663-7090

This island getaway, centered around a cedar lodge built on pilings over the water, draws serious fisherfolk from all over the world. April Point also offers activities such as bicycle, scooter, and kayak rentals; helicopter tours; and whale- and bear-watching trips. The 49 spacious units range from large houses to lodge rooms and comfortable cabins; some have jetted tubs, living rooms, and kitchens, and all have sundecks with water views. At the restaurant in the main lodge, seafood (including sushi) is the focus; wraparound windows and a sunny deck offer dramatic water views. Take advantage of the on-site Aveda Spa, located within the blissful gardens. *$$$; AE, DC, MC, V; no checks;* www.aprilpoint.com; *10 minutes north of ferry dock, or accessible by free water taxi from Painter's Lodge in Campbell River.*

Hollyhock / ★★⯪

**MANSON'S LANDING, CORTES ISLAND;
250/935-6576 OR 800/933-6339**

Hollyhock is one of those institutions better known internationally than locally. Set into the woods at the southeast end of Cortes Island, this holistic healing–renaissance center draws guests for retreats that focus on alternative or natural health and human potential. Stay in comfortable accommodations that range from bunk beds to cozy cabins; all meals (vegetarian plus seafood) are included, and yoga, forest and beach walks, library reading, and hot tub soaking occupy the time. *$–$$; MC, V; no checks; www.hollyhock.ca; on Highfield Rd 11 miles/18 km from ferry dock.*

T'ai Li Lodge / ★★★

BOX 16, CORTES BAY; 800/939-6644 OR 250/935-6711
Bound on three sides by the ocean, Desolation Sound, and coastal mountains and surrounded by forest on a rocky peninsula that forms a secure deep-water anchorage, this gorgeous lodge feels like a wilderness retreat. T'ai Li has evolved over the years from a "water-access only" coastal camp to a comfortable, serene retreat, with yoga and kayaking opportunities available. The entire 1,600-square-foot/148.6 sq-m fully equipped home can be rented and includes a private tent-cabin with comfy king-size bed (which can be arranged as two singles) right on the ocean and overlooking the sound, and a small camping area. There's no paved or groomed forest footpaths; guests bring flashlights to navigate at night. As owner Steve Landon says, "You'll see constellations of stars that you probably have forgotten exist." *$$$–$$$$; MC, V; no checks; www. www.taililodge.com; on Cortes Bay, 12 miles/20 km from ferry dock.*

Tsa-Kwa-Luten Lodge and RV Park / ★★

1 LIGHTHOUSE RD, QUADRA ISLAND; 250/285-2042 OR 800/665-7745
Built on a 1,100-acre/445 hectare forest preserve by the Laichwiltach First Nation, this handsome ocean-view lodge was inspired by traditional long-house design. Native art is featured throughout. Stroll beaches to ponder ancient Native petroglyphs, visit the outstanding Kwagiulth Museum (45-minute walk; 250/285-3733), walk to nearby Cape Mudge Lighthouse, or opt for a massage. The lodge hosts First Nations cultural demonstrations and salmon barbecues monthly in summer. Stay in the main lodge's 30 varied rooms or five quiet waterfront cabins. In the Hamaelas dining room, seafood—sometimes including your own catch—and such First Nations–inspired dishes as cedar-baked salmon, breaded oysters, and steamed clam are the stars. *$$$; AE, DC, JCB, MC, V; no checks; closed mid-Oct–Apr; www. capemudgeresort.bc.ca; 15 minutes south of ferry dock.*

Port McNeill and Telegraph Cove

The major asset of the remote area near Vancouver Island's northeast end is its proximity to all things wild. The inspiring **U'MISTA CULTURAL CENTRE** (Front St, Alert Bay; 250/974-5403; www.umista.org) nearby is only a short ferry ride from the Port McNeill waterfront; learn about potlatch traditions of the local Kwakwaka'wakw people.

Whale-watching (June–Oct) is superior from Telegraph Cove, a village on stilts 13 miles/21 km south of Port McNeill. **STUBBS ISLAND WHALE WATCHING** (Telegraph Cove; 250/928-3185 or 800/665-3066; www.stubbs-island.com) offers cruises to view orcas. Old homes in Telegraph Cove have been revived as lodgings at **TELEGRAPH COVE RESORT** (in Telegraph Cove; 250/928-3131 or 800/200-4665; www.telegraphcoveresort.com).

LODGINGS

Hidden Cove Lodge / ★★

HIDDEN COVE; 250/956-3916
Sandra and Dan Kirby's waterfront retreat on 8½ acres/3.4 hectares is interspersed with walking trails and offers back-to-basics relaxation 20 minutes south of Port McNeill. Eight guest rooms with private baths are furnished in pine, and rates include home-cooked breakfasts such as eggs Benedict or pancakes. In summer (mid-May–mid-Oct), dinners of Dungeness crab, baby back spareribs, salmon, halibut, or other hearty favorites are served. The two two-bedroom waterfront cottages with fireplaces and full kitchens allow families to cook on their own. *$$–$$$$; MC, V; no checks; www.hiddencovelodge. com; take Beaver Cove–Telegraph Cove cutoff from Hwy 19.*

Port Hardy

A harbor-front promenade leavens your stay in this gritty town at the end of Hwy 19 near Vancouver Island's far northeastern tip. Logging, fishing, and mining have provided most of the employment, though they're fading. Travelers stop to catch the acclaimed 15-hour **BC FERRIES** (250/386-3431 or 888/223-3779; www. bcferries.bc.ca; reservations required) cruise north to Prince Rupert on the mainland or to Bella Coola and Bella Bella on the midcoast. Book summer well in advance: ferry passengers fill the hotels.

The famous Edward S. Curtis silent film *In the Land of the War Canoes* was filmed in nearby **FORT RUPERT** (off Hwy 19, 3 miles/5 km south of Port Hardy). The **COPPER MAKER GALLERY** (114 Copper Wy, Fort Rupert Village; 250/949-8491) is nice.

Remote **CAPE SCOTT PROVINCIAL PARK** (37 miles/63 km west of Port Hardy; www.env.gov.bc.ca/bcparks) is among the most beautiful places on earth. A 1½-hour drive over gravel roads west of Port Hardy and a 45-minute walk take you to its spectacular San Josef Bay; camping is permitted. A more challenging hike leads to the island's northern tip; the Port Hardy **VISITOR INFO CENTRE** (7250 Market St, Port Hardy; 250/949-7622; www.ph-chamber.bc.ca) has information.

SOUTHERN INTERIOR
AND THE KOOTENAYS

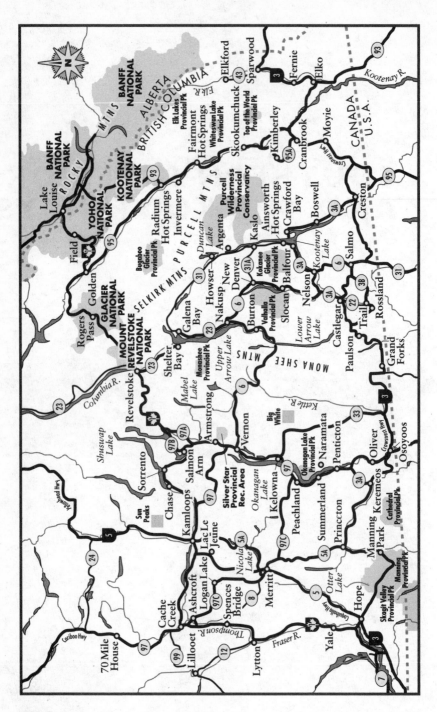

SOUTHERN INTERIOR AND THE KOOTENAYS

British Columbia's southern interior, a vast territory that extends east and north past Hope in the Lower Mainland, is one of the most diverse, scenic, and sometimes challenging landscapes on earth. Innumerable mountain ranges crowd up beside each other: the Cascades, the Monashees, the Selkirks, the Purcells, the Bugaboos, and the mighty Rockies. The West Kootenay lies in the central stretches of British Columbia's southern interior; to envision this area, imagine four mountain ranges furrowed together like an accordion.

The Interior Plateau—immediately to the east of the coastal mountain chain—has a much drier and more continental climate than in western BC, where the mountains act as a barrier to the moist westerly air flow. This means summers in the southern interior, including the Okanagan, Similkameen, and Thompson River valleys, are primarily warm and dry; winters are cooler but less moist. In fact, this is where you'll experience BC's hottest summers, with temperatures often ranging from 86°F to 102°F (30s Celsius), occasionally rising above 104°F (40°C). The region is a Mecca for adventure seekers and the gateway to remote mountain lodges. For an idea of distance from Vancouver, Kootenay Pass is about eight hours east of Vancouver, a good day's drive. Just over the mountains is the province of Alberta.

ACCESS AND INFORMATION

Almost every main road or highway in southern British Columbia intersects the **TRANS-CANADA HIGHWAY** (Highway 1) at some point. In this region, Hwy 1 covers 372 miles/600 km between Hope and Field on the BC-Alberta border. Other major highways here include **HIGHWAY 5** (the Yellowhead Highway), whose 130-mile/210-km Coquihalla Highway portion (drivers must pay a $10 toll) provides beautiful landscapes and the most direct route between Hope and Kamloops, 45 miles/73 km shorter than Hwy 1 between those two points; **HIGHWAY 97C**, linking Hwy 1 at Cache Creek to Kelowna in the Okanagan; **HIGHWAY 97** through the Okanagan between Penticton and Kamloops; and **HIGHWAY 3** (the Crowsnest Highway), which parallels the U.S. border for 491 miles/792 km between Hope and the BC-Alberta border east of Fernie.

KAMLOOPS AIRPORT (250/376-3613; www.kamloopsairport.com) is served by **AIR CANADA JAZZ** (888/247-2262; www.flyjazz.ca), **HORIZON AIR** (800/547-9308; www.horizonair.com), and **VIA RAIL** (888/842-7245; www.viarail.ca). **KELOWNA AIRPORT** (250/765-5125; www.kelownaairport.com) is served by Air Canada Jazz, Horizon, and **WESTJET** (800/538-5696; www.westjet.com). **PENTICTON AIRPORT** (250/770-4414; www.cyyf.org) is served by Air Canada Jazz. **CRANBROOK** and **CASTLEGAR** are served by Air Canada Jazz; the latter two airports are notorious for cranky winter weather, with flights frequently canceled by fog. **GREYHOUND CANADA**

SOUTHERN INTERIOR THREE-DAY TOUR

DAY ONE: Rise early for a walk along Kelowna's lakefront promenade, stopping to enjoy breakfast alfresco at the **GRAND OKANAGAN LAKEFRONT RESORT**. Drive over a unique floating bridge to **MISSION HILL FAMILY ESTATE** for a winery tour. Continue south along Lake Okanagan to **OSOYOOS**, stopping at the many roadside stalls to provision for a picnic with your favorite variety of fruits and freshly squeezed juices. Walk off lunch along the interpretive boardwalk at the **DESERT CENTRE**, protecting Canada's only true desert, and visit **NK'MIP DESERT AND HERITAGE CENTRE**. Enjoy an early dinner at **CAMPOMARINA ITALIAN RESTAURANT**, then make the three-hour drive through the wilderness of the Monashee Mountains to Rossland. Check in to your room at the **RAM'S HEAD INN**. For dinner, head to the **SONORA ROOM AT BURROWING OWL** in Oliver. Spend the evening curled up in front of a log fire with a good book.

DAY TWO: After breakfast at the Ram's Head, drive to Nelson for a self-guided walking tour of the historic downtown precinct. Grab lunch at the **RICE BOWL RESTAURANT** (301 Baker St, Nelson; 250/354-4129). Afterward, drive north on Hwys 3A and 31 to **AINSWORTH HOT SPRINGS**. Trade your clothes for a bathing suit and relax in the resort's public soaking pools. Drive the short distance

---

(800/231-2222; www.greyhound.ca) offers daily service along the Trans-Canada Highway, through the Okanagan and the Kootenays.

The Thompson Plateau

As the Trans-Canada Highway (Hwy 1) and the Coquihalla Highway (Hwy 5) climb and wind their separate ways north from Hope (see Lower Mainland British Columbia chapter) before crossing paths again in Kamloops, they pass through a variety of climates, from the arid canyons carved by the Fraser, Nicola, and Thompson rivers to the gently rolling highlands of the Thompson Plateau.

Merritt

The waters around Merritt (population 7,000) are famous for producing rainbow trout. Fly-casting is the fishing style of choice. Close to 50 percent of British Columbia's total **FRESHWATER SPORT FISHING** occurs in the Thompson-Nicola region: the Thompson and Nicola rivers are historic salmon-spawning tributaries of the Fraser River, and the smaller feeder streams are also where rainbow trout, Dolly Varden char, and kokanee (freshwater salmon) spawn. The Baillie House

along Kootenay Lake to **KASLO**. Find a table on the patio at the **ROSEWOOD CAFÉ** for an early dinner, and revel in your newfound sense of well-being. Enjoy the scenic evening drive on Hwy 31A between Kaslo and New Denver and Nakusp, and let your eyes do the work as you sightsee along Slocan and Upper Arrow lakes. Catch the ferry across Upper Arrow Lake from Galena Bay to Shelter Bay. It's only a short drive from Shelter Bay to **MULVEHILL CREEK WILDERNESS INN** south of Revelstoke.

DAY THREE: After a leisurely breakfast, head for the inn's beach on Upper Arrow Lake. When you're ready, drive into **REVELSTOKE** and stop at the 112 for a weekday lunch. Point your car's nose up the **MEADOWS IN THE SKY PARKWAY** in nearby **MOUNT REVELSTOKE NATIONAL PARK**. Have plenty of film ready to record the profusion of wildflowers. Look east toward Rogers Pass and the massive Illecillewaet Glacier. That's where you're headed once you return to the Trans-Canada Highway (Hwy 1). Pull over at the top of the pass for a visit to the uniquely shaped information center. Primed by your crash course in a century of mountaineering tradition in **GLACIER NATIONAL PARK** (West Glacier, Montana; 406/888-7800; www.nps.gov/glac), enjoy the descent past the peaks to **GOLDEN**. Drive on to **EMERALD LAKE LODGE** in **YOHO NATIONAL PARK** for dinner and the night.

operates **MERRITT'S TOURISM INFORMATION BOOTH** (2250 Voght St; 250/378-0349; www.bailliehouse.com or www.tourismmerritt.com), across from the city hall, and is a good source of information on the area. Every year in July, Merritt hosts a mammoth country music–themed event, the **MOUNTAIN MUSIC FESTIVAL** (www.mountainfest.com).

LODGINGS

Quilchena Hotel / ★★

HWY 5A, QUILCHENA; 250/378-2611

Visitors are forever parading into this heritage roadhouse's saloon to inspect the real bullet holes left by rowdy cowboys in the early 1900s. Thankfully things are much calmer today, offering visitors a unique experience with fine food, friendly surroundings, and a variety of leisure activities all in a tranquil setting. The 16 rooms and suites, some with private baths, are all different, high-ceilinged Edwardian marvels with period wallpaper and original furnishings that have been there since it opened in 1908. The Victorian dining room offers a savory blend of West Coast and ranch cuisine, and there's a coffee shop in the hotel. Located in the heart of one of British Columbia's largest working cattle ranches, it offers guests horseback riding, bike rentals, tennis, golfing, and ranch tours. *$$; MC, V; no checks; closed Nov–late Apr; www.quilchena.com; 12 miles/20 km east of Merritt.*

Cache Creek

Aside from a gas stop, quiet, dusty Cache Creek offers few other incentives to pause. The surrounding landscape, however, is one of the most striking in the province—wide-open views of sagebrush-covered mountainsides shaped by eons of weathering. Cache Creek is the junction of Hwy 97 (the Cariboo Highway; see Northern Mainland British Columbia chapter) and Hwy 1. From here, Hwy 1/97 leads 52 miles/84 km east to Kamloops.

Five miles north of Cache Creek, **HAT CREEK RANCH** (800/782-0922; www. hatcreekranch.com) is one of the province's finest heritage attractions, an original Cariboo Road way station whose buildings have been lovingly restored. Stroll into the tack barn, and the atmosphere seems the same as it must have been a century ago. Visitors can ride horses, gallivant around in horse-drawn wagons, or stay the night in miners' tents, cabins, or a *kekuli*, a traditional First Nations lodge.

RESTAURANTS

Horsting's Farm Market / ★

HWY 97, CACHE CREEK; 250/457-6546
Jars of Horsting's brand pickles, beets, fresh baked bread, home-grown produce, local honey, and other tasty treats line the walls of Ted and Donna Horsting's rambling fruit and vegetable store, café, and bakery. Best of all, nestled in the back is an eight-table restaurant in which soups, sandwiches, chili, bread, and pies comprise the modest menu. From March through November, this is the best place north of the Okanagan to buy fresh fruit and vegetables. *$; AE, MC, V; no checks; lunch every day; no alcohol; no reservations; www. horstingfarms.com; 1.2 miles/2 km north of town on east side of hwy.* &

LODGINGS

Sundance Ranch / ★★

KIRKLAND RANCH RD, ASHCROFT; 250/453-2422 OR 800/553-3533
Set in high, semi-desert plateau country southeast of Cache Creek, surrounded by sagebrush and cottonwood, the guest ranch of the Rowe family offers sweeping views of the Thompson River Valley. It's a ranch-resort hybrid with a heated outdoor pool, tennis courts, horseshoe pitch, and movie lounge. The real attraction here is the corral, where wranglers assemble 80 to 100 horses for daily rides (included, along with all meals, in the hotel room fee). Immaculate guest rooms are divided between an adult and a kids' wing (though kids can bunk with their parents) and two separate sports lounges. Saturdays, there's a much-anticipated cowhand hoedown. *$$$$; MC, V; no checks; closed Nov–Mar; www.sundanceguestranch.com; 5 miles/8 km south of Ashcroft.* &

Kamloops

Kamloops (population 80,380), the largest city on the Trans-Canada Highway between Vancouver and Calgary, Alberta, sprawls across the weathered benches above the Thompson River's north and south forks. The town's name is taken from this important geographical intersection; it translates from the local Secwepemc language as "where the rivers meet."

Nearby **SECWEPEMC NATIVE HERITAGE PARK** (E Shuswap Rd; 250/828-9779; www.secwepemc.org) features traditional pit-house dwellings and a huge wooden structure dubbed the "pow-wow arbor." Tall timbers thrust above the rounded arbor's square-shingled roof, which at its center opens to the sky. The **KAMLOOPS POW WOW**, held here in August, is a spectacular expression of the Secwepemc heritage, featuring more than a thousand performers and craftspeople.

Fly-in fishing lodges are on many of the area's 700 lakes, where anglers cast for Kamloops trout. The **KAMLOOPS VISITOR INFO CENTRE** (1290 W Trans-Canada Hwy; 250/374-3377 or 800/662-1994; www.tourismkamloops.com) offers more information.

RESTAURANTS

Brownstone Restaurant / ★★

118 VICTORIA ST, KAMLOOPS; 250/851-9939
Located in the stately Canadian Imperial Bank of Commerce building (an official heritage building built in 1904), Brownstone features fine dining and great service in an elegant setting. Dale and Connie Decaire's cozy, intimate dining room, as well as an outdoor patio, offers skillfully prepared international dishes with an emphasis on using local produce. The osso buco, as well as the duck served three ways, are two of the chef's best. They also host wine tastings on the fourth Sunday of every month. *$$$; AE, MC, V; no checks; dinner Wed–Sun; full bar; reservations recommended; www.brownstone-restaurant. com; downtown at 1st Ave.* &

LODGINGS

Riverland Inn & Suites / ★

1530 RIVER ST, KAMLOOPS; 250/374-1530 OR 800/663-1530
Centrally located, the Riverland offers quick access to major highways, and attractions are within walking distance. The motel's 58 standard rooms are spotless and pleasantly furnished, all with refrigerators. Though kitchen units are available, the adjacent Storms Restaurant features a full menu of creative pastas, seafood, ribs, and racks, best enjoyed on the sheltered patio overlooking the river. *$–$$; AE, MC, V; no checks; www.riverlandinn.kamploops.com; Hwy 1 exit 374 toward Jasper, then first left.* &

South Thompson Inn / ★★★

3438 SHUSWAP RD, KAMLOOPS; 250/573-3777 OR 800/797-7713
Poised on the north shore of the South Thompson 20 minutes outside Kamloops, this imposing inn looks like an overgrown cotton-plantation mansion, with white dormers, a long covered porch overlooking the river, and a broad lawn sweeping down to the water. "Kentucky style," the inn advertises itself, and life does seem more genteel here. All rooms offer vistas of the river or the mountains to the north; golf, swimming, and equestrian activities occupy guests here. *$–$$$; AE, MC, V; no checks; www.stigr.com; Hwy 1 exit 390 (LaFarge), north across river, follow signs east along north shore 4 miles/6 km.* &

Sun Peaks Resort

Sun Peaks has outgrown the early buzz that declared it the "next Whistler," an identity it no longer wishes to assume. Today it is a family-oriented winter-sports resort, with three separate mountains to ski and a world of other activities. Eight slope-side hotels anchor a village of chalets, condos, townhomes, and bed-and-breakfast inns. Most offer true ski-in, ski-out access to the lifts. In summer, a ski lift transports hikers and cyclists to high alpine meadows, while golfers stride the fairways of the golf course.

Located 30 miles/50 km northeast of Kamloops on Hwy 5 and Tod Mountain Road, Sun Peaks takes about 45 minutes to reach from Kamloops, much of it a pleasant drive beside the North Thompson River. Aside from the lodgings listed below, hundreds of condos and rental homes are available, all with excellent access to the slopes. Once you arrive at the resort, you won't need your car, though groceries are sparse. Contact **SUN PEAKS RESORT CORP** (3250 Village Wy, No. 13; 250/578-7710 or 800/807-3257; www.sunpeaksresort.com) for a variety of homes and condos available to rent as well as summer and winter vacation packages.

LODGINGS

Father's Country Inn / ★★

TOD MOUNTAIN RD, HEFFLEY CREEK; 250/578-7822
A stay at Father's Country Inn, a bed-and-breakfast hideaway 4 miles/7 km west of Sun Peaks Resort, confirms that no matter how far you roam, you'll still find surprises. Proprietor David Conover Jr. markets not only his resort but also the images his father took of Marilyn Monroe, whom Conover Sr. befriended while he was on a photo shoot for the U.S. Army in Los Angeles during World War II. At the inn, nestled on a hillside overlooking meadows and streams, you can relax in the outdoor hot tub, have a refreshing swim in the heated indoor pool, or just enjoy the view and fresh mountain air from the patio overlooking the valley below. *$–$$; MC, V; no checks; www.bedandbreakfastkamloops.com; Hwy 5 exit at Heffley Creek/Sun Peaks to Tod Mountain Rd, follow signs.*

Nancy Greene's Cahilty Lodge / ★★

3220 VILLAGE WY, SUN PEAKS RESORT; 250/578-7454 OR 800/244-8424

After perfecting their hotel skills at Whistler in the 1980s, Nancy Greene Raine and her husband, Al, migrated east in 1996 to Sun Peaks and opened the Cahilty Lodge, named for a local pioneer ranching family. This full-service condominium hotel's amenities range from rooms with modest cooking facilities to fully equipped suites that sleep eight. A hot tub and an exercise room, plus a ski and mountain-bike room, share the downstairs with Macker's Bistro (250/578-7894; www.mackersbistro.com), one of the most consistent restaurants at Sun Peaks. Adjacent to the lodge is the resort's sports center with swimming pool and weight room, outdoor skating rink, and tennis courts. Service here regularly outperforms guest expectations. *$$–$$$; AE, DC, MC, V; no checks; www.cahiltylodge.com; east on Creekside Wy to Village Wy.* &

The Okanagan Valley

Beloved for a mild, nurturing climate with more than 2,000 annual hours of sunshine and an unparalleled landscape that ranges from desert to snowcapped peaks, the Okanagan has something for everyone: swimming, boating, golfing, biking, hiking, skiing and snowboarding, and innumerable orchards and vineyards. Mediterranean-themed Osoyoos, at the valley's southern end, lays claim to the title of warmest resort area in Canada, with the warmest lake. Hwys 1 and 97 divide at Monte Creek, 19 miles/31 km east of Kamloops. From there, Hwy 97 runs south to the head of Okanagan Lake at Vernon in the North Okanagan, where it links with Hwy 97A. (Hwys 97A and 97B lead south from the Trans-Canada at Sicamous and Salmon Arm, respectively; near Enderby, Hwy 97B merges with 97A.) From Vernon, Hwy 97 follows the lake south to Penticton, then on to Osoyoos and Hwy 3.

Numerous orchards and vineyards testify to the fact that this is some of the most productive fruit- and vegetable-growing land in the world, while dozens of parks surround 79-mile/128-km-long Okanagan Lake. As you pass through the lush South Okanagan and Similkameen regions, near the U.S.-Canadian border, remains of old mining settlements along Hwy 97 have been replaced by innumerable fruit and produce stands. Travel information on the entire region is available from **THOMPSON OKANAGAN TOURISM** (800/567-2275; www.totabc.com). The region is painfully popular in July and August, when visitors must book coveted accommodations months or even a year ahead.

Vernon and Silver Star Mountain Resort

For decades, Vernon (population 36,000) was one of the largest fruit-producing towns in the British Empire, thanks to the abundance of freshwater for irrigation. One of many farms surrounding the city, **DAVISON ORCHARDS** (Bella Vista Rd;

SKIING THE SOUTHERN INTERIOR

The Northern Europeans who settled Rossland in the 1890s well knew how much snow fell in the area since they spent considerable time in those mountains mining. Olaus Jeldness, a Norwegian who'd prospected all over the West, decided to organize a race—even though he complained that it was "far too steep and the snow conditions too extreme"—for a satisfactory race. More than a century later, **RED RESORT SKI AREA**, a utopia for skiers who take their sport seriously, was built in the same area. With two mountains now, and mountains of snow each winter to blanket them, Red Resort draws skiers from around the world, just like the rest of British Columbia's southern interior.

Skiers who think only of Whistler when they think of BC are missing a lot. Whistler has the top-of-the-heap international reputation, but there are dozens of primo ski areas elsewhere in the province, which is why, in fact, British Columbia is Canada's ski capital.

"In the past," says Olympic gold medalist Nancy Greene Raine of **SUN PEAKS RESORT** near Kamloops, "this was perceived as a place where a small group of rugged, wild-and-woolly skiers went to enjoy some of the best powder skiing in the province." But Sun Peaks has transformed itself into a three-mountain, family-friendly resort with a lovely base village, exceptional intermediate skiing, and plenty of nonski activities, such as dogsledding, to keep the entire family occupied. Says Greene Raine, who grew up and learned to ski at Red Resort,

250/549-3266; www.davisonorchards.ca), welcomes visitors with a self-guided walk, wagon tours, a petting zoo, and a country gift shop as well as a café, a bakery, and fresh produce. Contact **VERNON TOURISM** (701 Hwy 97S; 250/542-1415 or 800/665-0795; www.vernontourism.com) for more information.

High above Vernon, **SILVER STAR MOUNTAIN RESORT** (Silver Star Rd, 12 miles/22 km east of Hwy 97; 250/542-0224 or 800/663-4431; www.skisilverstar. com) is the outdoor hub of the North Okanagan, and it's usually called the area's best family resort (though critics carp, somewhat understandably, about its garish faux-Victorian architecture). Forested trails link the resort with adjacent **SOVEREIGN LAKE SKI AREA** (250/558-3036; www.sovereignlake.com) in **SILVER STAR PROVINCIAL PARK** (www.env.gov.bc.ca/bcparks), where the Nordic lodge sells tickets and has a café, wax room, and rental shop.

Once at Silver Star, whether you stay at a condo on Knoll Hill—where Victorian Gaslight–replica homes are decorated in four or five exterior hues and trimmed with cookie-cutter moldings—or in a hotel on Main Street with wraparound verandas, everything is within walking (or skiing) distance. The **BUGABOOS BAKERY CAFÉ** (250/545-3208) and its companion, Francuccino's, are noted for robust coffee, serious strudel, and ambrosial cinnamon buns made of croissant dough.

"More visitors are coming to Canada on a two-week ski holiday. They spend a week at Whistler, then they want to come to a resort like ours where you can actually meet people."

Just as Sun Peaks has evolved into a world-class family resort, so have numerous others in the interior. **BIG WHITE SKI RESORT** (near Kelowna) and **SILVER STAR MOUNTAIN RESORT** (near Vernon) in the Okanagan both draw families for extended vacations; **APEX MOUNTAIN RESORT** near Penticton is a training Mecca for serious skiers. **WHITEWATER SKI & WINTER RESORT** near Nelson is legendary for knee-deep light powder, and **KIMBERLEY ALPINE RESORT** has its own pseudo-Bavarian village.

In the Rockies, **FERNIE ALPINE RESORT** doubled its size in 1999, adding to the legendary appeal of its light powder snow. Nearby **PANORAMA MOUNTAIN VILLAGE**, at Invermere, is a very big destination resort tucked into a valley in the Purcell Mountains with a charming village and amenities such as an outdoor hot-pools complex. **KICKING HORSE MOUNTAIN RESORT**, outside Golden, is another big area adding facilities, including a unique top-of-the-mountain guest suite whose occupants have an ironclad first-tracks guarantee when they wake up in the morning. The Okanagan's and the Kootenays' top-notch destination resorts have excellent snow, large mountains, and fully developed base areas with complete visitor amenities.

—Eric P. Lucas and Andrew Hempstead

RESTAURANTS

Eclectic Med Restaurant / ★★

2915 30TH AVE, VERNON; 250/558-4646
Andrew Fradley's Eclectic Med Restaurant has been winning the hearts (and palates) of epicureans in the North Okanagan since 1996. Fradley's culinary inclinations lean to Caribbean, Thai, and East Indian influences. Tuscan tuna, Moroccan lamb, Salmon Tropicana, and Calypso pork top the extensive menu. Combinations hark back to North African–born Fradley's dozen years in Portugal. *$$; AE, MC, V; no checks; dinner every day; full bar; reservations recommended; at 29th St.* &

LODGINGS

Pinnacles Suite Hotel / ★

SILVER STAR MOUNTAIN; 250/542-4548 OR 800/551-7466
The Pinnacles Suite Hotel, poised on the open slopes above Silver Star's mountain village, has the best seat in town. Each of the 18 suites has a private entrance, spacious living area, full bath, kitchen, and ski locker. Relax in a

rooftop hot tub after a day on the slopes. The adjacent Kickwillie Inn, Silver Star's original day lodge, is now renovated to hold seven suites. *$$; AE, MC, V; checks OK; www.pinnacles.com; 14 miles/22 km northeast of Vernon.*

Kelowna

Sprawled alongside Okanagan Lake's hourglass waist, Kelowna ("grizzly bear" in the native Okanagan dialect) is the largest (population 106,000) and liveliest city in the valley and one of the fastest-growing in Canada. The **CENTRE FOR THE ARTS AND KELOWNA ART GALLERY** (1315 Water St; 250/762-2226; www. galleries.bc.ca/kelowna) and 8,000-seat **PROSPERA PLACE** (1223 Water St; 250/979-0888; www.skyreachplace.com), home of the Western Hockey League's Kelowna Rockets and a live music venue, herald a renaissance fueled by an influx of young professionals, many of whom work for the 200 tech firms based here. Wineries also thrive.

In the heart of downtown, the Okanagan's oldest winery, **CALONA WINES** (1125 Richter St; 250/762-3332; www.calonavineyards.ca), is a good starting point for a wine-country tour. **MISSION HILL FAMILY ESTATE** (1730 Mission Hill Rd, Westbank; 250/768-7611; www.missionhillwinery.com), perched atop a ridge on the west side of Okanagan Lake, offers one of the best views. **SUMMERHILL** (4870 Chute Lake Rd; 250/764-8000 or 800/667-3538; www.summerhill.bc.ca), overlooking city and lake from a bench south of Kelowna, is a pioneer in organic wine-making, aging many of its wines in a massive pyramid. Its restaurant specializes in using Okanagan foodstuffs such as apples and other fruit, and summertime diners enjoy an unsurpassed vantage of the valley.

Kelowna is a jumping-off point for outdoor recreation, from cycling the **MISSION CREEK GREENWAY** or **KETTLE VALLEY TRAIL** to kiteboarding at a lakeside beach, to exploring the surrounding Monashee Mountains. **MONASHEE ADVENTURE TOURS** (1591 Highland Dr N; 250/762-9253 or 888/762-9253; www. monasheeadventuretours.com) rents bikes and offers guided cycle tours. Kelowna also boasts 16 of the 39 **GOLF COURSES** (www.golfkelowna.com) between Vernon and Osoyoos, including some of Canada's highest-rated, such as Predator Ridge.

And the lake has its own version of the Loch Ness monster: **OGOPOGO**. No one has yet claimed the $2 million reward for proof it exists, but its statue in downtown Kelowna is one of the most-photographed sights in the Okanagan. Contact the **KELOWNA VISITOR INFO CENTRE** (544 Harvey Ave; 250/861-1515 or 800/663-4345; www.tourismkelowna.com).

RESTAURANTS

Doc Willoughby's Downtown Grill / ★★☆

353 BERNARD AVE, KELOWNA; 250/868-8288
Darren Nicoll and Dave Willoughby (the restaurant is named for his grandfather) stripped this 1908 downtown landmark to the walls, then rebuilt with wood salvaged from a heritage site in Vancouver. Hardwood floors, maple

tables, cozy booths, and a floor-to-ceiling bar provide atmosphere; upscale pub fare and regular live music define the flavor. The veggie burger was voted one of the best in the city. *$–$$; AE, MC, V; no checks; breakfast Sat–Sun, lunch, dinner every day; full bar; no reservations; near Pandosy St.* &

Fresco / ★★★★

1560 WATER ST, KELOWNA; 250/868-8805
Renowned chef Rod Butters and his wife, Audrey Surrao, arrived in 2001 via a string of notable British Columbia restaurants, including the Fairmont Chateau Whistler. The downtown heritage building was emptied to its frame and trimmed with light clear fir. The menu, which changes with the seasons, has a strong focus on local and organic foods and fuses Asian flavors, a dash of European flair for presentation, and a hint of Canadian wry humor. Highlights on the menu are Chef Butters' signature dishes, which are each a culinary adventure not to be missed, particularly his sensational version of caesar salad with sun-dried olives and double-smoked bacon. Oenophiles relish Fresco's award-winning wine list with more than 120 wines, many of them from the top local BC and Okanagan winemakers. *$$$; AE, MC, V; no checks; dinner Tues–Sun (closed Jan); full bar; reservations recommended; www.frescorestaurant.net; 2 blocks from Harvey Ave.* &

LODGINGS

Casa Loma Lakeshore Resort / ★★☆

2777 CASA LOMA RD, KELOWNA; 250/769-4630 OR 800/771-5253
Its location alone would make Casa Loma one of the most appealing accommodations in the Kelowna area. Not only is it right on the lakeshore, in a quiet corner across the water from the city's hubbub, but it also borders beautiful Kalamoir Park. The 20 cottages and villas are the best, with kitchens, living rooms, and decks, which are staggered to assure privacy. The 20 units in the main lodge are suites, too, but not as appealing. Minimum three- or seven-night stay required in summer. *$$$; AE, MC, V; no checks; www.casaloma.com; 1 mile/1.6 km south of Hwy 97C on east lakeshore.*

The Grand Okanagan Lakefront Resort / ★★★

1310 WATER ST, KELOWNA; 250/763-4500 OR 800/465-4651
The Grand's modernist design harkens back to Kelowna's Mission past and complements the city's burgeoning cultural and entertainment center. Rooms in the 10-story main tower have panoramic views. Standard rooms have full-length windows that open onto Romeo-and-Juliet balconies. For longer stays, two-bedroom condo suites are great. Amenities include a spa, hot tubs, saunas, and a pool. Three restaurants, two lounges, a pub, and the Mind Grind Internet Café share the main floor with the Lake City Casino (www.lakecitycasinos.com). *$$$$; AE, MC, V; no checks; www.grandokanagan.com; 5 blocks north of Hwy 97.* &

Manteo Resort / ★★★

3762 LAKESHORE RD, KELOWNA; 250/860-1031 OR 800/445-5255

The brightly colored, four-story Manteo looks sunny even on cloudy days. Opened in 2000, the resort has 78 hotel rooms and 24 private villas in an intimate setting on the shore of Okanagan Lake. Quiet and arty, the Tuscan-style lobby sets the right vacation tone. Thoughtful touches, such as fruit baskets, abound. The resort is otherwise designed to keep every family member occupied. Their Wild Apple Grill features monthly specials inspired by fresh produce. Service throughout is superb. *$$–$$$$; AE, DC, MC, V; no checks; www. manteo.com; 4 miles/6.5 km south of downtown at Pandosy St.* &

Big White Ski Resort

Less than an hour's drive southeast of Kelowna via Highway 33, on the perimeter of the Monashee Mountains, is **BIG WHITE SKI RESORT** (Big White Rd, 14 miles/ 23 km east of Hwy 33; 250/765-3101 or 800/663-2772; www.bigwhite.com). Set at the highest elevation of any winter resort in British Columbia (5,760 feet/1,755 m), Big White is one of the largest ski-in/ski-out resort villages in Canada.

The **HAPPY VALLEY ADVENTURE CENTRE** and theme park offers tubing, dogsledding, ice skating, and snowmobiling. Visitors can hop on a horse-drawn wagon as it trots by, then sit on a hay bale and let the team of Percherons do the rest. More than a dozen restaurants—**SNOWSHOE SAM'S** (250/765-5959; www. snowshoesams.com), **COPPER KETTLE GRILL** (250/491-8122), and the **KETTLE VALLEY STEAKHOUSE AND WINE BAR** (250/491-0130) are best bets—dot the village. The Village Centre Lodge's wood-fired bakery has cinnamon buns with enough icing to rival the snow on the slopes.

LODGINGS

White Crystal Inn / ★★

BIG WHITE RD, KELOWNA; 250/765-8888 OR 800/663-2772

This classic four-story chalet has grown with the mountain and now offers 49 rooms spread between two wings. So successful was the original design that it was copied for Chateau Big White nearby. But they couldn't replicate the White Crystal's intimacy or its impeccable location next to the resort's gondola and Bullet Express quad chair. All rooms are outfitted in cedar and slate. On the lodge's main floor are the stylish Copper Kettle Restaurant and a more casual bistro. *$$; AE, MC, V; no checks; www.bigwhite.com; on right as you enter resort, next to Village Ctr.* &

Penticton and Apex Mountain Resort

Penticton, the "Peach City" (population 30,985), might just as easily be called Festival City. There's always some serious fun going on in this town spread between Okanagan and Skaha lakes, including **FEST-OF-ALE** (www.fest-of-ale.bc.ca) in

April; weeklong **WINE FESTIVALS** (250/861-6654; www.owfs.com) in May and October; the May **MEADOWLARK FESTIVAL** (250/492-5275 or 866/699-9453; www.meadowlarkfestival.bc.ca), which celebrates the environment; a campy **BEACH BLANKET FILM FESTIVAL** (www.beachblanketfilmfest.com) in July; the **AUGUST PEACH FESTIVAL** (250/493-4055 or 800/663-5052; www.peachfest. com), now in its sixth decade; and the **PENTASTIC JAZZ FESTIVAL** (www.pentastic jazz.com) in September.

Athletes from around the world turn out for **IRONMAN CANADA** (www. ironman.ca), the swim-bike-run triathlon held here in August annually. Some of the best **ROCK CLIMBING** in BC occurs at the **SKAHA BLUFFS** on the town's southeastern outskirts. **SKAHA ROCK ADVENTURES** (113-437 Martin St, Penticton; 250/493-1765; www.skaharockclimbing.com) guides climbers on many of the bluff's 120 cliffs.

Contact the **PENTICTON VISITOR INFO CENTRE** (888 Westminster Ave W, Penticton; 250/493-4055 or 800/663-5052; www.penticton.org) for details. For a wine tour, visit the **BC WINE INFORMATION CENTRE** at the same location (250/490-2006; www.bcwineinfo.net).

APEX MOUNTAIN RESORT (on Green Mountain Rd, Penticton; 250/292-8222 or 877/777-2739; www.apexresort.com) is 21 miles/33 km west of town. Lift lines are virtually nonexistent, and the powder snow is dry and sparkling. On-hill accommodations are limited to one wonderfully cozy lodge: the **SADDLEBACK LODGE BED & BREAKFAST** (115 Clearview Crescent, Apex Mountain; 250/292-8118 or 800/863-1466; www.saddlebacklodge.com). Most visitors stay in Penticton, a half-hour drive away. A shuttle bus that makes the rounds of local hotels provides handy access to the slopes.

RESTAURANTS

Bogner's Restaurant / ★★★

302 ECKHARDT AVE, PENTICTON; 250/493-2711

One of the Okanagan's oldest fine-dining restaurants is also one of the most consistent: great food, great location, and desserts that alone make the trip worthwhile. Diners relax in front of the rambling 1912 Arts and Crafts–style fireplace. A restaurant maxim states that the eyes eat first—nowhere more so than at Bogner's, where chef Peter Hebel's entrées arrive garnished with an eye for color and shape. His bouillabaisse is a bargain and a meal in itself. *$$; MC, V; no checks; dinner Tues–Sat (in summer); full bar; reservations recommended; www.bogners.ca; 2 blocks south of Main St.*

LODGINGS

God's Mountain Estate / ★★★

4898 LAKESIDE RD, PENTICTON; 250/490-4800

It's difficult to adequately describe God's Mountain Crest Chalet, where Ulric Lejeune and his wife, Ghitta, have created the Club Med of B and Bs, a wonderful romantic getaway in the heart of Okanagan wine country. The white Mediterranean-style mansion overlooks the Lejeunes' vineyards,

Skaha Lake, and the Okanagan Highlands. Inside the 12-room inn—some rooms with shared baths, others with private baths—is an eclectic blend of antiques and religious iconography. Quiet pervades, even at breakfast, when guests gather for sumptuous buffets. A large swimming pool and hot tub (perfect for late-night stargazing) are surrounded by gardens. If you enjoy sleeping under the stars, the roofless rooftop room lets you gaze at shooting stars from the in-room hot tub or lie in bed with the blue sky and clouds as a ceiling. *$$; MC, V; checks OK; www.godsmountain.com; 3 miles/5 km south of Penticton.*

Naramata

North of Penticton off Hwy 97, the picturesque village of **NARAMATA** (www. discovernaramata.com) is surrounded by wineries. Rugged Naramata Road leads north through slopes and headlands that jut out into the lake. You can easily spend a day and visit only half the wineries. Two that shouldn't be missed are **LANG VINEYARDS** (2493 Gammon Rd; 250/496-5987; www.langvineyards.com) and **RED ROOSTER WINERY** (910 Debeck Rd; 250/492-2424; www.redrooster winery.com). Naramata (population 2,000) lies 10 miles/16 km from downtown Penticton; turn east from Main Street (Hwy 97) onto Jermyn Avenue and follow the signs.

LODGINGS

Naramata Heritage Inn & Spa / ★★★

3625 1ST ST, NARAMATA; 250/496-6808 OR 866/617-1188
This 1908 landmark hotel, long vacant after midcentury life as a girl's school, has been lavishly restored into the Okanagan's most elegant heritage inn. The stucco exterior calls to mind Northern California inns of the period; the long porch pulls in morning sun, and trees shade the grounds. Inside, clear fir floors and dark wood beams set off Mission-style furniture. The Rock Oven dining room offers a five-course dinner. *$$$; AE, MC, V; checks OK; www. naramatainn.com; downtown.* ゟ

Sandy Beach Lodge & Resort / ★★

4275 MILL RD, NARAMATA; 250/496-5765
Sandy Beach's dozen log cabins are so popular that in July and August they are often completely booked two years in advance. That said, six B and B rooms in the restored 1940s main lodge—the real deal at this Okanagan Lake retreat—are usually still up for grabs. Each has its own covered veranda overlooking the lake. May and September are pleasant months to visit, when competition is less fierce and the waters are almost as inviting as they are in summer. *$$–$$$$; MC, V; no checks; www.sandybeachresort.com; end of Mill Rd at Okanagan Lake.* ゟ

Oliver and Osoyoos

The South Okanagan is a wondrous produce basket. Travelers on the 12-mile/ 20-km stretch of Hwy 97 between Oliver (population 4,500) and Osoyoos (population 4,750) pass the most bountiful agricultural land in the entire valley. Since the 1990s, this has become a prime region for growing classic European varietal grapes such as pinot noir and merlot, all of which thrive in the warm climate. The industry has grown to the point that Oliver has reconstituted itself as a "resort municipality," like Whistler, and small inns and bistros are planned throughout the area.

The **DESERT CENTRE** (west on 146th Ave off Hwy 97, Osoyoos; 250/495-2470 or 877/899-0897; www.desert.org) protects a "pocket desert," where less than 12 inches/30.5 cm of precipitation fall annually and cacti, prickly pear, sagebrush, and rattlesnakes survive in the dry, sandy environment. Back roads on the east side of the valley lead past several award-winning wineries, including **BLUE MOUNTAIN VINEYARDS AND CELLARS** (RR1, S3, C4, Okanagan Falls; 250/497-8244; www.bluemountainwinery.com; by appointment only), often cited by connoisseurs as the best of all British Columbia wineries.

From there, drivers and cyclists enjoy a unique perspective on the eroded west side of the valley. This is also the site of fledgling **SOUTH OKANAGAN NATIONAL PARK** (www.parkscanada.ca) as well as the Okanagan Indian Band's **NK'MIP DESERT AND HERITAGE CENTRE** (1000 Ranch Creek Rd, Osoyoos; 250/495-7901 or 888/495-8555; www.nkmipdesert.com), a Native interpretive center adjacent to the Spirit Ridge resort and winery. Contact the **OLIVER VISITOR INFO CENTRE** (36205 93rd Ave, Oliver; 250/498-6321; www.oliverchamber.bc.ca) and the **OSOYOOS VISITOR INFO CENTRE** (Hwys 3 and 97, Osoyoos; 250/495-3366 or 888/676-9667; www.destinationosoyoos.com) for details.

RESTAURANTS

Campomarina Italian Restaurant / ★

5907 MAIN ST, OSOYOOS; 250/495-7650
Friendly and courteous service is the hallmark of the Campo Marina, where variety, great food, large servings, and moderate prices add up to good value at this self-defined "funky" eatery. The menu blends continental and Mediterranean flavors. Antiques and collectibles festoon the walls and tables, with an Okanagan vineyard ambience. *$$; MC, V; checks OK; dinner every day; full bar; no reservations; www.campomarina.com; across from Dairy Queen.*

Sonora Room at Burrowing Owl / ★★★

100 BURROWING OWL PL, OLIVER; 250/498-0620 OR 877/498-0620
After years of service with Pan Pacific hotels in Southeast Asia, British Columbia native Glenn Monk has returned home to lend a distinctly Asian air to the bistro at one of the Okanagan's best wineries. Not surprisingly, some of his preparations evince Malaysian or Indonesian touches, such as the Balinese prawn *satay* or wild salmon poached in coconut broth. The balcony tables

have a smashing view of a wetland. *$$$; AE, MC, V; no checks; lunch, dinner every day; full bar; reservations recommended; www.bovwine.com; off Hwy 97, 7 miles/13 km south of Oliver.* &

LODGINGS

Spirit Ridge Vineyard Resort / ★★

1200 RANCHER RD, OSOYOOS; 250/495-5445 OR 877/313-9463
Poised between vineyards and the desert beyond, this resort's stucco buildings house 30 bright suites and villas, all furnished in desert hues with views, all with kitchenettes and patios. The Spirit Ridge winery is next door. Behind the resort, a short walk takes you to the biggest undeveloped stretch of desert in the South Okanagan. *$$$; AE, MC, V; no checks; www.spiritridge.ca; on east side of Osoyoos, 1 mile/1.6 km north of Hwy 3.*

The Kootenays

The Kootenays occupy the entire southeast portion of British Columbia. Winter sunlight barely brushes the valleys of the West Kootenay. Residents head to lively towns, such as Nelson, or to local ski areas. The majestic **COLUMBIA RIVER** winds through it all. Transportation in the Kootenays is by road. Time zones shift between Pacific and Mountain from one town to the next, and some areas don't switch to daylight time. Get information (www.bcrockies.com) before visiting.

Rossland and Red Resort Ski Area

Rossland (population 3,278) is in the Monashee Mountains close to **RED RESORT SKI AREA** (on Hwy 3B, 3 miles/5 km northwest of Rossland; 250/362-7384 or 800/663-0105; www.redresort.com). In the 1890s, when Rossland was at the peak of its gold-mining boom, Red Mountain hosted the first Canadian ski racing championships. The mountain has since produced two of the best skiers to ever represent Canada. Today the resort is a cult favorite. Recently bought by Southern California tycoon Howard Katkov, the resort is undergoing significant expansion but intends not to go the Whistler route—it's focusing on condo accommodations rather than hotels, for instance. The **BLACK JACK CROSS-COUNTRY SKI CLUB** (Hwy 3B, Red Resort; 250/364-5445; www.skiblackjack.ca) lies at the base.

The heritage buildings that line many of Rossland's streets reflect the boom times of a century ago. Rossland's **WINTER CARNIVAL**, first held in 1897, is going strong the last weekend in January. Sometimes referred to as "Canada's Mountain Bike Capital," Rossland hosts the annual **RUBBERHEAD MOUNTAIN BIKE FESTIVAL** near Labor Day. Contact the **ROSSLAND VISITOR INFO CENTRE** (Columbia Ave and Hwy 3B, Rossland; 250/362-7722 or 888/448-7444; www.rossland.com; May–Sept) for details.

RESTAURANTS

Sunshine Café / ★

2116 COLUMBIA AVE, ROSSLAND; 250/362-5099
Everyone takes a shine to Rossland's favorite little café, where you can sit in the front of the restaurant to do some people watching or walk past the kitchen to the back room. The food doesn't try to be fancy, just good, and there's lots of it. Huevos rancheros is a breakfast favorite. Mealtimes are crowded. *$; MC, V; no checks; breakfast, lunch Wed–Mon; beer and wine; reservations recommended (ski season); just east of Queen St.*

LODGINGS

Ram's Head Inn / ★★★

RED MOUNTAIN RD, ROSSLAND; 250/362-9577 OR 877/267-4323
What sets the Ram's Head Inn apart is its cozy size—12 guest rooms, 34 guests maximum—and little touches, such as chalet slippers at the door. The inn's location at the foot of Red Resort Ski Area doesn't hurt, either—it's the only traditional lodging at the area's base. Rooms are cozy affairs with warm wood decor. Guests gather for a complimentary breakfast or relax on an overstuffed couch beside the granite fireplace. *$$–$$$; AE, MC, V; no checks; www.ramshead.bc.ca; off Hwy 3B at Red Mountain Rd.* &

Nakusp

Nakusp (population 1,500) occupies a wide bench in a crook of the arm of Upper Arrow Lake, set squarely between the Monashee and Selkirk mountains. This is **HOT SPRING COUNTRY** (see "Some Like It Hot"). Along Highway 23 between Nakusp (at Hwy 6) and Galena Bay at the northern end of **UPPER ARROW LAKE** (near Hwy 1) are two commercial and four wilderness springs. You can't drive to the wilderness springs in winter (back roads aren't plowed); reach them on snowshoes or skis. Contact the **NAKUSP VISITOR INFO CENTRE** (92 6th Ave NW; 250/265-4234 or 800/909-8819; www.nakusphotsprings.com) for details.

LODGINGS

Halcyon Hot Springs Resort / ★

HWY 23, NAKUSP; 250/265-3554 OR 888/689-4699
In 1999, like the proverbial phoenix, Halcyon Hot Springs Resort rose from the ashes of its predecessor, which operated here on the shores of Upper Arrow Lake between the 1890s and 1950s. The 24 cabins and chalets sleep up to six. A restaurant is in the main building. Halcyon in Greek means "calm, serene," and that's how one feels after bathing in the two hottest pools, which share a vista of Arrow Lake with the main swimming pool. *$$; AE, MC, V; no checks; www.halcyon-hotsprings.com; 20 miles/32 km north of Nakusp.* &

Kaslo

Kaslo, a former mining hub on **KOOTENAY LAKE**—almost 99 miles/160 km long, one of British Columbia's largest freshwater lakes—retains the flavor of its heyday, much like the gloriously restored sternwheeler **SS MOYIE** (324 Front St; 250/353-2525; www.klhs.bc.ca; 9:30am–4:30pm every day mid-May–mid-Oct). Kaslo, on Highway 31 between Hwys 3 and 1, remains the most appealing town on the lake. These days, it's best known for its jazz festival on the first weekend in August. Music lovers dig the tunes from dry land as the music flows from a stage anchored offshore. Contact **KASLO VISITOR INFO CENTRE** (324 Front St; 250/353-2525; www.kaslo.org; May–Oct) for details.

RESTAURANTS

Rosewood Café / ★★☆

213 5TH ST, KASLO; 250/353-7673 OR 888/875-7673

Smell the chicken, pork, and beef ribs long before you reach this café's white picket fence. Everything on the menu, right down to the mayonnaise, is made from scratch. The fact that chef Grant Mckenzie does much of his cooking outdoors on an 8-foot barbecue helps draw a crowd. There are about 17 specials every day, but Mckenzie's signature dish is a cedar-plank salmon topped with crab and shrimp béarnaise, served on a foot-long cedar plank. Gracious service, a gorgeous wine list, and sumptious desserts (particularly the chocolate pâté and the peanut butter pie) make reservations a must in summer. About half the seats are on a spacious patio overlooking Kootenay Lake. No wonder the Rosewood has a loyal clientele from as far afield as Washington state. *$$; MC, V; local checks only; lunch, dinner Tues–Sun, brunch Sun (closed Jan); full bar; reservations recommended; rosewood_cafe@hotmail.com; at east end of 5th St.* ♿

LODGINGS

Wing Creek Cabins Resort / ★★

HWY 31, KASLO; 250/353-2475

Nestled in a clearing above the upper end of Kootenay Lake, Wing Creek Resort is a beautiful place to bask in the serenity of the area and the stunning view of the Purcell Wilderness across the lake. The five cozy timber-frame cabins all have fireplaces and face a large hillside with a meadow and orchards; a trail leads to the private beach. In winter, heli-skiers lift off from the meadow. *$$; AE, MC, V; no checks; www.wingcreekcabins.com; 4 miles/ 6 km north of Kaslo.* ♿

Ainsworth Hot Springs

Ainsworth Hot Springs is a sleepy spot on Hwy 31, about 12 miles/19 km south of Kaslo and 30 miles/50 km north of Nelson. It was a boomtown during the heyday of silver, zinc, and lead mining in the 1890s. Today, if it weren't for the hot springs, few travelers would slow down on their way through the small community perched above Kootenay Lake.

LODGINGS

Ainsworth Hot Springs Resort / ★

HWY 31, AINSWORTH HOT SPRINGS; 250/229-4212 OR 800/668-1171

Ainsworth Hot Springs Resort boasts a former mine shaft into which steamy mineral springs are vented. Hot water drips from the granite ceiling and flows through a tunnel into the resort's large outdoor pool. A hop into the icy plunge pool will restore your senses. Upgraded in 1999, but still unremarkable, the three-story resort's accommodations range from standard hotel rooms to suites with kitchenettes. The draw is the hot springs. *$$; AE, DC, MC, V; no checks; www.hotnaturally.com; 10 miles/16 km north of Balfour.* ♿

Crawford Bay

The tiny community of Crawford Bay (population 300) across from Ainsworth Hot Springs on the east side of Kootenay Lake, accessible from Balfour on Hwy 3A via the world's longest free ferry ride, is home to many artisans, including Canada's only **MANUFACTURER OF TRADITIONAL STRAW BROOMS** (www.kootenaylake.bc.ca/Artisans.shtml). Crawford Bay is popular with golfers for the picturesque and challenging **KOKANEE SPRINGS GOLF COURSE** (16082 Woolgar Rd, Crawford Bay; 250/227-9226; www.kokaneesprings.com).

LODGINGS

Wedgwood Manor / ★★★

16002 CRAWFORD CREEK RD, CRAWFORD BAY; 250/227-9233 OR 800/862-0022

This lovely 1910 home, built on a 50-acre/20.23-hectare estate for the daughter of the renowned British china maker, is one of the finest lodgings in southeastern British Columbia. The four upstairs guest rooms open onto a reading room; the lakeview Charles Darwin Room and the Commander's Room receive afternoon sun. The fully furnished Wildwood Cabin provides a cozy escape and, unlike the inn's rooms, is available year-round. *$$; AE, MC, V; no checks; closed Nov–Mar; www.wedgwoodcountryinn.com; east of Nelson on Hwy 3A, take Balfour ferry to Kootenay Bay.* ♿

Nelson

Nestled on the shore of Kootenay Lake south of Balfour, Nelson (population 9,300) thrived during the silver- and gold-mining boom in the late 1890s and

SOME LIKE IT HOT

Its position on the Pacific Rim "Ring of Fire" means British Columbia is geothermally very active, providing the province with more than two dozen easily accessible hot springs (plus many more in wilderness locations known mostly to local residents). The area that has seen the greatest development of these natural spas is in the Kootenays, where hot mineral water flows out of the Rockies in numerous spots, several of which have been transformed into famous resorts.

AINSWORTH HOT SPRINGS RESORT is the most unusual of these. First used by Native inhabitants, then later by miners in the area, the 117°F (47.2°C) water is funneled first into an old horseshoe-shaped mine tunnel, which, after almost a century of mineral deposition, has become a cave. Bathers wade in through waist-deep waters to linger in nooks of the tunnel, which is in effect a steam bath. Committed enthusiasts can cool off in an icy plunge pool at the entrance to the tunnel; there is also an outdoor hot pool with sensational views across Kootenay Lake to the Purcell Mountains. The adjacent hotel offers lodging (see review) and a restaurant.

FAIRMONT HOT SPRINGS RESORT is a full-blown international destination with golf, skiing, tennis, horseback riding, hiking, and generally deluxe relaxation. A huge outdoor pool complex is open to the public; guests at the lodge (see review) have access to a smaller private pool. The resort drains the water each night, scrubs the pools, and then refills them, thus claiming its waters are "almost certainly the cleanest in North America." Hot-springs zealots won't be impressed by that, but the resort is a great place for a country club–style summer vacation.

retains its late-Victorian character, luring filmmakers to use its downtown as a set. More than 350 homes and buildings are designated heritage structures. Pick up a map, or join a free guided tour in summer, at the **NELSON VISITOR INFO CENTRE** (225 Hall St; 250/352-3433; www.discovernelson.com). Built on a hillside, Nelson has steep streets that demand you wear sturdy shoes for exploring on foot. The best vantage on Nelson is from **GYRO PARK** (corner of Park and Morgan sts). A pictorial exhibit is at the **NELSON MUSEUM** (402 Anderson St; 250/352-9813).

In summer the town turns into an art gallery, with the work of some 100 artists exhibited in shops, restaurants, and galleries during the **NELSON ARTWALK** (250/352-2402; June–Aug). Art and crafts are displayed year-round at the **CRAFT CONNECTION** (378 Baker St; 250/352-3006; www.craftconnection.org). Visitors to Nelson come not only for the city's arts and culture but also its health and wellness opportunities.

A culture of outdoor adventure permeates the region too. Whether it's a hike downhill to **OSO NEGRO COFFEE** (8-512 Latimer St, Nelson; 250/352-7661; www.osonegrocoffee.com) for Kootenay-roasted, fair-trade coffee or a day hike in the **SELKIRK MOUNTAINS** surrounding Nelson, there's plenty to keep you on

Just up the road from Fairmont, **RADIUM HOT SPRINGS** is within Yoho National Park, tucked in a narrow creek canyon. The big bathing pool's 103°F (39.4°C) waters have a higher concentration of sulphate and other minerals than most hot springs—beware the water's effect on dye colors in your bathing suit. The adjacent lodge overlooks the pools.

NAKUSP HOT SPRINGS (on Hot Springs Rd, 8 miles/12 km east of Nakusp; 250/265-4528; www.nakusphotsprings.com) is a complex operated by the village of Nakusp, along Arrow Lake. Its 130°F (54.4°C) source water is cooled to 108°F (42.2°C) and 100°F (37.7°C) in the two bathing pools; a campground and rental chalets give the complex a more laid-back atmosphere than other hot-springs resorts.

Also in this area is **HALCYON HOT SPRINGS RESORT**, an update of a colorful historic resort that burned down in the 1950s—the complex was operated for 30 years by General Frederick Burnham, a doctor who banned bathing suits, smoking, and drinking. Halcyon developed an international reputation as a place of healing. Today's resort has a small lodge, several cabins, and bathing pools of varying temperatures overlooking the lake.

In the Nakusp area, hot water runs deep: numerous undeveloped hot springs line the creek valleys in the region, to which residents might or might not offer directions if you ask nicely. Keep in mind the hot-springs code: no trash, no carousing, no pictures—and if you can't deal with nudity, don't go.

—Eric P. Lucas

your feet here. Outdoor enthusiasts shop at **SNOWPACK** (333 Baker St; 250/352-6411; www.snowpack.ca). The **KOOTENAY BAKER** (295 Baker St; 250/352-2274) stocks an excellent selection of healthy foods. Nelson's Baker Street is known for its restaurants and patios, but there is an array of excellent restaurants located just off the main drag.

The Selkirks are a magnet for hikers and backcountry skiers; a popular destination is **KOKANEE GLACIER PARK** (off Hwy 3A, 18 miles/29 km northeast of Nelson; 250/825-4421; www.env.gov.bc.ca/bcparks). **BALDFACE SNOWCAT SKIING** (250/352-0006; www.baldface.net) offers cat-skiing. **WHITEWATER SKI & WINTER RESORT** (on Hwy 6, 12 miles/19 km south of Nelson; 250/352-4944 or 800/666-9420; www.skiwhitewater.com) in the Selkirk Mountains is an old-school operation with four lifts. The high base elevation of 5,400 feet/1,640 m ensures plentiful light, dry powder. The rustic resort is also home to the Whitewater Nordic Centre.

RESTAURANTS

All Seasons Café / ★★

620 HERRIDGE LN, NELSON; 250/352-0101

This intimate café is great for a quick meal: you can sit near the bar, sip a microbrew, and enjoy an appetizer. Heavenly scented dishes emerge from the kitchen, and fresh sage-and-oregano bread arrives by the basket. To get in the full swing of All Seasons' "Left Coast Inland Cuisine," try the chèvre-stuffed Hills Farm chicken breast with a caramelized butternut squash–sided dish, followed by the ginger crème brûlée for dessert. *$$; MC, V; local checks only; dinner every day; full bar; reservations recommended; www.allseasonscafe. com; between Hall and Josephine sts.* &

The Outer Clove / ★

536 STANLEY ST, NELSON; 250/354-1667

After exploring the Selkirks, cap the day with a garlic martini and oven-roasted garlic cloves drizzled in Brie at this eclectic and cozy restaurant. Vampire jokes aside, the Outer Clove specializes in all things garlic: every item on the menu has garlic in it. Signature dishes include their cream of garlic and potato soup, the quasar burger (chicken burger with Brie), and any of their mouth-watering salad dressings. Great cozy ambience; there's live music every Wednesday at 7pm. *$$; MC, V; no checks; lunch, dinner Mon–Sat; full bar; reservations recommended on weekends; www.allseasonscafe.com; between Baker St and Herridge Ln.*

LODGINGS

Blaylock's Mansion / ★★★

1679 HWY 3A, NELSON; 250/825-2200 OR 888/788-3613

With this estate's exquisitely decorated theme rooms, 13 acres/5.26 hectares of manicured grounds and spectacular gardens, and another 35 acres/14.16 hectares of untamed land filled with wildflowers and old-growth trees, you can bask in the surrounding serenity. Every morning a dazzling breakfast awaits in the breakfast room: juice squeezed from organic fruits, platters of fresh fruits, organic granola or hot cereal, organic Arabic coffee, and a mouthwatering main course. At the on-site spa, guests can enjoy acupuncture, massage, and pedicures. There's also a billiards and snooker table room and a big-screen television room. This magnificent Tudor-style mansion perched above Kootenay Lake also gets more than a few spiritual encounters each year; guests have spotted otherworldly orbs in their photos of the mansion's interior. *$$$–$$$$; MC, V; checks OK; www.blaylock.ca; 3 miles/5 km east of Nelson.*

Cloudside Inn / ★★

408 VICTORIA ST, NELSON; 250/352-3226 OR 800/596-2337

Formerly called Inn the Garden, this centrally located B and B is where many Nelson residents book their out-of-town guests. In 2007 British nationals

Chris and Sally Drysdale immigrated to Nelson and took over as innkeepers of this beautifully restored six-unit early 1900s Victorian home, just a block from Main Street. The best bargain is the three-bedroom bungalow. B and B guests get a superb hot breakfast. *$$; MC, V; no checks; www.cloudside.ca; 1 block south of Baker St.*

Willow Point Lodge / ★★

2211 TAYLOR DR, NELSON; 250/825-9411 OR 800/949-2211
Mel Reasoner and Ulli Huber's three-story 1920 Edwardian home just outside Nelson occupies 3½ acres/1.4 hectares. Of the six guest rooms, the Green Room sports a private covered balcony overlooking the lake and mountains. Guests can stroll through the magnificent gardens and relax in the gazebo, or venture out for a little hike on a trail that leads to three waterfalls. After a day at Whitewater Ski Resort, soak in Willow Point's large outdoor hot tub. The lodge fills quickly in summer. *$$; MC, V; local checks only; www.willow pointlodge.com; 2½ miles/4 km north of Nelson.* &

Kimberley and Kimberley Alpine Resort

As with many foundering mining towns in the 1970s, Kimberley (population 7,300), on the west side of the broad Columbia Valley on Hwy 93/95, looked to tourism and—like Leavenworth, Washington—chose a Bavarian theme to bolster its economy. Accordion music is played on loudspeakers at the center of the **BAVARIAN PLATZL**, the town's three-block pedestrian plaza. For a quarter, a yodeling puppet pops out of the upper window of Canada's largest cuckoo clock. Pick up ingredients for a picnic lunch (or dinner at your condo) at **KIMBERLEY SAUSAGE AND MEATS** (360 Wallinger Ave; 250/427-7766).

At 3,650 feet/1,113 m, Kimberley is the highest city in Canada. From this height, views of the snowcapped Rockies are stunning. The **HERITAGE MUSEUM** (105 Spokane St; 250/427-7510) displays mining memorabilia. Gardeners shouldn't miss the **COMINCO GARDENS** (306 3rd Ave; 250/427-2293). A frenzy of expansion characterizes **KIMBERLEY ALPINE RESORT** (Gerry Sorenson Wy; 250/427-4881 or 800/258-7669; www.skikimberley.com), where a Marriott anchors the resort.

RESTAURANTS

Old Bauernhaus / ★★☆

280 NORTON AVE, KIMBERLEY; 250/427-5133
The Old Bauernhaus is a fine-dining restaurant with a very unusual history. Tony and Ingrid Schwarzenberger dismantled a beautiful 360-year-old Bavarian farmhouse and carefully shipped it from Germany to Canada, where they painstakingly reassembled it over 18 months. The menu reflects the Schwarzenbergers' Swiss-German roots: goulash soup, wiener schnitzel, raclette. In summer, they set patio tables out in the garden. *$$; MC, V; local checks only; dinner Thurs–Mon (closed 2 weeks Nov and Apr); full bar; reservations recommended; left off Gerry Sorenson Wy.* &

LODGINGS

House Alpenglow B&B / ★★

3 ALPENGLOW CT, KIMBERLEY; 250/427-0273 OR 877/257-3645
Merna Abel's three spacious and lovingly furnished guest rooms include the two-bedroom Sullivan suite with its private entrance to the outdoor hot tub and yard. After a complimentary plate of bratwurst and cheese on homemade bread, you won't be hungry again until supper. Kimberley Alpine Resort is several minutes uphill; the Old Bauernhaus across the road serves dinner. *$$; no credit cards; checks OK; www.bbexpo.com/alpenglow; west side of Gerry Sorenson Wy, near Trickle Creek Golf Resort.*

Fernie

An elegant stone courthouse anchors downtown Fernie (population 5,100), a mining and logging town on Hwy 3 with historic buildings. The craggy cleft of the Lizard Range above **FERNIE ALPINE RESORT** (5339 Ski Area Rd; 250/423-4655 or 800/258-7669; www.skifernie.com) is likened to an open catcher's mitt. The resort, along with Whitewater and Red Mountain Resort, is a legendary stop on British Columbia's powder circuit. An amazing 29 feet/8.84 m of natural snow blankets the ski area's impressive five alpine bowls. The prime parking at the bottom of the slopes is reserved for RVs from nearby small towns. With them in mind, Fernie provides a spiffy changing room, complete with showers.

The resort also offers sleigh rides (a handy way to get to the lifts from the parking lot), snowmobile tours, dogsledding, and snowshoeing, as well as a twice-weekly torchlight ski run. In summer, the hills draw horseback riders, mountain bikers, hikers, and adventure racers. Winter Olympic alpine gold medalist Kerrin Lee-Gartner settled here in 1999 to construct **SNOW CREEK LODGE** (5258 Highline Dr; 250/423-7669 or 888/558-6878; www.fernieproperties.com). Her medals and memorabilia are displayed in the lodge's lobby. Visitors are as likely to cross paths with the downhiller and her young family at **OUR CAPPUCCINO CORNER** (501 2nd Ave) as they are on the slopes. A good source for outdoor equipment is the **GUIDES HUT** (671 2nd Ave; 250/423-3650). Contact the **FERNIE INFO CENTRE** (102 Commerce Rd; 250/423-6868; www.ferniechamber.com) for details or consult www.fernie.com.

LODGINGS

Griz Inn Sport Hotel / ★★

5369 SKI AREA RD, FERNIE; 250/423-9221 OR 800/661-0118
When the Griz Inn opened in 1983, it signaled the beginning of a new era in tourism at Fernie Alpine Resort, which was primarily the preserve of locals. A sweeping list of new lodges and condos has joined in, but none supplants the Griz's prime location. Guests enjoy second-to-none views of the mountains and trails from private balconies. The largest suites sleep 16. The inn's Powderhorn Restaurant is a good bet. *$$; AE, MC, V; no checks; www.grizinn. com; off Hwy 3 west of Fernie.* &

Fairmont Hot Springs

Fairmont Hot Springs Resort, on Hwy 93/95 north of Kimberley, has accommodated both soakers and skiers since the 1920s, with the biggest outdoor thermal pool and the only private (guests only) ski resort in western Canada. Don't miss the view from the switchback road above the resort: from the Columbia Valley to the Selkirk and Bugaboo mountains, including the headwaters of the Columbia River. Viewpoints in the East Kootenay don't come any better than this.

LODGINGS

Fairmont Hot Springs Resort / ★★☆

FAIRMONT HOT SPRINGS; 250/345-6000 OR 800/663-4979
Fairmont Hot Springs Resort has odorless and sulfur-free thermal springs, in contrast to most. Many of its 140 units come with kitchens, and rooms have private balconies. The Olympic-sized hot-springs pool lies below, and lodge guests have their own pool. Rooms 492, 494, and 496 are the most private on the ground floor. The resort has a full-service dining room, coffee shop, and lounge. *$$$; AE, DC, DIS, MC, V; no checks; www.fairmont hotsprings.com; turn east off Hwy 93/95.* &

Invermere and Panorama Mountain Village

Just 2 miles/3 km west of Hwy 93/95 on Windermere Lake, Invermere (population 2,860) is the commercial hub, with a folksy main street, for the nearby towns of Radium Hot Springs and Fairmont Hot Springs. In summer, the beach at **JAMES CHABOT BEACH PARK** is the perfect place to swim and picnic, particularly if you've stopped at the **QUALITY BAKERY** (1305 7th Ave, Invermere; 250/342-9913; www.healthybread.com). Look for an enormous pretzel poised above its roof. Espresso coffee and Swiss pastries are the featured attractions. For information, contact the **COLUMBIA VALLEY VISITOR INFO CENTRE** (Hwy 93/95, Invermere; 250/342-2844; www.adventurevalley.com).

    PANORAMA MOUNTAIN VILLAGE (250/342-6941 or 800/663-2929; www.panoramaresort.com) lies at the end of a winding road 12 miles/20 km west of Invermere. Self-contained at its remote location in the Purcell Mountains, Panorama is a destination resort with dining, shopping, and outdoor hot tubs, plus several other unique attractions, including a wolf sanctuary and a three-car gondola that ferries guests up and down the village. The ski area itself is a massive layout with 4,000 feet/1,219 m of vertical, deep powder snow, and several large bowls that serve both intermediate and expert skiers. Cross-country skiers are catered to at the village's **BECKIE SCOTT NORDIC CENTRE** (250/341-4100), named for the Olympic gold medal winner. In summer, the action switches to golf at the **GREYWOLF GOLF COURSE** (1860 Greywolf Dr, Panorama; 250/341-4100 or 888/473-9965; www.greywolfgolf.com), tennis, horseback riding, hiking, fishing, and river rafting on Toby Creek.

Radium Hot Springs

Near the town of the same name, **RADIUM HOT SPRINGS** (on Hwy 93, 2 miles/ 3 km from junction with Hwy 95; 250/347-9485; www.radiumhotsprings.com or www.pleiadesmassage.com/radium) makes an ideal soaking stop at the base of the Kootenay Range. The hot springs, open to the public year-round and wheelchair accessible, are equipped with two pools: one heated, the other cooler for swimming.

Trans-Canada Highway, the National Parks, and Field

You can't go much farther east than Field, the modest commercial hub, as it were, of **YOHO NATIONAL PARK** (Field; 250/343-6783; www.pc.gc.ca/pn-np/bc/yoho), and still be in British Columbia. With adjacent Banff, Jasper, and Kootenay national parks, Yoho is part of a vast Rocky Mountain wilderness designated by UNESCO as a World Heritage Site. The Trans-Canada Highway (Hwy 1) parallels the Kicking Horse River through a valley as it winds down from its headwaters in the mountains. By the time the road reaches Yoho's headquarters in Field, 18 miles/30 km east of the park's west gate, the tone of the landscape shifts to glaciated peaks. Extensive hiking is found along 190 miles/300 km of trails in Yoho, a park characterized by rock walls and waterfalls. A highlight is the strenuous hike to the **BURGESS SHALE**, a world-famous site where mid-20th-century researchers unraveled the mysteries of a major stage of evolution. Access is permitted only with a registered guide from the **YOHO-BURGESS SHALE FOUNDATION** (800/343-3006; www.burgess-shale.bc.ca).

Contact the **FIELD VISITOR CENTRE** (250/343-6783; www.parkscanada.gc.ca/ yoho). **NOTE:** A pass, available at the visitor center, is required for all visitors stopping in national parks. Permits are good in national parks throughout Canada.

LODGINGS

Emerald Lake Lodge / ★★★

YOHO NATIONAL PARK; 250/343-6321 OR 800/663-6336
When Emerald Lake Lodge opened in 1902, it was one of the Canadian Pacific Railway's crown jewels. After falling on hard times, the lodge was restored to elegance in 1986. Set on a 13-acre/5.26-hectare peninsula that overlooks the lake, the lodge has 85 spacious guest rooms spread among 24 chalet-style buildings. (Unfortunately, some cabins are less than soundproof.) Rooms feature twig furniture arranged around fireplaces. Private decks open onto the lake and Presidential Range peaks. In summer, stop for afternoon tea on the main lodge's veranda or enjoy casual fare at Cilantro, an airy bistro. *$$$$; AE, DC, MC, V; no checks; www.crmr.com/emerald-lake-lodge.php; 6 miles/10 km south of Hwy 1.* &

Golden and Kicking Horse Mountain Resort

Much like its neighbor, Revelstoke, on the west side of Rogers Pass, downtown Golden (population 4,200) lies hidden from those passing through on the Trans-Canada Highway (Hwy 1). Not so for those exploring the Columbia Valley on Highway 95, which leads through Golden, at the confluence of the Columbia and Kicking Horse rivers. First came the railway, then logging. Now outdoor adventure draws people to Golden. Contact the **GOLDEN CHAMBER OF COMMERCE** (500 10th Ave N, Golden; 250/344-7125 or 800/622-4653; www.goldenchamber. bc.ca) for details.

KICKING HORSE MOUNTAIN RESORT (866/754-5425; www.kickinghorse resort.com), formerly called Whitetooth Ski Area, lies 7 miles/12 km west of Golden. The resort's Golden Eagle Express gondola deposits you at 7,710 feet/ 2,350 m elevation. The superb **EAGLE'S EYE RESTAURANT** demands a visit whether you intend to ski down or not, and the mountaintop lodge offers an accommodation unique in British Columbia: a deluxe suite in which guests can dine, stay overnight, and be absolutely guaranteed first tracks down in the morning.

LODGINGS

Hillside Lodge & Chalets / ★★

1740 SEWARD FRONTAGE RD, GOLDEN; 250/344-7281

A century ago, the Canadian Pacific Railway constructed several alpine-style chalets in Golden to house Swiss mountain guides. More recently, Hubert and Sonja Baier built similar cabins for guests in search of a tranquil retreat. Five cabins and a main lodge are beside a river. Each is furnished with a fireplace and Bavarian furniture. Guests share the 60-acre/24.28-hectare property with wildlife and the Baiers' llamas. *$$; MC, V; no checks; www.hillsidechalets. com; 8 miles/13 km west of Golden.*

Revelstoke

Revelstoke (population 7,500), nestled beside **MOUNT REVELSTOKE NATIONAL PARK** (250/837-7500; www.parkscanada.gc.ca/revelstoke), is a railway town beside the Columbia River, just the right size for a stroll; pick up a heritage tour brochure from the **REVELSTOKE VISITOR INFO CENTRE** (204 Campbell Ave; 250/837-5345 or 800/487-1493; www.revelstokecc.bc.ca). Steep-pitched metal roofs confirm the area's heavy snowfall, as does the **CANADIAN AVALANCHE CENTRE** (300 1st St W; 250/837-2435 or 800/667-1105; www.avalanche.ca) downtown. The 15-mile/25-km **MEADOWS IN THE SKY PARKWAY** (summer only) reaches the highest elevation of any public road in Canada, climaxing in a view of surrounding ice fields in Mount Revelstoke National Park.

RESTAURANTS

The 112 / ★★

112 1ST ST E, REVELSTOKE; 250/837-2107 OR 888/245-5523

Located in downtown Revelstoke's Regent Inn (built in 1931), the 112 is a unanimous favorite among locals. The dining room's cedar-paneled interior and historic ambience are great, but the food is its biggest draw. Chef Peter Mueller specializes in veal. (On Sundays, when the 112 is closed, the Regent Inn's pub menu has solid fare with a neighborhood flavor.) *$$; AE, MC, V; local checks only; lunch Mon–Fri, dinner Mon–Sat; full bar; reservations recommended; www.regentinn.com; beside Grizzly Plaza.* &

LODGINGS

Mulvehill Creek Wilderness Inn / ★★★

4200 HWY 23S, REVELSTOKE; 250/837-8649 OR 877/837-8649

Cornelia and René Hueppi, a dynamic Swiss couple, have created a remarkable wilderness retreat south of Revelstoke. The inn, with a small tower room, is nestled in a tranquil, brightly lit clearing and holds eight suites, each with wildlife artwork and painted in soft shades. The Otter's Burrow is the largest, with private deck and Jacuzzi. A yard and garden contain a heated outdoor pool and hot tub. *$$; AE, MC, V; checks OK; www.mulvehillcreek. com; 12 miles/19 km south of Revelstoke.*

CENTRAL BRITISH COLUMBIA

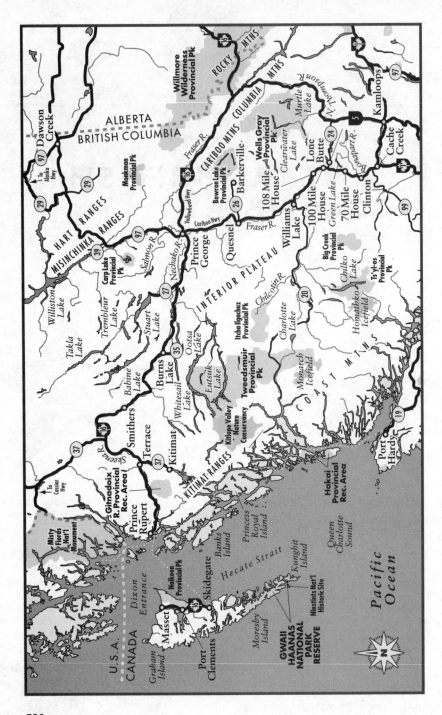

CENTRAL BRITISH COLUMBIA

From the mist-shrouded rain forests of the West Coast to the soaring peaks of the northeastern Rockies and on into the valleys of the natural resource–rich Peace River, central British Columbia encompasses a vast wilderness. Despite its size—think California and Oregon combined—the area is sparsely populated, and only a few roads intersect it.

Extending from Clinton (just north of Cache Creek) north to Prince George—an immense plateau shouldered by imposing peaks and drained by wild, free-flowing rivers—the Cariboo-Chilcotin region, as it's also known, was largely settled by Canadians and the British during the 1860s.

West of Prince George, the Pacific coast of British Columbia encompasses a huge system of fjords and rivers, as well as the archipelago called Haida Gwaii (pronounced "HI-dah gwhy"), also known as the Queen Charlotte Islands. Most of this remote area can be reached only by boat or air.

ACCESS AND INFORMATION

The central region has a very simple road system. Basically, there are Highways 5, 37, and 97, which run roughly north-south through central and northern British Columbia. **HIGHWAY 16** is the main east-west route, extending from the Rockies at Jasper (and points east) to Prince Rupert on the coast.

HIGHWAY 97 is the main road into the Cariboo-Chilcotin region from southern British Columbia (the highway is a continuation of US Highway 97 in Washington state's Okanogan). Many towns along Hwy 97 between Clinton and Quesnel (pronounced "kweh-NEL") are helpfully referred to by their distance from Lillooet (mile 0) north along the Gold Rush Trail, which preceded construction of the Cariboo Wagon Road. Thus 70 Mile House, for example, marks the distance between Lillooet and this point, the original site of a pioneer roadhouse. Note, however, that Lillooet itself lies 45 miles/75 km west of Hwy 97 on Highway 99. (See the Lower Mainland British Columbia chapter.)

From Prince George, a bit north of Quesnel, Hwy 97 winds northeast to Dawson Creek—mile 0 on the **ALASKA HIGHWAY**—and northwest to Watson Lake on the British Columbia–Yukon border, via Fort St. John and Fort Nelson, 737 miles/1,228 km in all. When venturing into this region, keep in mind that the highways of this huge, sprawling province are not very well suited to 70mph barreling-down-the-road travel. Plan itineraries accordingly.

HWY 5 runs between Hwy 97 and the Rockies, connecting Kamloops with Hwy 16 at Tete Jaune. **HWY 37** connects Kitimat and Stewart near the western end of Hwy 16, between Prince George and Prince Rupert.

PRINCE GEORGE AIRPORT (4141 Airport Rd-10, Prince George; 250/963-2400; www.pgairport.ca) is served by **WESTJET** (888/937-8538; www.westjet.com), **AIR CANADA JAZZ** (514/393-3333 or 888/247-2262; www.flyjazz.ca), and **HORIZON AIR** (800/547-9308; www.alaskaair.com), which provides nonstop service from Seattle, Washington.

PRINCE RUPERT AIRPORT (on Digby Island, Prince Rupert; 250/624-6274; www.ypr.ca), the coastal air transportation hub, has daily flights to and from Vancouver via Air Canada Jazz and HAWKAIR (250/635-4295 or 800/487-1216; www.hawkair.ca). Prince Rupert Airport is located on an island near the city; a 20-minute ferry trip links the city and airport.

Air Canada Jazz also flies from Vancouver to Sandspit on Moresby Island in Haida Gwaii, and to Terrace and Smithers, both located along Hwy 16. NORTH PACIFIC SEAPLANES (250/627-1341; www.northpacificseaplanes.com) has regularly scheduled flights from Prince Rupert to the Haida Gwaii communities of Sandspit, Queen Charlotte City, and Masset.

VIA RAIL's Skeena (888/842-7245; www.viarail.com) provides east-west passenger rail service from Jasper, Alberta, to Prince George, Smithers, and Prince Rupert. BC FERRIES (250/386-3431 or 888/223-3779; www.bcferries.com) sail between Prince Rupert and Skidegate on Graham Island in Haida Gwaii and south to Port Hardy on Vancouver Island. In summer, a popular ferry route takes a day to travel between Port Hardy and Bella Coola. The ALASKA MARINE HIGHWAY (800/642-0066; www.dot.state.ak.us/amhs) links Prince Rupert with Skagway, Alaska, to the north and Bellingham, Washington, to the south.

CENTRAL CARIBOO TOURISM in Williams Lake's Tourism Discovery Centre (1660 S Broadway, Williams Lake; 877/967-5253; www.visitcariboo.com) and CARIBOO CHILCOTIN COAST TOURISM (204–350 Barnard St, Williams Lake; 800/663-5885; www.landwithoutlimits.com) represent most of central British Columbia. NORTHERN BC TOURISM (1274 5th Ave, Prince George; 800/663-8843; www.northernbctourism.com) is a helpful source of information on the province north of the Cariboo-Chilcotin.

The Cariboo-Chilcotin Region

Clinton

Clinton (population 740) anchors mile 47 on the HISTORIC GOLD RUSH TRAIL. This frontier trading post's history can be vicariously relived at the SOUTH CARIBOO HISTORICAL MUSEUM (1419 Cariboo Hwy; 250/459-2442; May–Oct), located in a former schoolhouse. Framed by wrought iron and pine, the OLD CLINTON CEMETERY (7456 Cariboo Hwy) presents an apt gateway to Central British Columbia's past. Catch the town's WESTERN HERITAGE WEEK and MAY BALL RODEO (250/459-2261; www.clintonannualball.com), which kicks off with an annual dance that has taken place since 1867, making it the longest continually held event in British Columbia. For more information on Clinton, contact the MAYOR'S OFFICE (1423 Cariboo Hwy; 250/459-2261; www.village.clinton.bc.ca).

LODGINGS

Echo Valley Ranch & Spa / ★★★★

**BIG BAR RD OFF HWY 97 NEAR CLINTON;
250/459-2386 OR 800/253-8831**

An early pioneer in upscale ranches, this impressive collection of luxury accommodations includes 21 peeled-spruce-log cabins and lodges, a Thai therapy–focused spa, gourmet meals prepared by a master chef, sensational scenery, and activities like yoga and day trips to the legendary million-acre Gang Ranch, once the world's largest ranch and so dubbed because it was the first to use a double-furrowed gang plough from England. If you want to avoid the five-hour drive from Vancouver, Norm will hop into his DeHavilland Beaver to pick you up and deliver you directly to the ranch. *$$$$; MC, V; no checks; closed Nov–Mar except Christmas and New Year's Day; www. evranch.com; 30 miles/50 km west of Hwy 97 at Clinton.* &

Moondance Guest Ranch / ★★☆

**880 ISADORE RD OFF HWY 97 NEAR CLINTON;
250/459-7775 OR 888/459-7775**

In addition to three- to seven-night all-inclusive stays in four cheerful cabins, this guest ranch offers weeklong natural horsemanship sessions for serious horse enthusiasts and weekend packages in conjunction with the Clinton Rodeo (see section introduction). Fresh-baked breads and pastries made with organic grains will see you through hours of riding on the ranch's well-mannered steeds (one of the owners is a certified guide and trainer). *$$$$; MC, V; no checks; closed Nov–Apr except Christmas and New Year's; www. moondanceguestranch.com; 19 miles/30 km west of Hwy 97 at Clinton.*

Interlakes District

Head east off Hwy 97 at either 70 Mile House or 93 Mile House, using the Green Lake Road or Highway 24, and you'll find yourself in the Interlakes District. **GREEN LAKE** is the first of hundreds of lakes, large and larger, strung between Hwy 97 and Hwy 5, which parallels the North Thompson River. For a quick sample, drive the **GREEN LAKE SCENIC LOOP** north from Green Lake to Lone Butte on Hwy 24, which connects Hwy 97 and Hwy 5. Each lake boasts at least one guest ranch or fishing camp.

LODGINGS

Crystal Waters Guest Ranch / ★★

**N BONAPARTE RD OFF HWY 24 NEAR BRIDGE LAKE;
250/593-4252 OR 888/593-2252**

Rodeo veteran Gary Cleveland and his wife, Marisa Peters, offer seven log cabins—each sleeping from 2 to 12 persons—on the shores of Crystal Lake. With electric heat and tasteful Western-style decor, the cabins also have

<hr>

NORTHWEST COAST THREE-DAY TOUR

DAY ONE: Start your day in **PRINCE RUPERT** with a coffee and pastry at **COW-PUCCINO'S COFFEE HOUSE** (25 Cow Bay Rd, Prince Rupert; 250/627-1395), then a walk through downtown. Begin at the **MUSEUM OF NORTHERN BRITISH COLUMBIA** and join a guided walking tour of totem poles. Take the **KAIEN ISLAND CIRCLE TOUR** with **PRINCE RUPERT ADVENTURE TOURS** (207 3rd Ave E, Prince Rupert; 250/627-9166 or 800/201-8377; www.westcoastlaunch. com). Have lunch at the **COW BAY CAFÉ** before heading to the **NORTH PACIFIC CANNERY VILLAGE NATIONAL HISTORIC SITE** in nearby Port Edward. Late in the afternoon, check in to **EAGLE BLUFF BED & BREAKFAST** and relax to the sound of the ocean. Then set off for dinner at **SMILE'S SEAFOOD CAFÉ** (113 Cow Bay Rd, Prince Rupert; 250/624-3072).

DAY TWO: After breakfast at your B and B, head for the **BC FERRIES TERMINAL** for the all-day crossing to **HAIDA GWAII** (Queen Charlotte Islands), watching for whales, seals, and seabirds en route. Grab lunch on the ferry, then,

<hr>

refrigerators and a "cowboy outhouse." A modern central washhouse with separate toilets, showers, and laundry facilities is just a short walk from the cabins. Explore the 640-acre/259-hectare spread on one of the ranch's horses, soak away your worldly worries and sore muscles in a lakeshore hot tub. Fish for rainbow trout, go mountain biking, or paddle Crystal Lake. *$$$$; MC, V; checks OK; closed Nov–Apr; www.crystalwatersranch.com; 3 miles/5 km southwest of Hwy 24 at Bridge Lake.* &

Flying U Guest Ranch / ★★☆

N GREEN LAKE RD OFF HWY 97 NEAR 70 MILE HOUSE; 250/456-7717
Founded by rodeo star Jack Boyd in 1924, the Flying U is Canada's oldest guest ranch, its character embodied in the smoky whiskey smell that emanates from the lodge's stone fireplace. Flying U has remote quirkiness—there's no sign leading to the ranch gates. This is the only major guest ranch in the Northwest where clients can ride out unescorted. Vintage western movies, bonfires, hayrides, or square dances often follow dinner. *$$$$; MC, V; checks OK; closed Nov–Mar; www.flyingu.com; 12 miles/20 km east of 70 Mile House.*

100 Mile House

100 Mile House (population 1,740) is home to the 50K "classic technique" **CARIBOO CROSS-COUNTRY SKI MARATHON** in February, hosted by the 100 Mile Nordic Ski Society (www.100milenordics.com). Note how seriously locals take their sticks: at the entrance to the **SOUTH CARIBOO VISITOR INFO CENTRE** (422 Hwy 97; 877/511-5353; www.southcaribootourism.com) stands the world's largest pair

when you arrive at **GRAHAM ISLAND**, head up toward Masset to stay at the **ALASKA VIEW LODGE** (Tow Hill Rd, Masset; 250/626-3333 or 800/668-7544) for the night. Have dinner at the friendly **TROUT HOUSE** (9102 Tow Hill Rd, Masset; 250/626-9330) nearby.

DAY THREE: Enjoy breakfast in your lodge with your hosts, then dig your toes into the pristine, sandy beaches of **NAIKOON PROVINCIAL PARK** (Masset; 250/626-5115). Head south to lunch at the **RISING TIDE BAKERY & COFFEE SHOP** (37580 Hwy 16, Tlell; 250/557-4677) before visiting the **HAIDA HERITAGE CENTRE AT QAY'LLNAGAAY** just north of **SKIDEGATE**, where you can also sample traditional Haida fare at the center's **EATING HOUSE**.

Return south to **QUEEN CHARLOTTE CITY** and stroll the waterfront, enjoying the sunset over the ocean and a slice of homemade cheesecake from the deck at **HOWLER'S PUB AND BISTRO** (2600 Oceanview Dr, Queen Charlotte City; 250/559-8600) before heading to **SKIDEGATE LANDING** to catch the overnight ferry sailing back to the mainland at **PRINCE RUPERT**.

of skinny skis accompanied by a 30-foot/9-m pair of poles, pointing skyward. Arguably the best track-set cross-country skiing in British Columbia is found on the 120 miles/200 km of trails between here and 108 Mile Ranch. For information, contact **GUNNER'S CYCLE AND X-COUNTRY SKI SHOP** (800/664-5414) in 108 Mile Ranch. For a unique North Country experience, try your hand at mushing a team of purebred Siberian huskies at the **WOLF DEN DOGSLED ADVENTURES** (7665 Eagan Lake Rd; 250/397-2108 or 877/397-2108; www.nakitsilik.com).

RESTAURANTS

Trails End Restaurant / ★★

1871 Lodge / ★★

HWY 97 (HILLS HEALTH AND GUEST RANCH),
108 MILE HOUSE; 250/791-5225 OR 800/668-2233

The 1871 Lodge and the Trails End Restaurant are located at the Hills Health and Guest Ranch (see review). The Trails End dining room in the main lodge offers a menu of fresh, organic, and generously portioned Cariboo Country selections as well as lighter spa fare. The emphasis is on local meat, fresh seafood, and creative vegetarian dishes prepared by chef Anna Tanner, whose inspired touch also infuses the dinner menu at the 1871 Lodge. The 24-seat log lodge dining room surrounds you with windows to the wilderness, a fireplace, and fine linens. Highlights include all-you-can-eat fondue and hot-rock steaks that diners cook themselves. $$–$$$; AE, MC, V; checks OK; breakfast, lunch, dinner every day, brunch Sun; full bar; reservations recommended; www. spabc.com; east side of hwy just north of main intersection. &

LODGINGS

The Hills Health and Guest Ranch / ★★★

HWY 97, 108 MILE HOUSE; 250/791-5225 OR 800/668-2233
Taken with the Cariboo's natural splendor, free-spirited zeitgeist, and health-oriented milieu, Pat and Juanita Corbett began purchasing bare land in 1982, intent on creating Canada's first health-spa resort in a guest-ranch setting. Three "International Specialty Spa of the Year" awards later, this is a place where celebrities and others flock. All of the spacious three-bedroom chalets feature fireplaces and balconies. *$$$; AE, MC, V; checks OK; www.spabc. com; east side of hwy just north of main intersection.* &

Williams Lake

The most exciting time to visit Williams Lake (population 12,000) is on the last weekend in June, when this lumber and cattle town hosts the **WILLIAMS LAKE STAMPEDE** (250/398-8388; www.williamslakestampede.com), the second-largest rodeo in Canada. To learn about local cowboys and rodeos, drop by the **MUSEUM OF THE CARIBOO CHILCOTIN** (113 N 4th Ave; 250/392-7404; www. cowboy-museum.com), home to the BC Cowboy Hall of Fame and a collection of western art. The **WILLIAMS LAKE VISITOR INFO CENTRE** (1660 S Broadway; 250/392-5025; www.williamslakechamber.com) provides information on local accommodations and events.

Highway 26

In the mid-1860s, the Cariboo Gold Rush drew fortune seekers and entrepreneurs from all over the world, making Barkerville the largest town north of San Francisco and west of Chicago. It was a rough and vibrant community that included several boardinghouses, a theater, a literacy society, and a Chinatown where the many Chinese miners and service workers formed a cultural neighborhood. Today, **BARKERVILLE HISTORIC TOWN** (888/994-3332; www.barkerville.ca; closed Oct–Apr) is a heritage site featuring 130 original and reconstructed buildings, costumed interpreters, gold panning, performances, and stagecoach rides. Located at the end of Hwy 26, 55 miles/88 km east of Quesnel, Barkerville is the only heritage site in Canada that allows overnight guests, so don't miss the unique opportunity to stay in one of the town's B and Bs.

Combine your trip to Barkerville with a few hours of paddling at **BOWRON LAKE PROVINCIAL PARK** (800/435-5622; www.bowronlake.net), a world-famous canoeing destination, 24 miles/38 km farther along the highway.

Chilcotin Plateau and Bella Coola

From Hwy 97 at Williams Lake, **HIGHWAY 20** leads 274 miles/456 km west across the Chilcotin Plateau and the Coast Mountains to Bella Coola on British Columbia's central coast. A small section of Hwy 20 remains unpaved, like many smaller roads leading south into the heart of the plateau. Hwy 20 takes you through a small section of **TWEEDSMUIR PROVINCIAL PARK** (250/397-2523), one of the province's oldest and biggest, home of countless bears, wolves, and moose.

LODGINGS

Elkin Creek Guest Ranch / ★★★

SOUTH OF HWY 20, NEMAIAH VALLEY;
604/573-5008 OR 877/346-9378
Set in a beautiful, remote valley at the edge of the pristine Chilcotin Plateau, Elkin Creek Guest Ranch is an intriguing wilderness ranch. Seven elegantly furnished two-bedroom log cabins are tucked into an aspen grove overlooking a pasture leading to the creek; guests dine in the nearby main lodge. Stunning views of the Coast Range's snowclad peaks seal the deal. *$$$$; MC, V; checks OK; closed Nov–Apr; www.elkincreekranch.com; 56 miles/90 km south of Hwy 20 at Hanceville.*

Tweedsmuir Lodge / ★★

HWY 20, BELLA COOLA VALLEY; 250/982-2407 OR 877/982-2407
Located at the far inland end of the Bella Coola valley, this heritage lodge occupies a blissful spot overlooking a broad meadow that leads down to a river. Choose from six chalets and four cabins. Keep an alert eye out for grazing grizzlies from the vantage point of the outdoor hot tub or the main lodge's veranda. *$$$; MC, V; no checks; closed mid-Oct–May; www.tweedsmuir parklodge.com; within Tweedsmuir Provincial Park, 43 miles/70 km east of Bella Coola.*

Prince George

Prince George, the largest city in the British Columbia interior (population 72,400), sits near the geographical center of the province, but it's still considered by most as part of Northern BC. From here, Hwy 16 leads east to the Rockies and west to Prince Rupert; Hwy 97 leads northeast to Dawson Creek and the Alaska Highway. Dubbed "P. G.," or the "City of Bridges," the city sits at a crossroad of rivers, railroads, and highways. The mighty Fraser and Nechako rivers merge near old **FORT GEORGE** (south end of 20th Ave), which is now a historic park. The paleontology gallery at the **EXPLORATION PLACE SCIENCE CENTRE AND MUSEUM** (333 Becott Pl; 250/562-1612 or 866/562-1612; www.theexplorationplace.com) is worth a visit if you have dinosaur fans in the family; they can have their photo taken with a model of a *T. rex* skull and uncover fossils in the Dig Pit.

The **PRINCE GEORGE VISITOR INFO CENTRE** (101-1300 1st Ave; 250/562-3700 or 800/668-7646; www.tourismpg.com) provides information on the area. A pool, an art gallery, and a park are downtown close to the **COAST INN OF THE NORTH** (770 Brunswick St; 250/563-0121 or 800/716-6199; www.coasthotels.com), the best bet if you're overnighting.

Hazelton

If you're driving to Prince Rupert along Hwy 16, take a break from the road at Hazelton and visit **KSAN HISTORICAL VILLAGE** (on Hwy 62, north of Hwy 16; 250/842-5544 or 877/842-5518; www.ksan.org). Located where the Gitxsan First Nation's village of Gitanmaax stood for hundreds of years, it features replicas of traditional buildings, a museum, totem poles, and a café serving salmon and other Native foods.

The Northwest Coast

Prince Rupert

Prince Rupert is home to one of the best displays of **TOTEM POLES** on the West Coast. In summer, the **MUSEUM OF NORTHERN BRITISH COLUMBIA** (100 1st Ave W; 250/624-3207; www.museumofnorthernbc.com) offers guided walking tours, or you can take a self-guided tour beginning at the **PRINCE RUPERT VISITOR INFO CENTRE** (215 Cow Bay Rd; 250/624-5637 or 800/667-1994; www. tourismprincerupert.com).

Just south of town is **PORT EDWARD**, 7 miles/11 km southwest of Hwy 16, where you'll find the **NORTH PACIFIC CANNERY VILLAGE NATIONAL HISTORIC SITE** (1889 Skeena Dr, Port Edward; 250/628-3538; www.portedward.ca; closed mid-Sept–mid-May). Until the 1970s, it employed as many as 1,500 workers. Boardwalks link offices, stores, cafés, and homes to the West Coast's oldest standing cannery, perched at the mouth of the Skeena River.

RESTAURANTS

Cow Bay Café / ★★★

205 COW BAY RD, PRINCE RUPERT; 250/627-1212
Blending her British West Indies roots with her good old down-home cooking skills, Adrienne Johnston infuses her dishes with the essence of a culinary adventure. The curry flavors of her heritage are integrated into incredibly fresh seafood dishes with results that vie for honors as the best and most interesting menu in northern British Columbia—with a selected wine list to match. Where else are you ever going to try short-spine thorny-head? *$$; AE, MC, V; no checks; lunch Tues–Sat, dinner Wed–Sat; full bar; reservations recommended; in Cow Bay section of town.* &

LODGINGS

Eagle Bluff Bed & Breakfast / ★★☆

201 COW BAY RD, PRINCE RUPERT; 250/627-4955 OR 800/833-1550

The waves of Cow Bay lap beneath Eagle Bluff's pilings, providing a soothing setting and tantalizing waterfront views at this sweet B and B. The century-old house on the pier features five casually decorated guest rooms (think rustic elegance); a hearty full breakfast is included. Fireplaces in two of the rooms amp up the coziness during stormy weather. The two-bedroom suite is ideal for families. *$–$$; MC, V; no checks; www.citytel.net/eaglebluff; on harbor, 1 block west of Hwy 16.* &

Haida Gwaii (Queen Charlotte Islands)

Made up of 150 islands, this archipelago is considered by many travelers to be one of the most evocative landscapes in the world. Sometimes called Canada's Galapagos, it is home to a distinctive ecosystem and people, the Haida First Nation. Dubbed the Queen Charlotte Islands by an 18th-century British sea captain, this place's older Haida name is Xhaaidlagha Gwaayaai, or Haida Gwaii, "Islands at the Boundary of the World." It is known by both names today. The **VISITOR INFORMATION CENTRE** (3220 Wharf St, Queen Charlotte City; 250/559-8316; www.qcinfo.ca) can help you sort out must-sees—and there are plenty of them—as well as help you plan your visit.

The largest of the islands are Moresby and Graham. Ferries between Prince Rupert and Haida Gwaii dock at the BC Ferries' terminal at Skidegate Landing on **GRAHAM ISLAND**; the ferry crossing takes seven or eight hours. **QUEEN CHARLOTTE CITY** (population 1,046), with a serene waterfront, lies 2½ miles/ 4 km west of Skidegate on Hwy 16. Just north of the ferry terminal is the **HAIDA HERITAGE CENTRE AT QAY'LLNAGAAY** (on Second Beach Rd, east of Hwy 16; 250/559-7885), which celebrates the culture of the Haida with a museum, longhouse, teaching center, and cedar-carving house.

Tucked into a remote southern area of the islands, accessible only by boat or chartered floatplanes, is the **GWAII HAANAS NATIONAL PARK RESERVE AND HAIDA HERITAGE SITE** (250/387-1642 or 800/435-5622) and the UNESCO World Heritage Site **NAN SDINS ILLNAGAAY** (also called Ninstints), home to an awe-inspiring collection of 100-year-old carved mortuary poles. Natural treasures in this park include wildlife, birds (especially eagles and seabirds), and spectacular scenery at every turn. Most people visit the area on **TOURS** (www.placeofwonder. com); independent travelers must reserve in advance with park authorities.

Index

Best Places Northwest Report Form

Based on my personal experience, I wish to nominate the following restaurant, place of lodging, shop, nightclub, sight, or other as a "Best Place"; or confirm/correct/disagree with the current review.

_____
_____
_____

(Please include address and telephone number of establishment, if convenient.)

REPORT

Please describe food, service, style, comfort, value, date of visit, and other aspects of your experience; continue on another piece of paper if necessary.

_____
_____
_____
_____
_____
_____
_____
_____
_____
_____
_____
_____

I am not associated, directly or indirectly, with the management or ownership of this establishment.

SIGNED
_____

ADDRESS
_____
_____

PHONE   **DATE**
_____

Please address to _Best Places Northwest_ and send to:
SASQUATCH BOOKS
119 SOUTH MAIN STREET, SUITE 400
SEATTLE, WA 98104
Feel free to e-mail feedback as well: **BPFEEDBACK@SASQUATCHBOOKS.COM**

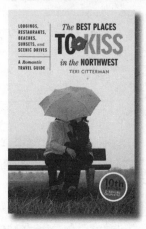